REACTIONS TO IRISH NATIONALISM

1865 - 1914

REACTIONS TO IRISH NATIONALISM

WITH AN INTRODUCTION BY
ALAN O'DAY

THE HAMBLEDON PRESS
LONDON   AND   RONCEVERTE

Published by The Hambledon Press, 1987

102 Gloucester Avenue, London NW1 8HX (U.K.)

309 Greenbrier Avenue, Ronceverte,
West Virginia 24970 (U.S.A.)

ISBN 0 907628 85 0

The publishers are grateful to the editors of all the journals in which
these essays first appeared for permission to reproduce them here.
In particular, they wish to express their gratitude to *Irish Historical
Studies*, the original source of seven contributions herein.

British Library Cataloguing-in-Publication Data

Reactions to Irish nationalism, 1865-1914.
  1. Ireland – History – 1837-1901
  2. Ireland – History – 1901-1910
  3. Ireland – History – 1910-1921
  I. O'Day, Alan
  941.5081   DA957

Library of Congress Cataloging-in-Publication Data

Reactions to Irish nationalism, 1865-1914.
  Includes bibliographical references and index.
  1. Ireland – Politics and government – 1837-1901.
  2. Nationalism – Ireland – History.
  3. Ireland – Politics and government – 1901-1910.
  4. Ireland – Politics and government – 1910-1921.
  5. Home rule (Ireland)
  6. Ireland – History – Autonomy and independence
    movements.   7. Irish question.
  I. O'Day, Alan
  DA957.R43 1987   941.508   87-100

Printed and Bound in Great Britain
by WBC (Printers) and WBC (Bookbinders), Maesteg

CONTENTS

Acknowledgements   vii

List of Contributors   ix

Introduction by *Alan O'Day*   xi

1   Symbols of Irish Nationalism   1
Peter Alter

2   Patriotism as Pastime: The Appeal of Fenianism
in the Mid-1860s   21
R. V. Comerford

3   Ireland and the Ballot Act of 1872   33
Michael Hurst

4   The Political Mobilization of Irish Farmers   61
Samuel Clark

5   The Tenants' Movement to Capture the Irish Poor
Law Boards, 1877-1886   79
William L. Feingold

6   The I.R.B. and the Beginnings of the Gaelic
Athletic Association   95
W.F. Mandle

7   Cardinal Cullen and the National Association of
Ireland   117
Patrick J. Corish

8   The Early Response of the Irish Catholic Clergy
to the Co-operative Movement   167
Liam Kennedy

9   The Roman Catholic Church in Ireland, 1898-1918   187
David W. Miller

10   J.S. Mill and the Irish Question: Reform, and the
Integrity of the Empire, 1865-1870   205
E.D. Steele

11   The Irish Question and Liberal Politics, 1886-1894   237
     D.A. Hamer

12   Home Rule, Radicalism, and the Liberal Party,
     1886-1895   259
     Thomas William Heyck

13   Rosebery and Ireland, 1898-1903: A Reappraisal   285
     David W. Gutzke

14   Irish Home-Rule Finance: A Neglected Dimension
     of the Irish Question, 1910-1914   297
     Patricia Jalland

15   Lord Randolph Churchill and Home Rule   319
     R.E. Quinault

16   The Ulster Liberal Unionists and Local Government
     Reform, 1885-1898   347
     Catherine B. Shannon

17   The Southern Irish Unionists, the Irish Question,
     and British Politics, 1906-1914   365
     P.J. Buckland

Index   393

ACKNOWLEDGEMENTS

The articles reprinted here first appeared in the following places and are reprinted by the kind permission of the original publishers.

1   *Studia Hibernica*, 14 (1974), pp. 104-23.

2   *Irish Historical Studies*, xxii, no. 87 (1981), pp. 239-50.

3   *Historical Journal*, viii (1965), pp. 326-52.

4   *Canadian Review of Sociology and Anthropology*, 12 (1975), pp. 483-99.

5   *Albion*, 7 (1975), pp. 216-31.

6   *Irish Historical Studies*, xx, no. 80 (1977), pp. 418-38.

7   *Reportorium Novum*, 3 (1961-2), pp. 13-61.

8   *Irish Historical Studies*, xxi, no. 81 (1978), pp. 55-74.

9   *Éire-Ireland*, iii (1968), pp. 75-91.

10 *Historical Journal*, xiii (1970), pp. 419-50.

11 *Historical Journal*, xii (1969), pp. 511-32.

12 *Journal of British Studies*, xiii (1974), pp. 66-91.

13 *Bulletin of the Institute of Historical Research*, liii (1980), pp. 89-98.

14 *Irish Historical Studies*, xxiii, no. 91 (1983), pp. 233-53.

15 *Irish Historical Studies*, xxi, no. 84 (1981), pp. 377-403.

16 *Irish Historical Studies*, xviii, no. 71 (1973), pp. 407-23.

17 *Irish Historical Studies*, xv, no. 59 (1967), pp. 228-55.

NOTES ON CONTRIBUTORS

Peter Alter, Deputy Director of the German Historical Institute, London and Professor of Modern History at the University of Cologne (West Germany).

Patrick Buckland, Reader in History, University of Liverpool.

Samuel Clark, Associate Professor of Sociology, University of Western Ontario (Canada).

R.V. Comerford, Lecturer in History, St Patrick's College, Maynooth (Ireland).

Fr Patrick Corish, Professor of Modern History, St Patrick's College, Maynooth (Ireland).

William Feingold taught History at Bellevue College (Nebraska, U.S.A.) until his death.

David W. Gutzke, Assistant Professor of History, Southwest Missouri State University (U.S.A.).

D.A. Hamer, Professor of History, Victoria University of Wellington (New Zealand).

T.W. Heyck, Professor of History, Northwestern University (Illinois, U.S.A.).

Michael Hurst, Fellow of St John's College, Oxford.

Patricia Jalland, Lecturer in History, Murdock University (Australia).

Liam Kennedy, Lecturer in Social and Economic History, The Queen's University of Belfast.

William F. Mandle, Head of the School of Liberal Studies, Canberra College of Advanced Education (Australia).

David W. Miller, Professor of History, Carnegie-Mellon University (Pennsylvania, U.S.A.).

Alan O'Day, Senior Lecturer in History, Polytechnic of North London.

Roland Quinault, Senior Lecturer in History, Polytechnic of North London.

Catherine Shannon, Professor of History, Westfield State University (Massachusetts, U.S.A.).

E.D. Steele, Senior Lecturer in History, University of Leeds.

FOR MARGARET PATRICIA PURCELL

INTRODUCTION

ALAN O'DAY

From the mid–1860s to 1914 the Irish problem was frequently the prime issue in British politics. Quantatively it absorbed more time and energy than any other question. There was little about Ireland which was not aired at length in the press, in Parliament and at the dinner tables of the British political elite. Fenianism obsessed British minds at the beginning of the period while at the end it seemed all too possible that Irish home rule would spark off the largest civil disruption in the British Isles since the seventeenth century. Throughout the late Victorian and Edwardian eras Ireland never drifted far from political consciousness. The importance of the Irish question in modern British history is undeniable. It remains a staple of schools and university history syllabuses. For many William Gladstone's long career, most of which had little connection with Ireland, was bound up with his mission to pacify the Emerald Isle. Charles Stewart Parnell, the Protestant nationalist who guided an essentially Catholic movement so triumphantly, has inspired the best in poetry and the worst of Hollywood. The Irish problem, understandably, has continued to excite interest and passion beyond any other issue of the time. Its ramifications are with us even today. Failure to resolve the Irish problem by 1914 left a bitter legacy and was a major factor in giving birth to the contemporary Northern Ireland violence.

That the Irish question played so considerable a part in later nineteenth and early twentieth century Britain is at initial glance very curious. Ireland was a small, relatively poor backwater on the fringe of the British Isles and western Europe. It possessed few significant resources and had little intrinsic importance. Scotland and Wales, lands of infinitely more value to Britain, attracted little concern by comparison though both had grievances and aspirations similar to those in Ireland. Moreover, neither the industrial workers of Britain's cities or the agricultural classes of the countryside were given the consideration devoted to the humblest of Ireland's Catholic peasantry.

Ireland's centrality is explicable in three principle ways. First, there was a range of outstanding Irish grievances which public opinion had been educated to understand demanded attention if the Catholics of the country were to consent freely to be part of a unified kingdom. Certain issues, then, were ripe for legislation. Secondly, a movement emerged which was able to galvanise the Catholic masses. It also proved effective in keeping Ireland to the fore in British life over an extended time.

Finally, matters of principle were raised in the Irish question pushing it beyond being merely a set of remedies for a particular problem. Potentially, the whole of the British Empire was effected by what happened in Ireland. Indifference to Irish claims was impossible – the stakes were too high.

Not surprisingly, an impressive academic literature has been spawned by the Irish problem. In recent years new evidence, fresh perspectives and demanding reinterpretations have illuminated the field. Worthy contributions have come from scholars working in a number of countries. Many important articles have been published in a considerable number of academic journals and have appeared over more than two decades. Some of this scattered material is relatively inaccessible. *Reactions to Irish Nationalism, 1865-1914* is the first attempt to bring together a selection of journal articles to make them more readily available.

The volume concentrates on the nature and development of nationalism and the reactions of British leaders and Irish|unionists to it. Those pieces included have been chosen for their quality, relevance to the book's theme, how they fit the time scale and out of a wish to have a variety of methodologies and approaches represented. Each article is reprinted without alteration excepting minor typographical emendations. Clearly, the volume is not a narrative of Anglo-Irish relations during the period but offers specific treatment in depth of certain issues. The first half (nine articles) examines aspects of nationalism while responses to it form the subject of the second portion (eight essays). No pretense of a value judgment about articles not included is implied.

Peter Alter's general investigation of the neglected topic of national symbols opens the volume. Control and manipulation of national symbols was, he shows, an ingredient in the formula for the legitimatization and dominance of one strand of nationalism. His piece draws attention to parallel developments in Continental countries showing that Irish nationalism did not function in a vacuum but was an integral part of broad developments. Nationalism, he reminds us, was not a plant left to grow wild but one carefully cultivated. A central part of his analysis concerns the way the Irish party, which dominated politics from the 1870s to 1914, adopted and created symbols like the flag, anthem, festivals, monuments and nomenclature for public places for its own purposes. Many of the symbols proved to be exclusive to the Catholic community thus tending to increase the distinction in Irish life between the majority and Protestants. Symbols, then, contributed to splits in Ireland as well as helping fortify the nationalists. His stimulating article originally appeared in a limited circulation journal and remains one of the few of the author's writings available in English.

If symbols have been neglected, Fenians cannot be said to have endured a similar fate. R.V. Comerford's succinct contribution looks at an old theme from a different angle. Whereas it has been usual to see Fenians as intensely committed revolutionaries aiming to mount an armed struggle, Vincent Comerford places the movement in the context of the social history of the British Isles. He notes that the young men who participated in this secret oath-bound society frequently engaged in flagrant public displays – an apparent paradox he explains by arguing that Fenianism possessed an organizational apparatus which provided members with a sense of personal fulfilment through identifying with a group of peers in autonomous social activities. It was an alternative form of recreation to that sponsored and supervised by the clergy. Fenianism, he suggests, was for some a means to assert independence from family and priests. It should be seen, he argues, as a section of the story of the rise in public leisure and participants as fairly typical mid-Victorians. His analysis gives a framework for understanding apparent problems of Fenianism like why it expanded and contracted so swiftly and how members were able to participate simultaneously in other organizations which competed with and were hostile to revolutionary ideas. He enhances an appreciation of why so many clergymen were able to condemn Fenianism but not its individual members. His is, above all, a severe slap at the myth of the bold Fenian men fighting a single-handed battle for Ireland's freedom. He pushes the discussion past the bounds of politics and into the realm of social psychology.

Expansion of nationalism coincided with the growth of democracy. It has been obvious that the more democracy Ireland received the stronger grip nationalism exerted. In particular, historians tended to see two pieces of legislation during the period – the Ballot Act of 1872 and the Franchise and Redistriction Acts of 1884-85 – as key factors in the sweeping nationalist tide. Michael Hurst has deflated the first assumption and subsequent writers have cast doubt on the second as well. He demonstrates that home rule candidates were regularly successful at the polls prior to the implementation of the secret ballot. Why then was it necessary and what, if any, effect did the ballot have? His response to the former is that the ballot had been necessary for the maintenance of law and order at elections, not for the sake of Irish freedom. To the second, he answers that the Act served mainly to give protection to unionist electors in predominantly Catholic districts. Nationalism, he observes, did not require institutional tinkering to triumph but succeeded because of its own appeal, organization and leadership. With the alliance of Liberals, priests and tenant-right supporters collapsing when the jam proved too thin, nationalist politicians were positioned to fill the void. This article, now more than twenty years old, has given a hoard of historians cause to pause and reconsider many time honoured and comfortable assumptions about Anglo-Irish politics.

Samuel Clark's article on the land war is complementary to that of Michael Hurst. He, too, examines a long accepted truism and finds it wanting. For long historians have accepted that the discontent arising from the agricultural crisis of the late 1870s was a decisive chapter in the rise of nationalism. As a transatlantic sociologist, Samuel Clark imposes a different vision on the assumed relationship between discontent and nationalism. He observes that discontent had existed in the past. What had changed by the late 1870s was that there was now a political movement capable of mobilizing discontent into an effective instrument. He sees the new situation as being the outcome of structural shifts in Irish life and its economy. The growth of literacy, spread of railways and integration of rural inhabitants in commercial transactions bridged the gulf between agrarian and urban communities. Modernization had enabled the emergence of a cooperative relationship between farmers and shopkeepers with the consequence that the peasant masses were open to the organization by, and leadership of urban politicians. All that was essential was an occasion to bring the two elements together in a political movement. In the land crisis a match touched combustible material. His treatment can be seen to affirm that the rise of an efficient national movement was not a chapter of accidents or the outcome of a series of errors and misjudgments of British politicians.

Nationalism conveyed a varied and complex message. At local level in Ireland it often spelt a means by which Catholic notables could elevate their status. William Feingold, who unfortunately died prematurely, concentrates on the use of nationalism as a force for democraticizing a key local institution, the Poor Law Boards. His analysis of the elective element of the Boards reveals that by the mid-1880s in about half of the country, particularly in the south and west, the previous dominance of the Ascendancy had been broken. In its place, local self-government by the Catholic nationalist tenantry was a reality. This rapid transition was a consequence of the polarization of Irish life. Nationalism provided a motif for the seizure of local power. Poor Law Boards in many parts of the country became organs of the prosperous farmers, shopkeepers and the rising professional classes. William Feingold notes that local self-government did not begin with the Act of 1898 and by then a Catholic elite had gained valuable experience and established itself ready for the day when further democratization would make additional advances possible. His treatment has three significant ramifications – he shows how the nationalist cause was interpreted locally; why local notables remained intensely loyal to the Irish party after 1891; and why Protestants, particularly in heavily Catholic districts, feared democracy.

William Mandle's tracing of the early origins of the most successful of institutions to spring from the cultural revival, the Gaélic Athletic Association, takes the study of nationalism in another direction. In many parts of central and eastern Europe cultural nationalism proceeded political organization. The obverse was true in Ireland. As a consequence of political nationalism certain forms of Gaelic culture were revived or invented from the middle of the 1880s. Despite being a minority concern at all points, cultural nationalism exercised significant influence in the years immediately proceeding the war. In Ireland nearly all forms of public expression became tied to the nationalist movement. At issue in the Gaelic Athletic Association was just which strand of nationalism would control sports. There was, as Vincent Comerford observed, a pool of young men yearning for fraternal association of the sort supplied by the G.A.A. Moreover, its rise corresponded with the development of sports clubs in Britain and elsewhere. Control of the G.A.A. was regarded as vital and hotly contested. Fenians won the battle but at the cost of opening wounds and intensifying a rift in the national ranks. The article is a pertinent reminder that though Fenianism had been eclipsed by the home rulers, its spirit was alive and, in certain conditions, could muster an impressive following. Furthermore, the ethos of the G.A.A. tended to be hostile to Protestants creating an additional barrier between the minority and majority. Refusal of the G.A.A. to allow policemen or soldiers to join or members to engage in so-called foreign sports differentiated the social experiences of Irish young men. Once again we can see that nationalism had many manifestations, not all following along the same path.

The next three articles examine the intimate links between religion and nationalism. Unlike in some parts of Europe, they were inseparable in Ireland. No national movement could flourish against the opposition of the Church but, on the other hand, clerics had to be sensitive to the feelings and aspirations of their flock. This symbiosis of clerics and political leaders was evident in the very meeting place of so many popular movements – churchyards after Sunday Mass. Only the Church possessed a durable institutional fabric situated in every Catholic parish. Relations between the clergy and national spokesmen were frequently delicate, even strained, but neither could function without reference to the other.

Father Patrick Corish's essay looks at the creation of the National Association of Ireland by Cardinal Cullen in response to the Fenian threat of mid-1860s. His article, by far the longest included, was first published in a short-lived, limited circulation journal and has not been accessible to many people. His treatment shows the central importance of Paul Cullen and how Fenianism induced him to enter more directly into politics and to work with Gladstonian Liberalism. Cullen's reluctant emergence into politics was a significant step because he and the Association laid the foundation for a constitutional organization and helped channel popular politics into forms acceptable to both Church and State. Cullen had the wisdom to see that political Catholicism could not seek only religious reforms such as Disestablishment of the Church of Ireland but had to link these to economic and political demands. If the National Association enjoyed only a brief tenure, its policy and approach survived as the corner-stone of the dominant strand of nationalism to 1914.

The co-operative movement in Ireland poses an enigma. It failed to develop so swiftly or firmly as in many parts of Europe. In theory its purpose was purely the economic betterment of Irish farmers. In practice, as Liam Kennedy's penetrating study shows, the very shirking of politics and its non-denominational character restricted growth in a community where nearly every vital aspect of life took on a political and religious colouration. At first, many priests were suspicious of the new movement and gave it little or only circumscribed endorsement. They were worried about the Protestant and unionist leadership and also about the potential impact on local traders, many of whom gave generously to Church funds, in provincial Ireland. Certainly, this article underlines the influence of the Church in every corner of the Catholic community. Only when the organizers of the co-operative movement secured local clerical support could it thrive.

David Miller's essay completes the portion of the book devoted to the growth of nationalism. He draws attention to the nature of the Irish Church, its internal divisions, how sensitive the clerical leaders were to grass roots opinion, and the balance which had to be maintained by an institution poised between the State, the Vatican and the people. The British State was a constant problem for churchmen. Westminster politicians were always selective in their consideration of Irish ecclesiastics. Moreover, British governments were seldom shy about appeals to Rome against Irish ecclesiastics or reluctant to exploit internal clerical divisions. David Miller also notes the considerable sympathy Irish-Ireland ideas enjoyed in the clerical ranks. Its stress upon creating a Catholic rather than a pluralist Irish society received a good deal of encouragement from some clerics, a factor tending to increase misunderstanding between the two religious communities in the country. His analysis shows that the clerical leadership helped shape nationalism while being, at the same time, a reflector of wider tensions within the Catholic community. Together the three articles on religion and politics widen understanding of the interaction between Church and people in the nationalist movement, a feature distinguishing Ireland from much Continental experience.

Responses to nationalism took many forms. E.D. Steele's reassessment of John Stuart Mill, a man who exerted a profound influence on British ideas about Ireland, introduces discussion of a major personality and reveals the limits to English reformers' sympathy for Ireland. Mill, as he demonstrates, could identify significant defects in how Ireland was managed by Britain. Yet, Mill's vision was clouded by dislike of Catholicism and also by his general complacency about the superiority of Britain's political and social institutions. He notes that Mill was a patriot and convinced imperialist, both affecting how he viewed Irish aspirations. If reformers like Mill displayed reservations about nationalist hopes, it is scarcely surprising that so many other intellectual and political leaders showed less enthusiasm for Irish claims. How in such an atmosphere could Irishmen feel anything but underprivileged outsiders in the British State? The article raises important points about Mill; it is also a valuable indicator of the crucial significance of ideas and attitudes in shaping political reactions.

, At one level the Irish problem was a contest of competing ideas but at another it was shaped by specific British political considerations. D.A. Hamer's pioneering article sought to place the debate on home rule between the mid-1880s and 1894 in the context of how Gladstone viewed the needs of the Liberal party. He argues that the Liberal chief had become concerned about the splintering of the party into sub-groups pursuing separate ends. What Gladstone believed was essential for restoration of cohesion was concentration on a single cause. Irish home rule, he argues, fitted Gladstone's requirement because it was timely and contained those elements of Liberal principles necessary to unite the party. Gladstone's desire for a single cause conflicted with Joseph Chamberlain's programme approach to Liberal politics. For Gladstone an advantage of home rule was that it would enable him to subdue Chamberlain and reassert control over the party. After 1886 home rule had an additional virtue being a convenient excuse for Liberal weakness. His treatment places the evolution of the Irish problem squarely within the perimeter of Liberal party considerations and not as the simple outcome of nationalist pressure or tactics.

Employment of statistical and computer methods is still relatively novel in studies of the Irish question. T.W. Heyck, using such methods, provides a riposte to D.A. Hamer's theme. In contrast, he asserts that home rule rather than imposing single issue politics on Liberals facilitated party dominance by Radicalism with its wide ranging package of reforms. Right wing Liberals deserted over home rule leaving the party in the hands of Radicals who, if fewer in number in the House of Commons after 1886, nevertheless made up a far higher proportion of Gladstonian M.P.s. As a consequence even Gladstone was obliged to accept a more progressive platform for his party. He counters those who have suggested that the eventual decline of Liberalism can be traced to the home rule commitment with an insistence that it was due mainly to the nature of the party itself. The two articles, in fact, share a good deal of common ground but provide differing and interesting perspectives on how Liberalism responded to the nationalist challenge.

After Gladstone retired in 1894 home rule occupied a less prominent place in the Liberal programme. Only in 1910 did it once again emerge as a priority. Lord Rosebery, in particular, has been seen as steering the party away from the home rule commitment. David Gutzke reassesses Rosebery's role. He stresses the divisions and doubts of Liberals on the Irish problem, the widespread absence of conviction on home rule, and the impact of John Redmond's demands in the late 90s in hardening resistence in the party. Rosebery was not so much initiating as reflecting generally held Liberal opinion.

Patricia Jalland's investigation of the financial sections of the home rule bill of 1912 explores a neglected but major subject. In addition to the specific points raised, she provides an insight into Liberal attitudes towards Ireland and nationalist politicians. The bill, like its two predecessors, contained embarassing flaws. It was virtually the same as the 1893 proposal which, in turn, was very similar to the 1886 bill. In the intervening years the difficulties of merging principles of devolution and imperial authority, and of insuring Ireland of adequate sources of revenue without a Dublin Parliament having to impose vast new taxation, were not resolved. In 1912, as she notes, Liberals did not lack for adequate advice on the financial aspect but the Cabinet chose to ignore the recommendations of the experts it had commissioned to study the matter. In the end the fiscal sections of the bill were the preserve of Herbert Samuel with others taking little interest. His scheme increased the difficulties, not least in failing to allow for separate provision for Ulster. Irish representatives were allowed little voice and obliged to accept what Liberals offered or risk rejection of home rule altogether. She shows that once more mistrust of Irish M.P.s was a factor in the way legislation was devised – a not entirely happy beginning for a supposed conciliatory bill. The bill, and particularly the fiscal provisions, offered an easy target or unionist critics and rendered resolution of the Ulster question even more treacherous. Her article, in common with others, is a valuable increment to the literature of British history as well as to Anglo-Irish affairs.

The Conservative party has had a bad press over Ireland. No doubt the generous whiff of anti-Irish sentiment emanating from so many Tories has made them appear an impediment to resolving tensions over Ireland. Possibly no single Conservative has been so damned as Lord Randolph Churchill, who if many writers are to be believed, played an unscrupulous game and inflamed Ulster in 1886. Roland Quinault argues that Churchill has been misjudged. Lord Randolph he sees as an enlightened unionist who was consistent in his attitudes. By careful analysis of Churchill's speeches, an underused resource of many leaders, he lays out evidence for his case. Churchill's experience in Ireland in the late 1870s when his father was Viceroy made him a convinced unionist reformer. He believed the union could only survive if Ireland was treated equally. Also, the article places the Ulster campaign in 1886 in context pointing out that Churchill's vigorous support for the Protestants in the province had its origins in family connections with the region. His treatment illustrates that ideology, personal predilection, kinship and other connections were important factors in shaping a man's stance in British politics.

Enlightened unionism was not exclusive to Churchill. Catherine Shannon examines the role of Ulster's liberal unionists in securing those reforms, including elective local government, which they hoped would undermine the home rule demand. Opponents of nationalism wished to secure economic cures which they believed essential to stem discontent with the union. After 1895, she suggests, the situation was more favourable to Tory sponsored reform. A Chief Secretary who had access to the highest Conservative councils pushed for major Irish legislation. His thrust was aided by liberal unionists in Ulster who saw reform as the last hope. Certainly there can be no doubt that nationalism sparked a constructive response from certain Tories who might not have given Ireland much thought otherwise.

Patrick Buckland's examination of southern Irish unionist activity in the years immediately proceeding the war concludes the volume. It would be fair to say that his work on unionists in the south of the country has created an appreciation of a group which had not commanded much respect from historians. Though southern unionists were few in number they were able to exercise immense influence. They held vital seats in the House of Lords and some sat for parliamentary constituencies on the mainland. A number of British M.P.s owed their election to the support of southern unionists. But, three additional factors were probably decisive – southern unionists were able to present their cause in a form acceptable to Tory opinion; they had access to the elite of the Conservative party; and there was not an alternative unifying issue available to the British Right. He argues that had there not been southern unionists, a Conservative compromise on home rule which would exclude Ulster was possible. It was, he believes, the southern unionists who made resolution of the Irish problem impossible before 1914. Patrick Buckland's stress upon the role of social proximity and access in political decision making is a major theme in interpreting the course of pre-1914 British politics.

Historical writing is never definitive. Changed perspectives and new evidence means that practitioners of the art are constantly reassessing others work and revising their own. The articles included in the volume represent an attempt by the authors to advance historical scholarship. In turn some of their views have been and will continue to be challenged and modified. Nor can it be pretended that the pieces selected cover all the possibilities for topics in Anglo-Irish relations. Each, however, does in a significant way inform us of an aspect of Irish problem. It may be that republication in collected form will rekindle interest in some, draw attention to those which have been overlooked, and stimulate the field as a whole.

SYMBOLS OF IRISH NATIONALISM
PETER ALTER

The significance of symbols as factors of political integration has received much attention from researchers of nationalism and nation-states in recent years.[1] The pioneering work of the historian Percy Ernst Schramm on medieval 'Herrschaftszeichen und Staatssymbolik'[2] gave, in particular, the impetus for a history and investigation of modern state signs and national symbols. In his conclusion Schramm makes the point that modern national symbols, in contrast to medieval symbols with their deep roots in the sphere of religion, are nothing but the result of 'conscious acts which take into consideration the psychological reaction of all classes of the community . . ., which—if necessary—use a biased historical account'.[3] When one considers the role which political symbols played in influencing the masses during the totalitarian regimes of the period between the world wars, then this observation of Schramm is certainly correct. But the question remains as to the extent to which Schramm's observation can also be applied to national symbols which, for the most part, came into existence in Europe and America during the nineteenth century. In other words: were these national symbols also manipulated from above as calculated creations for influencing the masses?

A recent study has answered this question negatively.[4] While the fascist movements had created consciously and according to plan a symbol cult for guiding and influencing the masses[5] examples taken

---

[1] See, for example, the following works: K. Loewenstein, 'The Influence of Symbols on Politics', in *Introduction to Politics* (ed. R. V. Peel and J. S. Roucek, New York 1946) 62-84; K. Loewenstein, 'Betrachtungen über politischen Symbolismus', in *Gegenwartsprobleme des internationalen Rechts und der Rechtsphilosophie. Festschrift für Rudolf Laun* (Hamburg 1953) 559-77; Th. Schieder, 'The German Kaiserreich from 1871 as a Nation-State', in T. D. Williams (ed.), *Historical Studies* viii (Dublin 1969); E. Fehrenbach, 'Über die Bedeutung der politischen Symbole im Nationalstaat', in *Historische Zeitschrift* 213 (1971) 296-357.

[2] P. E. Schramm, *Herrschaftszeichen und Staatssymbolik. Beiträge zu ihrer Ge'chichte vom dritten bis zum sechzehnten Jahrhundert*, 3 vols. (Stuttgart 1954-6).

[3] Ibid., iii, 1063.

[4] Fehrenbach, esp. 352, 356.

from the history of European nationalism demonstrate that national symbols in almost all cases originated from the spontaneous reaction of the people in a revolutionary situation, and that it was often possible to justify them later as having been derived from national tradition and history.[6] Quite obviously, there is a complicated underlying procedure in the course of which the spontaneity of the people plays just as important a role as the propaganda by a government or a political organization and its promotion of certain symbols which usually follows later.[7]

This paper, a sort of case study, deals with the origin and application of national symbols in Ireland—a country with one of the most active and efficient European national movements in the 19th and early 20th centuries. It concentrates on the political symbols of the Irish Parliamentary Party, symbols which were primarily party symbols and not symbols of the Irish nation. Yet it is legitimate to equate the symbols of the Parliamentary Party—as a result of their widespread dissemination, their exclusiveness, and their recognition—with the national symbols of Ireland in the period from about 1875 to 1916. The symbols of the Parliamentary Party were the Irish national symbols for the five decades of the Home Rule Movement.

The analysis of the symbols of the Irish Parliamentary Party will be concerned with three questions: 1. Which symbols had the party, the most important representative of Irish nationalism before independence, at their disposal?; 2. Under which historical circumstances did the symbols of the party come into existence?; 3. To what extent did the symbols of the party promote political integration among the Irish people?

I

In much the same way as since the beginning of the 1880s Nationalists, i.e. followers of the Parliamentary Party, penetrated

---

[5] See Loewenstein, 'Influence', 71: 'The history of the revolutionary period since the first World War reveals clearly the unspontaneous, artificial, manufactured, and above all scientific character of processes and techniques of political symbolism.'

[6] Here Fehrenbach (302-3, 356-7) differentiates the thesis of Carlton Hayes according to which national symbols have developed from the secularizing of religious cults—a process which repeats itself in all nations and at the same time explains the universality of the nation-state symbolism (*Essays on Nationalism* (New York 1926, reissued 1966) 103, 107-9, 117).

[7] The history of the *Marseillaise,* the first national anthem, and the French tricolour are classic examples of this process (cf. Fehrenbach, 303-5).

into Irish local administration and the Boards of Guardians[8] a process of 'nationalization' took place on the level of political symbols with the creation of the Home Rule Movement. In Irish as in other European national movements, well-known symbols received a national meaning and new symbols were created. The national history, in particular, became the source for national symbols, especially the period of Henry Grattan and the United Irishmen, of Daniel O'Connell, the Young Irelanders, and the early Fenian movement. From among the comparatively large number of symbolic forms used since about 1875 only the most important ones will be discussed here: the flag of the Party, its anthem, the 'national festivals' which the Party espoused, the O'Connell monument in Dublin, and the phenomenon of a national nomenclature for streets, squares, and bridges.

THE FLAG

The green flag with or without a golden harp was undoubtedly the most popular symbol of the Home Rule Movement. Reports in the Irish newspapers of that period show that the flag was conspicuous at any nationalist meeting or demonstration. At demonstrations of the National League, the organization of the Party in Ireland since 1882, or of the Party itself it was carried by the crowd and the speaker's platforms were decorated with it. At visits of the Irish members of parliament and especially of the Party's chairman Charles S. Parnell, occasions which often took on the character of public festivals,[9] the population decorated the streets with the green flag. During the Dublin National Exhibition, organized by the Nationalists in August 1882, it commanded the city,[10] and during the visit of the Prince of Wales to Ireland in the spring of 1885 the green flag was displayed in competition with the Union Flag in many places as an expression of national sentiment.[11] After the founding of the Irish Volunteers in 1913 it was the flag of this semi-military organization which was closely connected with

[8] See my book, *Die irische Nationalbewegung zwischen Parlament und Revolution. Der konstitutionelle Nationalismus in Irland 1880-1918* (München-Wien 1971) 127-37.

[9] See e.g. the newspaper reports on Parnell's visits to Cork (*Cork Examiner*, 3/10/1881, and 23/1/1885).

[10] *Freeman's Journal* (henceforth FJ), 16/8/1882.

[11] Cf. the report on the arrival of the Prince of Wales at Dublin in *Cork Examiner* (henceforth CE), 9/4/1885.

the Parliamentary Party for a period of time.[12] And when John Redmond, the Party's chairman from 1900, in the autumn of 1915 visited the European Front, Irish soldiers paraded in front of him with 'the green flag of Ireland'.[13] But then, in the aftermath of 1916, the green flag disappeared and the tricolour flag of green, white and orange emerged as the national flag of the Irish Free State, an interesting process of change which will be discussed further below.

The terminology of the contemporary Irish press and the literature of the Parliamentary Party leaves no doubt that from about the end of the 1870s the Irish population identified the green flag of the Party with the national flag of Ireland. It was designated as 'the National banner', 'the National standard', 'the national colours', 'the Irish national flag' or 'Nationalist flag' or simply as 'the Irish flag'.[14] By these designations and the use of the green flag as a symbol of the Parliamentary Party the fact can become obscured that the green flag was not a creation of the Party, but was recognized much earlier as a symbol of Ireland and of Irish nationality. The Young Irelanders used it as well as the Fenians whose green flag often showed the harp in the middle of a sunburst.[15] Indeed the flag was used since the end of the 18th century by Irish nationalists. It is not fully clear whether it was first used by Henry Grattan around 1780 or by the United Irishmen around 1798.[16] The motivation for the selection of the green colour is not clear. Until the middle of the 18th century blue, 'St Patrick's Blue', was the colour associated with Ireland.[17] Presumably green was selected in analogy with the shamrock which around 1700 became the emblem of the Catholic Irish in reaction to the anti-Catholic laws of William (III) of Orange and his

[12] See J. Carty, *Ireland from the Great Famine to the Treaty (1851-1921). A documentary record* (Dublin 1951) 111, and F. X. Martin (ed.), *The Irish Volunteers 1913-15. Recollections and Documents* (Dublin 1963) 130.

[13] D. Gwynn, *The Life of John Redmond* (London 1932) 453.

[14] See *United Ireland* (henceforth UI), 12/12/1885, 6/10/1883, 8/2/1885; CE, 3/10/1881; FJ, 7/8/1880, and M. MacDonagh, *The Home Rule Movement* (Dublin and London 1920) 263.

[15] See D. Ryan. *The Fenian Chief. A Biography of James Stephens* (Dublin 1967) 260, and O. Snoddy, 'Fenian Flags', in *The Irish Sword* 8 (1967) 1.

[16] Cf. *Encyclopedia of Ireland* (Dublin 1968) 171 ('The Constitution: National Symbols').

[17] Ibid., 171, and S. Leslie, *The Irish Tangle* (London n.d.) 64 ('A Note on the Irish Flag').

successors on the British throne.[18] This motivation seems probable in view of the fact that during the 19th century, especially in Ulster, green was generally recognized as the colour of Catholic Ireland which was identified with nationalist Ireland. In the tricolour of the Irish Republic, too, green is to symbolize the Catholic portion of the population.[19] It is obvious that the reasons for the change from blue to green as Ireland's national colour, which seems to have taken place at the beginning of the 18th century, still require a more exact examination.

Since the United Irishmen the flag was combined with the harp, the oldest heraldic symbol of Ireland and from its origins a dynastic symbol. The problem of continuity in Irish symbolism cannot be dealt with in detail here, but it would surely be a rewarding task to trace the history of the harp as a symbol since its first appearance and to show more specifically its connection with medieval Irish symbolism. It is quite certain, however, that the heraldic use of the harp can be traced back into the 16th century. During the reign of Henry VIII, who proclaimed himself king of Ireland in 1541, the harp appeared on coinage for the first time, and since 1603, with the accession of James I to the throne, it is also to be found in the Royal Standard as also in the flag of the Confederation of Kilkenny.[20] These official uses of the harp as symbol of Ireland find their continuation in the 19th century: for example, the standard of the Lord Lieutenant shows the Union Flag with a golden harp on a blue shield in the centre.[21] After 1801, in the Royal Standard the harp continues to appear in the third quarter.[22] The harp, therefore, is the only Irish symbol of the 19th century with a twofold function: it serves as dynastic symbol and at the same time as a symbol of constitutional nationalism.

Although the Union Flag, since 1801, contained an Irish symbol with the incorporation of the Cross of St Patrick it was not accepted

[18] Cf. G.-D. Zimmermann, *Songs of Irish Rebellion. Political Street Ballads and Rebel Songs 1780-1900* (Dublin 1967) 43. According to the legend St Patrick explained the nature of the Holy Trinity to the Irish by using the shamrock.

[19] *Encyclopedia of Ireland,* 171, and G. Campbell and J. O. Evans, *The Book of Flags* (London ⁵1965) 20.

[20] Leslie, 64. According to Campbell and Evans (8) the harp as the heraldic symbol of Ireland had been chosen by Henry VIII.

[21] E. MacGeorge, *Flags: Some account of their history* (London 1881) 71. Cf. also the Arms of the Republic of Ireland.

[22] Campbell and Evans, 9.

in Ireland during the Union as a flag of unity, representing the entire nation, which it, strictly speaking, originally was not intended to be,[23] but as the flag of a definite portion of the population.[24] The exhibition of the Union Flag meant, especially in the second half of the 19th century, the expression of Unionist and Protestant sentiment. The increasing gravity of the internal conflict in Ireland between Nationalist Catholics and Protestant Unionists since the turn of the century, in particular, caused the Union Flag to lose all power of integration in the sense of the concept of a more or less politically homogeneous United Kingdom. It was regarded, instead, as the symbol for a political attitude which was diametrically opposed to the nationalism of the vast majority of the Irish population.

THE ANTHEM

With much more justification than in the case of the flag the unofficial Irish 'national anthem' from 1880 until 1916, 'God save Ireland', can be viewed as a creation of the Parliamentary Party. The author of this song, which was sung to the melody of a then well-known American march, was Timothy D. Sullivan, editor of the famous Irish paper *The Nation*.[25] Along with 'God save Ireland' he published a series of popular songs with subjects taken from Irish history which caused him to be the most widely known Irish poet of this type of song in the second half of the 19th century.[26] He was the man who, according to a nationalist clergyman, 'gave to the Irish nation the national watchword, the symbol of their hopes and aspirations'.[27]

'God save Ireland' originated from an episode in the history of the Fenian movement. The song praises revolutionary nationalism, and according to Owen D. Edwards brought 'many to an unconscious acceptance of the justifiability of insurrection'. [28] In its four ballad-

[23] Ibid., 17: 'When the present design was made official in 1801, it was ordered to be flown on all His Majesty's forts, castles, etc.—and not by His Majesty's subjects.'' Cf. also E. M. C. Barraclough, *Flags of the World* (London and New York [2]1965) 43.

[24] Leslie, 65.

[25] T. D. Sullivan (1827-1914), Lord Mayor of Dublin in 1886 and 1887, MP since 1880.

[26] Cf. Zimmermann, 60, note 4, and P. S. O'Hegarty, *A history of Ireland under the Union, 1801-1922* (London 1952) 411.

[27] CE, 31/1/1885.

[28] O. D. Edwards et al., *Celtic Nationalism* (London 1968) 173. For the text see Zimmermann, 266-7, and P. Rose, *The Manchester Martyrs. The story of a Fenian tragedy* (London 1970) 130.

like verses the execution of the three Fenians William Philip Allen, Michael Larkin, and Michael O'Brien by the British is described. The so-called Manchester Martyrs had been found guilty of killing a policeman in 1867 in the attempt to free Fenians from a prison van.[29] Their last words from the scaffold were used several days later by T. D. Sullivan as the title for his song which, according to him, within a very short time had spread all over Ireland and forced into the background the most popular national songs until that time, 'A Nation once again' written by the Young Irelander Thomas Davis, and 'The Wearing of the Green', a song which had originated around 1800.[30] At about 1875 'God save Ireland' was already *the* national song of the Home Rulers,[31] and in the nationalist press of the 1880s it is unequivocally designated 'the anthem', 'the National Anthem', or 'the Irish national Anthem'.[32] The *Annual Register* also recognized this quality of 'God save Ireland',[33] and even the Royal Irish Constabulary described Sullivan as 'the author of what is known as the "Irish National Anthem"'.[34] Next to the green flag 'God save Ireland' was the best known and most popular symbol of the Parliamentary Party.

The song was sung until 1916 at every occasion on which the Irish gathered, no matter what the reason, not only in Ireland but also in America and other Irish settlements abroad.[35] Until 1916, which represents a definite break in the history of Irish political symbolism still to be discussed, political and social gatherings were concluded with the singing of 'God save Ireland'. Victories of nationalist candidates in parliamentary or municipal elections were celebrated with demonstrations and the singing of the 'national anthem'.[36] At demonstrations and meetings of the National League 'God save Ireland' belonged along with the green flag to the self-evident

[29] For the details see P. Rose, op. cit., and E. R. Norman, *The Catholic church and Ireland in the age of rebellion 1859-1873* (London 1965) 119-26.

[30] As to the origin of the song which was published on 7 Dec. 1867 in *The Nation* cf. T. D. Sullivan, *Recollections of troubled times in Irish politics* (Dublin 1905) 177-80.

[31] Cf. F. H. O'Donnell, *A History of the Irish parliamentary party*, i (London 1910) 137.

[32] Cf. UI, 1/12/1883, 1/3/1884, 5/12/1886; CE, 13/4/1885, 24/11/1885.

[33] *Annual Register* 1887, 201.

[34] State Paper Office, Dublin, Police Reports 1886-1915: List of Nationalist Members of Parliament and detailed Biographical Notes, 1887.

[35] Cf. Sullivan, 179; O'Hegarty, 457, and T. P. O'Connor, *The Parnell movement with a sketch of Irish parties from 1843* (London ²1886) 202.

[36] See, for instance, UI 5/12/1886, and CE 30/11/1885.

requisites. The eviction of tenants by the Royal Irish Constabulary was accompanied by the crowd of spectators with the singing of 'God save Ireland' and other 'popular songs'.[37] Demonstrations against the British government included the singing of 'the anthem' in front of the gates of Dublin Castle,[38] the seat of the Irish executive, or during the visit of the Prince of Wales in Ireland. But when at the arrival of the Prince at Mallow the band struck up 'God save Ireland' the nationalist press spoke of 'occurrences . . . of deplorable character' because such a reception lacked the 'respectful reserve and neutrality' which Parnell had recommended.[39] Moreover, the words 'God save Ireland' were used as the nationalist rallying cry which appeared on posters and in newspaper advertisements of the National League. They could be found on banners and flags and with them nationalist speakers concluded their speeches. Since the 1880s, in Ireland and in Irish circles abroad, but also among the Irish Members of Parliament in Westminster, 'God save Ireland' replaced 'God save the Queen' as a toast in order constantly to demonstrate that Ireland did not recognize the forced Union of 1801.

THE NATIONAL FESTIVALS

The executions of the three Fenians on 23 November 1867 at Salford Prison, Manchester, led to one of the two Irish national holidays at that time. Along with the traditional festival of St Patrick's Day the 23rd of November was used by the Nationalists to commemorate the Manchester Martyrs who were glorified by the populace and the Parliamentary Party,[40] because—as described in the nationalist terminology—they had sacrificed their lives for Irish freedom 'with the prayer on their lips of "God save Ireland".'[41] According to the reports in the newspapers and the police files both holidays were celebrated with large participation of the population well into the 1890s,[42] while the state celebrations and anniversaries were ignored by the Irish Nationalists and

[37] UI, 20/8/1881.
[38] Ibid., 19/8/1882.
[39] CE, 14/4/1885. Cf. also *Annual Register* 1885, 198-9.
[40] Cf. K. Loewenstein ('Influence', 76): 'The greatest emotional value is attached to martyrs who have suffered persecution or died for the "cause". No revolutionary movement passes up the opportunity to make use of a convenient martyrology. Where martyrs do not exist they are invented or made.'
[41] John Redmond in Cork (CE, 22/11/1882).
[42] Cf.e .g. State Paper Office, Dublin, Crime Branch Special, Divisional Commissioners' Reports (S. W. Division), Report of Dec. 1894.

often used for counter-demonstrations in the form of rallies and the displaying of national symbols.[43]

The manner in which the two memorial days of the Nationalists were celebrated shows certain differences. The memorial day of the Manchester Martyrs was celebrated in the 1880s, just as earlier, with torchlight processions in most of the provincial towns and larger villages which usually ended in the cemetery where memorial crosses were erected for the executed and memorial speeches were held. Green and black flags were carried by the crowd. In the cities memorial masses were held in the churches in addition to the processions and speeches.[44] When public demonstrations occasionally were cancelled as, for example, in Cork in 1885 at least some sort of celebration took place in an assembly-hall in the town.[45] The processions and celebrations were usually organized by the local branches of the National League. The direct participation of the Party was less evident, and no central celebration was held to complement the local gatherings.

Such a central celebration of the Parliamentary Party formed the high point of St Patrick's Day, the 'national festival', which was not a festival inspired by the Party because the custom to celebrate it was much older but which was given a political accent by it. This celebration took place in London, necessitated by the session of the House of Commons. Almost always all the Irish Members of Parliament participated in it. Parnell or one of the other leading representatives of the Party made a political speech in which the national aims of the Party were dealt with.[46] In Ireland processions, masses, and celebrations took place, but generally they did not attain the proportion and large participation of the population as was to be observed on the memorial day for the Manchester Martyrs. These gatherings exhausted themselves by and large in the demonstration of national

[43] On the occasion of the coronation of George V the Party declared: 'Ever since the foundation of the United Irish Party under the leadership of Parnell, it has been the settled practice and rule of the party to stand aloof from all Royal or imperial festivities or ceremonies, participation in which might be taken as a proof that Ireland was satisfied with or acquiesced willingly in the system under which, since the Union, she had been compelled to live' (L. G. Redmond-Howard, *John Redmond. The man and the demand* (London ²1912) 248).

[44] Examples: UI, 25/11/1882 and 1/12/1883. Cf. also the numerous 'Ballads of the Manchester Martyrs' which originated in the time to come (printed in Rose, op. cit. 129-135).

[45] CE, 25/11/1885.

[46] Cf. e.g. CE, 18/3/1882, 18/3/1885, 18/3/1886.

symbols,[47] especially the shamrock which was also recognized as a 'national emblem'.[48] The shamrock was 'the emblem of faith and nationality',[49] thus indicating that on St Patrick's Day national and religious feelings were united in a remarkable way. The Party which conceived itself as the representative of the *entire* Irish people saw this claim often threatened by the one-sided accentuation of the sectarian element on St Patrick's Day. Parnell, for example, deemed himself obliged in 1886 to write an open letter offering 'a word of advice and warning'. In this letter he wrote: 'It is at all times desirable that we should do nothing at any time to excite the irritation of the Orange section of our countrymen.'[50] Such a danger existed especially in Ulster with its strong Protestant-Unionist population.

THE O'CONNELL MONUMENT

The close interlocking of the national and the sectarian element which became apparent at St Patrick's Day celebrations can also be seen in its early stages in the erection of the monumental statue for Daniel O'Connell in Dublin. The preparations for the erection of a 'National Monument' for the 'Liberator', that is to say for the man who had won Catholic emancipation, not for the man who had demanded repeal of the Union, were underway since 1862. But it needed the efforts of the Parliamentary Party to achieve the completion of the statue on the occasion of the 100th anniversary of the day Grattan's Parliament was constituted which had proclaimed 'the birth of Irish freedom'.[51]

The initiative to build a monument for Daniel O'Connell in the centre of the city which was to be financed by the Irish people emanated from the then proprietor of the *Freeman's Journal*, Sir John Gray.[52] 'A National Monument', as was resolved by the *O'Connell Monument Committee* which was founded on 13 October 1862, representing Dublin liberal citizens and Catholic clergymen, 'to commemorate the services of O'Connell as the advocate of civil and religious liberty, and as the emancipator of the Catholic people

[47] Occasionally portraits of leading MPs were borne in the processions (see e.g. CE, 18/3/1882).

[48] CE, 18/3/1885.

[49] Ibid., 18/3/1882.

[50] Ibid., 16/3/1886.

[51] UI, 19/8/1882.

[52] J. O'Hanlon (ed.), *Report of the O'Connell Monument Committee* (Dublin 1888) xii.

of this realm, may be erected in the metropolis of his native land'.[53]
This resolution made plain that O'Connell's work for the repeal of
the Union was being ignored by the committee members. This veiling
of the historical reality did not remain without contradiction already
in 1862: the archbishop of Tuam, John MacHale, pointed to the
inadmissibility of the manipulation of historical truth by 'honouring
the Emancipator only and ignoring the Repealer'.[54] The curious
cleavage of the historical figure of Daniel O'Connell was a phenomenon which could be observed until Parnell's time: the picture of the
Liberator, resting on his work for Catholic emancipation, overshadowed that of the Nationalist and Repealer. It was not until
Parnell became the chairman of the Parliamentary Party that a
reversal of this interpretation was achieved. Now the party tried to
overcome the onesided emphasis on the emancipation aspect in the
political career of O'Connell by emphasizing his universal significance
for Irish nationalism.

The work on the memorial dragged out over almost twenty years.
The generous contributions by the Irish people made possible the
laying of the foundation-stone in August 1864,[55] but thereafter the
work came to a standstill for a couple of years. The planned unveiling
of the monument on the occasion of O'Connell's 100th birthday had
to be postponed. Not until 1879 did the work continue at a more
rapid pace.[56] In the spring of 1882 the Committee decided, under
the pressure of the Dublin Lord Mayor Charles Dawson, to have
the unveiling take place in conjunction with the National Exhibition
inspired by Dawson and other Nationalists,[57] which was to serve
the 'encouragement of Irish, in preference to British and foreign
manufacture'.[58] The Exhibition was opened on 15 August 1882, in a
large setting but without the participation of representatives of the
Irish government.

[53] T. D. Sullivan, *A. M. Sullivan. A memoir* (Dublin 1885) 88.
[54] Ibid.
[55] O'Hanlon, xlii.—In the period from 22 Sept. 1862, when the first call for
contributions was published in *The Freeman's Journal,* until 30 Oct. 1865, the
Irish people collected the large sum of almost 10,000 Pound Sterling which
consisted largely of very small contributions (cf. the subscription lists in O'Hanlon
1-146 and 149). Unfortunately the subscription lists do not contain the social
status of the contributors. If they had, they would have been a valuable source on
the social structure of the national movement.
[56] Cf. FJ, 21/6/1880.
[57] O'Hanlon, lxvii.
[58] Quoted in M. McCarthy, *The Irish revolution* (Edinburgh and London 1912)
189. For the history leading to the exhibition: *Annual Register* 1882, 192-3.

In contrast to 1862, the speeches which were held during the unveiling of the National Monument in the presence of numerous provincial mayors, town commissioners, aldermen, the bishops and clergy, the Irish Members of Parliament, the trades, and the delegations from all parts of the country,[59] make evident a definite shift in accent. On this occasion again one was reminded that the monument was erected 'in honour of O'Connell, the Liberator of his own people from penal chains",[60] but in the speeches of Parnell and other speakers the attempt is obvious to place the emphasis, with a glimpse at the 100th anniversary of the first independent Irish parliament, on the general meaning of O'Connell as an Irish nationalist.[61] 'In 1882, shall we forget the dream of Grattan', the Lord Mayor Charles Dawson asked, 'the first and the last love of O'Connell, the desire of the nation—our native legislature?'[62] And Parnell declared: 'The most endearing monument that we can erect to O'Connell is to strive to gain the ends to which he devoted his great life.'[63] In this vein the nationalist newspapers commented, too, so *The Cork Examiner,* when it wrote: 'The O'Connell Monument . . . is the symbol of the desire for legislative independence which is as strong today in the heart of the people as it was in the palmiest hours of the Repeal Association.'[64]

Behind these efforts to create a sort of O'Connell myth the unmistakable idea becomes apparent of making O'Connell the symbol of Irish nationality and Irish aspirations for autonomy. The Dublin monument is the most important expression of this intention, but it finds its continuation in the process of naming streets, squares, and bridges after O'Connell, a procedure which runs parallel to the penetration of Nationalists into the organizations of the Irish local administration.[65]

O'CONNELL STREET, DUBLIN

The name of O'Connell was to integrate the Irish nation and help to accomplish the identification of all Irishmen with the demands of

[59] See FJ and CE, 16/8/1882, and O'Hanlon, lxxii.

[60] See E. D. Gray as speaker of the O'Connell Monument Committee (FJ, 16/8/1882).

[61] Cf. the speeches of Parnell, Dawson, and O'Hanlon (FJ, 16/8/1882; UI, 19/8/1882).

[62] FJ, 16/8/1882.

[63] Ibid.

[64] CE, 16/8/1882.

[65] Compare with my book: *Die irische Nationalbewegung,* 127-37.

the Parliamentary Party. But the question remains as to what extent
the Party was conscious of the problem of such a national-
educational venture because the integrational effect of the name
O'Connell was limited to the Catholic Irish alone while the Protestants must have felt excluded from the outset. The Protestant portion
of the population, especially in Ulster, but also in Dublin, could
hardly be stirred by the name of O'Connell because his name, in
spite of all the Party's attempts to make him a central symbol of
national identification, stood foremost for the emancipation of the
Catholics. The anti-nationalist Protestants, for this reason, opposed
the advancement of an O'Connell myth. A good example of the
limited power of integration of the name of O'Connell can be found
in the stubborn resistance of the wealthy Protestant citizens of
Dublin who persistently refused to accept the renaming of the most
important street of the city, which was named after a Lord Lieutenant
of the 18th century, from *Sackville Street* to *O'Connell Street*.

This renaming was concluded by the Dublin Corporation with a
considerable majority in December 1884 with the explanation that
'the names of the thoroughfares of the chief cities of a nation should
be such as to recall events in its history and progress deserving
commendation'.[66] Some of the influential residents of the street had
recourse to the courts against this decision because from their viewpoint the renaming 'would cause them inconvenience, and considerable injury and loss of business'.[67] This somewhat superficial
argumentation was upheld by the courts,[68] so that the street had no
generally accepted name for over thirty years: the Nationalists named
it *O'Connell Street*,[69] whereas the Protestant citizens and the Unionists
held onto *Sackville Street*.[70] While, for example, the Party gave the
address of the Hibernian Bank where they had an account in their
papers as *O'Connell Street* the bank continued to use the designation *Sackville Street* on their commercial papers.[71] Similar double
designations of the street on other occasions can be found in large
numbers. Henceforth, the designation of the street as either *Sackville
Street* or *O'Connell Street* was able to give information as to the
political attitude of individual Irishmen. Still in 1916 the Unionists

[66] UI, 13/12/1884. See also *Annual Register* 1884, 47 (Chronicle).
[67] CE, 9/1/1885.
[68] J. Harvey, *Dublin. A study in environment* (London and New York 1949) 37.
[69] Cf. CE, 17/10/1885: 'O'Connell Street, Dublin—the new name . . . is, by
the way, now almost generally adopted.'
[70] Cf. McCarthy, *Irish revolution,* 364.
[71] See J. F. X. O'Brien Papers, MS. 9236 (National Library of Ireland).

continued to speak of *Sackville Street* just as they held on to the designation *Carlisle Bridge* for the bridge which crosses the Liffey at the lower end of *O'Connell Street*. The renaming of the bridge as *O'Connell Bridge* had been concluded by the Dublin Corporation under the Lord Mayor E. D. Gray in the early summer of 1880 when the old bridge, also named after a Lord Lieutenant, had been replaced by a new construction.[72] In this case, too, the Nationalists met with resistance. The refusal of the Dublin Port and Docks Board to remove the old tablets with the inscription *Carlisle Bridge* could not be overcome until after an inquiry of the Irish MP and later Lord Mayor Charles Dawson in the House of Commons.[73]

The process of 'nationalization' on the level of nomenclature, here more or less allusively described, took place, in conjunction with the progressive change of the majorities in the town councils all over Ireland in the 1880s. The old names of streets and squares, especially when they carried a definite English designation, were replaced by 'national' designations. In Dublin, in addition to *O'Connell Street,* numerous minor streets were given the names of figures from Irish history.[74] In the provincial towns bridges, streets, and squares were named first of all after Parnell and O'Connell. The process of 'nationalization' was extended in Dublin also to the designing of the city flag, and the accompanying circumstances should be mentioned here because they give, in a very picturesque manner, some of the atmosphere in which the conflict between Nationalists and Unionists took place at that time. Because, in 1885, the Lord Mayor of Dublin had publicly declared that he would haul down the city flag from the Mansion House at the impending visit of the Prince of Wales, the flag was carried off by students of Trinity College with the intention of preventing its demonstrative hauling down by the Nationalists and of carrying it instead in procession at the entrance of the Prince into the city.[75] The disappearance of the old flag, which showed three white castles on a blue background, was now used by the nationalist Corporation for designing a new flag because, after some perplexity, according to the *Annual Register*

[72] Cf. FJ, 21/6/1880; McCarthy, *Irish revolution,* 280, and O'Hanlon, lxvi. The official renaming took place on 6 Aug. 1880.

[73] FJ, 10/8/1880.

[74] Cf. McCarthy, 364: 'The titles of the Dublin streets illustrate the continuous loyalty of its Corporation to the English connection until the arrival of Parnell, being almost a complete index to the Lord Lieutenants.'

[75] *Annual Register* 1885, 197, and CE, 25/3/1885.

they came to the conclusion that 'out of evil cometh good'.[76] The new flag was 'a combination of National and civic emblems by exhibiting a harp on a green ground, and displaying in one quarter three white castles'.[77]

II

The types of symbols dealt with here possessed by and large unrestricted validity until the Easter Rising. Some older symbols began to earn new meaning from the turn of the century, such as the favourite song of the Sinn Féin movement 'A Nation once again', but that was simply a marginal phenomenon in the years before 1916.[78] How strong and unbroken the attraction of the Party symbols still were is demonstrated by the example of the Irish labour movement whose semi-military organization, the Citizen Army, hoisted in a ceremony, which has been the source of much discussion since then, the green flag with the harp as 'the sacred emblem of Ireland's unconquered soul' on top of Liberty Hall, the headquarters of the Irish Transport and General Workers' Union, just a week before the Rising.[79]

With the Rising of 1916 a break took place in national symbolism which was most visibly manifested in the national flag and the anthem which the young Irish nation accepted. The demise of the Parliamentary Party stands in direct parallel to the just as rapidly diminishing power of its symbols. The green flag and 'God save Ireland' began to be discredited as symbols of constitutional nationalism and, instead, the symbols of revolutionary nationalism gained popularity as the majority of the Irish people identified itself with the political aims of the Easter revolutionaries.[80] The use of symbols made apparent that the occurrences of 1916 initiated a new epoch in Irish history much in the same way as the Union of 1801 and the Famine of 1845-8 did.

Both the national flag and the national anthem of present-day Ireland derive origins directly from the Rising. At first it still

[76] *Annual Register* 1885, 197.

[77] FJ, 27/5/1885. Cf. also *Annual Register* 1885, 197-8, and UI, 30/5/1885.

[78] Cf. M. Freund, 'Die Nationalhymnen der Irländer', in *Die Neueren Sprachen* 27 (1919-20) 46.

[79] *Irish Times*, 17/4/1916, and D. Ryan, *The Rising. The Complete Story of Easter Week* (Dublin ⁴1966) 76. Cf. also C. D. Graves, *The Life and Times of James Connolly* (London 1961) 323, and R. M. Fox, *Green Banners. The Story of the Irish Struggle* (London 1938) 191.

[80] Cf. *An Bhratach Náisiúnta* (*The National Flag*) (Baile átha Cliath n.d.) 7.

appeared as if the revolutionaries would take over the old symbols because on the roof of the their headquarters, the Dublin General Post Office, a green flag with the harp was hoisted next to the republican tricolour although with the inscription 'Irish Republic'.[81] Even 'God save Ireland' was sung by the revolutionaries during Easter week.[82] But after the failure of the Rising and the subsequent executions of the leading revolutionaries the tricolour and 'The Soldier's Song' became more and more popular as symbols of the rebellion. 'Tricolour badges', it is said in an eyewitness report from the autumn of 1916, 'were worn on coats, caps, and hats; songs were whistled and sung. "The Soldier's Song" began to be known; soon one could hear it in the streets.'[83]

The republican tricolour, a revolutionary symbol and unequivocally modelled after the French example, consists of the colours green, white and orange whereby the green is said to represent the Catholic and the orange the Protestant section of the population while the white is to stand for 'a lasting truce' between the two denominations.[84] The origin of the tricolour is generally dated to the year 1848 when it was presented by a delegation of Young Irelanders to the citizens of Dublin after their return from Paris where they had conveyed the congratulations of the Irish people to the newly established republican government in France.[85] But it must be doubted whether the Irish tricolour is a creation of the Young Irelanders because it can be proved that it was used earlier. Documentary evidence indicates that the tricolour was known as early as 1830,[86] and Michael Toibin offers convincing evidence that the tricolour was displayed by the insurgents, at least in county Wexford,

---

[81] Cf. the eyewitness reports in R. McHugh (ed.), *Dublin 1916* (London 1966) 68, 87, 126, 159.

[82] Zimmermann, 68.

[83] Quoted in McHugh, 139-40. Cf. also L. O Broin, *The Chief Secretary. Augustine Birrell in Ireland* (London 1969) 190. The tricolour had been used as the national flag since then, but its official recognition as such was first anchored in the constitution of 1937 (Art. 7), cf. *An Bhratach,* 7.

[84] *Encyclopedia of Ireland,* 171. Cf. also Campbell and Evans, 20. According to the Protestant interpretation the orange is derived from William of Orange, King of England since 1689.

[85] T. F. O'Sullivan, *The Young Irelanders* (Tralee 1944) 78, 81, 200, and J. D. O'Donnell, *How Ireland is governed* (Dublin 1965) 150 (Appendix F: 'History of the National Flag', (150-52). See also R. Kee, *The Green Flag. A history of Irish nationalism* (London 1972) 265.

[86] P. O'Connor, 'The National Flag', in *An Consantóir. The Irish Defence Journal* 6 (1946) 141.

as early as 1798.[87] Since then it was looked upon as the symbol of revolution and after its short emergence in 1848 it appeared to find wide acceptance first at the beginning of the twentieth century as a symbol now frequently used by the Sinn Féin movement and—since 1913—by the Irish Volunteers which under the influence of Sinn Féin had split from the National Volunteers closely associated with the Parliamentary Party.[88]

The new national anthem, 'The Soldier's Song', was much younger. Its historical origin as a march and revolutionary song shows definite parallels to the origin of the *Marseillaise*.[89] Although 'The Soldier's Song' had already come into existence in 1907 and had been published in *Irish Freedom*, the journal of the I.R.B., in September 1912,[90] the song was known before 1916 only as a marching song of the Irish Volunteers and the Citizen Army.[91] As, however, numerous Volunteers and members of the Citizen Army belonged to the revolutionaries it became popular with the insurrection, so that by the end of 1916 it was 'the *de facto* National Anthem of Ireland'.[92] In July 1926 'The Soldier's Song' was made the official national anthem of the Irish Free State by government decree.[93]

III

This survey of Irish national symbols between 1875 and 1921 allows for some concluding remarks:

It emerges from the enumeration of Irish symbols that during the period in which the Parliamentary Party was the country's most important national organization Ireland already possessed the entire series of symbols which were to be found in all European nation-states with an astonishing similarity of form and use. Almost forty years before the achievement of national independence all the

[87] 'Enniscorthy and the National Flag', in *The Past* 7 (1964) 145, 148.

[88] *Encyclopedia of Ireland*, 171, and O'Donnell, 151. Some documents which give evidence to the use of the tricolour by the Fenians, especially after 1867, can be found in Snoddy, 'Fenian Flags', 9.

[89] For the origin of the *Marseillaise* cf. Fehrenbach, 303-9.

[90] Zimmermann, 68; S. de Burca, *The Soldier's Song* (Dublin 1957) 52-5, and P. Kearney, *The Soldier's Song and other poems* (Dublin 1928). The text was written by Peadar Kearney (1883-1942) and the melody by Patrick Heeney (1881-1911). Both were members of the Gaelic League.

[91] De Burca, 54, and O'Donnell, 153.

[92] De Burca, 55, and O'Donnell, 153.

[93] *Encyclopedia of Ireland*, 172; O'Donnell, 153, and P. Nettl, *National Anthems* (New York ²1967) 106.

typical symbols of the nation-state can be found in Ireland, especially
the four well-known basic elements of national symbolism created
by the French Revolution: the national flag, 'nationalism's chief
symbol of faith and central object of worship',[94] the national anthem
which replaced the traditional royal hymn or, at least, moved into
a competitive situation with it, the national holiday as 'nationalism's
holy day' according to the thesis of Carlton Hayes of 'nationalism
as a religion',[95] and lastly the national monument from which —
as Th. Nipperdey rightly stresses[96]—a constant initiative to win
and strengthen the national identity should emanate. The detailed
reports in the contemporary Irish press of the national agitation and
national gatherings in Ireland clearly demonstrate that these symbols
play an important, but much disregarded role in the history of Irish
nationalism and that they, analogously to the circumstances in other
national movements, received a meaning as factors of political
integration which can hardly be overestimated even though they are
very difficult to measure.

The example of Ireland demonstrates that national symbols
are not static, at least not in the politically instable period of a
national awakening which usually stretches over several decades,
but that they are, to a certain degree, capable of change. Established
national symbols can, under certain circumstances, even be replaced
by other national symbols. Traditional national symbols lose their
political integrating force and their credibility especially when the
national programme for which they stand loses its persuasive power
and is replaced by a different programme.[97] In the case of Ireland
investigated here this means more tangibly that certain symbols were
identified quite unmistakably with the Parliamentary Party and its
politics. When after the Easter Rising revolutionary nationalism
superseded constitutional nationalism new forms of symbols were
the logical result which, at the outset, competed with those of constitutional nationalism and finally superimposed themselves. The
favourable prerequisite for such a process of supersession is a
revolutionary situation, but it can also be observed very clearly in

[94] Hayes, *Essays on nationalism,* 107.

[95] Ibid., 108.

[96] Th. Nipperdey, 'Nationalidee und Nationaldenkmal in Deutschland im 19.
Jahrhundert', in *Historische Zeitschrift* 206 (1968) 582.

[97] This confirms Loewenstein's statement 'that no major political revolution
has ever been accomplished without a change in the set of political symbols'
('Influence', 80).

Ireland how this process had already gradually started around the turn of the century. Those symbols were excepted from the process which more or less did not stand immediately for a definite pattern of Irish nationalism. Several 'superior' national symbols, such as the harp, the colour green, St Patrick's Day, and the shamrock, retained their significance in the Free State while at the same time 'God save Ireland', the green flag with the harp, or the memorial day for the Manchester Martyrs disappeared almost completely. It was not until the conclusion of the national-revolutionary process that the symbols consolidated. Then, dynamic and revolutionary symbols—according to the classification of Karl Loewenstein[98]—became static and traditional symbols. There is, after all, no example in the history of European national movements for a replacement of national symbols after the achievement of national independence without a simultaneous and fundamental political upheaval.

The Irish national symbols can be divided into two categories. On the one hand, there are symbols which have long possessed a national meaning and which were taken up by the Parliamentary Party, were changed, given other meanings, and utilised to convey a particular interpretation of the history of the country. To this group belonged the green flag, the shamrock, and St Patrick's Day. Included in this group must be also those symbols whose spontaneous creation can still be traced back in detail and which were taken over at a later time by constitutional nationalism (e.g. 'God save Ireland', the memorial day for the Manchester Martyrs). After the turn of the century, for the revolutionary line of Irish nationalism, the procedure of taking over already known symbols can be similarly demonstrated by tracing the history of the Irish tricolour and the national anthem of the Free State. In addition, and this is the second category, there are several symbols in Ireland which, for the most part, can be looked upon as proper creations of constitutional nationalism. These symbols were knowingly composed and propagated by the Parliamentary Party. They are the expression of an attempt to place new symbols at the service of a certain national idea. In this category we may count the efforts of the Party to create an O'Connell myth, the renaming of streets, bridges, and squares after figures from Irish history, the creation of a new city flag for Dublin as well as, though with some qualified limitations, the erection of the O'Connell Monument in Dublin and similar monuments in other parts of the

[98] Ibid., 67.

country.[99] In any event, here one can recognize rudimentarily the predecessors and transitions to the later use of symbols in totalitarian states. It would be a rewarding undertaking of historical research to illuminate more closely, with the use of comparative methods, the creation and the history of these symbols of European nationalism which are perhaps less the result of the spontaneous reaction of the populace than the consequence of propaganda from above.

[99] It would be worthwhile to investigate the erection of the Parnell Monument in Dublin. The movement for this monument got under way in the autumn of 1898 on the initiative of the Parliamentary Party. The foundation-stone was laid a year later, and the monument was unveiled in 1911. Some useful information on its erection can be found in: *Souvenir of the Unveiling of the Parnell National Monument. Dublin, 1st October, 1911* (Dublin 1911).

2

PATRIOTISM AS PASTIME: THE APPEAL OF
FENIANISM IN THE MID-1860s
R.V. COMERFORD

There is general acceptance in recent writings that fenianism in its heyday — which is to say the middle 1860s — was espoused predominantly by members of lower-ranking social and occupational groups. It is not difficult to assemble supporting references and texts from well-placed contemporary observers. T. D. Sullivan writing privately to Thomas D'Arcy McGee in 1862 described the active but still anonymous organisation subsequently known as the 'I.R.B.' or the 'fenians' as drawing the bulk of its membership from among 'shopkeepers' assistants in our cities and chief towns who have a little smattering — often a very little indeed — of education', and from 'the very poorest and most ignorant people'.[1] By 1865 the term 'fenianism' was in extensive use and the thing itself was receiving widespread attention. Writing his diary for 26 June that year, W. J. O'Neill Daunt expressed the opinion that in his part of County Cork those implicated in fenian activities were 'country lads' and 'town shop-boys'.[2] At the same time, the mounting pile of constabulary reports from around the country provided more and more references to the infection of specific categories by fenianism: in one area, shopboys, artisans, servants and reduced farmers; in another, 'young men of the labouring class and also mechanics or tradesmen such as tailors, nailors, shoemakers'; elsewhere, subordinate employees on the railway. Less specifically, an alarmed detective visiting the Thurles area reported that the 'lower orders' thereabouts were fenians virtually to a man.[3] Cardinal Cullen believed that the fenians were mostly impoverished tradesmen.[4]

John O'Leary, one of the I.R.B. leaders, conceded the general point, however reluctantly, in his published recollections.[5] In private O'Leary was, apparently, more blunt. Returning to prison from a court appearance, after he had been arrested with most of the other fenian leaders in September 1865, O'Leary commented to his companion in the police van, Thomas Clarke Luby, on the social composition of their movement, expressing

[1]Sullivan to D'Arcy McGee, 18 Feb. 1862 (Ottawa, Public Archives of Canada, MG27. 1.E9).

[2]Journal of W. J. O'Neill Daunt, 26 June 1865 (N.L.I., MS 3041).

[3]Constabulary reports, 30 Aug., 1 and 6 Sept., 25 Oct. 1865 (S.P.O., fenian police reports, 1864-5, nos. 208, 214, 223, 239). All S.P.O. records referred to in this article belong to the 'fenian papers' section of the 'police and crime' division.

[4]Cullen to Tobias Kirby, 8 Mar. 1867 (P. J. Corish, 'Irish College, Rome: Kirby papers; guide to material of public and political interest, 1862-83' in *Arch. Hib.,* xxx (1972), p. 55).

[5]John O'Leary, *Recollections of fenians and fenianism* (2 vols, London, 1896), ii, 239.

disappointment that their men 'belonged so much to the riff-raff'. Or so Luby reminded him many years later.[6]

Scientific-minded curiosity for more precise and accurate information led to Dublin Castle officials being requested early in 1870 to establish on a statistical basis what were 'the classes amongst which fenianism prevailed'.[7] There was to hand among the records of the government's handling of fenianism a particularly good source for the information sought, namely the three volumes of 'Habeas corpus suspension act, abstracts of cases, 1866-8'.

The arrest of the fenian leadership in 1865 had left the movement largely unharmed, and with the escape of the chief conspirator, James Stephens, from Richmond Jail in November the government's *coup* had come to appear totally ineffective. More drastic measures were needed. In February 1866 an act was passed suspending the application of habeas corpus in Ireland so that persons could be lawfully arrested and held by the authorities on warrant of the lord lieutenant.[8] This enabled the police to arrest and detain known fenians, especially those against whom they did not have evidence of a kind that would support a criminal prosecution. Just over eleven hundred were arrested under the terms of the act, the great majority of them in 1866 and 1867 and the remainder in 1868. In Dublin Castle, where they were referred to as the 'H.C.S.A. prisoners', abstracts from the information filed on each of them were compiled in two volumes with an alphabetical index in a third.[9] Excluded were most of those fenians taken before the courts, such as the movement's small middle-class intellectual élite (the majority of whom were arrested in 1865) and the prominent Irish-American military men captured after the attempted rising of March 1867. That only served to make the list more representative of the generality of fenians. So did the exclusion of serving members of the crown forces, a marginal and not very typical element in fenianism whose importance has been exaggerated because John Devoy was involved with them.

The H.C.S.A. list provides a more satisfactory sample than another, and superficially more attractive, Dublin Castle source, 'Fenianism: index of names, 1866-71'[10] That includes virtually everyone suspected of political disaffection during the period, some of them strong opponents of fenianism such as A. M. Sullivan and John Martin. The superiority of the H.C.S.A. sample is supported by the decision of contemporary Castle officials to choose it in January 1870.[11]

The task of analysis was undertaken by Robert Anderson, a lawyer intimately acquainted with the government's anti-fenian campaigns and with

[6]T. C. Luby's recollections of the *Irish People,* communicated to John O'Leary, 1892 (N.L.I., MS 333) (hereafter cited as Luby, MS 333).

[7]William Neilson Hancock to the chief secretary, 3 Jan. 1870 (S.P.O., 'F' papers, 5477R).

[8]Habeas Corpus Suspension (Ireland) Act, 29 & 30 Vic., c. 1.

[9]Habeas Corpus Suspension Act, abstracts of cases, 1866-8 (S.P.O., police and crime records, fenian papers).

[10]In S.P.O., police and crime records, fenian papers.

[11]However, the genuinely fenian element in the more comprehensive list is sufficiently strong for analysis to show up the same general patterns, even if they are less decisive; see Samuel Clark, *The social origins of the Irish land war* (Princeton, 1979), p. 203.

the archives they had produced. Among the items recorded on each H.C.S.A. prisoner's file was his occupation, usually, it seems, as given by himself after arrest.[12] Anderson was able to satisfy himself about the occupation or status of each of 1086 prisoners. (A scrupulous researcher working now on the surviving evidence might exclude a few score of these from consideration but without significant effect on subsequent calculations.) Almost 500 of his total Anderson classified as 'tradesmen, artisans, millworkers, etc'. As they were designated only by the trade in which they worked ('tailor', 'shoemaker', 'nailor', etc), there was no way of distinguishing between proprietors and wage earners, but everything known about them suggests that they were predominantly the latter. In any case, their number constitutes impressive evidence for the social bias in the composition of the movement. The addition of 23 bakers to this category — which seems logical though they are listed separately by Anderson for no obvious reason — brings the total of skilled workers to 520 (47.8 per cent). This figure is so impressive that his other findings serve largely as commentary on it.

Townsmen of the labouring class, including 19 porters, account for 69 arrests (6.4 per cent) suggesting that fenianism drew its main strength from the lower classes but not the lowest. Occupations to which young men of humble origins might aspire on the basis of an affinity for the 'three Rs' and good character references account for a significant 9.1 per cent of the arrests (made up of 57 'clerks and commercial assistants', 29 'national school masters' and 13 'school teachers and tutors'). These were people in a social and economic position comparable with that of the artisans. Here, too, should be noted Anderson's category of 'shop assistants and shopkeepers' sons' totalling 39 (3.6 per cent).

Shopkeepers (52) and publicans (37) amount together to 8.2 per cent of the total, a quite high figure for this group in relation to its overall size. The contrast with the representation of farmers is striking: from this large and prominent sector of the population only 39 actual farmers and 21 farmers' sons are included (5.5 per cent). Agricultural labourers totalled 58 (5.3 per cent). Self-confessed veterans of the United States army (47) together with ex-members of her majesty's army and navy (21) and dismissed or pensioned constabulary (7) constitute 6.9 per cent of the arrests. A number of other occupations are represented but none accounts for more than 1 per cent and their combined total comes to just over 6 per cent.[13]

Whatever contemporaries may have thought of them, there is no doubt that a significant proportion of the rank and file was sufficiently prosperous to have money to spend on leisure. According to John Devoy ninety per cent of the thousand or so Dublin fenians under the command of one Mathew O'Neill, a

[12]'Summary of the occupations of the prisoners in custody under the lord lieu-tenant's warrant', 12 Jan. 1870 (S.P.O., 'F' papers, 5477R). The date is that of compila-tion: the last of the H.C.S.A. prisoners had been released by late 1868.

[13]A sample of 523 H.C.S.A. prisoners is subjected to a series of interesting analyses in H. H. van der Wusten, *Iers verzet tegen de staatkundige eenheid der Britse eilanden, 1800-1921: een politiek-geografische studie van integratie- en desintegratieprocessen* (Amsterdam, 1977), pp 84-99. In particular Dr van der Wusten demonstrates, by reference to the occupational statistics in the 1861 census, the great under-representation of farmers and of labourers of all kinds and the over-representation of the trades, schoolteachers and publicans.

builder, earned thirty shillings per week.[14] And even if we must treat all Devoy's statistics with caution, there is no gainsaying the evidence his statement provides concerning the comparative prosperity of many fenians. Further evidence comes from Luby who found that as a gentleman in straitened circumstances he was unable to hold his own financially with the smart young wage-earners who filled the fenian ranks in Dublin. Accordingly he was much relieved to be able to pass a great part of the burden of maintaining regular social contact with them on to Joseph Denieffe, who was employed at the time at a good salary as a foreman-cutter in a merchant tailoring house. 'So he could now meet and associate with youths like my recruits as often as he liked on equal pecuniary terms, incurring no humiliating obligations.'[15]

Fenianism in the mid-1860s appealed, then, predominantly to 'respectable' wage earners and some of the urban lower-middle class. The higher-middle and professional classes who had been so prominent — with the artisans — in Young Ireland days gave virtually no support. More striking still, the farming population, that most important element in post-famine Ireland, remained almost totally aloof. The fenian newspaper, the *Irish People,* took the line that the 'people' — as opposed to the middle classes and gentry — had a near-monopoly of altruistic patriotism.[16] This was an implicit acknowledgement of the limited appeal of the I.R.B., but it is not of much use as an explanation. Certainly James Stephens did not intend to have his following confined to the lower ranks of Irish society. He had canvassed support at every level.[17] How is the bias of the response to be explained?

Unlike those in the upper-middle class, most of the people attracted to fenianism had no direct access to parliamentary politics. Neither, however, had most farmers, and even those who had can have gained but little satisfaction from it between 1852 and 1868. The period of most spectacular movement into the fenian ranks, 1863-6, coincided with years of particularly high emigration,[18] and it is reasonable to postulate a connection between the two trends. However, the principal Irish economic crisis of the period was in agriculture and primarily affected those who showed least interest in fenianism.[19] In short, purely political or economic factors cannot, alone or together, satisfactorily explain the appeal of the I.R.B. at this time. We must consider also the social role of the organisation.

The age structure of the H.C.S.A. prisoners provides a suggestive start on this subject. The ages of 746 of them are recorded in the index. They range from 15 to 70, but the arithmetic mean was very much nearer the lower figure, just 27 years in fact. Altogether 87 per cent were aged under 36.[20] In selecting

[14]*Irish Freedom,* Mar. 1913.

[15]T. C. Luby's recollections of early fenian events, communicated to John O'Leary, 1890-92 (N.L.I., MS 331) (hereafter cited as Luby, MS 331).

[16]*Irish People,* 5 Dec. 1863, 23 Jan. 1864.

[17]Desmond Ryan, *The fenian chief: a biography of James Stephens* (Dublin and Sydney, 1967), chs 7-15; Luby, MS 331.

[18]W. E. Vaughan and A. J. Fitzpatrick, *Irish historical statistics: population, 1821-1971* (Dublin, 1978), p. 261.

[19]See J. S. Donnelly, Jr, 'The Irish agricultural depression of 1859-64' in *Irish Economic and Social History,* iii (1976), pp 33-54.

[20]'Habeas Corpus Suspension Act, abstracts of cases, 1866-8' (S.P.O.).

suspects for arrest the authorities are unlikely to have been unduly biased towards youth, and so these figures show fenianism as a young men's movement.

'After a while the secret part of the business was wearing away and we were making ourselves known pretty freely to one another.' Thus wrote John Daly of Limerick recalling after an interval of nearly forty years his experience of fenianism before 1867.[21] Much contemporary evidence exists to show that a great proportion of the brotherhood departed at an early stage from Stephens's blueprint for a perfect secret society organised into independent cells with the individual member being known only to his immediate superior. When in 1859 Stephens arranged for American drill-masters to come over for the purpose of instructing the fenians he was implicitly abandoning the cellular system; even in Stephens's imagination men could not drill together without knowing one another. However, he still obviously intended the I.R.B. to keep itself well hidden from all outsiders. So, drill was to be conducted with all possible secrecy. John Daly recalled that he and his friends initially learned drill in the fields at night, but that after a while they began boldly to hold their exercises on Sundays.[22]

Stephens's lieutenant Thomas Clarke Luby visiting Carrick-on-Suir with another officer during a tour of inspection in 1860 felt called upon to remonstrate with local leaders for apparent lack of progress. Next day as the visitors were boarding a car for Clonmel 'a crowd of the boys' in military order marched into view, determined to impress the visitors with a spectacular farewell. Luby was greatly relieved that the car moved off at once, for he had no desire to receive such a potentially embarrassing compliment.[23] What interests us here is the evidence that in one of the strongholds of the organisation fenians were accustomed to marching and considered it proper to make a public display of their prowess.

Undoubtedly the same 'boys' were involved when, on a Sunday morning in October of the same year, a group of 'about fifty persons mostly of the class of shop-assistants and tradesmen' arrived in the village of Kilmoganny, County Kilkenny, from Carrick-on-Suir, travelling on a convoy of eight horse-drawn vehicles with green ribbons in their coats, and to the accompaniment of a drum and some musical instruments.[24] When challenged by a constabulary officer they explained that they were on their way to engage groups from Kilkenny city and Callan in a cricket match. They then proceeded to Dunnamaggin and duly met up with the other contingents. An unconvincing pretence of playing cricket was put up for a short while, to be followed by some hours of convivial conversation between the members of all three groups. There were conflicting reports as to whether the conviviality occurred inside or outside a public house. On the way home the Carrick men were shouting slogans of strong political import.[25]

There is no doubt that this was a fenian outing. A hostile local newspaper comment on the episode was headed 'Supposed political meeting at

[21]*Irish Freedom*, Feb. 1912.
[22]Ibid.
[23]Luby, MS 331.
[24]*Irishman*, 20 Oct. 1860.
[25]Ibid.

Dunnamaggin' and remarked, pointedly, that in the Carrick district the Phoenix Society (under which name the I.R.B. was first uncovered by the police late in 1858) was well known to have many supporters, and that 'instead of dying away it has been nurtured and carefully propagated'.[26]

A gathering held at Dunnamaggin in October 1864 (again under the guise of a cricket match) was reported in advance to Dublin Castle by Pierce Nagle, a well-placed informer, who indicated that it was a totally fenian project.[27] On this occasion contingents came from Carrick-on-Suir, Kilkenny, Callan, Clonmel and Mullinahone, all strong fenian bases.[28] Cars were used for transport; the travellers were sustained by fife and drum music; ribbons, neckbands and hatbands of green were much in evidence, while many green boughs were carried. At their meeting place the excursionists began a cricket match but most of them soon lost interest and scattered around the field in groups. The highpoint of their day was a picnic meal of which about four hundred of them partook. As they ate they were clearly distinguishable from an even larger number of locals who flocked to the field attracted by the excitement. The vigilant constabulary noted the prominent part played by individuals known to them — and to us — as local fenian leaders.[29]

What are we to make of such demonstrations by an allegedly secret society? They were not alone contrary to official I.R.B. policy, but they contributed in no way to the achievement of the organisation's supposed aim of preparing secretly for armed rebellion: in fact they were most likely to dissipate effort and invite unwelcome attention. Fenianism had been converted to a social purpose for which it had not been intended. It was providing young men with a forum for fraternal association and communal self-expression, even to the detriment of its formal conspirational objective.

The internal history of the I.R.B. down to March 1867 is largely the story of James Stephens's struggle to keep the movement under his control and to prevent it from metamorphosing into a loose network of autonomous social clubs with strong but vaguely-defined nationalist inspiration. That was the direction in which the inclinations of a number of leading fenians tended. This was especially true of Jeremiah O'Donovan Rossa. Indeed his Phoenix Society, founded in Skibbereen in 1856, should be seen as the precursor not of the silent army that James Stephens hoped to establish but of the means of social expression for smart young artisans and clerks which, to a large extent, Stephens's organisation actually became.[30] The arrest of Rossa and other 'Phoenix' men in West Cork and Kerry in December 1858, some months after their movement had been absorbed into the I.R.B. by Stephens, may have been made possible partly because of the habit of openness encouraged by Rossa himself. If so, the fact made little impression on him, for some months after his release in July 1859 he was making public statements on national organisations.[31] He directed a number of public demonstrations in 1863, including one (in support of the Polish rebellion of that year) that involved a large body of men in military array and with flags and lighted torches

[26]*Kilkenny Moderator*, quoted in *Irishman*, 20 Oct. 1860.
[27]Police report, 24 Sept. 1864 (S.P.O., fenian police reports, 1864-5, no. 68).
[28]Constabulary report, 3 Oct. 1864 (ibid., no. 66).
[29]Ibid.
[30]See Seán Ó Lúing, *Ó Donnabháin Rosa I* (Dublin, 1969), pp 81-2.
[31]*Irishman*, 5 Jan. 1860.

marching through Skibbereen in defiance of six magistrates.[32] The demonstration may not have been composed entirely of fenians, but every available fenian under Rossa's influence was involved. Is it any wonder that Stephens later in the year grasped the opportunity to remove Rossa from Skibbereen to Dublin by making him business manager of his newly-founded weekly the *Irish People*?

In Dublin Rossa was under supervision but unrepentant. Stephens's absence in America in early summer 1864 provided the opportunity for the Corkman to display his organisational talents once more. The occasion he chose was a public celebration for the rededication of a catholic church in Kilkenny city on 22 May. Following arrangements made by Rossa and John Haltigan, contingents of fenians travelled on the various special excursion trains to Kilkenny and joined with local members of the brotherhood to form a separate and flamboyant section of the procession to the church. A few high-spirited Dublin fenians attempted to uncouple the last carriage of their home-bound train — just for a laugh among the boys.[33]

But the most typical outdoor manifestation of fenian camaraderie was drill and marching. Certainly, even the most circumspect programme of drill meetings would risk occasional discovery by a vigilant police force. However, the large number of cases noticed by the constabulary in 1864 and 1865 can only be explained by the fact that many fenian groups felt and behaved not merely like part of a secret army but as cliques of young men discovering personal identity and achievement in group display.[34] On a few occasions enough evidence was available to justify charges in court.[35] After one such case had resulted in a number of convictions the *Irish People* remarked that 'surely there is a time and a place for all things, and midday marching before a police barrack is neither rational as to time or place'.[36] At all times the *Irish People* sought to inculcate silence, patience and circumspection. In a particularly striking flight of fancy a leading article declared that 'Irishmen' (clearly meaning the fenians) 'could now, like the people in the streets of Warsaw, see their brethren shot down and remain sternly silent till the moment and opportunity of vengeance would arrive'.[37] That was a vain hankering after the discipline of the ideal secret society.

Camaraderie inculcated self-esteem and undermined traditional deference. Pierce Nagle, when asked by the police in 1864 if the I.R.B. had any passwords or signs, replied that it had not. 'But', he continued,

the members often know each other in general by wearing their beard, and at the same time they meet each other by a stern look, and if met by the same they are ninety-nine out of a hundred fenians; for a stern look in the eye will cause a man who is not up to this mark to look some other way. The general exception to this are the [gentry][38] and government officers and these the fenians know well to avoid.

[32]Ó Lúing, *Ó Donnabháin Rosa I*, pp 132-7.
[33]Luby, MS 333; *Irishman*, 28 May 1864; John Devoy, *Recollections of an Irish rebel* (New York, 1929), pp 50-51 (where the date is wrongly given as 15 Aug.).
[34]Constabulary reports (S.P.O., fenian police reports, 1864-5, passim).
[35]*Irishman*, 20 Feb., 19 Mar. 1864, 9 Sept. 1865.
[36]*Irishman*, 26 Mar. 1864.
[37]*Irish People*, 12 Mar. 1864.
[38]In the MS copy in which Nagle's reply survives the word here is 'sentry' but the sense suggests it is a transcriber's error.

A fenian, Nagle explained, will not salute a nobleman or a clergyman, even if he happens to know him, unless he also happens to be in some way subject to him. All of this is done in conscious imitation of the 'yankee' fashion, 'as far as can be by those who never were in yankee-land'. And Nagle added another interesting qualification: 'in out-of-the-way rural districts this rule will not hold good, but in towns and cities it is correct'.[39] In May 1865 Superintendent Ryan of the Dublin police put on record another report in the same vein:

I am informed that at present nearly all the drapers' assistants in Dublin have assumed an air of careless independence that renders them almost unmanageable by their employers, who are grown quite timid and almost afraid to rebuke them. In many cases they openly express their political sentiments and their minds seem imbued with revolutionary and democratic ideas.[40]

An officer on special duty in Kilkenny some months later reported that a great number of men in the city were fenians and that they had 'a lot of swagger' about them.[41]

Fenianism, then, appealed most strongly to sections of the population that were ready for an organisation that would provide members with a sense of personal fulfilment through identifying with a group of their peers in autonomous social activities. So it flourished in Dublin and in many of the towns and villages of Leinster and Munster, among young men who very often were already in contact with one another through their employment but had previously lacked any specific pretext for fraternisation in their free time. The rural population for the most part was not yet ready for advance in this sphere.

Fenianism provided townsmen and villagers with a vehicle for more rapid and visible progress in a direction in which the trend of the times was drawing them in any case. The 1860s witnessed in Britain a notable rise in public leisure activity on the part of working men, and the progressive development of recreational institutions (railway excursions, brass bands, and the music hall, to mention a few) that responded to the felt requirements of ordinary people rather than to 'what benevolent superiors thought was their need and ought to be their interest'.[42] Much work remains to be done on the extent and pace of Irish participation in this development, but fenianism is certainly a significant part of the story.

If fenianism filled a social vacuum, as suggested here, it follows that a movement with less radical nationalist objectives, or no nationalist objectives at all, could just as easily have satisfied this social need. On the other hand, all the evidence suggests that in the mid-nineteenth century any popular organisation among Irish catholics whatever its initial or nominal purpose was likely to become a vehicle for nationalist feeling, more or less quickly depending on its degree of popularity.

In Dublin city in the 1860s the I.R.B. was not the only society offering working men the opportunity of self expression and independence through association. There was also a flourishing collection of 'trade associations' co-

[39]Police report, 19 Aug. 1864 (S.P.O., fenian police reports, 1864-5, no. 44A).
[40]Police report, 8 May 1865 (ibid., no. 157).
[41]Police report, 21 Sept. 1865 (ibid., no. 203).
[42]Geoffrey Best, *Mid-Victorian Britain, 1851-70* (2nd ed., London, 1979), p. 220.

operating loosely from 1863 under the umbrella of the United Trades Association.[43] The trades — as they were generally referred to — provided fraternity, a certain amount of conspiracy, and, on suitable occasions, pageantry, with the members of each association, bedecked with badges, marching in order behind their own bands and banners.[44] All of this was the very stuff of popular nationalism. In 1864 Pierce Nagle, under circumstances that encouraged exaggeration, estimated that fifty-five per cent of the members of the Dublin trades were fenians.[45] Given the overlap of social functions, an overlap of membership was not surprising, but the I.R.B. did not dominate the trades.

Fr Mathew's temperance campaign in the years 1839-45 provided an earlier example of how a movement with a specifically 'moral' objective could be drawn irretrievably into nationalist politics.[46] A small revival of that movement in Cork city and county in 1863 gave rise to excursions and displays by St Finbarr's temperance band (wearing green and gold caps) and public meetings that were 'more political than temperance'.[47] Interestingly, the Phoenix Society, in its first stage, enjoined teetotalism on its members.[48] Charles J. Kickham always felt that fenianism and temperance went hand in hand. The wish being father of the thought, he wrote enthusiastically about the improved sobriety noticeable among young men where the *Irish People* was most read.[49] A common pledge of teetotalism could certainly consolidate the fraternal spirit, but so also could the conviviality of the public house. Indeed, most fenian business, especially recruitment and initiation of new members, appears to have been conducted in public houses. The pub provided excellent cover, but to see fenian recourse to the pub as a merely accidental matter of convenience would be to miss the point: public house conviviality was part of the very fabric of fenianism. The vitality of fenianism and the rising sales of liquor were both products of a modest prosperity.[50]

Not surprisingly, in view of its social dimension, fenianism is frequently mentioned in contemporary sources in connection with games and popular pastimes; what is surprising is the wide range of activities involved. References to cricket we have already seen. The constabulary reported from west Cork in the autumn of 1858 that suspected Phoenix Society organisers were constantly travelling the country engaged in coursing — 'a good means of meeting young fellows'.[51] An American fenian officer on one occasion reviewed the Limerick city I.R.B. on the local racecourse, where they were assembled in small groups

[43]*Irishman*, 12 Dec. 1863.

[44]*Irishman*, 16 Nov. 1861; Breandán Mac Giolla Choille, 'Dublin trades in procession, 1864' in *Saothar: Journal of the Irish Labour History Society*, i, no. 1 (May 1975), pp 18-30.

[45]Police report, 19 Aug. 1864 (S.P.O., fenian police reports, 1864-5, no. 44A.)

[46]See Elizabeth Malcolm, 'Temperance and Irish nationalism' in F. S. L. Lyons and R. A. J. Hawkins (eds), *Ireland under the union: varieties of tension* (Oxford, 1980), pp 75-7.

[47]*Irishman*, 29 Aug., 26 Sept. 1863.

[48]Statement of Robert Cusack, undated (S.P.O., Reports on secret societies, 1857-9).

[49]*Irish People*, 17 June 1865.

[50]See J. J. Lee, 'Money and beer in Ireland, 1790-1875' in *Econ. Hist. Rev.*, 2nd series, xix (1966), pp 183-7.

[51]Constabulary reports, Bantry, 24 Sept. and 25 Oct. 1859 (S.P.O., Reports on secret societies, 1857-9).

posing as sightseers inspecting the jumps.[52] After a number of convictions for illegal drilling in the vicinity of Cork city had inculcated the need for some caution, it was noticed that suspect groups of young men meeting near Glanmire carried a football with which they played whenever a stranger was approaching near enough to observe their activities.[53] A police raid on a Dublin premises where fenians had been meeting in large numbers at evening times, uncovered evidence of swordstick play, gymnastics and boxing.[54] Commenting on a hint that footrace meetings near Millstreet, County Cork, were being organised for fenian purposes, a senior constabulary officer declared sweepingly that he was 'quite confident that those persons going through the country as strolling players, and most of those attending races, football and cricket matches, etc., are connected with fenianism'.[55] When the Mullinahone fenians went on a Sunday outing in the summer of 1863 some of them occupied themselves at 'leaping and stonethrowing'. Others took to dancing 'all the dances . . . except waltzing and the polka' with a group of local girls.[56] (This is one of the very few references to female participation in fenian social activity that I have come across.)

Clearly the fenians used sport as a cover for other business, but as in the case of the public house there was also a stronger link. For fenianism in its social aspect was filling in many Irish towns and villages the function which in the mid-nineteenth century organised sport was beginning to perform in various European countries. This particular aspect of fenianism was grasped in 1865 by a County Cork aristocrat, Lord Fermoy, whose insight was sharpened by his fear of imminent political and social upheaval. He declared that one of the reasons for the progress of the dreaded organisation was 'the want of amusement or rational employment of their leisure hours experienced by the young shopmen and such like of the country towns. We have no national game or sport, and cricket does not seem to go down well, and consequently in a country town there is no resort for the young shopman or artisan but the public house.'[57] He had got to the heart of the matter, even if he was seeing it the wrong way round: any nominally sporting alternative to fenianism would also have been a vehicle of nationalist feeling and propaganda, so that the end result, from Lord Fermoy's point of view, would not have been greatly improved.

Most of those who exercised 'social control' during the decades after the famine — clergymen, landlords, magistrates, policemen — discouraged organised popular sport in the interests of peace and public order. At least as early as 1858 this policy was criticised from a nationalist viewpoint by a leader-writer in the *Irishman* who lamented especially the neglect of hurling.[58] When he went on to advocate the establishment of an organisation based on

[52]*Irish Freedom*, Feb. 1912.

[53]Constabulary report, 13 June 1865 (S.P.O., Fenian police reports, 1864-5, no. 179).

[54]Police report, 2 Dec. 1864 (S.P.O., fenian police reports, 1864-5, no. 87).

[55]Constabulary report, 4 Nov. 1966 (S.P.O., 'F' papers, F1423 and F3192).

[56]*Irishman*, 11 July 1863. For a convincing evocation of a Cork fenian Sunday afternoon see Maura Murphy, 'The working classes of nineteenth-century Cork' in *Cork Hist. Soc. Jn.*, lxxx (1980), p. 48.

[57]Lord Fermoy to Lord Palmerston, 1 Sept. 1865 (Broadlands, Palmerston papers, GC/GR 2577) (used by permission of the Broadlands Trust).

[58]*Irishman*, 2 Oct. 1858.

parish clubs for the fostering of native pastimes he was advocating a specifically Irish version of what was already coming to pass in British sport, and he
was anticipating the Gaelic Athletic Association of a quarter century later.
The *Irish People* of 15 October 1864 carried a leading article — anonymous,
but in the unmistakable style of C. J. Kickham — under the title of 'National
sports'. This made the case in defence of those popular pastimes, 'hurling,
football and even dancing', that were being discouraged by the authorities. If a
score or two of young men and women meet on Sunday afternoon, Kickham
complained, they were likely to be interrupted by magistrates and policemen.
If they then refused to disperse they were harrassed, names being taken and
tenant farmers getting the hint next day from the bailiffs to keep their sons at
home. Kickham rejected the pretexts offered to justify this regime — 'respect
for the sabbath and fear of vice and immorality' — and affirmed the
determination of youth to have its fling: 'our fathers and grandfathers hurled
and leaped and danced, and we cannot see why we should not do the same'.
However, editorial policy called for the inculcation of secrecy, and accordingly Kickham continued his article with an exhortation that sports meetings
should not be turned into political demonstrations. There was no need, he
declared, for any public demonstrations whatsoever. But there is no mistaking
where his heart was, just as there is no doubting how faithfully his evocation of
the recreational aspect of fenianism reflected the feelings of a great many of
the rank and file.

The particular susceptibility of farmers and their sons to external social discipline partly explains their lack of support for fenianism in the 1860s. By the
same token, the decline in the social influence of Irish landlords as a consequence of the land war must have had a bearing on the rise of the Gaelic
Athletic Association later in the century. Farmers' sons could now beard the
gentry as boldly as artisans or town shopboys.

The catholic clergy were even more concerned with social control than were
the landlords. The full intensity of clerical opposition to fenianism in the 1860s
can only be understood in terms of a struggle to maintain the dominance of the
parish priest over certain areas of parochial life.[59] By endeavouring to institute
new modes of social intercourse — or perhaps even to revive old ones —
socialising fenians disturbed all guardians of the status quo.

The catholic church made no concerted effort to satisfy the social need that
fenianism was meeting: the ecclesiastical attitude was predominantly
defensive. The only widespread organisation under church auspices offering
young men the opportunity of social expression was the Catholic Young
Men's Society. It had come into existence in Limerick city in 1849 under the
guidance of the Reverend Dr Richard O'Brien, later dean of Limerick.[60] In
subsequent years it spread widely, if unevenly, throughout Ireland and among
Irish communities in Britain. Branches held regular meetings, marched in
formation with banners to church on Sundays, and arranged lectures, *soirées*
and amateur theatricals.[61] Ostensibly, the C.Y.M.S. was a resolutely non-

[59]R. V. Comerford, *Charles J. Kickham: a study in Irish nationalism and literature*
(Dublin, 1979), pp 68-9.
[60]*Irishman*, 5 Feb. 1859.
[61]Constabulary report, 8 Dec. 1858 (S.P.O., reports on secret societies, 1857-9);
Irishman, 28 Dec. 1861, 24 Jan. 1863, 25 Mar. 1865.

political organisation and its regulations actually outlawed discussion of political topics.[62] However, as we have seen, social organisation tended to drift into nationalist expression and the C.Y.M.S. was no exception. When John Mallon, a future detective chief, came to Dublin in November 1858 to work in the Castle, he was impelled, as a serious-minded young catholic, to join the C.Y.M.S. However, he soon found that his fellow members tended to let their conversation 'drift upon dangerous political lines', and in fairness to them and to himself he felt obliged to resign.[63] Dr O'Brien was himself a highly politicised priest and in 1868 he was to launch a celebrated declaration in favour of repeal.[64] The working of his society's ban on politics can be judged from the following words of a branch secretary to a speaker being engaged for a lecture:

You will of course know how to combine the avoidance of all party politics, to which our society is pledged, with the healthy and manly national tone which we have steadily tried to impress on all our proceedings.[65]

As early as November 1858 O'Brien issued a circular to all branches of his organisation warning against secret societies. That is a good indication that he had received reports of members having been tempted.[66] When six suspected Phoenix Society men (fenians) were arrested in Callan, County Kilkenny, two months later, five were found to be members of the Catholic Young Men's Society.[67] The society did not present the church with a safe alternative to the I.R.B. On the contrary, the occasions for fraternisation that it provided, and many of the attitudes and practices that it fostered, served only to make its members more susceptible to fenianism.

The I.R.B. in the mid-1860s spread political ideas and made preparations for an expected rising. However, the military preparations proved less than thorough and the extent to which republican theory (as distinct from nationalist feeling) was successfully propagated may have been equally unspectacular. It is doubtful if truly *doctrinaire* republicans were more numerous in Ireland than in contemporary England. And it would be difficult to prove that Queen Victoria was more unpopular in Ireland in the 1860s than she was elsewhere in the United Kingdom before Disraeli rescued her from retirement. However strongly they may have repudiated allegiance to the queen in their initiation oath, the fenians we have been looking at here were from the point of view of social history easily recognisable and fairly typical mid-Victorians.

[62]*Nation*, 28 Feb. 1863.

[63]F. M. Bussy, *Irish conspiracies: recollections of John Mallon (the great Irish detective) and other reminiscences* (London, 1910), p. 17.

[64]Thornley, *Isaac Butt*, p. 56.

[65]J. MacCarthy to J. P. Leonard, 25 Aug. 1862 (N.L.I., Leonard papers, MS 10,505).

[66]*Irishman*, 20 Nov. 1858.

[67]*Irishman*, 8, 15 Jan. 1859.

3

IRELAND AND THE BALLOT ACT OF 1872*
MICHAEL HURST

IT is almost a commonplace nowadays that the passing of the Ballot Act of 1872 revolutionized Irish politics. Sir Robert Ensor is quite categorical: 'But where the act had revolutionary consequences, which its authors had neither foreseen nor intended, was in Ireland.'[1] The authority quoted is Charles Stewart Parnell, who had insisted: 'Hitherto the Irish voter, powerless against the intimidation of his social superiors, had returned members to one or other of the two English parliamentary parties' and now with secret voting 'need do so no longer'.[2] By way of conclusion Ensor goes so far as to reflect: 'that but for the undesigned gift of this act, the whole of his meteoric career, with its profound reactions upon English history for half a century, might never have occurred'.[3] Elsewhere he attributed the emergence of the classic Irish party to agricultural depression and Parnell's magnetic leadership, though without in any way specifically retracting the ballot point.[4] Barry O'Brien explained the circumstances of Parnell's placing so much faith in it:

In 1872 Parnell...returned to Avondale. Vote by ballot had just been extended to Ireland. The measure drew Parnell's attention once more to politics. He thought it was of greater practical importance than either the Irish Church Act or the Land Act, for it emancipated the voters. 'Now', he said, 'something can be done if full advantage will be taken of this Ballot Act.' His sympathies had gone out to the Fenians after the Manchester executions. But he did not see how Fenianism was practically to be worked. The Ballot Act first suggested to him a mode of practical operation. The Irish voter was now a free man. He could send whom he liked to Parliament. He was master of the situation. An independent Irish party, free from the touch of English influence, was the thing wanted, and this party could be elected under the Ballot Act.[5]

Respect for this view is severely undermined when O'Brien goes out of his way to stress that Parnell was 'utterly ignorant of political affairs in 1872'. 'His whole stock of information about Ireland' being 'limited to the history of the "Manchester Martyrs"', absolute reliance upon any opinion offered would be foolhardy. Admittedly, he stuck to the point eighteen years later before the Special Commission. Still, that in itself does not prove experience had borne out his hunch. Public men are all too fond of sticking to nostrums

---

* The election results used in this article are drawn from F. H. MacCalmont, *Parliamentary Poll Book* (1911 ed.).

[1] Sir R. C. K. Ensor, *England, 1870–1914*, p. 24.

[2] Ibid.   [3] Ibid.

[4] Sir R. C. K. Ensor, 'Some Political and Economic Interactions in Later Victorian England', *Transactions of the Royal Historical Society* (1949), pp. 24–5.

[5] R. Barry O'Brien, *The Life of Charles Stewart Parnell*, I, 56.

in the face of evidence they choose to ignore, and the new model Irish party had been going long enough for its leader to afford romantic notions as to its origins. Moreover, the 'Independent Opposition' movement of the 'fifties had given him the idea for this party, and his failure to see that it had succeeded without secret ballot was scarcely a sign of having thought the matter through.[6]

No less a person than J. L. Hammond subscribed to what may be termed the Parnell line, and Mrs O'Shea, John Morley and E. Strauss did likewise.[7] Even very recent writers like W. B. Gwyn, H. J. Hanham, L. J. McCaffrey, C. C. O'Brien, C. O'Leary, D. Thornley and J. H. Whyte tend to swallow it or ignore the problem altogether.[8] Some of the earlier commentators thought rather differently, generally contenting themselves with modest statements of what was undoubtedly true—that broadly speaking, 'A workman or a tenant could no longer be punished because he did not vote according to the will of his employer or landlord';[9] that under the secret ballot tenants

[6] Ibid. pp. 72 and 229.

[7] J. L. Hammond ignores the question in *Gladstone and the Irish Nation*, but see J. L. Hammond and M. R. D. Foot, *Gladstone and Liberalism*, pp. 123–4. See also Katherine O'Shea (Mrs Parnell), *Charles Stewart Parnell*, I, 128; John Morley, *Life of Gladstone*, II, 370; and E. Strauss, *Irish Nationalism and British Democracy*, pp. 184–5.

[8] W. B. Gwyn, *Democracy and the Cost of Politics*, p. 133, assumes Irish nationalism needed the protection of the secret ballot. H. J. Hanham, *Elections and Party Management: Politics in the Time of Disraeli and Gladstone*, mentions the pre-Ballot Act successes of Home Rule, yet seems to accept Parnell's assessment both in the introduction, at p. xiv, and in the main text, pp. 182–3. L. J. McCaffrey in ['Home Rule and the General Election of 1874 in Ireland',] *I[rish] H[istorical] S[tudies]*, IX, makes no mention of the Ballot Act except in dealing with the actual events of 1874, although the developments in the years from 1870 have been given almost six pages (see pp. 190–6). Again in his ['Irish Federalism in the 1870's: A Study in Conservative Nationalism',] *T[ransactions of the] A[merican] P[hilosophical] S[ociety]*, new series, LII, part 6, bold claims are made for the effects of the Act on the 1874 election, pp. 17–23. For the period from 1870 to the election there is one casual mention of the secret ballot on p. 12. C. C. O'Brien, *Parnell and his Party, 1880–1890*, p. 34, places great stress on the importance of secret voting, claiming the nationalist electors had no real confidence in the system in 1874. If this were true the Home Rule success of that year demonstrated the superfluity of the secret ballot. If not, the argument about confidence in it leading to the change in the social complexion of Home Rule members falls to the ground. C. O'Leary, *The Elimination of Corrupt Practices in British Elections, 1868–1911*, does not discuss the issue. D. Thornley, ['The Irish Conservatives and Home Rule, 1869–1873',] *I[rish H[istorical] S[tudies]*, II, has no mention of the secret ballot except as part of Liberal policy in the Monaghan by-election of 1871 (see p. 213). His new *Isaac Butt [and Home Rule]* shows scant consistency on the point. On p. 27 he claims the secret ballot helped radically to alter the nature of the Irish representation. Presumably, because numerous electors acquired a new security and felt able to promote and support candidates of less elevated social position and more radical views. Clearly, this is the Parnell interpretation. Later, on p. 133 he expresses no preference between the Parnell view and the one claiming the secrecy would guard against mob rule. Still further on, at p. 205, he appears to come closer than anyone else to the heart of the matter. Commenting on the differing expectations from the Act, he says: 'Some, perhaps wisest of all, expected matters to remain much as they were before.' J. H. Whyte, ['The Influence of the Catholic Clergy on Elections in Nineteenth-Century Ireland',] *E[nglish] H[istorical] R[eview]* (1960), only mentions secret ballot on p. 256 in connexion with allegations of feigned illiteracy during the Parnellite versus Anti-Parnellite rows of the 1890's.

[9] Sir James O'Connor, *History of Ireland, 1798–1924*, II, 32.

'voted for landlords who were Home Rulers' and 'against others who were not';[10] and that there was still a loophole, for 'Some landlords, knowing or strongly suspecting, that their tenants would vote for a candidate distasteful to the ruling caste, have prohibited them from voting at all, under the ancient penalty of landlord displeasure'.[11] Nor would anyone wish to quarrel with O'Neill Daunt's statement: 'Of the multitude of tenants expelled from their holdings it is commonly believed that a large number have been punished by eviction for voting at elections against the will of their landlords.'[12] But the crucial question is not the ending or extent of evictions for political acts. It is whether a secret ballot was necessary for the emergence of a fully independent Irish party, and if not, why not? Or, in other words, did the act revolutionize Irish politics, and if not, what did?

This can be answered by examining the course of Irish politics from both a short- and a long-term viewpoint relative to 1872. From a short term, to see the effects of Fenian and Federalist currents on affairs just prior to and after the passing of the Ballot Act. From a long term, to judge of the general nature of the political behaviour of the Irish popular party at the constituency level. Of the former, it will be shown that 'the movement' for a fundamental change in the constitutional relationship between Great Britain and Ireland 'spread rapidly by one of the surest tests which can be applied to any political movement—the test of elections', before the vote became secret.[13] Of the latter, that 'In Ireland...notwithstanding the terrible and frequent exercise of landlord power, it was not so easy to drive electors like swine to the market' because of their strong 'spirit of constitutional independence'; and that 'They have more frequently voted, in proportion to their numbers, in accordance with their political preferences'.[14]

Because developments from the Fenian rising of 1867 to the onset of the agricultural depression in 1877 left no very great impact upon the British scene it is all too often assumed to have been 'almost, for Ireland, a period of calm between storms'.[15] Rather was it a period of storm between two hurricanes. A false sense of security arose in Britain even before Gladstone's victory at the polls late in 1868. It sprang from a consciousness of good intentions at a time when Ireland's national movement appeared to have suffered an irreparable reverse. Speaking at Bristol, Lord Stanley described the Irish problem as 'one which I suppose at the present moment is hardly ever absent from the mind of any person who takes part in public affairs...' and again 'supposing', went on to say 'there never was a time when Englishmen of all parties and all classes were more anxious to give all reasonable

---

[10] F. H. O'Donnell, *A History of the Irish Parliamentary Party*, 1, 92.
[11] O'Neill Daunt, *Eighty-Five Years of Irish History*, p. 151.
[12] Ibid. p. 150.
[13] Ibid. p. 151.
[14] Ibid.
[15] Bernard Holland, *The Life of the Duke of Devonshire, 1833–1908*, 1, 84.

satisfaction to Irish demands, and even, as far as can be done without national injury, to humour the feelings and prejudices of the Irish people'.[16] The impressive showing of the Liberal party in Ireland at the general election seemed to confirm that all might yet be well. The special circumstances contributing to it were nevertheless of a kind unlikely to be repeated. The ecclesiastical and agrarian legislation about to be delivered would, when in operation, destroy the very common ground the prospect of its coming had created. Catholic priesthood and Tenant Righters alike might, and indeed did, find the 'jam' too thin. The Church Disestablishment Act of 1869 and the Land Act of 1870 actually did little to end the religious and agrarian aspects of the Irish question. On the contrary the education and land owner-ship issues were the more starkly delineated.[17] Then again, Fenianism and the 'Independent Opposition' nationalism would not again suffer from the same disadvantages, if the Catholic Church decided against an all out effort for Whig Liberalism. The former might have to be tolerated by the priests, and the latter would stand a good chance of receiving their positive help and encouragement. However much the hierarchy might hate the Fenians, they could not be anathematized out of existence. If their leaders were released from prison, elections would possibly appeal to them as a channel for tough political action. Leadership of the open national movement would then be in question and the priests would have to look to their laurels.[18] Events were also likely to benefit the gentler national groups. All in all, unqualified support for Liberalism among the priesthood would tend to lessen sharply on both idealistic and materialistic grounds, except for certain older, con-servative-minded sections. At best the Liberals could hope for a divided Catholic hierarchy and clergy; at worst, virtual desertion.

What George Borrow wrote of Anglo-Welsh relations applied with vastly added force to Anglo-Irish. 'The English have forgot that they ever con-quered the Welsh, but some ages will elapse before the Welsh forget that the English have conquered them.'[19] For Lowe[20] to maintain that Fenianism should be left out of sight in discussing the Irish question and had no con-nexion with the Church or Land issues was sheer stupidity.[21] Social and

---

[16] *Annual Register, 1868*, p. 3.

[17] Though hopes of what might come from Gladstone in the way of educational concessions kept some of the Catholic hierarchy and their priests behind official Liberalism well into 1873, thoughts of attacking the Liberals on educational policy were voiced during the 1868 General Election. The *Galway Vindicator* (12 Aug. 1868) contended that immediately dis-establishment was passed Irish Catholic members 'would very probably find themselves in opposition to the Liberal party on the subject of education' (Thornley, *Isaac Butt*, p. 33). How Gladstone could ever have thought his first Land Act would solve Irish agrarian prob-lems is difficult to understand.

[18] W. Bence Jones in his *A Life's Work in Ireland*, p. 64, believed the priests had never before had 'so hard a game to play'.

[19] George Borrow, *Wild Wales*, p. 293.

[20] Sir Robert Lowe, Chancellor of the Exchequer, later 1st Viscount Sherbrooke.

[21] *Annual Register, 1868*, p. 51.

economic discontent fed the fires of national grievance. A Fenian leader spoke the truth when claiming that

The suppression of the rising in 1867 and the imprisonment of our people did not damp our energies a bit. We kept working away just the same as ever, with this difference, that we had thousands of sympathisers in 1870 who would not touch us at all in 1865. In fact we had a stronger hold on the country after the rising than we had before.[22]

The motive force came, according to the veteran 'Independent Brigade' leader, George Henry Moore, from the conviction which had been 'gradually growing upwards—from the starving to the needy, from the needy to the struggling classes, from the struggling classes to all above, those who are still left in Ireland—that the Government under which we live is a very bad Government for our country'.[23] Whether or not the actual process went exactly like that, there is no doubt of Fenianism's having 'entered into the hearts of the people'.[24] An all-important part of its significance, especially in relation to events prior to the agricultural depression, was the absence of any great leader.

It germinated almost simultaneously in different parts of Ireland and spread silently from one centre to another....But Fenianism was democratic; it was organised by shopboys and artisans with no help or encouragement from the leaders of public opinion. The bishops and priests used every effort, moral and spiritual, to defeat it, but their influence had waned during the years they had supported the traitors and they found their counsels produced no effect. The Young Irelanders and the Constitutionalists opposed the physical force party, but their position was difficult, and when some of the Fenians were arrested, they were denounced as 'Felon Setters'.[25]

The sentiment flourished among large sections of the population, electors and non-electors. So often in history there must come a chain of events to exploit such revolutionary feelings for practical ends. Here the release point for this purpose was provided by the Constitutionalists.

Not all the members of Parliament called Liberal in 1868, nor the men supporting them, could be regarded as firm adherents of Gladstone. Others were only conditionally so. Whilst true that the Catholic clergy had exerted themselves with great success to exclude 'nationalist deviationists' from Liberal candidatures, exceptions had been made. For example J. T. Hinds might suffer at their hands in County Meath, but the same did not apply to G. H. Moore in County Mayo. Within the province of Tuam, under Archbishop MacHale, Catholicism carried its national feelings more on the left. Aided by the clergy, Moore demonstrated something crucial to the true appreciation of the role of the Ballot Act. Without professional agents, without the ex-

[22] R. Barry O'Brien, op. cit. p. 64.
[23] M. G. Moore, *An Irish Gentleman: George Henry Moore*, p. 361.
[24] Ibid. p. 320.
[25] Ibid.

penditure of money, 'with nothing to rely upon but the inspiring influence of the clergy, acting under the inspiration of the greatest Irishmen in the world (Dr MacHale) and the pluck and resolution of the people, we made our adversaries pass under the Caudine Forks before the day of nomination'.[26] Blake, the Whig candidate, withdrew; so formidable had the nationalist Liberals proved. Moore's basic aim had been to settle the question whether 'one lord shall drive a hundred human souls to the hustings, another fifty, another a score; whether this or that squire shall call twenty or ten or five as good men as himself, his voters, and send them up with his brand on their back to vote for an omadhaun at his bidding'.[27] An unopposed return along with a Conservative might seem a confused answer to receive. In fact it was not. Moore had no running mate and drove the other 'popular' candidate from the field. The electorate was narrow, yet the Conservative got in really because no one else was there to stop him. He was a relic of what Moore termed the 'two donkey'[28] system whereby each United Kingdom party had a seat each to avoid a contest. County Mayo was at once a warning and a promise. So too, was County Cork where M. Downing, a man of Moore's outlook, got in. In both places the clergy had sided with the successful candidates. A warning to the Liberals and a promise to the nationalists. A promise gained under a system of open voting and a narrow franchise. The direction of politics could be changed when such a release of 'popular' sentiment was proved possible. Naturally, the Fenians were not slow to see elections as a means of hitting at the British and soon took action.

Eleven months later, in October 1869, the newly formed Amnesty Association held a two hundred thousand strong gathering at Cabra, near Dublin. In the chair was its President, Isaac Butt, Conservative critic of the Ascendancy and a prominent lawyer. The release of Fenian prisoners was at this time the main Fenian interest, though the ecclesiastical and prospective land legislation of the Liberal party owed its official adoption to the dread in which they were held. Meetings on a nationwide scale pushed the prisoners' case right to the fore. Land prices might rise from as low as ten years' purchase to twenty-six or even twenty-seven;[29] trade and agriculture generally might show an upward trend; only twenty-four out of eleven hundred arrested for treasonable practices might have been genuine occupiers of land;[30] and at the top of Catholic society nationalism might appear moribund, but already contrary forces were stirring. The old 'Orange' versus 'Green' quarrel was of course inherent in the 'unmeasured violence'[31] against the Church of Ireland at Liberal election meetings, and, ironically enough, reforms aimed at the Ascendancy had the unexpected effect of pushing an important section of the 'Orange' party into the 'Green' camp on the question of self-government.

[26] Ibid. p. 334.
[28] Ibid. p. 325.
[30] Ibid. p. 38.

[27] Ibid. p. 323.
[29] Earl Grey, *Ireland*, p. 41.
[31] Ibid. p. 82.

During 1869 moves were made towards the foundation of a Home Rule organization—moves which were to culminate in the famous Bilton Hotel meeting in May of the next year. When Bishop Moriarty of Kerry wrote to William Monsell, in March 1868, claiming that 'The minds of the Irish people are in the hands of the Irish priests',[32] he was badly out of date. Had he been correct, however, it would not, as we have seen, necessarily have secured the Liberal party or the Union. Chichester Fortescue himself admitted, at almost the same date, that 'the revolutionary movement was more formidable'[33] than in the past, yet seemed fundamentally at one with Moriarty in his optimism as to the future. 'The forces of law and order were much greater' and included the Catholic clergy and those of their faith 'connected with the land, the mercantile, professional and almost the whole middle class'.[34] What he failed to appreciate was that the path of constitutional revolution, pursued through elections, would make the Fenians 'anxious to follow the new movement carefully'[35] and that sympathy for sufferers in the national cause would cause a man like Butt to praise them. 'A people who have renounced their allegiance' and knew 'no patriotism except hatred for their rulers'[36] was not to be won to 'Unionism' by half-hearted reforms, especially with 'the habeas corpus act still in suspension and the gaols full from the Fenian rising'.[37] When habeas corpus was restored in the following year, outrages increased fivefold.

Such was the background to the victory of the Fenian, O'Donovan Rossa in the Tipperary by-election of November 1869. Far from waiting for the release of prisoners, the erstwhile revolutionaries ran a convict for Parliament. A man who had spent most of the summer of that year with his hands tied behind his back. His election horrified the British press. All the newspapers expressed astonishment that Ireland was not completely satisfied with the 'generosity' of the proposed legislation. *The Times* bewailed the result as betokening 'the revival of the Fenian spirit in Ireland, without any visible cause or favouring circumstances'.[38] Quite baffled, it resigned itself to the whole disappointing business being 'just one of those Irish paradoxes, which Englishmen find it hard to understand'.[39] Moore, already thinking of taking the Fenian oath, saw the event as useless—because Rossa was disqualified from sitting—except as the shadow 'coming events cast before them'.[40] What a shadow it was! Later Lord Hartington was to claim 'the Irish voter was the last person who was expected to have any influence over his own

---

[32] J. H. Whyte, ['Select Documents XVIII. Bishop Moriarty on Disestablishment and the Union, 1868',] I[rish] H[istorical] S[tudies], x, 195. Gladstone Papers. B.M. Add. MS. 44152, fos. 98–113.

[33] Hansard, 3rd series, cxc, 1594.   [34] Ibid.

[35] R. Barry O'Brien, op. cit. p. 64.

[36] J. H. Whyte, *I.H.S.* p. 198.

[37] D. Thornley, *I.H.S.* p. 200.

[38] M. G. Moore, op. cit. p. 359; *The Times*, 28 Nov. 1869.

[39] M. G. Moore, op. cit. p. 359.   [40] Ibid. p. 362.

vote, and that it was a struggle, between the landlord and the priest, who should take him to the poll'.[41] Well here was a marked exception. Landlord and priest had together failed to defeat Rossa, failed on a narrow franchise exercised under a system of open voting.[42] Had not Parnell and those who thought or think like him forgotten Tipperary as they forgot that other radical county—Mayo?

The contest is worth a more detailed examination. The Liberal candidate was a well known and popular barrister, named D. C. Heron, selected by a joint meeting of laymen and Catholic priests. He himself was a Catholic. Late in the day, Rossa was put up by his friends as a 'protest against Whiggery to rally the Fenians'.[43] 'To the amazement of the Loyalists'[44] he was elected by 1131 votes to 1030, a pathetic Conservative receiving a paltry 12. The poll was approximately 23 per cent. A very low figure indeed, considering the priests had been active for Heron and that on polling day 'the usual priest-led cavalcades of voters were to be seen going into the five polling towns'.[45] J. H. Whyte finds there were some 'good excuses...for the clerical defeat on this occasion'.[46] He argues that 'Rossa's candidature came as such a complete surprise that no previous arrangements had been made on Heron's behalf'.[47] Surely, however, the very lateness of Rossa's appearance put his followers at an even graver disadvantage and the very privileged social position of the priests would enable them to overcome the surprise with rapidity? The argument that, as Heron assured everybody, he would be elected whatever the vote—Rossa being ineligible to sit—the priests did not exert themselves unduly, is too much to swallow. Apart from the lack of proof, is it really feasible to suppose the clergy would risk public humiliation at the hands of the feared and hated Fenians on the promise of their man creeping into the House of Commons on a technicality? If anything, Heron had such advantages as generally weighed in Irish elections of the 'sixties firmly on his side. Over 1100 voters saw fit to flout the landlords and the priests and brave the consequences. It was most interesting too that their action won at least the qualified approval of a priest-lover like Moore.

To anticipate a little so as to complete the picture—when Heron proved wrong and a second by-election took place in the following February, the priests left no stone unturned. Although the poll rose by some 10 per cent and Heron, running for a second time, got in, the majority was a mere 4 votes scored against a divided Fenian camp. Over 1600 voters showed that the priests were not universally recognized as 'the mind of the Irish people'.[48]

---

[41] Bernard Holland, op. cit. p. 93.
[42] Convincing evidence that a secret ballot was not necessary for a change in the type of parliamentary representative.
[43] R. Barry O'Brien, op. cit. p. 64, n. 1.   [44] Ibid.
[45] J. H. Whyte, *E.H.R.* p. 253.
[46] Ibid.   [47] Ibid.
[48] J. H. Whyte, *I.H.S.* p. 195.

Kickham, the Fenian, declared he would never sit in the 'English Parliament'[49] and yet lost by so few against a fully prepared opponent. Many of his own side did not approve his standing and held that they ought to have rested content with Rossa's demonstration. Despite the pulpit and the press the 'popular' groups in Irish politics were soon showing a strong indisposition to being tied to the Gladstonian juggernaut. There appeared in one county at least enough hardy material for the creation of an uncompromising national party. The accident of a by-election had shown it. Without an extreme candidate the strength of extremism could not have been revealed.

Why had the first Tipperary election also been the first shock to the new Liberal 'ascendancy'? Eleven more by-elections had preceded it, ten going to the Liberals and one to the Conservatives—an exact repeat performance of the General Election. No attempt had been made by either Liberal nationalists, the emerging Home Rule Conservatives or Fenians to queer the pitch. So far as the Conservative seat was concerned there was nothing surprising in this. County Antrim, as an Orange stronghold, was hardly the place to fight for these causes. Even the orthodox Liberals made a poor showing. Moreover, August 1869 was rather premature for much action by any disruptive force. The same applied to all but one of the Liberal seats, the exception being Waterford City, fought one week before Tipperary. No fewer than eight Liberals were returned unopposed. Of these, six had had to resubmit themselves to their constituencies after receiving governmental appointments. The remaining two stood in seats where the General Election return had been declared void on petition. At Yougal in May the Liberal retained the seat against a Conservative in another election brought on by the same cause; while in Waterford two Liberals fought each other. This last is the only vacancy where trouble might have arisen, but Waterford was not Tipperary. The forces of loyalism and the Catholic clergy were exceedingly strong and the necessary knot of local Fenian activists was not forthcoming, or did not choose to chance its arm. At the same time Liberal nationalism and Conservative Home Rule had not yet decided to take electoral action.

Hard on Rossa's victory came an attempt by an old campaigner, John Martin, to end Whig supremacy in County Longford. Although much more of a constitutional politician than Rossa, he found himself *persona non grata* with the local priests. Not only had an exclusively clerical meeting nominated 'a youthful whig',[50] Reginald Greville-Nugent, as the official Liberal candidate, but the clergy regarded Martin as an ancient adversary of the great Daniel O'Connell. But the lack of any helpful links with the clergy did not prove an absolute liability. Ripples of local resentment against alleged

---

[49] R. Barry O'Brien, op. cit. p. 64, n. 1.
[50] J. H. Whyte, *E.H.R.* p. 253.

'clerical dictation' over the choice of Greville-Nugent led a group of the laity under a Catholic provision merchant, James Murtagh, into putting Martin up. Naturally, ripples alone were not enough to break up the Liberal control and he was beaten by 1478 to 411 votes, on a poll of some 67 per cent. The by-election had come when the Catholic Church was still satisfied with the government. No groups of the younger priests had then decided to act against it, and no members of the hierarchy were actively encouraging them to do so. Martin was too left wing a nationalist to create a temptation, but his vote alarmed their bishop and at the second by-election, following the unseating of Greville-Nugent on petition, the clergy were instructed to take no lead. Encouragement of Fenian-tainted nationalism by seeming to over-play their status had to be stopped forthwith. 411 men openly challenging their lead were 411 too many.[51]

On 19 May 1870 the Home Government Association was founded at the Bilton Hotel, Dublin. Immediately beforehand the Fenians promised at least benevolent neutrality towards the 'open movement'.[52] Events in that year, before and after that crucial day, pointed to the resuscitation of constitutional and the strengthening of unconstitutional nationalism. Ensor regarded the 1870 Land Act as establishing a reign of peace in Ireland destroyed only by the advent of agrarian distress, but Isaac Butt's address in the Bilton Hotel and the earlier meeting of his Tenant League were unequivocal signs to the contrary on the constitutional level. And Hartington hit the nail on the head about direct action in 1871: 'No one but a fool could have supposed that the disestablishment of a Church, or the alteration of the position of the stronger tenants by the Act of 1870 would prevent village ruffians from committing outrages', though 'this was no argument against the intrinsic merit of that legislation'.[53] That the Liberals feared what was afoot in Ireland is amply proved by the passing of a Peace Preservation Act.[54] Ribbonism was active against men like Moore, not to speak of the less 'Green' landlords. At first the Home Government Association had in it more Protestant Conservatives, smarting under the impact of disestablishment and the prospect of changes in the land system, than Catholic nationalists, Liberal or otherwise. Within a matter of months the tendency was clearly the other way and continued so, but what proved of vital importance for the future was the failure to build up numerous branches all over the country. The Association aimed at uniting men on one issue—Home Rule. Its composition put an accompanying programme on Tenant Right, education and amnesty right out of court. This meant each group of nationalists in the constituencies had

[51] Ibid.

[52] R. Barry O'Brien, op. cit. p. 65, n. 1. For a discussion of an alleged compact between Butt and the Fenians, see Thornley, *Isaac Butt*, pp. 87–8. For many Home Rule was Repeal in disguise (W. Bence Jones, op. cit. p. 61).

[53] Bernard Holland, op. cit. p. 87.

[54] Ibid.

to fend for itself. At first, this was a blessing from a genuine nationalist viewpoint, for it meant that priests and other Liberal nationalists were not kept out of local organizations as disillusionment with Gladstone's government mounted. Their distrust of and dislike for the Association lasted to some extent until its transformation into the Home Rule League in December 1873, although the University Education crisis had done much to destroy any hostility based on positive friendship for orthodox British Liberalism. The disadvantage of incomplete coverage was scarcely felt so long as electoral activity was restricted to by-elections, in which outside help could be improvised. Later the lack of ready means for coping with a snap General Election was to irk the Home Rule League. There was insufficient time between its foundation and the 1874 dissolution to repair previous neglect. For the Conservative latter-day nationalists an early extension of Association activity might have proved an advantage. Once enthusiasm got going, however, nothing would have sold them to the Catholics. Butt himself was different. He had ceased to be a Conservative save on external affairs. The nationalist element risked association with the Conservatives to further the Home Rule, or Federalist, cause. The course of events justified their conduct, not least because of the flexibility in the constituencies.

Of the eight by-elections held in 1870, seven occurred before the formation of the Federalist committee. It cannot be stressed too much that the trend of the elections depended greatly upon whether or not a local cadre of activists in the nationalist cause happened to have come together in the particular constituencies affected, or whether or not outside interference by other nationalists looked like paying dividends. If the electorate had no Home Rule candidate it could not oust the British-linked parties. If the electorate had a Home Ruler whose *bona fides* it suspected the Liberals tended to get the benefit of the doubt. Tipperary was a Liberal gain, but a remarkable tribute to lay nationalist strength; Mallow a narrow victory for the Liberal over the Conservative; Queen's County an unopposed Liberal return and Dublin University an unopposed Conservative one. Longford and Waterford City were fought by men soon to be associated with the Home Government Association, but won by the Liberals. Mayo kept up the Moore tradition by returning a Home Ruler unopposed, the first gain for a constitutionalist nationalist. Dublin City polled two months after the Bilton Hotel meeting. The Liberals gained the seat from the Conservatives, there being no orthodox candidate on their behalf. The same Home Ruler as had contested Longford fared badly here.

Both Longford and Dublin City showed the essential futility of the new 'Orange' and the growing strength of the 'Green' Home Rule movement. The Catholic electorate preferred Liberals and mild reform to the services of those whose very Home Rule opinions had been adopted to try and bring to an end the existing trends towards the things the masses of the south and west had long craved for. Home Rule propaganda by Major Knox in the *Irish Times* during the Mallow by-election cut no ice for E. R. King Harman, contesting Longford as a Conservative-Liberal, or Home Ruler. Nor did other efforts by sundry Conservative Home Rulers, not even the statement by a Protestant clergyman that the Queen's crown should be thrown into the River Boyne.[55] Whilst cautious, the priesthood openly condemned him, as did the Liberal press, including the *Freeman's Journal*, which deplored 'the insidious attempt made to seduce them from their allegiance to their country and drag them into the mire of Toryism'.[56] His defeat by G. F. Greville-Nugent, brother of Reginald, decisive though it was, could not be viewed with much pleasure in Liberal or clerical circles. 1217 to 932 was a lot less impressive than 1478 to 411. Of course King Harman had some orthodox Conservative votes, but it was certainly not without significance that Longford was a county where the Conservatives were very weak, and that an 'Orange' landlord had persuaded more than double the number of voters in a predominantly Catholic constituency to support him than had supported a 'Green' nationalist the year before. Some Catholics at least were prepared to snub their priests openly by voting for a Home Ruler whatever his pedigree. Nor had any effort been spared by either side. The poll was 77 per cent. Still, King Harman had been standing on his head. 'Green' Home Rule was the real beneficiary.

Dublin provided some brisk electioneering. Sir Dominic Corrigan, the Liberal candidate, had narrowly missed election in 1868. When fully backed by Whigs and nationalists together he polled 5379. His fellow Liberal, Jonathan Pim, was elected with 5586 and the top man, the Conservative, Sir A. E. Guinness, received 5587. In the by-election Corrigan scored only 4468 against King Harman's 3444. The *Dublin Evening Mail* admitted that 'the Liberals had rejected' the latter 'as a Tory' and 'the Tories for their part disowned him as subversive'.[57] Certainly, as in Longford, some Conservatives had not disowned him and the 'Orange' Home Rulers had quite a following in Dublin, but allowing for these things, 3444 votes was quite an achievement and the drop of about 1000 in the Liberal vote at a time when a demonstration of strength must have been highly desired not without importance for the future. This was the first by-election since the launching of the Home Rule programme and the government needed a knock-out victory. In fact their success was rather hollow. Voting for King Harman required real moral courage in 'patriot' electors. Apart from the material risks to be run there was the danger of being branded a 'Tory' for lending countenance to an 'Orange' landlord. That so many did it testified to the inherent strength of the Home Rule appeal under even so unattractive a guise. That such

[55] D. Thornley, *I.H.S.* p. 203; M. G. Moore, op. cit. p. 355.
[56] D. Thornley, *I.H.S.* p. 209; *Freeman's Journal*, 15 April, 12 May, 1870.
[57] Ibid.

success as this landlord had was mainly due to his being a means to an end cannot be overstressed.

To come within 8 of winning Waterford City and to carry Mayo un-opposed, both with no-nonsense nationalist candidates—these were the real triumphs of the sentiments later to sustain Parnell. Individual nationalists could achieve a great deal simply by putting up their colours. Large portions of the electorate and even larger proportions of the non-electors welcomed them with open arms. P. J. Smyth had fought Waterford back in February. George Browne was returned for Mayo just one week before the Bilton Hotel meeting. It therefore met with one member of Parliament elected under the banner to be espoused, besides William Shaw of Bandon and Philip Callan of Dundalk who had been returned as Liberals and could not be absolutely sure of re-election. The Catholic priests loathed all Conservatives, but were beginning to regret their long flirtation with the Liberals, or rather, very many of them were. The obvious beneficiaries from the change would be the old nationalists, Liberal nationalists and tamed Fenians. The combina-tion between those experienced manipulators of votes—the priests—and the spontaneous nationalism of masses was again within sight. Under skilful leadership it had scant need of secret voting to flay the landlords of 'Unionist' persuasion. Under no leadership at all, or scarcely any, it could get a long way, even when imperfectly formed. Whig priests were to be taught that they at least were not 'the mind' of the Irish 'people'.

The next year the Home Rule movement spread much more rapidly and the initiative passing to its hands was never again lost. Ribbonism had taken over in some parts of the country when direct action Fenianism petered out. A crop of agrarian outrages in County Westmeath and 'neighbouring dis-tricts' eventually obliged the government to suspend Habeas Corpus there. 'Experience shows that' such crimes 'could not be sufficiently dealt with under the ordinary law, reinforced though it was by the provisions of the Peace Preservation Act. It was impossible to obtain evidence or secure convictions against the evil-doers.'[58] Indeed, so serious did things become that the Cabinet asked Parliament to appoint a Select Committee to 'inquire secretly' into 'the nature, extent and effect of a certain unlawful combination and confederacy'. On the strength of its findings, Hartington spoke of an 'intolerable state of terrorism, based upon murder[59] and reluctantly intro-duced the Bill for dispensing with Habeas Corpus. In August a highly unfortunate clash broke out in Phoenix Park between the police and a large crowd of nationalists which had defied the forbidding of an amnesty meeting. With the Prince of Wales and Prince Arthur staying at Viceregal Lodge the whole affair took on a particularly sinister character. The subsequent release of the Fenian prisoners still 'confined to English dungeons'[60] seemed like a

[58] Bernard Holland, op. cit. p. 84.
[59] Ibid. p. 88.
[60] Ibid. p. 89.

surrender to violence, and did little or nothing to appease nationalism, while alarming loyalists. When Lord Dufferin defended the release of certain Fenian prisoners in March, declared Fenianism had failed and claimed that Ireland was 'in a condition of peace and political tranquillity from one end of the country to the other',[61] he was either thinking wishfully, or relying on the force of the Peace Preservation Act. Gladstone was busy at the year's end pooh-poohing trouble. Speaking at Aberdeen he defended the Union with considerable warmth and smugness, designating University Education the only remaining Irish grievance. Parliament had to set itself right with the national conscience, but he refused to admit that Ireland was not going to be conciliated. In his conceit, little did he realise what small effect his refusing to do 'this or that' was going to have for some time upon the Irish scene.[62]

Seven by-elections went on against this background. Home Rulers won four, the Conservatives two and the Liberals just one. With such results the non-nationalist priests and Liberals had seriously to consider whether support for the Home Rule cause might not be essential for the full maintenance of spiritual and social influence in the one case and political and social influence in the other. At the same time the nature of Home Rule support, the role of the old nationalists and the behaviour of Butt disgusted the 'Orange' Home Rulers. When the leader of the Home Government Association spoke out constantly for Tenant Right and state maintenance of denominational education their world seemed on the edge of destruction. In the first of the by-elections—County Meath—John Martin of Longford fame beat G. Plunkett by 1140 to 684 on a 50 per cent poll. As in Longford the Liberal had been underwritten by the priesthood before Martin's appearance upon the scene, but this time no firm front was maintained against him. Evidently the spontaneous feelings of the majority of the electorate were strong enough to prevent any spiritual blitzkrieg, albeit Plunkett was both Whig and Catholic, while Martin was an Ulster Presbyterian and sometime editor of the *Irish Felon*! For what the *Freeman* termed an 'improvised raid'[63] the vote was extremely impressive, and this it admitted. 'The Meath election is a great fact. It may eventuate in nothing important, but even should it be so, it is still a great fact. It may, however, prove to be the beginning of the end.'[64] Like in Tipperary and Mayo, but unlike the second Longford and Dublin elections, Meath gave no openings for anti-Home Rule propaganda based on anti-Conservatism. The discomfiture of Whiggery was there for all to see, and, in the words of the *Nation*, it looked as though 'Henceforth the spell-word of self-rule must be the "Open Sesame" to the constituencies'.[65]

[61] Sir Alfred Lyall, *The Life of the Marquis of Dufferin and Ava*, I, 187.
[62] *Annual Register, 1871*, p. 105.
[63] D. Thornley, *I.H.S.* p. 211; *Freeman's Journal*, 2 Jan. 1871.
[64] D. Thornley, *I.H.S.* p. 211; *Freeman's Journal*, 6 Jan. 1871.
[65] D. Thornley, *I.H.S.* p. 211; *The Nation*, 6 Jan. 1871.

The next four elections were unopposed. At Newry the Liberals ran no candidate and allowed the Conservative, Viscount Newry, to gain a seat for his party. In County Limerick the Liberals retained the seat, with an unopposed return. William Monsell had just been made Postmaster-General and evidently no one on the nationalist side felt confident of his being disposed of as was the unfortunate Vesey Fitzgerald in Clare back in 1828. Certainly the priests would have fought hard for him, and there were, of course, always the government's education plans to bear in mind. Too much antagonizing might not pay, and failure to bring off 'an improvised raid' would have boomeranged hard on an up and coming cause. February saw Mitchell Henry returned for Galway with a programme of 'denominational education, "the dignity and independence of the Pope", and home government'.[66] Although he did not join the Home Government Association until 1873, and supported the government over the Westmeath inquiry there is no doubt of his nationalism. Curiously enough it was in Westmeath where the next vacancy arose. Again Home Rule, represented by P. J. Smyth, had a victory. The new member of Parliament combined an impeccable nationalist record with an unerring support for the political policies of the Catholic Church and had received the blessing, however reluctant, of the local ecclesiastical arm. The bishop told a disappointed Whig aspirant for this favour that he and his priests had been 'afraid to oppose the popular feeling that would be evoked' had Smyth not been sponsored. He added that in Meath such priests as had given strong support to Plunkett were now aware of 'an antagonism' between themselves and their flocks.[67] Nevertheless, allowances must be made for the circumstances under which these statements were made. Whereas Cardinal Cullen deplored the Meath result, Archbishop MacHale had welcomed it. The younger and less officially favoured priests had many genuine nationalists in their ranks and there is no reason for supposing the counties of Meath and Westmeath were exceptional and had none resident within their borders. Popular pressure doubtless served as an excuse for them to brave the displeasure of their superiors, and anyway, what could a superior say against championing Home Rule when he was himself trimming before its mighty wind to avoid upsetting 'popular feeling'? Besides the shift in clerical policy occasioned by such feeling, there is the force of intimidation from below to consider. In Westmeath it was obviously quite considerable and far outweighed any terrors landlord retaliation might have. If anything a loyal tenant rather than a disloyal one had to look out for himself under the open voting system. In 1870, Moore had pointed out that 'the utterance of disaffection in Ireland is no longer treason, it is the expression of the long-considered and matured judgment of the whole nation'.[68]

[66] D. Thornley, *I.H.S.* p. 212; *Freeman's Journal*, 10 Feb. 1871.
[67] D. Thornley, *I.H.S.* p. 212; J. A. Dease to W. Monsell, 14 and 15 June 1871, Monsell Prs. Nat. Lib. Ire. MS. 8317.   [68] M. G. Moore, op. cit. p. 361.

In 1871 that utterance of disaffection did not always have to go as far as individual declarations in contested elections. The general will was sometimes keeping the non-Home Rule landlords at home and bringing off unopposed returns of leading agents of constitutional protest.

If further proof of current trends had been needed, it was more than provided by the County Monaghan contest. While pressures were being exerted on Butt himself to contest the seat, a Conservative Home Ruler, John Madden, backed by a number of prominent 'Orange' and 'Green' Home Rulers, came forward. His supporters appealed to Protestants not to vote Conservative and to Catholics not to support the Liberal, one H. O. Lewis, 'who had already addressed the county for the ballot, denominational education and the defence of the Pope'.[69] Immediately, the Catholic Liberal nationalists were up in arms. Not for Madden the fate of King Harman—he never reached the poll. The key fact to understanding the inherent weakness of 'Orange' Home Rule was that once Madden withdrew and Butt came forward to save the day, the priests, most Liberals and the *Freeman* straightway left Lewis in the lurch. The fight was finally directly between Leslie, the orthodox Conservative and Butt. The former won. The figures were 2521 and 1528 and the poll was just over 73 per cent. Not a surprising result for that partially Protestant county, yet a firm demonstration of nationalist strength and the true nature of Irish nationalism, openly given and scored on a restricted franchise. Butt concentrated on Tenant Right. Nevertheless, Home Rule was not hidden from view. There was no gathering in of votes by false pretences.

Nor were any punches pulled in his successful bid for the representation of Limerick City two months later. Right from the start he spoke out for 'a Catholic University and denominational education, in addition to his well-known radical views on Tenant Right'.[70] The 'Orange' Home Rulers might bewail the adulteration of their cause, 'here by an Ultramontane, there by a Fenian ally',[71] but in that so-called adulteration lay the heart of popular Irish nationalism. However much his programme was disliked by 'the Quality', its fear of 'the Quantity' gave Butt an unopposed return to Westminster. With two new recruits from the Liberal members of Parliament —John Maguire of Cork City and McCarthy Downing of County Cork— there were as the year closed 9 Home Rulers among the 103 representatives of Ireland.

During the first months of 1872 excitement continued to mount. In Britain serious doubts had arisen 'as to that new era of peace and goodwill' in Ireland 'which Mr Gladstone had foretold as a response to the legislative

[69] D. Thornley, *I.H.S.* p. 213; *The Nation*, 15 July 1871.

[70] D. Thornley, *I.H.S.* p. 214; *The Irish Times*, 5 Sept. 1871.

[71] D. Thornley, *I.H.S.*, *Dublin Evening Mail*, 12 Sept. 1871. W. Bence Jones (op. cit. p. 62) alleges 'sympathy with Fenianism, and nothing else' was the 'true characteristic' of the Limerick City by-election.

benefits which he had been shedding upon her'.[72] Whig Liberalism, which 'thanks to the support of the clergy had hitherto been the dominant policy'[73] there, was suffering a rapid decline. Electors and non-electors were together making it perfectly plain that 'Home Rule had a great hold upon the mass of the Irish people'.[74] Later, nationalists of the new model party were to regard men of the Mitchell Henry and P. J. Smyth stamp with some hostility, but, as one of them put it,

at the time when Home Rule was still in its dawn, the election of Mr P. J. Smyth and the election of Mr Mitchell Henry were hailed with jubilation as proof of the amount of vitality in the country. The election of Mr John Martin for Meath and of Mr Butt himself for Limerick gave fresh impetus to the advancing movement, which now began to be regarded with equal enthusiasm in Ireland and indignation in England.[75]

He might have added the victories of Captain Nolan in Galway and of R. P. Blennerhassett in Kerry, the last startling contributions to Irish electoral history in the years before the secret ballot.

They took place against a background of rising prosperity, even in the west of the country, and showed how little the 'political chimeras' had 'been dispelled by recent legislation'.[76] Both provide classic evidence on the misconceptions of the Parnell school as to the necessity of the secret ballot. Galway was an instance of the landlords versus the rest, with an orthodox Conservative as the 'unionist' aspirant.

Mr Justice Keogh, in one of the less abusive parts of his judgement on the subsequent petition, denounced the election as 'the most astonishing attempt at ecclesiastical tyranny which the whole history of priestly intolerance afforded'.[77] Naturally, this cannot be regarded as anything other than a ludicrous exaggeration. Yet there is no denying that, from the archbishop of Tuam down to the meanest curate, the Catholic clergy excelled themselves in zeal for Nolan. They would have preferred him to Henry at the previous by-election because of his strong views on the temporal restoration of the pope. Yet the simple 'Orange' versus 'Green' battle really determined their basic position for them, and the outlook and initiative of MacHale made it a remarkably active one. Indeed, had he been primate of Ireland, Parnell might well have found his part in the country's history much smaller than it turned out to be. As a landlord who had of his own free will 'submitted to an arbitration award which restored a number of his evicted tenants to their holdings',[78] Nolan was anathema to most of his class. Many a Whig land-

---

[72] Lady Gwendolin Cecil, *Life of Robert, Marquis of Salisbury*, ii, 38.
[73] L. Paul-Dubois, *Contemporary Ireland*, Introduction by T. M. Kettle, M.P., p. 79.
[74] J. McCarthy, M.P., *Ireland Since the Union*, p. 216.
[75] Ibid.
[76] *Annual Register, 1872*, p. 11.
[77] Ibid. p. 80.
[78] D. Thornley, *I.H.S.* p. 216.

owner therefore found himself supporting E. le Poer Trench, the Conservative. Land bulked large in the contest, joining with nationalism and religion
to create the violent emotional force necessary to blast the control landlords
almost invariably tried to exercise over the way in which their tenants voted.
The result would show beyond doubt whether the 'popular' side could use
this force to best advantage. The result was: Nolan 2823, le Poer Trench 658;
almost a 70 per cent poll. Had all the remaining 30 per cent voted Conservative, Nolan would still have won.

Kerry was a much more complicated affair. There, the Home Ruler was
a Protestant and his Whig opponent a Catholic. Unlike Galway, it was not
under the jurisdiction of MacHale and the local bishop was none other than
Moriarty, an enthusiastic Whig. The clergy were badly split and the Fenian
contribution a good deal beyond the 'benevolent neutrality' promised before
the Bilton Hotel meeting, as, of course, it had been at by-elections in the
previous year as well. Moriarty was to see at first hand the involvement of
his younger clergy with a nationalist movement 'tainted with the revolutionary
spirit'.[79] Four years before he told William Monsell: 'The clergy will preach
against rebellion on account of the evils it will bring on the people, but I am
sure that their almost unanimous opinion is, that if there was a fair chance of
success, it would be lawful, nay "dulce et decorum".'[80] Now, with 'the
whole constitution...in their hands',[81] the masses were using it 'for their
own purposes'.[82] Given the possibility of a revolution in slow motion, their
priests tended more and more to preach it.

Reporting three weeks before the polling took place, Lord Kenmare told
Hartington: 'I feel confident that, although the fight will be a *very tough* one
indeed, we shall win. Blennerhassett's agents openly confess that they rely
on mob intimidation and that our voters will be afraid to come to the Poll.
Their mobs are aggressively Fenian. We shall have to take every precaution
to ensure protection of voters.'[83] Bishop Moriarty had abandoned the
optimism of 1868 and was especially worried about denominational education.
He poured out his thoughts, this time to Hartington: 'We are in for a very
hard fight in Kerry. All territorial influence at one side, a foolish people
led astray by a bad press on the other.'[84] How different from the old claim
that the priests ran extensively read newspapers and 'the people read no
other'![85] He continued:

Your Lordship's speech at Knighton has increased our difficulty. Priests who were
with me in advocating Mr Dease's return have been turned over. They do not

[79] The words are Cardinal Cullen's. See J. H. Whyte, *I.H.S.* p. 194.
[80] Ibid. p. 198.
[81] M. G. Moore, op. cit. p. 362.   [82] Ibid.
[83] Lord Kenmare to Lord Hartington, 14 Jan. 1872, Devonshire Papers 340. 483.
[84] The Bishop of Kerry (Moriarty) to Lord Hartington, 10 Jan. 1872, Devonshire Papers
340. 482.
[85] J. H. Whyte, *I.H.S.* p. 195.

complain of the policy you enunciate, but of the insult your expression conveys. They never asked that the education of Ireland should be handed over to them. When the landlords and parsons refused or neglected to cooperate with the National Board, the priests at great personal sacrifice built the schools of three provinces. Your speech will make some and confirm many Home Rulers. I do not know whether it is possible for your Lordship to say anything in explanation.[86]

It was, but confusion became only the worse confounded. A letter of Hartington's attempted to smooth down the priests, but repeated that 'the demands of the Catholic Bishops' were 'such as Parliament could not grant'.[87] Moriarty felt its publication 'would prejudice the election contest'[88] further.

Meanwhile the bishop had felt constrained to address a 'solemn warning' to the electors. 'You do not always know your friends,' he admonished.

Stand by a Legislature which has given to your property a security and prosperity which your fathers never hoped for...farmers of Kerry, beware! It is not the place of Parliament which these agitators so much desire to change. It is the representation of the country which does not please them. If you give them their way, you will have household suffrage, and then manhood suffrage; and then your labourers and servant boys, and the journeymen of your towns, will choose your representatives and become your masters, and then—.

As deliberate a piece of oligarchical self-esteem as any Whig ever gave voice to; and it ended with the assurance that in her present state of disunion, self-government would bring only 'a war of faction and class' to Ireland.[89] An attempt by John Bright to aid Dease by a letter denouncing Home Rule only got him ridiculed in the *Irishman* as 'our fat friend', 'politically narrow and politically selfish—a social revolutionist, and not a statesman'.[90] A charge coming ill from that quarter.

It was hardly surprising that Blennerhassett's agents relied on intimidation. As demonstrated, the mob was the most effective answer to landlord pressures, especially where the clergy was divided. That a fair election did not ensue does nothing to prove the 'popular' side needed a secret ballot. On the contrary, their opponents seemed to need it more in the face of priest-cum-Fenian counter attack. Requests for military protection were, as always, from what ironically had now become the anti-popular side. The night of Kerry was almost frantic with anxiety lest a gunboat should not be sent to Valentia and Kenmare implored Hartington to see troops 'should be in the county a week before' polling, as 'The intimidation is tremendous and their presence would give confidence'.[91] He deemed it absolutely essential 'that it should become well-known that the voters will be amply protected'.[92]

[86] The Bishop of Kerry (Moriarty) to Lord Hartington, 10 Jan. 1872, Devonshire Papers 340. 482.
[87] Ibid. 19 Jan. 1872, Devonshire Papers 340. 484.
[88] Ibid.
[89] *Annual Register, 1872*, p. 12. [90] Ibid. p. 13.
[91] Lord Kenmare to Lord Hartington, 27 Jan. 1872, Devonshire Papers 340. 487.
[92] Ibid.

Whiggery was in very low water indeed when the Whig lord lieutenant of the one county in Ireland where his party outstripped the Conservatives in its following among the landowners had to admit 'the intimidation and the *terror*' coming from an independent left was 'almost incredible'.[93] Naturally, many electors could not be evicted for voting Home Rule, and they knew it.[94] But social unpleasantness of high intensity could be heaped upon them by revengeful landlords. Moreover, while true that non-electors did not vote, their activity during the election could still be duly noted and acted on afterwards. Intimidation was a highly necessary part of the rise of a fully effective Irish party, just as in British industry militant trade unionism proved essential to the creation of extensive Labour representation. Perhaps one of its most effective achievements was in causing Whig, or rather landlord finances to reach breaking point. In this particular election, Dease had been chosen because of his financial resources. 'Castlerosse and he' were said to be able 'to stand the shot which no one else, certainly of the natives, was prepared to do'.[95] 'The shot' was estimated as likely to be £1500, it finally exceeded £6000, a sum not easily to be found. Apart from the transport costs arising out of getting voters to the poll,[96] there was the question of bribery. It looked as though the landlords just could not raise enough to make men brave Fenian violence. Violence which was not simply a matter of a few weeks before and during the election, but something likely to prove dangerous in the months after it was over, and the 4000 soldiers were no longer there. And this raises the added point that military protection could but be temporary, however genuine the need. Large numbers could not be given constant personal protection *ad infinitum*. When sentiment and safety coincided to favour the 'popular' cause, very large sums indeed were needed for bribes. Kerry showed that a large sum just was not enough. Yet how could bigger ones ever be raised, and how could a party as poor as the Liberals fight a whole country on that basis? When Parnell acquired money he was able to dispense with 'the Independent gentlemen, who would not be certain to take orders'.[97] He had not needed it to throw out the opponents of Home Rule.[98]

A result giving Blennerhassett 2237 votes and Dease 1398 derived from conditions rather different from those obtaining in Galway. With the transfer

[93] Ibid.

[94] Because of the nature of their land tenure. Of course, landlords with long memories might later decline to renew leases. Non-electors also stood to lose if noticed as part of the anti-landlord campaign. The fact of their not having votes would not necessarily mean their contribution to landlords' discomfiture had not been significant.

[95] Lord Kenmare to Lord Hartington, 27 Jan. 1872, Devonshire Papers 340. 487.

[96] The Whigs hired a special train for the purpose (*Annual Register, 1872*, p. 14).

[97] W. B. Gwyn, op. cit. p. 135.

[98] Blennerhassett had money, but others had done as well without it. Nevertheless, Lord Kenmare was right to count the fact a Home Rule advantage in Kerry, however exaggerated his view that it supplied 'the only thing wanting for the full development of their (i.e. the Home Rulers') mischief'.

of priestly favour and influence to the 'popular' side incomplete, the high
Liberal vote did not necessarily represent a marked degree of successful
landlord pressure, though some there undoubtedly was. Curiously enough
the issue was considered doubtful till the last, 'when great pressure was put
on, and the popular excitement increased as the non-electors saw the preparations which were made for bringing Mr Dease's friends to the poll under
military escort'.[99] Kenmare declared that as far as he knew 'nothing…
could be better than the arrangements made by the Government for the protection of the voters; there was', he believed, 'ample force in the county'.[100]
The news of Nolan's victory probably made up any deficiency in the local
propaganda and had 'some effect upon the wavering and timid voters. Some
were emboldened to oppose the wishes of their landlords, and others feared
to encounter the resentment of the people, who were lashed into a state of
frenzy by the incessant appeals of the Home-Rule orators. The polling,
however, was carried on without any of the rioting which brought disgrace
upon many former elections in the South'[101]—a sure sign Kenmare's assessment of the military was correct. Several priests actually led in their flocks
to vote for Blennerhassett.

The poll was 66 per cent and some Whigs were left dazed by the size of
the Home Rule majority because of the announcements as to the number of
pledged supporters made by Dease's committee, headed by Sir James
O'Connell. Very sensibly they drew the conclusion that some had been persuaded not to vote, and others to break their promises, but rather disingenu-
ously put it all down to genuine fear of 'the indignation of the multitude'.[102]
That men had seized at an excuse for abstention or desertion does not seem
to have crossed their minds. Kenmare said, 'every considerable landlord'[103]
came out for Dease. Another account that 'The influence of the landlords
was not all thrown into the scale, for several owners of property, including
some Conservatives, were favourable to Mr Blennerhassett, or remained
neutral, a position which in a contest of this kind is favourable to the popular
candidate'.[104] The two are consistent if all the 'popularists' and neutralists
were small men, and, anyway, unpromised votes could not desert. The
collapse of much of the landlords' hold itself entailed the breaking of a multitude of promises. This was where using popular pressure as an excuse came
in. Some examples of what happened have been recorded, for example:

Mr Denny had appointed seven o'clock in the morning to meet eighty tenants at a
certain cross-road and come into Tralee with them to vote for Mr Dease. He was
there at the time named with a strong escort, but there were no tenants, and he had

[99] *Annual Register, 1872*, p. 14.
[100] Lord Kenmare to Lord Hartington, 13 Feb. 1872, Devonshire Papers 340. 494.
[101] *Annual Register, 1872*, p. 14.
[102] Ibid. p. 15.
[103] Lord Kenmare to Lord Hartington, 13 Feb. 1872, Devonshire Papers 340. 494.
[104] *Annual Register, 1872*, p. 15.

to return alone; for the Rev. Eugene O'Sullivan, P.P. of Spa had made an appointment with them for the same hour to meet him at another place and vote for Mr Blennerhassett. A contingent, numbering 200 electors from Castleisland, Brosna, and other adjoining parishes, came in about twelve o'clock, accompanied by a band, and voted in a body for Mr Blennerhassett. They had been canvassed by their landlord, the Hon. Mr Wynne, for Mr Dease, and dinner had been provided for them; but at a signal they rose almost to a man and left him, after handing a written refusal to vote as he desired. Only eighteen of the party voted for Mr Dease. It is reported that the mob wrecked his house at night, and that he was obliged to secrete himself to escape personal violence.[105]

So secret did the populace wish their vote to be; so impossible was it to run an independent Irish party without the secret ballot! Evidence of a more negative kind came from Lenagh, where '*none* of Vintney's tenants were able to vote'.[106] Small wonder that Moriarty had asked for cavalry.[107]

The worthy bishop had even had faith in the weather as a general damper on proceedings,[108] but the Home Rule enthusiasm proved a stronger force. Kenmare stressed that: 'In recounting the causes of Dease's failure (and 'no possible local candidate would have conciliated the same amount of support')[109] I must not omit to mention the fascination exercised by the Home Rule cry over every class of the community save the landlords', and went on:

I believe that the idea entertained of its meaning is revolutionary, that it means the transfer of power and property from the present holders and a severance of the British connection. Under the circumstances, the election was carried by a vast amount of intimidation applied in every conceivable form, guided from Dublin, through the instrumentality of itinerant orators, local and imported Fenians ('spreading', as Moriarty phrased it, 'terror amongst the farmers and raising the hopes of the terrorist boys'),[110] the whole popular press and the unsurpassed energy of a powerful section of the priests, who combined to fan the Home Rule sentiment into a frenzy.[111]

Compared with such events the gain scored for Home Rule at Wexford Town in April and another Liberal victory at Mallow—both significant—passed scarcely noticed, and the Ballot Act came into force on 18 July.[112] Between the 1868 General Election and then eight Home Rulers had won by-elections.

---

[105] Ibid.

[106] Lord Kenmare to Lord Hartington, Feb. 1872, Devonshire Papers 340. 493.

[107] Bernard Holland, op. cit. p. 92; The Bishop of Kerry (Moriarty) to Lord Hartington, 1 Feb. 1872, Devonshire Papers 340. 491.

[108] Ibid.

[109] Lord Kenmare to Lord Hartington, 13 Feb. 1872, Devonshire Papers 340. 494.

[110] The Bishop of Kerry (Moriarty) to Lord Hartington, 1 Feb. 1872, Devonshire Papers 340. 491.

[111] Lord Kenmare to Lord Hartington, 13 Feb. 1872, Devonshire Papers 340. 494.

[112] It was to expire on 31 Dec. 1880, unless extended by Parliament. It was, but remained subject to renewal until 1918, when it acquired permanency.

Petitions had been lodged against the victors of Galway and Kerry, one with a notorious success, but what was more, the general conduct of the elections had finally convinced the government it should sponsor the secret ballot. On purely partisan grounds the Liberals seemed to have little to gain or lose in Ireland from the change. *Qua* government they longed for law and order. Troops were not only unsatisfactory from a practical angle. They were also a severe embarrassment to any British administration, especially one of the left. Hartington pointed out to Kenmare over Kerry that it was 'essential that, in making such extraordinary and exceptional preparations for an election, we should be able to show, if called upon, that we have only done what was necessary in order to preserve freedom of election, and that nothing has been done in the interest of either party'.[113] The smoother running of elections was Gladstone's main aim, and reassured about the prospects of increased priestly influence, he was relieved to find an answer. Not that other powerful factors did not weigh with him, Ireland just happened to be the most pressing. Home Rulers had demanded the secret ballot, but so had many Irish Liberals, and only one of them voted against it. Ideally, of course, abolition was the best guarantee that landlord pressures would end. Nevertheless, despite patches here and there, the Home Rule movement had in general already put paid to them.

In November Londonderry City, the first Irish contest since the Act was passed, was a Conservative gain. A small Home Rule vote split the left forces, and the Liberal Solicitor-General for Ireland suffered public humiliation. Almost a month later J. P. Ronayne won Cork City in a straight fight with a Conservative—another Liberal seat lost without as much as a token resistance, and Ronayne 'a raging Fenian'.[114] 1873 had but one contested by-election—in County Tyrone. County Armagh and Lisburn returned Conservatives, and Counties Roscommon and Waterford Liberals; far from dramatic sequels to what Parnell thought a significant new-found freedom. Subsequent events were to prove there was more in the last two than met the eye. A sitting member of Roscommon, The O'Conor Don, had already, along with Kenelm Digby, Queen's County, and Sir Rowland Blannerhassett, Galway City, subscribed to the Home Rule line during the year since Kerry. Only the last actually joined the Home Government Association and the other two remained nominally Liberals. The new member for Roscommon was in exactly the same position, being a Home Rule, Tenant Right and denominational education supporter. Down in Waterford the new member was also a fellow-traveller; so was his colleague, Sir J. Esmonde, who stood as an open Home Ruler in 1874. For one reason or another—sincere nationalism, tacking before the wind and a Catholicism enraged by Gladstone's University Bill among them—many a Liberal member of Parliament was

[113] Lord Hartington to Lord Kenmare, 28 Jan. 1872, Devonshire Papers 340. 488.
[114] Frederick Clay to Lord Hartington, 14 Nov. 1872, Devonshire Papers 340. 512.

reconsidering his position *vis-à-vis* Home Rule. Mathew D'Arcy of County Wexford was the last one individually to approve of it.[115] Bigger things were about to happen. On 21 November the Home Rule League, an unequivocally 'Green' nationalist body, was formed. Butt had taken the initiative in throwing off the embarrassments of the Home Government Association for good and all. Twenty-five members of Parliament were founder members,[116] the majority being Liberal. Admittedly, the 'green' had its pale patches, yet the masses found in them better expression of their national aspirations than any men since the end of the Repeal movement. It is vain to argue that secret voting had done all this. The signs that it would happen were unmistakable before July 1872 and have been demonstrated to have been such.

County Tyrone was the key as to where the Ballot Act would change the shape of politics, so long as the electorate remained narrow. In the by-election there, with a predominantly Protestant electorate, J. E. Macartney, a Tenant Right Conservative, failed by a mere 36 votes (3139 to 3103) to gain the seat from the orthodox Conservative. In 1868 both Conservatives had been unopposed. The usual champions of Tenant Right in Ulster were Radical Liberals. Armagh and Lisburn were difficult propositions and there had not been time for preparations to be made. A champion happened to be at hand in Tyrone and cut down the delay in attacking the landlords. The 1869 by-election and 1874 General Election figures for Antrim have only to be compared for the force of this point to be appreciated. Whereas in the by-election the Conservative majority had been 3294 on a 67·5 per cent poll, in 1874 it was 133 on a somewhat higher one. Exactly how much higher is difficult to determine because there were three candidates for two seats, but as both Conservatives received about the same number of votes there must have been a rise of roughly 5 per cent. While the Liberal vote almost doubled, the Conservative fell by 1200. This upsurge of Radicalism was but an instance of the trend throughout almost the whole of Ulster. Home Rule had beaten the Whigs on its own steam before the Ballot Act. Only by joining in the stream were most of them able to save themselves before as well as after 1872. Yet Ulster Radicalism had needed secrecy of voting to flourish. Why? In an area enjoying Ulster Tenant Right a sturdy independence in voting habits might have been expected. The answer probably lies in the lack of any supreme emotional rallying cries among the tenant farmers to combat social pressures. Neither nationalism nor Catholicism sparked them off, except into bitter hostility. A 'unionism' and Protestantism held in common with the aristocracy and gentry worked very much to the advantage of the

[115] Mathew D'Arcy was not member for County Waterford as stated by L. J. McCaffrey, *T.A.P.S.* p. 14.

[116] For a list of the twenty-five, see L. J. McCaffrey, *I.H.S.* Appendix A. A list of Irish members of Parliament who contested their seats as Home Rulers in 1874 can be found in Appendix B.

latter. Solidarity meant 'follow the leader' and most of the leaders were Conservative.[117]

In face of all the evidence, Parnell's assessment of the likely effect of the secret ballot cannot be upheld for the years which saw the beginnings of the Home Rule movement. With or without the help of the hierarchy, with or without the help of priests, and even in face of a strong clerical opposition, large sections of the Catholic Irish had shown the spirit behind independent opposition. In face of their enthusiasm the landlord interest had avoided or been beaten in open battle. Secret ballot had been needed for the maintenance of law and order, not for the sake of Irish freedom. And in the long run, before 1868 and after 1873, how did the 'spirit of constitutional independence'[118] show itself among the Catholic Irish? Generally speaking, it showed itself fairly strongly in the earlier periods and exceedingly so in the later ones. Before 1868 the basic fault in the Irish national movements would appear to have been at the top. Any people needs leading. With nothing to turn to except local authority, it will become politically malleable and concerned with its own petty parochial squabbles. This happened to the Catholic Irish before 1826. Then the priesthood formed a bridge between the Catholic middle-class nationalists and the masses. Landlords found themselves openly deserted by their tenants, who turned to other more liberal Protestants of property, prepared to champion Catholic Emancipation. At the beginning, a supply of rich Liberal Protestants was absolutely essential to the Catholic cause, for despite his famous victory in County Clare,[119] O'Connell was no more able to take his seat than O'Donovan Rossa forty years later. That very victory depended a lot on O'Connell's personal authority; had he not stood fewer voters would have taken risks for their cause. Indeed, the whole Emancipation and Repeal movements drew an enormous amount of strength from his directing hand. It was a truly remarkable thing that in a country so cursed with land hunger voters defied the preponderantly 'unionist' landowning class with so much tenacity. The Lichfield House Compact and elections fought hand in hand with the Whigs naturally blurred the national cause, but a new movement was emerging just as the famine virtually crushed the capacity for self-assertion. Within four years the 'Independent Brigade' idea was a reality. A quarter of a century had seen the emergence of the first 'Christian Democratic' party in the world, and its eventual failure under the impact of calamity and the fleshpots. It saw the recreation of that party in the 'Brigade' and a second failure under the impact of hierarchical displeasure and the fleshpots. What can the ordinary voter do, when lacking money, he has to rely on a church leadership that gives up the struggle and

[117] The admission of the more dependent labourers to the franchise in 1884 did much to restore Conservative fortunes in the region at the General Election of 1885.

[118] See n. 14.

[119] In 1828. Thus proving the formidable 'underswell in the Irish people' (W. E. H. Lecky, *Leaders of Public Opinion in Ireland*, II, 101).

representatives who choose to break their pledges? Before the abolition of the property qualification for members of Parliament in 1858 mere lack of funds was not the only problem. Small wonder that a period of demoralization set in.

The unconstitutional spirit of independence revived first, and, in the late 'fifties and early 'sixties, nationalist Irishmen came to regard Fenianism as their prime hope. The constitution seemed to have failed them and for many years the Liberals benefited from the efforts of the tough and tougher men (and women).[120] Evidence taken in inquiries over the 1868 General Election revealed their full importance. First the genuine surviving remnants of the 'Brigade', led by Moore, and then the Home Government Association changed all this. How, has been explained. Through all these vicissitudes the width of the franchise was often a factor, but never the prime one. The will to win more than survived the Irish County Franchise Act of 1829. Nationalism was reviving before the extension of the county vote in 1850. Home Rule grew up on the basis of that law, as the Reform Act of 1868 had little impact in a country with so few borough seats.[121] So long as Catholic or nationalist Protestant voters were on the register in any number the 'spirit of constitutional independence' thrived when well led. Individual priests there had always been on the national side, even at its lowest points, but it was Parnell's good fortune to inherit a popular movement backed by the Church. Through the power and example of the lay leaders the hierarchy itself began to work for the nationalist cause. In 1874 the transference of support was nearly complete. Nationalism had a reasonable leadership and scored heavily in the General Election. Butt had boasted Home Rule could win eighty seats at the next General Election at a time when it looked as though it would be fought on an open voting system.[122] As things turned out it did not exceed sixty, perhaps because of the strain put upon an embryonic central organization by a sudden dissolution. If the electorate had no faith in the Ballot Act as a means of preserving their secrets and yet that faith was necessary for the defeat of rampant landlordism, those holding the Parnell view have some explaining to do.[123] Moreover, if the electorate disbelieved in the Act's efficacy in 1874 and believed in 1880, why was so little ground gained by Home Rule in the General Election of the latter year?

[120] For the activities of the women in the Kerry by-election, see *Annual Register, 1872,* p. 15.
[121] Bernard Holland's claim in his biography of Devonshire (I, 91) that the extension of the urban franchise in 1867 'gave birth to a new democratic movement in Ireland' is palpable nonsense, and, in any case, the Irish Second Reform Act was passed in 1868. Its provisions were scarcely far-reaching. In borough constituencies the new law laid down £4 instead of £8 as the poor rate qualification for the franchise. As under the kindred British legislation, lodgers were given the vote subject to certain time and tenancy conditions. The county qualification remained unchanged. The rating had to be £12 or above.
[122] See L. J. McCaffrey, *T.A.P.S.* p. 13.
[123] See the comments on the views of C. C. O'Brien in n. 8.

They also forget that a national movement cannot be completely clandestine. Men need more than the secret vote to hide their politics. The use of the illiteracy clause must in some cases have been an attempt to avoid the danger of being dubbed a 'landlord's man'.[124] Boycotting was scarcely a secret occupation. In short, the Ballot Act was a minor matter in the history of Irish nationalism![125] Very often it was a protection to the unionist elements.[126]

What then made the new model Irish party? Most important was the 'spirit of constitutional independence' prevalent amongst the nationalist Irish. This spirit was fierce against the parliamentary party elected in 1874, many months before the agricultural depression began. Then there was a leader—Parnell—the first really outstanding layman since O'Connell. Add to these the supply of American money and the friendship of the church and all the essential ingredients are there. It might be argued the priests were not absolutely necessary, but without them the movement would have been short of educated men in the constituency parties during the first years. Agrarian distress merely accelerated the 'Butt Must Go' campaign, it did not create it. A wider franchise simply gained a few seats and increased majorities. But as for the party it was made, like Butt's, on the 1850 statute. The county constituencies were its backbone.

Historical myths are so easy to launch into a thing so permeated with emotion as the Irish question. Destroying them is never an easy proposition. This particular myth about the Ballot Act does the Irish nationalists less than justice, though, of course, it makes the British appear 'bloody, base and brutal'. Should not the picture be corrected, not only for the sake of truth, but for the sake of Irish self-esteem?

[124] The two main schools of thought on this are well represented by John Morley, op. cit. III, 254, and *The Liberal Unionist*, no. 19, where J. Gordon McCullagh had an article called 'Parnellism and Illiteracy'. Bernard Holland claims: 'It was, probably, one effect of the substitution of voting by ballot that in Ireland the secret power of the priest and of the masked secular intimidator prevailed over the terrors of the landlord. In any case these elections made it evident that future Irish governments might have to deal with something different either from occasional Fenian risings or from chronic subterranean anarchy' (op. cit. p. 93). On the other hand, the Committee on the secret ballot was convinced by the Catholic Bishop of Limerick that 'if secret elections were introduced no priest could bring pressure to bear on a penitent to make him say in the confessional how he voted: and not only that: if a penitent told a priest in confession how he had voted, nothing and nobody could make the priest tell it to anyone else' (Stanley Hyland, *Curiosities from Parliament*, p. 185).

[125] For an interesting corroboration of the main argument of this article, see the new novel *Thy Tears Might Cease*, by M. Farrell, at pp. 87–8. Whether right or wrong it bears out yet again the truth of W. S. Trench's assertion in *The Realities of Irish Life* (at p. 343) that a country election in Ireland was the 'most odious of all odious calamities'.

[126] Home Rule by-election losses during the 1874–80 parliament, like the one in Cork City in 1876, also went to show how unimportant the Ballot Act was. When there was zest Home Rule won. When there was not, it might or might not win. These criteria applied before and after the Act came into operation.

4

THE POLITICAL MOBILIZATION OF IRISH FARMERS
SAMUEL CLARK

This paper seeks to explain why an agrarian rebellion broke out in Ireland in the late nineteenth century. Although the level of discontent in rural Ireland was certainly high when the rebellion broke out, such a situation was not unprecedented. Discontent had been just as intense at earlier points in time (most notably during the first half of the nineteenth century) without similar political consequences. In order to understand why it was in the late nineteenth century that Irish rural tenants rebelled, we have to recognize that in the decades preceding the rebellion there had developed a new set of social conditions that facilitated rural political mobilization. Without exhausting the subject, the author suggests that these conditions consisted of leadership provided by the nationalist movement and an organizational base, provided by a number of structures, among which special emphasis is given to the cooperative relationship that emerged in the postfamine period between rural tenants and a segment of the town population. The study gives support to the mobilization rather than to the discontent thesis for the study of social protest.

In the late nineteenth century, Irish tenant farmers rebelled against their landlords. They took part in mass demonstrations, refused to pay their normal rents, resisted evictions, and in other ways challenged the existing system of land tenure. It was not the first time they had fought with their landlords, but it was the first time that the contest took on the proportions of a large-scale rebellion. Previously, agrarian protest in Ireland had been either limited to a small segment of the rural population or, if inclusive of many tenants, at a low, almost passive, level of participation. In the late nineteenth century, however, a large and broad sector of the farming population actively participated in a revolt against the land system. The revolt is popularly known among the Irish as the 'Land War.'

The agitation began in the spring of 1879 in the western province of Connaught, the poorest

* A shorter version of this paper was presented at a session of the Eighty-First Annual Convention of the American Psychological Association, Montreal, 27 August 1973

and most economically backward of the four Irish provinces. It quickly spread to other regions, and by 1880 the only part of Ireland into which it had not successfully penetrated was the province of Ulster. Initially, the aims of the movement were to reduce rents and to prevent evictions, but gradually tenants came to demand that the government abolish the landlord system entirely and undertake to finance the transfer of land holdings to their occupiers. The agitation raged off and on for two decades, reaching its peaks in 1879–82, in the late 1880s, and finally in 1898–1902. Although the first of a series of legislative measures that effectively assured the transfer of land to occupiers was not passed until 1903, the earliest of these three periods was nevertheless the most tumultuous and the most eventful phase of the Land War. For most of the period between 1879 and 1882 Irish tenants were organized in a large political association known as the Land League, under whose guidance a greater number of rural inhabitants actively engaged in political agitation than at any other time in Irish history.

THEORETICAL APPROACHES TO
REBELLION

In this paper I shall try to explain why the Irish Land War broke out when it did. In doing so, I shall make an effort to utilize theories of social protest developed by social scientists. For the kind of problem with which I am concerned, two distinctly different theoretical approaches are available. The first, which I shall call the *discontent thesis*, says that social protest occurs when there is an increase in popular dissatisfaction with some aspect of existing social arrangements. Researchers who lean towards this view have concentrated their energies on explaining why and when this kind of dissatisfaction experiences such an increase. The second approach, the *mobilization thesis*, says that social protest occurs when new political resources are being mobilized. Researchers who prefer this approach have concentrated their efforts on identifying factors that facilitate political mobilization.

Of the two, the discontent thesis has been the more popular. Probably most students of political unrest consider discontent to be the primal cause of rebellious behaviour. They typically begin with the 'common-sense assumption' that 'political turmoil is the consequence of social discontent' (Feierabend, et al., 1969:634). And

it is possible to find books on 'why men rebel' that contribute primarily to our understanding of what makes them angry (Gurr, 1970; Davies, 1970). Indeed, the study of discontent has been going on so long, and has been pursued with such energy, that we can claim considerable sophistication in our understanding of it. The principal refinement that has been made is the realization that discontent is as much a function of people's expectations as of their objective situation. Thus, it is very rare today to find social scientists explaining rebellions simply in terms of absolute level of deprivation. But it is quite common to find them attributing rebellions to a gap between the expectations people hold and their actual achievements.

The intellectual origins of this approach can be traced to scholarly giants such as de Tocqueville and Durkheim. Both men sought to explain social unrest as a function of rising expectations (de Tocqueville, 1888: especially, 152; Durkheim, 1951:246–7). In recent years, the most celebrated formulation of the theory of rising expectations is James Davies' J-curve. Davies (1962 and 1969) has argued that revolutions are most likely to occur when a prolonged period of objective economic and social development is followed by a period of sharp reversal. This reversal, even if it does not bring people to their former low levels, can create tremendous dissatisfaction because expectations acquired during the prosperity are disappointed. Other recent writers have argued that a gap between expectations and achievements can be produced under a variety of conditions, ranging from rising prosperity to declining prosperity (Geschwender, 1968; Gurr, 1970:46–56).

The second theoretical approach differs from the above by treating rebellion as a function of the mobilization of political resources. Social unrest occurs, it is argued, when the power of established political groups is challenged by new political collectivities. Carried to the extreme, the mobilization thesis states that discontent is always present in sufficient intensity to cause rebellion, but only does so when the discontented are mobilized. Not surprisingly, few of those who stress mobilization have made the argument in this extreme form. They almost always allow that an increase in discontent can significantly raise the probability of social unrest. But they frequently assert, to quote Charles Tilly, that 'men grow angry far more often than they rebel' (1970:144; see also

Snyder and Tilly, 1972). Thus, if we want to understand why they rebel, and when they may be expected to do so, we should consider other factors besides discontent, and, more specifically, we should direct our attention to those factors that tend to facilitate their mobilization.

It is rather difficult to indicate precisely the intellectual origins of the mobilization thesis. It can perhaps best be traced to Marx and more recently to Ralf Dahrendorf (1959). But there has been considerable disagreement, among students of mobilization, over what social conditions underlie this process. Indeed, there are those who explain mobilization in a way that comes pretty close to a discontent argument. For example, some writers relate mobilization to new political expectations, whose rise they trace to such things as the evolution of more egalitarian concepts of citizenship (Ortega, 1961; Mannheim, 1940:44–9; Bendix, 1964). Other writers argue that political mobilization occurs when individuals seek to overcome the rootlessness and alienation of mass society (Kornhauser, 1959). And still others link political mobilization to any set of changes that tend to break down old patterns of behaviour and make people available for new patterns (Deutsch, 1961). Yet there is at least one line of reasoning in the mobilization thesis that contrasts sharply with the discontent thesis. The two approaches differ most when students of mobilization stress the importance for rebellions of a *source of leadership* (Oberschall, 1973:119) and an *organizational base* (Pinard, 1968; Tilly, 1969:35–41; Oberschall, 1973:102–45).

We can briefly review some of the reasons that have been given for emphasizing these variables. One of the foremost justifications for stressing the importance of a source of leadership is that discontented groups generally have a scarcity of persons with the skills, experience, and economic security necessary to lead a revolt against established institutions. As a result, the leadership for rebellions often comes from strata outside, or at least marginal to, the strata from which the main support is drawn. It is usually crucial to the probability of rebellion that there be available some external group of persons who not only possess leadership skills but are also willing to take up the cause of the discontented group and are able to establish the social connections with this group that are required to provide it with leadership.

The importance of an organizational base is derived, at least in part, from the necessity for channels of communication among potential supporters of a rebellion, and between these supporters and the leadership. An organizational base is also important in so far as it provides a network of cooperative relationships that can effectively serve to motivate people to support a rebellion. An organizational base may consist of communal bonds founded on ties of kinship, community, tribe, or region, or it may consist of associational bonds founded on occupational, religious, political, economic, or other special-interest groups. The mobilization thesis (at least the version I am describing) contends that the probability of rebellion is greater if organizational bonds of this kind exist, if these bonds are strong, and if they are sufficiently independent of established institutions that they can be adapted to serve the purposes of rebellion.

It should be made clear that the mobilization thesis does not in any way deny that discontent is a necessary condition for social protest. No one disputes the fact that, in order to explain rebellions, we have to explain why people get angry. Since this is what the discontent theorists have been trying to do, it would seem to be a relatively simple matter for students of rebellion to combine the two approaches into one comprehensive theory. Doubtless, if we were merely interested in enumerating the social conditions that underlie protest, the differences between the discontent thesis and the mobilization thesis would cause no problem. We would simply list both discontent and mobilization as necessary conditions. But most students of rebellion are less interested in a comprehensive list of conditions for protest than they are in explaining why rebellions occur in certain places and at certain times. Why does social order occasionally break down? Why do people challenge governments, ruling classes, and even social systems that they did not challenge before? Faced with these questions, it is more difficult to integrate the discontent thesis and the mobilization thesis. Inevitably, discontent theorists will acknowledge the importance of mobilization but will explain the timing of rebellions in terms of increased discontent, while mobilization theorists will acknowledge the importance of discontent but will explain the timing of rebellions in terms of mobilization.

It is unlikely, therefore, that a genuine integration of these approaches is imminent. I certainly shall not seek to integrate them in this paper. My objective is a more limited one: to assess the relative usefulness of the two theories for explaining the timing of one particular rebellion. In doing so, I shall make a special effort to put the discontent thesis to a test more severe than it is normally required to withstand. Too often discontent theorists are satisfied with demonstrating the presence of a high level of discontent at the point in time that a rebellion breaks out. They suppose that if they explain this high level of discontent they have ipso facto explained the rebellion. For example, Davies (1962 and 1969) believes that he has provided empirical support for his theory by showing that various revolts he has studied were immediately preceded by conditions that conform to his J-curve. Yet he presents almost no evidence to refute the hypothesis that similar conditions may have existed in earlier periods without revolutionary consequences. Similarly, the Feierabends (1969) believe that they have explained political unrest during the transitional stage towards modernization simply by explaining why such a transition might generate discontent. Like Davies, they consider it unnecessary to demonstrate that discontent was actually absent when and where political unrest did not occur. They assume that whenever discontent is intense it will inevitably make itself noticed by generating instability in the political system. However, if one uses a much broader historical focus to study rebellions, one often finds evidence suggesting that assumptions of this kind are unwarranted. In the course of this paper, I shall try to evaluate the two theoretical approaches outlined above, not just by examining social conditions in the years immediately prior to the Land War, but also by examining, in a necessarily general way, social conditions in Ireland during the entire nineteenth century.

ORIGINS OF THE IRISH LAND WAR

Let me begin, then, with some preliminary observations on the structure of Irish society in the early nineteenth century. In order to understand why an agrarian rebellion could occur at all in Ireland, we must be aware of the social cleavages that plagued the country in this period. There are three that are critical for our purposes. First, there existed a belligerent relationship between landlords and tenants. Irish landlords were notoriously bad landlords. A high rate of absenteeism was probably the most

common charge levelled against them, but this shortcoming was merely one aspect of their general failure to perform services in return for the rents they collected. They did not, as a rule, make improvements to their land, nor did they provide buildings, fences, and so on. This was normally left up to the tenant who was rarely compensated for the improvements he had made if and when his tenancy terminated. To make matters worse, the frequency with which tenancies terminated increased dramatically in the first half of the nineteenth century. Landlords began to take steps to reduce the number of small tenants on their land because they believed these tenants were economically inefficient and because many small tenants were so poor they were often not able to pay their rent. Although it is impossible to specify the exact date at which relationships between Irish landlords and tenants degenerated into conflict, it is clear that with the close of the Napoleonic Wars in 1815 their relationships took a turn for the worse, and that by the third decade of the nineteenth century a fierce struggle had developed between the two groups. Landlords fought to collect rents and to evict tenants who were not paying, while tenants resisted payments and, above all, resisted evictions.

The second social cleavage was a religious one. For several centuries Ireland had been religiously stratified, with persons of the Protestant faith enjoying higher status than those of the Catholic faith. This difference in status had been a source of conflict in the eighteenth century, but it became far more contentious in the early nineteenth century when two Catholic elites rose to challenge the supremacy of the Protestant establishment. These two Catholic elites were the Catholic clergy and the Catholic urban middle class. The significance of this religious cleavage, from our point of view, is that eventually it created a situation in which a source of leadership became available for an agrarian movement.

The third social cleavage was between town and country. Historically this cleavage could be traced to the fact that Irish towns were largely the creation of foreigners, first the Danes and then the English. But in the eighteenth century a significant growth in trade and domestic industry led to the development of many strong relationships between townspeople and country people. It was actually the tremendous expansion in population and the industrial decline of the early nineteenth century that brought about a separation of the two, especially in western districts and especially for the lower orders of the population. In the Ireland of the early nineteenth century, a vast number of rural inhabitants were so poor that they lived barely at a subsistence level and enjoyed few, if any, stable economic relationships with people living in towns and cities. The significance of this particular cleavage was not that it contributed to an agrarian rebellion in Ireland but that for a period of time it helped prevent one.

It was the first of these cleavages, of course, that was responsible for rural discontent. The underlying hostility existing between landlords and tenants insured that agriculture adversities would invariably be accompanied by an increase in dissatisfaction with the land system. Both crop failures and a decline in agricultural prices subjected a tenant to greater deprivation; they also threatened his ability to pay his rent, thus encouraging landlords to evict. Later in the century, it was precisely this kind of situation that precipitated the Land War. The Land War began during an agricultural depression brought on by crop failures and aggravated by a collapse of butter prices and low cattle prices. This depression followed a prosperous period for Irish agriculture – in fact, the most prosperous period since the Napoleonic Wars. Thus, in one sense at least, the timing of the Land War conforms remarkably well to Davies' J-curve of rising and falling satisfactions. Indeed, we have good reason to believe that expectations not only rose before the Land War but actually rose to an unrealistic level. During the prosperity, many small farmers got themselves heavily into debt, confident that the future would bring even better economic returns. When the exact opposite course of events ensued, not a few farmers were left in serious financial straits. In 1880, an authority on Irish agriculture, testifying before a Royal Commission, described how the prosperity had raised the expectations of farmers and had enticed them into debt: "People have been from a variety of remote causes deficient in thrift. Then came the great bound of modern prosperity. The growth of wealth led to the establishment of a great many banks; the banks gave money on easy terms to shopkeepers, and then the shopkeepers, as it were, forced a system of credit upon the small farmers; and all of a sudden that has collapsed. That collapse took place last year" (House of Commons, 1881a:89).

Thus, if the question we are asking is what social conditions precipitated the Land War, the most reasonable answer is that it was primarily the agricultural depression of the late 1870s. This depression raised the level of discontent by disappointing expectations created during the previous period. By studying discontent, we are able to explain why the Land War began in 1879. Focusing on discontent also enables us to explain broad regional variations in the strength of the agitation. The agitation not only originated but also generally remained strongest in Connaught, the poorest region of the country and the hardest hit by the depression.

However, a far more important question cannot be answered by focusing on levels of discontent. Studying discontent does not tell us why Irish tenants rebelled against their landlords in the late nineteenth century whereas no comparable rebellion had ever occurred before. Increased discontent may explain why the Land War broke out in the particular *year* that it did, but it does not explain why it broke out in the particular *period* that it did. After all, hostility between landlords and their tenants was hardly a new development. There was just as much discontent in many earlier periods.

It was especially before and during the great famine that rural discontent was intense. The country was then plagued by overpopulation, by frequent crop failures, and by one long deflationary period lasting from 1813 to 1836. These conditions regularly aggravated distress among tenants; they did so in a number of ways, but most of all by making rents difficult to pay and by increasing the number of evictions. Disappointments caused by unfulfilled rising expectations, however infuriating, could never provoke an Irish tenant as much as the possibility of losing his holding could. Prefamine tenants may have had modest wants, but they were, if nothing else, determined to hold onto their land. They could become uncontrollably discontented when this right was threatened. Although good statistical evidence is not available, it is clear from all we know that after the close of the Napoleonic Wars and in the early 1820s, the 1830s, and above all during the great famine, tenants were ejected in numbers that make the evictions of 1879–82 look like minor relocations by comparison. G. Locker Lampson (1907:208) reports a claim that there were 150,000 evictions in a five-year period from 1839 to 1843. However, he fails to give his source and truly reliable statistics are available only from the year 1849. Yet it is worth noting that there were 16,686 evictions (23 per 10,000 persons) in 1849, while there were only 1238 evictions (2 per 10,000 persons) in 1879, and only 2110 (4 per 10,000 persons) in 1880, the first two years of the Land War (House of Commons, 1881b).

An additional source of discontent among prefamine tenants were tithes, that is, taxes paid to the established Protestant church. These taxes fell on Catholic as well as Protestant tenants and were paid either in kind, by a fixed annual payment based on acreage, or by 'view' of the crops, in which case the tithe varied according to the output. A common arrangement was the payment of 10/–an Irish acre for wheat and potatoes and 7/–to 8/– for oats (Macintyre, 1965:170). In the early 1820s some effort was made to reform and regularize the collection of tithes and further legislative changes were made in the 1830s; but the burden of payment remained.

Prefamine tenants regarded the collection of tithes as another evil of the land system, along with rents and evictions. They fought against all three in mobs and in gangs that terrorized the rural society. This violence never assumed the rebellious proportions of the Land War since it was sporadic, disorganized, and locally based. There was little coordination between one gang and another and only a limited number of persons actually participated (Lewis, 1836:190–3, 213). Nevertheless, the violence did reflect the prevailing dissatisfaction with the land system. It enjoyed widespread sympathy among the lower orders of the rural population (Lewis, 1836:193–201, 250–3). The fact that it was an almost permanent feature of the society induced the government to pass or reenact, between 1800 and the great famine, no less than thirty-five coercion acts directed at Ireland and, in most cases, directed specifically at rural unrest in Ireland (Lampson, 1907:637–638). Whatever we can say about tenants who took part in the Land War, we cannot say that they were angrier than their ancestors had ever been. This is especially true for those in Connaught. For generations, peasants in Connaught had suffered greater hardships than those in other regions. But until the Land War they had been the most politically passive. Why, then, did they rebel in the late nineteenth century?

I would suggest that this question can only be answered by understanding how Irish peasants acquired a greater capacity to mobilize their political resources. Without going into great detail, I shall now outline the major factors that I believe must be considered in order to appreciate how this change came to pass.

First, we want to know why there was no large-scale agrarian rebellion in the prefamine period. In searching for a reason, we are immediately struck by the nature of hostilities within the tenant population at this time. The agrarian violence referred to above was actually inflicted by tenants on one another rather than on the land-owning class (Lewis, 1836:119–20, 223). A number of factors contributed to this internal strife among tenants but by far the most significant was the extensive system of subletting land. Most tenants did not rent their holdings directly from a landowner but more often from a landlord who was also a tenant (Freeman, 1957:21–23). The prefamine tenant population consisted of a variety of social classes, one of the largest being a 'cottier' class. Members of this class held small plots of land and paid their rent in labour, usually to a large farmer. The result of this subletting system was that the hostility felt by aggrieved tenants towards their landlords was actually hostility towards other tenants. It also meant that those who sublet land were as much afraid of the threat from below as of the oppression from above. In prefamine Ireland, there were many tenants who could identify their interests with neither the tenant class nor the landlord class because they were, in fact, members of both. Under these circumstances, it is not surprising that agrarian discontent was spent in warfare among tenants themselves.

Also helpful for understanding the absence of an agrarian rebellion in the prefamine period is the recognition that prefamine tenants had no adequate source of political leadership. Large farmers were not sufficiently numerous that they could provide political leadership for the tenant population. More decisive still was the fact that large farmers did not have the same economic interests as the majority of rural tenants; they were foremost among those caught in the position of being both landlords and tenants. Outside the tenant population, there existed some very obvious sources of leadership, namely, the Catholic clergy and the Catholic urban middle class. Elements within both were politically organized and were challenging the supremacy of the Protestant establishment. Many Catholic clergymen were becoming increasingly involved in politics on an individual basis; they were also involved through the Church hierarchy, which was beginning to campaign actively to eliminate the last vestiges of political discrimination against Catholics and to undermine the established position of the Protestant Church of Ireland.

By the Catholic urban middle class I mean primarily those Catholics engaged in mercantile and professional occupations in cities and in large towns. Because this class was closely associated with Catholic landowners, it would be useful to include the latter in the same social group. Catholic landowners, however, were small in number as a result of Protestant domination of landownership. Thus, the secular Catholic elite was largely urban. It was from this stratum that support was drawn for a number of Catholic political organizations in the prefamine period, all of which were led by Daniel O'Connell: (1) the Catholic Association of the 1820s, which sought the 'emancipation' of Catholics, that is, their right to hold high judicial and political posts including the right to sit in Parliament; (2) the Irish Party, which represented Irish Catholic interests in parliament in the 1830s and 1840s; and (3) the Repeal Association of the 1840s, a nationalist organization which sought a greater amount of political autonomy for Ireland.

However, neither the Catholic clergy nor these middle-class Catholic organizations provided leadership for a tenant movement. They did, it is true, muster peasant support for their own political ventures, and the fact that they were able to do so is a further indication of the intensity of social discontent in the prefamine rural population, but the peasants were merely used by the Catholic elites for their own purposes. They obtained no benefits and were passive rather than active participants. They were rounded up by the clergy and brought to mass meetings. They were spellbound by O'Connell's charisma. They were induced to believe that great benefits would result. Yet in a manner that is perhaps analogous to followers of millenarian movements, they were led to expect

that these benefits would be miraculously delivered to them rather than won through their own hard efforts. In no sense were they organized to help themselves.[1]

This is, of course, not surprising. The Catholic elites were as afraid as anyone of the revolutionary consequences that grass-roots organization would ultimately have had. In addition, a large segment within the Catholic elite had no satisfactory way of making contact with the rural population. This was not true of the Catholic clergy, but it was true of most members of the Catholic urban middle class. It is here that the social cleavage between town and country becomes relevant. Since most rural inhabitants were too poor to engage directly in commercial transactions, social bonds between town and country were weak, and only a minority in the rural population were available for direct political organization by urban groups. Consequently, inasmuch as the politically organized segments of the Catholic middle class were largely urban, they were at a serious disadvantage when they sought to mobilize rural inhabitants at the grass-roots level. Thus, even if they had been willing to organize tenants to help themselves, they could only have done so in those areas that enjoyed relatively close contact with urban society. It is significant that on the one occasion (before the Land War) when some Catholic politicians did take an interest in leading a tenant movement, their success was limited mainly to areas of the country that were situated close to Dublin and where a comparatively large share of the rural population was engaged in commercial transactions. The movement to which I am referring made its appearance in the closing years of the great famine. It was supported by an association called the Tenant League, founded largely by nationalists who had formerly belonged to the Repeal Association. The core of the leadership came from a radical faction that had broken from the Repeal movement and were known as the Young Irelanders. But the movement was a complete failure, realizing none of its goals and

---

[1] The only possible exception to this statement was the Tithe War of the early 1830s. The impetus for this movement came from Catholic clergymen and large farmers. It sought the abolition of tithes paid to the established Protestant church. Even in this case, however, only peasants in a small number of eastern counties were active, and they opposed tithes using their traditional violent methods with little direct leadership from the elites. There was no local organizational structure to which large numbers of tenants could belong. The outcome of the tithe agitation was not the abolition of tithes but their conversion into rent-charges. This meant that landowners were obliged to collect the tithe as part of their rent but were permitted to retain 25 per cent as compensation for their trouble. Hardly a victory for tenants. For historical accounts of this movement, and the others mentioned above, see Reynolds (1954), Macintyre (1965), Nowlan (1965), and Maher (1951).

only briefly mobilizing a small number of tenants in the eastern counties. It was noticeably
least successful in remote areas, especially in
Connaught.[2]

What happened in the interval between the
great famine and the Land War was that this
cleavage between rural and urban Ireland was
bridged. It was bridged partly by a tremendous
advancement in the literacy rate, partly by the
construction of a national railway system, but
most of all by an increase in the proportion of
rural inhabitants engaged in commercial transactions. This extension of commercial transactions took the form of a shift from tillage to
pasture and an increase in livestock. As prices
in England soared for livestock, the cattle and
sheep population in Ireland rose from approximately four million in 1841 to approximately
eight million in the late 1870s, despite a sharp
decline in the number of rural tenants over the
same period (House of Commons, 1843 and
1877). The sale of this livestock brought a larger
segment of the rural population into a cash
economy; more concretely, it brought them into
towns. They came to town to sell their livestock
at fairs and to patronize shops and public
houses. This was even true of small farmers in
the west of Ireland, who specialized in breeding
and selling young cattle.

As I shall suggest later, these social and
economic changes had a number of consequences that eventually contributed to the political mobilization of Irish farmers. In this paper,
I shall focus primarily on the one that my research to date has led me to regard as the most
critical: the rise in social importance of a small
business class consisting mainly of shopkeepers
and publicans. Some indication of their new
importance in the postfamine period is afforded
by examining their numbers. While the total
population of Ireland was declining rapidly, the
number of shopkeepers and publicans remained
fairly constant. Unfortunately, it is impossible
to say exactly how many there were, since the
1881 census does not provide a separate
classification for traders and business proprietors. It does, however, provide a separate
category called 'persons working and dealing in
food and lodgings,' nearly all of whom were

shopkeepers and publicans, though, of course,
only a portion of all shopkeepers are covered by
this group. In 1841, there was one person in
this category for every 166 persons in the country; in 1881, there was one for every 78 persons
in the country. The change was less striking in
Connaught, but in view of the smaller number
and size of towns in that province, it was still
substantial: in 1841 one person fell into this
category for every 246 persons in Connaught,
while in 1881, there was one for every 175 persons (House of Commons, 1843, 1882b, and
1882a).

The significance of this small business class
(except in large towns and in cities) lay in the
cooperative relationship that most of its members had with farmers. There was, first of all, a
kinship bond. Most townsmen had relatives
who were farmers. Indeed, of a sample of
seventy-five traders and business proprietors in
one western district, no less than 40 per cent
were actually farmers' sons.[3]

Second, there was a commercial bond; shopkeepers and publicans came to depend almost
entirely on the farming population for custom-
ers, while farmers came to depend on these
shopkeepers and publicans to provide credit.
Although not altogether uncommon before the
famine, it was between the famine and the Land
War that the much debated credit system became fully developed in Ireland. The essential
feature of this system was that farmers remained perpetually in debt to one or two shopkeepers with whom they kept a running account. Such a system undoubtedly generated a
certain amount of strain and, in some cases, it
led to serious conflict. Nevertheless, in the majority of cases, its far more important effect was
that it encouraged a stable relationship between
a particular farmer and a particular shopkeeper
and so contributed to the development of a social tie between the two. As a rule, the terms of
credit were not extortionate, and the amount of
credit given, especially in hard times, was liberal, sometimes 'beyond all conception' (Congested Districts Board, 1898:381). For most
small farmers the securities they had to offer
were so limited that their shopkeeper was the
only person willing to give them the credit they

2 This conclusion is based on accounts of the Tenant League's activities provided by its leaders, particularly
Duffy (1886), and also on what is known about where most of the League's branches were located (Whyte,
1958:6).
3 The sample consisted of all traders and business proprietors whose marriages were registered in the superintendent registrar district of Roscommon between 1864 and 1880 (Registry of Births, Deaths and Marriages).

needed to carry on the operation of their farms (House of Commons, 1914:76). The point is not that there developed a perfectly harmonious economic relationship between shopkeepers and farmers but that there developed a *cooperative relationship* based on their mutual interdependence.

Finally, it should be noted that shopkeepers and publicans became the principal sources of information in the rural community; they were receivers and transmitters of anything from trivial gossip to news of major consequence, not only because they were in contact with farmers, but also because they enjoyed relatively greater contact with the larger society.[4]

Another important development in the post-famine period was the reorientation of political groups drawn from the Catholic urban middle class. Although technically this class could be defined so as to include townsmen, politically organized groups in the Catholic population were to be found only in some of the larger towns and were primarily concentrated in cities, particularly Dublin. Over a period of time (actually commencing in the early 1840s with the Repeal Association) many members of the Catholic urban middle class became involved in a nationalist movement (or, more precisely, two nationalist movements) seeking a larger measure of political independence from England. In principle, nationalist leaders were unwilling to espouse popular grievances[5] and for a long time this principle kept them from trying to provide tenants with leadership. For this they needed a broader base of support than the Catholic urban middle class. What is essential to recognize is that they could not get this additional support from the landed upper class, largely as a result of the religious cleavage to which reference has already been made. Although there was some increase in the number of Catholic landowners during the postfamine period, the majority of landowners were still Protestant. And Protestants were separated from Catholics, not only by religious bigotry and differences in social status, but also by a conflict of interests. Because they constituted a numerical minority, Protestants believed that their social position depended on the preservation of the British connection.

For these reasons a political alliance between members of the Catholic urban middle class and members of the mostly Protestant landowning class proved impossible. Actually, some effort was made to form such an alliance. In the early 1870s, the more moderate faction in the nationalist movement (the so-called constitutionalist faction) endeavoured to attract both Catholic and Protestant landowners to the nationalist cause (McCaffrey, 1962). However, the effort failed, and its failure, together with the overall weakness of the nationalist movement owing to its lack of rural support, led some nationalist politicians to argue that they should adopt a program that would appeal to agrarian interests.

The initiative was taken by a group of Fenians, the name usually given to the extreme faction in the nationalist movement. In November of 1878, John Devoy, the most influential Fenian in America, sent a now famous telegram to C.S. Parnell, the leader of a new aggressive group within the constitutionalist faction. In this telegram Devoy proposed an alliance between the Fenians and these more aggressive constitutionalists. He specified that one of the terms of this alliance would be that the new movement embark on vigorous agitation of the land question (*Nation*, 16 November 1878:6). In the following year, Michael Davitt, an associate of Devoy, persuaded a handful of Fenians to help him organize a series of mass meetings among farmers in Connaught. These meetings were held in the spring and summer of

4 This special relationship between town and country survived long after the period we are discussing. When Arensberg and Kimbal (1968) studied the west of Ireland in the 1930s they found that the bond between farmers and townsmen was still strong and they argued that the credit system contributed to maintaining this relationship. Indeed, Arensberg has claimed that the credit system, far from being evidence of a conflict between shopkeepers and farmers, is actually evidence of a close social tie. For a shopkeeper to foreclose, or for a farmer to clear his debt, would be a declaration of intent to terminate their friendship. Thus, according to Arensberg, the credit system functions as a symbol of their personal bond (Arensberg, 1968:155–9). Whether or not one accepts Arensberg's argument, it is clear that the credit system did increase the mutual interdependence of shopkeepers and farmers. Arensberg and Kimbal also found that townsmen provided crucial centres for local social interaction. As Arensberg has written: 'The shop and the pub was and is the countryman's metropolitan club' (Arensberg, 1968:161).

5 This was true of both the moderate and the extreme wings of the nationalist movement, although the extreme wing was far more explicit. See Moody (1968).

1879. Parnell, who was trying to rejuvenate the constitutionalist wing of the movement, was induced to speak at some of the meetings. Gradually he too became involved in the protest. Under Parnell, the agitation was extended beyond the borders of Connaught, and a national association called the Irish National Land League was formed. The executive of this association consisted entirely of nationalists, both Fenian and constitutionalist. Nationalist politicians also spoke quite regularly at rallies, large numbers of which were held throughout the period of agitation. Finally, nationalist politicians provided farmers with a band of parliamentary candidates who ran almost exclusively on a tenant-right platform and endeavoured to present the tenants' case in parliament.[6]

A careful study of the Land War reveals that nationalist politicians could not have provided the leadership they did if a segment of the town population had not been available and willing to bridge the gap between the nationalist movement, which was largely urban, and the rural population. In an earlier paper (Clark, 1971), I was able to show that, although the Land War was fought mainly by farmers, it was fought with the assistance of townsmen. Some measure of the latter's contribution is provided by an analysis of arrests made in 1881–2 when the government suspended habeas corpus. The Protection of Person and Property Act of 1881 was passed for the specific purpose of suppressing the land agitation; under its provisions 955 persons were arrested and detained without trial. Occupational data are available for 845 of them. Townsmen were overrepresented in the list of arrests relative to their number in the society. Indeed, the commercial and industrial sector was the only occupational sector substantially overrepresented. This was especially true in Connaught: 35.5 per cent of the 268 suspects arrested in Connaught belonged to the commercial and industrial sector while only 15.4 per cent of the male labour force in Connaught belonged to this sector. By way of contrast, 60.1 per cent of those arrested in Connaught belonged to the agricultural sector, while a larger percentage, 75.5 per cent, belonged to this sector in the male labour force. The corresponding percentages for the country

as a whole were 36.8 per cent (of the suspects) and 31.7 per cent (of the male labour force) for the commercial and industrial sector, and 57.8 per cent (of the suspects) and 57.4 per cent (of the male labour force) for the agricultural sector (Irish Crimes Records, 1881; House of Commons, 1882a and 1882b).

Information on the particular function that townsmen performed is more difficult to obtain, but there are at least two generalizations that can be made with some degree of confidence. First, it is clear that initially townsmen acted as *contacts* for nationalist politicians. By this I mean that it was to townsmen, more than to farmers, that nationalist politicians went in the first few months of the agitation in an effort to reach the farming population and to get a movement going. To be more concrete, if we examine in detail the early meetings in Connaught promoted by Davitt and his Fenian associates, we find that these meetings were organized with the help of local groups consisting of both farmers and townsmen but mostly of townsmen (Clark, 1971:458–462).

The second generalization that can be made is that townsmen were willing to instigate acts of violence, but they did not, as a rule, engage in violence themselves. In order to explain this phenomenon, it is necessary to outline the main techniques of agitation employed by the Land League. Their attack on the land system consisted of an effective combination of violent and nonviolent activities. The most noteworthy nonviolent activities were mass meetings and boycotts. Mass meetings were used to mobilize support for the movement and to articulate its goals; boycotts were used to punish people for violating Land League rules or for opposing the League. In addition, both mass meetings and boycotts provided a means, indeed the principal means, of pointing the finger at enemies of the League. The most common to be labelled as enemies were: (1) land agents, bailiffs, and process servers and (2) 'landgrabbers,' that is, persons who took land from which the previous tenant had been evicted. But almost anyone who did not support the League could be declared an enemy, and it was by denouncing an individual at mass meetings or by issuing a boycott against him that these declarations were made. In this way nonviolent agitation

---

6 These statements can be verified by examining the two major historical accounts of the agitation: Davitt (1904: chapters 11–18) and Palmer (1940: chapters 6–8). See also Moody (1949).

TABLE I

PERCENTAGE OF SUSPECTS ARRESTED FOR NONVIOLENT ACTIVITIES UNDER THE PROTECTION OF
PERSON AND PROPERTY ACT, 1881, BY OCCUPATION

Occupation	Percentage suspected of nonviolent crime	Total number of arrests
Farmers	66.1	324
Farmers' sons	46.5	131
Other agricultural	31.4	16
Traders and business proprietors	80.8	94
Shopworkers and clerks	75.0	28
Innkeepers and publicans	80.9	68
Artisans and nonfarm labourers	41.9	86
Unspecified labourers	14.4	35
Newspaper editors and correspondents	92.9	14
Total	61.0	796

NOTE: Nonviolent crimes consist of a variety of activities such as making seditious speeches, issuing threatening letters or notices, and participating in illegal meetings as well as other kinds of nonviolent intimidation, such as boycotting. I have omitted from this table occupations contributing less than 1.5 per cent to the total arrests. Whenever an individual's activities included both violent and nonviolent activities, he was coded according to whichever seemed to be the primary reason for his arrest.
This table has been adapted from Table 4 in my paper (Clark, 1971). The source is Irish Crimes Records, 1881.

provided direction for those who sought to oppose the land system through violence. Many, if not most, violent attacks were made on people who had been cited at a mass meeting or were being boycotted. Thus, under the Land League, agrarian violence was no longer disorganized and sporadic, as it had been in the prefamine period, but instead was a coordinated part of a much broader assault on the land system.

What evidence we have suggests that townsmen were primarily active in nonviolent activities. Table 1 is based on the list of arrests made under the Protection of Person and Property Act, 1881. For each occupational group, it gives the percentage who were arrested on suspicion of having committed nonviolent crimes. Most town occupations are distinctly overrepresented. For example, 80.8 per cent of the traders and business proprietors were arrested for nonviolent activities while a much smaller percentage, 61.0 per cent, of all arrests were for activities of this kind. Shopworkers and clerks, innkeepers and publicans, and newspaper editors and correspondents are similarly high in the percentage they contributed to nonviolent

activities. The only town occupations that were relatively low were artisans and nonfarm labourers as well as unspecified labourers (that is labourers for whom it was not known whether they were farm or nonfarm workers).[7]

This finding is consistent with the conclusions to which the author came as a result of an intensive study of the Land League in two localities in Connaught, the Castlebar, and Roscommon districts. For these districts, I was able to form a subjective impression of the functions townsmen performed. By carefully reading issues of the *Connaught Telegraph* and the *Roscommon Journal* I became familiar with the major personalities in the movement in these two areas. In both, townsmen functioned as local leaders. They organized demonstrations, solicited support from nationalists in Dublin, identified enemies of the movement, and even went into the countryside to instruct farmers on how to organize a Land League branch. Although not the first branches to be formally constituted, the Land League branches in these towns were the most important in their districts. In Roscommon, the town branch was made the

7 My earlier paper (Clark, 1971) gives a more detailed analysis of the list of arrests under the Protection of Person and Property Act. Some of the problems encountered in analysing these data are also discussed.

central branch in an official manner by including delegates from the countryside (*Roscommon Journal*, 18 December 1880:2).[8]

Townsmen, of course, were not involved in every aspect of the movement. We should not, therefore, overlook certain postfamine changes that may have contributed to the capacity of rural tenants to form their own organizational base. Perhaps the most important change was the increase in size of holdings. Between 1841 and 1876, the median size of agricultural holdings in Ireland rose from 12.8 acres to 18.5 acres (House of Commons, 1843 and 1877).[9] As a result, a larger proportion of the agricultural labour force came to be made up of economically independent farmers. As mentioned above, most rural tenants in the prefamine period were cottiers. They were extremely poor, lived on small plots of land, and were employed by farmers. The combined effect of the great famine and postfamine emigration was to greatly reduce the size of this class. Tenants who lived primarily off their own holdings (and did not have to rely on additional outside employment) now became the largest single occupational group engaged in agriculture, comprising almost half of the agricultural population. The census commissioners reserved the terms 'farmer' and 'grazier' for economically independent tenants of this kind, and the number of persons enumerated as farmers or graziers rose from 25.4 per cent of the agricultural labour force in 1841 to 44.3 per cent in 1881. The statistics for Connaught are 22.0 per cent in 1841 and 51.5 per cent in 1881 (House of Commons, 1843, 1882b and 1882a). It is likely that this development alone would have had the effect of producing a more sophisticated and politically enlightened tenant population.

In addition, it is reasonable to assume that greater literacy, the construction of railways, and the growth in the proportion of tenants engaged in commercial transactions must have broadened the range of contacts enjoyed by rural inhabitants in more ways than simply through the intermediation of townsmen. These developments probably increased the level of social interaction among tenants themselves and in doing so may have strengthened tenant solidarity, especially since there was also an enormous decline in the practice of subletting land. The practice, it is true, could still be found but, as a result of the drastic decrease in the number of cottiers, it was much less common in the postfamine period for tenants to sublet their holdings from other tenants. In this way, a major source of class hostility within the tenant population had been partially, if not entirely, eliminated.

If these changes in postfamine rural society had the political consequences I am speculating they may have had, we should be able to observe some concrete manifestation of an increased organizational capacity among tenants themselves. By far the most noticeable manifestation was the emergence of a small group of politically organized large farmers. In the late 1860s and in the 1870s, several dozen farmers' clubs were established in some southern and eastern counties. Their members were tenants with extremely large holdings of grazing land. One of the most active clubs, and the one for which the most information is available, was the Limerick and Clare Farmers' Club, whose members were proud to admit that they were 'big graziers' (*Limerick Reporter*, 18 June 1878:3). Despite this class affiliation, the members of these clubs found that their interests were consistent with those of most farmers. They sought to promote reforms of the land

---

8 The hard core of active Land Leaguers in Roscommon consisted of a half-dozen townsmen, who were well known to authorities and were regarded as responsible for activities often carried out by others (*Roscommon Journal*, 5 February 1881:1). Townsmen in Roscommon were especially active in boycotts, sometimes trying boycott victims in Land League courts held in the offices of the *Roscommon Messenger* (*Roscommon Journal*, 19 March 1881:2). For examples of townsmen in the Roscommon district helping farmers organize Land League branches, see *Roscommon Journal* (4 September 1880:2) and *Nation* (2 October 1880:13). In Castlebar, townsmen assisted Davitt in the early months of the agitation (Clark, 1971:460) and also organized the first large demonstration in that district (*Connaught Telegraph*, 20 September 1879:5). Their Land League branch was clearly the most important in the district, assisting tenants who were being prosecuted or evicted and issuing speaking invitations, on behalf of the district, to prominent nationalists. See, for example, *Connaught Telegraph* (20 March 1880:4; 25 September 1880:3; 30 October 1880:2, and 6 November 1880:4).

9 These medians have been computed from grouped data. They actually refer to the median size of holdings over two acres in 1841 and over one acre in 1886. The 1841 data have been corrected according to Bourke (1965) in order to compensate for errors made by the census takers and discussed in detail by Bourke. This correction simply entails doubling the median for the 1841 data.

system, specifically to persuade parliament to pass legislation that would provide tenants with greater security of tenure. Their main method of attack was to become involved in the constitutionalist wing of the nationalist movement. During the early 1870s they tried to persuade this movement to take up their cause. The effort was only partly successful because the constitutionalists, as we already know, were at this time also soliciting the support of the landed upper class.

The farmers' clubs played no part whatsoever in the initial organization of the land agitation in Connaught since there were almost no clubs to be found in that province. Nevertheless, they provided a crucial organizational base for the Land War. As early as January 1879, four months before Davitt began to organize meetings in Connaught, some clubs were holding land demonstrations; by June most clubs were holding frequent meetings as word spread that agitation was building in the west (*Nation*, 18 January 1879:6; 25 January 1879:3; 21 June 1879:7). It has already been mentioned that, under Parnell, the agitation spread beyond the borders of Connaught. This feat was greatly assisted by the base provided by the farmers' clubs. Indeed, one of the main political advantages Parnell had over Davitt was a closer affiliation with these clubs as a result of the earlier involvement of the clubs in the constitutionalist wing of the nationalist movement. When Parnell founded the Irish National Land League in October 1879, he was aided by the farmers' clubs, many members of which can be found among the list of names comprising the founding committee of the Land League (Committee members at first meeting of the Irish National Land League).

One other organizational base that deserves mention is the Catholic Church. The participation of many local clergymen in the Land League is well known. To be sure, there are some serious objections that could be raised against placing a great deal of emphasis on their role. First, their participation suffered from severe limitations. Catholic clergymen were constrained by the institution to which they belonged. Especially during the Land League phase of the Land War, many members of the Church hierarchy were not in support of the agitation. Thus, the level of clerical participation that was permitted varied greatly from region to region depending on the attitude of the local bishop or archbishop. Secondly, one

might argue that, in so far as the clergy did assist the agitation, there was nothing very new about this role. Catholic clergymen had always been the political leaders of their parishes and had, even in the prefamine period, organized the tenant population in political struggles, most notably in the emancipation campaign of the late 1820s.

However, as was pointed out above, in these prefamine movements tenants were not actually organized at the grass-roots level; they were merely mustered as political support for movements that promoted the interests of the Church and of the Catholic urban middle class. Furthermore, although the bond between local clergymen and their parishioners had always been strong, recent historical research has shown that in the prefamine period the Catholic Church was relatively disorganized; most Catholic clergymen were persons of little education and some of questionable morals; and considerable conflict existed between clergymen and their parishioners, especially over the question of clerical dues (Larkin, 1972). The same research has demonstrated that in the decade or so before the famine, and in the postfamine period, the Catholic Church became wealthier and better organized; the morals and education of the clergy improved; the priest to population ratio rose; the contributions of Irish Catholics to building religious edifices became larger; and, most important of all, the formal religiosity of Irish Catholics increased greatly. Thus there is every reason to believe that the bond between Catholic priests and their parishioners, although always strong, was even stronger in the postfamine period, and that the quality of leadership that clergymen were capable of providing was vastly improved.

In any case, it is possible to establish beyond a doubt that in many areas Catholic clergymen did make a significant contribution to the agitation. Especially after Parnell took over the leadership, many clergymen, and a few archbishops and bishops, were active supporters of the tenants' cause. For example, 13 of the 57 members of the Land League's founding committee were Catholic clergymen (Committee members at first meeting of the Irish National Land League). In addition, research on rural branches discloses that clergymen were energetic in these local bodies. Many branches were, in fact, established at meetings held in chapel yards after mass, and the geographical unit on which many rural branches were based was the

Catholic parish. A further indication of the role of clergymen in local branches is provided by a still extant collection of reports sent by branches to the central executive in Dublin. Of a sample of 115 branches, 32.2 per cent submitted reports that were signed by at least one clergyman acting as president, vice-president, or secretary of the branch (Irish National Land League Papers). Clearly, if there were some districts in which the clergy remained aloof from the agitation, there were many others in which they did not. The role played by the clergy, therefore, can hardly be dismissed as inconsequential.

Although I have discussed several different organizational bases, it has not been my purpose to provide the reader with a conclusive statement of how Irish farmers got politically organized. Such a statement, along with an assessment of the relative importance of the various factors that contributed to their mobilization, will have to await further research. My intention has been simply to demonstrate that there is sufficient evidence to support the claim that, in one form or another, a stronger organizational base was present in the late nineteenth century than in the prefamine period.

DISCUSSION

The question I have been asking in this paper is why the first large-scale agrarian rebellion in Ireland broke out in the late nineteenth century. I have tried to argue that the best answer is that, in the postfamine period, Irish tenants acquired a source of leadership and an organizational base. Unquestionably the leadership came from the nationalist movement. The organizational base appears to have had a number of sources, but for the time being it is probably wisest to stress the special relationship that evolved in the postfamine period between rural tenants and townsmen. Although discontent was certainly a necessary condition for the Irish Land War, studying variations in the level of discontent contributes little to our understanding of why Irish tenants rebelled against their landlords in the late nineteenth century on a greater scale than they had ever rebelled before.

While broad similarities with other rebellions can be noted, we should be very careful about drawing conclusions from the Irish Land War and applying them to social unrest in general. The factors that determine when men will rebel depend on the structural conditions present in a particular case. One structural condition in Ireland, the social cleavage between landlords and tenants, determined that an agrarian rebellion would most likely erupt during an agricultural depression when landlord-tenant hostility was at a peak. Depressions made it difficult for tenants to pay their rents and so encouraged landlords to evict. In other societies, even other peasant societies, discontent will, of course, be generated in a different way and may, as a result, have quite different consequences. Similarly, the source of leadership that ultimately became available to Irish tenants was a direct function of the particular relationship that existed in Ireland between major social elites. The urban middle class was forced to ally with the tenant population, rather than with the landed class, because of religious divisions in the society. If Catholics in Ireland had managed to break into the ranks of the landed class to the same extent that they had succeeded in breaking into urban society, a political alliance between the landed elite and urban elites may have materialized and Irish tenants may never have obtained satisfactory political leadership. Finally, increased contact between town and country only facilitated an agrarian rebellion in Ireland because the potential source of leadership for tenants was largely urban. Again, in other peasant societies, under different structural conditions, increased contact between town and country could have tremendously different consequences.

Even the importance of mobilization itself depends on certain conditions. It is not always true that factors facilitating mobilization are better predictors of when people will rebel than are factors enhancing discontent. In the case we have been examining, mobilization was more important because a high level of discontent was present on numerous occasions, whereas the capacity for mobilization was not. In other societies, particularly in industrialized societies, the situation may be the reverse. As Dahrendorf (1959) suggests, once industrial classes have been fully formed, people may possess the capacity for political mobilization, but they may become discontented only occasionally. Under such circumstances, studying discontent would, indeed, be a better way of predicting when they will rebel.

However, during the transition from nonindustrial to industrial society the conditions for mobilization are certainly as important as are those causing discontent, perhaps more important. One may observe, as the Feierabends have, that political unrest is relatively common during this transitional phase of modernization. Many social scientists have been quick to explain this finding by arguing that modernization raises expectations to an unrealistic level in its early stages (Ridker, 1962; Feierabend, *et al.*, 1969). Others have explained the relationship by stating that modernization breaks down the traditional mechanisms of social solidarity that hold traditional societies together (Durkheim, 1933; Hauser, 1963). Still a third possibility is that modernization promotes social protest by increasing social communication and cooperation among the discontented and by producing new middle-class groups that are in a position to provide the lower classes with political leadership. Let us assume, for the sake of argument, that modernization does indeed have this effect. If it could also be shown that discontent is often just as intense before modernization as during the initial stages of modernization, then we would be forced to conclude that the association between early modernization and social protest is primarily a consequence of the facilities for mobilization that modernization can bring to already discontented people.

Whatever is true in general, this is the conclusion to which I have been led in my efforts to account for the Irish Land War. Although Irish rural tenants certainly experienced a rise in expectations during the postfamine period, the social changes that raised their expectations also enhanced their capacity for mobilization. But their increased expectations did not, even when disappointed, generate greater discontent than they had ever felt before. In order to understand why Irish farmers rebelled in the late nineteenth century, one must go beyond the immediate conditions that precipitated their rebellion and do more than just explain why they were angry. One must explain how they were mobilized.

REFERENCES*

Arensberg, C.M.
1968　The Irish Countryman. New York: Natural History Press
Arensberg, C.M., and S.T. Kimbal
1968　Family and Community in Ireland. Cambridge, Mass.: Harvard University Press
Bendix, Reinhard

1964　Nation Building and Citizenship. New York: Wiley
Bourke, P.M. Austin
1965　'The agricultural statistics of the 1841 Census of Ireland: a critical review.' Economic History Review. Second series 18:376–91
Clark, Samuel
1971　'The social composition of the Land League.' Irish Historical Studies 17:447–69
Congested Districts Board
1898　Base Line Reports of Inspectors for Congested Districts Board, 1892–8. Trinity College Library
Dahrendorf, Ralf
1959　Class and Class Conflict in Industrial Society. Stanford California: Stanford University Press
Davies, James C.
1962　'Toward a theory of revolution.' American Sociological Review 27:5–19.
1969　'The J-curve of rising and declining satisfactions as a cause of some great revolutions and a contained rebellion.' In H.D. Graham and T.R. Gurr (eds.), The History of Violence in America. New York: Bantam
1970　(Ed.) When Men Revolt – And Why. New York: Free Press
Davitt, Michael
1904　The Fall of Feudalism in Ireland. New York
Deutsch, Karl, W.
1961　'Social mobilization and political development.' American Political Science Review 55:493–513
Duffy, C.G.
1886　The League of North and South. London
Durkheim, Emile
1933　The Division of Labour in Society. Translated by George Simpson. New York: Free Press
1951　Suicide: A Study in Sociology. Translated by John A. Spaulding and George Simpson. New York: Free Press
Feierabend, Ivo K., Rosalind L. Feierabend, and Betty A Nesvold
1969　'Social change and political violence: cross-national patterns.' In H.D. Graham and T.R. Gurr (eds.), The History of Violence in America. New York: Bantam
Freeman, T.W.

* References to newspapers are given in full in the text and are not repeated here.

1957 Pre-Famine Ireland: A Study in Historical
     Geography. Manchester: Manchester
     University Press
Geschwender, James, A.
1968 'Explorations in the theory of social
     movements and revolutions.' Social
     Forces 47:127–35
Gurr, T.R.
1970 Why Men Rebel. Princeton, N.J.: Prince-
     ton University Press
Hauser, Philip
1963 'The social, economic and technological
     problems of rapid urbanization.' In Bert
     Hoselitz and Wilbert Moore (eds.), Indus-
     trialization and Society. The Hague:
     Mouton
House of Commons
1843 Report of the Commissioners Appointed
     to Take the Census of Ireland for the Year
     1841 (504): xxiv
1877 Agricultural Statistics of Ireland for the
     Year 1876 [c 1749]: lxxxv
1881a Minutes of Evidence Taken Before Her
     Majesty's Commissioners on Agriculture
     [c 2778-I]: xv
1881b Return ... of Evictions Which Have
     Come to the Knowledge of the Con-
     stabulary in Each of the Years From 1849
     to 1880 (185): lxxvii
1882a Census of Ireland, 1881: Part I ... Vol. IV,
     Province of Connaught [c 3268]: lxxix
1882b Census of Ireland, 1881: Part II, General
     Report [c 3365]: lxxvi
1914 Report of the Departmental Committee
     on Agricultural Credit in Ireland [Cd
     7375]: xiii
Kornhauser, William
1959 The Politics of Mass Society. New York:
     Free Press
Lampson, G. Locker
1907 A Consideration of the State of Ireland in
     the Nineteenth Century. London: Con-
     stable
Larkin, Emmet
1972 'The devotional revolution in Ireland,
     1850–75.' The American Historical Re-
     view 77:625–52
Lewis, G.C.
1836 On Local Disturbances in Ireland, and on
     the Irish Church Question. London
McCaffrey, L.J.
1962 'Irish federalism in the 1870's: a study in
     conservative nationalism.' Transactions
     of the American Philosophical Society,
     New Series 52. pt. 6

Macintyre, Angus
1965 The Liberator: Daniel O'Connell and the
     Irish Party, 1830–1847. New York: Mac-
     Millan
Maher, J.
1951 'The repeal movement and the land ques-
     tion.' Bulletin of the Irish Committee on
     Historical Sciences, No. 63
Mannheim, Karl
1940 Man and Society in an Age of Reconstruc-
     tion. New York: Harcourt, Brace and
     World
Moody, T.W.
1949 'The new departure in Irish politics,
     1878–9.' In H.A. Cronne, T.W. Moody,
     and D.B. Quinn (eds), Essays in British
     and Irish History in honour of James
     Eadie Todd. London: F. Muller
1968 'The Fenian movement in Irish history.'
     In T.W. Moody (ed.), The Fenian Move-
     ment. Cork: Mercier Press
Nowlan, Kevin, B.
1965 The Politics of Repeal: A Study in the
     Relations Between Great Britain and Ire-
     land, 1841–50. London: Routledge and
     Kegan Paul
Oberschall, Anthony
1973 Social Conflict and Social Movements.
     Englewood Cliffs, N.J.: Prentice Hall
Ortega Y Gasset, José
1961 The Revolt of the Masses. London:
     Unwin Books
Palmer, N.D.
1940 The Irish Land League Crisis. New
     Haven: Yale University Press
Pinard, Maurice
1968 'Mass society and political movements: a
     new formulation.' The American Journal
     of Sociology 73:682–90
Reynolds, James
1954 The Catholic Emancipation Crisis in Ire-
     land, 1823–1829. New Haven: Yale Uni-
     versity Press
Ridker, R.G.
1962 'Discontent and economic growth.'
     Economic Development and Cultural
     Change 11:1–15
Snyder, David, and Charles Tilly
1972 'Hardship and collective violence.'
     American Sociological Review 37:520–32
Tilly, Charles
1969 'Collective violence in European perspec-
     tive.' In H.D. Graham and T.R. Gurr
     (eds.), The History of Violence in
     America. New York: Bantam

1970 'The changing place of collective violence.' In Melvin Richter (ed.), Essays in Theory and History: An Approach to the Social Sciences. Cambridge Mass.: Harvard University Press

Tocqueville, Alexis de
1888 The State of Society in France Before the Revolution of 1879. Translated by Henry Reeve. London: John Murray

Whyte, J.H.
1958 The Independent Irish Party. Oxford: Oxford University Press

Manuscript sources
Committee members at first meeting of the Irish National Land League, 21 October 1879. National Library of Ireland, MS 9281
Irish Crimes Records, 1881. State Paper Office
Irish National Land League Papers. National Library of Ireland
Registry of Births, Deaths and Marriages. Custom House

5

THE TENANTS' MOVEMENT TO CAPTURE
THE IRISH POOR LAW BOARDS, 1877-1886*
WILLIAM L. FEINGOLD

There is a well-established notion among Irish and British historians that local self-government began in Ireland in 1898, when the Local Government Act created the system of elective county councils to replace the old grand jury system in the government of the counties. The grand juries, it is well-known, were instruments of the Irish "landed interest"—the gentry and aristocracy—whose dominance over these bodies was protected by a rigid system of property qualifications and appointing procedures that admitted only trustworthy landowners to the jury seats.[1] Since only the juries were empowered to levy and expend the county tax known as the "cess," they were therefore also able to dominate the lesser county authorities, the county and baronial presentment sessions, through control of the purse. When the 1898 act abolished this aristocratic system and replaced it with a new system of representative county and district councils, the result was a *de facto* transfer of power in local government from the old landowning class to the peasantry. This view, which was first promoted by the founders of the 1898 act, has been repeated by numerous historians since then, and for lack of evidence to the contrary it prevails today.[2]

Willian O'Brien, the nationalist M.P. and editor of the Parnellite newspaper *United Ireland,* might well have disputed this view if he were alive today. As a practicing politician who understood well the

---

*This article is based on the author's doctoral dissertation, "The Irish Boards of Poor Law Guardians, 1872-1886: A Revolution in Local Government," University of Chicago, 1974. A different version of the article was presented to the Midwest Conference on British Studies, University of Minnesota, October 26-27, 1974. Maps by David M. Thorndike, Department of Geography, Bellevue College, Nebraska.

[1] A good brief description of the constitution and functions of the grand juries, boards of guardians, and other local government bodies in Ireland toward the end of the nineteenth century may be found in William F. Bailey, *Local and Centralised Government in Ireland,* (London, 1888).

[2] For the classic statement see Ernest Barker, *Ireland in the Last Fifty Years, 1866-1916,* (Oxford, 1917), p. 22.

ways in which power can be exercised, he was more inclined to look at the practical operations of public bodies rather than their constitutions to determine which party held the real power. In his *Recollections,* which were published in 1905, O'Brien reminisced about the turbulent years of the great "land war" of 1879-1882 and recalled how, in 1882, that historic struggle between Irish landlord and tenant for control of the soil focused for a time in a struggle for control of the Irish boards of guardians, the 163 bodies which administered the Irish poor law in the localities.[3] Constitutionally, the boards were a hybrid between elective and appointive bodies. Half of their members were elected, in annual elections, by the ratepaying public, which included all owners of property and all occupiers whose holdings were valued above £4. The poor law franchise, which was at the time the most liberal franchise of any governmental institution in Ireland, qualified over 500,000 people to vote in poor law elections.[4] The other half of the membership were ex-officio appointees who were drawn, as stipulated by law, from the highest-rated justices of the peace presiding in the counties.

These provisions made for an interesting social admixture at the boards. Since the highest-rated justices were almost invariably aristocrats or country gentlemen, the ex-officios were all landlords of varying stature. The elected members, on the other side, were almost all men without property; tenant farmers mostly, but also shopkeepers and publicans, and a substantial number of "landlords' men"—land agents and bailiffs.[5] Most of the elected guardians were tenants of one or another of the ex-officios. Each board, in short, was a microcosm of the surrounding community, but with the landlords raised to a level of numerical equality in spite of their small minority in the community. This composition, which was peculiar to the boards of guardians in Ireland, contained an inherent potential for political conflict, especially in the midst of a land war.

At the time of the poor law election mentioned by O'Brien the land war had been in progress for three years. Only a few months earlier the government had enacted the first truly effective land act, which granted the Irish tenantry what amounted to a partnership

---

[3]William O'Brien, *Recollections,* (New York, 1905), p. 413.

[4]Great Britain. Parliamentary Papers *(Commons),* 1874, vol. 56 (Accounts and Papers, no. 253). "Return from each Poor Law Union in Ireland, of the number of persons entitled to vote in each such union for Poor Law Guardians...," p. 927.

[5]For the social composition of the boards in the 1870s see chapters 1 and 2 of the author's dissertation, *Supra.*

status in the land tenure. Although this act might have been expected to calm the agitation, its salutary effects were negated by a second act, a coercion act, which had been enacted as a punitive corollary to the land act to enable the government to imprison suspected agitators without trial. At the time of the poor law elections in March, 1882 about 800 suspects were or had been in prison, most of them local and national leaders of the tenant organization, the Land League.[6] Charles Stewart Parnell, the president of the League and leader of the Home Rule Party in parliament, was in Kilmainham jail together with most of his party aides. The Catholic tenantry were in a defiant mood, and some kind of anti-government demonstration seemed to be in order. But from which quarter would it come, with all of the leaders in prison? It came, O'Brien tells us, in the poor law election, for when the elections were held during the last week of March, "as if by one universal impulse the country rose...swept the landlords form their old ascendancy at the Poor Law Boards, and put the most advanced of suspects in their places."[7]

If O'Brien was right, and the landlords had been "swept" from their "old ascendancy," it would appear that a revolution of sorts occurred in that election, a transfer of power from landlord to tenant in a very important local government institution. If that were so, then what is to be made of the claim that the Local Government Act of 1898 initiated local self-government? Obviously, the answer would depend upon what one accepts as the definition of local government before 1898. Unfortunately, little notice has been taken of the boards of guardians in that respect, although they were important rivals to the grand juries throughout the last half of the nineteenth century. Before the enactment of the Irish poor law in 1838, local government in Ireland was shared by the Municipal corporations in the cities and the grand juries in the rural districts. The poor law act created the boards of guardians to administer the workhouse system established under the same act, empowered the boards to levy a separate poor relief tax known as the poor rate, and superimposed over the existing county administration an entirely new administrative structure based on the territorial unit of the poor law union. Each of the 130 unions (163 after a redrawing of the boundaries in 1847) was administered by a board of guardians.

[6]Sam Clark, "The Social Composition of the Land League," *Irish Historical Studies,* 17 (September 1971), pp. 451-57.

[7]William O' Brien, *Recollections,* p. 413.

The boards were responsible to a five-man Poor Law Commission which answered to parliament through the Chief Secretary for Ireland. In 1872 this commission was converted into the Local Government Board in a move that was designed to increase the efficiency of local government in Ireland. The boards of guardians were the chief administrative wing of the Local Government Board, and their activities were carefully supervised by a talented group of local government inspectors.[8]

Beginning with the Great Famine of 1845-1847 the grand juries underwent a rapid decline, as parliament, appreciating the value of the boards as an efficient administrative network that was more amenable to its control than the juries, assigned the poor law administration a great many new responsiblities in areas other than poor relief. By 1872 these responsiblities included such diverse functions as the operation of the dispensary system; cattle, food, and workshop inspection; vaccination; the fostering-out and education of orphaned children; emigration assistance; and dog-catching; as well as related functions such as the registration of eligible voters, and the hiring, firing, and pensioning of personnel under their control. The bureaucracy for which they were responsible included workhouse masters and assistants, doctors and nurses, cooks, teachers, inspectors, and clerks of various kinds, and their patronage extended also to the giving out of contracts for food and fuel, medicines, ambulances, and public works projects relating to health and welfare. Their taxing powers expanded accordingly. Beginning with an annual budget of about £200,000, the guardians' expenditures rose by 1872 to £668,000, and by 1890 to £1,099,000. The 1890 figure represented about thirty-six percent of the total local government revenue that year, as compared with thirty-nine percent for the grand juries and twenty-five percent for the municipal and town authorities.[9]

These facts and figures demonstrate that fiscally and functionally the boards of guardians were an institution of at least equal importance to the grand juries, and growing in importance when the Local Government Act of 1898 abolished the juries and subsumed the boards as committees of the new urban and rural district coun-

[8]An excellent short discussion of the boards of guardians' history and functions to about 1880 may be found in Richard O'Shaughnessy, "Local Government and Taxation in Ireland," in J. W. Probyn, ed., *Local Government and Taxation in the United Kingdom,* (London, 1882).
[9]T.W. Grimshaw, *Facts and Figures about Ireland* (Dublin, 1893), p. 49.

cils. Whether the boards were technically representative bodies would be difficult to say, because of the appointive element in their constitution. But for political purposes they must certainly be considered representative bodies if it could be shown that the elective element possessed the actual power prior to 1898. The constitutional makeup of the boards in this case is of little help in defining the political reality.

How then would one test O'Brien's claim about the landlords' ascendancy being swept away? Can political ascendancy be measured for bodies of men in 163 localities spread out over the whole of Ireland? On the face of it, the problems would appear to be insuperable—among others, the problem of defining "ascendancy" and finding ways to identify it, when the individuals involved are obscure persons about whom little if any documentation has survived. Quantity is also a factor, since the average board membership numbered about fifty—twenty-five each of elected and ex-officio guardians—and the annual number of guardians in the system as a whole was about 7,300.[10] Fortunately, the problem is simplified greatly by the existence on each board of three officers, who were elected by the board members and who, by the very fact of their election, may be taken to reflect the preferences of the majority of the board. The officers were a chairman, a vice-chairman, and a deputy vice-chairman, who were, in effect, alternate chairmen empowered to occupy the chair in the order mentioned whenever the holder of a higher office was absent. As posts of honor and power, these offices were naturally given out to the most influential members of the board. But the political condition of Ireland, divided as it was between two conflicting social classes, was such that the measure of a candidate's influence was based not so much on his administrative qualifications as on his stature as a landlord or a tenant. Since this point is important to the present study, it will require some elaboration.

The election mentioned by O'Brien was not an isolated incident. It was a single episode in a broad tenants' movement during the 1870s and 1880s to gain control of all representative positions that were open to tenants. On the parliamentary level the attack was led by the Home Rule party, first under the leadership of Isaac Butt,

[10]Great Britain. Parliamentary Papers *(Commons)*, 1884, vol. 68 (Accounts and Papers, no. 335). "Return of the number of attendances of Poor Law Guardians at the board meetings of each Poor Law Union in Ireland, in the year ended 25th March 1884, pp. 55-59.

then under Parnell, Butt succeeded in winning fifty-nine out of the hundred Irish constituencies for the party in the general election of 1874; Parnell, whose posture was more defiant and therefore more popular, raised this number to a clean sweep of the Irish constituencies outside of the Protestant centers in Ulster, in the general election of 1885. To accomplish this feat, Parnell constructed, between 1882 and 1885, the National League, a political machine of uprecedented complexity and effectiveness, whose branches numbered over 1,200 at the time of the 1885 election.[11] Reports in the press indicate that a similar movement developed in the municipalities and towns, led by nationalists who were determined to unseat the Liberals and Conservatives who had been entrenched in the seats of the urban bodies for decades.[12]

The same movement extended to the boards of guardians, which were politically much more important to the nationalists than the urban authorities, since they extended over both urban and rural districts, had a great deal more patronage at their disposal, and were, in the rural districts, the only public bodies with a representative element. As early as 1872, attempts were made by poor law guardians connected with the nationalist and land reform movements in the unions of Roscommon and Kilmallock, to unseat the ex-officio officers of their boards. In both cases the offices had been held by ex-officios since the founding of the poor law.[13] The Kilmallock nationalists succeeded, and the ex-officios never again won an office at the board; the Roscommoners failed because they did not yet have sufficient support among the electorate to win the number of seats necessary for a clear majority. Nevertheless, the Roscommon proceedings came to the attention of the editor of the *Nation,* the widely circulated nationalist journal, who urged nationalists in other unions to emulate the Roscommon patriots. Such a movement, the editor suggested, would permit the nationalists to use the poor law elections to publicize their cause, while electoral victories would demonstrate to the government the extent of nationalist support in the country. The electoral campaigns would also give the branches of the Home Rule Association an opportunity to develop their political skills between parliamentary elections.[14]

[11]Conor Cruise O'Brien, *Parnell and His Party, 1880-1890,* (Oxford, 1957), pp. 127-132.
[12]See, for example, *Freeman's Journal,* April 12, 1880.
[13]*Roscommon Journal,* May 25, 1872; *Limerick Chronicle,* April 6, 1972.
[14]*Nation,* August 15, 1874.

This suggestion was not taken up immediately, except in a few unions where tenant political organizations were especially active. These isolated attacks were not expanded to the level of a national movement until after the flareup of agitation in the West of Ireland in 1879, and the founding of the Land League in November that year. For the next seven years the local branches of the Land League and its successor, the National League, focused their attention on the poor law elections each March in a concerted drive to capture for the tenants, first the elected seats, then the offices, of the boards in their unions. In 1881 Parnell lent his enormous prestige to the movement by publishing an open letter in the *Freeman's Journal* just before the poor law election, urging the Land League branches to "see that all exertions are made to secure the return of Land League candidates as poor law guardians, and to drive from office the agents, bailiffs, and landlord nominees who have hitherto been allowed to fill these important posts."[15]

Whenever Leaguers of a union managed to secure a majority of the elected seats, they immediately challenged the ex-officios for control of the board offices at the first meeting of the new board. Their task was often simplified by the fact that the ex-officio ranks were filled with absentee landowners who often lived outside of the union and rarely attended meetings. Even with this handicap the ex-officios put up strong resistance. They could usually count on the support of a few of the elected guardians and were able to increase their own numbers, at least for the single election meeting, by calling in absentees residing in distant places. The strategies of the tenant party, and the names of the party's nominees, were usually decided at a meeting of the local League branch. In some cases, as for example in the Roscommon union in 1881, nominating conventions were called to select the popular nominees. These maneouverings on both sides were covered in the local and national press with a zeal that was normally typical of parliamentary elections, and the measure of success was the extent to which the one party or the other was able to place its candidates in all three, or at least two, of the board offices. Sometimes the majority party, as a gesture of conciliation, allowed the minority members to name one of the officers, usually a man acceptable to the majority side.[16]

---

[15] *Freeman's Journal,* March 1, 1881.
[16] These elections are discussed extensively for each year in the author's dissertation, *Supra,* Prologue-Chap. 5.

Because the role of the offices in the rivalry was crucial, the office-holders are an excellent source for identifying party ascendancy. And because the parties were divided along clear social lines (allowing for a small number of landowners and tenants who were associated with the opposite side), the landholding status of the officers—whether they were owners or tenants—can be taken as an indication of their party affiliations. It would not be inappropriate to assume, therefore, that the proportion of owners to tenants in the offices of a given board, or all boards taken together, should yield a fairly accurate index of the relative strength of either side. If such an approach were valid, one would expect to find a very high percentage of landowners in the board offices in some year before the opening of the land war, and a similarly high percentage of tenants after 1882, assuming that O'Brien's analysis was correct.

In order to test this hypothesis I surveyed the 489 men who held the board offices in 1877, a year which I judged to be representative of conditions during the years just before the land war, to ascertain whether each was a landowner or a tenant-occupier. I then did the same for each year from 1879-1886, the peak years of the land war and Parnellite agitation. The names and addresses of the officers were obtained from the annual editions of *Thom's Directory of Ireland*.[17] The landholding data was derived from two sources used in combination: the 1876 parliamentary paper known as the "Domesday Book,"[18] which listed all persons owning more than one acre of land in Ireland; and the land valuation records of the period, which gave the names of the occupier and immediate lessor of every holding in Ireland.[19] All persons shown in the valuation records as occupiers who did not appear as the immediate lessor or in the "Domesday Book" as an owner, were classified as tenants. About fifteen to twenty-five percent of each annual group were persons whose names did not appear in either the "Domesday Book" or the valuation records. But on closer scrutiny these men were discovered to be justices of the peace listed in the *Thom's* lists of magistrates. Their omission from the landholding records at first presented a perplexing problem, until I discovered the probable reason for their omission: many justices of the peace were sons of

[17]First published under the title of *Thoms's Irish Almanac and Official Directory* (Dublin, 1844-).

[18]Great Britain. Parliamentary Papers *(Commons)*, 1876, vol. 80 (Accounts and Papers). C. 1492. "Return of Owners of Land, of one acre and upwards in the several counties, counties of cities, and counties of towns in Ireland...."

[19]Valuation Records, General Valuation Office, Dublin.

aristocrats and gentry who resided on their fathers' estates but did not hold title to land in their own right. Since they neither owned nor occupied a separate holding, they would not have appeared in either of the reference documents used. To place this group in with the tenants, or even to omit them from the statistics, would have unduly biased the results so as to give the appearance of less landowner representation than was actually the case, since these justices were members of landowning families. Therefore for the purposes of analysis, these unidentified justices were placed in the category of landowners. Now to the results of the survey.

The 1877 statistics completely supported O'Brien's statement regarding the "landlords' old ascendancy." That year 87 percent of the 489 offices were occupied by landowners. Within the three officers classes they had a virtual monopoly of the two higher offices, with 99 percent of the chairmanships (161 out of 163), and 93 percent of the vice-chairmanships (152 out of 163). Of the 59 tenants in the 1877 group, all but thirteen were in the lowest office, the deputy vice-chairmanships. Yet even in that office landowners held 69 percent of the seats. If this prevalence of landowners in the offices may be taken as a measure of their influence at the boards, one would have to conclude that the term "ascendancy" was appropriate for the landowners' position before the land war.

The percentages for 1879-1886 reveal a dramatic decline of the landlords influence, but not as complete a decline as O'Brien's statement implied. The percentages of tenants in all three offices combined are plotted for these years on the graph in Fig. 1. The graph shows clearly that the tenant gains did not occur entirely in 1882, but were spread over the seven-year period. The greatest period of absolute change came in 1879-1882, when seven percent of the offices changed hands each year. These tenant incursions were undoubtedly a product of the highly volatile political climate and strong anti-landlord feelings that were generated by the land war and the organized activities of the Land League. The coercion act, as has already been mentioned, was the principal motivation in the 1882 election. The movement suffered a decline in 1883, probably because of Parnell's deliberate attempts, following the so-called Kilmainham Treaty of April 1882, to stem the revolutionary tide and redirect the agitation toward the constitutional struggle for Home Rule. Throughout 1883 the Parnellites were busy building up the political machine in preparation for the next general election, and most of their activities were carried on behind-the-scenes. The

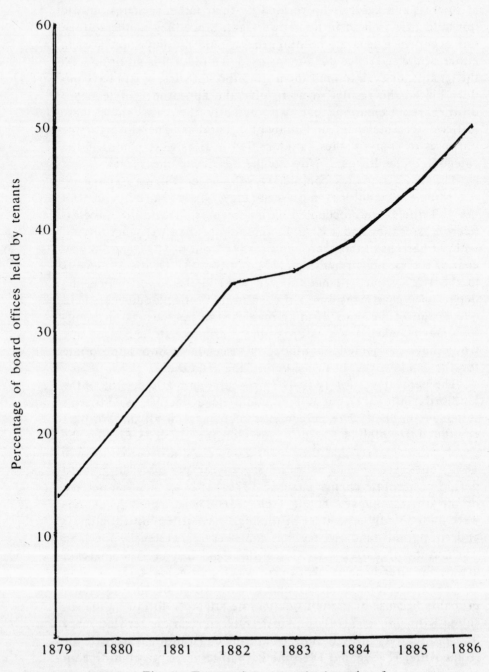

Fig. 1. Tenant increases in boards of
guardians offices, 1879-1886

resurgence of tenant office captures resumed in 1884 and carried through to 1886. These new gains were probably connected with the revival of organized political activity in the localities under the newly-formed branches of the National League. But the 1886 election was undoubtedly influenced also by the Parnellite sweep of the Irish constituencies in the general election, which took place only three months earlier. 1886 was by far the best year for the tenants in the boards of guardians elections. Although the absolute increase of tenant officerships was only six percent the *relative* increase was much larger than the seven percent of the early years, because there were many fewer offices remaining to be captured.

A second significant fact to emerge from the survey is that the tenants had possession of only half of the offices by 1886. For reasons of methodological consistency, the survey was not carried beyond 1886.[20] However, there is good reason to believe that 1886 was the last year of any substantial increases in tenant officeholdings. After that election the press lost interest in the poor law elections, and the National League turned its attention to the renewal of the land war in the "Plan of Campaign." Even a cursory glance at the listings of board officers in *Thom's* for the next five years reveals few changes in those offices that were held by landowners in 1886. Many of the ex-officios who occupied those offices were still in office in 1898, when the boards were brought into the new county government and the ex-officio element was abolished altogether. Therefore, the 1886 statistics probably represent close to the sum total of the officer changes. The final balance sheet shows that half of the total offices were held by tenants and half by landowners, with tenants occupying thirty-five percent of the chairmanships, forty-eight percent of the vice-chairmanships, and sixty-nine percent of the deputy vice-chairmanships.

It would be an exaggeration to say that the tenantry, with half of the offices, had completely destroyed the ascendancy of the landlords at the poor law boards. Clearly, the landlords retained a good

[20]After 1886 the land act of 1881 and the Land Purchase "Ashbourne" Act of 1885 began to have an increasing effect on land tenure relationships, as large numbers of tenant-occupiers began to take over the title to their holdings and themselves became owners. Thus the distinction between owner and tenant, which was useful for the earlier years as a way of distinguishing between the two groups politically, became less useful. In other words, the fact that a man was a landowner did not necessarily signify that he was also a member of the old landed interest. For this reason, I thought it best to terminate the survey in 1886, rather than run the risk of distorting the data by the introduction of a new variable.

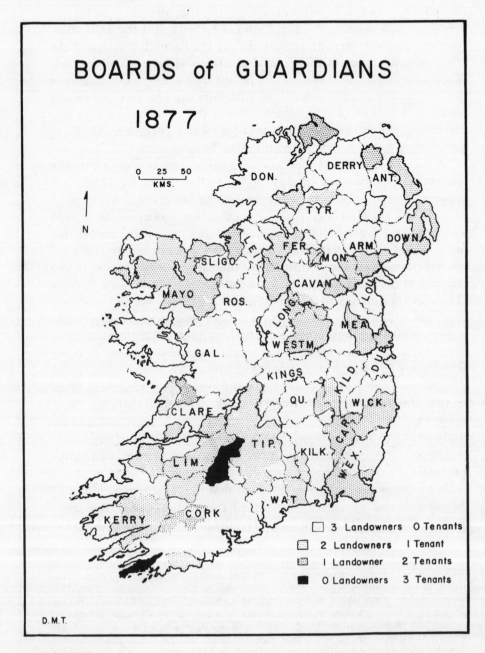

Fig. 2

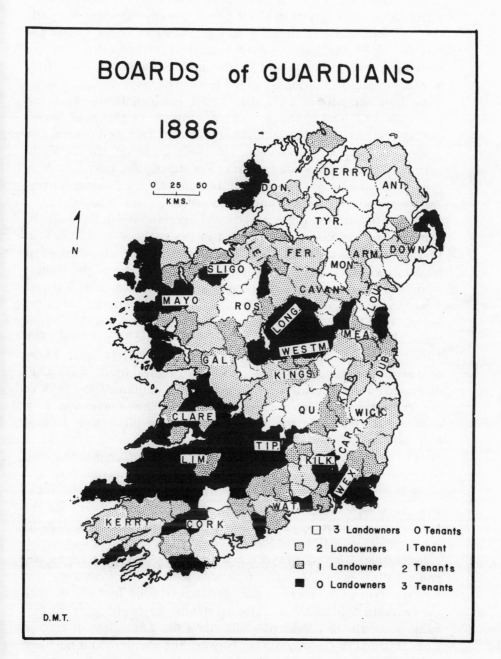

BOARDS of GUARDIANS

1886

0 25 50
KMS.

N

DON
DERRY
ANT?
TYR.
FER
MON
ARM
DOWN
SLIGO
CAVAN?
LOU
MAYO
ROS
LONG.
MEA
WESTM.
GAL
KINGS
DUB
CLARE
QU
KILL
WICK
TIP.
CAR?
LIM
KILK.
WEX
KERRY
WAT.
CORK

☐ 3 Landowners   0 Tenants
▨ 2 Landowners   1 Tenant
▦ 1 Landowner   2 Tenants
■ 0 Landowners   3 Tenants

D.M.T.

Fig. 3

deal of their influence. But how strong was the influence they did retain? Does the fifty percent figure represent a compromise in which both sides agreed to share power equally? Or does it signify that the landlords' ascendancy still prevailed at about half of the boards, while the tenants were ascendant in the other half? A possible answer is suggested by the manner in which the offices were allocated on a union-by-union basis. The maps in Figs. 2 and 3 show how the offices were distributed between landowners and tenants in 1877 and 1886. In both maps, unions or groups of unions having respectively three landowning officers, two landowners, one landowner, and no landowners (or three tenants), are shown in various shades from white to black. For descriptive purposes these groups of unions are designated respectively as "conservative," "moderate-conservative," "moderate-radical," and "radical."

Fig. 2 illustrates quite clearly the pattern of landlord domination of offices that was described in the analysis for 1877. That year all of the boards in Ireland but six were in the conservative or moderate-conservative categories, meaning that most of the tenants who held an office were on boards where the two other officers were landowners. The six boards with tenant majorities were in the unions of Kilmallock, Co. Limerick, and Castletown, Co. Cork (radical); and Scariff and Corofin, Co. Clare; Inishowin, Co. Donegal, and Newtownards, Co. Down (moderate-radical). Many of the moderate-conservative (two-landowner) boards were concentrated in the southwestern region which contained the bulk of the radical and moderate-radical boards. This suggests a less-conservative tendency among the guardians in this region even at that early date.

The 1886 map (Fig. 3), illustrates the dramatic change that had occurred in the interim, but also reveals that the changes followed some distinctive regional patterns. Most of the boards in the counties south of a line drawn from Wicklow to Galway were on the radical side of the spectrum, except for a small strip along the southern coast of Cork which remained conservative or moderate-conservative. The boards in the southwest which were moderate-conservative in 1877 were now completely dominated by the tenants. Two other areas of radical concentration in 1886 were in the northern Midlands—a region stretching westward from the east coast of Louth to Longford—and along the west coast of Ireland from Donegal to Galway. But in between the southern and northern radical areas was a conservative center which embraced large portions of the counties of Dublin, Wicklow, Carlow, Queens and Kings. The southern coast of Cork around Cork city was also conservative. But the most conspicuously conservative region was the far north, which incorporated all of Ulster with the exception of a few unions on the peripheries.

The existence of these distinctive patterns to a large extent proves the validity of using the landowning and tenant officers to determine party influence. If the decision of the guardians to elect one, or two, or three tenants was arbitrary, then we would expect to find the radical and conservative unions distributed randomly throughout the country. The fact that they were grouped in distinct pockets of three-landowner and three-tenant unions, and that these pockets were in most places separated by "buffer" areas of two-landowner and two-tenant unions, suggests that the number of owners or tenants holding office on a board was determined by a conscious political decision. It is unlikely, in other words, that the guardians of a number of adjacent unions would elect to have the same number of owners or tenants in their offices, unless the number in itself was in some way significant. We may therefore assume that the unions with three tenant officers were controlled entirely by that element which represented the tenant electorate, whereas the three landowner unions were still dominated by the propertied classes. We can be less certain about the moderate "buffer" unions, but may conjecture with a fair amount of assurance that the number of owners or tenants was also significant there. Since these unions were on the periphery of the extreme areas, the majority party probably had a smaller majority and had to compromise with the opposition party. No doubt the dominant party in these unions was the party which held two of the offices.

We may conclude from these maps that the fifty percent figure for 1886 did not represent a compromise in the distribution of power, but represented, rather, an ascendant influence exercised by landlords and tenants in separate territorial regions. In the northern third of Ireland, and in two regions of the south, the "landlords' ascendancy" still prevailed. But throughout most of the southern two-thirds of the country—an area comprising about half of territorial Ireland—this ascendancy was broken and local self-government by the tenantry was a reality. This being the case, the Local Government Act of 1898 did not, as is commonly supposed, initiate local self-government in Ireland. It only completed a democratizing process which had already begun without any change in the laws.

The development of representative local government in Ireland was a slow process which had begun in the 1830s with the Municipal Corporations Act and the Irish poor law act. Although it took sixty more years for the process to be completed legally, the Irish tenantry in the interim gained a valuable education in local self-government in the urban bodies and boards of guardians. By the time the county councils were established in 1898 there was a plentiful supply of experienced administrators and politicians among the tenantry who were ready to step in to the new county seats without any loss of continuity. It is in this context, as an educational experience for the tenantry, that the movement to capture the boards of guardians is most significant. From this experience they gained valuable lessons in the operation of the political process and the techniques of managing public institutions. Most of all, they could not help but gain a respect for constitutional action, which they carried with them into the new Irish state after 1921. Therefore, the conflicts in the board rooms in the 1880s may be regarded as a significant episode in the political apprenticeship of the Irish people.

6

THE I.R.B. AND THE BEGINNINGS OF
THE GAELIC ATHLETIC ASSOCIATION

W. F. MANDLE

The G.A.A. was founded as a consequence of an article, ' A word about Irish athletics ', that appeared in *United Ireland* on 11 October 1884. The writer, almost certainly Michael Cusack, a Dublin teacher, bewailed the fact that traditional Irish games had been abandoned because of English rule : ' the hated and hitherto dominant race drove the Irish people from their trysting places at the cross-roads and hurling-fields back to their cabins'; the Irish had become effete, pursuing fripperies and fashion, or, if they still practised athletics, did so under the control of an alien English Amateur Athletic Association where the main objective was to degrade the Irish by forcing them to compete in, and be defeated at, sports unfamiliar to them. The remedy was for ' the Irish people to take the management of their games into their own hands '.[1]

Cusack was then aged thirty-seven. He was the principal of a coaching academy in Gardiner's Place that specialised in cramming candidates for the civil service. He habitually wore a big black hat, knee-breeches, and carried a blackthorn stick. James Joyce caught the tone of his appearance and vocabulary in his portrait of the Citizen in *Ulysses*. He was reputed to have been a fenian in his youth and he was an almost exaggeratedly romantic nationalist as his account of how and why he had come to take up the cause of Irish athletics shows. He stated that in a dream the assorted shades of Wolfe Tone, Napper Tandy, Thomas Davis, Kickham, ' Speranza ' and Famine had come to him, braving ' leering fiends '. Finally Thomas Meagher ' darted up from the Missouri on a ray of the morning star and fiercely asked what had become of Irish hurling? ' Cusack, ashamed at the answers he would have had to give, then swore to Mother Erin, another of the shades in attendance, that ' I'll take hold of the first caman that comes my way, call the boys together, make a beginning,

[1] Research for this article could not have been undertaken without the assistance of the Australian Research Grants Commission. I am also indebted to Professor Oliver MacDonagh for his help and advice.

and ask the avid people to join us'.[2] There was a prompt response to his
'word'. The following issue of *United Ireland* carried a letter from
Maurice Davin, a noted member of a noted athletic family, welcoming
Cusack's call and suggesting the early drawing-up of official rules for
the distinctively Irish games and sports.[3] Cusack replied the next week
suggesting a meeting of interested persons at Thurles, County
Tipperary, on 1 November.[4]

At 2 p.m. on that Saturday eight men met at Miss Hayes's Hotel
and founded the Gaelic Athletic Association for 'the preservation and
cultivation of national pastimes'. Davin, one of the eight, was elected
president, and Cusack one of the three honorary secretaries, while
Croke, Davitt and Parnell were invited to become patrons.[5] It might
have seemed pretentious for eight men, armed though they were with
nearly sixty apologies for absence,[6] to have approached three such
august figures, and what is more, to have their approaches recipro-
cated, but the rapid spread of the G.A.A. justified such pretensions.
The unwritten memoirs of Cusack and the unpublished records of the
I.R.B. might also tell us the reason, for among the eight was a
suspiciously high proportion of fenians.

This was not surprising as fenians had recently been trying to
organise Irish games in Dublin and elsewhere. There had been
meetings of I.R.B. men P. N. Fitzgerald, P. J. Hoctor, John Menton

[2] See David Greene, 'Michael Cusack and the Rise of the G.A.A.' in
Conor Cruise O'Brien (ed.), *The shaping of modern Ireland* (London,
1960), p. 77, *Sixty glorious years of the G.A.A.* (Dublin, 1947), pp 9–10,
T. F. O'Sullivan, *Story of the G.A.A.* (Dublin, 1916), p. 3, James Joyce,
Ulysses (London, 1960), pp 380–448, P. J. Devlin, *Our native games*
(Dublin, [1935]), pp 7, 16–18.

[3] *United Ireland* (henceforth *U.I.*), 18 Oct. 1884. See Pat Davin,
Recollections of a veteran Irish athlete (Dublin, [1939]), pp 40–42 for
the achievements of his brother Maurice, described as a 'big reachy
man', six feet tall, fifteen stone in weight, and forty-seven inches across
the chest. At one time in the 1870s he held the world's record for the
hammer throw. See *60 years*, p. 8.

[4] *U.I.*, 25 Oct. 1884.

[5] There is a report of the meeting in *Freeman's Journal* (henceforth
F.J.), 3 Nov. 1884. See also S. P. O'Ceallaigh, *History of the Limerick
G.A.A. from the earliest times to the present day*, Part I, 1884–1908
(Tralee, 1937), pp 29–30 and O'Sullivan, *G.A.A.*, p. 7. Davitt sent an
apology for his absence together with his acceptance of the invitation, see
Cork Examiner, 3 Nov. 1884. Croke and Parnell also accepted, see *U.I.*,
27 Dec. 1884

[6] James Hurley, 'The founders of the Gaelic Athletic Association' in
Capuchin Annual, 1960, p. 197.

and James Boland at Blackrock, County Dublin, earlier in 1884 to consider the formation of a nationalist athletic movement, and in August a deputation consisting of Cusack and I.R.B. members J. P. McCarthy, John Sweeney, P. J. Kelly and James Lynam called upon the nationalist Bishop Duggan of Clonfert to obtain his patronage of a Gaelic athletic association. He declined, suggesting they consult the younger Archbishop Croke.[7]

The eight who met at Thurles (the figure generally given is seven, but it seems likely that the presence of F. R. Moloney, a noted fenian, was concealed at the time for fear of bringing suspicion upon the Association) were Cusack, Davin, John Wyse Power (a Dublin journalist then 'with the extreme section of the Irish nationalists'), John McKay (a Cork journalist), J. K. Bracken (a Templemore, County Tipperary, stonemason and I.R.B. man), P. J. Ryan (a solicitor of Thurles), St George McCarthy (a member of the R.I.C. stationed at Templemore who, his real purpose perhaps accomplished, took no further part in the organisation — he later played Rugby football for Ireland), and Moloney.[8]

The principles and meaning of the G.A.A. have been the subject of fleeting if favourable historical comment,[9] most seeing it as a populist precursor of the Gaelic League, founded in 1893. But it had its own *raisons d'être*. First, it was intensely Anglophobic. Cusack called rugby football 'a denationalising plague [carrying] on through winter the work of ruin that cricket was doing through the summer',[10] and *United Ireland* saw English games as 'the demoralising and prostrating tide that is rushing up to our doors through the ill-concealed sewers which are the homes of vile and treacherous things that work during the night'.[11] Archbishop Croke's letter of acceptance

[7] G.A.A. Golden Jubilee Supplement *Irish Press*, 14 Apr. 1934, pp 44, 56; Mark Tierney, *Croke of Cashel* (Dublin, 1976), pp 192–3.

[8] For Wyse Power see S.P.O., Crime Branch Special (henceforth C.B.S.) 11207/S; for McKay see R. Smith, *Decades of glory* (Dublin, 1966), p. 15; for Bracken see S.P.O., C.B.S., 12844/S and Andrew Boyle, *Poor dear Brendan* (London, 1974), pp 19–20; for Ryan and McCarthy see *60 Glorious years*, p. 10; for Moloney see S.P.O., C.B.S., 126/S.

[9] See, e.g., F. S. L. Lyons, *Ireland since the famine* (London rev. ed., 1972,) pp 225–7; Oliver MacDonagh, *Ireland* (New Jersey, new ed. (1977), pp 72–3, and C. Cruise O'Brien, '1891–1916' in idem. *Shaping*, pp 15–17.

[10] Brendan MacLua, *The steadfast rule: a history of the G.A.A. ban* (Dublin, 1967), p. 96.

[11] 3 Jan. 1885. This could have been written by Cusack, but William O'Brien, the editor's, style was not dissimilar.

which became a manifesto of the G.A.A. was bitterly anti-English and flamboyantly pro-Irish. All things English—fashion, accent, literature, music, dancing, mannerisms, games and pastimes—were attacked, all things Irish, those 'racy of the soil,' were praised.[12]

The timing of the G.A.A.'s foundation reflected fears that the new organised sports of the late nineteenth century would, if directed from England and integrated into a United Kingdom pattern, further weaken distinctive Irish culture. Association football had come under the control, in 1880, of an Irish Football Association, modelled on the English F.A., and using its laws. Rugby football in Ireland grew up in the 1860s around a Trinity College, Dublin, club which formed the Irish Football Union in 1874 with another Dublin club, the Wanderers, which had been founded by an English ex-public schoolboy.[13] There was also a class element in the movement. Cusack himself was particularly keen to extend sport to the workers,[14] and Davin spoke of the need for games ' especially for the humble and hard-working who seem now to be born into no other inheritance than an everlasting round of labour '.[15]

Given such attitudes, the G.A.A. could hardly avoid being political. As the *Irishman* put it, ' if any two purposes should go together they ought to be politics and athletics. A political people we must be; the exigencies of our situation force us into perpetual war with England . . . our politics being essentially national so should our athletics '.[16]

Within a few months of its foundation the G.A.A. was at war on the athletics front in a struggle which demonstrated its nationalist principles. Despite the fact that probably only one meeting under G.A.A. auspices had been held before January 1885,[17] and that no

[12] *U.I.*, 27 Dec. 1884.
[13] It was not until 1881 that the Dublin and the independently formed Belfast clubs (the first in 1868) combined to form the Irish union that drew its rules and its opponents from the rest of the United Kingdom, see W. J. Morgan and Geoffrey Nicholson, *Report on rugby* (London, 1959), pp 97–8.
[14] See, e.g., *F.J.*, 3 Sept. 1885.
[15] 'Hurley Founders', p. 205; *60 Glorious years*, p. 13; *U.I.*, 18 Apr. 1885.
[16] Quoted in O'Sullivan, *G.A.A.*, p 12.
[17] At Tuomes, County Cork, see *F.J.*, 19 Nov. 1884. This meeting consisted of foot races only. The first major meeting did not take place until May 1885 at Blarney, County Cork, see *F.J.*, 4 May 1885 and the first football game was at Callan, County Kilkenny, early in February, see *60 Glorious years*, p. 14.

G.A.A. rules for football, hurling, or athletics were published until February 1885,[18] those then in charge of Irish athletics recognised a threat. There was no Irish Amateur Athletic Association at the time,[19] but steps were speedily taken to form one once the G.A.A. committee announced on 17 January 1885 that, after St Patrick's day, no athlete would be allowed to compete at a G.A.A. meeting if he competed elsewhere under other rules.[20]. Five days later the Irish Cycling Association met and one delegate called for cyclists to unite with other Irish athletes ' to quash the G.A.A.'.[21] Within a couple of days of this appeal, a meeting of representatives of athletics', harriers', cyclists', and footballers' clubs was held in Dublin and arranged for a further meeting to form an Irish Athletic Association on 21 February.[22]

Cusack turned up to this meeting and became at once the centre of a storm. Davin had written a letter asking that Cusack be permitted to attend, but he spurned the courtesy. He would not risk betraying the G.A.A., he said. He then refused to be accounted another delegate from the G.A.A., McKay and F. O'Crowley, the association's official handicapper,[23] being already there in that capacity. Finally he chose to remain as a member of the press. Eventually the representatives of the twenty clubs present went on to form an Irish Amateur Athletic Association.[24] The two rival associations now began a struggle that lasted for just over a year, until April 1886, when it had become clear that, far from being ' quashed ', the G.A.A., which had on its side all the advantages accruing to an organisation avowedly nationalist, ostentatiously Irish, and, crucially, church-supported, was by far the stronger of the two.

The first test of strength came on Sunday 17 June 1885, at Tralee. The County Kerry Athletic and Cricket Club had advertised a

[18] See *U.I.*, 7 Feb. 1885 for first football and hurling rules, 14 Feb. for weight-throwing, and 21 Feb. for jumping.

[19] Lyons, *Ireland*, p 225 suggests that there was, but he seems to be in error, for the foundation meeting was not held until 21 Feb. 1885, see below.

[20] *U.I.*, 24 Jan. 1885. This was the beginning of the famous 'ban '.

[21] *F.J.*, 23 Jan. 1885.

[22] *F.J.*, 29 Jan. 1885.

[23] O'Crowley was an Advanced I.R.B. see S.P.O. C.B.S. 126/S, Return of Advanced I.R.B.s and F.B.s who attended Thurles G.A.A. Convention, etc. (henceforth ' Return ').

[24] *F.J.*, 24 Feb. 1885; *U.I.*, 28 Feb. 1885; *60 Glorious years*, pp 13–14. The G.A.A.'s representatives opposed the decision.

meeting under I.A.A.A. rules to be held on that date. The G.A.A. organised a rival meeting inviting Irishmen ' to choose between Irish and foreign laws '.[25] The I.R.B., led by an old fenian, William Moore Stack, played its part, as did the clergy, a local priest, Fr McMahon, opening the meeting with a claim that the G.A.A.'s existence showed that the ' soul had come back to Ireland '. Special trains and carriages brought spectators and competitors from all over the south-west of Ireland, and while between ten and fifteen thousand persons watched over 450 athletes competing under G.A.A. rules, a few hundred in a nearby field attended the disastrously out-faced I.A.A.A. meeting.[26] Nothing thereafter that summer could halt the rapid progress of the G.A.A. On 11 July *United Ireland* announced that it could no longer carry reports of all G.A.A. meetings because they had grown too numerous, and on 8 August the *Freeman's Journal* began printing lengthy lists of prospective meetings. The clergy joined with the National League and even, probably, unknowingly, with the I.R.B., as at Tralee, in fostering the growth of the organisation.

It was noted in April 1885 that six priests were on the Gort, County Galway, committee and in September that the clergy were present in large numbers at the Ashford, County Wicklow, sports. At Queenstown Father Murphy became president of the G.A.A. club and clerical support was reportedly strong in Drogheda. The first school to have a G.A.A. club was the Carmelite college at Terenure, County Dublin, which formed one in October 1885. The National League and the Land League were particularly active in Kerry.[27]

By August 1885 Cusack claimed that the G.A.A. had ' hundreds ' of clubs, but at the convention of March 1886 only sixty-eight clubs had paid affiliation fees, not in itself a totally definitive indication of numbers, but one that suggests Cusack's figure was an exaggeration.[28] The I.A.A.A., which claimed it had twenty-nine clubs by the same month,[29] attempted to counter this surge of support by imposing a counter-ban to become effective on 1 September 1885,[30] but the spectacle of the Irish athletics world so divided moved Croke to

[25] *U.I.*, 30 May and 13 June 1885.

[26]*U.I.*, 27 June 1885; O'Sullivan, *G.A.A.*, p. 22; T. S. O'Sullivan papers (N.L.I. MS 15385).

[27] *U.I.*, 4 Apr., 29 Aug., 26 Sept., and 17 Oct. 1885; *F.J.*, 1 June and 26 Oct. 1885; O'Sullivan, *G.A.A.*, pp 18, 22; ' PF ' (Patrick Foley), *Kerry's football story* (Tralee, 1945), p. 31.

[28] *F.J.*, 6 Aug. 1885 and 1 Mar. 1886; *U.I.*, 6 Mar. 1886.

[29] *F.J.*, 29 Mar. 1886.

[30] *F.J.*, 19 Aug. 1885.

suggest ' toleration ' in a letter to the first annual convention of the G.A.A., held on 31 October at Thurles;[31] and after a dispute over an I.A.A.A. proposal for amalgamation, which the G.A.A. indignantly rejected,[32] the bans were lifted by the G.A.A. in February 1886, and by the I.A.A.A. in March.[33] One of the major issues in the contest had been accusations that the G.A.A. had too close a link with the national movement. No matter how much the G.A.A. denied these accusations, calling them ' as vile a production as has ever been evolved ',[34] it was a charge that had substance, as the evidence showed, and as such statements as ' the Gaelic Athletic Association is not a political association although it is a thoroughly national one '[35] failed to refute. The very names of the clubs spoke of the nature of the association. There were many Young Irelands, there was an Erin's Hope, a Bray Emmet's, a Dublin Kickham's, and there were clubs named after Biggar, Davitt and Parnell.[36] The green flag with the gold harp floated over G.A.A. sports meetings,[37] and the whole association revelled in its links with a specifically Irish tradition.

The G.A.A. from the start took great pains to emphasise the distinctiveness and the long history of Irish games and sports. Irish football was claimed to have separate origins from the Anglo-Saxon versions. Hurling was traced back to the days of Cuchulain and vested with legendary grandeur, and Irish athletics were said to be coeval in origin with those of Greece. As *United Ireland* put it on 5 September 1885, the G.A.A.'s ' ideal Ireland was dotted all over with miniature armies of hurlers, bowlers, jumpers, weight-throwers, merry dancers and joyous singers '.

The nationalist and political implication of such attitudes engaged the increasing attention of Dublin Castle and it is to its records that we owe much of the evidence of the I.R.B.'s successful attempt to make the G.A.A. its own. The problem of using such evidence is apparent, but the public record of events, as detailed in the press, confirms the police analysis. Moreover the general impression to be gained from the reports, both at the local and central level, is of

[31] *F.J.*, 2 Nov. 1885 and *U.I.*, 7 Nov. 1885.
[32] *F.J.*, 5 and 8 Dec. 1885 and 9 Mar. 1886.
[33] *F.J.*, 1 and 29 Mar. 1886; *U.I.*, 6 Mar. 1886.
[34] *U.I.*, 15 Nov. 1884.
[35] O'Sullivan, *G.A.A.*, p 23.
[36] Carbery ' (P. D. Mehigan), *Gaelic football* (Dublin, 1941), p. 89; O'Ceallaigh, *Limerick*, p 35; *U.I.*, 6 Mar. and 11 Nov. 1886.
[37] *U.I.*, 26 Sept. 1885.

matter-of-fact reportage rather than of hysterical paranoia. Final judgment must rest with the reader as he watches the story unfold.

In nineteenth-century Ireland, no organisation such as the G.A.A. could avoid a political dimension. As a Dublin Castle report put it, early in 1888, ' the question was not whether the association was a political one, but only to what particular section of Irish national politics it could be annexed '.[38] The advantages to whatever section did annex the G.A.A. had rapidly become obvious as the association grew in strength during 1885. From the very outset, some had regarded the G.A.A. as a creature of the I.R.B. Inspector Waters went so far as to state that the G.A.A. had been founded by the I.R.B. He explained that the success of the Land League, followed by that of Parnell and the National League, had split the ' old fenian ' movement into those who ' more or less honestly supported the policy of Parnell, and accepted home rule as a settlement of the Irish question ' and those ' who retained their original determination to be satisfied with nothing less than absolute independence '.

This latter party, accepting the general assurance that home rule, as defined by the other section, would become an accomplished fact, cast around for a means whereby they could in such an event be in a position to control and direct the Irish executive to their own ends; and with this object, the idea suggested itself of combining the muscular youth of the country into an organisation, drilled and disciplined to form a physical power capable of over-awing [sic] and coercing the home rule government of the future.

The moderates and the clergy, either through ignorance, or confidence that they could keep the I.R.B. in check, supported the new association.[39]

The I.R.B. influence in the executive of the G.A.A. was maintained at the elections to office at the 1885 convention. Davin remained president, Cusack, McKay and Wyse Power secretaries. The vice-presidents were Bracken, J. E. Kennedy (an 'advanced I.R.B. man'[40] from Cork), J. F. Murphy, J. Stewart and W. Barry. F. O'Crowley remained official handicapper. There were therefore five fenians on the ten-man executive. During the year Murphy, McKay and Cusack left the executive. Cusack's going was, inevitably, the stormiest. His extreme statements had hampered negotiations with the I.A.A.A.

[38] ' The political aspect of the Gaelic Athletic Association in Ireland ', P.R.O. C.O. 904/16.

[39] Inspector A. W. Waters, 11 Nov. 1887, in S.P.O., C.B.S. 126/S.

[40] ' Return ', loc. cit.

In January 1886, at quite a delicate stage in the discussion, he had publicly called it a 'ranting, impotent, West British abortion',[41] and the previous June he had successfully sued its president, J. Dunbar, for libel.[42] Then in March 1886, as a result of the *Freeman's Journal* delaying the report of a speech of Croke's on the topic of amalgamation, Cusack had written a fiery letter to Croke declaring that he would 'face out' both him and the *Freeman*. Croke angrily replied that it was he who had requested the *Freeman* to delay publication of his speech so that he might vet its text. He added that 'if Mr Michael Cusack is allowed to play the dictator in [the G.A.A.'s] counsels, to run a reckless tilt with impunity and without rebuke' then he, Croke, could not continue as patron.[43] He was in trouble again in June, being rebuked by the executive for criticising the Dublin Grocers' Assistants club for appointing its own and not the G.A.A.'s official handicapper.[44] Then, in July, Wyse Power sent a letter of complaint to Davin about Cusack's secretarial incompetence. A special meeting was at once called for Sunday, 4 July, and in Davin's absence, Frank Moloney took the chair. Cusack's rather pathetic efforts to defend himself (he took a sheaf of letters and postal orders, some of them, on later evidence, revealed to have been uncashable because they were seven months old, from his pocket to demonstrate his mastery of the correspondence) failed, and he was expelled from his position by 47 votes to 13.[45] Cusack's tempestuous behaviour had finally persuaded his colleagues of the necessity to be rid of him; as he saw it he was being persecuted.

The I.R.B. confirmed its utilisation of the G.A.A. in September 1886. John O'Leary was invited to become the fourth patron of the Association, and it was decided to set up committees to organise memorials to C. J. Kickham who had died in 1882.[46] At the elections to office at the 1886 annual convention held at Thurles on 15 November the I.R.B. virtually took over the executive. The convention of 1887 has generally been seen as the one in which the I.R.B. made its bid for power in the G.A.A.,[47] but examination of the men who were

[41] *F.J.*, 9 Jan. 1886.
[42] *F.J.*, 5 June 1885.
[43] *F.J.*, 9, 19, 20 and 23 Mar. 1886.
[44] *F.J.*, 5 and 7 June 1886.
[45] *F.J.*, 5 July 1886, 3 and 4 April 1889, *U.I.*, 10 July 1886.
[46] *F.J.*, 30 Sept. 1886.
[47] See, e.g., Greene, 'Cusack', p. 83 and Nicholas Mason, *Football!* (London, 1974), p. 81.

elected in 1886 bears out the truth of an I.R.B. leader's remarks to
a police agent in November 1887 that the priests who had come to
oppose the I.R.B. were 'about a year too late'.[48] Davin remained
president, but the new vice-presidents were Bracken, Kennedy, P. T.
Hoctor and Frank Moloney. Patrick Hoctor was from Limerick, a
great friend of a leading I.R.B. man, P. N. Fitzgerald, and a very
active worker on behalf of the brotherhood.[49] The new treasurer was
Patrick Hassett of Ahane, Co. Limerick, an advanced I.R.B. man.,
and the four secretaries were all members of the I.R.B.—Wyse Power,
Tom Riordan or O'Riordan of Cork, J. B. O'Reilly of Dublin, and
James Butler of Thurles.[50] F. B. Dineen replaced O'Crowley as
official handicapper. The I.R.B. triumph was rounded off by
O'Leary's acceptance of the post of patron. Just as the initial choice
of Croke, Davitt and Parnell as patrons reflected the balance within
the orthodox nationalist forces at its inception, the addition of John
O'Leary showed how the balance was tilting after only two years of
existence.

Following this convention the I.R.B., almost wholly in control of
the centre of the G.A.A., began its efforts to extend that control into
the provinces. On 27 February 1887 the new executives met at
Wynn's Hotel in Dublin. Davin was unable to be present and the
chair was taken by Bracken. Every one of the others present was also
a member of the I.R.B.—Kennedy, Hoctor, Dineen, Hassett, Wyse
Power, O'Reilly and O'Riordan, together with three coopted
members, Anthony Mackey, P. J. O'Keeffe and P. C. Kelly.[51] The
meeting made a number of rulings that under the terms of article 14
of the constitution were completely illegal. Members of the Royal
Irish Constabulary were banned from competing at G.A.A. meetings;
county committees had to sanction all proposed meetings and, most
importantly, henceforth all members of the executive were to be

[48] F. B. Dineen speaking to Const. O'Reilly, see S.P.O., C.B.S., 126/S.
[49] For Hoctor see S.P.O., C.B.S. 1128/S and P.R.O., C.O.
904/17/351.
[50] For Hassett and O'Riordan see 'Return', loc.cit.; for O'Reilly
S.P.O., C.B.S., Report of district inspector, crime special, on secret
societies (henceforth S.S.), Northern division, Sept. 1887; for Butler see
S.P.O., C.B.E., 9500/S and 9692/S, and *Gaelic Athlete,* 10 July 1915.
[51] For Mackey, I.R.B. county centre for Limerick, see S.P.O., C.B.S.
9000/S and P.R.O., C.O. 904/18/713; for O'Keeffe, county centre for
Kilkenny, see S.P.O., C.B.S. 5404/S and P.R.O., C.O. 904/18/821; for
P. C. Kelly (not to be confused with P. J. Kelly, also of Galway) see
S.P.O., C.B.S. 5528/S and P.R.O., C.O. 904/18/647.

ex officio members of all county committees with powers to vote. In other words the I.R.B. ascendancy at the centre could be extended if necessary and at will to any provincial part of the organisation.[52]

Davin, when sent a copy of these new rules, was horrified, and protested at an executive meeting held in Limerick on Easter Monday, 11 April. His protests were unavailing, and so on 18 April he sent in a letter of resignation. He later explained that he felt he had two courses open to him, either to call for a special convention with all the political dissensions it would arouse, or to resign and ' see how things went on '.[53] At another ' packed ' executive meeting held at Limerick on 28 May, his resignation was considered and accepted. The presidency lay vacant and the I.R.B. monopolised the executive.

During the summer the new executive strove both to exert its authority and to demonstrate its adherence to the more extreme brand of Irish nationalism. It did this, in sporting terms, by trying to dictate to two leading Dublin athletic clubs, the Grocers' Assistants and that of the *Freeman's Journal,* who should handicap their major meetings. But the issue ranged further and was seen to range further than one of athletics pure and simple.

On 28 May the executive ' proclaimed ' the Grocers' Assistants meeting set down for 10 July. The full County Dublin committee responded on 8 July with a critical attack on the new executive.

Such vexatious and tyrannical reading of the rules as the central committee have adopted they believe will do more harm to the G.A.A. than all the coercion acts could possibly do, and they trust that before it is too late those who have the carrying out of the rules will give a more liberal interpretation of them . . . as if not districts that are thoroughly Gaelic will be found floating the flag of the I.A.A.A.[54]

The meeting went ahead, despite a hail of posters, distributed by supporters of the executive, which underlined the political realities of the dispute :

The Gaelic Athletic Association.
Nationalists of Dublin!

Down with dissension ! Discountenance disunion ! Support not the would-be wreckers of the G.A.A. ! Down with the men who would disgrace the association that has for its patrons the tried, true, and illustrious Irishmen—Archbishop Croke, C. S. Parnell, Michael Davitt, and John O'Leary.

[52] O'Sullivan, *G.A.A.,* p. 43.
[53] *F.J.,* 2 Nov. 1887.
[54] *F.J.,* 9 July 1887.

Who are those men who try to prove that Irishmen are not worthy
of self-government?

   The Grocers' Assistants Sports Committee.

Do not by your presence at their meeting commit an act of treason
to Ireland.

   God Save Ireland.[55]

The success of the meeting, despite the executive's warnings,
emboldened the *Freeman's Journal* athletic club, convenor of the
largest regular athletics meeting in Ireland, set down in 1887 for
10 September, to announce its intention of bypassing the official
handicapper. On the day that decision was announced, 3 July, the
executive, meeting at Limerick Junction, took the extreme step of
expelling the Grocers' Assistants club from the G.A.A., expelling all
members of the County Dublin committee who had supported the
club, and suspending for three months all athletes who had taken
part in the meeting. The chairman, Hoctor, said that an attack upon
'the national feeling of the country' was being made. All those present
at this meeting were I.R.B. men—Hoctor, Kennedy, Bracken,
Moloney, Frewen, Dineen and O'Riordan—who, as well as imposing
suspensions and expulsions, claimed that the G.A.A. was Ireland's first
home rule association, and criticised Dublin for its sneers at 'gentlemen, no matter how estimable, from remote districts'.[56]

   The campaign was stepped up as the date of the sports meeting
neared. On 3 September *The Gael*, the G.A.A.'s official newspaper
edited by Hoctor, carried an announcement 'proclaiming' the meeting and threatening suspension from the G.A.A. of all competitors
and even spectators who chose to show 'their preference for a half-
day's pleasure to the exclusion of that spirit of true national independence'. An editorial called for action on behalf of 'two hundred
thousand true-hearted Irishmen' against a weak minded, dissentient
clique, acting under the control of the worst form of the West British
element. On the one side is independence; on the other, treachery'.[57]
Matters had clearly gone far beyond the question of who should be
handicapper at the sports. The meeting took place successfully, claimed
the *Freeman's Journal* of 12 September, perhaps inevitably, but the
police had some reservations.

---

[55] *Irish Times,* 11 July 1887.
[56] *F.J.*, 9, 23 and 27 July 1887.
[57] Cuttings from *The Gael* (no copies of which appear to have survived) in S.P.O., C.B.S. 126/S.

Although the sports were very well attended by the respectable classes, they were I believe on the whole a failure in a monetary point of view . . . The stand and enclosures were no doubt extremely well filled, but free passes to those places were very freely given, and even Mr E. D. Gray M.P. brought large numbers into the grounds on several occasions . . . without paying . . . The fenian element was completely absent, and there were very few of the artisan and labouring classes present.[58]

The dispute had proved bitter enough for Croke to try to intervene late in July. He said that when the G.A.A. was founded he feared three things: drink, the ' desecration of the Sabbath', and 'bad blood'. Those fears had proved largely groundless, but now a new danger, that of ' dictation', had arisen to cause ' unseemly squabble or contention'.[59] His statement led to suggestions that he should be called upon to mediate, but *The Gael* snubbed him : ' we do not want one or all of our patrons as judges. We want them to remain in their high and dignified position of honour'.[60]

In private, about this time, Croke was also displaying signs of disquiet. In conversation with ' a fenian' he was reported as saying ' The country is in a worse state than ever I remember it'. He had confidence only in Parnell and when ' the fenian' said to him, ' we will get nothing from England but by force of arms' Croke replied ' I hope you will never have anything to do with the like'.[61]

During the autumn, as the time for the convention neared, there was mounting criticism. A South Tipperary and Limerick convention resolved to oppose the re-election of Bracken and Moloney in November, in Wexford a convention condemned ' Bracken and all those scoundrels', and at Clonmel, Co. Tipperary, a meeting called for the restitution of Davin as president. But not all opinion was critical. At a Cork meeting Davin was called ' a renegade', and his name, together with that of the *Freeman* and of the *Celtic Times*, was hissed. A meeting of the expelled Dublin clubs, held on 4 November, indicated to what extent the athletics aspect of the dispute was merely a symbol of deeper discord. The meeting resolved to deprecate ' in the strongest possible manner any action tending to bring the Gaelic Athletic Association into conflict with the Irish national movement'.[62]

[58] Report of Supt Reddy, D.M.P., 13 Sept. 1887 in S.P.O., C.B.S. 126/S.

[59] *F.J.*, 26 July 1887.

[60] Quoted in O'Sullivan, *G.A.A.*, p. 46.

[61] S.P.O., C.B.S., S.S., South-east division, Aug. 1887.

[62] *F.J.*, 10, 17, 24 and 31 Oct., 5 and 7 Nov. 1887; O'Sullivan, *G.A.A.*, p. 46.

The events of the year had not escaped the attention of Dublin Castle. The results of the G.A.A. elections of November 1886, when so many familiar names appeared in new, sporting roles, caused police interest in the association to quicken. It found much to be disturbed about. In Clare ' a good opportunity of a general communication of all the leading conspirators in the county ' was afforded by the sudden growth of the G.A.A., which existed to ' enable leading members of the I.R.B. to consult together' and to recruit young men who marched to and from their games in military order and were defiant to the police.[63] From Tipperary came reports of P. N. Fitzgerald travelling through the county in May, ostensibly as a commercial traveller but carrying no samples. He was accompanied by J. E. Kennedy, and after they had left a local I.R.B. man told a police agent that the G.A.A. would be ' a useful thing to keep us together . . . if our organisation was failing '.[64] By June the police feared that the extremists were eroding ' the good influence of the priests and that the growth in the G.A.A. was hardly to be accounted for by a sudden love of athletics '.[65]

By the summer the G.A.A. was well enough organised in Clare to be able to ' take over as the leading nationalist organisation ' if the National League were proclaimed (as it was in August).[66] P. J. McInerney, an I.R.B. man with suspected connections with the Invincibles,[67] was running the G.A.A. from Ennis as ' a cloak under which meetings of the dangerous characters can take place whenever the National League may be suppressed '.[68] Some doubts were nonetheless being expressed as to exactly how loyal was the G.A.A. to the National League,[69] but the constant activity of the I.R.B. in the association was not in question. Dineen and O'Reilly were busy recruiting and organising G.A.A. clubs throughout Louth, and by October the movement was spreading into Armagh and Monaghan with large crowds attending the matches.[70] In Queen's County I.R.B.

[63] S.P.O., C.B.S., Divisional commissioners' and county inspectors' monthly report (henceforth monthly report) south-western division, Mar. 1887.

[64] S.P.O., C.B.S., S.S., south-east, May 1887.

[65] Ibid., June 1887.

[66] S.P.O., C.B.S., monthly report, south-west, June 1887.

[67] S.P.O., C.B.S. 1224/S.

[68] S.P.O., C.B.S., monthly report, western, Aug. 1887.

[69] E.g. S.P.O., C.B.S., SS., south-east July 1887 and monthly report, western, July 1887.

[70] S.P.O., C.B.S., SS., northern, Sept. and Oct. 1887.

' orders' had come through in July to start twenty-one G.A.A. branches, and in the west each I.R.B. centre was reported to have received instructions to attend all local hurling matches in order to recruit young men to the Brotherhood.[71]

Police reports only confirmed what the public prints demonstrated; that the G.A.A. was becoming a political organisation of a particular cast, in which athletics played only a minor role. There would be much to discuss at the convention. ' Wait till November!' had been a cry as early as July,[72] and by November the topics for discussion had multiplied. The association's ex-president had condemned the executive on the eve of the convention, expressing fears for the safety of delegates in the prospective overcrowding at Thurles;[73] Archbishop Croke had been snubbed; the County Dublin committee and almost all the city's clubs had been expelled; and through the country there had been expressions of disquiet.

The I.R.B., aware that a conflict was in the offing, laid its plans to ensure that the convention would afford support to the executive. There were by now over 600 clubs in the G.A.A., each with the right to send two delegates to the convention; hence the fears of Davin and others. The very number of clubs, many of recent foundation, gave an opportunity to rig the convention that the I.R.B. did not neglect. Afterwards, a parish priest from Roscrea, County Tipperary, complained that men not known in his district had represented clubs that did not exist.[74] From Tipperary it was claimed that there were no such clubs as Nenagh Castle, Ferryglass, Cloughprior or Drominagh, yet ' delegates' from them were at the convention, and a Templemore club, which sent no delegates, was surprised to discover that two men had represented it at the convention. A delegate from Wexford, an I.R.B. man, George Keegan, who was elected to the executive, had never even been seen at a match in the county.[75] An anonymous letter from Cork explained how things had been done there.

There are about 20 clubs in the city, many of whom could not afford the cost of sending delegates to the convention. They were, however, relieved of all anxiety on this hand by gentlemen from two 'philanthropic'

[71] S.P.O., C.B.S., SS., south-east, July 1887; monthly report, western, Sept. 1887.
[72] *F.J.*, 13 July 1887.
[73] *F.J.*, 2 Nov. 1887.
[74] *F.J.*, 29 Nov. 1887.
[75] *F.J.*, 17 Nov. 1887; for Keegan see Return, loc.cit.

societies in the city volunteering to represent them gratis. The clubs readily consented, and handed over their admission cards . . .; two other gentlemen . . . represented a hurling club that does not exist . . ."[76]

Non-existent clubs, unknown delegates and proxy representation demonstrate the reprehensible sophistication of the I.R.B.

The brotherhood made other preparations. On 1 November, eight days before the convention was due to meet, a select meeting of county centres and others was held at Limerick ' to arrange for the Thurles Convention to support the executive, and exclude all but I.R.B. men '.[77] On the eve of the convention Hoctor and Fitzgerald ('walking very fast here and there quite pale with anxiety ') reached Thurles, and the next morning met their allies as they arrived at the station. From there they moved into the streets of Thurles through which from time to time contingents of delegates from country clubs ' marched in perfect military order '.[78]

Between seven and eight hundred delegates crammed themselves into the small Court House where the convention was to be held. At 1.30 p.m., amid much noise and confusion, the meeting opened and Alderman Horgan of Cork (and of the I.R.B.)[79] proposed Fitzgerald as chairman. Hoctor seconded, but amid a storm of cheering and hissing Fr Scanlan, a Tipperary priest, proposed a Major O'Kelly. Fitzgerald, who had taken up, without any apparent justification, the position of chairman on the bench where the executive sat, ruled the nomination out of order because O'Kelly had been expelled from the G.A.A. As delegates hooted, shouted and whistled from the gallery and floor of the Court House, Fr Scanlan cried out ' it will give a very questionable appearance to the outside public if Mr P. N. Fitzgerald is elected to the chair '. There were shouts of ' he suffered for Ireland ', and insults were hurled at the many priests in the gathering. At one stage in the noisy confusion that followed, Fr Scanlan and a group of priests advanced towards the bench and something like a free fight developed, sticks being raised and collars grabbed. Hoctor then leapt onto a table and began an impassioned defence of Fitzgerald:

[76] *F.J.*, 19 Nov. 1887.
[77] Insp. Bourchier to Capt. Slacke, 5 Dec. 1887 in S.P.O., C.B.S. 126/S.
[78] Reports of Const. O'Halloran, Acting-Sgt. Murphy and Const. McNulty in ibid.
[79] Ibid.

I come today to the rescue of an Irishman who has been insulted in the most gross and slanderous manner, for no other reason than that he ' has run the outlaw's bold career' (cheers). It is an outrage on Irish freedom and a disgrace to Ireland (cheers) that the people of Ireland will not forget for centuries to come.

Fitzgerald's history justified such controversy. He was a Cork publican, later a commercial traveller, in 1887 aged thirty-nine. He was the leading I.R.B. organiser for the south of Ireland, a member of its supreme council and a close friend of both Kickham and O'Leary. Suspicions of violent conduct surrounded him, Davitt had suspected him of placing bombs under his (Davitt's) platform at a Sligo meeting, and he was tried but acquitted of participation in the Crossmolina conspiracy.[80]

After Hoctor's speech hostility to the priests mounted and Fitzgerald threatened, ' we will have to make it rough if this goes on. A voice—Rough we will make it (cheers)'. Separate altercations and shouting matches were going on all over the hall, tables collapsed and pressmen fled for cover clutching their notebooks. A semblance of order being restored, Fitzgerald threaten to remove Scanlan and told him that his priest's cloth was no protection. As Scanlan continued to argue that Fitzgerald was illegally in the chair, he was assailed by cries of ' Balfour's pensioner'. So finally, at about a quarter to three, he marched out of the Court House, to be followed by about two hundred supporters.

Outside, Fr Scanlan told them ' the association was being made a fenian organisation for the purpose of putting down the National League'. He went on : ' Goodness knows we have enemies enough without fighting against ourselves, but I can tell you that these men are going in for breaking up the National League, and we must put them down '.[81] The meeting then surged into the market-place where Scanlan announced, to cheers for Parnell, that a new athletic association, which would support the National League, would be formed. He and his followers continued on to Hayes's Hotel, cheered by local townspeople, to form this new body. Scanlan took the chair and the meeting became a political rally on behalf of O'Brien and the National League. There was much talk of the bond between priests and people, and Croke was upheld as a symbol of Irish

[80] S.P.O., C.B.S. 5786/S; P.R.O., C.O. 904/17/251–2; William O'Brien and Desmond Ryan (eds), *Devoy's post-bag 1871–1928*, vol. ii (Dublin, 1953), p 22; *F.J.*, 7 Oct. 1907.
[81] *F.J.*, 10 Nov. 1887.

freedom. A motion that he be requested to become a patron of the new association was proposed by Fr Moloney, another priest from Tipperary, and seconded by, of all people, J. K. Bracken.

Bracken's change of heart, if it were genuine, for he was observed consulting with leading fenians before he left the Court House, was apparently due to a denunciation by his local priest that he was ' worse than a protestant, or even an atheist '. Possibly for religious reasons, possibly because he felt his business might suffer—he was, after all a monumental mason—he began to moderate his ways, thus incurring the wrath of local fenians who unsuccessfully lay in wait for him one night. Kennedy was another surprising attender at Hayes's Hotel, there, so he said, because ' if he openly sided with P. N. Fitzgerald's faction he would . . . have suffered severely in his business position '.[82]

Back in the Court House, the convention proper continued. O'Riordan read his secretary's report, and the meeting then passed to the election of officers. Hoctor and J. C. Ford of Cork proposed Edmond Bennett of County Clare as president. Bennett was in the words of the police, ' a broken down farmer of bad character. He was a '67 fenian. He is a bad lot '.[83] Originally Fitzgerald himself had contemplated standing, but he was so taken aback by the fierceness of the opposition to him that he chose to put forward a less controversial figure. He ' never thought things would become so hot at the convention . . . never dreamt that the priests would come so boldly to confront him '. At one point he exclaimed, " By G— the whole thing will bust and we will all be destroyed. You may look for a shower of informers now from those fellows " '.[84] The I.R.B. was not allowed to get away with the easy election of a puppet. Maurice Davin's name was put forward, and

amid very great confusion a show of hands was taken. It was now growing dark; the air was most oppressive and warm; some of the delegates were smoking, a few were disputing. The *debris* of what had been once the petty sessions clerk's desk was strewn about in front of the reporters.

The show of hands proved indecisive, despite some of Bennett's supporters raising two. An attempt to divide the still cramped house proving equally indecisive, after a hurried discussion on the platform

[82] Reports of Acting-Sgt. Murphy and Inspr. Waters in S.P.O., C.B.S. 126/S.

[83] Minute of Inspr. Turner to Const. O'Halloran's report, loc.cit.

[84] Inspr. Bourchier to Capt. Slacke, 11 Nov. 1887 in S.P.O., C.B.S. 126/S.

Fitzgerald proposed that supporters of each candidate pass out into the courtyard through separate doors to be counted. There followed a cunning comedy. At first, only Davin's supporters' door was opened, and out they poured into the yard. Then, suddenly, it was shouted that only Bennett's supporters were to go outside. As the Davinites tried to get back into the Court House, they found their way blocked and only a proportion of them were able to do so. The door was then locked, and in the gloom, for it was now five o'clock, all those outside the building, Bennett supporters and excluded Davinites alike, were counted as voting for Bennett, those inside for Davin. Despite protests the result was then declared as 316 for Bennett, 210 for Davin.[85]

After that, things ran fairly smoothly for the I.R.B. Hoctor was elected a vice-president, as was Hogan. Patrick O'Brien of Nenagh and William Troy of Fermoy, County Cork were also elected as vice-presidents.[86] Another clutch of I.R.B. men, Dr Jeremiah Nally, R. J. Frewen, P. J. O'Keeffe and George Keegan were elected committee-men, and three more I.R.B. members became secretaries—O'Riordan, O'Reilly and James Weldon of Drogheda.[87] F. B. Dineen was re-elected as official handicapper, to be assisted by P. O'Shea of the intensely nationalistic Kickham club, Dublin. J. A. Bradley, a journalist from the *Cork Examiner*, a man without any known I.R.B. connections, became records secretary.

Their control confirmed, the I.R.B. indulged in a few delicate finesses, one of which was to cost them dear. They rescinded the rule by which executive members were *ex officio* members of county committees, and they abandoned the one which declared that the official handicapper should officiate at all large meetings. They then substituted for the rule that the association should not approve any political movement one that the association should be non-political. This last decision caused the trouble. It was moved from the floor, with what artifice it is impossible to say, that a resolution of sympathy should be carried in favour of William O'Brien. There could have been no shrewder choice of name. O'Brien was at the time in Tulla-more jail, ' pale and delicate ', refusing to wear prison clothes there because of the coercion act, his nationalism, and his advocacy of the Plan of Campaign. He was also, of course, a leading member of the National League. To the motion Bennett said : ' we are after passing a resolution, not to take part in politics, and I rule such a motion out

[85] *F.J.*, 10 and 15 Nov. 1887.
[86] For O'Brien see Fr. Scanlan's denunciation in *F.J.*, 10 and 15 Nov. 1887; for Troy see S.P.O., C.B.S., SS., south-west, Sept. 1888.
[87] For Weldon see S.P.O., C.B.S. 5403/S.

of order'. Those in the Court House were not yet so quiescent as to accept that. There were cries of 'we'd die for O'Brien' and counter cries of 'you're out of order' as the proposer declared that he would move anyway 'that we tender to that pure souled patriot, Wm. O'Brien, our heartfelt sympathy in his present trying position'. There was more shouting and Bennett resolved the dispute by leaving the chair, thus closing the meeting. It was then seven o'clock.

Reactions that night to the day's events were varied. Sergeant Collins reported that one I.R.B. man told him : ' they were proud the priests were put out; that the Club was composed of fenians, and not of rotten nationalists, and if the priests had left long ago they would have less trouble in organising their men '.[88] ' Bendigo ', an informer, accompanied Hoctor to the post office and saw him send a telegram to John Torley of Glasgow which read ' victory all along the line '.[89] As for the priests, most of them left Thurles soon after the meeting at Hayes's Hotel had ended. They felt that 'they had the honest hurlers . . . and left the tail end of a fenian society behind them in the Court House'. From now on it was likely that the G.A.A. would be attacked ' from every altar '.[90] Fitzgerald himself had been disturbed by the vehemence of the priests' opposition and it was rumoured that some of his colleagues in the I.R.B. leadership felt that he had been ' too hasty and outspoken '.[91]

Hoctor's exultant telegram was premature, for the real struggle had yet to be joined. As one delegate sat in the train that was taking him that night from Thurles, he was goaded by Constable Reilly from Naas who posed as a Fitzgeraldite. The delegate finally turned on him : ' I came here to support the priests against fenianism, and puppies like you who come from Dublin and elsewhere spreading it . . . I'll do my best to stop it, as I know well what it is, and what the result of it was to a first cousin of mine, who died suffering by the work of such ruffians, and the priests are well aware of what's going on too, and will and must stop it.[92]

And, for a time, they did stop it. Archbishop Croke gave his support to a reconstruction convention that met on 4 January 1888 at Thurles. Of the eighty delegates who met there, elected by county conventions

---

[88] Bourchier to Slacke, 14 Nov. 1887 in S.P.O., C.B.S., 126/S.

[89] Torley was the Scottish representative on the supreme council of the I.R.B., see S.P.O., C.B.S. 533/S and 5757/S; Bourchier to Slacke, 5 Dec. 1887, loc.cit.

[90] Report of Const. O'Halloran, loc.cit.

[91] Bourchier to Slacke, 5 Dec. 1887, loc.cit.

[92] Report of Acting-Sgt. Murphy, loc.cit.

on the basis of the number of clubs in the county, only eighteen can definitely be identified as members of the I.R.B., although its voting strength seems to have been closer to thirty.

During the often stormy meeting P. N. Fitzgerald gave vent to prophecy. During the voting for officials when the nomination for records secretary produced a glut of names (among them Balfour from James Lynam), and a row, Fitzgerald protested against ' the unseemly nature ' of some of the nominations and added :

He had the proofs in his hand that the convention was ' rigged ' (cries of ' no, no '). Still they were all Gaels, and though they might be beaten, still, perhaps in twelve montns or two years they might rise again. Mr Dundon (Limerick)—No, sir.[93]

Mr Fitzgerald—I don't like these drunken interruptions (cries of 'withdraw '). No doubt all conventions are rigged by caucuses, still if we were in a majority we would not trample on the right of a minority.
Mr Dundon—Who is ' we? ' (cries of ' order ').[94]

Whoever ' we ' were, they justified Fitzgerald's optimism. Determined work throughout 1888 and an increasing tendency on the part of the local clergy to discourage participation in the G.A.A. enabled the I.R.B. to regain full control at the 23 January 1889 convention. They were never again to relinquish it. The increasing hostility of the hierarchy and the priesthood, which mounted to a climax during 1891 when the G.A.A. strongly supported Parnell, served only to diminish the numerical strength of the association. In 1889 there were 777 clubs affiliated to the G.A.A. In 1890 there were 810, of which 191 were controlled by the clergy, 497 by the I.R.B., and 122 were unattached. The respective memberships were about 9,000, 26,000, and 5,000. By 1891 there were only 66 ' clerical ' clubs and 273 I.R.B. ones, with a total membership of about 15,700.[95] As debate grew less rancorous and the political climate less harsh the long dormant G.A.A. began again to stir and as it did so left no one in any doubt as to where its allegiance lay. To explain how and why the I.R.B. came so early to hold such a strong place in the counsels of the G.A.A. has been the purpose of this study. The pattern set was not to change.[96]

[93] *F.J.*, 5 Jan. 1888.
[94] Ibid.
[95] S.P.O., C.B.S. 296/S and 464/S; P.R.O., C.O., 904/16.
[96] An essay by the author, ' Sport as politics : the Gaelic Athletic Association 1884–1916 ', forthcoming (1978) in Michael McKernan and Richard Cashman (eds), *Sport and history* (Brisbane) deals in more detail with events covered in this epilogue.

7

CARDINAL CULLEN AND THE NATIONAL
ASSOCIATION OF IRELAND
PATRICK J. CORISH

IN THE following pages I have tried to trace the story of an almost forgotten movement in Irish history. The story of the decade after 1860 has been written almost entirely in terms of Fenianism, but in fact that same decade saw the rise of a constitutional movement, the National Association of Ireland, which prepared the way for the first considerable legislative achievements for more than thirty years. In a sense, the times were propitious for such a movement, for Irish aspirations could count on a measure of genuine sympathy and support from the rising Liberal party in England. On the other hand, the urgent necessity of providing some effective alternative to the Fenian movement meant that the Irish party had to be built up over the four difficult years before Gladstone's first government came into office, a period of such uncertain allegiances in the House of Commons that no government commanded a majority sufficiently firm to contemplate seriously the introduction of controversial Irish legislation.

I have confined this study to these four difficult years between the foundation of the National Association at the end of 1864 and Gladstone's taking office at the end of 1868. Between these limits, I have felt it necessary to go into matters in some considerable detail, for the problems are complex and largely unexplored. The Fenian question is, naturally, ever-present during these years, and must have its part in this story, if only because it was the spur which led to the foundation of the National Association, and made its founders determined that in spite of difficulties it must succeed. As far as possible, however, I have tried to confine any discussion of Fenianism to what is necessary as a background to understanding the history of the National Association.

The point of greatest interest in this history is probably that which concerns the political opinions of Cardinal Cullen.[1] Cullen had come from Rome to Ireland convinced that a Catholic bishop should not directly concern himself with party-politics. Fifteen years' experience of Irish problems led him to modify that opinion. In the development of the National Association his own political

---

[1] Created Cardinal-priest of S. Pietro in Montorio at the consistory of 22 June 1866.

opinions emerge rather clearly, and, perhaps surprisingly to people who may have judged them solely in terms of his uncompromising opposition to Fenianism, they were not, in any accepted sense of the word, conservative.

In regard to sources, the newspapers are, of course, essential to any study of the period. I have based my work here on the *Freeman's Journal*,[2] which contains the fullest reports of the progress of the National Association ; other newspapers are used to supplement it on particular issues. The newspapers, of course, do not provide the whole story ; especially for the judgment of motives behind men's public actions it is essential to have access to their private correspondence. Here I am under a great debt in particular to the Irish hierarchy and to Mgr. Herlihy, rector of the Irish College, Rome, for permission to consult the Kirby correspondence in the College archives ;[3] to his Grace the archbishop of Dublin for permission to consult material in the Dublin diocesan archives,[4] and to those who helped me there, especially Mgr. O'Regan and Fr. Kingston ; and to Professor Dudley Edwards, who put at my disposal his notes on the Manning correspondence in the archives of the Oblates of St. Charles, Bayswater.[5]

I

The year 1860 saw the affairs of Catholic Ireland in a disorganized and depressed state. In the previous decade, the Tenant League had planned to send an Irish party to Westminster to pursue a policy of complete independence in opposition to any English party which should not commit itself to satisfactory legislation for Ireland. The aim was a bold one in the circumstances of the time, and it had not succeeded. The Catholic clergy had taken a prominent part in the organization of the Tenant League, and its failure had left them a legacy of divisions and recriminations. Among the people, the failure to establish a political party devoted effectively to bettering conditions in Ireland inevitably nurtured the belief that nothing could be expected from constitutional methods. It seemed utterly impossible to reconstruct a united political party, and in these circumstances the Fenian programme of armed revolution could appear more effective than it ever really was.

The divisions among the Catholic clergy enabled the Tories to increase their representation steadily, both in by-elections and in the general election of 1857.[6] Relations between the Catholics and the

[2] Cited as *FJ*.

[3] This great collection of correspondence between Mgr. Kirby, rector of the Irish College, Rome, and nearly all the Irish bishops and a number of priests, can run to 500 letters a year. The letters are arranged chronologically, and for this period those of each year are numbered independently, so that a reference to the number and date of a letter identifies it fully.

[4] Cited as DDA.

[5] Cited as Bayswater, OSC.

[6] Whyte, *The Independent Irish Party*, pp. 169 ff. On the much-exaggerated effect of the synodal legislation of 1850 and 1854 on " priests in politics " see the

Whigs, severely strained since the Ecclesiastical Titles Bill, erupted into bitter and open warfare as a result of developments in Italy in 1859 and 1860, particularly because of Lord John Russell's outspoken diplomatic despatch of 27 October 1860, in which he had proclaimed that the governments of the Pope and the kingdom of Sicily provided so ill for the welfare of their people that their subjects looked to their overthrow as a necessary preliminary to any improvement.[7] Politically, the despatch shocked every conservative in Europe ; the Irish Catholics were as deeply shocked as any, though the chief menace they saw in the declaration arose from the threat it contained to the Pope's position as a religious leader. Though it was easy, on the political level, to make the obvious comment that Lord John's concern could have found examples of really bad government nearer home, the only people who could press the point without any inhibitions were the Fenians.

There can be little doubt that an important factor contributing to the great increase in Fenian recruiting in Ireland, especially after the funeral of Terence Bellew MacManus in November 1861, was the widespread conviction that no action in parliament could possibly induce any government, Whig or Tory, to give serious attention to the problems of Ireland, nor could anyone seriously believe that the Irish members had either the quality or the cohesion to supply the necessary stimulus. The Repeal agitation had dwindled into the National League, which, as even its leader, John Martin, admitted, was making little or no progress. While its policy, repeal of the Union, was clear-cut, it seemed to have no clear idea as to what means it should adopt to gain this end,[8] apart from holding meetings at which the speakers were often carried away into an expression of sentiments which made it hard to distinguish their views from Fenianism, even though the League's policy ruled out the use of physical force.

Some of the fieriest speeches to be heard at these meetings came from priests whose sympathies had been with the Young Ireland movement. The Tenant League priests were also among John Martin's supporters, though their hopes were directed rather to the revival of an Independent Opposition party in parliament, which should have Repeal as part of its programme. The leading figure in this group was John MacHale, archbishop of Tuam.[9] MacHale was as convinced as ever that no British government could resist a genuinely united Irish opposition, and that even from a religious point of view, to secure the real fruits of Emancipation, Repeal was

---

comments and examples ibid., pp. 121 ff. The legislation was not directed at " keeping priests out of politics," but at controlling some abuses which could arise from the large part they in fact took in politics in Ireland.

[7] Cf. Morley, *The Life of William Ewart Gladstone* (ed. Lloyd, London, 1908, 2 vols.), i. 485.

[8] *Irish People*, 13 August 1864, 20 August 1864 ; *FJ*, 20 August 1864 ; and cf. letter of John Martin, *Irish People*, 3 December 1864.

[9] See his letter to John Martin, 3 August 1864, *FJ*, 10 August.

necessary.[10] He was convinced that the instrument he had helped
to forge in the 1850s, the Independent Irish Party, had been an
instrument suited to his purposes. Now that this had failed, there
was not much he could do politically, apart from writing long and
threatening public letters to Lord Palmerston,[11] and lending his
support in whatever way he could, usually not very effectively, to
the cause of " popular politics ".[12]

Another serious cause of weakness and division arose from the
fact that MacHale was convinced that Archbishop Cullen of Dublin
had a heavy responsibility in destroying the Independent Irish Party,
and he was not a man who found it easy to forgive. This estrangement between the two archbishops had been one of the gravest
legacies of the dispute. The personal feud between these two natural
leaders of Irish Catholicism was all the more unfortunate because
there was a great measure of substantial agreement in their aims.
While it was true that MacHale's approach had more of a political
tinge than that of Cullen, which meant, for one thing, that he
attached great importance to repeal of the Union, which for Cullen
was a secondary consideration, both were agreed that the urgent
task was to secure for Catholics that just share in their country,
which, in spite of the repeal of the Penal Code, they were far from
possessing in fact, the poorer classes especially. Indeed, in the
depression and despair of the early 1860s the prospects seemed
worse than ever ; and in this despair the straightforward solution
proposed by Fenianism had many attractions.

This sense of depression and impotence can be traced very clearly
in the extensive correspondence of Mgr. Kirby, the rector of the
Irish College, Rome. " We are in a sad, puzzling condition indeed,"
the bishop of Elphin wrote, " and it is a very hard thing not to
become a declared rebel amidst the scenes that are rending our
hearts ".[13] The bishop of Kilmore wrote that the archbishops of
Dublin and Tuam were working for Catholic education and tenant-
right, but could make no impression on the government or any
person of influence, and that there seemed little hope of improvement,
as many Catholics opposed the bishops.[14] The archbishop of Cashel
declared that the government had no intention of changing the land
laws, as they were only too happy to see the flood of Catholic
emigration continue.[15] The more occasional letters from priests are
usually more outspoken. In letters of 1865 Fr. O'Leary of St.

[10]O'Reilly, *John MacHale, Archbishop of Tuam*, i. 480; Broderick, *The Holy See
and the Irish Movement for the Repeal of the Union with England*, p. 150.
[11]E.g., *FJ*, 20 Sept. 1861, 20 Feb. 1862.
[12]See his letter to Bishop Kilduff of Ardagh enclosing a subscription towards
expenses in connexion with the Longford election petition, *FJ*, 9 May 1862. He
sends also subscriptions from the bishops of Killala, Clogher, Clonfert, Derry,
and Achonry. In the same issue is a letter from Bishop Keane of Cloyne, also
sending a subscription.
[13]Gillooly to Kirby, 10 Jan. 1863, no. 13.
[14]Browne to Kirby, 12 March 1863, no. 85.
[15]Leahy to Kirby, 27 March 1863, no. 101.

Colman's College, Fermoy, clearly showed that his sympathies were with the Fenians.[16]   The country, he wrote, was wasting away ; the people had lost confidence in all but a few of the bishops ; they could not or would not understand the condemnation of societies, secret or otherwise, directed against the state : " 'tis a sad thing to see the people separating from the priests and souls remaining in sin because, as they say, bishops violated the articles of '52 to which they put the sign of the Cross." The people, he wrote in a further letter, asked no more than neutrality from the priests in the Fenian question, and surely the priests owed nothing to a heretical government. " It is ", he declared, " an uprising of the Irish race against Saxon domination. There is no irreligious tendency in it no matter what may be said. . . . rise they will and if opposed by the hierarchy they will make no difference between government officials and clergymen. Would to God they could smash the first heretical power on the globe and destroy the great bulwark of the devil." O'Leary's bishop, Dr. Keane of Cloyne, gave testimony in a letter a few months later to the continuing attractiveness of the Fenian programme.[17]   The very schoolchildren, he said, were Fenians, not because they wished to give up their faith, but because they hated the Fenians' enemy, England, the enemy of their country, their creed, and the Pope. The people's faith, he felt, was being dangerously strained ; they had been complaining for some years past that the clergy were interested only in the upper-class Catholics, and were neglecting the interests of the poor.

It was, indeed, a dangerous and explosive situation, from both the political and the religious point of view. It was very accurately summed up by David Moriarty, the bishop of Kerry, in a long letter to William Monsell dated 2 March 1868, which Monsell felt was of sufficient importance to forward to Gladstone, in whose papers it has survived.[18]   The bishop wrote :

> In fine we are in a sad state. I do not fear revolution or rebellion or even sedition. I do not fear repeal of the Union ! ! But here we are in the midst of a people who have renounced their allegiance, and who know no patriotism except hatred for their rulers. I think this a far deeper evil than rebellion itself.
>
> The clergy will preach against rebellion on account of the evils it will bring on the people, but I am sure that their almost un-animous opinion is that if there was a fair chance of success it would be lawful, nay, *dulce et decorum.*
>
> I do not speak disrespectfully of them. I look on them as the key of the position. The British treasury could not bribe them. They can be gained only by justice to the people. If I differ much in opinion with them it is because I have lived in other lands and studied other laws and I saw none like our own.

[16]O'Leary to Kirby, 28 July 1865, no. 172 ; 5 Oct. 1865, no. 218.
[17]Keane to Kirby, 6 Feb. 1866, no. 24.
[18]Edited by Whyte in *Irish Historical Studies*, x. 194–9 (Sept. 1956).

While Moriarty was alone among the Irish bishops in defending the Union on purely political grounds,[19] there could be no real difference of opinion expressed in the public pronouncements of Catholic bishops on Fenianism at the time. Whatever modifications in practice the solid Catholicism of Ireland might introduce into a revolutionary movement, it was hardly to be expected that the Church could judge other than in the light of revolutionary movements in Europe generally, and this judgment was bound to be adverse, especially in view of the revolutionary threat to the Papal States. Any possible temptation to give a benign interpretation to revolution in Ireland was ruled out by the statements of some of the Fenian leaders, notably James Stephens, who had certainly come back from Paris a convinced revolutionary socialist, and who certainly did not play down his contacts with revolutionary circles there. Strange as it may seem, there was in Rome about the time of the MacManus funeral, in some circles at any rate, a certain enthusiasm for the *movimento Irlandese*, but it was prompted merely by satisfaction in seeing the discomfiture of England facing at home a movement of the same kind as Palmerston and Lord John Russell had done so much to encourage in Italy. The more sober judgment, specifically that of Cardinal Antonelli, was that Fenianism must be linked with the European revolution ; he claimed to have information that French agents were active in Ireland as they had been in Hungary and Poland. The Holy See, he said, had been left in a very perplexed condition in consequence of the active part taken by the clergy in revolutions in these countries. They had been approached by the Russian government to restrain the clergy of Warsaw. They had refused, on the grounds that the issue was a political one, but this had not prevented the exile of the archbishop of Warsaw together with great numbers of his clergy. Antonelli approved the action taken by Cullen in connexion with the MacManus funeral, and expressed the hope that the clergy in general would follow his example.[20]

In their Lenten pastorals of the following year a number of bishops issued a condemnation of secret societies, the bishop of Clogher,[21] for instance, the archbishop of Dublin and the bishop of Ossory.[22] The matter was considered at a bishops' meeting in May, from which the following resolutions were issued :

That we have heard with deep regret that in some parts of the country persons have been known to administer unlawful oaths,

---

[19]See his letter to the people of Kerry, *Irish Times*, 12 Jan. 1872. Cullen was notoriously suspicious of Isaac Butt's Home Rule Movement, but his opposition was not to Home Rule in principle, but to certain aspects of this particular movement. Even in this case, he carefully refrained from making any adverse public pronouncement. See the very interesting letter, Croke to Kirby, 28 March 1881, no. 83.

[20]DDA, Kirby to Cullen, 6 Dec., 14 Dec. 1861 ; Moran to Cullen, 14 Dec. 1861.

[21]*FJ*, 5 March 1862.

[22]*Ibid.*, 10 March 1862.

and to entice foolish men to enter secret associations dangerous to religion and society.

That we earnestly, and with all paternal affection, warn Catholics against all such combinations, whether bound by oath or otherwise, and especially against those that have for object to spread a spirit of revolution, which, in other lands, is now producing such disastrous results.

That while we warn our people against those unlawful associations we cannot be blind to the many injustices they suffer, and the manifest inequality before the law which inspires some individuals with a spirit of alienation from authority and of resistance to public order leading in some cases to crimes which we and all good men deplore.[23]

The bishops' meeting in August of the following year was even more specific. The second resolution of this meeting condemned the Fenians by name, or rather under the name of the Brotherhood of St. Patrick, an organization which claimed to be " open and unsworn ", but which undoubtedly worked in such close alliance with Fenianism that the two bodies were not easily distinguishable. The Brotherhood, which is described as " having for its object the support and defence by arms of what is called in the oath of membership the Irish republic ", and all similar societies, " though sometimes not bound by oaths ", were condemned by the assembled bishops, as also was " the publication of any defence of them under any pretext ".[24] The following year, 1864, saw the publication of the first Roman decision on Fenianism in the form of a decree of the Holy Office.[25]

The above is a bare outline of the steps by which the Irish episcopate took up a definite attitude towards Fenianism. There is no doubt that Cullen took the initiative all through, but there is, almost equally, no doubt that, though there may have been some misgivings over the decision to issue a formal condemnation, once such a condemnation was proposed there were no suggestions of any possible alternative action.[26] It was, in a sense, an unfortunate accident that the Fenian question became the occasion of another public personal clash between the archbishops of Dublin and Tuam. This arose from the case of Fr. Patrick Lavelle.

Again, it is possible to give only the briefest outline. A full account would call for a book, many passages of which might be

---

[23]*Ibid.*, 27 May 1862.

[24]*Catholic Directory*, 1864, pp. 285 ff. Again, the bishops called on the government for legislation and called on the people to organize petitions, especially for tenant-right.

[25]Text in *I.E.R.*, 1864, p. 38.

[26]On 9 August 1863, the day after the meeting ended, Cullen wrote to Kirby saying that the decision to issue a condemnation of Fenianism had been unanimous. The letter goes on to describe the opposition raised by the bishop of Clonfert and especially the archbishop of Tuam on a matter arising directly out of the condemnation, the case of Father Lavelle—Cullen to Kirby, 9 Aug. 1863, no. 203.

very entertaining were it not for the grave scandal involved. Lavelle was parish priest of Partry in the diocese of Tuam, a poor area much troubled by proselytizing societies. He was zealous, courageous, and devoted to his people, but outspoken, headstrong, and defiant. In defiance of Cullen's ruling, he had delivered the funeral oration over the grave of MacManus, and both before and after he had attacked Cullen insultingly in the public press. He was vice-president of the Brotherhood of St. Patrick and stuck to his post even when it came under episcopal condemnation. Cullen was insistent that Lavelle be punished for grave breaches of ecclesiastical discipline, and before long the case of the parish priest of Partry had become an issue of personal prestige between the two archbishops. Cullen made every effort to have Lavelle suspended, but resolutions of bishops' meetings, decisions of Propaganda, and even a personal intervention by the Pope, were ineffective in the face of MacHale's dogged determination not to be bested in the matter.

In this way, then, the Fenian issue became the cause of further public estrangement between MacHale and Cullen. This in turn meant that the task of finding some acceptable political alternative to Fenianism was made very much harder. It was made harder still by Cullen's tenacious conviction that politics as such was not the direct concern of a bishop. Politics, he felt, should be left to the politicians, who could be guided indirectly by organized Catholic public opinion. The quarrels which ended the Tenant League strengthened his conviction that ecclesiastics should not be directly involved in political movements. Yet his own programme for bringing pressure on the government had produced no results, which indeed was not altogether surprising in view of the attitude of the English government and the lack of cohesion among Irish representatives.

However, the attractions of Fenianism made the devising of some political organization an urgent necessity. The attempt was made at the end of 1864, with the founding of the National Association, and the story of how this became possible is very largely the story of Cullen's reluctant acceptance of the necessity of taking a more immediate part in politics. It was a decision to which he moved with a genuine reluctance, and even after reading through his private correspondence for the period it is not possible to do more than indicate what seem to be the main factors influencing him in making it.[27]

According to A. M. Sullivan, the new departure in Irish political life came about as a result of contacts between " some Irish

---

[27]Direct references to the formation and progress of the National Association scarcely exist in Cullen's correspondence for this period, which may indicate the reluctance with which he approached the project. A passing reference in a letter to Kirby (undated, but no. 20 in the letters of 1865, indicating a date towards the end of January—it seems to be a reply to DDA, Kirby to Cullen, 5 Jan. 1865) is very revealing : " The Association is going on slowly. It is hard to keep laymen right, especially on the education question ".

ecclesiastical and lay politicians " on the one hand, and " certain prominent English Liberals " on the other.[28] There are reasons to suspect that Sullivan exaggerates the direct part played by ecclesiastics in these negotiations, and one can be almost certain that Cullen took no part in them. In the events leading to the foundation of the National Association, his primary concern, as always, was with the interests of religion. Since the Ecclesiastical Titles Bill he had the deepest suspicions of the Whigs, and any possible hopes that Liberalism might be transforming the party must have been severely shaken by the reception given to Garibaldi when he visited England in April 1864.[29]

Yet it cannot be denied that the Liberal programme did hold some attractions for him, especially as it began to appear that the matter in which there seemed to be the most immediate hope of fruitful co-operation was a proposal for the disestablishment of the Church of Ireland. Nevertheless, Cullen's approach towards some form of alliance with Liberalism must have been slow and full of hesitation. Almost certainly the two key figures in getting his co-operation were James Kavanagh and Peter Paul M'Swiney.

Kavanagh had been a senior inspector of the National Board of Education, but had clashed with its policy when he published an outspoken defence of certain actions taken by Cullen in the matter of mixed education. For Cullen, there could be no stronger re-commendation, for he consistently held that the securing of Catholic education was the most important political question of the day, and never tired of pointing out how many other problems were, as he saw it, the direct consequences of the mixed system.[30] M'Swiney was Lord Mayor of Dublin in 1864. He too came close to Cullen's ideal of the Catholic politician,[31] all the more, perhaps, because he was so frequently the target of Fenian attacks.[32] He was prominently associated with the committee planning the erection of the O'Connell monument, and in fact the plans for the National Association may well have taken shape at the meetings of this body. Certainly the list of speakers at the banquet held on 8 August to celebrate the laying of the foundation-stone includes many of those who at the time were active in the work for the new political movement—the

---

[28]*New Ireland*, p. 301.

[29]Cf. Cullen to Kirby, 5 April 1864, no. 78, 15 April, no. 86 ; DDA, Cullen to Moran, 12 April 1864.

[30]Kavanagh lost his post with the National Board and in 1859 he was appointed professor of elementary mathematics in the Catholic University—McGrath, *Newman's University*, pp. 30, 31, 39 ; Devoy, *Recollections of an Irish Rebel*, p. 12.

[31]See, for instance, DDA, Cullen to Moran, 7 Nov. 1864, praising M'Swiney for attending the opening of the academic year at the Catholic University and afterwards holding a banquet in the Mansion House at which the Pope's health was proposed before the queen's.

[32]For an example of a very sharp attack, see the *Irish People*, 9 Jan. 1864.

Lord Mayor, the archbishop of Cashel, the bishop of Ross, J. F. Maguire, Sir John Gray, and John Blake Dillon.[33]

For some years it had indeed been inevitable that the name of O'Connell should be prominently in the minds of those who were seeking some workable political alternative to the Fenian programme of armed revolution. There is evidence that O'Connell was coming to occupy a very prominent place in Cullen's mind too. Two interesting letters from his friend and confidant, Mgr. Kirby, recall O'Connell's name in urging on Cullen the importance of providing a vigorous and constitutional means whereby popular agitation could express itself against injustice. The English government, Kirby wrote, would never do justice to the Catholic religion or to the Irish poor unless it were forced to do so. O'Connell, though he vigorously condemned secret societies, exposed the fraud of the government with equal vigour, and compelled it to a measure of justice to Ireland. No matter how vigorously the clergy might denounce secret societies, he went on, they could not hope for permanent success as long as the government continued to deny justice to the country and to the poor, for so long as this was denied the revolutionaries had a permanent pretext to lure the people to their destruction.[34]

Cullen was certainly convinced that the Fenians were in fact luring the people to destruction. " God help the poor who are so easily duped ", he wrote to Kirby somewhat later, " the savages of England would treat the poor people, if disturbances were got up, just as Muravieff treats the Poles ".[35] More important, his pastoral letter of May 1862 contains very definite echoes of the ideas Kirby had been putting forward.[36] His denunciation of Fenianism followed the usual lines, drawing a parallel with the anti-Catholic tendencies of secret societies in Europe, and insisting that the Fenian plan for rebellion had no hope of success—it "would bring ruin and desolation to our poor country, making her position worse than it is," but he spoke too of how Irish leaders had in the past successfully kept the people from secret societies — " many prelates and several distinguished laymen, and among others the ever-lamented Liberator, Daniel O'Connell, publicly denounced them, and succeeded in preventing their spread in the country ".[37] He also, though with some caution, voiced Kirby's positive recommendations :

It is our duty to call on the public authorities to relieve public distress, and to petition for such measures as may prevent its

[33]*FJ*, 9 Aug. 1864. The speech of the archbishop of Cashel is especially interesting in its references to O'Connell and the obligations of the clergy to speak out against injustice.

[34]DDA, Kirby to Cullen, 11 Jan., 14 Dec. 1861.

[35]Cullen to Kirby, 18 Dec. 1863, no. 331. The *Irish People* (7 May 1864) attacked Cullen for inconsistency in showing sympathy with revolution in Poland and denouncing it in Ireland.

[36]Moran, *The Writings of Cardinal Cullen*, ii. 134 ff. Extracts from the pastoral in *FJ*, 26 May 1862.

[37]Moran, op. cit., pp. 144-5.

periodical recurrence. . . . Without preaching up sedition or violence, we can and ought to love Ireland, and prove the sincerity of our love by seeking for measures of practical utility, such as the freedom of education, encouragement and protection for agricultural industry, a proper administration of the poor laws, and relief from the burden of the Protestant establishment.[38]

This reference to love of country is further developed in another passage in the same pastoral, and it indicates a further train of ideas working on Cullen's mind at the time, and which must have had its influence in persuading him of the need to take a more active part in political affairs :

> With regard to Ireland, her literature, her history, her antiquities, her ruins, her victories, her heroes, her sages, everything connected with her glories, ought to be the subject of our pride. But nothing should be so dear to us as the memories of our saints and martyrs who died for their religion, and who handed down to us the most precious of all inheritances, the Catholic faith ; and it should be our greatest ambition to preserve a profound veneration for our ancient Church, which has withstood the storms of so many ages, and is now rising up so glorious from her ruins.

Cullen was intensely Irish, but his patriotism, in marked contrast with that of, say, Thomas Davis, rested on a complete identification of Faith and Fatherland ; his interpretation of past history, which is the basis of all patriotism, was dominated by the fact of Irish attachment to the Catholic faith. For him, this was not an idea of recent growth,[39] but there are indications that just about this time he was particularly preoccupied with it. One reason was the publication of J. H. Todd's *St. Patrick, Apostle of Ireland* in 1864. This was a work at the same time scholarly and controversial, and Cullen was anxious that its strong confessional bias should be met by an adequate Catholic reply. He had no great hopes of an effective reply from home sources—from Maynooth, where McCarthy and Gargan were working on historical questions, or from the *Dublin Review*, which, he wrote, " now becomes altogether English—Dr. Manning and I know not who are to be the future editors. The theologian or professor of theology in the Cardinal's seminary, Mr. Ward, is to

---

[38]*Ibid.*, pp. 147–9. The *Irish People* (7 May 1864) professed to see in Cullen's May pastoral of that year (Moran, op. cit., ii. 254 ff.) the first suggestion of a constitutional alternative to their programme. A comparison of the two documents shows that the later pastoral is no more explicit than the earlier one. The attitude of the *Irish People* in May 1864 probably represents an attempt to embarrass or destroy the growing measure of agreement on the launching of a constitutional movement. Cf. the comments on a speech of Bishop Butler of Limerick, *Irish People*, 16 April 1864.

[39]See for instance the very interesting address which he delivered on 2 July 1846 to the Roman Accademia di Religione Cattolica on the connexion of the early Irish Church with the Holy See, printed as an appendix in Moran, *Writings*, iii. 790 ff.

be the principal. You may guess how Irish it will be ".[40] In these circumstances he eagerly encouraged the work being done by his nephew, Patrick Francis Moran, vice-rector to Kirby in Rome, supervising the printing in Dublin of the *Essays on the Early Irish Church* and the *History of the Catholic Archbishops of Dublin*, both published by Duffy in 1864,[41] and planning, or at least suggesting, a very ambitious programme :

> Would it not be a good thing if a project were set on foot to print all the documents printed or in manuscript that relate to Irish history—such works as those of Dr. French and the bishop of Ossory [David Rothe] and Dr. Lynch's are useful. Colgan's and Fleming's and such other works should also be published.[42]

His reading of the *Life of Archbishop Whately*[43] prompted the comment, again in a letter to Moran, that in his education policy Whately had two objects : first, to banish from the schools every recollection of Ireland, and second, to shake the people's faith by giving them only rationalistic views, and thus setting them to question its foundations. Though he failed in his second object, he succeeded very largely in his first, by omitting all reference to Ireland, her history or her church, in the text-books of the National Schools.[44] It is, in fact, easy to find in this correspondence with Moran in 1863 and 1864 indications that Cullen's reflections on religion and nationalism should be leading him, however reluctantly, towards more active participation in an urgently-needed political movement.

II

The support of the archbishop of Dublin was valuable to the new Association ; so too was the support of John Blake Dillon, who agreed to join it in the Autumn of 1864. While there is no doubt that Dillon's motives were, essentially, the same as Cullen's, namely, the wish to provide some alternative to what he regarded as the dangerous and futile Fenian conspiracy,[45] it was nevertheless an extraordinary development to see Archbishop Cullen working together with one of the men of 1848. However, there were many who did not find it possible to follow the example of Dillon, a man of very even temper and exceptionally controlled emotions ; there were a number of Irish political figures who simply could not bring themselves to work with Cullen after the recriminations of the fifties.

---

[40]Cullen to Moran, 29 May 1863, Kirby correspondence, no. 156.

[41]These writings of Moran, though inevitably bearing traces of the controversial atmosphere in which they were written, were, especially the latter, invaluable pioneering work in showing how much of Irish Catholic history was to be found in the papal archives.

[42]DDA, Cullen to Moran, 20 May 1864.

[43]Also published in 1864.

[44]DDA, Cullen to Moran, 20 July 1864.

[45]See Gavan Duffy's account of his conversation with Dillon on this matter, *My Life in Two Hemispheres*, ii. 266.

George Henry Moore, in particular, was altogether embittered and unforgiving. Gavan Duffy, who paid a visit to Ireland in 1865, was less bitter, but still could not bring himself to sit at the same table as Cullen, even though, he admitted, he received a number of indications of the archbishop's goodwill.[46] John Martin, though undeniably impressed by the course John Dillon had taken, decided that, though it was possible to have friendly relations with an association which aimed at securing just laws at Westminster, the National League, which had a single aim, repeal of the Union, would have to continue to adopt a separate platform.[47]

John Dillon, then, was the only prominent political figure among the Irish laity who gave wholehearted support to the new Association. Matters were quite different among the bishops, where there was only one who completely dissented—MacHale. MacHale had so identified himself with the political programme adopted more than ten years previously that it was hardly to be expected that he would revise his stand sufficiently to allow him to join a party with which Cullen was so prominently associated. Though he was no Fenian, he was by nature a fighter, and the programme which had been laid down for the Independent Irish Party in the fifties was in some ways more suggestive of the armed camp than of the opposition benches. It was not surprising then, that when he was approached by Dillon his answer gave little room for compromise, all the more as he insisted on turning this answer into a political manifesto by having it published.[48] The objects of the proposed association, he wrote, were most important—so important that his only surprise was that there had been such a long silence about them. He expressed himself altogether sceptical, however, of the adequacy of the means now proposed, and made it quite clear that the only political association which could expect his support was a revival of the Independent Irish Party. He further made it clear that he was not prepared to work with anyone whom he believed to have been guilty of treachery in the past without formal public repentance. Otherwise, the old game would begin all over again. If I thought you and a few others I have confidence in could stop it, he wrote to Dillon, I would give you my support; but as I feel the only effective means is an unambiguous renunciation of past error by a number of people associated with the new movement, I can have no part in it.

MacHale's opposition, though it received little support, if any, among his fellow-bishops,[49] was a serious handicap, all the more so as the new Association had no lack of other enemies. The Protestant

---

[46]*Ibid.*, ii. 267–8.

[47]Letter of John Martin, *Irish People*, 3 Dec. 1864.

[48]MacHale to J. B. Dillon, 6 Dec. 1864, published in *FJ*, 22 Dec., with the note that it is published at MacHale's request.

[49]See the list of bishops who appended their names to the notice requisitioning the meeting to inaugurate the National Association, *FJ*, 21 Dec. 1864. There are 23 names in all, and the absentees are not the noted political supporters of MacHale, all of whom signed their names.

Vigilance Committee threatened " to set the Liffey on fire " if any such Popish meeting were held. The serious and prolonged outbreak of rioting in Belfast which had been sparked off by the O'Connell procession in Dublin the previous August stood as a warning that this might be no empty threat, and almost certainly is the explanation of the fact that five of the ten episcopal names missing from the notice calling the inaugural meeting of the National Association are those of bishops or coadjutors of sees in Ulster, though the two bishops from Belfast, Dr. Denvir and his recently-appointed coadjutor, Dr. Dorrian, signed the requisition. From the opposite quarter, Fenian hostility to the new organization mounted steadily as the date of its inauguration drew nearer. Quite rightly, the Fenians saw in the Association a plan to provide an alternative to their own programme, which they could only regard as a weakening of the national effort. Its supporters, wrote the *Irish People*,[50] are not merely place-seekers, but place-holders ; Judge Keogh could hand in his name without a qualm. Small wonder, seeing that it was led by his friend, Archbishop Cullen. The " honest priests " who had been the supporters of tenant-right were holding aloof. (These same " honest priests ", of course, regularly came under the lash of the *Irish People*, especially such of them as were addicted to making belligerent speeches at meetings of the National League, but just now they could be usefully invoked to discredit Cullen.) As for John Blake Dillon, the *Irish People* concluded, " we are curious to see how a rebel of '48 will play the part of lay-leader to this new brass band ".[51]

All things considered, it was something of an achievement that the meeting was held on 29 December 1864 and the Association got under way without any outbreak of violence or rioting from one side or the other. Seven bishops attended—the archbishops of Dublin (Cullen) and Cashel (Leahy) ; the bishops of Cloyne (Keane), Ardagh (Kilduff), Ross (O'Hea), Elphin (Gillooly), and the co-adjutor bishop of Meath (Nulty). The two archbishops, with the bishops of Cloyne and Elphin, together with a number of laymen, addressed the meeting.[52] Finally, a number of resolutions were moved and adopted.

First, it was resolved that an association be founded, to be known as the National Association of Ireland, having for its objects a land bill to secure compensation for tenants' improvements, a bill to disendow the Established Church, and a bill to secure free and equal education rights for all denominations. The second resolution made it clear that the new association was not to be regarded as a political party, but was to seek its objects indirectly, by working on and

---

[50]*Irish People*, 26 Nov. 1864.

[51]*Ibid.*, 24 Dec. 1864.

[52]Full report in *FJ*, 30 Dec. 1864. Cullen's speech in full in Moran, *Writings*, ii. 283 ff. See also DDA, Cullen to Moran, 30 Dec. 1864.

informing public opinion. This and the following resolution were the cause of so much wrangling that they are best given *verbatim* :

2. The Association will seek to realize its objects by convincing, as far as possible, all men of their fairness and utility, by fostering a rational and intelligent patriotism, by uniting the people for mutual aid and protection, and by placing in representative positions, both imperial and local, men from whose principles and character they may anticipate a disinterested and effective support.

3. The Association will not support any political party which shall not in good faith co-operate with it in establishing by law the tenant's right to compensation, or in procuring the disendowment of the Established Church. Neither will it recommend, or assist in the election of, any candidate who will not pledge himself to act on the same principle.

The fifth resolution provided for the setting-up of a committee to manage the affairs of the Association, from which charges later arose that the whole direction of affairs was being deliberately kept in the hands of a narrow clique. Some substance for these charges might appear from the tenth resolution, which laid down that a fee of £1 was to be paid by each member on joining, with an annual subscription of a shilling thereafter ; there was, however, provision for associate membership at an annual fee of a shilling.

The new Association had set itself the task of winning and moulding public opinion. The task was not easy. There was point in Cullen's remark : " the people cheer anything that is menacing to the English government, though it may be sheer nonsense. It is hard to do anything right ".[53] For the moment at any rate the Association offered little scope for cheering or political excitement, for there was no widespread support for its plans to work in close alliance with the Liberal group in England. Popular opinion in Ireland at this stage does not seem to have made any distinction between the Liberals and the Whigs, and the Whig administrations since the time of O'Connell, or more accurately since the death of Thomas Drummond in 1840, had sown such distrust in Ireland, culminating in the Italian policy of Russell and Palmerston, that many Irish Catholics were inclined to the Tory alternative, though this was so unpromising that the only thing possessing real popular attraction was the call for " independent opposition ". The National Association was an attempt to find a way out of this dilemma, but it was not going to be easy to convince people that the Liberals were a real alternative to the Whigs.[54]

---

[53]DDA, Cullen to Moran, 30 Dec. 1864. The remark was occasioned by Cullen's opinion that Dr. Keane, the bishop of Cloyne, had brought " a little Young Irelandism " into his speech, and seemed anxious to get a good cheer.

[54]Cf. Dorrian to Kirby, 6 Feb. 1865, no. 28 : " It was unfortunate that the priests were for a time withdrawn from politics. The people were thus driven in despair to combine illegally, when they saw that nothing was to be done but sell them for sops to place-hunters. The new Association is sound at heart, but the

The Fenians, as might be expected, assailed the new Association continuously and not altogether scrupulously ; the *Irish People* is full of scathing attacks, especially on Cullen personally.[55] A. M. Sullivan, in a move which further worsened his already bad relations with the Fenians, came out strongly and immediately in support of the new movement.[56] The Association could of course count on the steady support of the *Freeman's Journal,* whose proprietor, Sir John Gray, had been one of the leaders in the movement towards an alliance with the Liberals.[57] Among the bishops, Cullen followed up the implications of his appearance at the meeting of 29 December by addressing a letter to his priests in which he commended the new organization, and urged them to take part in it in so far as they had the time to spare. Certain difficulties in his position appear when he warns them that their interest in politics must not lead to neglect of duty, or to any action unbecoming the ecclesiastical state, and reminds them of the synodal legislation of 1854 regulating the political activities of the clergy ; [58] in private, he made no secret of his belief that to make the Association an effective political instrument would be a delicate and difficult task.[59] Other bishops took the occasion of their Lenten pastorals to recommend the movement to their people ; [60] but MacHale took the same occasion to show himself as unbending as ever.[61]

It was in the diocese of Meath, however, that trouble came to a head. Here, both bishop and clergy had taken a prominent and well-organized part in the Tenant League agitation of the fifties.[62] The coadjutor bishop, Dr. Nulty, had been present at the meeting in Dublin on 29 December, but his Lenten pastoral for 1865 had contained a sweeping and not altogether discriminating attack on the slavery of Irish members of parliament to the Whig Party.[63] It soon became clear that the pastoral only reflected growing dissatisfaction in Meath at the differences becoming apparent between the National Association and the Tenant League and Independent Opposition of the previous decade. This dissatisfaction grew until a secession of the Meath clergy threatened.

country will be a long time in coming to believe that, after having been so often betrayed. However, I hope it will work its way and do good in time ". (I have used the term " Whig " to describe Liberals of the Palmerston school, reserving " Liberal " for the forces which came to power in Gladstone's first government. This terminology is not completely satisfactory, but no terminology can be altogether accurate for these years in which the Liberal party was being transformed under the influence of Radicalism.)

[55]E.g., *Irish People,* 7 Jan., 14 Jan., 4 Feb., 18 March 1865.
[56]*Nation,* 30 Dec. 1864 ; and cf. *Irish People,* 7 Jan. 1865.
[57]See, for instance, the leading article in *FJ,* 3 Oct. 1864.
[58]Letter to the clergy of the diocese of Dublin, 23 Jan. 1865, Moran, *Writings,* ii. 326.
[59]Cullen to Kirby, January 1865, no. 20. On the dating of this letter, see above, note 27.
[60]E.g., Elphin (*FJ,* 1 March 1865) ; Galway (*ibid.,* 3 March). See also MacEvilly to Kirby, 10 March 1865, no. 53 ; Gillooly to Kirby, 12 April 1865, no. 80.
[61]Pastoral in *FJ,* 1 March 1865.
[62]Whyte, *The Independent Irish Party,* pp. 118, 121, 154.
[63]See Cullen's comments in his letter to Kirby, 10 March 1865, no. 52.

The differences were patched up at a private meeting in Dublin on 28 April 1865. As this meeting was not reported in the press, it is by no means easy to find out exactly what happened at it. The only accounts available are a letter to Kirby from Dorrian, the coadjutor bishop of Down and Connor, written a few days after the meeting,[64] and references made to it during the debates at a general meeting of the Association on 19 June.[65] The meeting of 28 April was attended by the committee of the Association, the archbishop of Dublin and some Dublin priests, the bishops of Ross and Elphin, the coadjutor bishop of Down and Connor, the coadjutor bishop of Meath and representatives of his clergy, and, in the chair, the bishop of Cloyne. After a long discussion, it was agreed, apparently with only one dissentient voice, that certain amendments be introduced into the rules, rule (3) of the meeting of 29 December to be replaced by two new rules, these to read :

That this Association pledges itself to the policy of entire and complete parliamentary independence, and that—inasmuch as the reform of the law of landlord and tenant is a question of pressing exigency, and can only be accomplished by its advocates in parliament voting, on all questions involving confidence in the ministry, in opposition to government which will not adopt and make a cabinet question a measure of effectually securing compensation to the occupier of the soil for all improvements by which the annual letting value is increased—this Association will not support any candidate who will not pledge himself to adopt that course.

That the acceptance of place or the solicitation of favours from government is incompatible with an independent attitude towards the ministry ; and therefore it shall be a recommendation from this association to all Irish constituencies to bind their representatives to accept no place and to solicit no favour from any government which, by the foregoing rule, they shall be bound to oppose ; and to bind their representatives, further, to take counsel with the party in the House of Commons who hold the same principles, and to act in accordance with the decision of the majority.[66]

A comparison of these rules with the original shows that they represent a marked gain for the " independent opposition " party. Unfortunately, the meeting which drew them up, while it was reasonably amicable, seems to have been conducted in some confusion, and the new draft showed traces of being what Dillon was later to describe as " a document prepared by twenty or thirty persons at the same time, all taking an active part in the process ; one man suggesting a phrase should be inserted here, another that a word should be omitted there ".[67]

---

[64]Dorrian to Kirby, 2 May 1865, no. 93.   [65]Reported in *FJ*, 20 June 1865.
[66]Cited by MacCarthy Downing at meeting on 19 June, *FJ*, 20 June 1865 ; substantially in Dorrian to Kirby, 2 May 1865, no. 93.   [67]*FJ*, 20 June 1865.

Certainly, Cullen was convinced on maturer reflection that the rules as now proposed were open to much criticism.[68] His criticism is to be found in a memorandum apparently submitted to a further meeting of the committee sometime towards the end of May, a draft of which has been preserved in the Dublin diocesan archives. It is a long document, but obviously much thought-out (as is evident from the many corrections and modifications introduced in the draft), and is worth summarizing in some detail.

He began by expressing regret that it had been thought necessary to introduce any changes into the rules, as the discussions of 28 April had convinced him that there were no real differences of opinion, and any formal change after so short a time might well leave the Association open to charges of instability or fickleness. Nevertheless, he declared that he was satisfied in general with the proposed alterations, as expressing more exactly the sense of the meeting at which the original rules were drawn up.

He went on to some criticism in detail. He agreed that parliamentary policy must be one of complete independence. Neither Whigs nor Tories were deserving of any commitment. Nevertheless, support should not be refused to any measure of justice for Ireland, no matter what quarter it came from, even though, as things stood, there were no indications that very much would be found worthy of support. He approved of the use of the phrase " parliamentary independence " instead of " independent opposition ", because the latter phrase, rightly or wrongly, had been construed as meaning blind and indiscriminate opposition. Although this sense had been disavowed by leading clergy and laity, the phrase had in fact been extensively used as the watchword of an extreme, unsound and morally indefensible plan of action, and as the sole test of the integrity of a public man.

He approved also of the decision to restrict the obligation of voting against a government adverse to the aims of the Association to votes of confidence in the ministry, for this explicitly recognized the incontestable right, and, as he saw it, the bounden duty, of members to vote on other matters according to their conscience. A test so infrequently used as to be in danger of being inadequate was better than a test which was unsound.

Cullen further expressed his pleasure at the enunciation of the objects of the Association, and hoped it would now be free of charges of ambiguity.[69] He pointed out, however, that in the rule as it now stood there was danger of a new ambiguity—that it might oblige the Association to oppose a candidate committed, for reasons which

---

[68]Proposed, for, according to the rules of the Association, a rule could be changed only if the change were discussed and approved at two successive committee-meetings called for the purpose, and confirmed by a general meeting of the Association (*FJ*, 30 Dec. 1864).

[69]The reference is to the prominence given in the revised rules to the need for land-legislation—a matter in which the committee, drawn predominantly from Dublin, had been accused of showing insufficient interest.

he and his constituents judged sufficient, to only a part of its pro-gramme, a candidate who might in fact be a member of the Association. Again, it was a restriction on the right of members to do their best in accordance with conscience, and this further ambiguity—clearly arising from the long and awkward parenthesis in the draft of the rule—would have to be removed.

Cullen now addressed himself to the second of the proposed new rules. It was even more difficult ground than the first, by reason of the commonly-accepted view that the Independent Party of the previous decade had collapsed because of the treachery of Sadlier and Keogh, and because of the episcopal support they had received after their betrayal, support for which Cullen, it was commonly believed, had a heavy responsibility. While the latest authoritative examination of the facts comes to the conclusion that the defection of Sadlier and Keogh was by no means decisive,[70] and while every new piece of evidence goes to show that Cullen's " commitment " to Sadlier and Keogh had never really existed except in the minds of Lucas and Gavan Duffy and in the propaganda of the *Irish People*,[71] he was, nevertheless, believed to be associated with those who had taken office at the price of principle. This popular misjudgment did not modify Cullen's views on the right of Catholics to accept public office ; neither did the fact that the promotion of Catholics was a prominent part of Whig policy. He had enunciated his principles in this matter some years previously in a public letter to Thomas O'Hagan : [72]

I do not censure Catholics for seeking or taking office, and I am very far from joining in the outcry that everyone doing so must be a traitor to his religion or an enemy to his country. Catholics, in my opinion, have a full right to share in the government of their own country, a right which is still scandalously withheld from them. . . . Were men who act in a truly Catholic spirit, and do honour to our country by their lives and their virtues, raised to office, I would commend them for accepting it, and rejoice in their promotion. As to Catholics who either seek to gain office by denying the principles or practices of their religion, or who, having obtained office through Catholic influence, betray their promises and pledges, it is not my business to throw the first stone at them. I leave them to the judgment of their country and their God.

---

[70] Whyte, *The Independent Irish Party*, pp. 175–6.

[71] The following extracts from Cullen's correspondence with Kirby may be of interest : " Judge Keogh is said to be in Rome. Don't let him get a grand audience. *E un cattivo mobile*. The wife is very pious." (Cullen to Kirby, 25 Feb. 1867, no. 63) ; " If you can do anything to convert Judge Keogh it would be a charity to do it. He is the worst enemy of Catholicity we have under the name of a Catholic " (same to same, 1 March 1867, no. 70) ; " I hope you were able to see Judge Keogh and tell him some truths whilst he was in Rome " (same to same, 6 March 1867, no. 74).

[72] Published in the *Catholic Telegraph*, 20 June 1863 ; reprinted in Moran, *Writings*, ii. 180 ff.

The whole question was overshadowed by the betrayal of Sadlier and Keogh, but it nevertheless remained a real problem because, as long as a member of parliament drew no salary or allowance, there was little alternative to the possession of private means except the acquiring of some office of profit. Cullen could see the dangers— they were indeed obvious—but again his memorandum insists that the distinction must be drawn between the corrupt acceptance of office for private advancement and the right Catholics had as citizens to a due share in the public administration, indeed their obligation to accept such a share.

On the final clause in the second rule he commented that in recommending a mutual understanding between candidates and constitutents, the terms used might be better if they indicated less distrust of the candidates. Neither should too much reliance be placed on pledges or verbal engagements. The only real guarantee that a candidate would keep his promises if elected was the candidate's moral character.

Finally, in regard to the proposal that majority decisions of the party were to be binding, he argued that while a united party was very desirable, and hitherto very lacking, unity must not be insisted on down to the smallest detail. Again, room must be left for the conscientious discretion of the individual. While it could be insisted that the party must be united on the basic principles of the Associa-tion, and while the duty of taking common counsel should also be demanded, and it should be clearly understood that each departure from a majority decision was a proper subject for enquiry, any insistence on absolute unanimity of action in all things was an extreme and unsound test of public morality, which might deter men who might be very useful to the Association from joining it, and could easily lead to fatal disputes.[73]

Danger now threatened from another quarter. The rules proposed at the meeting of 28 April were given to the press. There is no direct evidence to show who was responsible, but there is no doubt that it was done by some of the " Independent Opposition " party, to guard against any danger that they would be watered down.[74] The *Irish Times* immediately commented that the new rules indicated that the Association had dropped disestablishment from its pro-gramme, and in view of the very bad drafting of the first of them this was an inference which could not easily be refuted. It made the case for some revision of the draft still stronger.

At this stage the Association was in real danger of going the same way as the Independent Party of ten years before, and for rather

---

[73]The break-up of the Independent Irish Party had shown that this last point was a real consideration (cf. Whyte, op. cit., p. 176) ; that it remained such became evident from Dillon's discussions in London with some of the Irish members, who flatly told him they would have nothing to do with such an unreasonable pledge— *J*, 20 June 1865.

[74]See Dillon's remarks, *FJ*, 20 June 1865.

similar reasons. The problem was urgent, for a general election was due in July. There now began an all-out effort, led by John Dillon, to hold the Association together. Again, it is impossible to fill in all the details, but the discussions resulted in a circular being sent to all who had been present at the meeting of 28 April, with the proposal :

This Association pledges itself to the policy of complete parliamentary independence, and will support no candidate for parliament who will not pledge himself to vote for all the objects of the Association, and further, to vote (on all questions involving confidence in the ministry) in opposition to any government that will not adopt and make a cabinet question a satisfactory measure of tenant compensation ; that question being deemed by the Association as of pressing urgency.[75]

In this latest version, the drafting is noticeably tighter. However, the rejection of any acceptance of place or favour and the demand that majority decision be binding have gone, except in so far as they may remain by implication. As might be expected, there was a storm, Dillon and the committee being freely accused of a breach of faith with those who had attended the meeting of 28 April. The general meeting, planned for 5 June, had to be postponed for a fortnight, and when it finally met on 19 June it was clear that it was going to be a difficult one.[76]

It began by M'Swiney giving an account of what the Association had done since its foundation. Committee meetings had been held every week, petitions to parliament had been organized when matters arose which concerned the interests of the Association. He pointed out, as a first achievement, that on their initiative a bill to abolish oaths obnoxious to Catholics had been introduced, and was advancing in parliament. Public opinion in England and Ireland was rallying to the Association, whose policy, the constitutional policy of O'Connell, uniting priests and people, should appeal to all Irishmen. He concluded with remarks clearly inspired by Cullen. The presence or absence of a pledge in the Association's programme, he said, was not a decisive factor. Pledges of independent opposition had proved useless in the past. What mattered was to return representatives who could be trusted.

Dillon now rose to propose the election address of the Association. It proposed, first, that a committee of electors should be set up in each constituency to judge whether candidates who proposed themselves should be given the support of the Association. Sitting members were not to be too hastily or rashly rejected, but there was to be no tolerance of deliberate treachery or corruption. It was essential that the election-results should produce an effectively-independent party.

---

[75]Quoted by MacCarthy Downing at the meeting of 19 June, *FJ*, 20 June 1865.
[76]Reported in *FJ*, 20 June 1865.

So far, the meeting seems to have proceeded in ordered silence. Everyone was waiting for the same thing, and Dillon now turned to it. It was a difficult speech. He took the line of pointing out the problems which had arisen in consequence of the bad drafting at the meeting of 28 April, and proposed that the formal revision of the rules should be postponed until there was an opportunity for further discussion. In any case, he said, there was a procedural difficulty which made a postponement inevitable. The rules as drafted on 28 April were admittedly so full of ambiguities as to be unacceptable. Yet he could not propose the amended form because of the objection raised that it was a breach of faith with the committee responsible for the first draft, and in any case inadmissible as the rules of the Association demanded that a change of rule be considered at two meetings of the committee before being submitted to the general meeting. The election address, if adopted, was, he claimed, a sufficient indication that the Association was committed to a truly independent policy.

The speech was as skilful as could be made in the circumstances, but it could hardly hope to escape challenge. The spokesman of the challengers was MacCarthy Downing, who began by complaining, with some reason, that he found it hard to be sure exactly what Dillon meant. The essential fact, as he saw it, was that according to the rules of the Association, the changes proposed at the meeting of 28 April should be put to the general meeting now convened. There was nothing to be gained by postponement; unless this issue was faced now the Association was dead.

At this stage the peacemakers took over. They were helped by the fact that no one was willing to contemplate a complete breakdown. After a number of speeches stressing the worth of the cause and the integrity of all concerned, the proposal was made:

> That the resolutions agreed to at the conference on 28 April last be affirmed, subject to such amendments as a committee hereafter to be appointed may deem necessary, preserving the principles therein enunciated.

This proved a sufficiently acceptable compromise.

The scene now shifts to the bishops' meeting at Maynooth.[77] Here, the initiative seems to have been taken by Dorrian, and gradually people were brought together.[78] A number of the bishops agreed to meet Dillon in Dublin next day (22 June) at Coffey's Hotel—Derry (the bishop of Clonfert), Keane, Nulty, and, rather unexpectedly, MacHale.[79] That night Dorrian and Dillon went to Cullen, who also agreed to attend.

---

[77]For what follows, see Dorrian to Kirby, 27 June 1865, no. 141.

[78]Dorrian's words are: " a little private talk amongst a few of us showed good symptoms ".

[79]There is no evidence to show why MacHale agreed at this stage. It seems a reasonable inference that the other three named were in close contact with him, and, once persuaded that they could usefully attend the meeting, succeeded in persuading MacHale to attend as well.

The meeting was held as arranged, the bishops of Elphin and Ardagh being present in addition to those already named. Agreement was reached in the following terms, which, this time, were given to the press :

The Association pledges itself to the policy of complete parliamentary independence ; and the electors shall in all cases be urged to bind their representatives, not only to vote for all the objects of the Association, but also to oppose any government which shall not incorporate with its policy, or otherwise efficiently support, a satisfactory measure of tenant compensation—that measure being deemed one of pressing exigency and paramount importance.

That as it is impossible to give an honest and efficient advocacy in parliament to measures and at the same time to incur personal obligations to a minister who is opposed to these measures, the electors should bind their representatives to accept no place or honour for themselves, and incur no personal obligation to any minister who shall not support a satisfactory measure of tenant compensation.

That there should be an understanding between the electors and their representatives that the latter should take counsel together, so as to secure a general uniformity of policy and a combined action for the ends of the Association.[80]

This agreement bears all the marks of a hard-fought compromise, but the meeting seems to have been amicable and even cordial.[81] MacHale, however, refused to join the Association, at least for the present. He said that he would do so at once if it consisted only of those present, but that he would have to wait and see if it followed the policy now agreed on. To Dorrian's suggestion that he might make a public statement formally approving this policy, he would go no further than to say that he would do this " at some proper time ".[82]

On 27 June Dillon reported his success to the committee of the National Association. He naturally took particular satisfaction in having secured the support of MacHale.[83] The satisfaction did not last beyond that same evening, when Dillon took the chair at a dinner in honour of Gavan Duffy, who had returned to Ireland on a visit. At this dinner a number of letters of tribute to Duffy were read. Among them was one from MacHale, dated Tuam, 24 June, in which he made it quite clear that if he were to join the National Association he would not be satisfied with the compromise expressed in the resolutions agreed to at the meeting of 22 June. His letter ran :

---

[80]*FJ*, 24 June 1865.
[81]Dorrian's letter stresses the unexpected cordiality, especially between Cullen and MacHale.
[82]Dorrian to Kirby, 27 June 1865, cit.
[83]*FJ*, 28 June 1865.

Nothing short of the pledge of independent opposition, in all its plenitude and vigour, can save the country, with the exercise of greater vigilance on the part of electors to see this pledge carried out by their representatives. . . . Owing to the deteriorating influence exercised these years past by an unfaithful party, " independent opposition in a foreign parliament " is the highest grade of patriotism to which our best men have ventured to aspire as a test for parliamentary candidates. However, at the election following the. next they will, I trust, again remember our anti-union history by referring to the examples of Australia and Canada, and kindling a desire to bring back our exiled people to share the prosperity which, in Ireland as well as in those countries, must ever be the fruit of native legislation.[84]

Shortly after this letter was read G. H. Moore rose to speak. Moore had emerged as the leader of the Independent Opposition party by the election of 1857, and had become a close associate of MacHale. He was a gifted man, but lacked almost every quality needed to hold a party together. He throve on controversy, in which, unfortunately, he was always offensive.[85] Now, in a speech of great power and bitterness, he deliberately opened every old wound of the controversies of the previous decade.[86] " He scoffed at the attempt of certain persons, meaning Dr. Cullen and his associates, to revive a national movement, after having betrayed and destroyed one of the greatest national movements Ireland ever possessed ".[87] It took all Dillon's tact to carry the festivities to an outwardly peaceful conclusion.

Four days later, Saturday, 1 July, A. M. Sullivan made a bitter attack in the *Nation*, accusing the Association of " excessive amiability " in admitting undisguised Whigs and place-hunters to membership, and attacking Cullen personally for his " disastrous mistakes " as a politician and his " fatal incapacity of judging public men ".[88] Whatever be the explanation of the sharpness of the attack—and Sullivan was certainly playing a devious game in which personalities counted as well as principles—it was another indication that the controversies of the fifties were still sufficiently alive to prejudice the National Association's plans for co-operation with the English Liberals,[89] and certainly sufficiently alive to prejudice its chances of effective intervention in the coming elections.

---

[84]*Ibid.*

[85]Whyte, op. cit., pp. 154 ff.

[86]Speech reported in *FJ*, 28 June 1865.

[87]Gavan Duffy, *My Life in Two Hemispheres*, ii. 268.

[88]See *Nation*, 1 July 1865 ; *Irish People*, 8 July ; *Catholic Telegraph*, 8 July; *FJ*, 10 July.

[89]For the continuing opposition of the politicians and priests of the Tenant League see Gavan Duffy, op. cit., ii. 268 ff.

III

The election results, as might be expected, were inconclusive. It was clear that the programme of the National Association was tainted with "Whiggery" in the eyes of many of the Catholic electors.[1] John Dillon was returned as one of the members for Tipperary, but the opposition was weak and the electorate apathetic;[2] the only excitement came from Fenian obstruction. In a review of the general result the National Association could only claim that

> the number of members returned to parliament who are pledged more or less to our policy is considerable. Nearly all the new members have declared for some part of our programme. If the number of those who have subscribed to our entire programme be not as large as it ought to be no one will deny their power and influence.[3]

There was still a long road to be travelled before an effective parliamentary party could be formed.

The development of such a party was made easier by the growing strength of English Liberalism. In October 1865 Lord Palmerston died. If ever the phrase "end of an era" was justified, it was justified here. He had sat in parliament for nearly sixty years; he had been a minister for nearly fifty. Abroad, his name had always been associated with constitutional reform, but at home, especially as he grew older, he had resisted any change in existing institutions. On 18 October Lord John Russell succeeded him as premier. This raised the hopes of the reform-party in England, but in Ireland the distrust arising from the Ecclesiastical Titles Bill and his Italian policy was still strong.

Nevertheless, within a very short time the new government had made an approach to the Vatican on Irish affairs. A. H. Layard, under-secretary for foreign affairs, made his appearance in Rome. Mgr. Kirby, rector of the Irish College, was able to report, from information supplied by Cardinal Antonelli and Mgr. Talbot, that Layard had informed the Vatican that his government was definitely resolved to abolish the Church Establishment in Ireland, and that in general it was prepared to grant the Irish Catholics all their just demands, now that Palmerston, the great obstacle to any such concessions, was dead. To Antonelli, Layard gave a firm assurance that a Catholic education system would be provided in Ireland, the government insisting only on control of the examinations. That, Kirby remarked to Antonelli, might be a very important reservation. Antonelli agreed. In writing to Cullen, Kirby recorded his impression that Layard had spoken clearly and unambiguously; while time alone could tell if he spoke truly, all the indications were

---

[1] For an analysis of the results, see *FJ*, 26 July·1865.
[2] See the *Irish People*, 22 and 29 July 1865.
[3] P. P. M'Swiney, reported in *FJ*, 26 July 1865.

that he did. Kirby's conclusion was that the government was badly frightened by Fenianism, and hoped to weaken its influence by concessions.[4]

Another important factor in the new political developments was the steady rise of Gladstone as the man capable of forming a united party out of the Whig and Liberal elements. Gladstone, though a member of Palmerston's administration, had openly championed radical opinions in the house even at the cost of incurring his premier's anger.[5] By the autumn of 1864 his plans for reform were extending to include the problems of Ireland,[6] and in the spring of 1865 in a debate on another private member's bill involving the disestablishment of the Irish Church he again defied Palmerston and spoke in favour of disestablishment as a measure of abstract justice, though he was equally definite that it could not yet be considered as a matter of practical politics.[7]

The problems of Italy, however, were still a barrier between Gladstone and Catholic opinion. The defence of the Pope's temporal power by French bayonets was a genuine scandal for him. He shared the wave of pro-Italian feeling on the arrival of Garibaldi in England, though not with some misgivings at the "attentuated beliefs" of "the soldier who bore the sword for human freedom."[8] Among those who attempted to drive home the contradiction between reform and anti-Christian revolution was Henry Edward Manning, since 1857 provost of the chapter of Westminster. Gladstone, Manning warned, was in all honesty attacking what he believed to be evils in the administration of the Papal States, but what he said and wrote was being used by those whose real purpose was revolution. If he did not dissociate himself from such people, he would be used as a tool and must face the consequences.[9]

There was a genuine mutual esteem between the two men, and Manning's nomination to the archbishopric of Westminster on 30 April 1865 naturally added weight to what he had to say. Unfortunately this link did not, immediately at any rate, bring Gladstone into any closer relations with the Irish hierarchy, because Cullen distrusted Manning, quite simply, it would seem, because he regarded him as "too English", too ready to be on friendly terms with the government.[10] From the available correspondence it is clear that from the beginning of his episcopate Manning set out to establish co-operation and unity of action between the English and Irish

[4]DDA, Kirby to Cullen, 29 Nov., 11 Dec. 1865.
[5]See the account of Gladstone's support of a private member's bill for the extension of the franchise, 11 May 1864, Morley, *Gladstone*, i. 569.
[6]See Morley's comment on Gladstone's speech at Manchester, 13 Oct. 1864, op. cit., i. 574.
[7]*Ibid.*, i. 580 ff.
[8]*Ibid.*, i. 554 ff.
[9]Manning to Gladstone, 28 Nov. 1862, 25 April 1864, 24 Oct. 1864—Bayswater, OSC.
[10]He supported Errington for the see of Westminster. (Leslie, *Henry Edward Manning*, p. 153.)

hierarchies, on the basis of a demand for the cessation of English anti-Roman policy, a demand for full and perfect equality of rights for Catholics, and a recognition of the integrity of the United Kingdom.[11] Cullen was suspicious of this offer of co-operation; the first reply I have been able to trace is dated 7 February 1867,[12] and in it, while he recognises the value of Manning's advocacy, he makes no reference to his concrete proposals.

In Ireland, Cullen's projects were not meeting easy weather. On 10 October 1865 he issued a pastoral letter against Fenianism, or rather against what he regarded as the two extremist secret societies in Ireland, the Orange Order and the Fenian Brotherhood. The Orange organization he condemned as a menace in itself and in a real sense the parent of Fenianism, for as long as those in power were allowed to form secret societies, it was hard to blame the poor for doing the same. Yet this did not excuse those who took the Fenian oath. They had been warned by their Church, and they should have been warned by the character of the movement, a secret society whose leaders were said to be infidels and who were certainly dangerous, as was proved by the ideas circulated by the *Irish People*.[13] The movement was impotent for all the dangerous ideas it circulated. It had won no great following among a deeply-religious people. The leaders of this "secret society" were so inept as to conduct their affairs in public, and now its members were at the mercy of the English, who would show little mercy, in spite of their adulation of the revolutionary Garibaldi, even though it was this adulation, together with the unjust government of Ireland, which had caused and encouraged Fenianism.

In contrast, the Catholic attitude to revolution was clear and unambiguous; so too was Catholic approval of the lawful and available means of fostering what it had always proclaimed to be the virtues of rational liberty and love of country. These means were the election of suitable members to parliament and the use of a free press to call attention to wrong and injustice. They had been effective before, and could be effective now.[14]

The pastoral was well received in the English Liberal press. *The Times* summed up the conservative reaction by denouncing Cullen's claim that English misgovernment of Ireland had been the cause of Fenianism as "a most impolitic, not to say dangerous, doctrine". At home, it was not easy to make the "lawful and available means" effective. From the very beginning, it was obvious that the question on which it was going to be most difficult to find common

---

[11]See Manning to Cullen, 8 Dec. 1865, 5 Feb., 3 April, 26 April, 29 May 1866, ed. by Leslie, " Irish Pages from the Postbags of Manning, Cullen and Gladstone " in *Dublin Review*, no. 331 (1919), pp. 163–5.

[12]Leslie, art. cit., pp. 165–6.

[13]Suppressed by the government on the occasion of the Fenian arrests a few weeks before this pastoral was issued.

[14]Text in Moran, *Writings*, ii. 388 ff. The same ideas recur in his Lenten pastoral for 1866, *ibid.*, 484 ff.

ground between Irish Catholics and English Liberals was education. Liberal opinion in England found it very hard to see how disestablishment and Catholic education could fit into the same programme. Disestablishment was Liberal, sectarian education was not. There could be little doubt that if the government should get the idea of introducing an education-bill satisfactory to Catholics, they would, especially in the very fluid state of party allegiances, lose enough radical votes to the Tories to bring about certain defeat.

In these circumstances, the divided views of the Irish bishops were hardly a decisive factor, but the division did not help what slight prospects existed. When the government raised the education question with them in the summer of 1865, their difficulties at once became apparent. Cullen was not disposed to accept any substantial compromise on his Catholic university; MacHale was not prepared to help him in this matter, not of course because he was in any way in favour of mixed education, but because he regarded the Catholic University as Cullen's university. In consequence, when the bishops met on 22 August to consider the education question, there were no formal proposals from the government to put before the meeting, because, so Cullen claimed, MacHale had obstructed the steps necessary to get such information.[15] It is certain at any rate that the government would have given details of its proposals if asked, for two bishops—Butler of Limerick and MacHale himself—were able to communicate these details to the meeting, having got them privately from members of the government. The proposal, Cullen wrote to Kirby,[16] was to establish a new Royal University, which was to be an examining body for degrees in medicine, law and arts, with a senate to consist of sixteen Catholics and sixteen Protestants. The government hoped that the Catholic bishops would agree that some of their number would accept nomination among the Catholic members.

Cullen felt it would be difficult to get Roman approval of bishops sitting on the senate of a neutral university, nor did he view the idea himself with any great favour, though he reflected that at Louvain students appeared before a state examining board and that the French *Conseil d'Enseignement* included rabbis as well as Cardinals.[17] In any case, as these proposals were not formally before the meeting the only decision which could be taken was that the four archbishops should meet representatives of the government and report to a further meeting. The meeting with the government seems to have been fairly encouraging, in spite of Cullen's fears that the differences between himself and MacHale would be so obvious that the only answer they could expect would be a request to compose their own differences first.

[15]Cullen to Kirby, 14 Aug., 25 Aug. 1865, nos. 180, 189.
[16]25 Aug. 1865, no. 189.
[17] Cullen to Kirby, 27 Aug. 1865, no. 191.

The delegation reported to a bishops' meeting in the middle of December. MacHale did not attend. In his absence, Cullen's views met little opposition, and the meeting drew up a petition asking for a charter for the Catholic University. While they did not reject the government proposals directly, they declared they could not accept them if they entailed mixed education.[18] They did not declare whether the proposal that bishops should be members of the senate of the Royal University was acceptable or not; this decision, Cullen felt, would have to be left to Rome.[19] Getting the decision took time,[20] and with the delay the "unanimity" of the bishops' meeting showed signs of breaking down. MacHale had refused to sign the memorial to the government issued by the meeting.[21] Later Moriarty left no doubt that he would settle on terms much less exigent than Cullen's.[22] In its final form, the government's bill did no more than confer a supplemental charter on the Queen's University, empowering it to examine for degrees students other than its own, and to confer its degrees on them if successful. The senate of the Queen's University was to be increased by the addition of members favourable to Catholics. The bill was passed in June 1866, but even these meagre provisions were not put into effect, for an injunction was obtained by those opposed to denominational education setting the supplemental charter aside as invalid and the whole scheme collapsed.

The land-question was also the cause of trouble in the second half of 1865. In November, the bishop and clergy of Meath finally wi hdrew from the National Association. Their grievance was still the same as that which had threatened a break earlier in the year, namely, that the Association was not sufficiently serious in its demand for land-reform. The bishop and clergy met on 6 November and decided to establish a tenant-right society. At this meeting too they decided to draw up an address, which was published on 29 November. The address was by no means complimentary to Cullen's programme, notably his October pastoral denouncing Fenianism, and to the programme of the National Association in general. It declared that the Meath clergy claimed little share in the congratulations being widely offered to the Irish clergy for their denunciation of conspiracy. There had been little conspiracy in Meath because there the clergy and people had always stood together on the only question which really counted, the land question. As so little could be expected from the present Irish members in this matter, they hoped that their example in founding a tenant-right society would

---

[18]Cullen to Kirby, 22 Dec. 1865, no. 297, 16 Jan. 1866, no. 8.
[19]Letter of archbishops and bishops of Ireland to Sir George Grey on the National system of education, Jan. 1866, Moran, *Writings*, ii. 443–50; same to same, on University education, *ibid.*, 450–63.
[20]DDA, Kirby to Cullen, 2 Jan., 4 Jan. 1866; Cullen to Kirby, 20 Jan. 1866, no. 12.
[21]Cullen to Kirby, 16 Jan. 1866, no. 8.
[22]Same to same, 15 May 1866, no. 109.

be followed by the establishment of such societies all over the country, which should look for guidance to Ireland's best friend, the man who had always held a steady course, John MacHale.[23]

Bishop Dorrian of Down and Connor, who had taken the initiative in mending the earlier crisis, was also growing discouraged. The National Association, he felt, had failed to win popular support because of the "great folly" of even indirect support of the Whigs, of which some of the bishops were guilty.[24] While there is no indication that he broke openly with the Association, it is clear that he felt it was no longer worth working hard for. Bishop Keane of Cloyne too showed indications of being discouraged at the failure of the Association to win popular support,[25] and while he still believed in the essential soundness of its programme, he made it quite clear that he expected it to get down to business, in particular to work for a satisfactory measure of land-reform.[26]

The one gain of these six depressing months must be credited largely to the tact and patience of John Dillon. Some time after the election the National Association met to discuss how to draw some profit from the rather meagre success it had brought them. Dillon urged that they should try to secure some kind of united action from the Irish members who in one way or another had indicated their support of the Association, by arranging a meeting with them in Dublin as soon as possible.[27] His negotiations must have run into difficulties, for at a later meeting of the Association in October we find him urging the episcopal members present, the archbishops of Dublin and Cashel and the bishop of Elphin, to proceed cautiously, in order to give the impression that the conference should come about through pressure of public opinion, not because the Association wished to impose conditions on members of parliament.[28] It took another six weeks to conciliate what seems to have been a touchy sense of independence, but the meeting when finally held on 5 and 6 December was quite successful. The twenty-two members who attended agreed to adopt a common policy on the Land, Church and Education questions, and, in the knowledge that its "advanced" section shared their views, to co-operate with the Liberal party in matters of common interest.[29] It was a small nucleus, roughly one-fifth of the Irish representation, a little less than one-half of those who called themselves "Liberals", but if it could be held together it might well be effective in the House of Commons as then constituted.

This was one clear gain for the National Association, to offset the open defection of some and the secret questionings of more.

[23]*FJ*, 4 Dec. 1865.
[24]Dorrian to Kirby, 28 Sept. 1865, no. 216 ; 10 Dec. 1866, no. 341.
[25]Keane to Kirby, 1 Jan., 6 Feb. 1866, nos. 1, 24.
[26]See his Lenten pastoral, *FJ*, 12 Feb. 1866.
[27]*FJ*, 30 Aug. 1865.
[28]*Ibid.*, 19 Oct. 1865.
[29]Resolutions of the meeting in *FJ*, 8 Dec. 1865.

It was now more than ever the only alternative to Fenianism, for John Martin's National League was moribund.[30]   In a series of meetings in the spring of 1866, plans were drawn up to make the committee more widely representative, for there was some discontent arising from a feeling that it was drawn too exclusively from a small group in Dublin.[31]   The committee also kept up pressure for remedial legislation through contacts with the English Liberals, John Bright in particular, by the organisation of petitions to the government, by further emphasis on Cullen's argument that Fenianism was an inevitable product of Irish discontent, which could be met only by removing discrimination and injustice, specifically the discriminations still imposed on Catholics.[32]

The Church Establishment inevitably appears as the great example of anti-Catholic discrimination, but in deference to popular pressure most of the practical effort was directed to a consideration of the land-question.   The defection of the diocese of Meath and the Lenten pastoral of the bishop of Cloyne were only two of many indications that this problem was widely held to be the most urgent one. A committee was set up, with John Dillon as chairman, to draft a Land Bill to be introduced in the Commons.[33]

The draft produced by this committee was considered at a meeting on 20 March. It got a mixed reception. From many quarters it was criticized as not securing the vital issue, the tenant's right to compensation for improvements he had carried out, but Dillon defended it on the ground that in this respect it compared very favourably with the 1860 bill and that it was the most they could hope to carry. He argued further that some success was essential now because feeling in Ireland was growing increasingly restive at the continuing inaction of the government. It was essential, however, that they should continue to support the administration, for it offered the only hope, and he believed it to be a real hope, of remedial legislation. After a debate the draft was grudgingly approved as expressing the minimum of the tenants' just demands.[34]

The question as to whether support of the government should be continued became more acute as it began to appear that the Extension of the Franchise Bill would provide the Irish Liberal members, if they so wished, with an opportunity of putting it out of office. At the end of April the second reading was carried by five votes only, in spite of the still solid support of the Irish Liberals.[35] A week or so before this a meeting of the committee of the National Association showed indications that even here the commitment to the government

---

[30] See reports of meetings in *FJ*, 7 Feb., 8 Aug. 1866.
[31] *FJ*, 24 Jan., 21 Feb., 1 March 1866.
[32] *FJ*, 14 Jan., 24 Jan., 21 Feb., 1 March, 7 March, 21 March 1866. From the reports of these meetings it is clear that the initiative and control lie with Kavanagh and M'Swiney, and that they are the spokesmen for Cullen's views.
[33] *FJ*, 21 Feb. 1866.
[34] *Ibid.*, 21 March 1866.
[35] *Ibid.*, 28 April 1866.

was under severe strain,[36] which was very little eased when the Tenure and Improvement of Land (Ireland) Bill was introduced on 30 April. It met Conservative criticism even on the first reading, and in Ireland there was much disappointment at its inadequacies, particularly the provision for tenant-compensation in clauses 29 and 30. These clauses ran into heavy criticism, especially from the bishop of Elphin, in the committee of the National Association,[37] and at further meetings on 25 May and 12 June all Dillon's persuasiveness was called for to secure a vote of continued support for the government.[38] Meanwhile, the debate on the second reading had been opened and adjourned on 17 May. Before it could be resumed the government had fallen. The increasing restiveness of the Irish Liberals led to a defection of eight of them in a crucial vote on an amendment to the Reform Bill. There was a majority of eleven against the government.[39] Lord John Russell immediately forwarded his resignation to Balmoral. The queen was unwilling to accept it, for war between Austria and Prussia had just broken out, but the prime minister insisted and on 6 July Lord Derby accepted the request to form a Tory ministry in circumstances which suggested that the new government would be even weaker than its predecessor. On 25 July the debate on the second reading of the Irish Land Bill was resumed, and ended, inevitably, in the Bill being withdrawn.

IV

The new government was so essentially a minority one that it could hope to remain in office only by professing to please everyone and doing as little controversial as possible. It promised reform-legislation for Ireland, but the National Association determined to continue the policy of co-operation with the English Liberals, now in opposition. John Dillon had been chiefly responsible for insisting on this policy, and it was a great shock to his followers when the news came of his sudden and unexpected death on 15 September at the age of 51.[40] His death meant a by-election in Tipperary and an immediate trial of strength, for White, the Liberal candidate, was opposed by Waldron, who argued that " the government should be given a fair trial " in view of the promises it had made.[41] The Catholic bishops concerned—Cashel, Killaloe and Waterford— openly declared their support of White,[42] and he was returned, though not by a great majority, after an election-campaign which

---

[36]*Ibid.*, 19 April 1866. Even within the meeting, the slogan of " independent opposition " was heard.
[37]*FJ*, 16 May 1866.
[38]*FJ*, 26 May, 14 June 1866.
[39]*Ibid.*, 19 June 1866.
[40]*Ibid.*, 17 Sept. 1866.
[41]*Ibid.*, 5 Oct. 1866.
[42]*Ibid.*, 11, 12, 15 Oct. 1866.

drew protests of " clerical intimidation " from the Tory papers.[43] By-elections later in the year gave mixed results. In Waterford, in the first contest since 1852, the Liberal candidate had a convincing majority, even though, at least in Cullen's eyes, the campaign showed that the conservatives could dispose of rather direct methods of intimidation too.[44] In the Wexford by-election, the contest lay between two Derby supporters, the Liberals not being able even to put a candidate in the field, due, Cullen commented, to the folly of the " Young Ireland " priests, strong in Wexford as in Meath, who had thwarted the wish of their bishop, Dr. Furlong, to put forward a Liberal candidate.[45]

In spite of reverses of this kind, the set of the tide was towards co-operation between the Irish Liberals and the English reform-party. This was emphasized by the reception given to John Bright on his visit to Dublin. On 30 October he was entertained to a banquet which was attended by many of the clergy, including prominent clergy of the diocese of Dublin. Though no bishop was present, all had been invited, and eighteen, including the three archbishops,[46] sent letters of apology which were read at the banquet, in which they took occasion to praise Bright and his associates as defenders of the people's rights.[47] The speeches on the occasion, however, underlined the fact that the education-issue still raised difficulties.[48] While there was agreement on the Church and Land questions, it was very hard to get the English radicals to see the demands of the Irish Catholics in regard to education as demands for free education rather than for sectarian education.

Even though the alliance prospered, little could be done while the Liberals were in opposition, and the continued deferment of hope helped only the Fenians. As the year closed, fears were expressed on all sides that a rising was imminent, and the government, supported by the demands of the conservative press, continued to strengthen its garrisons. Cullen saw developing under his eyes the situation he had always feared, the danger he had for years consistently warned against, a Fenian rising which, because it was doomed to failure, must inevitably strengthen the forces of conservatism and destroy the hopes for a bettering of the people's lot which had been raised by the Liberal alliance of the last few years.[49] A pastoral

---

[43]The figures were : electorate 8,996, White 3,419, Waldron 2,865. *FJ*, 22–23 Oct. 1866.

[44]Election results in *FJ*, 31 Dec. 1866. " At Dungarvan the lancers charged the poor people, killing one and wounding nineteen. Of course they were acting for the Beresfords." Cullen to Kirby, 2 Jan. 1867, no. 3.

[45]Results in *FJ*, 20 Nov. 1866 ; Cullen's comment in Cullen to Kirby, 2 Jan. 1867, cit.

[46]Armagh was at this time vacant.

[47]Letters in *FJ*, 31 Oct. 1866.

[48]See especially the speeches of Bright and M'Swiney, *ibid*. Irish guests at a reform-banquet in Manchester on 20 November reported signs of a better understanding—*FJ*, 13 Dec. 1866.

[49]See Cullen to Kirby, 27 Nov. 1866, no. 323, 2 Dec., no. 329, 7 Dec., no. 339 ; DDA, Kirby to Cullen, 9 Jan. 1867 ; Cullen to Manning, 7 and 13 Feb. 1867 Leslie, art. cit., pp. 165–7.

issued for the feast of the Immaculate Conception repeated what
were by now familiar warnings[50]—that revolution was not merely
wrong but could not hope to succeed, that the long list of Irish
grievances, tenant-right, disendowment, improvement of the poor-
laws, Catholic education, could be redressed only by lawful and
constitutional means, the success of which was guaranteed, not only
by the very justice of the claims, but by the growing sympathy of
a large section of the English people.[51]

In the end, patience did not prevail and the insurrection came in
1867. Shortly after the premature and abortive outbreak in Kerry
on February 11, Cullen had to speak at a gathering of a kind which
he did not frequently attend. It was a banquet given by the
Protestant Lord Mayor of Dublin to mark the work of the inter-
denominational committee which had administered relief during the
great cholera epidemic of the previous year. The Lord Lieutenant
sat immediately to the Mayor's right, Cullen immediately to his
left, a tribute to his enhanced status since he had received the
Cardinal's hat the previous year, and which, it seems, made it
necessary for the Protestant Archbishop Trench to remain away, so
as not to have to yield precedence.[52]

The Lord Mayor rose to propose the toast of the Cardinal,
praising his " learning, devotion to his country, his unceasing efforts
to alleviate the calamities of cholera ". The choice of theme to reply
to such a gathering could be difficult. Cullen chose to speak on
charity and works of charity. He was thankful, he said, to find his
name coupled with the charitable works of Dublin. The people of
Dublin were untiring in works of charity. The Catholics in particular
had performed miracles of charity over the past thirty years, in
building churches, schools and institutions. People of all faiths
had come together in works of charity during the cholera epidemic ;
the relief fund had been impartially administered by the inter-
denominational committee. Only the day before he had had the
pleasure of hearing eloquent speeches by two Protestants in support
of the Mater Hospital. It all showed that while there were many
things on which Catholic and Protestant could not agree, outside
these there was a " vast neutral ground " where all could work
together in alleviating the miseries of the country. There were signs
that better times were coming. In a speech of a few moments before,
the Lord Lieutenant had made them promises. If these promises
were carried out, the false patriotism of which they had seen examples

[50]Moran, *Writings*, iii. 20 ff.

[51]Some indications of the growing bitterness of Irish conservative opinion
can be seen in the comment of the *Evening Mail* that Cullen and Stephens had
identical interests ; both favoured the destruction of property and the establishment of communism, Stephens by revolution, Cullen by a land-bill and outdoor
relief for the poor. (Cited in *FJ*, 20 Dec. 1866.)

[52]The Cardinal's precedence prompted a question in the House of Commons by
a Tory member. The reply was that the function was not a diplomatic one, that
the Cardinal got his due precedence as a prince of his Church, and that the presence
of Catholic bishops at such functions was to be encouraged. *FJ*, 26 Feb. 1867.

in the last few weeks would lose its appeal. The Irish people would respond to justice, but only to justice. True patriotism and true charity lay in working together for the good of the country.[53]

The speech made a considerable impression. Its immediate result was a message from the Lord Lieutenant to the Cardinal assuring him of the desire of the administration to satisfy the bishops, and pressing him to attend at the Castle.[54] The reply was courteous but firm : that the bishops sought only justice for the country, and that for the present he must decline the invitation to the Castle. As he wrote to Kirby, if he were to attend state functions there he could be held up as a Castle hack and would lose his influence with the people. In such difficult times it was best to do one's duty to the government without seeking favour or recompense. Castle Catholics and liberal Protestants would be glad to see the bishops accept government patronage, not to strengthen their influence but to lessen it.[55]

One motive of Cullen's choice of subject for his speech had obviously been the need to bring calm in what was generally believed to be the aftermath of an unsuccessful Fenian rising.[56] Events soon showed that the outbreak in Kerry had not been the main effort. A much more widespread insurrection broke out on March 5, but met with no better success. In a pastoral dated 12 March Cullen underlined the warnings he had already so frequently given, the latest in his Lenten pastoral a few days before, insisting on the conscientious duty of allegiance, the obligation of adopting constitutional means of redress, the Mazzinian and Garibaldian affinities of the Fenian leaders, and ending by asking the government to act with clemency.[57]

The government did not show the clemency Cullen hoped for, but even when death-sentences were passed he still had good hopes they would be commuted.[58] In the trials of those taken in arms, two men, Burke and Doran, were sentenced to death, with a recommendation to mercy in the case of Doran.[58a] Eleven days later, on 12 May, Doran received news of the commutation of his sentence.

[53]Speech reported in *FJ*, 20 Feb. 1867. See also Cullen to Kirby, 22 Feb. 1867, no. 59, 18 March 1867, no. 100 ; Moran to Kirby, 5 March 1867, no 73.

[54]The Irish bishops had not attended at Castle functions since Cullen came to Dublin ; before this numbers of them attended regularly. The occasion for the change was the Ecclesiastical Titles Bill.

[55]Cullen to Kirby, 22 Feb., 18 March 1867, nos. 59, 100 ; Moran to Kirby, 5 March 1867, no. 73.

[56]For the same reason, he was annoyed by the bishop of Kerry's denunciation. Moriarty had declared in a sermon after the rising in Kerry that " Hell was not hot enough nor eternity long enough " to punish the Fenians. " He is very much blamed," Cullen commented, " for so foolish an exaggeration . . . I wish he could be called to an account for it." Cullen to Kirby, 22 Feb., 18 March 1867, nos. 59, 100.

[57]*FJ*, 15 March 1867. See also the pastoral of the archbishop of Cashel, 12 March 1867, *ibid.*, 14 March, and also the letter from the bishop of Cloyne, dated 25 March 1867, read at the meeting of the National Association a few days later (*FJ*, 28 March 1867), and his letter to Kirby, 18 March 1867, no. 99.

[58]Cullen to Kirby, 10 May 1867, no. 170.

[58a]*FJ*, 2 May 1867.

The silence in regard to Thomas Burke could well be construed as an indication of the government's determination to carry out the sentence in his case. The country was deeply agitated ; there had been no such execution in Ireland since 1803. The reform-party in England was prominent in the demand for mercy—there was in fact general agreement in the English press that the sentence should be commuted. A small section of Irish conservative opinion was alone in demanding blood. A meeting at the Mansion House drew up a petition to the Lord Lieutenant. The Dublin clergy were prominent among the organizers of the meeting, and a letter from Cullen was read supporting their petition and saying that an execution would cause him the deepest pain.[59] The deputation was not received until 24 May, and Burke's execution had been fixed for May 29.[60] However, everyone was confidently expecting a reprieve, and, in the circumstances, it was a reasonable hope. The government, however, seems to have attached very much weight to the need to meet the demand of the Irish conservatives, and when the deputation waited on the Lord Lieutenant they learned that the cabinet had decided there should be no reprieve. He could not, he said, hold out the slightest hope. The interview seems to have been equally painful and embarrassing for both sides. Everyone had been expecting a reprieve. There was a general shocked disappointment, spreading even to those who had earlier been insistent that the sentence be carried out.[61] A deputation of 40 or 50 Irish members of parliament waited on Lord Derby on Saturday May 25 ; should this interview fail, a smaller deputation was ready for a night journey to Balmoral to the queen. The deputation felt that Lord Derby had not quite closed all hopes. It is hard to be sure how right they were in this, for they were now prepared to grasp at shadows, and time was pressing. That same Saturday afternoon in Dublin the Cardinal went to the Castle.

It was understood, the *Freeman* reported,[62] that the Cardinal had urged that all the bishops and clergy, who had done so much to restrain Fenianism, wished for the commutation of the sentence, and that the Lord Lieutenant had been deeply moved by his representations and had promised to telegraph the cabinet immediately. It was public knowledge that Cullen's personal intervention would certainly carry great weight ; what was not public knowledge, of course, was that the Cardinal was now putting to the test the specific and personal undertaking the Lord Lieutenant had proffered earlier in the year, and which he had then rejected. Dublin and the country waited through Sunday, and at three o'clock on the afternoon of Monday 27 May the news arrived from London that Burke had been reprieved. The Lord Lieutenant immediately sent word to the

[59]*FJ*, 15 May 1867.
[60]*Ibid.*, 24 May 1867.
[61]*Ibid.*, 25 May 1867.
[62]*Ibid.*, 27 May 1867.

Cardinal and the Lord Mayor.[62a] It is impossible, naturally, to weigh with finality the motives which had led to the reprieve, but there can be little doubt, considering all the circumstances, that Cardinal Cullen's first visit to Dublin Castle had been a very important factor.[63]

The meeting of the Irish bishops, held in the opening days of October, issued a further warning against the " criminal folly " of secret societies, together with a declaration to the government that there would never be peace in Ireland without disestablishment, free education, and land-reform.[64] The immediate background to this new pronouncement on Fenianism had been the rescue of Colonel Kelly at Manchester, in consequence of which men were once again to stand trial for their lives. The story is too well known to need even recapitulation—the insistence in pressing a charge of murder, the completely unsatisfactory nature of the evidence to show that any of the prisoners had fired the fatal shot, the breakdown of the case implied in the unconditional pardon of Maguire and then the commutation of Condon's sentence because of American intervention. Again, it was a time of tense hopes and fears in Ireland, but this time, in spite of all the petitions and memorials, in which bishops and clergy joined,[65] there was no reprieve, and Allen, Larkin and O'Brien were hanged in Manchester on the morning of 23 November 1867.

This time Cullen did not intervene. The circumstances were very different from those of the preceding May, when his approach was to the Lord Lieutenant, who had given some indications that he was anxious to oblige him ; the matter then was primarily an Irish one, and only a small and daily decreasing body of public opinion called for the execution. Now it was an English matter, and English public opinion of all classes was inflamed at the idea that the Fenians could strike in the English cities, and was determined to have blood for blood.

A few days before the executions, the queen's speech at the opening of parliament had referred, in pointedly different terms, to the revolutionary movements in Italy and in Ireland :

> A band of Italian volunteers, without authority from their own sovereign, having invaded papal territory and threatened Rome itself, the Emperor of the French felt himself called upon to despatch an army for the protection of the sovereign and his dominions. That object having been accomplished, and the defeat and dispersion of the volunteers having relieved the territory from the danger of external invasion, I trust that his imperial majesty

---

[62a] *Ibid.*, 28 May 1867.

[63] The only reference I have been able to find in Cullen's private correspondence is two brief sentences : " The Fenians are now all reprieved. I went to the Lord Lieutenant to plead their cause ". Cullen to Kirby, 6 June 1867, no. 219.

[64] Resolutions of the bishops in Moran, *Writings*, iii. 89.

[65] See, e.g., the list in *FJ*, 19 Nov. 1867.

will find himself enabled, by an early withdrawal of his troops, to remove any possible grounds of misunderstanding between his majesty's government and that of the king of Italy.

The treasonable conspiracy, commonly known as Fenianism, baffled and repressed in Ireland, has assumed in England the form of organized violence and assassination. These outrages require to be vigorously put down ; and I rely for their effectual suppression upon the firm administration of the law and the loyalty of the great masses of my subjects.[66]

The reference to Garibaldi's latest foray into the papal states, which had ended with his defeat at Mentana, was in the direct line of Lord John Russell's famous despatch of October 1860, and led to a debate on the Roman question in the Commons which provided the predictable tirades against Popery. No one could read the reference to Fenianism without recognizing that it gave the highest sanction to the English demand for vengeance and killed all possible hopes of a reprieve.

Cullen's private thoughts were bitter. On 22 November, the day before the executions, he wrote to Kirby :

The queen has been very kind in her speech to the Garibaldians. She calls them Italian volunteers. Lord Stanley, minister of foreign affairs, was also very friendly to them, and also Lord Russell. *Che razza di vipere!* They are hanging Fenians who are *galantuomini* when compared with the Garibaldians whom they praise and encourage.[67]

The Manchester Martyrs immediately became the heroes, almost the saints of Ireland. Public demonstrations were organized, and public High Masses celebrated for the repose of their souls. In spite of his bitter reflections on English inconsistency and hypocrisy in the Manchester executions, Cullen could not approve. It was, he recognized, a right, even a duty, to pray for men who had died in the Catholic faith, but the public demonstrations and even the Masses were being organized for political reasons or at least being used to serve the political ends of Fenianism. In consequence, he felt obliged to take the same attitude as he had taken in regard to the MacManus funeral six years before, and there were no High Masses in Dublin.

V

Fenianism had provided all the drama in 1867, and neither its prominence nor its failure was a great help in winning support for the constitutional party. While it is true that the Fenian outbreaks did shock England into some realization of the problems of Ireland,

---

[66]*FJ*, 20 Nov. 1867.
[67]Cullen to Kirby, 22 Nov. 1867, no. 423.

the immediate response was anger. There were few in England in the autumn of 1867 who were prepared to comment so dispassionately as Gladstone :

> But for the lives that have been so sadly lost I could almost be pleased with the Manchester outrage. For the English people are deep sleepers and no voice will awaken them except one that is trumpet-tongued.[1]

Yet in spite of the disturbances at home and popular hostility and a Tory government in England the constitutional cause did make some progress during 1867. On 8 January the National Association held an important meeting. The chairman, M'Swiney, reviewed the progress which had been made, underlining the fact that it would have been far greater had it not been for the number of those who held aloof, some because the Association was too radical, some because it was too conservative. Their policy had been summed up in John Dillon's decision to support the Land Bill, not as final justice, but as a first instalment. If this had been given twenty years ago, there would now be less discontent and conspiracy in Ireland, but so long as the Tory government remained in office there was little hope of an instalment of justice.

Letters which were read from the Cardinal, the archbishop of Cashel, and the bishops of Cloyne and Ross had clearly provided the main lines of M'Swiney's speech, and they shaped the debate and resolutions which followed. On the Church question, a resolution was adopted to the effect that the Association reject any proposal of equal endowment of the churches and demand the voluntary principle for all.[2] Further resolutions were carried demanding tenant-right and a fair share of the public revenue for Catholic education. A series of resolutions on Reform pledged the Association to support reform in principle, to co-operate with the English Reform-party, to accept its support in return, and to organize a monster reform-petition.[3]

The queen's speech at the opening of parliament had promised the suspension of emergency powers in Ireland as soon as possible, and the speedy introduction of a Land Bill to promote the improvement of land by tenants and to facilitate the grant of leases.[4] Cullen was sceptical that anything could be expected from the government,[5]

---

[1]Gladstone to Manning, 11 Oct. 1867. Bayswater, OSC.
[2]This issue had arisen because of the publication of a pamphlet by the convert, Aubrey de Vere, proposing equal endowment for all. This solution had attractions, not merely for those who felt that religion should be endowed in some way by the state, but also to many who were seeking a compromise between the Tory defence of the *status quo* and the Radical policy of complete disendowment.
[3]*FJ*, 9 Jan. 1867. Shortly afterwards the Association rejected a proposal from John Martin, that it add repeal of the Union to its aims and associate itself with the National League, on the grounds that continued co-operation with the English Reform-party was essential to its programme. *Ibid.*, 16 Jan., 7 Feb. 1867.
[4]*FJ*, 7 Feb. 1867.
[5]Cullen to Kirby, 13 Feb. 1867, no. 53.

and the Fenian outbreaks were naturally a set-back to any hopes which may have existed. While these outbreaks could be used, and were used, to drive home to the government the need for remedial legislation in Ireland,[6] they were undoubtedly an obstacle to the introduction of any such legislation, and of course they prolonged indefinitely the suspension of *habeas corpus*. When the promised Land Bill was introduced, its proposals proved very disappointing.[7] In the event, it was not possible to get even this attenuated measure through the Commons. There were few regrets in Ireland when its withdrawal was announced.[8]

The Church-question was also clarified during the year. As has already been noted, a proposal was put forward to use the existing ecclesiastical property for the equal endowment of all the churches. The initiative had been taken in this proposal by the convert poet, Aubrey de Vere ; he got support from Catholic Whig politicians such as Monsell, and found one strenuous defender among the bishops, Dr. Moriarty, the bishop of Kerry.[9] Though Moriarty excluded any use of this property for the direct support of the Catholic clergy, Cullen opposed any suggestion that it should be put directly at the disposal of the Catholic Church at all. To do so would, he felt, introduce a fundamental change in a system which had worked so well in Ireland, would put the Church under a heavy obligation to the State, and might easily lead to its incurring the odium of the people. Further, there were practical objections—in any division he expected that the Established Church would get the lion's share, and in any case he saw no prospect of getting such a scheme through a parliament in which the Tories wished to retain the *status quo* and the Radicals wished to disendow all the Churches. He would prefer to see parliament use the property to establish a fund for general charitable purposes.[10]

With the backing of Cullen and other like-minded bishops, the National Association began to campaign for the voluntary principle.[11] Moriarty expounded his views in a pastoral which was answered by an article in the *Irish Ecclesiastical Record*, and some discreet Roman pressure was brought to bear through Kirby.[12] In this matter Cullen was inclined to suspect even Manning's good offices— this might at least be deduced from two of his letters to Manning

[6]See Cullen to Kirby, 5 April 1867 ; Cullen's pastoral, 12 March 1867 (*FJ*, 15 March) ; Keane to Kirby, 18 March 1867, no. 99 ; Keane to National Association, 25 March 1867 (*FJ*, 28 March) ; O'Hea (bishop of Ross) to Kirby, 28 March 1867, no. 117.

[7]*FJ*, 20 Feb. 1867. See also the discussion of the bill at a meeting of the National Association, reported *ibid.*, 28 March.

[8]*FJ*, 21 June 1867.

[9]See his pastoral letter to the clergy of Kerry, 17 March 1867, which was circulated in pamphlet form. Printed also in *FJ*, 20 March 1867.

[10]Cullen to Kirby, 2 Jan., 22 March, 5 April 1867, nos. 3, 108, 128.

[11]*FJ*, 9 Jan., 24 April, 29 June 1867.

[12]Cf. Moriarty to Kirby, 8 April 1867, no. 131.

about this time,[13] and seems confirmed by a letter from Moran to Kirby dated 12 April 1867.[14] He was not prepared to see the independence of the Catholic Church in any way imperilled, nor did he wish to see the continued endowment of the Established Church even in an attenuated form.

In the summer of 1867 the bishops of the world were assembled in Rome to commemorate the nineteenth centenary of the martyrdom of the Apostles, and on this occasion the Irish hierarchy received a definite ruling in favour of the voluntary principle. While this ruling emanated from Cardinal Antonelli, it is not difficult to see Cullen's guiding hand in it. From their meeting at the beginning of October the bishops published a series of resolutions, in which they demanded the disendowment of the Established Church; repudiated, " in accordance with Irish practice and traditions," any state-endowment for the Catholic Church; and expressed the wish that existing church-property should be used to establish a fund for charitable purposes. As might be expected, there was little discord at the meeting. MacHale at first proposed that they should express no opinion at all on the subject, and Moriarty showed some hankering after his earlier views, but neither was in a position to press his point.[15]

The bishops' meeting in October also discussed the third and thorniest problem, that of education. Exchanges so far between the government and the bishops had been concerned with the questions of recognizing as denominational the great number of primary schools where the pupils were in fact all Catholics, and the granting of a charter and endowment to the Catholic University. As has been seen, the university measure proposed by the previous government had been altogether unacceptable to the Catholics and had been successfully resisted by their opponents.[16] Negotiations continued with the Tories, and reached a point where the National Board was so obviously in difficulties in finding a reply to the bishops' demands for primary education that the ministry felt that the only solution was the appointment of a Royal Commission of Enquiry.[17]

At their meeting, the bishops repeated earlier resolutions on National Education, and decided to send a petition to parliament asking for "such a change in the existing National system of education as may afford the Catholics of Ireland all the advantages to which they are entitled ".[18] They also considered the government proposals to appoint two Catholic ecclesiastics among the seven Catholic members—half the total of fourteen—to be nominated to the Powis Commission on education. The government wished to appoint Dr.

---

[13]Cullen to Manning, 8 April, 17 Aug. 1867, Leslie, art. cit., pp. 167–8.
[14]No. 136.
[15]Resolutions in Moran, *Writings*, iii. 85–6; see also Moran to Kirby, 1 Oct. 1867, no. 356; Cullen to Kirby, 10 Oct. 1867, no. 368.
[16]See above, p. 145.
[17]The Powis Commission, appointed January 1868.
[18]Education Resolutions in Moran, *Writings*, iii. 87–9.

Moriarty, the bishop of Kerry, and Dr. Russell, the president of Maynooth. Cullen would have neither, for he suspected that they were not wholeheartedly in favour of denominational education. Finally, the meeting decided that no Catholic bishop or priest should sit on the Commission, but that the archbishop of Cashel and the bishop of Clonfert should be deputed to treat with the government on the University question.[19] The bishops, in fact, were not quite so united in the matter of education as they had been on the problems of the Established Church ; in particular, MacHale was still unwilling to indicate any public support for the Catholic University. Cullen, who always held that education was the most pressing of problems, was particularly insistent on it during the coming months,[20] but, once again, his hopes were to be disappointed.

It was now three years since the National Association had been founded. Though some progress had been made in building up an Irish parliamentary party, and some progress also in linking it with the English Reform-party, nothing concrete had in fact been achieved, and, given the composition of the English parliament, there was little hope of any immediate achievement. Fenianism, though it too had failed, was still strong. " My fear is not of revolution, sedition, or even repeal of the Union," the bishop of Kerry wrote to Monsell on 2 March 1868, " I fear worse, a people who have renounced their allegiance and who have no patriotism except hatred for their rulers ".[21] It is easy to see reasons for a growing impatience, such for instance as prompted the clergy of the diocese of Limerick to come together and issue a declaration, which soon won wide support, demanding Repeal as the only effective remedy.[22] Cullen's pastoral for the feast of St. Brigid[23] contained the usual warnings against Fenianism and the usual exhortations to avail of all constitutional and lawful means of redress, but he was forced to admit that there were no indications that anything would be soon achieved. The reaction of the English conservative press was hostile—Cullen was declared to be playing up grievances which in fact were far less than he claimed them to be, and in this way he was inciting to violence and playing the Fenian game : " if ever there was a time when the professed upholders of law, order, and the constituted authority were heavily bound over to keep silence on Ireland's grievances, it is now ".[24] If such comment was in any way seriously meant, it is an indication of a very deep misunderstanding of the reasons behind episcopal condemnations of

---

[19]Moran to Kirby, 4 Oct. 1867, no. 359 ; Keane to Kirby, 6 Oct. 1867, no. 361 ; Dorrian to Kirby, 7 Oct. 1867, no. 364 ; Cullen to Kirby, 10 Oct., 18 Oct. 1867, nos. 368, 384 ; Cullen to Manning, 17 Aug. 1867, Leslie, art. cit., p. 181.

[20]See especially the report in *FJ*, 19 and 20 Dec. 1867, of the meeting of the clergy of Dublin, with the resolutions there adopted.

[21]Ed. by J. H. Whyte in *Irish Historical Studies*, x. 194–9 (Sept. 1956).

[22]*FJ*, 3 Jan., 21 Jan. 1868.

[23]*Ibid.*, 27 Jan. 1868.

[24]*Morning Herald*, 30 Jan. 1868. See also *The Times* of the same date.

Fenianism, which were incisively summarized in the Lenten pastoral of the bishop of Cloyne.[25] Like Cullen, he described the country as being in a wretched state. He called his people's attention to the resolutions of the bishops' meeting of the previous October, condemning secret societies, and setting out demands in the matter of the church, the land, and education—" an epitome of all our problems ". English inconsistency, he said, condemns the Fenians as criminals and supports " revolutionary and infidel enthusiasts " in Italy, though the Pope's subjects are much better treated than the Irish are. Irish grievances, admitted by unbiassed English observers, called urgently for a settlement, or Irish disaffection would grow. The Irish were now a literate people, and the affairs of the whole world were in the press for them to read. They knew the neglect of their country, they knew that there was dissatisfaction in America because of it, they knew the help given by England to foreign revolutionaries. Though it was attacked by extremists from both sides, the·Catholic Church alone was consistent in its attitude to revolution.

He urged his clergy to try to get the people to sign petitions to parliament, even though the people called the petitions a mockery. They had not been far wrong, he commented, but now " the passionate earnestness of disaffected men " had created a situation in which petitions would be more favourably received. The time was now ripe for the success of a truly independent and united Irish party. The bishops had been urging such a policy since 1859 ; it was not just " episcopal policy," though it was frequently so referred to, but a true national policy, which might have been effective even earlier had it got steadier support.

In the meantime, private negotiations between the bishops and the government seemed to be making some progress in the matter of University education, though, as is the case with everything during this period of political confusion, it is not easy to say how much was being seriously offered and how much was being put forward to help other political ends without any real intention of granting it. In this case, there are rather solid grounds for thinking that the offer was not seriously meant.[26] Though Manning and Cullen were reasonably in one another's confidence on the question, Cullen did not share Manning's belief that the Tory proposals, put forward by Lord Mayo, the Chief Secretary for Ireland, were sincere, nor his view that they gave the bishops a guarantee of sufficient control over the University.[27]

---

[25]*FJ*, 24 Feb. 1868.   [26]Cullen to Kirby, 24 Oct. 1867, no. 391.
[27]As well, there was a lingering feeling that Manning's good offices, though valuable, and appreciated, introduced further complications into an already very complex situation, which Manning, Cullen felt, did not fully appreciate. See Cullen to Manning, 11, 15 and 20 March 1868, Bayswater, OSC ; Manning to Cullen, 14, 24 Jan., 20, 21, 29 Feb., 11, 14 March 1868, Leslie, art. cit., pp. 182-3. Cullen's doubts were not fully shared by Mgr. Woodlock, rector of the Catholic University—see Woodlock to Kirby, 15 April 1868, no. 128 ; DDA, Woodlock to Cullen, 14 March, 24 March 1868.

The University negotiations were still at a very indecisive stage when another political move completed the confusion in parliament. On 23 March 1868 Gladstone[28] gave notice of his intention to move three resolutions concerning the Irish Church : [29]

1. That, in the opinion of this House, it is necessary that the Established Church of Ireland should cease to exist as an Establishment, due regard being had to all its personal interests and to all rights of property.

2. That, subject to the foregoing considerations, it is expedient to prevent the creation of any new personal interests by the exercise of any public patronage, and to confine the operations of the Ecclesiastical Commissioners of Ireland to objects of immediate necessity, or involving individual rights, pending the final decision of Parliament.

3. That an humble Address be presented the Her Majesty, humbly to pray that, with a view to the purposes aforesaid, Her Majesty would be graciously pleased to place at the disposal of Parliament, Her interest in the temporalities of the Archbishoprics, Bishoprics, and other Ecclesiastical Dignities and Benefices in Ireland, and in the custody thereof.

Again, the move was designed to gain political advantage, to embarrass the government and concentrate the Liberal strength, and the question on which this issue was to be forced was shrewdly chosen. Yet it was not altogether a political manoeuvre ; for some months past Gladstone's commitments to the Irish demands for reform had been explicitly formulated in public speeches, and were being assiduously encouraged by Manning in private correspondence.[30]

The government opposed the resolutions, and Gladstone moved that the House go into committee to discuss them. A vote was taken after four nights' debate. Gladstone had a majority of sixty.[31] The debate in committee took place on 27, 28 and 30 April, after which Gladstone's first resolution was carried by a majority of 65. A week later his second and third resolutions were carried without a division.[32]

This decisive political victory was also, of course, the first firm indication that the Irish reforms could be carried. Cullen was naturally jubilant. He saw in the successful vote on disestablishment a vindication of his view that the only hope of success had lain in the policy he and Antonelli had agreed on the previous summer, of

---

[28]Now leader of the opposition. Lord John Russell had retired at the end of 1867 ; Disraeli was prime minister since the resignation of Lord Derby on 25 February 1868.

[29]*Hansard*, series 3, cxci, col. 33 ; *FJ*, 23, 24 March 1868.

[30]Morley, *Gladstone*, i. 655 ff. ; *FJ*, 20 Dec. 1867. See also Manning to Gladstone, 20 Dec. 1867, 11 Feb. 1868, Leslie, art. cit., pp. 169–70 ; *FJ*, 17 March 1868 (Manning to Grey).

[31]*Hansard*, cxci, 495 ff., 575 ff., 790 ff., 837 ff. *FJ*, 4 April 1868.

[32]*Hansard*, 1338 ff., 1466 ff., 1583 ff., 1949 ff. *FJ*, 1, 8 May 1868.

refusing anything in the way of endowment from the state.[33] He was convinced that this refusal was not merely a political necessity, but also in the best interests of the Catholic Church, in order to preserve its independence of the State. In consequence, he insisted on his refusal, even when it became clear that the Liberal leaders, specifically Bright and Gladstone, were prepared to consider some form of concurrent endowment,[34] taking the form of disestablishment and disendowment of the Protestant Church, its property to be distributed proportionately as a lump sum between the Catholic, Anglican and Presbyterian churches, all three being declared completely independent of the state.[35] Moriarty still hankered after such a solution, though he had given up hopes of it—" liberalism is the new religion and there is no seeking justice except through its help ".[36] Cullen would not have it, and through Manning he impressed on Gladstone that the Catholic Church would accept nothing.[37]

After its heavy defeat on the Irish Church resolutions, the government existed only on sufferance, an agreement being reached whereby it remained in office to complete the programme of the session, general elections being due in any case before the end of the year. In these circumstances, it was impossible even to consider any contentious legislation, which meant the end of the University proposals. Shortly after the government's defeat on Gladstone's first resolution, the negotiations with the archbishop of Cashel and the bishop of Clonfert were broken off. Though an attempt was made to blame the bishops for the breakdown, the situation in the Commons was explanation enough.[38]

With the carrying of Gladstone's resolutions, Ireland could indulge in a long-delayed mood of optimism. The country was already in this mood when the Prince of Wales made a visit to Dublin in April. The comment of the bishop of Cloyne was to the point : [39]

> In truth a great change has taken place, and for the better, in English opinion and feeling. As Cardinal Antonelli said to the Irish bishops last summer, " le Fenianisme est bon pour quelque chose ". Whatever other causes may have brought about the

---

[33]Cullen to Kirby, 15 April, 10 May 1868, nos. 126, 154 ; DDA, Kirby to Cullen, 10 April 1868.

[34]Of course, he may not have been wrong in his belief that such a measure could not have been got through any English parliament. The issue was never tested.

[35]Manning to Cullen, 30 March, 2 April 1868—Leslie, art. cit., pp. 171–3.

[36]Moriarty to Kirby, 24 March 1868, no. 105 ; cf. also Moriarty to Monsell, 2 March 1868, cit.

[37]Manning to Gladstone, 8 April, 8 May 1868, Leslie, art. cit., p. 173 ; Gladstone to Manning, 9, 18 April 1868, Bayswater, OSC ; Manning to Cullen, 15 May 1868, Leslie, art. cit., p. 170.

[38]Cf. Cullen to Kirby, 10 May 1868, no. 154. After the breakdown of negotiations the bishops released to the press their correspondence with the government ; it is printed in *FJ*, 23 May 1868.

[39]Keane to Kirby, 24 April 1868, no. 137.

change, fear has had its fair share. The London *Times* admits that Fenianism, if not the cause, is the occasion of intended concessions.

In Dublin, the Cardinal received the ecclesiastical place of honour at functions attended by the prince at the Castle and the Royal Dublin Society. He drew criticism from *The Times* for refusing an invitation to be present in St. Patrick's Cathedral for the prince's installation as a Knight of St. Patrick, though Catholics were present with his approval, and one would like to see how *The Times* would have drawn up the order of precedence had he chosen to attend. From the other side, he was criticized in a number of Irish papers for attending any of the functions. While his ingrained pessimism at government intentions does find expression in some of his letters to Kirby at this time, there is no doubt that he regarded the royal visit, particularly the fact that the prince included in his programme such Catholic institutions as the Mater Hospital, the Catholic University, and Maynooth, as some indication at any rate of more tangible benefits to come.[40]

The National Association had suspended its meetings during the winter, some apparently urging that it had done its part in presenting the evidence and that all that could be done now was to wait and see if the government would act. It began committee-meetings again on 20 March, at Cullen's instigation, it would seem.[41] A further meeting on March 27 adopted an address to the people of Ireland on the Church question. The land problem came to the fore again in consequence of a letter from the bishop of Cloyne read at a meeting on 14 April, but by the time the general meeting convoked for 12 May had assembled, at which a series of resolutions on church, land, and education were adopted, it was clear that the main interest had switched to preparation for the general election.[42]

This topic makes its appearance on the agenda of the committee-meeting of 26 May, when it was decided to prepare an address to the constituencies.[43] Before long a very active organization had come into being in Dublin.[44] Cullen's letter approving of these activities, read at a meeting of the committee on 14 July, was one of his last public acts for some time, for on 16 July prayers for his recovery from a very serious illness were asked by the vicars-general of the diocese.[45] For some time his life was in danger, and he did not return to work in Eccles Street until 8 October.

---

[40]Cullen to Kirby, 15, 17, 27 April, 1 May 1868, nos. 126, 131, 142, 147 ; Moran to Kirby, 8 May 1868, no. 153a.

[41]At the beginning of March Cullen had been writing to Manning expressing doubts as to the sufficiency of the government's proposals on University education —see above, p. 55. Report of this meeting in *FJ*, 21 March 1868, with letter from Cullen to M'Swiney read on the occasion.

[42]Report of meeting in *FJ*, 13 May 1868.

[43]*FJ*, 27 May 1868.

[44]*Ibid.*, 15 July 1868.

[45]*Ibid.*, 17 July 1868.

By then, the election campaign had reached its full momentum, and the tide in favour of Gladstone and reform was sweeping everything before it in Ireland. In Meath, the bishop and clergy found it necessary to explain that the course they had taken some time ago did not mean that they were opposed to disestablishment.[46] In Wexford, where, as Cullen had previously noted, the clergy were little disposed to give support to parliamentary agitation, they came forward prominently in support of the two Liberal candidates, even though their speeches were at times in terms stronger than Cullen would have approved of.[47] In Dublin, Cullen associated himself publicly and unreservedly with the Liberal cause.[48] Even MacHale, though he refused to associate himself with the movement, and though after the election he issued warnings that the deceits of 1852 must not be repeated, was nevertheless prepared to admit that the results gave some ground for the people to have confidence once again in their parliamentary representatives.[49]

The Irish results gave the Liberals 66, the Conservatives 39. More important than the gain of nine seats was the fact that the Liberal representation was now much more unified and with a definite programme. Further, Gladstone, the new prime minister, was deeply committed to that programme and had a majority of 112 in the House. The new Liberal party had come to maturity and was in a position to govern.

Ireland had every reason to expect the promised legislation. As things turned out, because of the real and deep differences between Irish Catholic and English Liberal, not all that had been expected was achieved. Disestablishment gave the least difficulty, for here both sought the same end, if for different reasons. The Land Bill of 1870 was only an instalment; it was to take much more time before it became clear in England that English and Irish land-problems required radically different treatment. It was, nevertheless, the first real instalment—" it did not prevent evictions, but it rendered them a costly legal undertaking to the landlord, while it likewise laid a foundation of legal protection for tenants—a tentative, halting protection—which was to point the way to the great charter of emancipation from landlord injustice to be won by the Land League in the Land Act of 1881 ".[50]

Education, where Catholic and Liberal ideas were so widely divergent, provided the greatest problem. The crisis came in the spring of 1873, when Gladstone's Education Bill faced a decisive vote. The bishops had already made clear their dissatisfaction. On

[46]*Ibid.*, 5 Sept., 11 Nov. 1868.

[47]Report of convention to select the two Liberal candidates for Wexford, *FJ*, 22 Sept. 1868. Reports of subsequent meetings frequently during the campaign.

[48]See his letter to the aggregate meeting of the Dublin Liberals, *FJ*, 3 Nov. 1868; letter to diocesan clergy, 14 Nov. 1868, *FJ*, 16 Nov.

[49]*FJ*, 16 Nov., 26 Nov., 10 Dec. 1868.

[50]Davitt, *The Fall of Feudalism in Ireland*, pp. 77-8.

9 March Cullen flatly declared his opposition to the bill. The division was taken at 2 a.m. on the morning of 12 March. Thirty-five Irish Liberals voted against the bill and it was defeated by three votes.

This was the end of the experiment in co-operation between Cardinal Cullen and the English Liberal party. The 1874 elections returned a substantial conservative majority, and the government then formed was still in office when the Cardinal died. In the Irish constituencies, the Liberal representation had shrunk to little more than a dozen; there were 58 Home Rulers, making it very clear that a new chapter had been opened.

Yet the chapter which had just closed had been productive of the first tangible benefits to Ireland for a long day, and there is no doubt that the National Association had had a considerable share in winning them. The Fenian outbreaks were certainly important in shocking English opinion into a realization of the needs of Ireland, but had it not been for the co-operation between Irish Catholic and English Liberal organizations the machinery for remedial legislation for Ireland would not have existed. It had been genuine co-operation in spite of genuine difficulties and differences. It had been genuine, I would suggest, because it was based on a common factor for which there seems to be no better name than "radicalism". Certainly it was in many ways the antithesis of conservative.

Cardinal Cullen was personally associated with this programme of the National Association of Ireland. His first commitment to party politics was, as has been seen, a very reluctant one, but, once made, it was definite and positive. The evidence examined goes to show that he was a real force behind the approach made by the National Association to English Liberal and Radical opinion. Cullen came to Ireland from Rome convinced that a bishop ought not to participate directly in politics, but the history of the 1860s shows that he was prepared to learn from his experience of Irish needs.[51] There was a real, if not immediately obvious, affinity between Irish Catholic and English Radical, because the Catholic Church in Ireland had no *Ancien Regime* splendours to regret, because it was the church of a people who had to struggle for a fair share and equal citizenship, but it is nevertheless a tribute to Cullen's courage as well as his perceptiveness that he was prepared to work with men like Bright and Gladstone. He had no real illusions as to the limits of the agreement which could be achieved; even in the case of Gladstone, the

---

[51]Dr. Murray of Maynooth, who had been on very intimate terms with Gavan Duffy, and whose personal relations with Cullen, partly in consequence of this, were by no means happy, commented in his diary on 25 Oct. 1878, the day after Cullen's death: " He came here as archbishop of Armagh with very strong views, which he often put forward in very strong forms. Very much to his credit, however, it must be said that for many years back those views had been greatly moderated, some of them entirely abandoned." (MS Diary, Maynooth College Library.)

Roman question was always a reminder of what real differences existed. Indeed, if Cullen's political efforts had been dominated solely by the exigencies of the Roman question, he would have found Disraeli and the Tories more sympathetic than Gladstone. Yet while he was prepared to negotiate with the Tory government for any concessions which might be had from that quarter, he was willing to try the experiment of positive political co-operation with Gladstone and the Liberals. Although he had an ingrained and not altogether unjustified pessimism as to what Ireland might expect from any party at Westminster,[52] he was nevertheless ready to work with a movement which promised a more lively consideration for his Catholic people.

---

[52]Cf. Woodlock to Kirby, 29 July 1892 (the Kirby letters for these years have not yet been numbered). Woodlock had been rector of the Catholic University at the time of Gladstone's first government, and he had been much more optimistic than Cullen that Gladstone would make satisfactory provision for Catholic higher education. In this letter, written in his last years, he gives news of Gladstone's latest electoral victory, and expresses the hope that it will lead to some good for Ireland. He adds the interesting comment : " At the same time I must confess that every day's experience confirms me more and more in the wisdom of the axiom which was constantly on the lips of our late beloved Cardinal Cullen— *nolite confidere in principibus* ".

8

THE EARLY RESPONSE OF THE IRISH CATHOLIC
CLERGY TO THE CO-OPERATIVE MOVEMENT[1]

LIAM KENNEDY

THE primary aim of this paper is to assess the role of the Roman Catholic clergy in agricultural co-operative development, drawing on evidence from the last decade of the 19th and the early decades of the 20th century. It is hardly possible, however, to treat such activity in isolation from the manifold preoccupations of rural society, as in practice no clear demarcation existed between economic and non-economic activity. An attempt is made to place such clerical activity in the cultural context of rural society, while simultaneously paying attention to the specific ideological, pastoral and economic pre-occupations of the clergy, and while treating the latter as a distinctive social category with affiliations both within and beyond the rural community.

The importance of the clerical response in influencing the prospects of any social or economic development in rural Ireland requires no amplification. Because of the democratic nature of co-operative organisation—requiring as it does mass participation by sections of a rural community—their strategic importance is likely to have been even more heavily underlined. In some areas clerical acquiescence was probably a necessary condition for co-operative progress in the formative period. Moreover, clerical numbers had increased steadily from about 5,000 priests, monks and nuns in 1850 to over 14,000 in 1900—despite a falling lay population.[2] In addition another key social category was increasing in relative terms in the late 19th century: the traders, publicans, shopkeepers, dealers in agricultural inputs and outputs. After the

---

[1] The writer acknowledges his considerable intellectual debt to E. W. Cooney, Reader in Economic History, University of York. Professor Cyril Ehrlich, Queen's University, Belfast, kindly commented on an earlier draft of this paper. Neither, of course, are responsible for any defects in the final product.

[2] Emmet Larkin, ' Economic growth, capital investment, and the Roman Catholic church in 19th century Ireland ' in *A.H.R.*, lxxii (1967), pp 864-5.

clergy, the traders formed the most influential non-farming element in rural society.

The institutional church: economic and social ideals
Rerum Novarum[3], published in 1891, signified Pope Leo XIII's willingness to attempt a reconciliation between the catholic church and modern industrialising society. Leo XIII's stricture to ' bridge the abyss between the priest and the people '[4], believed to have risen out of the twin processes of industralisation and urbanisation, was unnecessary in the Irish case. Industralisation in Ireland was limited and showed a high degree of regional concentration, and in rural Ireland a reverse process had been under way. Thus for the greater part the church operated within a socio-economic environment which traditionally had proved conducive to catholic orthodoxy.

The Irish hierarchy was delicately poised between the institutions of British civil authority and those of the nationalist (predominantly catholic) population, extracting advantage from both.[5] At parish level the identification of chapel and cabin was more complete. Given that catholicism and nationalism were almost perfectly correlated, that the social origins of the Irish clergy lay to a very considerable extent in rural Ireland[6], and that both priests and laity subscribed to a common, though highly selective and sometimes misleading, view of Irish history, the unity of priest and people is not unexpected. Factors which reinforced these bonds were the exclusion of the local clergy from the more prestigious (usually protestant)

[3] Leo XIII: *Rerum Novarum.* See the English translation in Sydney Ehler and J. B. Morrall (eds.), *Church and state through the centuries* (New York, 1967). In Europe the alliance of altar and throne precluded the church from adopting anything but an extremely cautious, if not actually reactionary, role in relation to social reform. While Social Catholicism had manifested itself in various forms and on a limited scale over the 19th century, it was only in the closing decade or so of that century that it received considerable encouragement from the papacy.

[4] A. R. Vidler, *A century of social catholicism 1820–1920* (London 1964) p. 127.

[5] A detailed assessment of relationships between the catholic church, the state and the institutions of Irish nationalism is contained in D. W. Miller, *Church, state and nation in Ireland 1898–1921* (Dublin, 1973).

[6] No systematic analysis of the social origins of the Irish clergy has been undertaken but the general consensus of opinion favours this interpretation. See Connell, *Irish peasant society*, pp 123–6 and 148–9.

segments of society and a pervasive sense of being bounded by alien institutions, regarded as inimical to Roman Catholicism.[7] As L. Paul-Dubois commented in 1908: ' The catholic clergy have never ceased to regard their flock as the object of the snares set by protestantism. '[8]

The position of the catholic church on economic policy may be briefly and somewhat crudely summarised as follows: maximise the numbers of people on the land as this is more conducive to the ' good ' life[9] and where possible develop alternative employment opportunities to stem emigration and its associated hazard of losing the faith. A practical implication of this was large scale redistribution of land, and population flows from areas with un-favourable man-land ratios—generally the western regions of the country—to areas less densely populated. In a joint pastoral letter in 1900, the bishops signified their support for such a land policy: ' . . . the great grass plains that are at present worthless to their owners, and are economically lost to the country ' should be returned to the poverty stricken Irish peasant.[10] Political constraints, however, ruled out any massive structural changes in Irish agriculture. The Congested Districts Board (C.D.B.) operated a policy of land redistribution on a modest scale, and this had the support of the Irish bishops. A C.D.B. scheme of land division on Clare Island, for instance, had the moral and financial backing of the Archbishop of Tuam, Dr McEvilly.[11]

[7] In a characteristic outburst, the *Irish Catholic* leader-writer (31 Aug. 1895) declares that the civil administration, ' so long as it rejects our national demands, can only be regarded as the enemy of Ireland and of her people '.

[8] L. Paul-Dubois, *Contemporary Ireland* (Dublin and London, 1908), p. 501. Even Paul-Dubois who was distinctly sympathetic to catholic aspirations could remark, (p. 481) that ' in no country does the secular arm show more respect for religion, and its ministers '.

[9] The Irish clergy's view of the moral decadence of industrial society, especially that of England (' pagan England ') is brought out in a number of books, pamphlets and statements. See, for instance, Rev. J. Guinan, *The Soggarth Aroon* (Dublin, 1905), p. 201, and Rev. M. O'Riordan, *Catholicity and Progress* (London, 1906), chapt. iv. It may be the case as one writer puts it—Arnold Schrier, *Ireland and the American emigration 1850–1900* (Boston, 1958)—that the clergy were less forceful than Irish nationalists in protesting against emigration, but their unease at the process, and the so-called moral dangers implicit in it are not in doubt.

[10] *Freeman's Journal*, 1 Oct. 1900.

[11] W. L. Micks, *History of the Congested Districts Board* (Dublin, 1925), p. 103. For generally favourable comments on land redistribution by

Striking confirmation of the effectiveness with which the notion of the superiority of rural life was communicated to the lay catholic is furnished by this extract from a taped interview with a townsman who is now approaching eighty years of age. Referring to Dr Kelly, Bishop of Ross and an acknowledged specialist on economic matters, and to Dean White, P.P. of Nenagh, he recalls: ' they regarded the land, you see, as the great asset of the country, which it was, and that character, (pause) that even character was formed by the land. ' Continuing, he suggests that the clergy of this period were not opposed to industrial development, rather they wished to see it ' allied to the economy of the country ' and that between agriculture and industry there should be ' a good balance, but the land should be the greater '.

Nor were all forms of economic development welcomed uncritically, by some of the clergy at least. A Belfast or a Birmingham might not be intrinsically 'hostile to the spirit of the catholic church', according to the Rev. T. F. Macken,

but it is emphatically not the ideal to be striven after and attained in this country. If we are to look abroad for examples, it is to be hoped that Ireland will develop after the model of Belgium or Denmark rather than on the lines of those countries where the land is deserted, and where the toiling millions are congregated in large cities and towns, and leading lives of moral and physical degradation . . . The farm is known to be the best place to bring up worthy sons and daughters . . . And so in Ireland the land industry must be cultivated first of all, and other industries must be brought to the homes of the people . . .[12]

Clearly the pattern of development favoured by many of the clergy was at variance with the experience, and probably the requirements, of modern industrial societies. It is interesting to note, though, that agricultural co-operatives would seem to fit almost perfectly within the framework of clerical preferences regarding organisation and type of economic activity. If the clerical response to co-operation was shaped solely by church social ideals then a uniformly favourable reaction is to be anticipated. But then life is rarely that simple, even for men whose kingdom lies elsewhere.

---

prominent clergymen see *Record of the Maynooth Union 1898-99* (Dublin, 1899) pp 31-4; *Record 1899-1900,* p. 40; *Record* 1900-01, pp 66-7; *Record 1901-2,* p. 50; *Record 1902-3,* p. 69.
[12] Rev. T. F. Macken, ' After the Land Purchase Acts ' in *Record of the Maynooth Union 1902-3* (Dublin, 1903), p. 75.

Two hypotheses and some evidence

In relation to the formation of co-operative societies it is possible to envisage two polar positions on the part of the catholic clergy.[13] One might hypothesise that the clergy in general sought actively to promote the cause of agricultural co-operation. A second hypothesis is that the clergy worked actively to impede such developments. The consensus of opinion is in favour of hypothesis one.[14] The orthodox interpretation lauds the widespread participation of clergy in co-operative endeavour.

The evidence in favour of this interpretation is impressive. Horace Plunkett in a brief reference in *Ireland in the new century* (p. 119) notes that of the co-operative societies organised by the Irish Agricultural Organisation Society ' there are no fewer than 331 societies of which the local priests are the chairmen, while to my own knowledge during the summer and autumn of 1902, as many as 50,000 persons from all parts of Ireland were personally conducted over the exhibit of the Department of Agriculture and Technical Instruction at the Cork Exhibition by their local clergy '. Other writers, while not providing quantitative evidence of this kind, carry a similar theme of constructive clerical involvement.

Further, such co-operative developments were congruent with the church's social thinking and its interest in stabilising the rural population, and promoting smaller scale industry where possible. The *Irish Catholic* newspaper spoke in approving terms of the Irish Agricultural Organisation Society (I.A.O.S.). ' It is simply the truth to say that the work of the Irish Agricultural Organisation is planned exactly on those lines of co-operation which the sovereign

[13] It is not my intention to give the impression that the protestant clergy played no part in the formation of co-operatives. Indeed they played an important role in some areas, particularly in the more northerly half of Ireland, and sometimes alongside their catholic brethren. However their overall significance in relation to co-operative development as a whole is not great.

[14] Accounts of the historical development of Irish co-operation devote little space to this point which is surprising and somewhat perplexing given the importance of the priest in rural society. One looks in vain for anything more than brief comments in such works as Horace Plunkett, *Ireland in the new century* (London, 1904); L. Smith-Gordon and L. Staples, *Rural reconstruction in Ireland* (London, 1917); The Horace Plunkett Foundation, *Agricultural Co-operation in Ireland* (London, 1931). James Johnston, author of *Agricultural Co-operation in Northern Ireland* (London, 1965) does not refer to this point, although pressure of space may have been the chief constraint here.

pontiff, Leo XIII, has so strongly commended to the workers of the world. It is eminently gratifying to be able to infer from the course of the proceedings at the Conference, that the counsels of the pope are destined to bear permanent fruit in the country . . . '[15] The first annual report of the I.A.O.S. states that in many districts its success is largely due to the help of the catholic clergy.[16]

The obvious point of departure in subjecting these claims to more detailed scrutiny is the private diaries of the leading co-operator, Horace Plunkett, (referred to hereinafter as the Plunkett Diaries). That Plunkett was sensitive to the temporal power of the clergy there can be little doubt. His diaries indicate that as a co-operative pioneer (and also as a member of the C.D.B.) he made a special effort to try and enlist their support for his work. The organisation of local meetings was sometimes preceded by a call on the local clergy or, on occasion, by a visit to the bishop. Plunkett did not hesitate, for instance, to approach Bishop Coffey in Killarney to ' get his assistance with the priest at Listowel '.[17] Bishop Dwyer of Limerick, in whose area much early co-operative development took place, became a respected acquaintance, although it should be noted that he was a very independent-minded prelate and regarded as somewhat of a tory politically. Dr O'Donnell, bishop of Raphoe, entertained Plunkett during a co-operative organising tour of Donegal in 1893, but the relationship appears to have declined at a later stage.[18]

Viewing the first three years of co-operative propagandising through the medium of the diaries, i.e. 1889–91, it appears that at four of the public meetings recorded the clerical reaction was favourable and at two it was negative. In this period one finds about 35 references to different public meetings arranged to promote the formation of co-operative societies for farmers and/or rural labourers. (There is

[15] *Irish Catholic*, 13 Nov. 1897, in a report on the third annual meeting of the I.A.O.S. McKevitt in his essay ' Epilogue: Modern Ireland ' in Corish, *Irish catholicism* (Dublin, 1970), is probably correct in claiming that a detailed interpretation by Irish churchmen of *Rerum Novarum* never proceeded very far. Yet it is unlikely that it failed utterly to produce some modification of the clerical world view. It could on occasion serve as a vague source of legitimation for innovations and alterations to existing practices, as illustrated in the *Irish Catholic* report for instance.

[16] I.A.O.S. Annual Report 1895, p. 4.

[17] Plunkett Diaries, 1 May 1891, (Plunkett Foundation for Co-operative Studies, Oxford).

[18] Plunkett Diaries, 5 April 1910.

some degree of arbitrariness involved in determining what meetings fall into this category; I have tried to eliminate references to the organisation of urban workers and to meetings of co-operative committees, or small groups of farmers that appear to be of a semi-private nature.) It seems significant that of these 35 meetings, a clerical presence, favourable or otherwise, is recorded in only six instances. (There is no indication of a clerical presence at the other gatherings excluded from this count.) This would appear to indicate that the dominant clerical reaction at local level was one of non-participation. Allowing for the high degree of selectivity and under-reporting involved in making diary entries, it still seems difficult to inflate our rough index of active clerical involvement—about 17%, or 11% if one includes favourable references only—to a figure which might compel an alternative interpretation. Nor was Plunkett normally indifferent in his diary entries or elsewhere to those who were present at meetings. An entry in the summer of 1891 reads: ' At 10 a.m. met the conference of delegates from 15 dairy co-op. societies, and Fingall, Monteagle, Anderson, Stokes, Gibson, Cleeve, Beamish, two priests and 1 clergyman and a few others—over 60 in all'. Again, the number of catholic clergy present as a proportion of the total gathering is tiny.

Moving forward to 1895, when a central organising body (the I.A.O.S.) was in existence, one finds two prominent catholic clergymen on its committee, Dr O'Donnell, bishop of Raphoe, and Fr Finlay S. J., of whom M. Digby[19] commented in her biography of Horace Plunkett: ' he was one of the few catholic clergy of high standing who from first to last gave Plunkett active support and valuable counsel '.

Again, turning to clerical participation in co-operative activity at national level, an analysis of the delegates at the first General Conference of the Irish Co-operative Dairy and Agricultural Societies in September 1895 reveals that of 60 delegates (representing 29 societies) present, two were catholic clergymen.[20] Another rough index of clerical interest in the central organising body of the co-operative movement is provided by a breakdown of the annual list of voluntary financial subscribers to the I.A.O.S.[21] In 1895, there were fifteen clergymen among the subscribers, representing

[19] M. Digby, *Horace Plunkett* (Oxford, 1949), p. 55.

[20] I.A.O.S. Annual Report 1896, appendix E.

[21] I.A.O.S. Annual Reports, 1895, 1905, 1915.

4% of the total. A decade later this number had increased to 64, or roughly 13% of the total. By 1915 the number of clergymen had declined to a mere nine, or 6% of all subscribers. These levels of clerical support are further deflated when it is considered that they also include a minority of protestant clergymen. From this it would appear that enthusiasm for the co-operative movement as a significant national force did not rise to any great level, and this impression tends to be reinforced by a reading of the I.A.O.S. a.g.m. debates between 1896 and 1920. As reported in the relevant annual reports, these debates do not appear to have induced many clerical contributions—if one excludes the addresses of Fr Finlay who was vice-president of the I.A.O.S. over this long period. A firm impulse to the co-operative movement, *as a movement,* does not appear to have been forthcoming in contrast with the experience of co-operative pioneers in some European countries, most notably Belgium, where the clerical response would appear to have been more wholehearted.

Thus in the initial stages of local co-operative endeavour clerical reaction was mixed, and clerical participation not nearly so marked (either at local or national level) as former accounts suggested. Nor, where there is evidence of non-involvement, is it safe to conclude that this indicated indifference. It is unlikely that many clerics did not play some role at parish level, that at the very least a sense of approval or disapproval was communicated. The involvement of the clergy in political and social affairs requires little substantiation, especially during the period immediately prior to and after the fall of Parnell.[22]

So far we have merely considered in a fairly abstract and rather incomplete way some measures of the extent and direction of clerical activity. No explanatory scheme embracing the probable determinants of such behaviour has been offered. We possess some observations but lack a theory. *Why should the clergy show anything but favour to the new movement?*

Conflict of economic interests

The three social categories identified in our introduction as being of central significance, in terms of the present inquiry, were

[22] One general instance, which has the merit of being quantitative, may suffice to illustrate this point. C. C. O'Brien estimates that the county conventions for the selection of parliamentary candidates in

the peasant farmers, the clergy, and the traders. There is over-whelming evidence from many parts of Ireland to suggest that the last were generally opposed to co-operative developments. The early writers on co-operation in Ireland whose works have been cited, Plunkett, Smith-Gordon and Staples, Johnston are consistent on this point. So also are M. Digby,[23] C. C. Riddall,[24] and Paddy the Cope.[25] Newspapers in the 1890s such as the *Skibbereen Eagle, Wexford People, Waterford Star, Cork Constitution,* and, on occasions, the *Freeman's Journal* and the *Cork Examiner* railed against the co-operative societies. Written communications[26] from twenty-one societies indicate that in over half of these cases opposition to local co-operative development was evident, and that, in some instances, it was very bitter indeed. Twenty of these are dairy co-operatives, and in seventeen of these twenty cases later expansion into non-dairying activities induced a hostile reaction.

This evidence suggests that the co-operative movement repre-sented a disruptive force which exposed latent contradictions in the rural social structure. In a small community characterised by many face-to-face relationships the local clergy would have found it well nigh impossible to insulate themselves wholly from the newly emerging social tensions.[27] The nature of their dilemma in such situations is well summarised by Dean White, parish priest of Nenagh and a prominent figure in North Munster agrarian and political circles. Having reluctantly accepted the chairmanship of a public meeting to discuss co-operation he warned his audience that his presence should not be misinterpreted as signifying approval of

---

1885 'consisted on average of 150 laymen and 50 priests'—C. C. O'Brien, *Parnell and his party 1880–90* (reprinted ed., Oxford, 1974) p. 130 While the comparison is somewhat unfair, this ratio of priests to laymen contrasts unfavourably with those we have calculated in relation to the co-operative movement.

[23] Digby, *Horace Plunkett.*

[24] C. C. Riddall, *Agricultural Co-operation in Ireland* (Dublin, 1950).

[25] P. Gallagher, *Paddy the Cope: my story* (revised ed., Tralee, n.d.).

[26] See appendix.

[27] Clearly the clash of economic interests and the consequent tensions varied very considerably from area to area. In remote areas where there was little if any concentration of traders the problem was likely to be less acute or non-existent. Also, of course, traders were sometimes part-time farmers. Further, in cases where co-operative endeavour was unlikely to result in competition with traders, such development could be of mutual benefit. For these reasons, and also possibly as a form of insurance, traders in some areas took shares in local dairy co-operatives.

co-operative enterprise. Observing that most of the traders were absent from the meeting and that they were generally very uneasy regarding the movement, he defined his position as follows: ' when it is made clear to me that the traders and shopkeepers have nothing to dread from the spread of this agricultural co-operative movement, I will have neither difficulty nor hesitation in giving the movement my support, but until I am satisfied on that point my position will be a neutral one '. He is further quoted as saying: ' any effort that would be calculated to weaken the trade's influence and interest in towns would, I think, be very dangerous '.[28]

The economic prerequisites of church activity are often ignored or naïvely assumed not to exist; yet this economic dimension— the revenue needs of the catholic church—is a relevant variable in considering clerical behaviour. Some crude estimates of the revenue needs of the church and the consequent burden imposed on its members have been made for the nineteenth century by Emmet Larkin.[29] While one may have little confidence in the calculation of this burden, his pioneering work at least illustrates the incontrovertible point that church financial demands were of a substantial order of magnitude. Given extensive belts of near-subsistence farming and the frustration of income expectations in Irish agriculture in the 1880s and the 1890s, it is most probable that the middle strata of rural society—big farmers, large and medium sized commercial interests, members of the professions— contributed much more per capita than the relatively less prosperous peasant farmers. This is especially likely in relation to items of capital expenditure, be it the provision of a stained glass window or a new church school.

In rural Ireland, then, such financial dependence on traders, shopkeepers and publicans would ensure that their interests were not lightly forgotten by the clergy. The correspondence reproduced in Larkin's article indicates the intensity with which the clergy sought revenue; any development which endangered revenue is unlikely to have received an unambiguous welcome. And, as we have seen, commercial interests were quite vociferous in publicly denouncing the co-operative movement as a threat to ' legitimate ' business.

[28] Descriptions of this meeting appeared in the *Irish Daily Independent* 27 Jan. 1896, the *Eagle and County Cork Advertiser* 1 Feb. 1896 and a long account in the *Cork Examiner* 18 March 1896. One report was aptly titled ' Agricultural co-operation on trial in Tipperary '.

[29] As note 2.

Large farmers, particularly graziers, stood to gain little from co-operative organisation and no doubt they also constituted important sources of clerical funds, but here the priest's dilemma was softened to the extent that conflict centering on the co-operative system impinged less directly on the interests of large farmers.

Oral testimony from a former chairman of a dairy co-operative society (situated in a medium-sized village) claims that clerical opposition to his society was motivated by a desire on the part of the local clergy to protect their revenue sources among the local traders. The most vivid description we have of clerical opposition to a co-operative enterprise is in Paddy Gallagher's autobiography.[30] Unfortunately he does not state explicitly why priests and traders were both strongly opposed to his pioneering efforts to establish Templecrone Co-operative society in 1906. Private communications (see appendix) from four other co-operative societies (situated in east Cork, mid-Tipperary, Tipperary-Limerick border, and Co. Roscommon respectively) state that while the clergy were interested, and in some cases active in the formation of purely dairy co-operatives, expansion into retailing brought clerical opposition. Three of these communications imply that observations of opposition on this point are not limited only to the co-operative society in question. Thus one such communication reads: ' the shopkeepers accepted the co-operative up to the time when the stores started and at that time in most places the parish priest was the man to show his disapproval and in nearly all cases he sided with the shopkeepers '. Another reads: ' . . . as in the last 30 or 40 years many local clergy were either directly related to or fairly closely related to retail traders, they did as a matter of ordinary personal reaction tend to work in their local community against the idea of the co-operative developing into retail trading '.[31] This suggests that, on occasion, kinship ties may have played a crucial role in determining behaviour and it is also suggestive of the social origins of the clergy.

[30] As note 25.

[31] This comes from the general manager of a large multi-purpose co-operative society with a trading area extending over several counties. There is a problem here in that this evidence relates to a somewhat later period. However, if one accepts that there is little reason to believe that rural society or its social composition was changing dramatically and that a group's position vis-à-vis another social group tends to be fairly enduring then such evidence is admissible. Certainly in the case of traders a consistent pattern (although of diminished intensity) is discernible from the early period until recent times.

The Plunkett Papers[32] contain an interesting exchange of letters between Horace Plunkett and the Bishop of Elphin, Dr Clancy. Plunkett opens by commenting: '. . . . I understand that you are letting it be known that you are opposed to the co-operative creameries which have been widely established in your diocese'.[33] Dr Clancy replies that he has been misinterpreted as denouncing such ventures, when in fact he denounced certain listed abuses associated with co-operative creameries and one is left in little doubt as to the extent of Dr Clancy's enthusiasm for such creameries. One such abuse may be significant in the context of clerical sensitivity to commercial interests.

Many of our Irish towns possessed, some few years ago, a flourishing butter market, and when the farmer sold his butter, he expended the money he received in purchasing food stuffs and clothing for the needs of his household. This meant a large circulation of money in our towns, and commercial interests of every kind were in flourishing condition. . . . Thus the destruction of the local butter trade has been followed by the decay of many subsidiary forms of industry, and nothing has taken their place.[34]

Quite apart from these possible economic implications of co-operative development, the political implications must be considered. Most members of the Nationalist party saw, or affected to see, co-operation as yet another Tory instrument designed to smother home rule aspirations with kindness. Prominent Nationalists like John Dillon and Michael Davitt were especially bitter in their denunciations. There can be little doubt that some of the clergy responded to these strictures. One parish priest consulted his M.P

Note the acidic comment of Patrick D. Kenny—the priest 'petted the child of the wealthy publican and ignored or intimidated the child of the poor peasant'—'Pat', *Economics for Irishmen*, (4th edition, Dublin, 1907), p. 148. Kenny further alleges that the clergy often opposed co-operation because it generated local lay catholic leaders who were seen as a threat to clerical leadership in secular affairs.

[32] *Plunkett Papers*—papers of Sir Horace Curzon Plunkett, (Plunkett Foundation for Co-operative Studies, Oxford).

[33] Plunkett to Clancy, 2 June 1908.

[34] Clancy to Plunkett, 9 June 1908. In a somewhat similar, though more antagonistic, vein note the testimony of the Rev. M. Kane to the *Royal Commission on congestion in Ireland: sixth report of the commissioners* [Cd. 3747] H.C. 1908, xxxix, Q. 34860.

about the I.A.O.S.,[35] and was advised to steer clear of it as its purpose, according to the M.P., was merely Plunkett's own political aggrandisement.

Under a newspaper heading of February 1896 (' Vigorous Condemnation of the Co-operative Association by the Borrisokane Nationalists ') one finds co-operation denounced as a landlords' plot to extract further benefits from tenant farmers. The meeting registered a protest against co-operative projects in the region and was chaired by a parish priest.[36] Indeed this is indicative of the divisions that sometimes occurred within clerical ranks under the impact of conflicting loyalties.[37] Within this very region, and at this time, there were a number of priests deeply involved in local co-operative societies.[38]

Margaret Digby, Plunkett's biographer, and a member of the Plunkett Foundation team which carried out a county by county survey of agricultural co-operation in Ireland in 1930, states that her impression is that by and large the clergy were suspicious of and/or antagonistic to co-operators in the early, formative years.[39] While this impression is not based on any systematic collection of data, it cannot be easily set aside as Miss Digby had personal access to most of the leading co-operative pioneers and is arguably one of the leading living authorities on Irish and European agricultural co-operation. This reaction, she feels, may be explained partly in economic terms, partly in terms of certain shared characteristics between clergy and the stronger traders—relatively high status in the community, and

[35] Plunkett Diaries, 9 Sept. 1897. It is also true that some clergy shared the popular notion that political reforms were preconditions for economic development. See, for example, the comments of Canon O'Mahony and Bishop Healy in the *Record of the Maynooth Union 1897-8*, pp 35-7.

[36] Literary Cuttings: Early History of the I.A.O.S., (Plunkett Foundation for Co-operative Studies).

[37] Such divisions could also occur sometimes between priests associated with different co-operative societies. See Plunkett Diaries, 4 June 1898.

[38] For example, Rev. J. Gleeson, P.P., Kyle Co-operative Credit Society, and Fr Crowe, Ballywilliam Co-operative Dairy Society. Rev. Fathers McKeogh and Magrath were involved in efforts to establish co-operative creameries about this time. For a description of conflict between a priest co-operator and his bishop see R. A. Anderson, *With Horace Plunkett in Ireland* (London, 1935), pp 92-3. The bishop is alleged to have opposed co-operation because of his kinship ties with traders.

[39] Interview with Margaret Digby, 1973; written communication, Feb. 1975.

interests which extended beyond the local and the mundane. Thus local clergymen, who incidentally were excluded by virtue of their religion from other high status groups in Irish society, would tend to gravitate towards elements in the local community who approximated more closely to them in terms of prestige, economic status, and world view. This accords reasonably well with our depiction of rural society. If one excludes the large farmers, the clergy and the traders were the only significant groups who might be described as possessing a cosmopolitan outlook, with formal links (either ecclesiastical or trading) extending outwards and upwards from an intensely community orientated, parochial setting. Economic bonds between the clergy and the stronger traders are also compatible with this interpretation.

Further evidence and attempted synthesis

A narrative *solely* in terms of the original assumption of favourable clerical reaction is clearly inadequate. Nevertheless clerical support and/or active participation in the launching of co-operative societies was an important factor in a significant number of cases.[40] Clearly no neat synthesis is possible, but can we in some instances attempt a partial synthesis of the conflicting evidence subject to the further check that such a synthesis meshes with evidence on other aspects of rural life? Let us take the case of one mid-Tipperary co-operative creamery, founded in 1908, and located in a medium sized village. Local farmers with long associations with the co-operative speak of the major role of the parish priest in establishing the society. This is confirmed by the minutes of meetings of the management committee.[41] However it is claimed privately that the original committee of management had to promise him that the creamery would largely confine itself to milk processing and not engage in any business activity which might bring it into competition with the village traders.[42] If this off-the-record assurance was given, and my

---

[40] If one divides the co-operative movement into its three major elements, credit, creamery, and agricultural store societies, it is probable that the first posed the fewest problems for the clergy, the second could in certain situations be controversial, while the last appears to have attracted little, if any, support.

[41] These are now in the possession of the writer.

[42] One informant, possibly adding a dash of colour to his narrative, claims that the parish priest ' made the committee-men go down on their knees and promise not to open a store in the creamery, ' It is worth noting that this clerical response to co-operation is consistent with the

personal assessment is that these informants are quite reliable, then the priest/chairman was instrumental in blocking potential developments of a controversial nature. Holding a key position on the farmers' management committee and combining with this role the further role of spiritual leader of the local community—embracing *both* villagers and country-folk — he was in a powerful position to determine what activities were the legitimate concern of what particular social groups. He, it would appear, legitimised co-operative activity in one direction, thus facilitating realisation of the farmers' main objective—an improved system of milk processing. In turn he protected the interests of the village traders who were dependent in part on the sale of agricultural inputs and consumer goods and the purchase of certain agricultural outputs, but were unconcerned with milk processing. Thus a direct clash of economic interests was avoided, stress points in the social structure eased, and the integrated nature of this microcosm of Irish society reaffirmed.

It is impossible to assess how general this experience may have been. It is certainly compatible with much of our knowledge of the role of the priest in Irish society and it would show our two fundamentally diverging sets of experience in a different and less contradictory light. Without doubt the clergy entertained a general sympathy for any attempts that might appear to promote the economic prosperity of their congregations, provided there were no adverse side-effects as viewed from the vantage point of the catholic church.[43] Evaluating a new social movement and determining the appropriate reaction was unlikely to be a hasty process. The presence of landlord and protestant elements in the co-operative movement

---

strictures of Bishop O'Donnell a decade earlier. ' It seemed to him that co-operation was in itself a sound and healthy plant . . . . But, in the first place, it seemed to him that they had to take care to bestow upon that plant careful cultivation, so that it would not protrude its branches into the windows, or its roots under the foundations of the shops of the country . . . as a friend of the movement he would warn its promoters to beware of promoting throughout Ireland any general system of co-operative stores. He need not enlarge upon the reasons which would at once alienate from the movement the sympathy of the clergy if a programme of that kind were adopted . . .' *Record of the Maynooth Union 1897–8,* p. 33.

[43] The various works on Roman Catholicism cited in this paper substantiate this point, as do leading articles from the *Irish Catholic,* and the observations of writers only incidentally concerned with religious topics.

and the hostility of most nationalist politicians compounded the problems posed by the natural antagonism of the traders. If the direct and indirect evidence we have adduced in favour of a reinterpretation of the clerical role is correct, then it appears, initially at least, that many of the clergy stood coldly aloof from co-operation. This in itself would prove quite an effective damper on co-operators' organising moves. A more sophisticated development, however, would have involved channelling co-operative enterprise, as the movement gathered momentum, along more acceptable lines, thus deflecting its socially disruptive thrust. This *via media*, as illustrated in the case of the mid-Tipperary co-operative, is exactly analogous to the strategy adopted by the clergy in the Land League agitation a decade or so earlier.[44]

Taking another area of rural economic life—that relating to the labourers and their struggle to win economic concessions—the clerical mediating role between distinct socio-economic groupings is perceptible. Thus the Rev. E. M'Swiney, presiding over a monthly meeting of the Enniskeen (Co. Cork) branch of the Democratic Labour Federation, is careful to refute the suggestion of some farmers that ' the labour agitation was an attack upon themselves '. Nothing, he claims, could be more absurd than this, ' because the labour movement was as much in favour of the farmers as the labourers '.[45] This parish priest then develops a skilful, though rather dubious, argument which serves to accommodate all interests. Devising a solution to the land question and the problem of the rural labourer involves transferring the land to the tenant farmers at low prices, thus leaving the new proprietor in a sound economic position—one in which he will be able to employ rural labourers. By contributing to the tenants' agitation the labourers can bring the land struggle to a successful conclusion thus ensuring their own employment prospects within a prosperous peasant proprietary. Viewed in this light their respective struggles are complementary.

[44] One recalls that only ten years before the founding of the first co-operative creamery Michael Davitt was setting up the Land League in Co. Mayo, in spite of strong clerical warnings of communist and socialist influences. Yet priests were later quite active in forwarding and channelling Land League agitations. Thus the fact that by 1903 or so there was considerable clerical involvement in local co-operative societies is not in itself quite so significant as might first appear. Nor is it necessary to assume a conscious strategy; a mere clerical presence on committees of management would imply certain constraints.

[45] *Eagle and County Cork Advertiser*, 10 March 1894.

At a 'monster meeting' of the representatives of the trades and labourers of Skibereen in 1894, the priest presiding notes the growing strife between capital and labour at home and abroad. He regrets that the 'friendly relations that should exist between workmen and employer are being strained, and are beginning to snap asunder'.[46] He goes on to emphasise the necessary interdependence between capitalist and labourer and the need for mutual co-operation and good-will.

In almost identical vein, one might note the address of the reverend chairman to a labourers' meeting in Nenagh in December 1894.[47] The role of mediator in economic affairs is illustrated in a more active sense by Bishop Dwyer's intervention in the strike of bacon curing workers in 1890, affecting Limerick, Waterford and Cork, and in the Limerick and Waterford railworkers strike of 1891.[48] The exercise of a similar function by the clergy in relation to land disputes involving tenant farmers is generally recognised. This further dimension of clerical activity, as revealed by comparative analysis, enhances our understanding of the clerical conception of social organisation and the appropriate social relationships between different classes. The reality of social stratification is recognised and accepted. The ideal society is conceived as a system of interlocking, mutually interdependent parts functioning smoothly in the interests of all. Although non-egalitarian, it is essentially a harmony model of society, as opposed to, for instance, the marxist conflict model. Conflict between different socio-economic groupings, be it between farmers/co-operators and traders, or farmers and labourers represents deviation from the social ideal of a harmony of classes, or what continental clergymen knew as *la paix sociale*.

In the light of this ideological orientation it is hardly surprising that the priest should play an important part in the management and resolution of conflicts within rural society. His role in settling land disputes between neighbours and agro-industrial disputes between employers and employees, and his reaction to rural labourers' claims and to co-operative developments displays considerable consistency. Certain forms of social conflict were to be deprecated as these introduced tensions which disturbed the stability and cohesion of

[46] *Eagle and County Cork Advertiser,* 1 Sept 1895.
[47] *Nenagh News,* 22 Dec. 1894.
[48] *Limerick Reporter* and *Tipperary Vindicator,* 1890–91. See also Fr Ryder's address to the Archconfraternity (Limerick) urging conciliation in the bacon industry dispute, referred to in the issue of 7 Feb. 1890.

Roman Catholic communities.[49]   Social deviants such as co-operative pioneers had to be reintegrated into community structures if the old clerical power and authority patterns were to be maintained intact.   Participation of clergy in co-operative societies would have gone a long way towards achieving this.

Evidence of joint action on the part of priests and traders in a number of instances is somewhat unexpected and suggests some interesting lines of enquiry.   While interpretation of such an association is extremely tentative, considerations of social status, revenue and kinship links suggest themselves as possible explanatory factors.

Conclusion

From our review of the available evidence it appears that clerical reaction to the co-operative movement took three main forms.   Firstly, reserve or actual opposition for a variety of motives, this being most apparent where co-operative development threatened the social equilibrium in rural communities.   Reserve and suspicion are likely to have been more general in the innovative period, sometimes crystallising into opposition where co-operator and trader groups adopted hostile postures vis-à-vis each other.   A very different reaction and one gaining momentum through time was that of active promotion of co-operative enterprises.   The third approach, which is really a refinement of the second, involved conditional and selective promotion of such enterprises e.g. purely milk processing as opposed to multi-purpose co-operatives.   Approaching the end of the first decade of co-operative propagandising, the second reaction or perhaps some refinement of it represents the dominant pattern.   Instances of hostility might manifest themselves occasionally from now on, but the co-operative form of organisation had established itself as a permanent feature of rural Ireland.   Clerical participation and interest in the central organs of the co-operative moment and, by inference, in the more visionary aspects of the co-operative ideology, cannot be viewed as noteworthy and would appear to have declined from a peak in the early years of this century.   The publication in 1904 of Plunkett's controversial book, *Ireland in the new century,* cannot have helped in attracting

---

[49] While the point is not developed here it is fairly obvious why these generalisations cannot be stretched to embrace the landlord element in rural society.

and maintaining clerical support. The subsequent renewal of nationalist attacks on co-operation as well as a general preoccupation with political issues and remedies after the liberal electoral triumph of 1906 were probably more significant factors. In view of these, one may wonder if the co-operative movement would have been even more successful in attracting the energies of local clergymen had it assumed a somewhat sectarian character or adapted itself to the political currents of the time by transforming itself into a vehicle for nationalism. A survey of co-operation in 1931, for instance, noted in passing that priests and schoolteachers, who in other countries had provided much of the local leadership for credit societies, had not performed a comparable role in Ireland.[50] European co-operative movements, it may be noted, tended to have strong identifying characteristics of a religious or national kind (infusing them, perhaps, with the ' vital heat ' George Russell found so conspicuously lacking in the Irish movement).[51] It seems reasonable to conclude that in certain fundamental respects the movement in Ireland fitted less than easily into the emerging social and political patterns of pre-independence Ireland. It retained its non-political and non-denominational character, but probably only at the cost of reducing its appeal for certain non-farming groups—the Roman Catholic clergy in particular.[52]

APPENDIX

Three distinct information gathering techniques were used in compiling evidence for this paper. While the main emphasis was placed on analysis of conventional documentary sources, this was supplemented by use of the technique of oral history and by the social survey technique of postal questionnaire. A few comments on the postal questionnaires (or private

[50] The Horace Plunkett Foundation, *Agricultural co-operation in Ireland: a survey* (London, 1931), p. 385.

[51] George Russell, *The building up of a rural civilization* (Dublin, 1910), p. 3. It is interesting to note that the Irish language movement, itself contemporaneous with the co-operative movement, evolved a radically different approach to the issues of language and nationality. It is hardly coincidental that the language revival campaign succeeded in gaining substantial clerical backing, especially among the younger clergy.

[52] In general it seems that, of the broadly political and economic roles open to him, the Irish *soggarth* found the former the more congenial of the two.

communications) may be in order. Using the 1912 list of co-operative dairy societies as a sampling frame 68 societies were randomly selected. Simple questionnaires seeking information on, among other things, trader and clerical reaction to the co-operative in its formative period were distributed to each society. It was specified in each case that written communications were desired only from individuals, either co-operative staff or past or present members of the management committees, who were intimately associated with the local co-operative society and felt they possessed reliable historical information.

It is difficult to assess precisely the response rate as quite a number of these 1912 societies are no longer in business; others replied that they felt unable to provide information. In all 25 completed returns were obtained, giving a wide geographical spread, 18 of which were useful within the context of the present paper. (In some instances interesting replies were followed up with oral interviews.) It should be noted in this brief review of procedure that the emphasis is on treating and presenting evidence supplied by private respondents as historical source material which must be subjected to the historian's checks. No broad social survey type claims are made, or intended.

9

THE ROMAN CATHOLIC CHURCH IN IRELAND, 1898-1918*

DAVID W. MILLER

DURING THE TWO DECADES from 1898, when the Irish Parliamentary Party began to recover from the chaos of the Parnellite split, until 1918, when that Party was decisively rejected at the polls, the Catholic Church was forced to adapt to a new role in Irish politics. By examining the Church's response to the political events of these years I hope to indicate how it accommodated itself to the revolutionary forces which achieved Irish independence.

In the early 1890's the Church, under the leadership of William Walsh, Archbishop of Dublin since 1885, and the veteran nationalist prelate Thomas Croke, Archbishop of Cashel, had seemed capable of regaining the extraordinary position in political affairs which it had enjoyed before the rise of Parnell. The Church's seeming success in the struggle against Parnellism, however, was a hollow victory.[1] Dissatisfaction on the part of leading Antiparnellites — notably William O'Brien and John Dillon — with the role clergymen were playing in political affairs contributed to a rift within the Antiparnellite party itself. Moreover, although the Church could still function quite efficiently in politics on the diocese and parish level, the machinery of political decision-making for the whole hierarchy had suffered serious damage in the Parnell debacle. Walsh, by all odds the ablest man in

* This essay is a slightly revised version of a paper read at the 1968 ACIS Conference at Cortland, New York, May, 1968.

1 See Emmet Larkin, "Mounting the Counter-Attack: The Roman Catholic Hierarchy and the Destruction of Parnellism," *Review of Politics*, XXV (April 1963), 157–182, and "Launching the Counterattack: Part II of the Roman Catholic Hierarchy and the Destruction of Parnellism," *Review of Politics*, XXVIII (July 1966), 359–383.

the hierarchy, had failed to gain Rome's confidence and had been denied the cardinal's hat in favor of Michael Logue, the much less imaginative Archbishop of Armagh. Though Logue was incapable of leading the hierarchy with the skill and sensitivity Walsh had exhibited in the difficult years of Parnell's ascendancy, he spoke for a significant number of clergymen who hoped to sustain the extraordinary political influence derived from their predominant role among "priests and people" of the rural parish. These hopes led many of these clergymen to support T. M. Healy's faction of the Antiparnellites, for Healy, by championing the rights of constituencies at the expense of strong central leadership in the Party,[2] was offering the Church the opportunity to influence politics at the level at which it was best equipped to do so.

The reunification of the Party was a process which began with the founding of the United Irish League by William O'Brien in 1898 and ended with the general election of October, 1900, after which Healy remarked that O'Brien had created "two united Irish Parties — of which I am one."[3] As friends of Healy who stood against official U.I.L. candidates in a number of constituencies were usually backed by solid phalanxes of priests, the import of the League triumph was clear: Henceforward the voices of laymen would dominate the councils of the national movement. Some ecclesiastics — notably Logue, who continued for a decade to sponsor Healy's political claims — still hoped for the return of rather heavy clerical influence in politics. Most clergymen, however, came to accept Healy's fall from power, and the rise of John Redmond, the former Parnellite leader who had been elected to nominal leadership of the reunited Party. Redmond gradually assumed effective leadership and worked to balance clerical and anticlerical forces within the national movement. Throughout large areas of Ireland, particularly in the West, where League candidates had not faced Healyite or clerical opposition in the election, the ecclesiastical authorities had already come to terms with the new League before 1900.[4] Both

2 F. S. L. Lyons, *The Irish Parliamentary Party, 1890–1910*, Studies in Irish History, Vol. IV (London, 1951), pp. 42–44.

3 Quoted *ibid.*, p. 98.

4 The spread of the League and its relations with the ecclesiastical authorities can be followed in considerable detail in the police intelligence notes for 1898–1901 in the Public Record Office, London, C.O. 903/8, a source which must, of course, be used with caution.

before and after its anti-Healy activities of 1900 the League's primary function was agrarian protest. Most of the western bishops were able to foster ties between their clergy and local League branches while carefully guarding against the kind of attack from Rome which had so complicated their task a decade earlier. Moreover, clergymen found the U.I.L. program, which gave high priority to division of the grazing farms among land-hungry peasants, particularly attractive, for it seemed to promise an end to emigration to British and American cities where dangers to faith and morals were thought to be much greater than in rural Ireland.[5] Though the League agitation failed to obtain such massive land redistribution, it did win the 1903 Land Purchase Act. Genuine clerical sympathy with the League's program between 1898 and 1903, and the tradition of clerical involvement in agrarian protest to moderate excesses, fostered much healthier relations between clergymen and the Party than had been apparent during the angry clashes of the 1900 general election.

The support of many, perhaps most, individual churchmen for the Party, however, did not constitute support by the Church as an institution. Although Patrick O'Donnell, Bishop of Raphoe, had become a trustee of the Parliamentary Fund and actively involved himself in the Party's internal affairs, the hierarchy as a body did not immediately follow his lead. The lack of a general ecclesiastical policy toward the Party did not result from any fundamental disagreement with the Party's stated goal of Home Rule or its "constitutional" methods for achieving that goal. Except for John Healy, Archbishop of Tuam, who despite fairly advanced views on the land question was unenthusiastic over Home Rule,[6] all the bishops regarded themselves as nationalists. Given Logue's antipathy toward the Irish Party, however, only Archbishop Walsh was in a position to lead the hierarchy into a working relationship with the Party. Immediately after the reunion Walsh's

5 Rev. Joseph Canon Guinan, *The Soggarth Aroon*, ninth printing (Dublin, 1946), an autobiographical novel by an Irish priest who had returned to Ireland from a parish in England, provides a revealing picture of clerical attitudes toward emigration. The Church's position on the division of the grazing lands is set forth in the joint pastoral of the 1900 National Synod (*Freeman's Journal*, October 1, 1900) and a resolution of the hierarchy published in *The Tablet*, July 5, 1902.

6 Archbishop Healy once told a congregation they were not yet "fit for Home Rule." (*Irish Catholic*, February 27, 1909.)

relations with Redmond had become quite cordial,[7] and one might
have expected him to assume this role. By 1903, however, the Archbishop was devoting his best political energies to obtaining a Catholic
college within the University of Dublin as a settlement of the University question. Since few bishops shared Walsh's enthusiasm for such
close ties with Trinity College, his leadership capacity was severely
taxed simply to maintain the appearance of episcopal unity on this
issue.[8] He was in no position to undertake the additional task of
winning over such prelates as Logue to support for the Party.

At this stage, a long-standing feud between the Party's organization
in Belfast and the Belfast Catholic Association — a political machine
controlled by Henry Henry, Bishop of Down and Connor, and heartily
approved by Logue — was becoming particularly acrimonious.[9] Moreover, resentment against the vestiges of Protestant ascendancy in urban
economic life had produced an "All Ireland" Catholic Association
which, though it explicitly disavowed political ambitions, might well
have precipitated in other regions conflicts similar to that raging in
Belfast. Fortunately for the political health of the country, Walsh
unilaterally condemned the Catholic Association in his archdiocese in
January, 1904,[10] at a moment when the sectarian animosities it was
arousing threatened to undermine the delicate negotiations for his
University scheme. Although Walsh succeeded in crushing the "All Ireland" Catholic Association, his negotiations with the Government for
the University settlement miscarried — an event which actually worked
to the benefit of the Party. It was now clear that the Unionist Party,
which had been dangling a University settlement before the bishops
since the late 1880's in hopes of winning them away from the popular
movement, would not actually deliver the settlement. Feeling betrayed
in a matter to which they attached the highest importance, the hierarchy as a whole now recognized the need for a working relationship

7 See correspondence between Walsh and Redmond during 1900 and 1901
in the National Library of Ireland, Redmond Papers.

8 See, e.g., Bodleian Library, MacDonnell Papers, MS Eng. hist., c.
351/149-150, Walsh to Sir Antony MacDonnell, January 7, 1904.

9 The controversy can be followed in the Party organization's Belfast organ,
the *Northern Star*, and in the *Irish News and Belfast Morning News*, which
generally supported the Association. Logue's attitude is revealed in a speech
reported in the *Irish Catholic*, April 28, 1900.

10 *The Times*, January 18, 1904.

with the Irish Party. Moreover, during 1904 Party leaders improved their standing with the bishops by conspicuous opposition to proposals which might reduce clerical influence in Irish primary education.[11] Early in 1905, the Standing Committee of the hierarchy, in a long statement on the University question, called upon "the whole country" to "rally round our Parliamentary representatives, and give them the whole strength of the nation's support in their endeavor to secure ordinary civic rights for Irish Catholics in educational and all other matters." [12] This admonition was backed up by individual expressions of support from some of the most recalcitrant of the Party's episcopal enemies. Subscriptions to the Party Fund were received from Cardinal Logue and from two prelates long regarded as "Castle bishops" — Archbishop Healy and Edward Thomas O'Dwyer, Bishop of Limerick.[13] Bishop Henry still hoped to salvage his political machine, but Party leaders, backed by substantial clerical opinion in his own diocese, forced the Bishop virtually to liquidate the Belfast Catholic Association. What Bishop O'Donnell called "the flowing tide" [14] was running strongly in the Party's favor — a fact which was dramatized in April, 1905, when Redmond was cordially received at the Vatican and granted a two-hour private audience with the Pope.[15]

The promising share of ecclesiastical confidence achieved by the Party in 1905 was gradually eroded in the succeeding years by forces which were perhaps inherent in the fact that, although a land settlement had been enacted in 1903, the Party's other traditional object — Home Rule — did not convincingly enter the realm of possibility until about 1909. Serious attention to the Home Rule question almost inevitably drew the Party into a closer relationship with the only English Party which could not conceivably grant Home Rule — the Liberals. Though Liberals tended to be sympathetic to Irish national claims, they were, at this time, preoccupied with programs toward which Irish ecclesiastics were, at best, apathetic, and, at worst, implacably hostile.

---

11   See statement by the hierarchy in *Freeman's Journal*, June 23, 1904, and speech by Dillon at Ballaghadereen in *Freeman's Journal*, October 10, 1904.

12   *Ibid.*, January 18, 1905.

13   *Ibid.*, February 13, 1905; *The Tablet*, February 11, 1905; *Irish News and Belfast Morning News*, February 14, 1905.

14   Redmond Papers, Bishop O'Donnell to Redmond, February 17, 1905.

15   Denis Gwynn, *The Life of John Redmond* (London, 1932), pp. 112–113.

In particular, the Liberal Government which came to power late in 1905 was committed to rescinding the financial benefits which the Conservatives had conferred on denominational schools in England in 1902. During 1906 Redmond established a healthy working relationship with the sensitive and pragmatic Archbishop of Westminster, Francis Bourne. Despite efforts by Tory Catholic spokesmen to associate the Catholic Church with the House of Lords' intransigent position on the Liberals' Education Bill, Bourne privately sanctioned a course of action by which the Irish Party secured meaningful concessions on most points directly affecting Catholic interests.[16] The Party was thus able to avoid alienating the Liberals and vote with the Government to reject the wrecking amendments of the House of Lords. This action, however, elicited a most abusive public letter from Bishop O'Dwyer of Limerick, who used such terms as "canine servility" to describe the Party leaders' relationship to the Liberals.[17] The Party's defense of Catholic interests in earlier deliberations on the Bill had been, in his view, "an elaborate imposture," for now "the screw is put on, and the Irish Party, by a vote that will never be forgiven, rat upon themselves, and forswear their own professions." An immediate public defense by Bourne of Redmond's actions forestalled further episcopal attacks, but it did not dispel from O'Dwyer's mind the belief which had been growing since early 1906 that the Irish Party had sold its soul to English secularists. O'Dwyer's intemperate outburst is of interest not because he spoke for any large, well-organized body of clerical opinion — he had long been a maverick within the hierarchy — but because it foreshadowed the clerical component of a more general tendency to regard the Party as out of touch with the genuine currents of opinion in Catholic, nationalist Ireland in later years. In an ominous passage of his letter on the Education Bill, the Bishop of Limerick wrote, "If just now they [the Irish Party] could separate themselves from Mr. Birrell and Mr. Lloyd George and the rest of the Eighty

16 The Redmond Papers contain extensive correspondence with Bourne during 1906. See especially the statement accompanying Bourne to Redmond, December 4, 1906. For Bourne's own account of the critical events see Archives of the Archdiocese of Westminster, Bourne Papers, copy of Bourne to Duke of Norfolk, January 6, 1907 (item 12 in pink folder marked "II Duke of Norfolk on Education almost all 1907.") The Bourne Papers were used by kind permission of His Eminence Cardinal Heenan, Archbishop of Westminster.

17 *Freeman's Journal*, December 15, 1906.

Club, and come over to Ireland and inquire why the fine generation of young Irishmen that is growing up is turning away from them en masse for the Gaelic League, or Sinn Fein, or some other policy, they would learn some salutary truths."

Within a few months there was a striking illustration of the way in which religious and secular objections to the Liberal alliance might reinforce each other. Augustine Birrell, who after the defeat of the Education Bill had been transferred from the Presidency of the Board of Education to the Irish Chief Secretaryship, brought forward the Government's Irish Council Bill in May, 1907. To "the fine generation of young Irishmen" to which O'Dwyer had alluded, the Bill was bitterly disappointing because it did not offer full Home Rule. To churchmen, however, the Bill was positively menacing, for it seemed the culmination of official efforts begun several years earlier under the Tories to introduce more democratic control into the Irish educational system.[18] When a Nationalist convention, heavily attended by clergymen, rejected the Bill out of hand, Birrell of course dropped it. More significant, however, he reconsidered his entire political position in the light of two major defeats in the first eighteen months of his Cabinet career. He instituted new, generous financial policies toward Irish primary education,[19] which for several years had been deliberately starved for funds as part of efforts to force the reforms which the Church opposed. Moreover, he abandoned the idealistic University scheme which his Liberal predecessor, James Bryce, had revived with Walsh's concurrence, in favor of a more pragmatic scheme which accorded better with the desires of the average ecclesiastic.[20] Though Birrell's actions helped to stave off temporarily any widespread clerical

18 As there is no published account of the bitter controversy over educational reform in this period, one must rely chiefly on newspaper accounts. For this purpose, a collection of press cuttings kept by the Irish Education Office and now available at the Public Record Office of Ireland (call number: 2C-64) is particularly useful. For ecclesiastical response to the Irish Council Bill, see especially *Irish Catholic*, May 11, May 18, 1907; *Freeman's Journal*, May 13, May 17, May 25, 1907.

19 *Freeman's Journal*, November 23, 1907, June 24, July 3, July 28, 1908. *Parliamentary Papers*, 1919, Vol. XXI Cmd. 60, "Report of the Vice-Regal Committee of Inquiry into Primary Education in Ireland," I, 37.

20 Augustine Birrell, *Things Past Redress* (London, 1937), pp. 200–203. MacDonnell Papers, MS Eng. hist., c. 350/15-16, Birrell to Sir Antony MacDonnell, August 25, 1907.

reaction in Ireland against the Liberal Government, the Chief Secretary did not, indeed could not, prevent the corrosive effects of the Liberal alliance upon clerical opinion of the Irish Party. As the Universities Act of 1908 seemed more the product of long years of ecclesiastical agitation than the fruit of the Irish Party's policies, the Party had no great successes comparable to the 1903 Land Purchase Bill with which to deflect attention from its strategies at Westminster.

Moreover, after 1903, agrarian agitation was an inadequate means of maintaining popular enthusiasm behind the Party and its current leadership. The Party's organization was augmented by Joseph Devlin's capture of the Ancient Order of Hibernians — a benefit society based on feelings of Catholic solidarity similar to those manifested in the Catholic Associations. Though the A.O.H., whose primary strength lay in Ulster, tried to obtain ecclesiastical sanction, it was not so willing as the U.I.L. had been to accept clerical influence. By 1909 the Order became a standing source of friction between many Ulster churchmen and the Party.[21] The A.O.H. was only one element of a "Tammany Hall" image which the Party was acquiring in these years. The delicate negotiations for Home Rule, which now became the Party's principal occupation, necessitated the concentration of authority in relatively few hands so that Party leaders might deal as plenipotentiaries with Cabinet ministers. Shifts in Irish public opinion had to be taken into account, but efforts to encourage such shifts were understandably regarded by Party leaders as a species of treachery. Therefore, when William O'Brien left politics in 1903 over a disagreement with Dillon and then tried to return to public life in the following year by calling for a drastic revision of nationalist objectives and strategy, Redmond, Dillon and other Party leaders turned the organization he had done much to create against him. In doing so, they disregarded many fine points of stated League and Party procedure (as O'Brien himself had done several years earlier in driving Healy into isolation). Though they prevented O'Brien from becoming more than an annoyance in nationalist politics, in the process they forfeited the confidence of Archbishop Walsh, whose legalistic mind recoiled at the breaches of estab-

21 C.O. 904/117, 904/118, 904/119, *passim.* Emmet Larkin, *James Larkin, Irish Labour Leader, 1876–1947* (London, 1965), pp. 313–314.

lished procedures which were employed to fight "factionism." [22] From about 1906 Walsh became thoroughly disillusioned with the Party, ceased to contribute to its funds and tended to restrict his political activity to direct dealings with Government officials.

The strategies adopted by the Party in the wake of the 1903 Land Purchase Act — the Liberal alliance in England and "machine" politics in Ireland — paid dividends in the period from 1910 to 1914, when the Irish Party was able to obtain a Home Rule Act "on the statute book." During these years when Redmond held the balance of power at Westminster, those churchmen whose confidence in the Party was waning wisely refrained from striking at the man who was now in a more commanding position than Parnell had ever been. William O'Brien, despite his alliance with T. M. Healy, failed miserably to obtain for his "All-for-Ireland League" the clerical backing which he hoped would result from his opposition to the Liberal alliance and to the Ancient Order of Hibernians.[23] Nevertheless, the hierarchy as a body did not rally round the Party. When, in 1910, the Party tried to persuade bishops to double their usual subscriptions to the Party Fund as an indication of their renewed support in this critical period, Cardinal Logue observed with pleasure that only nine of some twenty-eight prelates made the gesture.[24] The lack of a coherent ecclesiastical policy toward the Party had certain advantages for Redmond and his colleagues. The firm friendship of two prelates — Dr. O'Donnell and Denis Kelly, the Bishop of Ross — together with the routine support of many others, protected them from any allegations that the Church opposed the Party. A closer working relationship with the hierarchy as a body might have aroused the suspicions of secularist members of the Liberal Party whose fears that Home Rule might really mean Rome Rule were a constant source of anxiety to Redmond and Dillon.

The need to allay English Protestant misgivings had led the Party leaders to enunciate a broad, tolerant concept of Irish nationality.[25] The

22 Redmond Papers, Walsh to Redmond, December 3, 1905. *Irish Catholic*, August 17, 1907.

23 See leading article in O'Brien's mouthpiece, the *Cork Free Press*, December 22, 1910.

24 National Library of Ireland, O'Brien Papers, MS 8556/3, T. M. Healy to O'Brien, May 13, 1910.

25 See Redmond's speech at Leeds convention of United Irish League of Great Britain, *Irish Catholic*, June 13, 1908.

independent Ireland for which they worked would be a nation of diverse creeds in which the tradition of Swift, Grattan, Davis and Parnell would be as highly revered as that of O'Neill, O'Connell, MacHale and Davitt. Though few nationalists actively engaged in politics would have taken issue with this definition of Ireland, a very different nationalist ideology was also in circulation in this period. For D. P. Moran, editor of *The Leader*, Ireland was above all a Catholic country in which Protestants would be made welcome, but only on Catholics' terms.[26] The Irish Ireland movement (a term coined by Moran) came to rest on this ideological base, toward which clergymen were rather more sympathetic than they were toward the Irish Party's concept of Irish nationality. To be sure, the Gaelic League, the most broadly-based component of Irish Ireland, loudly proclaimed its non-sectarian, non-political status, but from about 1899 the League moved in a direction which made most Protestant members distinctly uncomfortable and precipitated their withdrawal. Priests voted for the Irish Nationalist Party, but the nationalism that captured their affections was to be found not in the columns of *Hansard*, but in the columns of *The Leader*.[27] Despite occasional friction between Irish Ireland and the Church, the movement's leaders, especially Douglas Hyde and Eoin MacNeill, were well suited to the task of maintaining clerical confidence.[28] Moreover, after the settlement of the land question, language

26 See, e.g., *The Leader*, July 27, 1901: "If an English Catholic does not like to live in a Protestant environment let him emigrate; if a non-Catholic Nationalist Irishman does not like to live in a Catholic atmosphere let him turn Orangeman, become a disciple of Dr. Long, or otherwise give up all pretence to being an Irish Nationalist. . . . We can conceive, and we have full tolerance for a Pagan or non-Catholic Irishman, but he must recognise, and have respect for the potent facts that are bound up with Irish Nationality."

27 Arthur E. Clery, "The Gaelic League, 1893–1919," *Studies*, VIII (September, 1919), 401–403. See also John Horgan, *Parnell to Pearse: Some Recollections and Reflections* (Dublin, 1948), p. 307.

28 See, e.g., MacNeill's letter to P. H. Pearse on the latter's plans for St. Enda's School: National Library of Ireland, MacNeill Papers, MS 10,883, copy of MacNeill to Pearse, March 4, 1908. The MacNeill Papers were used by kind permission of Mrs. Eibhlin MacNeill Tierney. On Hyde's relations with the Catholic clergy, see Donal McCartney, "Hyde, D. P. Moran, and Irish Ireland," in *Leaders and Men of the Easter Rising: Dublin: 1916*, ed. F. X. Martin, o.s.a. (Ithaca, N.Y., 1967), p. 51.

revival had tended to replace agrarian agitation as the leading corporate secular activity of the rural parish with which the parish clergy naturally associated themselves. Irish Ireland probably benefited from this circumstance in much the same way that the Irish Party had earlier profited from clerical involvement in the land agitation. Nevertheless, though Irish Ireland did include advocates of the "Sinn Féin" policy of abstention from Parliament, the movement in general was not really unified behind any program for political action. A second nationalist force outside the Party's control, the Irish Republican Brotherhood, did possess a well-defined political program but, because of the Church's explicit condemnation, was likewise not a real threat to the Irish Party. Toward the end of 1913, however, the growing threat of Ulster Protestant resistance to Home Rule called forth the Irish Volunteer movement — the first stage in an ominous coalition of the two nationalist movements outside the Party's control.

When, in the spring of 1914, the Volunteer movement began to seem formidable, many churchmen, though not the Church as a whole, responded according to the traditional ecclesiastical pattern of aiding the forces of constitutionalism in the face of a "physical force" threat.[29] The outbreak of World War I in August and Redmond's declaration of support for the war effort, however, altered the entire political equation. To be sure, the effects of the alarmed ecclesiastical reaction to the Volunteer movement were still perceptible as late as the end of 1914, when the police reported that "the Catholic Clergy throughout the country in general supported the policy of the Irish Parliamentary Party in relation to the war and recruiting."[30] Initial clerical sympathy with the war effort, however, declined fairly rapidly, as was illustrated when it became clear, late in 1915, that not enough Irish priests were volunteering to serve as chaplains to the forces.[31] In contrast to the "general support" for the war effort noted at the end of 1914, a police memorandum prepared two weeks before the Easter Rising stated that

29 C.O. 904/93, June 1914.

30 Chief Secretary's Office, Dublin Castle, *Intelligence Notes 1913–16, Preserved in the State Paper Office*, ed. Breandán Mac Giolla Choille (Dublin, 1966), p. 119.

31 See Cardinal Logue's appeal for chaplains in *Irish Catholic*, November 6, 1915.

"the R. C. Clergy as *a body* are, on the whole lukewarm on the subject of recruiting." [32]

It was against this background of growing clerical disillusionment with the Party's policy that the coalition of nationalist forces outside the Party thrust itself once more into national attention on Easter Monday, 1916. As there had been two years earlier, there was some strong ecclesiastical reaction against the physical force movement, which, it was argued, had mounted a morally and theologically unjustifiable rebellion. Seven prelates spoke out against the Rising on the two Sundays following its suppression. The majority of the bishops remained silent, perhaps waiting to consult their colleagues at the regular June meeting of the hierarchy. Two of those who did speak urged leniency toward the rebels, while Michael Fogarty, Bishop of Killaloe, tempered his condemnation with a strong note of extenuation. [33] There was not even a hint of condemnation, however, in the reaction of Bishop O'Dwyer. In a reply (which was quickly published) to a request from General Maxwell that he discipline two priests implicated in Irish Volunteer activities, the Bishop of Limerick denounced the General in unmeasured terms. [34]

In view of the very obvious threat of violent revolution, one might have expected the hierarchy to act quickly and decisively to shore up the existing constitutional movement. By placing his views on record in such an extreme form, before the hierarchy had even had an opportunity to meet, however, O'Dwyer had gravely complicated the already difficult problem of reaching a consensus among the bishops. Moreover, in the weeks following the Rising, the Party itself further alienated another section of the hierarchy by agreeing to accept a "temporary" settlement providing immediate Home Rule for the twenty-six southern counties. Two years earlier Redmond had found a surprising willingness among the northern bishops to accept a similar scheme for "tem-

32 *Parliamentary Papers*, 1916, Vol. XI, Cd. 8311, Royal Commission on the Rebellion in Ireland, "Minutes of Evidence and Appendix of Documents," p. 58.

33 *Irish Catholic*, May 13, May 20, 1916. John H. Whyte, "1916 — Revolution and Religion," in *Leaders and Men*, ed. F. X. Martin, p. 221.

34 Mainchín Seoighe, "Limerick and the Easter Week Rising," in *Cuimnionn Luimneac* (Limerick, [1966]), pp. 43, 45.

porary" exclusion of the four counties with clear Unionist majorities.[35] The new scheme, however, aroused episcopal fears not only by excluding a sizable territory with a Catholic majority, but also by spelling out, rather more explicitly than the 1914 proposal, plans for separate government authorities to administer the excluded area. Such suggestions immediately raised the specter of a Protestant-controlled Education Office in Belfast which might be especially hostile to clerical control of Catholic schools.[36] Unable to obtain any support from the bishops of the area to be excluded, Redmond nevertheless mobilized the Party's organization to secure acceptance of the proposals by a convention of Nationalists from the six northern counties, only to have the entire scheme torpedoed by a split in the Unionist camp. The Party thereby forfeited much of their standing with the northern bishops and permanently alienated Charles McHugh, the politically active Bishop of Derry, who had previously been quite friendly toward the Party. Moreover, they lost a golden opportunity to regain the support of Logue, whose dislike of the Irish Party was matched only by his terror of armed revolution. The June meeting of the hierarchy produced no public resolutions of any moment. When the hierarchy met again in October, it reportedly debated a group of resolutions opposing conscription and the continuance of martial law in Ireland but endorsing "the constitutional, as opposed to the physical force, movement." The resolutions were dropped after a segment of the hierarchy, including McHugh, Logue, Walsh and O'Dwyer, objected that such action might imply "satisfaction with and approval of, the policy, and course of action, of the Irish Party." [37]

During the year following the Rising, which the press dubbed the "Sinn Féin Rebellion," a shift of opinion in the rebel's favor resulted in the revival of the term "Sinn Féin" to cover almost any species of nationalist disenchantment with the Irish Party. In September, 1916, O'Dwyer, deprecating the Party's faith in the Liberals, proclaimed himself a Sinn Féiner.[38] By-election victories by two "Sinn Féin" candidates

35 Redmond Papers, Devlin to Redmond, March 5, March 6, "Saturday" [March 7], 1914. D. Gwynn, *Redmond*, p. 270.

36 See letter from Bishop McHugh, *Irish Weekly Independent*, June 24, 1916.

37 *Ibid.*, October 28, 1916. O'Brien Papers, MS 8556/11, T. M. Healy to O'Brien, October 17, 1916. I am indebted to Mr. John Whyte for calling the item in the *Weekly Independent* to my attention.

38 *Letters of the Late Bishop O'Dwyer* (n.p., n.d.).

in early 1917 demonstrated not only the waning popularity of the Party, but the growing willingness of younger clergymen to associate themselves with the ill-defined new political force even to the point of defying their ecclesiastical superiors. The hierarchy desperately needed a clear policy for dealing with the rapidly-changing pattern of political events but was paralyzed by divisions which had their roots in pre-War episcopal attitudes. At their June, 1917, meeting, the hierarchy did agree upon a stopgap policy in the form of an "instruction" to their clergy, which, beyond some platitudes about vaguely-defined national dangers, only restated standing regulations governing political activity by priests.[39] Some bishops perhaps hoped that the Irish Convention, to which they nominated four delegates at this meeting, might solve their difficulties by agreeing upon an Irish settlement. O'Donnell, who in effect led the delegation, found scope in that assembly for his leadership talents which had long been thwarted within the hierarchy.[40] The episcopal delegates, by consistent opposition to any form of autonomy for Ulster which might lead to Protestant control of Catholic education in the North, foreclosed the only avenue of compromise in which the Ulster delegates were interested. The Bishop of Raphoe pressed for a report demanding much fuller fiscal autonomy for Ireland than had been contemplated in the 1914 Home Rule Act. When the Southern Unionists offered a compromise fiscal scheme, which Redmond was inclined to accept in hopes of forcing the Government's hand, O'Donnell dramatically broke with the party leader, who, his health rapidly failing, retired from the Convention's deliberations. The Bishop of Raphoe, who moved easily into leadership of the Nationalist delegates, had virtually abandoned hope of reaching an immediate settlement but did hope to commit the Party and its followers to an extreme enough position to render the constitutional movement a viable competitor in Irish politics once again. In this hope he was disappointed, for a number of Nationalist delegates refused to endorse the extreme position and voted with the Southern Unionists for a compromise program.

39 *Irish Catholic*, July 7, 1917.
40 The fullest general narrative of the Convention is [Sir Horace Plunkett], "The Irish Convention: Confidential Report to His Majesty the King by the Chairman," a copy of which is available in Plunkett's papers at the Horace Plunkett Foundation for Co-operative Studies, London. Other material is contained in *Parliamentary Papers*, 1918, Vol. X, Cd. 9019, "Report of the Pro-

The Convention adjourned in March, 1918, without providing the hierarchy with a new basis for formulating an effective policy. Despite several by-election defeats, Sinn Féin was becoming more and more formidable, and the June "instruction" had proved practically valueless in asserting episcopal control over the younger clergy, who were flocking to the Sinn Féin standard. "Sinn Féin," however, remained an ambiguous phenomenon. Alongside members of the I.R.B., it contained many young men whose political education in the Irish Ireland movement had by no means alienated them from the Church. Though popularly associated with rebellion — past and future — in the present it was engaged in the unexceptionably "constitutional" activity of winning elections and it could point to an ideology purporting to be non-violent. By early 1918 it was becoming quite easy for churchmen to persuade themselves that Sinn Féin was not the kind of revolutionary movement upon which the theology textbooks had taught them to pronounce anathema. Though many ecclesiastics, of course, continued to prefer the Irish Party, the Church at last had an opportunity to resolve its fundamental problem.

The occasion for seizing this opportunity was the Government proposal, in April, to extend conscription to Ireland. The episcopal Standing Committee immediately denounced the measure, and on the following Sunday the administrator of Cardinal Logue's cathedral parish announced a series of demonstrations against Conscription. A nationwide anti-conscription movement with episcopal blessing and very prominent clerical participation was quickly organized.[41] By choosing to act on the conscription issue, the bishops avoided the kind of difficulties which had resulted in the 1880's from British government overtures at Rome. The Holy See was, of course, not anxious to compromise its neutrality by intervention in such a delicate matter.[42] The anti-conscription movement embraced both Sinn Féin and the Irish Party — a fact which was crucial to the hierarchy's new-found consensus. From this time until the

ceedings of the Irish Convention"; Stephen Gwynn, *John Redmond's Last Years* (London, 1919); D. Gwynn, *Redmond*; and Horgan, *Parnell to Pearse.*

41 *Irish Catholic*, April 13, April 20, 1018. Warre B. Wells and N. Marlowe, *The Irish Convention and Sinn Fein* (New York, n.d.), pp. 147–151. Dorothy Macardle, *The Irish Republic*, 1st Am. ed., (New York, 1965), pp. 249–251.

42 See Public Record Office, London, F.O. 380/17/201, Balfour to Count de Salis, May 20, 1918; F.O. 380/18/272, Cardinal Gasparri to de Salis, July 9, 1918.

general election in December, churchmen tried in vain to bring about a more general union of nationalist forces. After de Valera had been received, along with Dillon, by the hierarchy at Maynooth, however, no one could place upon Sinn Féin the stigma of theological unacceptability which was associated with most forms of rebellion. By the time of the general election no bishop used terms stronger than "unwise" or "impracticable" to describe Sinn Féin, and in expressing his preference for the Irish Party's policy of "non-abstention from Parliament" Archbishop Gilmartin of Tuam noted, significantly, that there were "good Irishmen and good Catholics" on each side.[43] Only in a few eastern constituencies and in Dr. O'Donnell's diocese of Raphoe did Irish Party candidates receive concerted clerical support. Elsewhere a few priests clung to their old allegiance to the Party, but in general it was clear during the election that Sinn Féin had won the support or acquiescence of most of the clergy.

The inability of the hierarchy to formulate a coherent policy for dealing with nationalist politics in the wake of the Easter Rising was a chronic, rather than an acute, condition. Since the early 1890's, the outlines of such a policy had emerged only briefly, in 1905, and after the formation of the Liberal alliance the hierarchy was unable to unite behind leadership which might carry this or any alternative policy into effect. Both Walsh and Logue held strong political views which were out of harmony with those of the average prelate, and neither was prepared to turn over political leadership to O'Donnell, the only bishop whose practical abilities rivaled those of Walsh. Lacking a working relationship with the Party and paralyzed by the dissent of a handful of prelates, therefore, the hierarchy did nothing in 1916 rather than act upon their only other real option — some form of condemnation of violent revolution. By thwarting united action in 1916, the episcopal dissidents were giving the revolutionary movement time to reconstruct and redefine itself in such a way that by 1918 ecclesiastics had the additional option of treating it as a constitutional movement. The primary achievement of the Church in this period, therefore, was not a decisive redirection of the course of political events such as had been attempted in 1891. By forcing the hierarchy to limit its goals, a minority of the bishops was compelling the Church to accept a more realistic role than

43 *Irish Independent*, November 28, 1918.

that which it had tried to play in the early 1890's. The achievements gained by accepting this role in 1918 were far from insubstantial. By acting as it did, the Church entered the revolutionary period, 1919–1923, passively, if not actively, associated with the revolutionary cause. If this had not been the case, the Church might well have suffered very serious repercussions in post-revolutionary Ireland. The bishops had taken a strong position from which to preserve the Church's influence in Irish society.

10

J.S. MILL AND THE IRISH QUESTION:
REFORM, AND THE INTEGRITY OF THE EMPIRE,
1865-1870

E.D. STEELE

I

THE first part of this study of Mill sought to show how much less radical he was on the subject of Irish land reform than is often supposed.[1] In the earlier editions of the *Principles of Political Economy* from 1848 to 1857 there were passages which constituted a terrible indictment of landlordism, and insisted on the need for legislation to convert the tenant farmers into joint owners of their holdings: but in another passage this harsh criticism was substantially withdrawn, and the demand for fixity of tenure effectively retracted. Although they continued to reproduce the criticism and the call for a drastic measure, the editions of 1862 and 1865 were more moderate still in their conclusions on Irish land. With the progress of the changes in the economy and society set in motion by the Great Famine, Mill became more strongly convinced that the country should be left to evolve slowly under the existing law of tenure, only slightly amended. One cannot imagine Mill saying, 'tenant-right...is equivalent to landlords' wrong':[2] but he and Palmerston were none the less in nearly complete agreement by 1865 on the degree of laissez-faire that was desirable in Ireland. For all his strictures upon aristocratic misgovernment and middle-class prejudice, Mill was too warm an admirer of British institutions to want to undermine their social basis over a wide area of the United Kingdom. The second part of this study deals with his action and his motives, in briefly advocating, without any reservations this time, the revolutionary land legislation from which he had always previously shrunk, despite his brave words written for the earlier editions of the *Principles*.

In October 1865 Mill was returned to Parliament for Westminster, the most notable radical success of that general election. Between then and the appearance of *England and Ireland* in 1868, his thinking on Irish land underwent little change, so that people were quite unprepared for the shock he administered in the pamphlet. At the same time he evinced a degree of insight into the nature of Irish unrest which reflected events since he wrote *Considerations on Representative Government* (1861). These three years, 1865-8, saw the Fenians' greatest activity in Ireland and in Britain, and the passing of the Second Reform Bill. Parliamentary reform and the popular feeling it generated aroused hopes among militant radicals of eroding the power of the ruling

---

[1] This paragraph is a summary of the article 'J. S. Mill and the Irish Question: The Principles of Political Economy, 1848–1865' in *Historical Journal*, xii (1969).

[2] Lord Palmerston in *House of Commons Debates*, 27 February 1865.

landed class in other ways. These hopes did not take any very definite shape, but they contributed to the profound uneasiness felt by many of the propertied classes, and not merely by the landed, when they contemplated their possible future under the new dispensation. Fenianism was really a revolutionary movement, with the elimination of alien landlords high among its objectives. There existed a genuine fear that the Fenians and British working-class radicalism were associated in planning to overthrow the established order in all its aspects.[3] There was, more reasonably, anxiety lest the growing political consciousness of the lower classes should be turned against the landlords of Britain by their sympathy with the grievances of the Irish tenantry, for which the Fenian outbreak had secured increased publicity.[4] Emboldened by the current optimism of progressives, Mill sought to exploit these apprehensions when he wrote *England and Ireland*.

He told J. E. Cairnes at the beginning of 1866 that he was 'disposed' to support a measure securing compensation to Irish tenants for their improvements, which should be drawn to give them a very wide claim against the landlords.[5] In the sixth edition of the *Principles* he had not troubled to consider what kind of basis such legislation ought to have. That he was being forced to revise his outlook on the Irish question emerged very clearly a few weeks later. His speech of February in the House of Commons on the suspension of Habeas Corpus in Ireland might fairly have been regarded as self-criticism, although it certainly did not have that sound. 'We were present', said Mill, 'at the collapsing of a great delusion. England had for a considerable number of years been flattering itself that the Irish people had come to their senses; that they had got Catholic Emancipation and the Incumbered Estates Bill, which were the only things they could possibly want; and had become aware that a nation could not have anything to complain of when it was under such beneficent rulers...'[6] He would not say so, but he had shared, almost to the full, the superficiality and complacency which he was now censuring. Not only in the latest edition of the *Principles*; the *Considerations on Representative Government* contained a passage at which the remarks just quoted might have been directly aimed.

No Irishman [he had written in 1861] is now less free than an Anglo-Saxon, nor has a less share of every benefit either to his country or to his individual fortunes, than if he were sprung from any other portion of the British dominions... There is now

---

[3] An example of this apprehension in official circles: Lord Strathnairn, Commander of the Forces in Ireland, discussed the possibility of such an alliance in a letter to the Duke of Cambridge, C.-in-C., Rose Papers (B.M. Add. MSS. 42824), 20 October 1867.

[4] Even before Fenianism captured the attention of this country, W. E. Forster, one of the leading representatives of a more advanced radicalism than John Bright's, issued a warning that the continued denial of agrarian reform to Ireland would have the effect of turning public opinion against the position of the landed class in England. *House of Commons Debates*, 31 March 1865.

[5] Mill–Taylor Collection, British Library of Political and Economic Science, (vol. LV), Mill to Cairnes, 6 January 1866.　　　　[6] *House of Commons Debates*, 17 February 1866.

next to nothing, except the memory of the past, and the difference in the predominant religion, to keep apart [the] two races...The consciousness of being at last treated not only with equal justice but with equal consideration, is making such rapid way in the Irish nation, as to be wearing off all feelings that could make them insensible to the benefits which...must necessarily derive from being fellow-citizens...[7]

While Mill derided the attitude towards Ireland which had seldom received such confident expression as in these words of his, he had, then and for some time afterwards, nothing really constructive to offer in its place. He told the House that foreign opinion would from now on see Ireland as restrained by 'brute force'. The description of British methods elicited cries of disapproval from Members, and he at once denied that he himself believed it to be justified. Next, however, he compared Great Britain and Ireland to the perpetrator and subject, respectively, of a flogging. The punishment might occasionally be necessary but he asserted that 'when any man... needed the instrument of flogging to maintain his authority—that man deserved flogging as much as any of those who were flogged by his orders'. The severity of this was weakened by his immediately adding that he would not vote against the Bill before the House, since the government had no alternative open to it, and by his acquitting ministers of responsibility not only for 'the misgovernment of centuries' but also 'the neglect of half a century' which he had newly discovered. He ended with the hope that when the Fenian threat had been overcome, '"We don't do it in England"' would not counter every suggestion of reform for Ireland.[8]

It was soon evident how little Mill had to suggest. His hostility to the educational concessions wanted by the Catholic Church in Ireland was determined. In May he explained his conception of agrarian policy in this challenging situation when speaking on the extremely mild tenants' compensation bill devised by the second Russell ministry, which did not get beyond the second reading. It was, in effect, a permissive measure: to reverse, prospectively, and in the absence of written agreement to the contrary, the presumption of law as to the property in improvements. No ministerial land bill since the modest and half-hearted series commenced in 1845 had been quite so careful of landlord rights, and quite so patently an empty gesture.[9] Mill nevertheless greeted it with resounding praise: 'It was in an auspicious hour for the futurity of Ireland, and of the Empire of which Ireland is so important a part, that a British Administration has introduced this Bill...nothing... any Government has yet done...not even Catholic Emancipation itself—has shown so true a comprehension of Ireland's needs...'

Coming from Mill, not from some hanger-on of the ministry's, this was

---

[7] J. S. Mill, *Considerations on Representative Government*, Everyman's Library edn. (1954), p. 365; hereafter cited as *Considerations*.

[8] *House of Commons Debates*, 17 February 1866.

[9] See the comments of J. E. C.[airnes] in *The Economist*, 12 May 1866, 'The Irish Land Bill'.

preposterous; except on the assumption that the bill was the precursor of a stronger measure. Though at first his arguments did appear to point in that direction, he made no such assumption. The speech seemed positively to exclude further legislation in the tenant's interest. Mill reminded the House of what was familiar to students of the *Principles*, that Ireland in respect of her small farms and her popular desire for a more permanent tenure conformed to the practice and opinion of those countries where the occupier was neither a serf nor a proprietor in the fullest sense; while the like of Britain's land system did not prevail in any other country. 'If we are making rules for the common case,' he asked, 'is it reasonable to draw our precedents from the exceptional one?' Fixity of tenure, he insisted, was indispensable if the Irish tenant-farmers were to prosper. Then he suddenly changed the tenor of his speech; continuing: 'Do I therefore ask you to establish...fixity of tenure as the rule...in Ireland? Certainly not. It is perhaps a sufficient reason that I know you will not do it; but I am also aware that what may be very wholesome when it grows up as a custom...would not necessarily have the same success if, without ever having existed as a custom, it were...enforced as a law.' Mill told Members that he regarded their wish to introduce the English structure of landholding in Ireland as 'very disputable' but added: 'I accept this is the thing you have got to do, and assuming it to be desirable, I ask how is it to be brought about?'.

There was only one way of proceeding: to help the most enterprising of Ireland's small tenants to grow into substantial farmers of the British type. 'You cannot evict a whole nation,' he commented, 'the country would be too hot to hold you and your new tenants if you attempted it.' The bill under consideration would give the tenants a vested interest in betterment, fostering the mutual confidence between landlord and tenant that was the natural thing in Britain but was conspicuously absent in Ireland. Mill had more to say about this lack of confidence. On the one hand, he said that 'one-half of the landlords, or some other proportion of them do not deserve confidence'. On the other hand, he remarked that the fact of large savings by Irish tenant-farmers in recent years did something to clear their landlords of the charge of extortion levelled against them. He conceded that at any rate 'a much greater number...than has often been supposed are neither greedy nor grasping'. The bill's machinery of adjudication upon disputed cases would enable trust to form between the two classes. Part of the speech was devoted to refuting the complaint that transfer of property in improvements was a violation of right. The theory of rights over land set out in the *Principles* was restated. Stressing the bill's very great moderation, its acceptability to the Irish Liberal M.P.s who spoke for the tenantry, and its value as an earnest of Britain's goodwill; he concluded by exhorting the House to rise above its ingrained prejudice against touching property.[10]

[10] *House of Commons Debates*, 17 May 1866.

Despite the tone of much of it, the aspersions it cast on the landlords, and its recognition of peasant discontent, Mill's speech did not really represent any significant advance on the *Principles* of 1865, either in his understanding of the Irish land question or in his conclusions about the policy which he thought Britain should pursue with regard to it. The fact that there were many tenants whom he anticipated would become large farmers with only the minimal help, and that chiefly psychological, afforded by the government's land bill, showed that he believed the 'misery' of which he had spoken to be far from universal, and testified to his underlying confidence in the British land system as a goal, on a realistic plane, of economic and social progress. Like most of his countrymen, Mill remained blind to the conviction of the Irish tenant that he was something more than a tenant. The speech made little impression on the House. The press, which saw the bill for what it was, deemed his theoretical excursion on the nature and scope of property-rights an unusual and interesting contribution to the debate in the Commons, but not one that improved the measure's unfavourable prospects.[11]

What is significant about this speech is that it showed no diminution of the new-found awareness of Irish nationality which Mill had displayed when speaking on the suspension of Habeas Corpus. In his opening words of extravagant commendation for the mildest of government land bills, he had referred to the importance of Ireland in the Empire. That reference explains the hyperbole. Mill was most anxious that Parliament should demonstrate to the Irish people its readiness 'to legislate... according to Irish exigencies and no longer according to English routine'.[12] To Mill, as to other politicians—he acknowledged the lead recently given by Gladstone—this was the condition of Anglo-Irish reconciliation. The hollowness of the bill did not matter: the legislative gesture was everything. Next year his concern that government should have the intelligence to be tender of Irish sentiment joined with his genuine sympathy for brave and sincere men when he was prominent among those who pressed for clemency to captured Fenians. He made great and successful public efforts to prevent in the case of the leaders of the abortive rising of 1867, what he called in a letter to Cairnes 'the gross blunder as well as crime of shedding the blood of Fenian prisoners'.[13] He spoke of them to a packed meeting on Parliamentary reform—not an audience to appreciate the reservation in his careful wording—as 'men who have been driven desperate by the continuance of what they think mis-government...'.[14] Not long afterwards, he was at pains to emphasize in the House of Commons that he considered the Fenians' activities 'greatly culpable, because... contrary to the general interests of society and of their country'. A statement worthy of

[11] E.g. the comments of the *Saturday Review*, 26 May 1866, 'The Irish Tenure Bill'.
[12] *House of Commons Debates*, 17 May 1866.
[13] Mill–Taylor Collection (vol. LV), Mill to Cairnes, 26 May 1867; M. St J. Packe, *The Life of John Stuart Mill* (London, 1954), pp. 462–4.
[14] Ibid. pp. 463–4.

the most fervent British patriot, typical of much less sophisticated minds in its identification of the national cause with what was best for humanity. He yet pleaded that the Fenians had shown themselves 'certainly not...likely to be guilty of ordinary crime and vice—rather...capable of heroic actions and lofty virtue'.[15]

However myopic he had once been, Mill now took Irish nationalism very seriously indeed. By contrast, his contemporaries were still widely prone to think of it as a menace, no doubt, but wanting the moral and political force of Continental nationalism. They were even capable of believing the Fenians to be adventurers and criminals who had suborned the poorest and least responsible elements of the population. Mill's defence of the revolutionaries from these imputations bespoke his grasp of Britain's difficulty in Ireland. It was only a matter of time before he perceived that the struggle between landlord and tenant was not just something which the nationalists could exploit but an integral part, perhaps the most important part, of popular resistance to the fusion of the two countries. The British press was, of course, generally hostile to Irish aspirations but gave them a great deal of publicity. The land question received a lot of attention but its real character did not emerge at all clearly from the protracted discussion which was severely limited by the ignorance of Irish realities and by the editorial tendency to pass over fixity of tenure as an impossibility, and concentrate on subsidiary issues like compensation for tenants' improvements and the substitution of written contracts for parole tenancies.[16] While the Irish peasants had considerable sympathy for Fenianism, they displayed very little inclination to take up arms. They responded in their own way to the excitement stirred up by the Fenians. Like the Continental peasants in 1848, they saw a chance of furthering their traditional hope, but did not want to fight for the abstractions of the revolutionaries. 'They are not loyal—but they are not Fenians...They...care little for anything but the land', wrote Lord Naas, Irish secretary in the Derby–Disraeli ministry.[17] The demand for fixity of tenure in one form or another was voiced more loudly than for many years past, encouraged by the conciliatory postures of the outgoing Liberal cabinet and viceroy. 'Fortescue's Land Bill and Kimberley's last speech have done an enormous amount of mischief'—Naas reported soon after taking office 'and even the most respectable among the farming class openly avow that tenant Compensation is all humbug, and 31 years' leases at low rents are what they must extract from the landlords'.[18] The twofold danger was that the agrarian unrest would grow

---

[15] *House of Commons Debates*, 14 June 1867.

[16] Underlying this tendency was the assumption voiced by *The Times*, 1 May 1867: '...the Englishman's view of the question is that which must prevail in the end, whatever temporary and partial expedients may be applied'.

[17] Mayo Papers, National Library of Ireland (MS 11, 144), Naas to Lord Derby, 23 December 1866.

[18] Derby Papers, Cnrist Church, Oxford (Box 155/3), Naas to Lord Derby, 15 August 1866.

in the unsettled atmosphere of Ireland; and that the Fenians would succeed where they had hitherto failed in harnessing this agitation to theirs. In Britain *The Spectator*, a journal which admired Mill and reflected his influence, had for some time been arguing the political case for fixity of tenure on the analogy of British India, maintaining that 'now in Ireland, as a hundred years ago in Bengal, the secret of order will be found in a Perpetual Settlement'.[19] The paper's championship of this policy was well known, and Mill must have been aware that he was following in its footsteps when he wrote *England and Ireland*. Thomas Hughes, another of the tiny band of advanced radical M.P.s, echoed *The Spectator* and anticipated Mill in a speech of December 1867 which elicited a sharply critical reaction. For Hughes was a respected figure, social reformer and philanthropist as well as author of an influential classic of moralizing fiction; a man whose pronouncements carried more weight than did those of *The Spectator* with its rather consciously literary and intellectual appeal.[20]

Mill wrote his pamphlet in the last months of 1867. He must have had in mind the Fenians' latest stroke and its aftermath. In September a group effected the audacious rescue of two captured leaders in the heart of Manchester. The incident, the trial of some of the rescuers, and the execution of three of them for killing one of the liberated men's police escort, had profound repercussions in Ireland where those hanged were remembered as the 'Manchester Martyrs'. It was demonstrated how very far Fenianism was from having suffered a fatal blow when its botched rising evoked little popular response and collapsed in February and March of that year. As Mill had foreseen earlier in the summer, the acquisition of political martyrs gave the movement fresh impetus. It was against this background that he composed his pamphlet. Before he had finished it over twenty people died in December, when the Fenians tried to blow up the wall of Clerkenwell Gaol, in a thickly populated district of London, in a bid to free one of their chiefs. There was a tremendous outburst of alarm and rage from all classes in Britain.[21] Mill related in his *Autobiography*, composed in the 1870s, that when he wrote, 'there were few who did not feel that if there was still any chance of reconciling Ireland to the British connexion, it could only be by the adoption of much more thorough reforms in the territorial and social relations of the country than had yet been contemplated'.[22] Manchester and Clerkenwell had a great

[19] The *Spectator*, 9 March 1867, 'The Insurrection in Ireland'.

[20] There is a short study of Hughes in Asa Briggs, *Victorian People* (London, 1954), ch. vi; it makes no reference to this speech, which attracted considerable notice. Hughes received a notable rebuke from *The Times*, 23 December 1867.

[21] *Papers relating to Foreign Affairs accompanying the Annual Message of the President to Congress*, 1868, pt. 1, p. 130. Charles Francis Adams, U.S. Minister in Great Britain, to William H. Seward, Secretary of State, 24 December 1867. Adams observed: 'It may be doubted whether at any time since the discovery of the scheme of Guy Fawkes there has been so much of panic spread...throughout this community as at this time...I think it would now be very unsafe for Irishmen to attempt to hold a meeting for any purpose in any great town in England.'

[22] J. S. Mill, *Autobiography*, World's Classics edn. (1955), p. 249.

deal to do with that mood; which he exaggerated, however, both at the time and in retrospect. Concessions to Ireland had always run up against the difficulty that they were not popular in this country, although politicians and newspapers might agree that they were necessary and just. This general feeling was naturally intensified for some little while by the Fenians' spectacular violence in their midst. Two months after the Clerkenwell explosion was not the most auspicious moment for Mill to launch his pamphlet, and in it to remind the public that 'Repressed by force in Ireland...the rebellion visits us in our own homes, scattering death among those who have given no provocation but that of being English-born'.[23]

Mill linked the absolute necessity of concession to Ireland with the political situation in Britain, as he pictured it, created by and to be anticipated from the future development of the changes of the last three years. During the struggle over Parliamentary reform some nervous and resentful conservatives had accused him of being associated with the Reform League in its extreme courses, real and supposed: whereas in fact he had exercised a restraining influence on that body at a critical juncture, and had maintained a distinctive position throughout.[24] His enthusiasm for the extension of the franchise was offset by insistence that the eventual realization of universal suffrage, of which he termed himself 'a strenuous advocate', must be accompanied by checks on the dominance of the majority that were more popular with his political opponents than with other advanced radicals.[25] He thus adhered to the line he had taken in his *Thoughts on Parliamentary Reform* of 1859 and in the *Considerations on Representative Government*. The severest censures he had attracted since entering Parliament resulted from his leading part in the attempt to secure the conviction of E. J. Eyre in the English courts for his actions as Governor of Jamaica in putting down the Negro rebellion of 1865 on the island. Too much has perhaps been made of this episode by those who would see Mill in their own image. His condemnation of Governor Eyre was not a condemnation of empire, but of its abuse. A good many people who were not radicals at all agreed with the substance of the charges brought by Mill and the Jamaica Committee against Eyre, while they did not think the circumstances justified a criminal prosecution.[26]

It came as a rude shock when Mill declared that 'the rising power in our affairs, the democracy of Great Britain' would not tolerate an Irish policy in

---

[23] J. S. Mill, *England and Ireland* (London, 1868), p. 6.

[24] M. St J. Packe, op. cit. pp. 457–62.

[25] See the speeches of Mill and Sir John Pakington in *House of Commons Debates*, 31 May 1866.

[26] H. S. R. Elliot (ed.), *The Letters of John Stuart Mill*, 2 vols (London, 1910); II, 68, Mill to David Urquhart, 4 October 1866: '...you see', he wrote, 'that I am not...standing up for the negroes, or for liberty, deeply as both are interested in the subject—but for the first necessity of human society, law'. B. Semmel, *The Governor Eyre Controversy* (London, 1962), pp. 178–9 eulogizes 'John Stuart Mill and his comrades' from the standpoint of a mid-twentieth-century liberal.

which steps to preserve the Union were negative in character and failed to include 'revolutionary measures' that struck at the roots of the Ascendancy. He called for the disestablishment of the Anglican Church in Ireland, towards which the Liberal party was, of course, already moving. Strong though this was, it paled beside the scope and the language of his demand for legislation against what he described as 'great-landlordism' in that country.[27] It was the period when even Bright's permissive land purchase scheme seemed fraught with hidden menace to worried landlords; when one sensible and liberal Whig politician, no alarmist, could write to another: 'We are entering...on a new and unquiet era of politics which will require very wary walking, especially for those who like ourselves are liberals by conviction, and large landowners ...'[28] Mill tried to take advantage of this current uneasiness among the propertied, and not merely the landed, classes; threatening them with the following dire prospect if they did not reform the Irish land system on Indian lines: 'An age when delegates of working-men meet in European Congresses to concert united action for the interests of labour, is not one in which labourers will cut down labourers at other people's bidding. The time is come when the democracy of one country will join...with the democracy of another, rather than back their own ruling authorities in putting it down.'[29] The reaction to this warning was powerful, if it was not what Mill had hoped. Taking the pamphlet in the round Mill never wrote anything so reckless of criticism, and so vulnerable to it.

II

Mill was possibly at his most eloquent in *England and Ireland*. He was clearly conscious of the pressure of events and was straining what has unkindly been called his 'power-loom prose',[30] to make an impact, to create a vivid awareness of the gravity of the Irish question, and to impart his strong conviction that there was not too much time left for Britain to come to terms with a people whom she had severely oppressed not so long ago and had persisted in misunderstanding and neglecting. Fervent and vigorous beyond his wont, Mill sacrificed candour and accuracy to the determination to make his case. He generalized as boldly as he had ever done, but without his usual care to qualify and balance the positive statement. The objections which he disposed of in these pages received cavalier treatment; others were simply not mentioned. All are weaknesses which should not be permitted to obscure the pamphlet's merits. He brought out the relationship between the political and agrarian

[27] Mill, *England and Ireland*, pp. 25, 43–4, 21.

[28] The Duke of Argyll told Gladstone in the autumn of 1866 that 'Bright's speeches are frightening all Whiggish Liberals into absolute Toryism', Gladstone Papers (B.M. Add. MSS 44100), Argyll to Gladstone, 4 November 1866; Ripon Papers (B.M. Add. MSS 43522), Lord de Grey to Lord Kimberley, 25 November 1867.

[29] Mill, *England and Ireland*, p. 26. The 'Congresses' are, of course, those of the First International.

[30] B. Willey, *Nineteenth Century Studies* (London, 1949), p. 161.

aspects of the Irish question, which was as little understood by the British public as it had been by Mill himself for many years. He set forth an effective indictment, in which there was much truth, of the lack of justice and imagination in Britain's treatment of a peasant society united with one of a very different character. Although the international odium and danger which Fenianism had revived and extended for this country had soon been keenly felt, Mill's minatory picture of the liabilities of our behaviour towards Ireland made a definite impression. These merits, however, are better appreciated today than they were by Mill's contemporaries. The fact of Irish national consciousness was conveyed too strongly to suit his avowed purpose. He sounded excessively sympathetic when portraying the feelings of the disaffected. The tone of *England and Ireland*, and the extraordinarily arrogant references to the stupidity as well as the perils of opposing its demands, militated effectively against its chances of securing a favourable reception.

It was thus on both political and economic grounds that Mill now argued for converting the Irish tenant into the substantial owner of his holding. The political reasons he adduced have already been mentioned and will be further discussed below. Consideration of the economic reasons he found to justify this tremendous change is not less important, and certainly not less interesting, for an assessment of Mill.

Three years earlier, in the last edition to date of the *Principles*, Mill had given an optimistic account of the progress and prospects of the Irish farmer, while expressing reservations about the condition of the landless labourer, and he had stated quite plainly that drastic land reform was no longer needed.[31] To judge from the pamphlet, he might never have written thus. He did not recant his opinions on these or any other matters on which he had before pronounced in a different sense: he simply disregarded them. '...In Ireland,' he now wrote, 'where the well-being of the whole population depends on the terms on which they are permitted to occupy the land, those terms are the very worst in Europe.' The context makes it clear that he was not merely referring to the legal insecurity of tenancy-at-will, with few parallels on the Continent. He was insisting that the state of rural Ireland at the time of writing fully demonstrated the validity of his dictum, which hitherto he had largely qualified away when applying it to Ireland, that where peasant farmers did not enjoy fixity of tenure or fixed rents, 'the social economy resulting is intolerable'. Not only did he assert that 'an average Irish landlord' entirely neglected to make any improvements on the estate; he alleged, 'so many landlords even of high rank' felt no shame in taking for themselves tenants' improvements or the value of them, by evicting or raising rents, that 'it is evident their compeers do not think it at all disgraceful'.[32] Here, by way of

---

[31] J. S. Mill, *Principles of Political Economy*, variorum edn. forming vols. II and III of the *Collected Works of John Stuart Mill* (Toronto, 1963–); II, 331–6; hereafter cited as *Works*, II or III.   [32] Mill, *England and Ireland*, pp. 14–20; quotations from pp. 15, 19, 17–18.

proof, he gave one spectacular example of landlord greed and lack of scruple; one that was to elicit a circumstantial rejoinder.[33] It was the only specific instance quoted of the tyranny ascribed to a whole class. An active and unwearying tyranny: for what else were Mill's readers to understand by this statement about the practical working of tenancy-at-will in Ireland? '...The bulk of a population dependent wholly on the land, cannot look forward with confidence to a single year's occupation of it...' Mill laid great stress on an obvious point, here strained for maximum effect: the weakness of an almost purely agricultural population, wthout any alternative means of getting a living at home, in bargaining with those in whose hands the ownership of land was heavily concentrated. The point was, of course, a valid one, but more impressive if it was understood, as he intended it should be, that the landlords in general exploited their advantage ruthlessly. Well might he then inquire: '...to what sympathy or consideration are those entitled who avail themselves of a bad law to perpetrate what is morally robbery?'.[34]

It may bear repetition that Mill was describing contemporary reality: he seemed oblivious of what he had written in 1862 and 1865, and had said in Parliament in 1866; the amelioration Ireland had experienced since the Famine was, apparently, a delusion. If Mill had then erred on the side of optimism about the Irish land system, this description of the Irish tenant's lot was absurdly overdrawn. How far did he believe in it himself? The question should be asked, and an answer will be propounded later.

When he put forward his remedy for the peasantry's melancholy condition, Mill could not overlook the familiar arguments against it and he dealt with them in a summary, not to say contemptuous fashion. They were swept aside with the words: 'Those who still believe that small peasant properties are either detrimental to agriculture or conducive to over-population, are discreditably behind the state of knowledge on the subject.' At the same time he fell into an oblique admission that the lot of the Irish peasant *had* improved considerably over the last twenty years. He was defending himself against the objection that the peasant was too wretched, too deprived, not to abuse the benefits of fixity of tenure. The relevant passage is too long to quote, but it opened with the revealing statement: 'All prognostics of failure drawn from the state of things preceding the famine are simply futile'.

The lessons of political economy in this context were reinforced by an appeal, for the first time in all Mill had written and said about Irish land, to the notions of property in land cherished by the peasantry, which were quite different from those embodied in the laws of the United Kingdom. In Britain, he conceded with perceptible reluctance, the absolute ownership vested in the landlord had not proved unacceptable to the people—'The traditions and

[33] Ibid. pp. 18–19 and footnote to p. 18; for the rejoinder by Viscount Lifford, an Irish landowner, see *House of Lords Debates*, 12 March 1868.
[34] Ibid. pp. 16–19; quotations from pp. 16, 19.

recollections of native Irish society', he wrote, more or less accurately, 'are wholly the contrary way...In the moral feelings of the Irish...the right to hold the land goes, as it did in the beginning, with the right to till it.' The agrarian secret societies of Ireland, he rightly insisted, were seeking to defend, not to violate, property. He invoked the British experience in ruling India, where they had risen above 'insular prejudices' and 'reconciled themselves to the idea that their business was not to sweep away the rights they found established...but...to protect...and use them as a starting point for... steps in improvement'. Although he remarked that it was one to embarrass 'our historical Conservatives', Mill did not, however, develop this line of argument. It was left to an Anglo-Indian admirer of his to take it further in the following years. These few lines were nevertheless the most perceptive, and the most prescient, in *England and Ireland*.[35]

Mill proposed a statutory commission with compulsory powers, charged to act expeditiously and commute present rents for fair and fixed levels and invest every tenant with a permanent right of occupancy, transferable to his heirs and assignees. Landlords should have the option of receiving the official rent directly from the tenant or in the form of interest on government bonds.[36]

Nothing short of this agrarian upheaval would serve to counter the attractions of revolutionary nationalism to the Irish; to satisfy the conscience of British democracy; and to meet the threat to the international security of this country from disaffection in Ireland. The last was an aspect of his subject which at the time excited grave apprehension. 'Neither Europe nor America would now bear the sight of a Poland across the Irish Channel.' Mill thus gave exaggerated expression to a danger of which Englishmen with a knowledge of the politics of power were uncomfortably aware. The Fenians had as one of their chief aims the enlistment of American sympathies through the agitation of the large Irish community in the United States. On the Continent, liberals and reactionaries were both far more inclined to take Ireland's part than England's. Mill did not believe in amity between the nations, as a matter of fact, and he asserted that his country with its scattered possessions and heavy dependence on overseas trade could only hold down a rebellious Ireland 'until the many enemies of British prosperity had time to complicate the situation by a foreign war'.[37]

In the *Autobiography* Mill described this pamphlet as written firstly to vindicate the Union and only secondly to make known his scheme of land reform.[38] The first of these aims was uncontroversial, and contemporaries fastened on the second. Nor has much notice been given since to the longest part of the pamphlet, setting out his arguments for the Union. They were a mixture of national self-interest and what may be called imperial altruism.

---

[35] Ibid. pp. 38–41, 9–14, 22–3; quotations from pp. 39, 40, 11–12, 22, 23, 13. For Mill's Anglo-Indian disciple see below pp. 234-5.　　　[36] Ibid. pp. 36–40.
[37] Ibid. pp. 21–6; quotation from p. 24.　　　[38] Mill, *Autobiography*, p. 249.

Mill did not underestimate the difficulty of combating the revival of Irish nationalism in the 1860s: but he was clear that it ought to be resisted for the sake of *both* peoples.

He seems to have thought, with good reason, that Fenianism had gone far to remove Irish unrest from the plane of religious and agrarian discontent to that of pure nationalism. The full realization of this dangerous prospect could not yet be averted. The idea and sentiment of nationality were formidable in themselves—he acknowledged that, and warned against the disposition to forget it—but he was optimistic that in the case of Ireland it was still possible to arrest their growth by remedying the complaints about other aspects of British rule than the constitutional. The crux of his whole argument was as follows: 'Rebellions are never really unconquerable until they have become rebellions for an idea...wait till all practical grievances have merged in the demand for independence, and there is no knowing that any concession, short of independence, will appease the quarrel.'[39]

What if the policy of redressing 'practical grievances', in which the great land reform was everything, did not have the desired effect? The possibility that Ireland might have to be allowed to go her own way was not a very real one to Mill. The peasantry would have received all they could hope to gain from a nationalist revolution; only grant them 'permanent possession of the land, subject to fixed burthens' and 'the difficulties of centuries in governing Ireland would disappear'. Indeed, the Irish already derived considerable benefits from the Union. An example was the opportunities they enjoyed in the political life and government of the Empire. Through her representatives at Westminster, Ireland was able to exert more influence in support of any cause favoured by her people than she might be expected to do as a small independent state or with, like Canada, internal self-government and no representation in the imperial Parliament. None of this implied that the Irish could safely be entrusted with the task of governing themselves. They could not. It was not merely the risk of civil war between inveterately hostile Protestants and Catholics, should the authority of Britain be withdrawn, that Mill had in mind. The Irish were deficient in the necessary attributes. This significant admission, which aligned Mill with unreconstructed Tories and sceptical Whigs, rounded off his case for the Union: he had been explaining why it was not feasible, as a compromise, to put the Anglo-Irish constitutional relationship on a similar basis to that of the Dual Monarchy. The Hungarians, he considered, had demonstrated 'a measure of the qualities which fit a people for self-government, greater than has yet been evinced by Continental nations in many other respects far more advanced. The democracy of Ireland', he observed tersely, 'and those who are likely to be its first leaders, have, at all events, yet to prove their possession of qualities at all similar.'[40]

[39] Mill, *England and Ireland*, pp. 7, 21–2, 42–4; quotation from p. 7.
[40] Ibid. pp. 21, 36, 30–5; quotations from pp. 21, 36, 35.

Mill's rejection of an independent or autonomous Ireland rested on more fundamental considerations than this unflattering estimate of the political capacity of her people. His opinion that she stood to gain nothing by breaking away 'except the satisfaction, which she is thought to prize, of being governed solely by Irishmen'[41] must be taken in the context of the theoretical solution he had formulated for the problem of small nations. In the *Considerations on Representative Government* he had compared the destiny of the Irish in the United Kingdom to that of the Bretons in France, and justified their absorption in these terms: 'When the nationality which succeeds in overpowering the other is both the most numerous and the most improved; and especially if the subdued nationality is small, and has no hope of reasserting its independence; then, if...governed with any tolerable justice...the smaller nationality is gradually reconciled to its position, and becomes amalgamated with the larger.' The absorption of smaller nations, in accordance with these desiderata, satisfied the ultimate moral requirement: it was 'a benefit to the human race'.[42]

Mill believed that this country had a special role in the progress of humanity; her strength and security were therefore of much more than national concern. These propositions he stated quite plainly and consistently. He even went so far as to assert that in respect of them 'the feelings of the élite of Europe would bear me out'.[43] With all that, in his opinion, cried out for reform in her political and social institutions, not only was England 'the Power, which of all in existence, best understands liberty', but she 'whatever may have been its [*sic*] errors in the past, has attained to more of conscience and moral principle in its dealings with foreigners than any other great nation seems either to conceive as possible or to recognize as desirable'. It scarcely needs to be pointed out that in being thus assured of his country's righteousness, Mill was expressing a very widely held view. The quotations above are taken from the *Considerations on Representative Government*;[44] six years later, in August 1867, Mill made it clear in a Commons speech that he did not shrink from the use of force against countries with which England had no quarrel, to safeguard her international position. He was attacking England's renunciation a decade earlier of her right to seize enemy cargo in neutral vessels, 'the natural weapon of a maritime nation...our main defence'. This had been the act of a Liberal ministry, and Mill felt obliged to censure his own side for its unwisdom. 'The bulk of the Liberal party acquiesced, silently or approvingly: and therein, I confess, we showed less knowledge of the subject, less understanding of the situation than the Conservative Leaders...' England was not responsible to herself alone. 'Great almost beyond calculation as are the British interests dependent on this issue,' he declared, 'it is on no narrow grounds of merely

---

[41] Ibid. p. 31.   [42] Mill, *Considerations*, pp. 364–5.
[43] *House of Commons Debates*, 5 August 1867.
[44] P. 380. He expressed himself similarly to J. E. Cairnes, who was an advocate of Imperial contraction, on more than one occasion, Mill–Taylor Collection (vol. LV), Mill to Cairnes, 15 June 1862 and 8 November 1864.

British patriotism that I...raise it...the safety, and even the power of England, are valuable to the freedom of the world, and therefore to the greatest and most permanent interests of every civilized people...' Like most Englishmen who watched the course of events in Continental Europe, he feared the inherent aggressiveness of its 'military monarchies'.[45]

Concern for 'the safety, and even the power' of his country figured prominently among Mill's arguments in *England and Ireland* for maintaining the Union in its present form. He laid greater stress, indeed, on this aspect of the matter than on his contention that the Irish were better off within the United Kingdom and on his belief that they were not fit for self-rule. The first of his stated aims in writing the pamphlet—'to show the undesirableness, for Ireland as well as for England, of separation...'[46]—may appear to us, as it apparently did to contemporaries, a superfluous labour in so far as it was directed to convincing Englishmen that their country could not afford to let the sister island go, which was the practically universal view here. In arguing thus, Mill placed himself in a long tradition of English statesmanship; but he was seldom willing to rely on inherited wisdom and he did not do so now. It is a reasonable surmise that he was squaring his sensitive conscience when he sought to reassure liberal opinion which was not oblivious of the question—could it be right to hold Ireland to the Union against her will indefinitely? That well-known public figure and advanced radical M.P., Thomas Hughes, who was politically connected with Mill, voiced this uneasiness in the speech mentioned earlier that attracted wide publicity and was delivered some two months before the latter's pamphlet came out. Although an ardent patriot, Hughes 'confessed that at times he thought it impossible that the two countries could go on in union. He could conceive a separation between them, and that England and Ireland should stand in the same relationship as Norway and Sweden, which were governed by the same sovereign.'[47]

Mill held some familiar language. The proximity of the two islands made for their union; if they did not form a single state, they would pose an unending mutual threat. He was patently committed to the English standpoint; although this was understandably not acknowledged: for he claimed to have transcended vulgar prejudice. Raising the old fear that an independent Ireland would fall victim to a rival power, would become 'a province of France', he inquired: 'I ask any patriotic Englishman what he would think of such a prospect...' There was another inescapable fact. Given their long and continuing history of antagonism, 'Parted...the two islands would be, of all countries in Europe, those which would have the most hostile disposition towards one another'. This, according to Mill, was decisive in excluding any relationship other than union: an alliance between independent nations; internal autonomy on the Canadian pattern; imitation of the recently concluded

---

[45] *House of Commons Debates,* 5 August 1867.
[46] Mill, Autobiography, p. 249. [47] *The Times,* 20 December 1867.

Ausgleich—were in turn ruled out. As regards the first, Ireland would be more inclined to ally with England's enemies. Then she could not be granted, nor would she be reconciled to, the degree of freedom enjoyed by Canada: because it was effectively open to the latter to decide whether or not she would take part in England's wars; because 'Canada is a great way off'; and because her actual status, compared with Ireland's under the Union, was 'a derogation, a descent...'. To adopt the solution found by Austria and Hungary was, Mill conceded, superficially attractive. 'In that there is nothing humiliating to the pride of either country': but he thought it was too new for any fair conclusions to be drawn from its functioning as yet. The overriding objection, however, was the same: this solution was not safe for England; 'the wrongs of centuries' had inspired such 'vindictive feeling' in the Irish people.[48]

The analysis of Mill's attitude to Irish nationalism would be incomplete if his strong dislike of Catholicism were left out of account. While he was not a Christian, his outlook on the religious issues that loomed so large in Victorian politics was scarcely distinguishable from that of the Nonconformist element in the Liberal party. He shared their wish to disestablish the Irish church, and also their obdurate resistance to the educational concessions persistently sought by the Catholic Church in Ireland. In their readiness to attack even the hint of such concessions, he and they showed themselves to be as righteously unsympathetic as any Orangeman to the sentiments of the majority of the Irish population.

Mill in his essay *On Liberty* had depicted the popular intolerance which evangelical Protestantism could evoke in England as something to be deplored and contained.[49] When the Liberal government of Russell and Gladstone was disposed to go some little way towards meeting the Catholic Hierarchy's objects in the field of eduction, he was prepared, if necessary, to excite that same popular emotion to compel ministers to abandon this part of the Irish policy which they were trying to fasion '...I am in hopes', he wrote to Cairnes, 'that the Catholic prelacy is showing itself so impracticable as to give the Government a fair ground for withdrawing any offers they may have made, if only they can be induced to think such a retraction desirable: and it must be the business of members of Parliament to try to make them think so ...Any tolerable stand made in the House will have powerful support outside from the mass of feeling in the country always ready to be called forth against any new concession to Catholics.'[50]

In *England and Ireland* he advocated the further development of 'a really unsectarian education...the most solid, and by far the greatest benefit we have yet conferred upon Ireland'. For this was the antidote to those errors of Catholicism which had the result mentioned in his pamphlet as a reason

[48] Mill, *England and Ireland*, pp. 26–35; quotations from pp. 29, 30, 27, 32–4.
[49] J. S. Mill, *On Liberty*, Everyman's Library edn. (1954), pp. 90–4.
[50] Mill–Taylor Collection (vol. LV), Mill to Cairnes, 6 January 1866.

against Irish independence—that 'the sympathies. . .of Ireland are sure to be on the same side as the Pope—that is, on the side opposed to modern civilization and progress, and to the freedom of all except Catholic populations held in subjection by non-Catholic rulers'. While he of course saw much that was good in Catholicism, he held, in common with most Englishmen of his time, that its claims were incompatible with freedom as that was understood by all shades of opinion in this country.[51]

Mill recounted in his pamphlet how a crowded meeting in London had responded with fervent denials to the inquiry: '"Do you think that England has a right to rule over Ireland if she cannot make the Irish people content with her rule?"'[52] Taking the pamphlet as a whole, it is clear enough that he did not seriously contemplate the possibility suggested by this question: that England might have to acknowledge herself unable to reconcile Ireland to the Union, and grant her independence in some form. The essential interests of England forbade it. The *Considerations on Representative Government* and his Commons speech on the maritime right of search explain what is left unsaid in the pamphlet: the moral justification for so obviously putting England's interests first. What was good for England in respect of her strength and security was good for the rest of the world. This is not a parody of Mill: the morality of Ireland's subjugation was all-important to him. He was nevertheless quite well aware that the rest of the world—'the élite of Europe' apart—did not see those essential interests of England in the same light, and the pamphlet was not the place to take issue with them. If he did not specifically refer to his theory of the destiny of small nations, his estimate of the Irish people, of their political maturity and of the religion to which they were so firmly attached, enabled him to represent the Union as offering the best future that any rational person could expect for their country.

Mill was sometimes critical of the doctrine, common in his day, that certain races or peoples were inferior to others in their aptitude for free and progressive institutions: but only when he thought it was being strained, and used in too deterministic a fashion.[53] His writings furnish examples of judgements on the basis of race or national character. There is a comment in *England and Ireland* which may imply an unfavourable opinion of Irishmen on such grounds, as distinct from their low level of political and religious development. Advancing his Indian solution to the land question, he observed: 'Persons who know both countries, have remarked many points of resemblance between the Irish and Hindoo character.'[54] One wonders whether any of those in Ireland who hailed the pamphlet reflected on these words. They might have noted that in the *Considerations* the 'Hindoos' were 'a people. . .unfit for more than a

---

[51] Mill, *England and Ireland*, pp. 42–3, 30; quotations from his speech in *House of Commons Debates*, 12 March 1868 and *E. & I.* p. 30.

[52] Ibid. pp. 25–6; M. St J. Packe, op. cit. p. 463.

[53] Elliot, op. cit. II, 44, 190, Mill to J. Boyd Kinnear, 19 August 1865, and to Sir C. Dilke, 9 February 1869.   [54] Mill, *England and Ireland*, p. 22.

limited and qualified freedom ...'.[55] In support of the suggested interpretation of this comment in *England and Ireland*—or at any rate as a further illustration of his view that the Irish were far behind the English in political civilization —there may be cited a letter written many years earlier, in which he avowed that 'I myself have always been for a good stout Despotism—for governing Ireland like India'.

In that letter Mill had continued: 'But it cannot be done. The Spirit of Democracy has got too much head there, too prematurely.' If 'Despotism' was impracticable, keeping Ireland within the United Kingdom in spite of herself was not, and now, thirty years afterwards, he was troubled by the necessity of confining that spirit. This feeling emerged strongly at the close of his pamphlet.[56] 'If, without removing this [the agrarian] difficulty,' he wrote, 'we attempt to hold Ireland by force ... we shall be in a state of open revolt against the universal conscience of Europe and Christendom, and more and more against our own.'[57] Hence the sweeping land reform; not only to bribe the peasant mass into a more positive acquiescence in British rule, but also to assuage the moral discomfort suffered by English liberals like himself at having to approve the forcible suppression of those who had turned their cherished principles of liberty and consent against them. Hence, too, the next remarkable feature of the pamphlet: his pretence that the condition of the Irish peasantry had not changed since before the Famine, blatantly ignoring what he had written in the *Principles* and said in Parliament on the subject between 1862 and 1866. He must have felt that he had to exaggerate their plight to recommend his extraordinary plan and that it was permissible to do so in the circumstances. Permissible also to play on topical fears by conjuring up the spectre of collaboration between the British and Irish commonalty against the selfish and the shortsighted who obstructed an act of manifest justice. Letters of March 1868 to Cairnes seem to confirm this hypothesis. The latter had expressed the hope that less drastic means of dealing with Irish land than the pamphlet advocated would suffice, and Mill replied: 'You will not find in it much argument, of a nature to remove any difficulties which *you* are likely to feel. The object was to strike hard, and compel people to listen to the largest possible proposal.' From everything that he had been able to learn, nothing less 'would now tranquillize Ireland, or reconcile the Irish people to the Union'.[58]

---

[55] Mill, *Considerations*, pp. 178–9.

[56] F. E. Mineka (ed.), *The Earlier Letters of John Stuart Mill 1812–48*, forming vols. XII and XIII of the *Collected Works of John Stuart Mill* (Toronto, 1963–); XII, 365, Mill to J. P. Nichol, 21 December 1837.

[57] Mill, *England and Ireland*, p. 44. This uncomfortable thought had been with him throughout. On an earlier page he had put a question which admitted of only one answer: 'On what principle did we act when we renounced the government of the Ionian Islands?' (p. 24). The cession of those islands to the weak, imperfectly civilized kingdom of Greece in 1863, notwithstanding the large claims that had been made for their strategic value, constituted an acknowledgement on the part of this country that she found a genuine and stubborn nationalism morally hard to repress, in a European people at any rate.

[58] Mill–Taylor Collection (vol. LV), Mill to Cairnes, 10 and 1 March 1868.

III

Mill overdid it in his desire to impress people with the urgency of the situation. He could have anticipated the emotion he elicited. His associate Thomas Hughes had been assailed for saying in his very recent speech, without reference to Mill's authority, that an Indian land settlement should be given to Ireland. It did not help Hughes that, as Mill was to do, he represented this to be dictated by the threat to England's place in the world. His suggestion that otherwise the Union might have to be dissolved was lost in the enormity of the proposed invasion of the rights of property. Mill suffered the same fate.

It has to be remembered that at this time the propertied classes, and especially landowners, in both Britain and Ireland were a prey to active fears as to what the future held for them. The Second Reform Act and its attendant circumstances had given rise to exaggerated gloom about the political strength of property, and above all of landed property, under the new dispensation. While Irish landlords were afraid of their being sacrificed to make British rule more acceptable to a refractory people, English landlords were now really apprehensive that a surrender of fundamental principles in Ireland would encourage the radical wing of the Liberal party and its working-class allies to exploit it against themselves.

Given the benefit of hindsight, these fears may appear to have been unreal: but they were reflected in journals like *The Economist* and the *Pall Mall Gazette*. The former under Bagehot can certainly not be accused of alarmism, and in fact both usually took a balanced view. *The Economist* urged the government in July 1868 not to leave Irish land to the next, reformed Parliament, which might not be inclined to deal gently with the owners. Recent history abroad exhibited the risk incurred by the postponement: 'that...a really popular assembly...manifested...very little, much too little, respect for proprietary rights. The same disposition may be shown by the new House of Commons...'[59] In a leading article of early February, headed 'The Attitude of the Liberal Party in the Coming Parliament', the *Pall Mall Gazette* complained that 'too many of our parliamentary politicians are holding language which implies...that "fixity of tenure" should be conceded...or that the State shall become "middleman" on a great scale, and purchase large estates...to create a... "peasant proprietary"'. The reference was to Bright and Hughes and their respective schemes: only they among English political figures of note had so offended—but they were enough in themselves to justify this concern. '...herein, according to our view' continued the *Pall Mall Gazette*, 'lie the danger and wrong of such language; that the politicians we speak of are giving a parliamentary status to projects hitherto entertained only by irresponsible agitators and reckless doctrinaires...They are acting as the Conservatives acted when they first pronounced the words "Household suffrage"; they

[59] *The Economist*, 25 January 1868, 'Lord Stanley at Bristol'.

are doing what can never be quite undone...'[60] The last illuminates the anxiety that Bright and Hughes, standing for the old and the new radicalism, had commenced an irreversible process of escalating the concessions demanded of landowners, similar to that which had so recently marked the course of Parliamentary reform.

In such an atmosphere as this, Mill's pamphlet dismayed and angered those who had been nervously awaiting a full-blooded attack on property. They had not supposed that it would come from him, from so respected and authoritative a quarter. The reaction was caused as much by his extremist language in the places that have been quoted as by the plan itself. The warning he gave that the masses in Britain and Ireland would make common cause against their rulers if the occupiers of Irish land were not speedily turned into its substantial owners seemed more than a threat which was calculated to be peculiarly disturbing, and appeared to imply a hope that this social revolution would not be confined to Ireland. One may instance the shocked surprise of a moderate Whig politician and Irish proprietor, Lord Bessborough, who later helped Gladstone with the provisions of the 1870 Land Bill and, as chief government whip in that House, with its passage through the Lords, 'Mill ought to be sent to penal servitude as a Fenian' he declared when acknowledging 'that wicked pamphlet' sent by his acquaintance Delane, the editor of *The Times*. To Bessborough's indignation at the 'plundering views' set forth was joined his natural resentment of the highly coloured picture of the Irish landlords and the condition of their tenantry. He was clearly worried about its effect in the light of the existing widely diffused prejudice against them. 'England in general', he wrote, 'believes that we are perpetually evicting wretched squalid people who have no resource but beggary.' He believed in the stock economic argument against fixity of tenure. Should the landlord's controlling hand be removed or paralysed by legislation, the tenants would assuredly revert to type, to the endless subdivision and primitive agriculture which had led inexorably to the Famine. Bessborough ended on the authentic note of the Ascendancy: '...if we ever expect to legislate to the extend of stopping agitators from speaking about the wrongs of Ireland, and the mob from believing and hallooing after them, we may legislate for ever and shall find ourselves just as near at the end'.[61]

The editorials and reviews which gave very full, if mainly adverse, publicity to *England and Ireland* show how disconcerting was Mill's conversion to fixity of tenure. *The Times*, after an initial passing reference to 'the sweeping interference with the rights of property contemplated by Mr Mill',[62] printed on the following day a long review that did not spare pamphlet and author. He was castigated for his style of advocacy: 'It is irritated and impatient, and seems

---

[60] The *Pall Mall Gazette*, 10 February 1868.
[61] Delane Papers (MSS of Times Newspapers Ltd.) (vol. 15), Bessborough to J. T. Delane, 22 February (1868).   [62] *The Times*, 19 February 1868.

to express a supercilious contempt for every one who is not a philosopher, or has not had the experience of an Indian official...His chief argument...is an appeal to our fears, and he seems to hope to goad us into agreeing with him by combining threats with taunts...'[63] The feeling thus expressed that he had abused his great influence as a savant was general. *The Economist*, which was kinder to him than most, reproached him with relying 'more than he should upon a sort of intellectual terror...'.[64] The conservative *Saturday Review* cried that 'the professional mouthers of revolutionary slang may salute with respectful admiration the successful competition of Mr John Mill...'.[65] It is only fair to note that in the opinion of the middle-of-the-road Liberal paper, the *Daily News*, 'He never wrote with more judicial calmness, gravity, and luminosity...'.[66]

Mill's theory of rights over land, said *The Times* reviewer, was the same as that of Proudhon—property was theft. For the rest, the comments ran along lines that were to become very familiar—Mill had grossly exaggerated the political unrest in Ireland; the case for peasant proprietorship was certainly not proved, particularly as far as that country was concerned; his plan would impel a flight of capital and the exodus of those on whom agricultural improvement depended; and if the provisions he had included against non-payment of rent and subdivision were enforceable, which was questioned, the reform would not get rid of the agrarian discontent. Surprisingly, the reviewer did not quote Mill's previous statements on Irish land against him.[67]

On the next two days *The Times* followed up this review with editorials. The first reiterated that the achievement of peasant proprietorship, by means of either fixity of tenure or state-assisted purchase, would do nothing but harm to Ireland.[68] The second of these editorials took what it saw as the vital issue raised by Mill's 'mischievous' scheme and warned that there could be no avoiding it. Urging the Parliamentary parties not to afford him any encouragement, *The Times* wrote:

Every man should make up his mind whether the received laws of property are to be upheld in the United Kingdom; or whether, beginning first with Ireland, we are to establish principles which would unsettle our whole social fabric...The first thing to be borne in mind is that every theory accepted for Ireland is accepted for England also, and that those who are now calling for 'exceptional' legislation would be, if successful, the first to declare that such legislation was not 'exceptional', but normal, and...should be applied in Great Britain...

Mill and those who put forward similar schemes must be made to realize that neither in Ireland nor in any other part of the Kingdom will the possessors of the soil be ousted in obedience to political theories...[69]

[63] Ibid. 20 February 1868, 'Mr Mill on Ireland'.
[64] *The Economist*, 22 February 1868, 'Mr Mill on Ireland'.
[65] The *Saturday Review*, 29 February 1868, 'Mr Mill on England and Ireland'.
[66] The *Daily News*, 18 February 1868.
[67] *The Times*, 20 February 1868, 'Mr Mill on Ireland'.
[68] Ibid. 21 February 1868.
[69] Ibid. 22 February 1868.

The same thing was being said privately. 'It is impossible not to see', wrote Lord Stanley, 'that what these men want is less to benefit the tenant than to drive out the landlord...'[70]

The Times returned to attacking Mill on two further occasions during the period of some three weeks between the publication of *England and Ireland* and the opening of the major debate on Irish policy in the Commons that began towards the middle of March.[71] The liberal Conservative *Pall Mall Gazette* did not differ essentially in its conclusions on 'Mr Mill's panacea': but its approach eschewed moral indignation in favour of practical reasons why 'we venture to disregard even his authority and resolutely to oppose ...'. The *Pall Mall* reaffirmed its Palmerstonian line that government and society as at present constituted in Ireland, should be left alone; and suggested an official inquiry into Irish land in the declared conviction that the policy it preached would be vindicated. Mill was commended for his exposition, described as the clearest and most powerful yet given, of the harm that would result to the empire and to Ireland from the dissolution of the Union.[72]

The weekly *Saturday Review*, which purveyed an intellectual conservatism, carried a violently hostile review of *England and Ireland*. Not only was Mill accused of pandering to 'the malignity of anti-English hatred' since there no longer existed any Irish grievance susceptible of legislative redress. He was the 'most recent and most thoroughgoing apostle of Communism'; and there was more in the same strain. This invective was in some measure provoked by the sheer unexpectedness of his display of fierce social radicalism after enjoying for so long quite another reputation. As is witnessed by the reviewer's concluding lament—'...that the great doctrine of Irish social problems is reducible to..."La propriété, c'est le vol" is one of those startling phenomena...which...occasionally reminds the human race of the follies of its wisest guides'. If absolute property in land was foreign to the Irish, so were representative government and a free press, which were equally of English provenance. Nor could the reviewer see any merit in the comparison between Ireland and India, derided as unflattering to the former. There was nothing distinctive about the remaining objections here made to Mill's plan, forecasting its breakdown under the social pressures of rural Ireland: but the whole article was a paean of indignation that such proposals should have emanated from 'a staid and sober politician in the nineteenth century....'.[73] The real cause of this furious anxiety was exposed by an editorial in the next issue, which provided a marked contrast in its dispassionate analysis of the conflicting tensions set up by the Irish question. There was in this country, in the judgement of the *Saturday Review*, a genuine desire to do something for

[70] Dufferin Papers, P.R.O. Northern Ireland (D 1071 H/B/F. 147) Stanley to Lord Dufferin, n.d. [March 1868].

[71] *The Times*, 28 February and 10 March 1868.

[72] The *Pall Mall Gazette*, 24 February 1868, 'Mr Mill and Ireland'.

[73] The *Saturday Review*, 29 February 1868, 'Mr Mill on England and Ireland'.

Ireland and thereby ease the pricks of conscience. This would take the form of an assault on the Irish Church, because à propos of Bright's and Mill's schemes, 'the great mass of English landlords, both Liberal and Conservative, hold that any change in the land tenure of Ireland would be a source of great danger, social and political, to England...'.[74]

The *Daily News* with its large popular circulation combined praise for Mill with grave doubts as to whether his plan could be justified in terms of agricultural improvement and social progress—doubts which it said 'seem to us, until better instructed, unanswerable'. The sympathetic praise was for his courage in treating it as of human, and not Divine, institution. The impression was left that Mill had gone far beyond the limits of practical politics. The *Daily News* thought that the pamphlet would have little effect except to promote greater understanding of 'the radical and national character of Irish discontent'.[75] The *Manchester Guardian*, prominent among provincial Liberal newspapers, simply said that the danger of an uprising in Ireland was not so alarming that Mill could secure the acceptance of the 'revolutionary measures' he asked for.[76]

The *Spectator* was naturally pleased Mill had abandoned the view that Ireland did not require 'heroic remedies', and had adopted the grand reform urged by itself for years. It attacked the *Pall Mall* for seriously underestimating Irish unrest, and criticized the 'unmeaning chatter' about property rights 'which no one proposes to invade except as they are involved by every Railway act'—this was worthy of Mill in his doctrinaire vein. The *Spectator* did not here deny the economic advantages of large farms, nor that their land system was still—'as yet, at least' it said—socially acceptable to the English people: but based its support of Mill chiefly on the generalization that the system was wholly unsuited to and unworkable in a country like Ireland without an indigenous aristocracy enjoying popular esteem. A gloss, seemingly, on a point of Mill's. The worst offenders among Englishmen who declined to recognize this truth, or to see that the incentives of ownership could transform the bad habits of Irish peasants were 'the economists who, of all Pharisees, are the most Pharisaic'.[77]

It was nevertheless *The Economist* that provided the most perceptive and balanced critique of *England and Ireland*. Observing that Mill's behaviour since entering Parliament was difficult to reconcile with what he had written before, it offered a qualified defence of his conduct. Mill's honesty was held to be beyond question, but he was portrayed as 'easily excitable and susceptible; the evil that is in his mind...seems to him the greatest...for the time nearly the only evil...'. Thus less than three years earlier, continued *The Economist*, his

[74] Ibid. 7 March 1868, 'Ireland'.
[75] The *Daily News*, 25 and 19 February 1868.
[76] The *Manchester Guardian*, 22 February 1868.
[77] The *Spectator*, 22 February 1868, 'Mr J. S. Mill on the Irish Land Question'.

conclusions on Irish land in the last edition of the *Principles* amounted to 'erasing and unsaying the most striking part of his first edition'. His temperamental reaction to the subsequent manifestation of Fenianism was accordingly to require 'a *most* heroic remedy'. Taking the picture he had just drawn of the Irish peasantry's wretched lot, this editorial pointed out that the changes in his proposals on Irish land between the first and last editions of the *Principles* explicitly reflected their altered condition. In the light of his statements in the edition of 1865, it was surely unnecessary to have to resort to a plan 'which is thought to be, and will have the moral effect of confiscation'.

The Economist recognized that Mill had been influenced mainly by political considerations. It could not accept that the plan would have the effect he predicted on Irish disaffection, because too strongly impressed with the arguments it proceeded to deploy, of the kind styled 'Pharisaic' by *The Spectator* and summarized here as: 'Our answer is that land . . . is a blessing only to those who can use it, and a poison to those who cannot'. Giving Irish land to the people, subject to a fixed rent, would appear to promise, not contentment, but increased wretchedness. The administration of the proposed settlement would involve the state in inextricable difficulties over the regulation and collection of rents. Continental and Indian examples of fixity of tenure were not really relevant: in those cases legislation had defined and determined what previously existed in the shape of old-established practice, as *The Economist* supposed it did not in Ireland. 'We are rather frightened', the article ended, 'by the glowing "Prospectus" of Mr Mill.'[78]

None of the journals whose reception of *England and Ireland* has been analysed at possibly excessive length was narrowly conservative. Between them they represented all shades of the broad, unifying liberalism that took in both parties and was characteristic of British politics in that age. Only the *Spectator* was approving. The rest concurred in regarding Mill's demands as impossible to accommodate within the social and political framework to which, if some, like the *Daily News*, professed to view it with an open mind, there was generally felt to be no desirable alternative. The avowedly Tory press was not more damning than *The Times* or *Saturday Review*.

In the first of two letters to Cairnes, dated 1 and 10 March, Mill put a brave face on the treatment he had received, saying: 'On the whole I have met with more approbation, and not more abuse, than I expected'. In both letters he referred to his motives for writing as he did in the pamphlet. The point has been made that his aim was to inspire the sort of action which was imperative, in his judgement, to preserve the Union. After going into the press reaction, it should perhaps be stressed that this was his aim, and not to shake society to its foundations. His explanation of the method he employed to that end has been briefly mentioned, and will now be given in full. 'I am sure', he wrote on 1 March, 'nothing less than some very startling proposal would have any

[78] *The Economist*, 22 February 1868, 'Mr Mill on Ireland'.

chance of whipping up the languid interest of English public men...and making them feel the critical nature of the situation...' On 10 March he told Cairnes 'if there is any intermediate course...its adoption is likely to be very much promoted by frightening the Government and the landlords with something more revolutionary...'.[79] While these remarks testify to his deep concern about the Irish question, and about the role of the agrarian problem in that question, they also hint faintly at the partial retraction which was to follow of his demand for universal fixity of tenure. The letters as a whole suggest that although he believed nothing else would have the hoped-for result, he was beginning to rationalize the acceptance of less. The barrage of criticism affected him more than he let Cairnes know.

The appearance of Lord Dufferin's 'Mr Mill's Plan for the Pacification of Ireland Examined' early in March served to prolong the criticism. This reply to Mill does not need to be discussed at any length. It rehearsed the arguments of the press, only more extensively.[80] Thus by the eve of the debate on Irish policy, 'the House of Squires' as the *Daily News* not unfairly called it,[81] was fortified, not in its aversion to invading property-rights, which could hardly have been stronger than it was to start with, but in its resolution to withstand the kind of pressures that Mill had brought to bear in his pamphlet.

Both the Liberal and the Conservative leadership had encountered acute difficulty with this Parliament of 1865–8 when their Irish land bills came before it. Lord Mayo introduced a bill in March 1867 to secure compensation for tenants' improvements which involved an element of compulsion upon the landlord, exercisable by a government commissioner, and which for that reason was very badly received, so much so that it was not proceeded with.[82] For the same reason Mill privately hoped it would pass, although he thought it was otherwise of little value.[83] When the Conservative cabinet decided to reintroduce Mayo's bill at the beginning of March 1868, the element of compulsion was left out as not being among 'those points of the controversy on which there begins to be a concurrence of opinion'.[84] Gladstone was no more confident than the Conservatives that the feelings of the Commons against any such measure could be overcome. He was anxious, two months before Mill's pamphlet saw the light, that the liberals should make 'every effort' to agree on a land bill with J. F. Maguire, who voiced in Parliament, with great

---

[79] Mill–Taylor Collection (vol. LV), Mill to Cairnes, 1 and 10 March 1868.

[80] Published in London. 'You have discussed like a gentleman and Mill has not argued like a philosopher', wrote an aristocratic friend of the author; Sir A. Lyall, *The Life of the Marquis of Dufferin & Ava*, 2 vols. (London, 1905); I, 167, Lord Arthur Russell to Dufferin, 10 March 1868.

[81] The *Daily News*, 25 February 1868.

[82] See the speeches of Mayo and G. M. W. Sandford, 18 February and 29 April 1867, and Mayo's reference to this bill on 10 March 1868 in *House of Commons Debates*; also the *Saturday Review*, 4 May 1867.

[83] Mill–Taylor Collection (vol. LV), Mill to Cairnes, 26 May 1867.

[84] Derby Papers (Box 146/4), B. Disraeli to Lord Derby, 4 March 1868.

moderation, the hopes and grievances of the tenants. At the same time he confessed that he did not know how the innocuous Liberal proposals of 1866 could be significantly extended. 'It would have been with the utmost difficulty' so he reminded his correspondent, Chichester Fortescue, the author of these proposals, 'that we should have got that Bill well supported by the Cabinet and our friends and a more ultra measure would only mean more splitting'. 'More splitting': this was a severely limiting factor in his calculations of the action it was possible to take on Irish issues. Not that he was inclined to underestimate the gravity of the situation. 'The Irish question...long... grave, is growing *awful*', he informed Fortescue. 'In my opinion this Empire has but one danger. It is the danger by the combination of the three names Ireland, United States, and Canada.'[85]

Gladstone's Southport speech of 19 December 1867, made a few days after writing this letter, publicized in less specific terms his awareness of the threat Ireland posed to Britain from without as well as from within. He did not need Mill to tell him how alarming it was.[86] The Commons' long debate between 10 and 16 March showed that other leading parliamentarians besides Gladstone were more alive than the press apparently was to the sapping of British power and influence by the Irish problem, and the concern of some was heightened by Mill's warnings on this head. A Conservative cabinet minister, Gathorne Hardy, felt impelled to state that if Mill were correct in his estimate of the problem, and more especially as to its effects on Anglo-American relations, 'then I say it may be necessary to resort to some measure which I do not now like to contemplate'.[87] The danger to which the empire was exposed furnished one of the debate's themes. Another was the rejection notwithstanding of Mill's truly radical land reform.

Mill and his pamphlet figured very prominently in the debate. The prevailing tone of the references to them was set by Charles Neate, a former professor of political economy at Oxford, in these words:

It might be thought work of supererogation to defend landlords in this House; but they must look a little to what was...said...elsewhere. He was chiefly addressing himself to a remarkable work which most Gentlemen had read, lately published by the honourable Member for Westminster.

Neate was, he said, 'quite taken aback' by the pamphlet; he could no longer acknowledge the author's 'excellent wisdom'. He likened him to the most dreaded type of social revolutionary—

It might appear startling to compare the two men; and a month ago he should have drawn a very unfavourable contrast between the violence and rapacity of Jack... Cade and the mild philosophy of the honourable Member...

---

[85] Strachie Papers, Somerset R.O. (H. 324/CP 1), Gladstone to Fortescue, 11 December 1867.

[86] *The Times*, 20 December 1867.

[87] *House of Commons Debates*, 12 March 1868.

He hoped that Mill's onslaught would rouse English and Irish landlords, who had thus been served with notice of their imminent extinction, to fight back.[88] There was inevitably a wealth of repetition as one speaker succeeded another with charges of 'confiscation' and prophecies of the misery that would ensue from conferring fixity of tenure upon those who would surely abuse it. Of the cabinet, Gathorne Hardy attacked Mill on both counts, and Lord Mayo[89] laboured the second in his speech. They pointed out, too, that the landlords constituted the strongest of Anglo-Irish ties. The government adhered to their main proposal on Irish land, of a royal commission on the question, which they had adopted at Delane's prompting before the publication of *England and Ireland*;[90] and like Delane they made it clear—Disraeli apart—that this was expected to vindicate the landlords. Of the Liberals John Bright did not believe that 'so vast and extraordinary a scheme' as Mill's could ever be relevant to Ireland, and he underlined the respect he had for property.[91] Gladstone observed with restrained irony: 'I have not daring sufficient to accompany my honourable friend...[in] what appeared to me to be the dismissal of the landlords of Ireland'. He voiced warm sympathy for the suffering alleged of the peasantry but limited the hope of legislative aid which he held out to an eloquent restatement of the Liberal bill of 1866. Predictably, he gave notice that the new departure which he thought was urgently required in Irish policy would be directed against the Protestant Establishment, and not the landlords.[92] This had the obvious advantage of uniting the large majority in all sections of his party.

The most powerful criticism of Mill—for so it struck the House and the press—came from Robert Lowe, whose formidable opposition to Parliamentary reform had been influenced by the firm view he took that it would undermine the whole structure of society. In a prognosis of the reform's baneful consequences given to J. T. Delane in December 1866, he had included an agrarian measure that 'would gravely injure Ireland, by inspiring apprehension, by diminishing the value [of] the land and by fomenting animosity'.[93] Over the past few years, Lowe had made something of a speciality of Irish land, in the Commons and in the leaders he wrote for *The Times*, taking the landlord's part on rigidly orthodox economic grounds, expounded with the lucid aggression characteristic of him.[94] The speech he now delivered was meant to eradicate any positive impression that Mill, whom he rated 'a great authority', might have made on English opinion. On the subject of

[88] Ibid. 10 March 1868.   [89] Ibid.

[90] Disraeli Papers, National Trust, Hughenden Manor (B/XX/S/796), Lord Stanley to Disraeli, 25 January 1868; Mayo Papers (MS 11, 164), Disraeli to Mayo, 7 February 1868; for Disraeli's speech see *House of Commons Debates*, 16 March 1868.

[91] Ibid. 13 March 1868.   [92] Ibid. 16 March 1868.

[93] Delane Papers (vol. 15), Lowe to Delane, 20 December 1866.

[94] See, for example, his speeches in *House of Commons Debates*, 27 February 1865 and 17 May 1866; his leaders are noted in the diary of contributors among the records of Times Newspapers Ltd.

landlord–tenant relations he was as disingenuous, with a contrary aim, as Mill had been in his pamphlet. Lowe asserted that the select committees of the Commons which had gone into this aspect of the question in recent years, and to which he had belonged, 'were entirely unsuccessful in discovering any case of real grievance'. This seems to have been in the narrow sense he first specified here: that witnesses before the committees did not identify concrete instances of landlord oppression—but the broad conclusion he suggested did not follow from their evidence. Classically, he saw Irish discontent as explicable almost wholly by rural over-population and the small farmer's impossible plight as the occupier of a holding which was quite uneconomic. There was, to his mind, no cure for the country's depressed condition but the establishment of a climate of confidence and physical security, to attract British capital. 'Reason and good political economy' taught that the owner of land should be completely free to do with it as he like. He pronounced it 'ridiculous to inveigh against a law...the same in Ireland as in England...whatever may be the difference between the two countries, it is impossible that there can be any fundamental injustice in a law which works with entire satisfaction in a country like this'. His detailed objections to Mill's plan were the usual ones: it was the assurance and incisiveness with which they were stated that was so telling.[95]

Mill's speech contained one passage that is well known to historians of economic thought—a measured rebuke to Lowe for treating political economy not as a theoretical science, a means to understanding, but as prescriptive, laying down certain unvarying propositions. It is not always remembered that his contemporaries thought Mill tended to fall into the same error, and especially when he wrote about peasant proprietorship.

In the remainder of the speech he was much less sure of himself. Not only was he now palpably on the defensive: he was trying to be conciliatory, and he made important concessions to his critics. These he did not mention as such in the *Autobiography*. While he repeated his view that Irish unrest gave cause for greater concern than ever before—because of its American dimension and its intensified national consciousness—there was no uncompromising insistence on his plan as the just and imperative response to the crisis. He opened with the acknowledgement that he had far outstripped public opinion.

When he reached his plan, he claimed, as in the *Autobiography*, that it had been misunderstood and misrepresented. There was after all 'a very great number of tenants who do not pay a full rent' under those landlords who were 'most moderate in their exactions...the best...the most improving...on the best terms with their tenants, and whom it is most important to retain in the country'. The savings amassed by Irish farmers were remarkable, and he was generous in his acceptance of the corollary: 'I must say...it reflects great

[95] *House of Commons Debates*, 12 March 1868.

credit on the landlords of Ireland, taken as a body, that the tenants should have been able to accumulate such almost incredible sums...' These passages in the speech could not be convincingly reconciled with his description of Irish landlords and tenants in the pamphlet. Since the plan strictly prohibited fixity of tenure at less than 'a full rent—fair...not...excessive, but still...full', he anticipated that many occupiers would prefer to retain their existing tenure under landlords who would be glad to accommodate them. It is not at all evident from *England and Ireland* that Mill had in mind this large exception to his plan; nor that there were a substantial proportion of tenants so fortunately placed, and a comparatively blameless landlord class.

Coming to 'the strongest argument I have...heard...against my plan'— that by it the government would incur unpopularity and get involved in the peculiar difficulties of Irish landlords—this was, he said, decisive if valid. He did not think the tenants could fail to be grateful and co-operative. Removing the landlords' option to convert their rents into Treasury bonds would, he suggested, save the government from embarrassment on this score. He ignored the objection that government still had the even more invidious task of settling the official rents.

Other, very significant, modifications of his plan considerably reduced its benefits, and consequently its attractions, to the Irish peasant. He mentioned here, exceeding his optimism in the last edition of the *Principles* on this point, that holdings were in general no longer too small to be viable: but if they were, the tenants would find themselves unable to pay the rent and they would be evicted—'a necessary part of my plan'—thus enabling the landlords to consolidate such holdings. Mill went further: possibly, in the case of occupiers below an acreage to be specified, fixity of tenure should be conditional upon improvement of the land. Pasture too might be excluded, to begin with, from the ambit of the scheme. In conclusion, Mill implied that he would not be unhappy if the House and his proposed land commission effected additional 'temperaments' as he called them, of his plan: its essence, he said, was 'not... that every tenant should have an actual perpetuity...only that every tenant who actually tills the soil should have the power of obtaining a perpetuity on an impartial valuation'. But not, presumably, the luckless occupiers of uneconomic farms.[96]

These far-reaching changes are termed 'explanations' in the *Autobiography*.[97] Mill had his share of vanity: nothing he wrote was so disrespectfully treated as *England and Ireland*. The amendments in this speech to his proposals were an admission that he had perpetrated an egregious blunder in pretending, if for patriotic reasons, that the Irish land system was so much worse than he had described it only three years earlier in his most authoritative work. There was not much left of the pamphlet after the speech, and Mill's intellectual

[96] Ibid.; Mill, *Autobiography*, pp. 250–1.
[97] Ibid. p. 251.

reputation had suffered. 'Mr Mill himself completed the work of demolition' said the *Pall Mall Gazette* 'partly by (for him) a singularly weak defence of his project, and partly by explaining much of it away'.[98] He did not care to record this unusual discomfiture for posterity.

IV

In the *Autobiography* Mill took to himself much of the credit for the 1870 Irish Land Act. 'It is most improbable', he wrote, 'that a measure conceding so much to the tenantry as Mr Gladstone's Irish Land Bill, would have been proposed by a Government, or could have been carried through Parliament, unless the British public had been led to perceive that a case might be made, and perhaps a party formed, for a measure considerably stronger.' Change, he fairly remarked, must be presented to the upper and middle classes of this country under the form of compromise, and other agrarian schemes appeared as such beside his.[99]

There may have been something in this claim; it cannot be dismissed as absurd. All the evidence suggests that it is very much exaggerated. In the first place, Mill had so modified his plan that, whatever its exact scope thereafter, it seemed to fall well short of universal fixity of tenure. Secondly, he dropped the subject of Irish land, to all intents, after his speech in March 1868. Fixity of tenure, however, continued to be demanded by the more outspoken leaders of the agrarian movement in Ireland, like Isaac Butt, Sir John Gray and some of the Catholic Hierarchy, and it was accordingly with them, and not with Mill, that this extreme was identified in the British mind. Thirdly, while Mill's plan did attract a little more support than it had initially received, that support represented additional strength in the quarter where he had found approval to start with—the intellectuals of advanced liberalism. Lastly, his plan is not considered in the mass of papers relating to the Gladstone cabinet's deliberations upon the Irish Land Bill in 1869–70, and there is mainly incidental mention of him in the very extensive journalistic debate at the time.

For the cabinet and the press the most influential single contribution to the overwhelming literature on the Irish land question was that made by a disciple of Mill's, but its approach was quite distinct from his. In *England and Ireland* Mill had made, but failed to develop, the point that the English and Irish notions of property in land were historically opposed to each other. The full relevance of this to the contemporary agrarian problem was shown by an Anglo-Indian admirer of his, George Campbell. In two remarkable pamphlets written in the summer and early autumn of 1869, Campbell exposed the pervasive influence of customary tenure in Ireland beyond the area where it flourished openly, and the way in which it circumscribed the operation of

---

[98] The *Pall Mall Gazette*, 14 March 1868, 'Irish Land Question in the House of Commons'.
[99] Mill, *Autobiography*, p. 250.

the law of landlord and tenant known to the courts. Legislation, he argued, should aim at constructing an agrarian code out of the custom of tenant-right. Effectively, this meant fixity of tenure; but Campbell's approach was much subtler and more profound than Mill's peremptory call for fixity. Advocating the extension as well as the legalization of Ulster custom was not new: Campbell's justification of it was. He demonstrated that in Ireland as in India fixity of tenure could be seen as the crystallization by government of practices which were integral to the fabric of native society. Gladstone tried, and failed, to induce the cabinet to accept a bill based on Campbell's proposals.

Campbell's two pamphlets, published in book form under the title of *The Irish Land*,[100] showed that the author was strongly influenced by Mill on property and society. Mill himself privately accorded Campbell high praise, but he was inclined to think, as in the *Principles*, that fixity of tenure should be limited to '*ryots*, or labourer-farmers',[101] which was to misunderstand, or to reject, the whole point of Campbell's book. The 1870 Land Act gave the force of law to tenant-right in Ulster and elsewhere only if the custom were shown to exist with at least the implied consent of the landlord. The large majority of tenants received a right to the value of their improvements, such as these were, and quite limited compensation for 'disturbance' on eviction.[102] Mill welcomed the bill in a *Fortnightly Review* article as 'a great step in advance, and a signal triumph of political necessity over inveterate prejudice' because it went a long way towards establishing security of tenure:[103] but in the preface to the 1871 edition of the *Principles* he inserted the cryptic statement that 'all notice, of the alteration made in the Land Laws of Ireland by the recent Act, is deferred until experience shall have had time to pronounce on the operation of of that well-meant attempt...'.[104]

A recent book on Mill seeks to show that 'the godfather of English liberalism...emerges...considerably less libertarian than is sometimes suggested ...emerges considerably more radical...'.[105] The present writer seems forced

[100] London, 1869. The foregoing paragraph is a summary of the present writer's article in the *Historical Journal* (1968), 'Ireland and the Empire in the 1860s. Imperial Precedents for Gladstone's First Irish Land Act'.

[101] Mill–Taylor Collection (vol. LV), Mill to Cairnes, 16 November 1869; printed in Elliot, op. cit. II, 229–30. In the following January Mill told Cairnes that he approved of the latter's article in the *Fortnightly Review* for that month, on 'Political Economy and Land', which endorsed Campbell's scheme, with the suggestion of certain minor changes. Yet while Mill thought the scheme was 'without doubt the utmost which there is any chance of obtaining at present from Parliament', he doubted whether anything less than the absolute security of 'fixity of tenure at a valuation made once for all' would content the Irish. Cairnes, whose views had undergone a marked change since he first wrote to the master about Irish land, was 'truly sorry to find you so desponding as to the efficiency of a measure such as Campbell has prepared'. Mill–Taylor Collection (vol. LV), Mill to Cairnes, 11 January 1870; ibid. (vol. LVI), Cairnes to Mill, 13 January 1870.

[102] In principle the 1870 Land Act was a measure of great moment: in practice it was much less significant. *The Times*, 10 August 1870.

[103] *The Fortnightly Review*, June 1870, 'Professor Leslie on the Land Question', p. 644.

[104] Mill, *Works*, II, xciv.

[105] M. J. Cowling, *Mill and Liberalism* (Cambridge, 1963), p. xii.

to conclude that Mill was less libertarian but less radical than is often sup-posed: because he very largely shared the complacency, if that is the right word, of his contemporaries about English political *and* social institutions: because he was a patriot and even—what is anathema to his most fervent admirers today—a convinced 'imperialist'.

11

THE IRISH QUESTION AND LIBERAL POLITICS,
1886-1894
D.A. HAMER

BETWEEN 1867 and the end of the nineteenth century the Irish question was one of the major issues in British politics. Between 1880 and 1893 in particular it achieved the status of the predominating issue, the great and abiding preoccupation of politicians. There would appear to be little difficulty for the historian in explaining why this was so. There were obviously abundant reasons in the Irish situation itself why politicians should have devoted so much of their time and effort to dealing with it—the urgent nature of Ireland's social problems, especially in relation to land-holding; the growth of Irish agrarian agitation so much better organized and supported than had hitherto been the case that it had to be met by a large and extremely time-consuming amount of coercion or land reform or a combination of both; the growing hold in Ireland of nationalism and of the demand for home rule; the new strength and cohesion of the Irish parliamentary party and its impact on British politics, both within the House of Commons and through the mobilisation of the votes of Irishmen in the non-Irish constituencies. Ireland clearly needed, and had the means of exacting, a very considerable amount of attention to its problems. The nature of the preoccupation with Ireland seems equally clear. The issues of land and local government reform, home rule, and coercion predominate in the thought and action of politicians with regard to the Irish question.

Most analyses of the situation concentrate on these aspects of it, and it cannot be denied that during this period the problems of Ireland constituted for politicians a major obstruction to progress in other areas of political interest. The reality of this obstruction having been acknowledged, there are, however, other questions which ought to be asked. There are other ways of considering the causes, the nature, and the significance of the great Irish preoccupation. What seems deserving of closer examination, for instance, is the reaction of the politicians to finding themselves preoccupied in this way. Did they resent it or did they welcome it? One has always to bear in mind that these were men elected by, and responsible to, a predominantly non-Irish electorate, an electorate greatly increased in 1867 and 1884 to include large numbers from the working classes, whom they were cultivating with policies and national campaigns and appeals. How did they present and explain their preoccupation with Ireland to these new voters for whose support they were appealing throughout this period and many of whom presumably expected that their acquisition of the vote would lead to greater attention to their own problems?

Associated with this is another important but neglected line of investigation. Was there any relationship between the Irish preoccupation and the other leading policy issues of the day more substantial than the fact that it prevented politicians from devoting enough time and thought to them? To what extent did it, as the concern of these politicians, acquire characteristics from the broader non-Irish context within which they principally operated? It would certainly be surprising if a preoccupation of such duration failed to acquire or have imposed on it some connexion with other, non-Irish aspects of the political life of the time. Even if one assumes that this concentration on Irish problems was inescapable for any leading politician during the period, one ought to recognize that he was still able, and indeed might have been obliged, to adapt or exploit the preoccupation to conform with the needs of his own particular non-Irish political situation.

Various theories have been put forward which suggest that the Irish preoccupation did develop in this way. There is, for example, the idea that it functioned as a safety-valve for the expression of feelings and the adoption of attitudes which were non-Irish in origin and nature but could not easily be manifested in the more general context. A recent biographer of A. J. Balfour calls it an 'escape vent for passions altogether too strong for their overt subject', a safety-valve for a body politic 'worried by signs of "democracy", murmurs of Socialism, fears of a declining economy'.[1] A variant on this is the idea that Ireland was a testing-ground for new political principles, such as state interference with contracts and with property rights, or that it was a battle-ground to which were transferred conflicts that really belonged in England. According to E. Strauss,[2] Ireland was 'an obvious field for the stratagems of mines and countermines between the two parties'. One of the Liberal arguments for home rule after 1885 was the desirability of ending a situation in which Ireland was treated as a cockpit for the struggles of the parties rather than in reference to its own special problems. John Morley, advancing this argument in a speech in 1891, remarked on how orators delighted to use Irish issues for the display of 'all the grand common-places of their art', such as '"Law and order" on the one side, "Reconciliation of the people" and "Freedom of a nation" on the other'. But he went further and claimed that

the man who hates change in England, the man who distrusts the look of present things and dreads the future, the man whose great object is to stem the democratic tide and to save his cherished inequalities and privileges, delights with his whole

---

[1] K. Young, *Arthur James Balfour: The Happy Life of the Politician Prime Minister Statesman and Philosopher, 1848–1930* (1963), p. 128.
[2] *Irish Nationalism and British Democracy*, (1951), pp. 184–5.

heart in keeping as long as he can, and for ever if he can, the two great political hosts of this country eternally clashing in the Irish ditch.[3]

Both this theory and the notion of the safety-valve raise the question of choice, of whether the preoccupation was always or completely involuntary and unavoidable. Did politicians deliberately either create or prolong and unnecessarily enlarge it in order that it might be a safety-valve or a battle-ground? What Morley was suggesting was that the Irish question was employed deliberately by certain politicians to distract attention from proposals for reform at home. This 'distraction' or 'diversion' theory is to be found in the works of some recent historians. C. C. O'Brien says that Tory coercion after 1886 'distracted attention from British domestic issues', and L. P. Curtis, Jr., remarks that, while neither Liberals nor Conservatives can be blamed for creating the Irish question, 'elements in both parties consciously allowed events in Ireland to obscure social and economic problems at home'.[4]

Space does not permit an examination of the relevance of these suggestions as to the nature and significance of the preoccupation with Ireland to all aspects of the Irish question in this period. I intend in this article to take one major episode—the devotion of the Liberal party to the policy of home rule from 1886 to 1893.

The origins of the preoccupation of the Liberal party with home rule after 1885 obviously lie mainly in the exigencies of the Irish question itself and in the development of the thinking of Liberals, notably Gladstone, on Irish policy in response to these exigencies.[5] The fact that little reference will be made in this article to these origins does not imply that they have been disregarded. What I have concentrated on doing is examining the preoccupation in relation to the development of the party itself and seeing what impact it had, or was made to have, on that development.

One of the major weaknesses that appeared in the Liberal party in the early 1870s was sectionalism. The party seemed to be simply a coalition of adherents to various reform interests each of whom believed that the reform which he favoured was the most important of all and the most deserving of attention by the party leadership. Professor Hanham has traced the growth of this 'faddism', as it came to be known.[6] It became a danger to the unity of the party, especially when the advocates of these reforms threatened to

[3] *The Times*, 22 Sept. 1891.

[4] C. C. O'Brien, *Parnell and His Party 1880–90* (Oxford, 1957), p. 210. L. P. Curtis, Jr., *Coercion and Conciliation in Ireland, 1880–1892: A Study in Conservative Unionism* (Princeton and London, 1963), p. 431.

[5] For a full account of these origins see D. G. Hoskin, 'The genesis and significance of the 1886 "Home Rule" split in the Liberal Party', Cambridge Ph.D. thesis, 1964.

[6] H. J. Hanham, *Elections and Party Management: Politics in the Time of Disraeli and Gladstone* (1959), chapter 6.

make support of their 'fads' tests for Liberal candidates. The National Education League, the Liberation Society, and the United Kingdom Alliance were among the most prominent of these pressure groups, but there were many more. As these competed for the attention of the Liberal leaders and reacted rebelliously if their demands were ignored or their interests damaged, the condition of Liberal politics became increasingly anarchic. Joseph Chamberlain remarked on 'the prominence of special questions' in the general election of 1874: 'The organizations of the Alliance, the Liberation Society, the National Education League, the Anti-Contagious Diseases Acts Association, the Home Rulers, the Women's Suffrage Association, and others —all consisting mainly of Liberals—were everywhere pressing their claims and striving to make their concession the crucial test.'[7] Gladstone too was at this time deploring the existence of so many reform questions, 'each with a group of adherents to a special view, but incapable of being pursued by common and united action'.[8]

Professor Hanham has suggested, however, that the Liberal defeat at the 1874 elections was a great shock to many 'faddists' and led to a more sober appreciation among them of the necessity in their own interest of maintaining the strength and unity of the whole party. Chamberlain is, of course, the outstanding example of a Liberal politician who behaved as a sectionalist before 1874 but after 1874 turned to building up the unity of the party. He saw the problem thus: 'At present there are only individual Radicals, each specially interested in some part of the whole...There are Leagues and Associations and Unions but no party...'[9] What the Liberals needed was some principle that would bind together all these Leagues and Associations and make a unified party. Mathew Arnold perceived the basic weakness when he wrote after the 1874 elections that the Liberal party had 'no body of just, clear, well-ordered thought upon politics' and would have to 'find a new basis'.[10] Liberalism as a political creed was no longer systematic enough; there was no general agreement among reformers calling themselves Liberals as to what the principles that should govern the political action of Liberals really were. What then were the alternatives?

For a time the development of party organization appealed to many Liberals, notably Chamberlain, as the answer to the problem of Liberal disunity, the cure for the Liberal 'disease'. In Birmingham Liberalism there had developed what could be called a mystique of democracy, a deep faith

[7] Chamberlain, 'The Next Page of the Liberal Programme', *The Fortnightly Review*, no. 94 (Oct. 1874), 413.
[8] J. Morley, *The Life of William Ewart Gladstone* (1903), II, 502–3. For examples of sectionalism, cf. A. W. W. Dale, *The Life of R. W. Dale of Birmingham* (1898), pp. 281, 285–6 and J. L. and B. Hammond, *James Stansfeld: A Victorian Champion of Sex Equality* (1932), p. 177.
[9] J. L. Garvin, *The Life of Joseph Chamberlain* (1932), I, 161.
[10] G. W. E. Russell (ed.), *Letters of Matthew Arnold, 1848–1888* (1901), II, 129.

in the possibility of establishing in political institutions the expression of a unified popular will.[11] The theory on which the 'caucus' type of organization and the National Liberal Federation were based was that the democratic principle could provide an effective integration of minority sections into unified party action. When Chamberlain and his supporters discussed the merits of the 'caucus' and the N.L.F., they laid great stress on the ending of 'faddism' as a disruptive force and on the harnessing of the energies of the sectionalists to the work of securing and maintaining a Liberal majority. Under the general organizational 'umbrella' the sectionalists would acquire the democratic instinct, develop a sense of wider loyalties, and be prepared to accept an order of priorities for reform legislation as decided by the majority. The basic problem was the establishment of these priorities, the evolution of order among the many diverse and competing reform interests. Through free and open discussion such order would emerge. There would be a consensus, a sense of a majority interest.[12]

The 'caucus' and the N.L.F. represented Liberal politics based on total comprehensiveness, the inclusion of all sections within the party organization. But quite the opposite attitude to the problem of securing party unity sometimes appears among the Liberal leaders. This was a disposition to seek or to welcome and exploit an opportunity for the purging of the party and its reconstruction on some narrower but more solid basis. Either electoral defeat or a split in the party over some clear issue of principle might actually be beneficial if what was left of the party was more coherent and compact. As early as 1866 Gladstone wrote: 'A general election, which should somewhat reduce the party, would be of great use, *if* it should also have the effect of [purging?] it.'[13] After 1873 in particular there emerged in the party a frame of mind that either assumed that a split was inevitable or favoured bringing on a split as a solution to the party's problems. Liberalism was seen by some as being in such a disorganized state that perhaps its only salvation lay in a reconstruction involving the cutting off of sections of the party. Hartington, who was prepared in 1875 to see the radicals and moderates go their own separate ways, said to Gladstone in 1885 that 'the point always urged upon him was, not to break up the Liberal party. But...can we avoid its breaking up, within a very short time after you retire, & ought this consideration

---

[11] Cf. A. Briggs, *Victorian Cities* (1963), pp. 188–227. For the sources of this mystique, cf. T. R. Tholfsen, 'The Origins of the Birmingham Caucus', *The Historical Journal*, II, no. 2 (1959), 161–84.

[12] Hanham, op. cit., chapter 7. R. S. Watson, *The National Liberal Federation from Its Commencement to the General Election of 1906*, 1907, esp. pp. 8, 15, 19, 20, 24. M. Ostrogorski, *Democracy and the Organization of Political Parties*, (1902), I, 175, 183. P. Fraser, *Joseph Chamberlain Radicalism and Empire, 1868–1914* (1966), pp. 29–32. J. Chamberlain, 'A New Political Organization', *The Fortnightly Review*, no. 127 (July 1877), 127–9; 'The Caucus', *The Fortnightly Review*, no. 143 (Nov. 1878), 726–7, 730, 734, 737.

[13] Gladstone to Russell, 20 June 1866, Russell Papers, P.R.O. 30/22/16, quoted in F. B. Smith, *The Making of the Second Reform Bill* (Cambridge, 1966), p. 114.

therefore to be regarded as of such very great force.'[14] Chamberlain, in spite of his claims to be setting up an all-inclusive party organisation, had the long-term strategy of expelling the whigs and establishing the ascendency of the radicals in a reconstructed party. The hope of seeing a split and a reconstruction on a new basis was, of course, characteristic of the attitude to the party of many advocates of particular reforms. The example may be given of W. E. Bear, a land-reform enthusiast, who wrote thus in 1879, when urging the party to 'take Free Agriculture for its watchword': 'It will be objected that to adopt this suggestion would be to divide the Liberal party. No doubt it would be; but the Liberal party can only be united by being divided. It is just now a nondescript body, without distinct aims, and without even a reason for existence beyond that of preventing the Conservatives from doing mischief...'[15]

Associated with this were certain other characteristics of late nineteenth-century Liberal politics—the growing aversion of some leaders from holding office, the recurrence of desperate attempts to find any excuse to leave office, the increasing inclination to court electoral defeat and exile from power. The leadership of a party plagued by the demands of sectionalists for attention to their reform interests naturally found itself in great difficulties whenever it constituted the government, for then the sections clamoured for action, and refusal or deferment of action at a time when the party held power only intensified their sense of grievance. Selection from among the reform proposals was a highly invidious operation. No guiding principles for this selection existed that were acceptable both to the reform advocates and to the party leaders. Power came to seem less and less attractive to those leaders who, upon acquiring it, had to try to organize reform legislation and restrain or satisfy the impatience of the sectionalists. Being in opposition was, at any rate, the best of all excuses for abstention from commitment and action. Events after 1885 have to be seen in relation to the decline of two Liberal governments from great election triumphs into a situation of disunity, incoherence, and longing for release from office.[16]

Controversy concerning the means of restoring order to Liberal politics tended to be focused on the question of the most desirable form of Liberal policy. Should the party adopt a wide programme of reforms or should it concentrate on a single major issue? The proponents of these two principles of action engaged in frequent debate during this period. The outstanding

[14] As reported in Gladstone to Granville, 22 Jan. 1885, A. Ramm (ed.), *The Political Correspondence of Mr Gladstone and Lord Granville 1876–1886*, II (Oxford, 1962), 326. For Hartington in 1875 see B. Holland, *The Life of Spencer Compton, Eighth Duke of Devonshire*, (1911), I, 141–4.

[15] W. E. Bear, 'The Liberal Party and the Farmers', *The Fortnightly Review*, no. 147 (Mar. 1879), 443.

[16] For 1873–4, cf. Morley, op. cit. II, 480–2. For the 'act of hara-kiri' in 1885, cf. Curtis op. cit. pp. 19–23.

advocate and practitioner of 'programme' politics, and indeed the man around whom much of the controversy centred, was Joseph Chamberlain. Yet even he had wavered. In the early 1870s he was very much a 'single question' politician with his involvement in the Nonconformist agitation against Forster's Education Act. Then in 1873 he produced his first programme—'Free Schools, Free Land, Free Church, Free Labour'. However, the chaotic multitude of 'special questions' which he saw Liberalism to be in the 1874 elections led him to look back to the electoral triumph of 1868 and conclude that the voices of the special interests were most likely to be silent whenever there was a 'larger issue' 'felt to be of sufficient magnitude to justify the postponement of all minor subjects'. By late 1874 he had decided that it was necessary to 'consider which of the many practical applications of Liberal principles has the first claim to be selected as the next rallying cry of the Liberal party'.[17] For a time, prompted by his friend John Morley, an ardent advocate of concentrating on one question, he looked to disestablishment as a possible rallying cry of this kind; but by 1877 he had reverted to his belief in programme. Organization now seemed to him capable of providing the essential cohesion.

But other Liberal politicians lacked his faith in organization. To them a programme was an unsuitable mode of political action because of the absence of generally accepted systematic principles that could hold together the various parts. A party that devoted itself to more than one reform issue at a time was doomed to incoherence and disunity if it had no underlying principles strong enough to bind these issues together. Gladstone, with his belief in great missions, was a notable practitioner of 'single question' politics. He was well known as having a 'one idea at a time faculty'.[18] John Morley and H. H. Fowler may be mentioned as prominent Liberals who theorized about the advantages of this mode of political conduct.[19] Particularly significant are references to John Bright's opposition to 'programme' politics.[20] In the 1870s Bright's influence in this regard was still being felt. At the inaugural conference of the National Liberal Federation in 1877 he made plain his antagonism to the type of political activity now being promoted by Chamberlain—and Chamberlain was very annoyed.[21] Ostrogorski quotes Bright's advice to a group of Lancashire Liberals who in 1874 wished to

[17] Chamberlain, 'The Next Page of the Liberal Programme' loc. cit. pp. 413, 418.

[18] Lord Houghton, quoted in J. L. Hammond, *Gladstone and the Irish Nation* (1938), p. 164.

[19] For Morley, cf. his correspondence with Chamberlain in Aug. 1873 in the Chamberlain MSS., Birmingham University Library, and in Garvin, op. cit. I, esp. pp. 146, 161. V. also Morley, *The Life of Richard Cobden*, I (1881), 203. For Fowler, cf. E. H. Fowler, *The Life of Henry Hartley Fowler, First Viscount Wolverhampton*, G.S.C.I. (1912), pp. 239–40.

[20] Fowler, op. cit. p. 384. Morley to Chamberlain, 18 Aug. 1873, and in a speech reported in *The Times*, 10 Dec. 1889.

[21] Cf. Chamberlain, 'A New Political Organization', loc. cit. pp. 127, 130; and Gladstone's recollection of the quarrel in F. E. Hamer (ed.), *The Personal Papers of Lord Rendel* (1931), p. 93.

revive the National Reform Union: that if they did so its programme should consist of one point, a single reform, and comments: 'In this he adhered to the old concept of popular Organizations formed for the realization of a distinct and specified object; in the pursuit of which men differing in opinion on other points might unite, resuming complete liberty of action as soon as the object was attained.'[22] For Bright had been involved in what was now the classic instance of successful 'one question' politics, the campaign of the Anti-Corn Law League; and both Fowler and Morley, for instance, stressed that in the conditions of British politics concentrating on one question at a time seemed to be the surest way to political success.[23] In the 1880s Liberals were given a renewed reminder of the effectiveness of that kind of political activity in Morley's biography of Cobden, published in 1881. Its advantages are referred to frequently in the book, both in Cobden's own words and in Morley's commentary.[24] A recent historian of the Anti-Corn Law League has traced the conflict in radicalism in the 1840s between those such as Cobden who advocated concentration on a single issue and those who would rather have agitated for a programme of reforms, and has suggested that 'an attack on the Corn Law was found an acceptable focus for Radical energies at a time when the Radicals were sadly in need of such a rallying point'.[25] The success of the League was a powerful argument in favour of a return to 'one question' radicalism—*if* such a unifying issue could ever be found again.

In order to understand why home rule became such an issue we must examine more closely the 'single question' politics of Gladstone. Since the early 1870s at least Gladstone had been very concerned about the disunited, factious condition of the Liberal party, its lack of a 'great positive aim', the fact that none of the reforms advocated by the various sections was supported by a 'clear and decisive majority' of the party or capable of 'being pursued by common and united action'.[26] Gladstone had little time for men with 'fads' and 'crotchets'.[27] And it is clear what remedy he favoured for the disorganization which they caused in the party—some 'positive force' that would 'carry us onward as a body', some issue that would serve for a time 'to mould the rest'.[28] He believed that the 'vital principle of the Liberal party, like that of Greek art, is *action*'. But effective action is possible only

[22] Ostrogorski, op. cit. I, 218.

[23] Fowler, op. cit. pp. 239–40. D. A. Hamer, *John Morley: Liberal Intellectual in Politics* (1968), pp. 94–5.

[24] Cf. Morley, *Life of Cobden*, I, 126–7, 142, 203–4; II, pp. 38–41, 112–13, 121, 384.

[25] N. McCord, *The Anti-Corn Law League, 1838–1846* (1958), pp. 16–17, 19–20, 41–3, 77–80, 111–12.

[26] Morley, *Life of Gladstone*, II, 457, 498, 502–3.

[27] Cf. his attitude to Leonard Courtney as reported in G. P. Gooch, *Life of Lord Courtney* (1920), p. 250.

[28] Morley, *Life of Gladstone*, I, 479.

if energies are concentrated. Therefore he searched constantly for some 'question of real magnitude likely to unite' the party.[29] When 'the great Irish question came up in force' in 1868, the action of the party had, he believed, been concentrated. Later his conduct in regard to the Eastern Question was influenced by a hope that here might be found the 'great question' that could bring about a Liberal revival.[30]

Never was the party more disunited than in 1885. The final split between the Chamberlainite radicals and the whigs seemed imminent. Gladstone's thinking on Irish policy meanwhile moved on its own lines towards acceptance of the home-rule solution. But his obsession with the Irish problem was not so complete as to prevent him from giving some thought to the problem of Liberal party unity—and the connexion between that unity and policy preoccupations and forms. In the election campaign the problem of order among reform questions and the notion of one question that would have a special, subordinating relationship to all others appear to have been very much on his mind. In a speech in Edinburgh on 11 November he said that political questions had a 'proper time' and a 'proper order' and that dis-establishment was not a mature enough subject to justify all others being thrust aside and cast into darkness for its sake.[31] In 1885 the greatest threat of Liberal disorganization came from the eruption of the other kind of Liberal politics in Chamberlain's 'radical' and 'unauthorized' programmes. There is some evidence to suggest that Gladstone saw a possible remedy in the re-assertion of 'single question' Liberalism. In mid-October Chamberlain wrote, after visiting Hawarden, that Gladstone

did not conceal that his present interest was in the Irish question, and he seemed to think that a policy for dealing with it might be found which would unite us all and which would necessarily throw into the background those minor points of difference about the schools and small holdings which threaten to drive the Whigs into the arms of the Tories or into retirement.

A few days later Gladstone wrote to Chamberlain: 'An instinct blindly impresses me with the likelihood that Ireland may shoulder aside everything else.'[32] In November Gladstone expressed the belief that Ireland would act on all other issues 'like the sun on a fire in the grate'.[33] The Irish crisis came first in influencing Gladstone's ideas on policy; but we can also see emerging in his mind the thought, obviously by no means unwelcome to him, that concentration on dealing with it might bring about the restoration of unity in Liberal action.

[29] Ramm, op. cit. I, 40, 42.
[30] Holland, op. cit. I, 149, 176.
[31] Morley, *Life of Gladstone*, III, 248.
[32] Chamberlain to Labouchere, 20 Oct. 1885, A. L. Thorold, *The Life of Henry Labouchere* (1913), p. 239. Gladstone to Chamberlain, 25 Oct. 1885, C. H. D. Howard (ed.), *A Political Memoir 1880–92 by Joseph Chamberlain* (1953), p. 132.
[33] S. Childers, *The Life and Correspondence of the Right Hon. Hugh C. E. Childers* (1901), II, 234.

Was Gladstone likely to be very worried if the prelude to the achievement of such unity was schism and purge in the party? We must bear in mind his own record in regard to party. He had been a Peelite; that is, he had once been involved in the disruption of a party over a great issue of principle. In addition, his own movement during his career across the party spectrum, and the way in which the Liberal party seemed to have grown up around him and to be dependent on his own personal appeal to the electorate, undoubtedly had left him rather less influenced that many others by 'ordinary' party considerations. He was in fact in the habit of distinguishing between 'party' questions and questions involving 'higher interests'. Thus when he voted in 1878 with a minority of Liberals for a motion condemning the calling out of the reserves he said: 'On these great questions, which cut so deep into heart and mind, the importance of taking what they think the best course for the question will often seem, even to those who have the most just sense of party obligation, a higher duty than that of party allegiance.'[34] It certainly seems that this distinction was again in his mind in 1885. In the speech at Edinburgh on 11 November he described himself as 'labouring with all my heart for the unity of the Liberal party' but then defined this unity as having to be 'founded upon common convictions as to the importance of the work to be done'. He agreed therefore that there might be 'a point which our convictions should part, if the questions at issue are of vital importance'. 'Conscientious motives' were 'higher than party motives', and if the need arose, he said, 'I hope the Liberal party will sever and split rather than sacrifice conviction and principle'. For a party ought to be 'an instrument for the attainment of great ends'.[35] In other words, the great cause came first, and a party ought to become its instrument even if a split resulted. And then, when the split over home rule did occur in 1886, Gladstone seemed to regard it as leading paradoxically to the emergence of a party more united and more capable of common and effective action.

One-third of the Liberal M.P.s elected in 1885 rebelled and repudiated Gladstone's leadership. But the split could be seen also as producing a purge and a reconstruction. The whigs and radicals who seceded over the Home Rule Bill may have made strange allies but they had this in common, that they had been the principal feuding elements in the party over the previous decade. Seceding, they left behind a party that, even if smaller and out of power, seemed much more united, and many Liberal leaders rejoiced in this. A comparison with the chaos of 1885 was implicit in Shaw-Lefevre's claim in 1887 that, if the two parties took up positions for and against home

[34] Gladstone to Granville, 12 Apr. 1878, Ramm. op. cit. 1, 70. On this preference for questions involving 'higher interests', see R. T. Shannon, *Gladstone and the Bulgarian Agitation 1876* (1963), pp. 96–7.
[35] *The Times*, 12 Nov. 1885.

rule, 'we shall, at the next general election, have no difficulties or dissensions in our own party', and in G. W. E. Russell's observation that in 1886, 'though we were heavily beaten, our state was, in one main respect, more gracious than it had been in 1885. We were no longer hampered by conflicting policies, or called on to decide between authorised and unauthorised programmes.'[36] A speaker at the National Liberal Federation council in 1887 called the party 'eager and united, better and stronger for its recent purge'.[37] John Morley claimed that the party had 'never been more united, more firm, more compact', while Campbell-Bannerman even thanked the Irish Nationalists 'for having invented an Ireland and an Irish question, which had been a source of so much good and so much strength to the Liberal party'.[38] Lord Rosebery, a very unenthusiastic advocate of home rule, was inclined to dwell on this aspect of the concentration on it. The party, he would say, had once been a 'disorganized multitude' with 'several leaders'; now it enjoyed 'union under one leader' and there was 'only one question of policy to be considered'. It was better to be a minority that was 'compact' and 'united by a principle' that a majority that was 'flabby' and 'disconnected'. Rosebery would describe what usually happened when there was a Liberal government. A certain number of Liberals would 'peel off' as reforms which did not satisfy their sectionalist interests were undertaken, and there was 'a process of waste, of deterioration' that 'never occurs, as far as I know, in the other party as it does among the more ardent minds of the Liberal party'. When the party had been 'enormously preponderant in the House of Commons' its very size had meant that 'it contained many schools of thought and still more numerous leaders'. Now there was only one policy and one leader.[39]

The basis of the Liberals' case as to the relationship of the home-rule policy to general British politics was the 'obstruction' argument, summed up in the slogan 'Ireland blocks the way'. They claimed that Ireland consumed, unavoidably, so much of the time and demanded so much of the attention of parliament and political leaders that no satisfactory progress was possible on any domestic reform question until Irishmen were enabled by the concession of home rule to attend to Irish affairs themselves. A manifesto issued by the National Liberal Federation in August 1886 declared that, until the Irish question was settled, 'no progress can be made with the ordinary work of the Liberal party'.[40] An image often used to describe the obstruction was that of a railway accident or a blocked railway line. Gladstone

[36] *The Times*, 12 Jan. 1887. G. W. E. Russell, 'The New Liberalism: A Response', *The Nineteenth Century*, Sept. 1889, p. 494.

[37] Watson, op. cit. p. 89.

[38] *The Times*, 13 Dec., 21 June 1888.

[39] Ibid., 20 Oct. 1886, 28 Apr., 21, 23 May, 18 Aug. 1887, 10 Oct. 1888. R. R. James, *Lord Randolph Churchill* (1959), p. 322.

[40] *The Times*, 9 Aug. 1886. Cf. Herbert Gladstone, 'Ireland Blocks the Way', *The Nineteenth Century*, June 1892, pp. 899 ff.

said that Ireland 'blocks the way' like a wrecked train, preventing anything else from getting through.[41] Spencer likened Ireland to an express train that 'stops the line': all other trains, 'laden with precious measures valued by the Liberal party', were 'blocked and shunted' until it had passed by.[42] Thus the home-rule preoccupation was associated with the maintenance of a general Liberal faith in progress. Progress remained inevitable, indeed mechanical. The *only* obstruction to it was the Irish question.

That the obstruction did exist there can be no doubt. What interests us here, however, is the bearing which its existence was made to have on general Liberal politics. Was the certain progress which the Liberals claimed that Ireland was obstructing itself a myth? For, quite apart from Ireland, there was another obstacle to development in Liberal politics—the confusion among Liberals as to what now constituted progress, their indecision as to what line of action to follow, their inability to agree on what reforms to promote and in what order. Irrespective of its accuracy, the notion of an Irish obstruction did enable the Liberals temporarily to find a scapegoat for these weaknesses within their own politics. If ardent reformers—or impatient voters—demanded to know why the Liberals were not acting on the reforms in which they had a special interest, here was the answer: Ireland rendered the Liberals 'impotent'.[43] What the Liberal leaders constantly implied in their speeches was that the removal of this obstruction was the key to the entire situation. Confusion would disappear, progress would resume. Gladstone put it thus: 'it is in the removal of that one great obstacle that the secret of all rational and effectual progress lies'.[44]

The home-rule preoccupation offered a temporary remedy for faddism, a temporary answer to the problem of fixing an order of precedence for action among the reform proposals. Clearing 'Ireland' out of the way was obviously the first duty of every reformer, no matter what his special interest might be. Progress on all other questions depended on the removal of the Irish obstruction. The home-rule issue thus became such a question as Gladstone had craved in 1873, one that would, if 'worked into certain shapes', 'help to mould the rest, at least for the time'. In the absence of a Liberal creed, this single great question functioned as a substitute, conferring a provisional order on the miscellaneous 'causes' of Liberal politics. To the promoters of 'particular subjects', to those organizations, 'in some respects competing', which had 'special and what might be called preferential interests in one or other' of these subjects, Gladstone gave this message: 'Your first interest is to get rid of the Irish question.' He asked them to appreciate that they could not get past this blockage on the line and that until they cleared the line their questions 'must continue in their present

[41] *The Times*, 18 Mar. 1887.   [42] Ibid. 27 Apr. 1887.
[43] Cf. Morley, *The Times*, 12 Feb. 1887   [44] Ibid. 25 Mar. 1890.

state of inaction and, for practical purposes, oblivion'.[45] The post-1885 career of W. S. Caine, the ardent advocate of temperance reform, shows how difficult such 'faddists' now found it to assert the primacy of their sectionalist interests in face of the absorption of political controversy in the issue of home rule. Much against his will, he was obliged to become categorized primarily in terms of *this* issue.[46] In 1886 Gladstone predicted that Ireland would 'control and put aside all other political questions in England';[47] and his prediction appeared to be fulfilled. According to Gladstone, Ireland became 'the key to the position of every English question and the real helm that steers the ship of politics', with the consequence that 'perhaps thirty or forty questions', 'all of them having large and intelligent bodies of men pushing them forward', had to remain in oblivion.[48] One cannot imagine that the thought of this alternative to the Irish preoccupation —the uncontrolled and uncontrollable 'pushing' of thirty or forty bodies of ardent reformers—filled Gladstone with pleasure. What was especially significant in this regard was the appearance in *The Nineteenth Century* of a series of articles by Gladstone entitled 'Electoral Facts', surveying the party's electoral progress since its commitment to home rule. In 1878 he had published a similar article, alleging that the enthusiasm aroused in the Bulgarian agitation had had a highly beneficial effect in checking 'the excesses of rampant and erratic individualism' and sectionalism in the party. Concentration on a single issue of this kind reduced the number of rival Liberal candidates considerably.[49] Nor did Gladstone's colleagues fail to see the advantage of the preoccupation in this light and to be anxious to see it maintained if the only alternative was chaos. Thus Rosebery told Gladstone in August 1889 that the only cure for a certain 'critical condition' in the party would be the knowledge that the leaders were once again devoting themselves to 'Irish policy & measures' as their first priority. He was worried about the growing interest in 'vague Socialistic schemes' and 'vaporous views which have at present no ripeness or consistency'. 'I am all', he said, 'for the free play of individuals in the party but not for chaos.' Only the Irish commitment gave the party 'faith & discipline'.[50]

The Irish preoccupation also represented a decision by Gladstone and those Liberals who supported him in favour of concentrated 'single question' politics as against dispersive 'programme' politics. The National Liberal Federation, which had been created as a vehicle of Chamberlainite

[45] Ibid. 18 Mar., 20 Oct. 1887. Hamer, op. cit., pp. 203–5.

[46] J. Newton, *W. S. Caine, M.P.: A Biography* (1907), pp. 167–8, 179–82. Lord Askwith, *Lord James of Hereford* (1930), p. 190.

[47] R. R. James, *Rosebery: A Biography of Archibald Philip, Fifth Earl of Rosebery* (1963), p. 191.   [48] *The Times*, 23 May 1888, 18 Mar. 1887.

[49] W. E. Gladstone, 'Electoral Facts', *The Nineteenth Century*, Nov. 1878, Oct. 1887, Dec. 1889, Sept. 1891.

[50] Rosebery to Gladstone, 11 Aug. 1889, Rosebery MSS., National Library of Scotland, Box 19.

'programme' politics, was temporarily transformed into an agency for promoting the alternative mode of political activity.

The attitude of the Liberal leaders to the Irish 'obstruction' was highly ambiguous. Frequently, of course, they cursed its existence and lamented the effect that it was having on reform politics. Yet at times they seemed to welcome it and to feel no strong desire for its removal. The preoccupation appeared to be doing the party so much good that they were reluctant to face up to the prospect of its coming to an end. Lord Ripon told the N.L.F. in 1887: 'They might rest in the shade of opposition, as long as Fox and Grey, but they would work on until they had accomplished...their policy.'[51] Rosebery promised that they would fight on until home rule was secured, 'however long their exile may be from power and from place'.[52] This kind of attitude set a deep gulf between the Gladstonian Liberals and the Liberal Unionists. To the latter such a willing acceptance of defeat and exile from office seemed little short of madness For example, Jesse Collings made what must have seemed to him a very practical and reasonable argument in favour of Liberal reunion at the end of 1886: 'The choice then seems to be Home Rule as the Liberal policy and certain defeat, or a Liberal platform (minus Home Rule for the present), and success with a restoration of the party to power.'[53] But the Gladstonians seemed actually to prefer the former of these alternatives. Power had lost its attractiveness for the time being.

Some Liberals moved on from talking about the 'obstruction' to praising the new electorate for having voluntarily taken up the cause of Irish reform. The voters were encouraged to believe that it was they, not the politicians, who were responsible for the preoccupation and that in assuming the responsibility they had shown great 'nobility of spirit', a 'wonderful record' of 'self-sacrifice'. It was an 'unselfish cause', one in which the new democracy had 'so little to gain', which 'did not affect its own interests'; and yet the democracy had taken it up.[54] In other words, it bore no direct relation to 'selfish' class interests. The alternative to the Irish preoccupation was attention by the new voters to *their own* needs, and such a prospect alarmed many Liberals.

The 'obstruction' argument and the concentration on Irish policy provided the Liberals with time in which to evolve new principles and policies that would be relevant to the voters' needs and would present a viable and safe alternative to 'selfish' 'Socialist schemes' such as Rosebery and others so feared. They provided an excuse for abstention from action that might be considered premature so long as such principles were not available to guide it. Some of the younger Liberals, such as R. B. Haldane, understood this

[51] *The Times*, 19 Oct. 1887.   [52] Ibid. 21 May 1887.
[53] Collings to H. H. Fowler, 27 Dec. 1886, quoted in Fowler, op. cit. p. 219.
[54] *The Times*, 7 Dec. 1887 (Arnold Morley), 5 May, 6 July 1892 (John Morley). J. Guinness Rogers, 'The Middle Class and the New Liberalism', *The Nineteenth Century*, Oct. 1889, p. 712. Hamer, op. cit., pp. 192–3.

aspect of the situation clearly. For example, in 1888 Haldane published two articles in the *Contemporary Review* on the theme of the need to be working now to prepare the Liberal future. He warned Liberals that 'there will come a time when the Irish question is out of the way, and when we shall fight on our general policy'. Unless that policy became more definite, the Liberal leaders would find themselves repeating the experience of 1885. Liberals should 'insist on the breathing space which the question of Home Rule has given us being used in making preparations' for the post-home-rule situation. They must counteract the efforts of 'the extreme Socialist party' 'to mould the new voters to its wishes'.[55] Haldane, A. H. D. Acland, and others felt that Chamberlain's attempt to raise social questions in 1885 had been premature because his ideas had been inadequately thought out. It was their aim to do the kind of work which would ensure that these subjects could be turned into useful legislation.[56]

But there were several consequences of the upheaval of 1886 which helped to diminish the usefulness of the 'breathing-space' for the reconstruction of the party and its policy. The secession of Chamberlain and other radicals removed valuable talent that would have been devoted to such work. What remained was the leadership of Gladstone, which was more than ever, in association with the Irish policy, the rallying-point for the many diverse elements of Liberalism. The Liberals were paralysed by the fact that so many people had followed Gladstone himself and accepted the home-rule policy principally because he recommended it.[57] Gladstone's authority remained paramount. The party as it existed after 1886 was a party shaped in his own image, constructed around his own decision to take up home rule. Because of this, and because he did not regard it as part of his responsibility after 1885 to help with the development of domestic policy, his leadership necessarily constituted a major obstruction to this development. He remained '*in situ* for the Irish question only'.[58] In 1885 he had made it plain that at his age he felt no further concern with the 'ordinary exigencies of party' and wanted to be troubled no more with the wide range of questions normally attended to by a party.[59] Thereafter he expressly absolved himself from participation in the discussion of the new ideas and policies that the party would so urgently need after the Irish interlude, and the party was paralysed by the lack of direction from the top on anything except Irish policy[60]—or issues such as Welsh and Scottish disestablishment where Gladstone saw commitment as necessary in the interests of the Irish policy.

[55] Haldane, 'The Liberal Party and its Prospects', *The Contemporary Review*, Jan. 1888, pp. 145 ff.; 'The Liberal Creed', ibid., Oct. 1888, pp. 461 ff.
[56] Cf. J. A. Spender, *Sir Robert Hudson A Memoir* (1930), pp. 21–2.
[57] For a good example of the attitudes of Gladstonian 'loyalists', see A. J. Mundella to Gladstone, 15 Dec. 1885, Gladstone Papers, B.M. Add. MSS. 44258, fos. 211–15.
[58] Morley, *Life of Gladstone*, III, 355.   [59] *Ibid.* III, 225–6. Ramm, op. cit. II, 405.
[60] Cf. Haldane's comments on this, *Contemporary Review*, Jan. 1888, p. 148; Oct. 1888, p. 474.

Another inhibiting factor stemming from the reconstruction of 1886 was the reviving in Liberal politics of the spirit of mid-nineteenth-century reform movements. The Liberal party seemed to have been forced to revert to the mode of reform agitation practised so successfully by the Anti-Corn Law League and imitated by the host of pressure groups that sought to promote the 'fads' of mid-Victorian Liberalism. But the essential characteristic of such agitation was that its aims were limited and that each organization formed was 'destined to come to an end with the triumph of the particular cause which had called it into life'.[61] The home-rule commitment represented a similar limited cause. But the Liberal party had to look to a future beyond the success or definitive rejection of that cause. The politics of the great reform movements were quite different in spirit from the politics of the permanent parliamentary parties. Perhaps the attempt to fuse them in 1886 reflected the attitude of men such as Gladstone himself who still understood party politics and reform movements mainly in terms of the pre-1867 situation. The Liberal party after 1885 was perilously close to being an anachronism. Chamberlain had appreciated the need for a framework that would allow flexibility and the simultaneous promotion of a variety of reforms and so be relevant to a changed political system. The problem was whether after 1885 the party had not acquired a form so rigid as to allow change only through dissolution, not through internal evolution.

Historians have been reluctant to acknowledge that at the time the Liberals' 'obstruction' argument was met by a considerable amount of criticism and disbelief. There were those who claimed—and perhaps their claims have not been attended to sufficiently since—that Ireland was not the only or the real obstruction, that there might be another obstruction to be sought in the fears and perplexities and deliberate diversion-creating tactics of the Gladstonian Liberals. Did Ireland, they asked, really need to be treated as obstructing progress on everything else?

Resentment of the monopolizing of Liberal politics by home rule, and disbelief that this was necessary, were among the bases of the Chamberlainite or Radical Unionist position. John Bright expressed their attitude well when he wrote in 1887: 'Mr Gladstone stops the way. He insists on an impossible legislation for Ireland, and insists upon it to the exclusion of legislation for the whole Kingdom'.[62] Chamberlain maintained afterwards that Gladstone had taken up home rule because 'there was nothing else for him except my programme' and 'to have adopted that would have been humiliating'.[63] When Chamberlain sought Liberal reunion in 1887, he tried

---

[61] Ostrogorski, op. cit. I, 132–3. Hamer, op.cit., pp. 269–70.
[62] G. M. Trevelyan, *The Life of John Bright* (1913), p. 443.
[63] F. W. Hirst, *In the Golden Days* (1947), p. 169. J. Amery, *The Life of Joseph Chamberlain*, (1951), IV, 511–12.

to confront Liberals with the choice of a different form of action, one in which 'all Liberal reform' would not be 'indefinitely adjourned' until the wishes of the Irish had been met.[64] Chamberlain saw the situation at least partly in terms of a counter-revolution by conservative Liberals, led by Gladstone, who feared what looked in 1885 like the imminent triumph of his radicalism. To him the adoption of home rule constituted a deliberate diversion.

Then, as Herbert Gladstone acknowledged in 1892, the Liberal leaders were 'frequently attacked by some of the more advanced members of the labour party for their insistence upon the paramount importance of the Irish question, and their determination to give it priority'.[65] The Fabians argued that the Liberals were trying 'to stifle English questions by an agitation about Irish grievances'.[66] According to Sidney Webb, workingmen felt 'a daily increasing suspicion that the Home Rule question is being used by Liberal landlords and capitalists, not to say by Mr Gladstone himself, as a means of staving off the far more deeply reaching social reforms which would otherwise have to be taken up by the Radical party'. They feared 'that the Liberal leaders are using the pretext that "Home Rule stops the way" as a cloak for their fundamental lack of faith in the possibility of social reform by legislative action'.[67]

Within the Liberal leadership itself Harcourt was a constant critic of the preoccupation with Ireland, maintaining that the party existed for something more than Ireland alone and must show that it did. Perceiving clearly and urgently the problem of the future of the party in the parliamentary system, he argued that it was wrong and dangerous for the party of progress to coop itself up within the confines of a single policy.[68]

But where else did order and cohesion lie? Beneath their discussion of the Irish policy Harcourt's colleagues, in particular Gladstone, showed a continuing consciousness of danger from faddism. They found great difficulty in resisting the demands for commitment to priority of attention from the advocates of Welsh disestablishment, for instance—except by using the pretext of the Irish obstruction.[69] The impatience of labour also worried them. The Liberal chief whip warned Gladstone in September 1890 of the danger of 'the very large and important class affected' by labour questions such as the eight-hour day 'being persuaded that their special interest ought to outweigh any considerations of the claims of Ireland in the votes they will be called upon to give'.[70] It is not surprising therefore that, while the

[64] Garvin, op. cit. (1933), II, 292.
[65] Loc. cit. p. 903.
[66] P. P. Poirier, *The Advent of the Labour Party* (1958), p. 32.
[67] S. Webb, 'The Moral of the Elections', *The Contemporary Review*, Aug. 1892, pp 282–3.
[68] *The Times*, 8 Feb. 1888, 24 Oct. 1889. Hamer, op. cit., pp. 228–30.
[69] K. O. Morgan, *Wales in British Politics 1868–1922* (Cardiff, 1963), pp. 90–1, 122–3, 139.
[70] Arnold Morley to Gladstone, 24 Sept. 1890, Gladstone Papers, B.M. Add. MSS. 44254, fos. 34–5.

Parnell divorce crisis with its weakening effect on the home-rule policy caused Harcourt to argue that now other questions should be attended to, his colleagues seemed more anxious about the possibility that the 'special interests' might be enabled to take charge and reintroduce anarchy into Liberal politics.[71] The notion of the home-rule preoccupation as an alternative to 'socialism' is seen in Lord Ripon's recommendation that the party 'firmly retain' home rule as its great policy because 'if it were displaced a whole series of labour questions would come to the front'.[72] The Liberal leaders examined the alternatives to the Irish preoccupation and found them inadequate and unattractive.[73] Tattered as it was, it had to remain. Even Harcourt had to acknowledge the difficulties. The 'selection of any particular subject for the first place' instead of home rule would, he wrote, 'cause discontent in the camp of those whose hearts like the Temperance people and the Welsh Noncons are mainly set on other topics'. He was prepared, therefore, to see the Irish preoccupation maintained, but now with an anti-coercion rather than pro-home-rule emphasis.[74]

The alarm in the party at the prospect of having to go to the electorate with so meagre a programme was so great, however, that the leaders deemed it expedient to adopt the resolutions passed by the National Liberal Federation at Newcastle in October 1891 as a vast 'omnibus' programme. Even Gladstone recognized the necessity of a wider reform commitment and, when returned to power in 1892, seemed at first ready to support legislative action on a broad front.[75] The home-rule issue soon took over, but the chafing and straining of Liberals at the curb which it imposed were very hard to contain. Liberals were described as 'famishing' for what they had not been able to get in the 'too many years in the wilderness', and Liberal M.P.s had promised the voters that there was 'no danger of a one-session Parliament, and a Parliament of one idea', but that English reforms would be carried as well as home rule.[76] The leaders realized that there was in the party 'no enthusiasm for Home Rule, and a desire to put foward at once other measures'.[77] Younger Liberals insisted on the importance of attracting to the party 'the confidence of that nascent body of opinion in the constituencies which cares little for

[71] Arnold Morley to Gladstone, 30 Dec. 1890, 1 Jan. 1891, B.M. Add. MSS. 44254, fos. 65, 67. Harcourt to John Morley, 19 Dec. 1890, 6 Jan. 1891, Harcourt Papers, Stanton Harcourt, Oxfordshire. John Morley to Gladstone, 31 Dec. 1890, B.M. Add. MSS. 44256, fo. 104. Hamer, op. cit., chapter 17.

[72] L. Wolf, *Life of the First Marquess of Ripon*, (1921), II, 196–200.

[73] Ibid. Morley, *Life of Gladstone*, III, 457. F. S. L. Lyons, *The Fall of Parnell 1890–91* (1960), p. 219. Memo. by J. Morley, enclosed in A. Morley to Harcourt, 30 Dec. 1890, Harcourt Papers. A. Morley to Gladstone, 30 Dec. 1890, B.M. Add. MSS. 44254, fos. 63–4. J. Morley to Gladstone, 31 Dec. 1890, 2 Jan. 1891, B.M. Add. MSS. 44256, fos. 103–4, 107.

[74] Harcourt to Gladstone, 3 Jan. 1891, B.M. Add. MSS. 44202, fos. 48–9.

[75] Gladstone to Harcourt, 14, 18, 22 July 1892, B.M. Add. MSS. 44202, fos. 157–8, 166–7, 176.

[76] F. A. Channing, *Memories of Midland Politics 1885–1910* (1918), pp. 129, 147.

[77] Wolf, op. cit. II, 200–1.

any Irish policy and concentrates itself on social questions'.[78] Any claim by Gladstone that 'English reforms were "subordinate" to Home Rule' was now reported to arouse 'a good deal of complaint' among Liberal M.P.s. According to Labouchere, because these men had won their seats by emphasizing non-Irish reforms, they dreaded 'the slightest possibility of these not being passed by the House of Commons before the next General Election' so that they would have to return empty-handed to the electors.[79]

There is evidence in Gladstone's correspondence after the Parnell divorce crisis in 1891 and after the elections in 1892 that he was aware of the need for the party to take up and attend to other reform questions.[80] But it is also clear that this need was seen by him mainly in relation to the strategy of promoting the home-rule policy. That policy remained the focus of all Gladstonian politics. As Campbell-Bannerman pointed out to Harcourt in August 1892, the government was 'formed for the special purpose of enabling Mr G. to carry out his ideas: it is in an unusual degree *his* Government'.[81]

The breakdown of the great Irish preoccupation came with the rejection of the second Home Rule Bill by the House of Lords and the decision of Gladstone's government not to make this rejection the subject of an appeal to the country. These developments dethroned the home-rule policy from its status of the great concentrating factor in Liberal politics. For behind it was revealed another obstruction on which it itself depended—the veto power of the House of Lords. Home rule had hitherto been represented as the policy that alone could end the paralysis in reform politics and ensure progress on the various causes that Liberals had at heart. This argument could no longer be used. Home rule was reduced to the level of other reform issues that appealed only to sections or minorities. Like them, it would have to wait until the Lords' veto could be effectively challenged on some issue which did appeal to a majority of the electorate. Until then it too was paralysed.

The new situation was made clear by Lord Rosebery in his declaration in March 1894 after becoming prime minister that home rule could not be conceded until there was a majority for it in England, the 'predominant member of the Three Kingdoms'. What Rosebery was expressing was both a reaction among Liberals against an era when non-Irish reforms had been subordinated to the home-rule policy and also a feeling that, in the interests of its survival, the Liberal party must try to re-establish contact with the moods and aspirations of the English electorate.

The brief and unhappy career of the Rosebery government in 1894–5

---

[78] Haldane to Sir A. West, 8 Aug. 1892, Haldane MSS. 5903, fo. 205, National Library of Scotland, Edinburgh.

[79] Labouchere to Harcourt, 9 Aug. [1892], Harcourt Papers; Labouchere to H. Gladstone, 27 Aug. [1892], Viscount Gladstone Papers, B.M. Add. MSS. 46016, fos. 156–8.

[80] Cf. above, note 75.

[81] J. A. Spender, *The Life of the Right Hon. Sir Henry Campbell-Bannerman, G.C.B.*, I (1923), 124.

reflected the consequences of the sudden removal of the two factors which had disciplined and concentrated Liberal politics over the previous eight years—Gladstone's leadership and the preoccupation with clearing the Irish 'obstruction'. Sectionalism appeared once more to be rampant and uncontrollable. 'Faddists' and other 'whose questions are hardly ready for immediate settlement' were observed to become 'impatient, and in their impatience exacting and impracticable'.[82] John Morley admitted that 'amongst the various interests which this Government represents there is a rivalry for priority'.[83] The Liberal leaders now lacked the means of imposing priority which the Irish 'obstruction' had provided. The question which occurred to many of them was whether they could find a substitute.

Although the events of 1893–94 did lead to a reaction against a primary concern with the problems of Ireland, there was definitely not also a reaction against the kind of politics which this concentration on a single issue represented. The multifarious commitments of the Newcastle Programme were blamed for much of the confusion and indiscipline in Liberal politics.[84] There was a yearning for a return to simplified 'single question' politics. In 1895 H. H. Fowler recalled Bright's warning 'that it was not possible to drive half a dozen omnibuses through Temple Bar at once', and remarked of the government of the previous three years: 'We tried to do that and we have failed.' The fact that the government 'at one and the same moment was working right and left, north and south' meant that it had 'diminished forces' and 'exhausted resources' and so could not resist the 'powerful combination' of 'all the sections' offended by the proposed reforms. He called for an end to 'Liberal programmes' and a return to conforming to the 'old-fashioned prejudice in this country in favour of doing one thing at a time, and doing it well'.[85] No one preached this message more vigorously than Rosebery himself. In the 1895 election campaign the theme which he tried to induce the party to take up was 'concentration'. He wanted the party to abandon the 'enormous and multifarious programme' which had burdened it since 1891 and to have instead a single aim. A programme with only one point in it was best 'for the purpose of a practical appeal to the English-speaking people'.[86]

The most obvious and most favoured substitute for the home-rule policy was a campaign against the House of Lords. This was a natural successor to the Irish question, since the veto powers of the Lords were now visible as a greater obstruction blocking the way to progress on all other reform

[82] J. Guinness Rogers, 'The Position of the Liberal Party', *The Nineteenth Century*, Feb. 1894, pp. 191–2.

[83] *The Times*, 22 May 1894.

[84] Cf., for example, Lord Rosebery, *The Pressing Question for the Liberal Party* (speech at Eighty Club), [1895]; *The Speaker*, 17 Oct. 1896, editorial on 'Party Discipline'.

[85] Fowler, op. cit. pp. 384, 441–2.

[86] *The Pressing Question for the Liberal Party*, pp. 9–11.

questions. Gladstone himself had wanted the party to concentrate on this issue after the rejection of the second Home Rule Bill; and Rosebery took it up as the single aim on which all Liberals should unite. In his speeches of 1894 and 1895 he again and again presented it in the classic form of the single great question, connected it with the principle of the 'concentration' of policy, and referred to it in terms very similar to those used by himself and other Liberal leaders about the Irish 'obstruction' between 1886 and 1893:

...when the dissolution comes, what will it be fought upon? Will it be fought upon Disestablishment, or Home Rule, or the liquor question?...the next election will be fought on none of these questions, but on one which includes and represents them all—I mean the House of Lords.

...[People may ask:] 'What is it you wish we should concentrate...? You say you will not present a dozen great questions in line. Is there one question that embraces and involves them all?' I say that there is. That question is the question of the domination of the House of Lords...That is a question which involves and concentrates in itself all those other causes, in which you specially may bear a particular interest.[87]

For a time, in 1894, other Liberal leaders and the Liberal rank and file seemed to manifest a similar enthusiasm for the issue.[88] But it soon became apparent not only that it was not an issue on which the Liberals were any more likely than they had been over home rule to gain the support of a majority of the non-Irish electorate but also that there was considerable variety of opinion on what should in fact be done about the Lords' powers. The appeal of the issue as a single, clear-cut, concentrating question waned rapidly.[89] In the 1895 election campaign there was no concentrating issue, in spite of Rosebery's efforts to make the Lords' veto into one. In its place there was a renewed willingness among the leaders to court defeat and the excuse for abstention from commitment and action that it would provide. 'I can't help feeling that defeat may be good for us,' wrote Herbert Gladstone at this time. 'We are plagued with obstinate faddists who are too strong for the leaders, and except for Ireland I could wish to get rid of them through defeat.'[90]

After the Unionist victory in 1895 Rosebery, although he had lost his premiership, was pleased that the party would now be forced to pass through a wholesome 'purgatory'. It had 'become all legs and wings, a daddy-long-legs fluttering among a thousand flames' and 'had to be consumed in order that something more sane, more consistent, and more coherent could take its

[87] Ibid. pp. 12–13. *Lord Rosebery's Speeches (1874–1896)* (1896), pp. 268–96, 347.

[88] See, for instance, the editorials in *The Speaker* during 1894, and also the reports of Liberal and N.L.F. activity in *The Liberal Magazine*, II (1894), e.g. pp. 46–7, 50, 166, 204–17.

[89] Cf. the complaints in editorials in *The Speaker* during the early part of 1895, e.g. 11 May and 6 July

[90] C. Mallet, *Herbert Gladstone: A Memoir* (1932), p. 156.

place'.[91] He devoted his own efforts henceforth to the task of 'consuming' what he regarded as the encumbrances of Gladstonian politics.[92] One of these was the commitment to home rule for Ireland which he became convinced was preventing 'the restoration of the Liberal party to what it was in richness, variety and strength before 1886';[93] and after 1895 he developed 'Liberal Imperialism' as a unifying and concentrating theme for all Liberals, including the Liberal Unionists.[94] Thus did Rosebery endeavour to cancel out the consequences of the reconstruction and purge of 1886 and start again with a 'clean slate' on which he intended to write a new constructive and 'purgative' principle.

In 1896 John Morley deplored the way in which 'the division of parties' was becoming 'to a very considerable extent also a division of classes', and then commented that 'he had never been able to see why that division should follow upon a difference of opinion as to what was the best form of government for Ireland, and he could not but think that before the new Home Rule policy was launched there must have been latent differences underneath.'[95] Now that the Irish preoccupation was gone, the 'latent differences' in both party and nation which it had overlaid were reappearing. The preoccupation had been no more than a temporary diversion. It had not been used creatively for the formation of new Liberal principles and policies. In 1888 Haldane had warned of the possible dangerous consequences of 'concentrating attention, not on the general purposes of the party, but on single questions'. The preoccupation with home-rule had led the leaders to neglect 'the general purposes', and nothing had been done to counter the development of the unjustified impression that the party was 'a class party, the party of the non-propertied class'. Liberals should 'insist on the breathing space which the question of Home Rule has given us being used in making preparations' for the coming political conflicts over social problems, in which the Liberals must be ready with a positive non-social programme of action. But, he complained, there was still 'an absence of such signs of preparation as one would like to see'.[96] These signs were still lacking in 1894. The systematic Liberal creed, for which the Irish preoccupation had been a temporary substitute, and on which the Liberals would depend in the long run for strength, purpose, and coherence in their action and the preventing of the disruption threatened by sectionalism and class antagonism, had not emerged.

[91] Rosebery to Canon Holland, 21 Aug. 1895, Rosbery MSS., Box 89.
[92] Culminating in his 'clean slate' speech at Chesterfield, 16 Dec. 1901.
[93] Cf. his memo. of 25 Aug. 1896, quoted in Crewe, *Lord Rosebery* (1931), II, 522-3.
[94] This theme can be found first enunciated in his speech at the City Liberal Club, 24 Apr. 1894. See *The Liberal Magazine*, II, 114.
[95] *The Times*, 5 Feb. 1896.
[96] 'The Liberal Creed', loc. cit. pp. 464-5, 474.

12

HOME RULE, RADICALISM, AND
THE LIBERAL PARTY, 1886-1895
THOMAS WILLIAM HEYCK

In 1887, Joseph Chamberlain wrote a letter to *The Baptist* in which he blamed the preoccupation of Liberals and Radicals with Home Rule for delaying social reform. "Thirty-two millions of people," he complained, "must go without much-needed legislation because three millions are disloyal."[1] Early in the 1890s, socialists and militant working-class spokesmen sometimes took up this cry to express their discontent with the Liberal party. And in later years, the Liberal-Radical commitment to Home Rule provided one of the main historical explanations for the founding of an independent working-class party; thus the dampening of Radicalism supposedly caused by Home Rule has been regarded as the source of the most important political transformation of recent British history. In the words of G. D. H. Cole:

> With Chamberlain's departure, and with the increasing pre-occupation of Gladstone with Home Rule, the Radical impulses of the 'seventies had died away. Some attempt was made to revive them when it had become plain that Liberalism was in serious danger of losing its working-class support. But the attempt was made too late, and the Liberal 'Newcastle Programme' of 1892 was only a very pale shadow of Chamberlain's 'Unauthorized Programme' of 1885.[2]

D. A. Hamer, in a recent article, takes essentially the same view, with some modifications. The Liberals, he says, took up Home Rule in a deliberate attempt to paper over confusion and disagreement within the party over other policies. In the 1880s, the Liberal party tended to be dominated by "faddists," who could not agree on the precedence to be given various reform proposals. By adopting Home Rule, they earned a period of "breathing-space," during which they could have worked out their problems. However, the Liberals wasted this opportunity because the "secession of Chamberlain and other radicals removed valuable talent that would have been devoted to such work." All that remained was Gladstone, whose leadership, committed as it was to Home Rule alone, paralyzed the party. Further, some moderate Liberals used the Home Rule issue to block the advance within the party of labor or

---

1. *The Baptist*, Feb. 25, 1887.
2. G. D. H. Cole, *British Working Class Politics* (London, 1941), pp. 82-83.

"collectivist" questions which came up in the latter 1880s. When Home Rule seemed to have been put aside in 1893 and 1894, the Liberals then adopted reform of the power of the House of Lords as another blockade against issues that might split the party.[3]

In one form or another, this interpretation of late-Victorian Liberal politics is the standard view. However, despite the paradigm's neatness and simplicity, another opinion expressed first in 1887 suggests that an alternative point of view must be considered. In that year Gladstone told the National Liberal Federation that Radicalism actually owed much to the advent of the Irish Question:

> After this Irish controversy is at an end the advanced Liberals, the Radical portion of the party, will have a vastly increased influence — not in consequence of the proposal of Home Rule, but in consequence of the resistance to that proposal, and of all of the influences and powers which that resistance will have brought into action.[4]

Even if Gladstone's prediction was only partly right, serious modifications of the standard interpretation would be in order. If the spirit of Radicalism were not dampened and its influence not decreased by the commitment to Home Rule, and if the Home Rule split did not deprive the Liberal party of its Radical element, then another view of the nature of the late-Victorian Liberal party must be adopted, and some other explanation of the militant working-class and socialist discontent with the Liberals must be found. If the nature of Radicalism after 1886 did not become less reformist, less concerned with its traditional issues, and if Radicals did not lose power within the Liberal party, then it might have been the substance of Radicalism itself with which so many working-class leaders became disenchanted.

What is needed to sort out these alternative explanations is, first, a hard look at the basis of working-class discontent; and second, an analysis of the Radical movement after 1886 and its role in the Liberal party. The first requirement is being supplied by Henry Pelling and other students of the labor movement. The second is to be provided by this article.

British Radicalism, especially since the 1850s, had always been a disorganized and crankish movement. Indeed, "faddism" was one of its defining characteristics. People became Radicals because

---

3. D. A. Hamer, "The Irish Question and Liberal Politics, 1886-1894," *Historical Journal* (1969); below, ch. 11. Hamer develops this thesis more thoroughly in his *Liberal Politics in the Age of Gladstone and Rosebery* (Oxford, 1972).

4. Quoted in National Liberal Federation, *Tenth Annual Report, 1887* (London, 1887), p. 48.

of one or another specific grievance at the hands of traditional, Anglican landowning society. Thus the Radical program in the late-Victorian period was largely one of abolishing privileges: the established churches, denominational influence in education, exclusive Anglican rights to parish burial grounds, a near monopoly in land ownership, and oligarchical political arrangements. The structure of the Radical movement was made up of a cloud of organizations and societies, each devoted, as the Anti-Corn Law League had been, to the accomplishment of a single goal. Moreover, the movement had two wings that were never successfully integrated — middle-class and working-class. Middle-class Radicals, organizing themselves in agencies like the Liberation Society, the National Education League, and the Reform League, liked to use the electoral influence of certain working-class organizers such as George Howell and Howard Evans, but they did not incorporate workingmen into their own structure of power.[5]

Yet there was an essential unity to the Radical movement, arising from a common sense of who the enemy was, from a common set of values, and from common ideas about the real and ideal British societies. Agreement on these things held the politically active workingmen in the Radical movement well into the 1880s.[6] All Radicals agreed that their enemy was orthodox, landowning society. To a remarkable degree, they thought that remnants of feudalism still dominated British society, with the result that independent, prudent individuals were prevented from full self-improvement. Of course, in this view they differed from Conservatives and Whigs, who believed that the landed orders already had seen their rights and institutions seriously eroded. But the Radicals also differed from moderate Liberals, who wanted not to destroy the landed orders but to bring about a balance of social forces, and who by the 1870s considered that only relatively moderate reforms were needed to finish the task. Radicals generally

---

5. For Radicalism, see T. W. Heyck, "British Radicals and Radicalism, 1874-1895: A Social Analysis," in R. J. Bezucha (ed.), *Modern European Social History* (Lexington, Mass., 1972), pp. 28-58. For Howell's career: F. M. Leventhal, *Respectable Radical: George Howell and Victorian Working Class Politics* (Cambridge, Mass., 1971). For Howard Evans: Howard Evans, *Radical Fights of Forty Years* (London, n.d.).

6. Heyck, "British Radicals and Radicalism," *passim*; Henry Pelling, *The Origins of the Labour Party, 1880-1900* (Oxford, 1965), p. 6; Trygve Tholfsen, "The Transition to Democracy in Victorian England," in *International Review of Social History*, VI (1961), 226-48; Royden Harrison, *Before the Socialists: Studies in Labour and Politics, 1861-1881* (London, 1965), *passim*. The bourgeois ideal, of which Radicalism was the epitome, is described very well in Harold Perkin, *The Origins of Modern English Society* (Toronto, 1967), Chap. VI-VIII.

wanted to establish no balance of forces, but a society in which bourgeois styles and institutions prevailed. Society would be orderly, but highly competitive. In effect, their social ideal was an extention of the middle-class Nonconformist value system.

In the 1870s and 1880s, most Radicals felt that their numbers and influence were increasing. Because of some internal disputes and a disenchantment with the Liberal party, Radicals did not fare well in the general election of 1874. Afterwards, they began to recover, slowly in the mid-1870s and rapidly thereafter. Through a statistical procedure called multiple discriminant analysis, which can use divisions in the House of Commons to distinguish between political groups, the number of Radical M.P.s can be set at about eighty for the parliament of 1874-80, and at about 120 for that of 1880-85. Radical M.P.s thus represented about one-third of the Liberal parliamentary party.[7] They were convinced that the proportion of Radicals among Liberals was very much greater outside the House than inside, and they expected the reform acts of 1884 and 1885 to uncover the true Radical power and enable them to sweep the Whigs from their traditional position of influence in the parliamentary party. However, the Radicals were disappointed at the results of the 1885 general election, as only about 160 were returned to parliament. Still, this number amounted to almost one-half of the Liberal M.P.s, a considerable advance over the two previous parliaments.

In the split over Home Rule which followed, the great bulk of Radical M.P.s supported Gladstone, and only a few dissented along with Chamberlain: 131 for Home Rule and thirty-two against. A greater proportion of Radicals voted for Home Rule than did the members of either the moderate or Whig sections of the parliamentary party. Because most of the Whigs and a substantial number of moderates abandoned the party over Home Rule, the Radicals were left in a numerical majority of the parliamentary Liberal party.[8]

This is not to deny that the group of Radicals who splintered

---

7. The statistical procedure on which these conclusions are based is described in T. W. Heyck and William Klecka, "British Radical M.P.s, 1874-1895: New Evidence from Discriminant Analysis," *The Journal of Interdisciplinary History*, IV (Autumn, 1973), 161-84. Lists of all Radical M.P.s, developed by using this procedure, can be found in the appendices of T. W. Heyck, *The Dimensions of British Radicalism: The Case of Ireland, 1874-1895*, forthcoming.

8. The Home Rule division is analyzed in detail in *The Dimensions of British Radicalism*, forthcoming, Chapter V, and in T. W. Heyck, "English Radicals and the Irish Question, 1874-1895" (Ph.D. dissertation, University of Texas, 1969), Chap. VI. See also, Donald Southgate, *The Passing of the Whigs, 1832-1886* (London, 1962), Chap. XV.

from the Liberal party was significant. As they included Joseph Chamberlain, easily the most outstanding Radical in England before 1886, the Radical Unionists inevitably were important. Yet in sheer numbers, the Radical Unionists were a small and declining faction from 1886 to 1895. During the Home Rule parliament, the Radical Unionists could claim thirty-three M.P.s, and shortly afterward, Chamberlain enlisted some fifteen thousand members for his new organization, the National Radical Union.[9] Neither section of unionist Radicalism ever amounted to as much again. The number of Radical Unionist M.P.s decreased to about twenty after the general election of 1886 and to eleven after 1892. The National Radical Union, founded for purely electoral purposes in 1886, faded away in 1888.[10]

Apparently, the reason that Radical Unionism declined was that Unionism put Radicals in an awkward and unnatural position. Chamberlain tried to use their weight to move the Conservative party toward progressive policies, but whenever the Conservatives were in danger of defeat, the Radical Unionists had to support them, regardless of the issue, in the interests of maintaining the Union. This sometimes entailed Radical Unionist support for the Tories on matters very distasteful to any Radical — coercion in Ireland and defense of the House of Lords, for example. A few Radical Unionists, among them G. O. Trevelyan and W. S. Caine, eventually found that their allegiance to Radical policies outweighed their doubts about Home Rule, and returned to the main Radical force.[11]

The vast majority of Radicals after 1886 belonged to the Gladstonian Liberal party; thus it is among the Liberal Home Rulers that one finds the men most appropriately called "Radicals." A careful examination of this group makes several important things clear. First, according to multiple discriminant analysis of the voting behavior of the Liberal parliamentary party, about 145 Radicals held seats in the 1886-92 parliament, some 9 percent fewer than in the Home Rule parliament, and about two hundred in the 1892-95 parliament. Second, despite an absolute decrease in the number of Radical M.P.s after the election of 1886, a higher proportion

---

9. Joseph Chamberlain, *A Political Memoir*, ed. C. H. D. Howard, (London, 1953), p. 228; Peter Fraser, *Joseph Chamberlain: Radicalism and Empire, 1868-1914* (London, 1966), p. 106; J. L. Garvin and Julian Amery, *Life of Joseph Chamberlain* (London, 1932-1969), II, 252.

10. Sir Ivor Jennings, *Party Politics* (Cambridge, 1961), II, 202.

11. For Radical Unionist policy, see Michael Hurst, *Joseph Chamberlain and Liberal Reunion: The Round Table Conference of 1887* (Toronto, 1967), *passim*, especially pp. 343 and 361-62.

of Liberal M.P.s voted 'Radically' than in the previous parliaments: over 70 per cent in both the parliaments from 1886 to 1895, as opposed to about 33 per cent from 1874 to 1885 and 48 per cent in 1886. And third, it becomes increasingly difficult even by fairly sophisticated voting analysis to distinguish the voting patterns of those M.P.s generally known as "Radicals" from those known simply as "Liberals"; thus the distinction between moderate Liberals and Radicals, which was plainly demonstrable through 1892 was much less so by 1895. Together, these observations show that, though the attachment to Home Rule slowed the advance of Radicalism in the House of Commons as a whole, it contributed to the progress of Radicalism within the parliamentary Liberal party. After 1886, Radicalism was by far the most important segment of parliamentary Liberalism.[12]

It should be emphasized that what multiple discriminant analysis shows is the increasing willingness of Liberal M.P.s to adopt measures that formerly had been the preserve of Radicals, and not the moderation of Radical policies. This point is confirmed by the recent findings of Hugh Berrington, who has used a different kind of voting analysis to understand the realities of late-Victorian politics. Berrington measures not only the frequency but also the direction of votes against party conformity in the late-nineteenth century, and, like Ostrogorski before him, finds that the unity of the parliamentary parties increased during the latter 1880s and 1890s. Unlike Ostrogorski, however, Berrington observes that on the Liberal side the characteristic rebellion against the party leadership had been by the Radicals; and it was this fractiousness that diminished after 1886. Further, the reason that Radicals rebelled less often after 1886 was that the party leaders acted in conformity to Radical wishes. Before 1886, the leadership of the two major parties often formed a consensus against the Radicals. However, the Home Rule issue drove so many Whigs and moderates out of the Liberal party that Liberal leaders had to look to the predominant Radicals for support. The results were an increase in Liberal party conformity and a Radicalization of the party.[13]

The social background of the Radical M.P.s after 1886 was generally the same as in the three earlier parliaments. From 1874 to 1885, most of the Radical M.P.s were wealthy middle-class men, about 80 per cent getting their incomes from bourgeois occupations.

---

12. Heyck and Klecka, "British Radical M.P.'s," *passim*.
13. Hugh Berrington, "Partisanship and Dissidence in the Nineteenth-Century House of Commons," *Parliamentary Affairs*, XXI (Autumn, 1968), 338-74.

The typical Radical M.P. in those years would have been someone like John Bright, Joseph Chamberlain, Samuel Morley or H. J. Wilson — hard-driving, self-made men who considered the landed orders to be non-productive parasites. The same was true after 1886:

TABLE I. OCCUPATIONS OF RADICAL M.P.s, 1886-95*

Occupation	1886-92	1892-95
Commerce and Industry	71	89
Law	35	53
Other Professions	4	4
Writing and Journalism	13	19
Teaching	5	7
Civil Service	3	3
Workers	10	11
Armed Forces	0	1
Land	9	6
Others	2	3
Unknown (No visible means of income)	7	11
Totals	159	207

*These figures represent the *total* number of Radicals who sat in the two parliaments, and not the number who held seats at any one time. Thus the actual Radical strength in both parliaments, as reflected in the text above, was somewhat lower than the totals given here.

It is perhaps surprising that Radicalism still recruited most of its parliamentary elite from the upper middle class at a time when big business was becoming increasingly important in British society. James Cornford has shown that by the 1880s the new suburbs were providing the path to Conservatism for many middle-class people.[14] Nevertheless, it is apparent that substantial numbers of bourgeois people still felt aggrieved by the privileges of the landed orders, and considered that British society did not reflect their middle-class Nonconformist ideal.

Another feature of the Radical M.P.s must be pointed out: the number of workingmen. Standing at nearly a dozen, the number of working-class Radical M.P.s was much higher than in 1874-80, when it was two, and 1880-85, when it was three. However, the

---

14. James Cornford, "The Transformation of Conservatism in the Late-Nineteenth Century," *Victorian Studies*, VII (Sept., 1963), 35-66.

number was not growing. In 1885, eleven working-class Radicals had been returned to parliament, the same number as in 1892. Moreover, a small number of socialists and workingmen emerged in parliament distinctly to the left of the Radicals. In 1886, R. B. Cunninghame Graham, an eccentric middle-class Fabian, won a seat; and in 1892 so did John Burns, Keir Hardie, J. Havelock Wilson, and Sam Woods, all of whom were militant working-class spokesmen.[15] Their presence indicated that as the working class became politically more powerful, Radicalism would have to compete with a new kind of rival for its support; the old attachment of politically-active workingmen to the Radical movement could no longer be assumed.

Nonconformity continued to be the rock of Radicalism. Nearly 75 per cent of the Radical M.P.s from 1886 to 1895 were Nonconformists, and a heavy majority of all Nonconformists in the House were Radicals. These facts suggest that, despite the severity of the dispute over Home Rule within Nonconformity, the Radical movement continued to recruit very well among Dissenters. Precisely how and where Home Rule cut through the Nonconformist community is hard to tell. It is possible that the number of Nonconformist M.P.s who adhered to the Gladstonian party was deceptively large. Nevertheless, John Morley thought that most Nonconformists did in fact support Home Rule:

> The attempt to kindle the torch of religious fear or hate was in Great Britain happily a failure. The mass of Liberal presbyterians in Scotland, and of nonconformists in England and Wales, stood firm, though some of their most eminent and able divines resisted the new project [Home Rule], less on religious grounds than on what they took to be the balance of political arguments.[16]

Other contemporary observations confirmed Morley's appraisal. *The Methodist Times,* for example, stated that the heavy vote by Methodist M.P.s in June 1886 for Home Rule (only two of seventeen opposed it) accurately reflected the feeling of English Methodists. If true, this remark would be doubly significant, for the Methodists were probably more divided over Home Rule than any other Nonconformist denomination.[17] *The Baptist,* which opposed

---

15. Burns, Hardie, and Wilson alike were known as socialists when they first entered the House. Burns turned out to be an orthodox Radical, and has been included here in the totals for working-class Radical M.P.s.

16. John Morley, *The Life of William Ewart Gladstone* (London, 1903), III, 323.

17. *Methodist Times,* June 10, 1886.

Home Rule, had to admit that at Baptist association meetings, the preponderance of opinion supported Gladstone.[18]

The general support rendered to Home Rule by Nonconformists is shown by a look at the constituencies from 1886 to 1895. As Henry Pelling points out, there is no evidence of a flight of Nonconformist voters from Liberalism to Unionism in these years.[19] The strongly Nonconformist areas of Britain remained Liberal and Radical, except in Cornwall and Birmingham, the former being explained by the proximity of Ireland and the consequent urgency of an imagined Irish threat, the latter by the influence of Chamberlain. The Radicals managed to increase their victories even in the election of 1886 in Wales and Scotland, where Nonconformity was exceptionally strong. Their losses occurred most in England, and in the big cities, where Nonconformity was not so influential. As Pelling has written, the larger the city, the weaker the Nonconformity.[20] One of the effects of Home Rule on Radicalism, thus on the Liberal party, was to increase the Radical dependency on the Celtic fringe. Realizing this, Scottish and Welsh Radicals pressed their demands forcefully, and successfully, on the Liberal party after 1886.

In England, nevertheless, there was one significant development in Radical representation after 1886. This occurred in London, where the Radicals since the 1860s had not won many seats. In 1885, Radicals won only eighteen of sixty-two metropolitan seats, and in 1886 only twelve. Between 1886 and 1892, however, Radicals in London engaged in strenuous organizational and propaganda work. They formed the core of a strong Progressive party that won control of the London County Council in 1894. In the general election of 1892, London Radicals won twenty seats in the House of Commons and had high hopes for more in the future. Their rising fortunes gave London much more importance in Liberal and Radical circles than at any time since the decline of the Philosophic Radicals. By 1890, London Radicals, who included some of the most modern and flexible of all Liberals, were one of the key groups competing for influence within the Liberal party.

---

18. *The Baptist*, June 18 and 25, 1886. Newman Hall, in a letter to the *Fortnightly Review*, admitted that as a Nonconformist opponent of Home Rule, he was in a "small minority." "Nonconformists and Unionism," *Fortnightly Review*, No. CCLXC, (Feb., 1891), 320-23.

19. Henry Pelling, *Social Geography of British Elections, 1885-1910* (New York, 1967), pp. 431-32.

20. *Ibid.*, p. 433.

For all the strength of Radicalism within the Liberal party after 1886, Radicals were hampered by inadequate leadership, and in this regard Hamer is right to count the loss of Chamberlain as a disaster to the Radical movement and to the Liberal party. The Radical prototype after 1886 would have resembled that of the previous two decades — a staunch, earnest, pious big businessman or lawyer — but it was precisely this kind of person who did not have a leader. Chamberlain formerly had provided the provincial democrats with aggressive leadership, but with him gone, the command fell to less well suited men. Many Radicals expected John Morley to assume Chamberlain's mantle. He was the chief writer of the faction even before 1886, and his early and enthusiastic devotion to Home Rule gave him an exceptionally strong position after 1886. Unfortunately, Morley's brilliant talents in editing and writing were accompanied by marked political weaknesses. He did not have the ability to perceive the country's increasingly complex social problems, still less the capacity to construct practical solutions for them. Essentially an intellectual of the 1850s and 1860s, Morley felt less and less at home in the world of the 1880s, and so clung to the one issue he understood and felt secure in — Home Rule. Moreover, Morley was a nervous man, hypersensitive, shy and vain; he did not strike blunt, hard men as a leader. Though a good platform speaker, Morley was a poor debater, too frequently slow, humorless and off the mark in the House. In July 1886, the positivist Frederic Harrison urged Morley to take the lead and form a party, much as Morley himself had once urged Chamberlain.[21] But the sure sense of the source and uses of power were not there; without it, Morley could never take Chamberlain's place.[22]

No one else rose to fill the void. The only Radical of any prior standing to enhance his reputation after 1886 was Henry Labouchere, who had wit and charm, but who was totally unfit by background, beliefs and temperament to lead the Radicals. After 1886, Labouchere attracted a following of malcontents by his ceaseless energy, by frequent attacks on the House of Lords, and by constant criticism of the expense of maintaining the royal family. He lacked, however, any steady plans or programs. The

---

21. British Library of Political and Economic Science, Harrison to Morley, July 24, 1886, Harrison Papers, Section A, Box 2.

22. The most recent biography of Morley is D. A. Hamer, *John Morley: Liberal Intellectual in Politics* (Oxford, 1968). But perhaps the best evidence of Morley's weaknesses is in Peter Stansky, *Ambitions and Strategies: the Struggle for the Leadership of the Liberal Party in the 1890's* (Oxford, 1964).

most promising young men among the parliamentary Radicals detested him. These made up the group later known as the Liberal Imperialists: H. H. Asquith, R. B. Haldane, Sir Edward Grey, Arthur Acland, Sidney Buxton, Augustine Birrell, and Tom Ellis. Receptive to new ideas, the little alliance was self-consciously progressive and had good relations with the Fabians.[23] Because these young men, known at the time as the "New Radicals" or "New Liberals," thought of themselves as constructive politicians, they sought to counter Labouchere's influence, which they regarded as all destructive. To this end they concerted their activities in parliament with Rosebery, Morley and H. H. Fowler.[24] But the "Articles Club," as the anti-Labouchere alliance was called, was flawed by some confusion of purpose. It clearly was not intended to divert the attention of the party away from Home Rule. The members tended to regard Morley as their mentor, yet he was among the strongest Home Rulers in the House. What held them together was a common desire to check Labouchere's frivolous, irresponsible kind of Radicalism and his annoyance of the Liberal front bench. Moreover, the Articles Club did not represent the provincial Nonconformist Radicals; most of them were too cosmopolitan, too "modern" to speak for the bulk of Radicalism. It was in regard to leadership that Radicalism suffered most heavily from the Home Rule split: Chamberlain did not take many Radicals out of the Liberal party with him, but he did take his own ability, and it was sorely missed.

II.

The Home Rule crisis had a marked impact on the organizational structure of both the Liberal party and the Radical movement. Before 1886, the structure of the party was quite separate from that of the Radical movement. The official headquarters of the party, the Liberal Central Association, attempted to coordinate the parliamentary activities of all Liberals, including Radicals, and engaged in electoral work as well; but it had no direct structural link with any of the various extra-parliamentary Radical organizations, including the National Liberal Federation. It had long been a concern of Radicals like Chamberlain and Dilke to get more

---

23. John Morley, *Recollections* (London, 1925), I, 323-24; A. M. McBriar, *Fabian Socialism and English Politics, 1884-1918* (Cambridge, 1966), pp. 253-57.

24. Dudley Sommer, *Haldane of Cloan: His Life and Times,* 1856-1928 (London, 1928), pp. 76-77; Roy Jenkins, *Asquith* (London, 1964), pp. 45-46.

influence for their persuasion within the Central Association.[25] The Radicals had no parliamentary agency of their own, though Chamberlain had tried to form one in the 1870s.[26] Consequently, Radical M.P.s tended to dissipate their strength in a kaleidoscope of temporary alliances. Outside parliament, the Radicals dominated a large number of special-purpose leagues and societies – the United Kingdom Alliance, the Liberation Society, the National Education League, the Land Tenure Reform Association, and the Peace Society, to name only a few – but they had no central organization to mobilize their forces. After 1886, the National Liberal Federation, still a Radical organization, was elevated to official party status and at the same time came to overshadow all the smaller societies. Liberal party agencies themselves became the chief organizations of and for Radicals.

The National Liberal Federation underwent a number of crucial developments after 1886, all tending to increase Radical influence within the Liberal party. The first changes originated in the Liberal defeat in the general election of 1886. The results of the election made it plain that Radicals fared better than moderate Liberals; consequently, many Liberals as well as Radicals expressed a desire for greater electoral control by the N.L.F., at the expense of the Liberal Central Association, in future campaigning.[27] In addition, Birmingham no longer being a congenial home for the N.L.F., Frank Schnadhorst, the executive secretary, moved the Federation headquarters to London in October 1886, into offices adjacent to the Central Association. Schnadhorst became secretary of the Association as well as the N.L.F.[28] These alterations effectively installed Radical views in the party's parliamentary command post. Distinctions between the parliamentary and extra-parliamentary organizations faded. Both Schnadhorst and the whips carried out electoral duties, and both advised Gladstone on party policy. Radicals were appointed whips for the first time: Arnold Morley, son of the influential Radical industrialist Samuel Morley, in 1886; and Tom Ellis, a popular Welsh Radical, in 1892. In 1887, the com-

---

25. BM, Memoirs of Sir Charles Dilke, Dilke Papers, BM 44,932, f. 17; 44,933, f. 71; 43,940, f. 16. Barry McGill, "Francis Schnadhorst and Liberal Party Organization," *Journal of Modern History*, XXXIV (March, 1962), 25.

26. This was the so-called "new party," consisting of Chamberlain, Dilke, L. L. Dillwyn, Joseph Cowen, Thomas Burt, John Morley and the Irishman E. D. Gray. BM, Memoirs of Sir Charles Dilke, Dilke Papers, BM 43,932, ff, 248-49.

27. A sample of Radical opinion is in BM, Henry Labouchere to Herbert Gladstone, July 9, 1886, Viscount Gladstone Papers, BM 46,016.

28. Barry McGill, "Francis Schnadhorst and Liberal Party Organization," *Journal of Modern History*, XXXIV (March, 1962), 29.

bined party headquarters established an office for official party propaganda, the Liberal Publication Department. It was controlled from the outset by Radicals who made up its management committee: James Bryce, James Stuart, Percy Bunting, and T. Wemyss Reid.[29] Furthermore, Schnadhorst's assistant (and successor), Robert A. Hudson, did administrative chores for both the Federation and the Central Association. Through Acland and Ellis he kept close contact with the young New Liberals, some of whom conducted a series of studies that contributed much to the Newcastle Program.[30] These steps amounted to a considerable advance of Radicalism in the party. In 1892 Arnold Morley rightly declared that the Central Office was "more efficient & more in harmony with recent developments of Liberal thought than it has been at any previous moment of its existence."[31]

Meanwhile the Federation vigorously expanded its organization outside the offices in Parliament Street. In October 1886, Schnadhorst set out to establish Liberal associations of the democratic type in every part of Great Britain, all to be connected by a network of regional federations or by direct affiliation with party headquarters. Federations of Liberal associations were formed in North and South Wales. Sixty-five associations were founded or newly affiliated with the London office, and 340 others were attached to the two Welsh federations. In 1886 and 1887, nine regional conferences were staged by the N.L.F. throughout England and Wales. By the end of 1887, hardly a locality outside of Scotland lacked a Liberal association affiliated to the Federation. The lists of their officers and representatives to N.L.F. conferences show that they were for the most part dominated by the "advanced men" so feared by the Whigs before 1886.[32]

Much the same kind of unifying process took place in Scotland. As Kellas has shown, Scottish Radicals before 1886 had their own organization, the National Liberal Federation of Scotland, while the Whigs and moderates controlled the Scottish Liberal Association. Rivalry between the two organizations in 1886 contributed to a number of the Liberal losses. Irish Home Rule was the key

---

29. National Liberal Federation, *Tenth Annual Report, 1887*, pp. 28-29.

30. J. A. Spender, *Sir Robert Hudson: A Memoir* (London, 1930), pp. 17-21.

31. BM, A. Morley to Gladstone, April 21, 1892, Gladstone Papers, BM 44, 254.

32. These lists precede each of the annual reports of the N.L.F. For the organizational efforts: National Liberal Federation, *Tenth Annual Report, 1887*, pp. 11-25; and Percy Corder, *The Life of Robert Spence Watson* (London, 1914), p. 244; Robert Spence Watson, *The National Liberal Federation: From Its Commencement to the General Election of 1906* (London, 1907), pp. 65-69.

issue at odds between the two organizations, the Scottish Federation strongly supporting Home Rule, the Liberal Association opposing. Late in 1886, Scottish Radicals, by permeating the Association, managed to carry a resolution for Home Rule at a conference of the Association. Their victory cleared away the main obstacle to unification. In December 1886, the Federation was merged into the Association, and Radicals soon won control over the policy-making conferences of the new joint Association. By October 1887, they had committed the Association executive to disestablishment; by 1892, to a full Radical program.[33]

Radical organizational power also increased markedly in London after the Home Rule division. As early as February 1886, the Radicals W. S. Caine (who later became a Unionist for a time) and Renwick Seager, secretary of the Liberal Central Association, were working to reconcile the rival moderate and Radical claims in various metropolitan constituencies.[34] However, at the time of the general election of 1886, most London Radicals were still divided into two competing associations, the London and Counties Liberal Union, and the London Liberal and Radical Council. Many constituencies had no local associations at all. Others had working-class Radical clubs, which remained independent of the larger bourgeois associations. Afterwards, through the efforts of James Stuart and R. K. Causton, two leading metropolitan reformers, the Liberal associations combined to form the London Liberal and Radical Union, with Radicals as officers: John Morley as president, Causton as chairman, Stuart as honorary secretary, and Seager as secretary. Decidedly Radical in both program and membership, the Liberal and Radical Union affiliated with the N.L.F. as one of its major subordinate units. For the area surrounding London, party leaders founded the more moderate Home Counties Division.[35]

It is important to note, however, that the formation of a substantially Radical organization in London did not end the old division between middle and working-class Radicals. Most of the Radical clubs, which had long been hostile to the bourgeois-dominated N.F.L., refused to be brought into the new Liberal and Radical union. Even though the Radical clubs wholeheartedly supported Home Rule, as did most working-class Radical organizations everywhere, they preferred their own Metropolitan Radical

33.   James G. Kellas, "The Liberal Party in Scotland, 1876-1895," *Scottish Historical Review*, XLIV (April, 1965), 5-14.
34.   *Times* (London), Feb. 18, 1886.
35.   National Liberal Federation, *Tenth Annual Report, 1887*, p. 26.

Federation to any middle-class agency, in which they would be treated as Indians and not chiefs. This was true in spite of the fact that some Fabians "permeated" various London Liberal and Radical associations; in 1889, for example, Sidney Webb was appointed to the executive committee of the London Liberal and Radical Union.[36] Class-consciousness, and not Home Rule, kept the middle and working-class wings of Radicalism in London separate.[37]

The structural problems in London were common to the Radical organizational experiences of the latter 1880s and early 1890s. During this period, the most crucial organizational problem that the Radicals faced was to respond effectively to growing demands by the working class for parliamentary representation, and consequently for positions of authority within the party structure. For decades, middle-class Radicals had claimed to speak for the working class, but from the mid-1880s, this claim no longer sufficed. The new working-class demand had nothing to do with Home Rule, and little to do with policies of any kind. Workingmen in increasing numbers were identifying themselves as a separate class and wanted to see their own kind in the House of Commons.[38] Schnadhorst and the other Radical leaders took the position that they would welcome the return of more working-class M.P.s, but that decisions to adopt candidates, whether middle or working-class, must remain with the local Liberal associations, which continued to be run by bourgeois Radicals. They felt that they could not deprive their loyal constituency chiefs of their time-honored right to choose candidates.[39] In the long run this response was inadequate, for it precluded large-scale working-class representation through Liberal institutions, even though Radicals now controlled those institutions.

One example illustrates the point. In November 1890, James Tims, secretary of the Metropolitan Radical Federation, formally asked Schnadhorst to have fifty Liberal candidates throughout the country withdrawn, so that labor candidates, with N.L.F. support, could contest the seats. Schnadhorst replied that the N.L.F. could

---

36.   McBriar, *Fabian Socialism and English Politics*, pp. 234-38.
37.   The best discussion of London Radicalism in this period is Paul Thompson, *Socialists, Liberals, and Labour: the Struggle for London, 1885-1914* (Toronto, 1967), Chap. V.
38.   Leon D. Epstein, "British Class Consciousness and the Labour Party," *Journal of British Studies*, I (May, 1962), 136-50. Henry Pelling, *Popular Politics and Society in Late-Victorian Britain* (New York, 1968), Chaps. 1 and 6.
39.   Pelling, *Origins of the Labour Party*, p. 59; National Liberal Federation, *Eleventh Annual Meeting, 1888* (London, 1888), p. 29.

not interfere with the local associations; furthermore, that working-class candidates would have to pay their own election expenses.[40] Under these conditions very few Liberal candidatures would ever be available to workingmen.

In earlier years, Schnadhorst had done good service for Radicals and Liberals, but he showed poor judgment throughout his dealings with socialists and laborites. He wrote to Gladstone of Sidney Webb:

> He is quite a new man & has little means of knowing the sentiments of London workmen. London to him & others means the few noisy impracticables who meet in a few Clubs, a class whom no programme can ever satisfy—they are the men who keep London Liberals divided and weak. Cooperation with them is almost impossible. There is a wide gulf between the sober, intelligent, hardheaded men of the provinces and these men. Sidney Webb is a socialist with little sympathy with us on the Irish question.[41]

This opinion reflected middle-class attitudes and interests, as the views of the Radical elite since the 1840s tended to do. Indeed, as the Radical structure after 1886 was given official Liberal party status, it became more impervious to working-class views and pressures. This tendency, rather than the commitment to Home Rule, would eventually deprive Radicalism and the Liberal party of working-class support.

III.

The improved numerical and organizational position of the Radicals, or at least the middle-class section of them, within the Liberal party naturally increased the influence of their policies. Thus the effect of Home Rule on the Radical program was to help promote it to official party policy. At the same time, however, Home Rule had no effect on the *nature* of the Radical program, and it was in this regard that Radicals, as well as moderate Liberals, failed to respond to new conditions. By 1886 the "Great Depression," whether economic historians think it substantial or not, was beginning to produce two related phenomena: aggressive, independent working-class activity, and socialist criticism of British society.[42] The pressures generated by these developments caused an important debate within Radical circles, and to a limited extent led to a modification

---

40. National Liberal Federation, *Proceedings of the Fourteenth Annual Meeting, 1891* (London, 1891), pp. 18-20.
41. BM, September 10, 1888. Gladstone Papers, BM 44,295.
42. Helen Merrell Lynd, *England in the 1880's: Toward a Social Basis for Freedom* (London, 1945).

of the Radical program; however, on the whole the Radicals held to their old individualistic and competitive ideology. Insofar as ideas were concerned, the roots of the eventual decline of Liberalism lay in this failure — an inadequate response caused much less by the commitment to Home Rule than by the nature of British Radicalism itself.

The main political objective of the Radicals had been to establish political democracy for men (women were another matter). They believed in majority rule on principle, and they expected it would destroy the power of the landed orders. Even after passage of the reform acts of 1884 and 1885, they gave high priority to proposals leading to democratic political arrangements: abolition of plural voting ("one man one vote"), simplified electoral qualifications and registration, payment from the rates of official electoral expenses, and shorter parliaments. Most of them also supported at least partial payment of M.P.s.[43] For local affairs, they wanted elective county, district, and parish councils.[44] But the political idea they talked most about was reform of the power of the House of Lords, though they could not agree whether to "end them or mend them." In 1894, when the Lords had rejected a number of Radical bills, the sentiment among Radicals for some kind of reform of the Lords was very strong, but they were frustrated by the ambiguity of Lord Rosebery and by disunity among party leaders. By 1895, reform of the Lords had become the leading rival to Home Rule itself for primacy in the Radical program. It would be wrong, however, to see this rivalry as a struggle between those who wanted to abandon Home Rule and those who threw up Home Rule as a diversion to reform of the Lords. It was rather a question of whether the House of Lords should be reformed before Home Rule was brought in again, or whether Home Rule should be taken to the electorate to get a mandate with which to override the Lords.[45]

Issues connected with religion provided important points in the

---

43. Andrew Reid (ed.), *The New Liberal Programme* (London, 1886), *passim*; *The Speaker*, Jan. 11, 1890, and April 2, 1892; Thomas Burt, "Labour in Parliament," *Contemporary Review*, LV (May, 1889), 681-82; J. Fletcher Moulton, "What Mr. Gladstone Ought to Do," *Fortnightly Review*, No. CCXIV (Feb., 1893), 265.

44. Reid, *New Liberal Programme*, *passim*; BM, Labouchere to Herbert Gladstone, Aug. 27, 1892, Vicount Gladstone Papers, BM 46,016.

45. See: Labouchere's motion in the House, *Hansard*, CCCXXIII, March 9, 1888, 763; E. A. Freeman, "The House of Lords and the County Councils," *Fortnightly Review*, No. CCLVII (May, 1888), 599; Alfred Russel Wallace, "How to Preserve the House of Lords," *Contemporary Review*, LXV (Jan., 1894), 114-17; *The Speaker*, Dec. 5, 1891; T. Wemyss Reid, "The Leeds Conference," *The Liberal Magazine*, XI (July, 1894), 200-02.

Radical program, as they had since the eighteenth century. The Radicals on principle opposed all established churches, but the influence of the Celtic fringe after 1886 pushed Welsh and Scottish disestablishment to the forefront and left disestablishment in England to the distant future.[46] Led by Stuart Rendel, Welsh Radicals were especially insistent, and by 1891, they had forced the leaders of the Liberal party to put Welsh disestablishment second only to Home Rule in the party platform. The temperance advocates, who wanted to make publicans go the way of the established churches, also gained in influence. Having finally agreed on a single plan—local option—they persuaded the party leadership to accept temperance as party policy; and this achievement got men like W. S. Caine to abandon Unionism and return to the fold.[47] Disestablishers and temperance advocates alike (very often they were the same people) remained strong Home Rulers. In 1894, it is true, four Welsh Radicals — Lloyd George, D. A. Thomas, Frank Edwards and Herbert Lewis — rejected the party whips in an effort to win attention to Welsh demands, mainly disestablishment. But they were not so much opposed to Home Rule as upset with the party's concern for claims other than their own.[48]

For decades the primary Radical social policy had been reform of the land laws. In the late 1880s, popular discontent with the land system began to wane, but Radicals continued to express great hostility to landlords. They still talked of establishing free trade in land through abolition of what they called entail and primogeniture, and of granting allotments of land through compulsory purchase of land by local authorities.[49] Increasingly, however, they concentrated on making landowners pay what they regarded as a fair share of social expenses — that is, to pay taxes at a rate equal to that borne by personalty owners.[50] They adopted from Henry George the idea that the full value of the "unearned increment" enjoyed by landlords ought to go to public authorities. In

46. Kenneth O. Morgan, *Wales in British Politics, 1868-1922* (2nd ed.; Cardiff, 1970), Chaps. III and IV; James G. Kellas, "The Liberal Party and the Scottish Church Disestablishment Crisis," *E.H.R.*, LXXIX (Jan., 1964), 31-46.

47. W. S. Caine, "The Attitude of the Advanced Temperance Party," *Contemporary Review*, LXIII (Jan., 1893), 47-60; Sir Wilfrid Lawson, "The Classes, the Masses, and the Glasses," *Nineteenth Century*, No. CXVIII (Dec., 1886), 795-804.

48. Morgan, *Wales in British Politics*, pp. 143-44.

49. Arthur Arnold, "The Land Transfer Bill," *Fortnightly Review*, No. CCXLVII (July, 1887), 113-14; BM, R. T. Reid to Schnadhorst, Sept. 16, 1891, in Gladstone Papers, BM 44,295.

50. *Star*, Nov. 11, 1890; BM, Labouchere to Herbert Gladstone, March 31, 1888, Viscount Gladstone Papers, BM 46,016.

response to urban problems, the Radicals after 1886 followed the Radical Program of 1885 in turning their criticism of the "unearned increment" to the cities. They wanted to give city authorities the right to tax the urban unearned increment, to take land for housing, sanitation, and beautification, and to force landlords as well as occupiers to pay the rates.[51] This was a thoroughly Chamberlainite approach, and shows conclusively that the Radicals after 1886 had not become less "radical."

The London Radicals in particular were the advocates of what was, to them, an advanced social program. They introduced into Radicalism a new emphasis on specifically metropolitan problems and a new rhetoric in criticism of rigid *laissez-faire* principles. Led by Professor James Stuart, a leader of the university extension movement, and J. F. B. Firth, Quaker barrister and president of the Municipal Reform League, the London Radicals sought to amalgamate the obsolete and complicated system of vestries, districts, and corporations of London into one representative government. They would use this central authority the way Chamberlain had used the Birmingham city council — to improve gas, water, and sanitation services, and to raise the standards of working-class housing. They would tax ground owners instead of occupiers, and would through "leasehold enfranchisement" enable occupiers to become owners. For the country at large, the London Radicals advocated improvement of the hours and wages of government employees and abolition of taxes on common items of the breakfast table.[52]

There can be no doubt that the social concern of the new Radicals or New Liberals and the London Radicals — the membership of these groups overlapped considerably — disturbed many other Radicals, as well as moderate Liberals. To some extent, this situation caused a debate among Radicals involving the attention that they should give Home Rule. But the substance of the debate within Radicalism was not about Home Rule, which they all supported, but about the relative merits of the new social issues versus the old Radical nostrums. By the latter 1880s in Britain, fundamental questions were being asked about the nature of industrial

---

51. A. J. Williams, "A Model Land Law," *Fortnightly Review*, No. CCXLIV (April, 1887), 558-72; J. Fletcher Moulton, "The Taxation of Ground-Rents," *Contemporary Review*, LVII (March, 1890), 412-20; *The Speaker*, Aug. 9, 1890.
52. McBriar, *Fabian Socialism and English Politics*, pp. 187-98 and 234-42; Thompson, *Socialists, Liberals, and Labour*, pp. 90-111; James Stuart, "The London Progressives," *Contemporary Review*, LXI (April, 1892), 521-32; H. W. Massingham, "The Government and Labour," *Contemporary Review*, LXIV (Dec., 1893), 770-75.

society itself. To some of the younger Radicals these questions demanded a more positive program than Radicals traditionally had pursued. Haldane, trained in German idealism rather than Benthamite empiricism, was the intellectual leader of the progressive movement. He wrote:

> The mere removal of obstacles which used to block the highway of human progress had been pretty well completed. We are face to face with a new kind of social problem. Liberalism has passed from the destructive to the constructive stage in its history.[53]

Implicit in the thought of the new Radicals was a new view of the world. Unlike Radicals of older generations, they did not believe that the unimpeded action of social and economic forces led necessarily to progress; indeed, they believed, most of the impediments were gone, and the social problem was greater than ever. Like all Radicals of the nineteenth century, the new Radicals wanted to establish the conditions in which an individual would have maximum freedom of self-development. But they now felt that positive action by the state would be necessary to bring about these optimum conditions. Thus they were severely critical of unrestrained capitalism and regarded some of the older Radicals as obsolete kinds of individualists. To some of them, for example, John Morley represented the 'individualist tail" of old-fashioned Radicalism; he was the "bondslave of Political Economy."[54]

Radicals like Morley and Bradlaugh, and many others, did not share this sense of urgency about urban social issues, and did not look upon the new spokesmen of the working class with much understanding. Morley wrote of the London Radicals:

> The anarchic follies of the London Radicals are playing the Tory game to a marvel. Indeed if these men are Radicals, I'm a Tory. We cannot win without accession of strength from the London constituencies, and that strength will never come so long as these blatant democrats persist in frightening the small shopkeeper, for one thing, and in standing aloof from organization for another.[55]

---

53. Haldane, "The Liberal Creed," *Contemporary Review*, LIV (Oct., 1888), 463.

54. G. W. E. Russell, "The New Liberalism: A Response," *Nineteenth Century*, No. CLI (Sept., 1889), 498. See also: L. A. Atherley-Jones, "The New Liberalism," *Nineteenth Century*, No. CL (Aug., 1889), 192; John Page Hopps, "The Nihilisms and Socialisms of the World," *Contemporary Review*, LVIII (Aug., 1890), 271-82; and J. Guinness Rogers, "Nonconformist Forebodings," *Nineteenth Century*, No. CCXIII (Nov., 1894), 790-806.

55. Morley to Chamberlain, Feb. 8, 1888, quoted in Garvin, *Chamberlain*, II, 515.

He regarded the Fabians as imprudent upstarts: "The Fabians interest and stimulate and suggest — but they are loose, superficial, crude, and impertinent."[56]

Yet if the old Radicals differed from the new Radicals in world view and in attitude towards socialist spokesmen, in both basic ideals and specific policies they differed very little. This is why one can speak of a Radical movement within the Radical tradition after 1886. The London Radicals, for example, built their plans on the municipal intervention and land reform so important to the older elements of the Radical program of the "civic gospel."[57] Further, all of the Radicals rejected the cooperative ideal underlying socialist programs and reaffirmed their belief in a competitive system. Arthur Arnold, a land reformer who stood at about the middle of the Radical spectrum, explained that Radicals wanted to regulate, not replace, the capitalist system: "We seek to establish well-ordered competition, because we find that in some form competition is the main-spring of production, and that moral and material stoppage and decline follow upon removal of this main-spring of society."[58] As Haldane put it, the state provides a civilized environment for capitalists, and the state has the right to charge "rent" for its services.[59] Haldane's sentiment was only an extension of Chamberlain's older doctrine of "ransom" to property of all kinds. Most Radicals could agree with it, and with Haldane's specific proposals: free education, release of charitable endowments through disestablishment, reform of land transfer laws, compulsory powers for local authorities for allotments, taxation of the unearned increment, and equalization and graduation of death duties on realty and personalty.[60] This was old Radical wine in new Radical bottles.

If the Radicals agreed in rejecting socialism, in terms of practical policies they could not agree on where to draw the line. The proposal of establishing the eight-hour day, which was the issue that most often divided Radicals from socialists, illustrates the point. In the belief that competition should operate throughout society,

---

56. National Library of Scotland, Morley to Haldane, Sept. 28, 1891, Haldane Papers, MS 5903.
57. The civic gospel is discussed in Asa Briggs, *Victorian Cities* (New York, 1970), Chap. 5.
58. "Socialism and the Unemployed," *Contemporary Review*, LIII (April, 1888), 561.
59. Haldane, "The Liberal Creed," *Contemporary Review*, LIV (Oct., 1888), p. 466.
60. *Ibid.*, pp. 462-74; and R. B. Haldane, "The Liberal Party and Its Prospects," *Contemporary Review*, LIII (Jan., 1888), 156-59.

Radicals like Morley, Bradlaugh, Mundella and even Thomas Burt (a former coal miner) rejected the eight-hour day. They would accept limitation of working hours only if it were proved to them that the health and safety of the workers was at stake — as they thought it was in the case of mining.[61] However, a number of Radicals, mainly from consituencies where the working-class electorate was large, supported the eight-hour day for all industries. It would be convenient for the historian if this issue had neatly divided old from new Radicals, but it did not. Haldane, for example, rejected the eight-hour day and held to the Radical policy of the 1870s — support for the development of well-run unions, which could obtain through free and fair bargaining all the legitimate demands of labor.[62] Clearly the issue troubled the Radical movement, for it set at odds the interests of capital and labor. The eight-hour day hit at the structural weakness in Radicalism just as did the problem of working-class parliamentary representation.

In what way was Home Rule related to these policies and programs? In the first place, it did not make Radical ideology or proposals any more or less "radical"; Radicalism remained after 1886 what it had been since the 1850s and 1860s. Second, the Radical program itself was one of the main reasons that Radicals had taken up Home Rule; that is, in an effort to clear the House of Commons of legislative blocks, the Radicals had by 1886 to support self-rule for the Irish.[63] Further, immediately after the general election of 1886, a number of Radicals, most notably Labouchere, had urged the Gladstonian leadership to sandwich Home Rule between Radical measures, in order to get the electorate to swallow it.[64] Others, however, were enthusiastic about Home Rule in itself, and felt in addition that there was no point in trying to pass any reforms until the Irish Question was settled. The Radical campaign for Home Rule was extremely enthusiastic from 1886 through 1889. It was not until the Parnell-O'Shea divorce rev-

---

61. Hamer, *Morley*, pp. 255-70; Charles Bradlaugh, "Regulation by Statute of the Hours of Adult Labour," *Fortnightly Review*, No. CCLXXIX (March, 1890), 440-54; Thomas Burt, "Mr. Chamberlain's Programme," *Nineteenth Century*, No. CXC (Dec., 1892), 868; Frederic Harrison, "The New Trades-Unionism," *Nineteenth Century*, No. CLIII (Nov., 1889), 721-32; *The Speaker*, Nov. 15, 1890; BM, Arnold Morley to Gladstone, Sept. 24, 1890, Gladstone Papers, BM 44,254.
62. R. B. Haldane, "The Liberal Creed," *Contemporary Review*, LIV (Oct., 1888), 468; and "The Eight Hours Question," *Contemporary Review*, LVII (Feb., 1890), 240-55.
63. See T. W. Heyck, "English Radicals and the Irish Question," Chap. VI.
64. For example: BM, Labouchere to Herbert Gladstone, July 9 and 28, 1886, Viscount Gladstone Papers, BM 46,016. (The letter of July 28 quotes Schnadhorst to the same purpose.)

elations that Home Rule was seen as an electoral albatross by a large number of Radicals. At that time, the Radical movement, like the Liberal party, became divided between those who thought that without electoral emphasis on Radical issues a majority of pro-Home Rulers could never be elected, and those who felt that until Home Rule was passed no Radical measures could be enacted. Thus the dispute was not whether Home Rule should be offered as a device to hold the party together or as a distraction from extreme collectivist proposals; it concerned the tactics most likely to win a majority sufficient to pass both Home Rule and the Radical program.[65]

IV.

It remains to be seen how the various Radical proposals fared within the official party after 1886. The evidence seems clear that the Radical program after 1886 enjoyed greater attention and support within Liberal circles than ever before. The Liberal party, as we have seen, relied heavily after the Home Rule split on the National Liberal Federation, and for all practical purposes, the party and the N.L.F. were the same. The party systematically adopted Radical policies between 1886 and 1892; insofar as the involvement with Home Rule affected this process, it caused Liberals, in search of support, to accept Radical policies they might otherwise have avoided for years. The Federation designed its series of political demonstrations in 1886 and 1887 to associate Home Rule with the reforms desired in each of the traditionally Liberal areas of England and Wales. This meant that the N.L.F. deliberately sought out and adopted Radical policies to build enthusiasm for Home Rule. In November 1886, for example, Asquith was the main speaker at a conference in Leicester of the Liberal associations of the midland counties. He took as his subjects Home Rule and the electoral registration laws. In Rhyl, Mundella spoke to the Liberals of North Wales about Home Rule, disestablishment of the Church in Wales and a Welsh "three F" land bill.[66]

---

65. Examples of the different sides in the dispute: Haldane told Edward Hamilton that social and labor questions would be forced to the front as a result of Parnell's disgrace. (BM, Sir Edward Hamilton Diaries, Dec. 14, 1890, Hamilton Papers, BM 48,654.) Morley wrote Gladstone to keep Home Rule in first position. (BM, Morley to Gladstone, Dec. 31, 1890 and Jan. 2, 1891, Gladstone Papers, BM 44,256.)

66. National Liberal Federation, *Tenth Annual Report, 1887*, pp. 17-25; R. Spence Watson, *The National Liberal Federation*, pp. 65-69.

Such meetings generated Radical policies which were added to the resolutions accepted at the annual conferences of the N.L.F. At the 1887 conference, held in Nottingham, the N.L.F. adopted Welsh disestablishment, London municipal amalgamation, abolition of the legislative power of the House of Lords, and equalization of real and personal property taxes.[67] At the 1888 conference, the N.L.F. added one man one vote, taxation of ground rents and mining royalties, better housing for the working classes, shorter parliaments, and public payment of election expenses.[68] In 1889 came payment of M.P.s, "the free breakfast table," Scottish disestablishment, and local option.[69] From 1889 through 1893, the list of policies remained substantially the same.[70] The 1894 conference added support for an employers' liability bill.[71] The 1895 meeting changed the order of proposals by moving reform of the House of Lords to a position second only to Home Rule, but otherwise left the program unaltered.[72] Home Rule stood at the top of the list every year.

Leaders of the parliamentary Liberal party accepted the full Radical program. The key men from 1886 to 1895 were Gladstone, Rosebery, Harcourt, and John Morley. Rosebery was one of the more progressive members of the party, and did not balk at the Radical program.[73] Harcourt, by birth and temperament more Whig than Radical, through most of his career moved to the left to keep up with party opinion. Caring little for Home Rule, he frequently urged his colleagues to adopt Radical policies to offset the unpopularity of the Irish cause.[74] At the N.L.F. conference in 1894 Harcourt went so far as to declare himself a "new Radical" and accept explicitly the complete Radical program.[75] John Morley was very uneasy about policies that to him smacked of socialism, and he resisted any attempts to ignore either Home Rule or the

---

67. National Liberal Federation, *Tenth Annual Report, 1887*, p. 9.
68. National Liberal Federation, *Eleventh Annual Meeting, 1888* (London, 1888), pp. 6-9.
69. National Liberal Federation, *Proceedings of the Twelfth Annual Meeting, 1889* (London, 1890), pp. 6-10.
70. National Liberal Federation, *Proceedings of the Thirteenth Annual Meeting, 1890* (London, n.d.), pp. 9-11; *Proceedings of the Fourteenth Annual Meeting, 1891* (London, 1891), pp. 7-8; *Proceedings of the Fifteenth Annual Meeting, 1893* (London, 1893), p. 6.
71. National Liberal Federation, *Proceedings of the Sixteenth Annual Meeting, 1894* (London, 1894), p. 5.
72. National Liberal Federation, *Proceedings of the Seventeenth Annual Meeting, 1895* (London, 1895), pp. 5-7.
73. Robert Rhodes James, *Rosebery* (New York, 1963), pp. 71-76; 197-99.
74. For instance, Harcourt to Gladstone, July 16, 1892, quoted in A. G. Gardiner, *The Life of Sir William Harcourt* (London, 1923), II, 179.
75. National Liberal Federation, *Proceedings of the Sixteenth Annual Meeting, 1894*, pp. 68-72.

alliance with the Parnellites. But Morley had long been a leading Radical, and he had no trouble in accepting the official Liberal-Radical program. In 1892, he campaigned for the full platform as well as for Home Rule.[76]

Even Gladstone accepted most of the Radical policies. Because he was seventy-seven years old in 1886, Gladstone insisted that Radical proposals would have to be managed and carried by younger men. He did not, however, stand in the way of the party's acceptance of them. He wrote Harcourt in 1886: "I will not break with the 200 (the Federation) or the Radical section of them if I can help it. But I am rather too old to put on a brand new suit of clothes."[77] Yet put on a new suit of clothes he did. After coaching by Arnold Morley, the Grand Old Man accepted the Radical program as it stood at the N.L.F. conference of 1887.[78] During 1888, he introduced into the House a motion to equalize death duties on real and personal property, and spoke and voted for payment of members.[79] In November 1888, he strongly advocated one man to vote.[80] In 1890 he adopted Welsh disestablishment.[81] And in 1891, by endorsing the Newcastle Program, Gladstone accepted a strong Radical program.[82] This is not the record of a man chaining Radicals to a moderate Liberal policy.[83]

It is clear, then, that the Radicals gained influence within the Liberal party as a result of Home Rule. Despite the setback in 1886 and the loss of Chamberlain, Home Rule on balance contributed to Radical power. Yet the years from 1886 to 1895 undeniably were a period when Radicals and Liberals began to lose the allegiance of some working-class and socialist leaders. The point to remember is that it was not the Radicals' involvement with Home Rule which caused them to turn a deaf ear to the new voices. Rather, it was that to listen would have required Radicals to violate the basic preconceptions and power arrangements within

---

76. See Morley's speeches reported in *Times*, June 15 and 20, 1892.

77. Nov. 16, 1886, quoted in Gardiner, *Harcourt*, II, 12.

78. BM, Arnold Morley to Gladstone, Oct. 4, 8 and 15, 1887, Gladstone Papers, BM 44,253; National Liberal Federation, *Tenth Annual Report, 1887*, pp. 67-75.

79. BM, Sir Edward Hamilton Diaries, April 25, 1888 and July 11, 1888, Hamilton Papers, BM 48,648 and 48,649.

80. BM, Hamilton Diaries, Nov. 6, 1888, Hamilton Papers, BM 48,649.

81. Morgan, *Wales in British Politics*, p. 90.

82. Gladstone's speech at the Newcastle conference is quoted in National Liberal Federation, *Proceedings of the Fourteenth Annual Meeting, 1891*, pp. 100-15.

83. The same general conclusion, from a different perspective, is argued in E. D. Steele, "Gladstone and Ireland," *Irish Historical Studies*, XVII (March, 1970), 58-88.

their movement — and at just the time when they had obtained preeminence in the Liberal party. To accept working-class and socialist demands, they would have had to alter their ultimate goals and ignore the vital interests of the main, distinctly bourgeois, element of their alliance. What seems to have happened after 1886 is that with most Whigs and many moderates gone from the Liberal party, and with Radical people, organizations and ideas elevated to official status, the conditions were created for middle and working-class Radicals to confront each other squarely — to recognize themselves and each other for what they were. The development of a separate, independent working-class party seems the inevitable result. None of these observations is meant to argue that Radicals, as well as moderate Liberals, did not debate the rank Home Rule should have in the Radical program, or the importance of the Parnellite alliance. These were important issues; but they are the subject of a different story.

13

ROSEBERY AND IRELAND, 1898-1903:
A REAPPRAISAL
DAVID W. GUTZKE

THE PROTRACTED DEBATE on Irish policy within the Liberal party following W. E. Gladstone's retirement has received considerable attention from historians. Most of them have focused on the contributions of the talented Liberal Imperialist group of Asquith, Grey and Haldane who successfully wrote their 'step by step' approach into the 1906 Liberal programme.[1] Less well scrutinized has been the policy of Lord Rosebery and his followers.

Emerging from retirement in late 1901, Rosebery gave his studied judgement on Ireland in a series of speeches which contemporaries and scholars alike have dismissed as 'purely negative' and opportunistic.[2] Yet Rosebery's Irish policy does not require an apologist, as his critics have mistaken its subtlety for opportunism. For Rosebery, while revealing pronounced scepticism about the expediency of home rule, did not repudiate this policy. Indeed he expounded a position in February 1902 compatible with Liberal home rule principles, which paradoxically precluded the eventuality of a subordinate Irish parliament. The inspiration for this policy in part derived from W. E. Gladstone's European perspective on the Irish question, and in part from John Redmond's extreme demands in 1898 and 1899 for an independent parliament. Whereas Gladstone had argued in the home rule debates that the successful European constitutional relationships furnished a 'precedent' for a more restricted Anglo-Irish arrangement, Rosebery stressed the difficulties subsequently encountered in the Norwegian-Swedish and the Austro-Hungarian unions to refute this contention. These two important developments since 1886 were united in Rosebery's argument that the concession of an independent Irish parliament would create the problems inherent in European dualism, and eventually lead to Irish separation. Converts he achieved, but the rival gradualist approach became official policy. The extent to which Rosebery's own enigmatic personality impaired the appeal of his policy must be considered.

The twelve years following the inauguration of Gladstone's alliance with the Irish had created a chasm across which the Irish viewed the Liberals with increasing distrust, especially when they detected any retreat from the 'Grand Old Man's' Irish priorities. For their part, the Liberals confronted a seemingly insoluble dilemma. To renounce home rule for office appeared to many Liberal supporters as an odious betrayal of principle, but to proceed with the Gladstonian approach that had already been twice defeated in parliament and at subsequent elections threatened to stultify the party. Other factors also contributed to the Liberal impasse. Liberals, for example, justifiably pointed to the quarrelsome Irish factions as an obstacle to the implementation of their

---

[1] M. E. P. Marley, 'Asquith, home rule, and the Gladstonian tradition' (unpublished Queen's University Belfast Ph.D. thesis, 1972); H. W. McCready, 'Home rule and the Liberal party, 1899–1906', *Irish Hist. Studies*, xiii (1962–3), 316–48; H. C. G. Matthew, *The Liberal Imperialists: the Ideas and Politics of a post-Gladstonian Elite* (Oxford, 1973). I am grateful to Professor Trevor Lloyd, my adviser, Professor Dave Healy, Mr. Craig Horle and Mr. Robert McCarron for their helpful comments and suggestions.

[2] McCready, p. 336; Marley, p. 284.

principles. In addition, so influential was the 1886 electoral realignment on Liberal expectations that a return to the over-all parliamentary majorities of 1868 and 1880 could not be anticipated. This gloomy situation was a recurrent theme throughout 1898 in the *Westminster Gazette*, the Liberal paper edited by J. A. Spender. While the Liberal party still adhered to the Gladstonian solution of home rule, the paper commented, 'there is no further benefit to be got by repeating the processes which failed in 1886 and 1893': the Irish 'cannot retreat', and the Liberal party, lacking a majority independent of the Irish to overwhelm the Lords, 'cannot go forward'. But the paper did not recommend a policy of despair. More than a year before the onset of the Boer War, the *Westminster Gazette* helped to give notoriety to Richard Haldane's 'step by step' policy first enunciated in 1896. Logically rejecting a third senseless onslaught on the entrenched Lords with the concomitant damage to the party's electoral prospects, the paper advanced 'Home Rule by stages' as a method of circumventing the Unionist veto.[3] It was only from July 1902 that this progressive newspaper—invariably eschewing party labels and disputes to pursue a self-appointed role as preacher of unity—would consistently advocate an instalment approach to home rule.[4] This four-year hiatus, nevertheless, should not obscure the important fact that a prominent Liberal daily newspaper was predisposed to the Liberal Imperialist policy before the heated debate of 1901–2. on Irish policy began in earnest.

Two events in 1898 fostered this uncertainty in Liberal thought about the Irish question. Many historians have rightly emphasized the significance of the Irish Local Government Act.[5] Henceforth Liberals argued that the nature of the Irish question had been fundamentally transformed, and to substantiate this view they frequently cited Lord Salisbury's 1885 dictum that the concession of Irish local government would be more dangerous than home rule. A more portentous event, later engendering bitter recriminations, involved an amendment to the address moved by John Redmond proposing the 'concession of an independent Parliament'. Defending this motion, Redmond, leader of the Irish Parnellite faction, characterized the two home rule bills as compromises rather than 'a full concession of the rights of Ireland'. He further rebuked the Liberals for their apostasy in not acknowledging the priority pledge inherent in the Irish-Liberal alliance. And John Dillon, the leader of the Irish faction dependent on this alliance, was castigated for deserting Charles Stewart Parnell in favour of fruitless Liberal co-operation. In response, Sir William Harcourt, then Liberal leader in the Commons, cogently demonstrated the contradiction between an independent parliament and the principles embodied in the home rule bills, the essence of which was the supremacy of the Westminster parliament. Liberal accession to Redmond's demand for an independent parliament, Harcourt asserted, would entail nothing less than the repudiation of every Gladstonian precept upon which the Liberals 'at least with the consent of the Leaders of the Irish Party . . . have founded a Measure or (*sic*) Home Rule'. Not surprisingly Redmond attracted little Liberal support, only three joining his sixty-five followers, several joining the 233 members in the opposition lobby, and most abstaining.[6]

For Redmond to have willingly confirmed his most vehement antagonists' worst suspicions appeared to be inexplicable. But the *Westminster Gazette* offered

[3] *Westminster Gazette*, 18 March, 19 July and 23 Aug. 1898. Matthew, pp. 268–9 discusses Haldane's speech.

[4] *Westminster Gazette*, 25 July and 22 Nov. 1902.

[5] F. S. L. Lyons, *Ireland since the Famine* (1971), p. 207; McCready, pp. 320–1.

[6] Hansard, *Parliamentary Debates*, 4th ser., liii, cols. 371–87.

three feasible explanations: party tactics, patriotism and Irish reunification. First, by composing an amendment unacceptable to the Liberals but difficult for Dillon, as a rival nationalist leader, to reject, Redmond had adroitly undermined the Liberal alliance. Second, given the ascendancy of Irish national pride in the centenary commemoration of the 1798 rebellion, the Irish parliamentary leaders felt compelled to placate their supporters. Last, the Redmond faction construed the alliance as an insurmountable obstacle to the reunion of Irish factions in the Westminster parliament. 'Without Parnell', the future biographer of Joseph Chamberlain remarked, 'the Irish Party ... is without the slightest influence upon the course of events'.[7] Even less hostile critics could not question this verdict, and, despite the presence of the other factors in Redmond's speech, this reconciliatory purpose appears the most compelling.

Harcourt's dismissal of Redmond's injudicious amendment might have successfully diverted public interest to other issues, had it not been for George Doughty, Liberal M.P. for Grimsby, who resigned his marginal seat in July 1898 and sought re-election as a Liberal Unionist. In a letter to his constituents, he queried the Irish commitment to home rule, concluding that separation was their objective. Doughty cited Redmond's motion as one reason for his conversion. On only a slightly diminished poll, he was re-elected in a three-way contest against Liberal and Conservative opponents, but significantly his majority rose from under 200 to over 1700. While the *Westminster Gazette* reproached his illogical defection from the Liberals who had dissociated themselves from Redmond's view, it reluctantly acknowledged that Doughty's letter was a manifestation of 'certain discontents which have a real existence in the Liberal Party'. Sir Robert Perks, a staunch if somewhat erratic nonconformist Liberal M.P. representing the adjacent Louth constituency, wrote to Rosebery that 'until we formally state, thro[ugh] the recognized leaders, that our Irish programme is something very different from Gladstonian Home Rule', the Liberals were susceptible to 'similar escapades like that of G. Doughty'.[8]

Perks did not hesitate to act on his own advice. Hitherto Perks's discontent with the Gladstonian approach had not prevented his adoption of the traditional Liberal posture of pledging adherence to home rule in theory while denying its practical application. Doughty's loss of faith brought about a remarkable transformation. By stating the position Rosebery would subsequently espouse early in 1902, Perks became the first public Roseberian. Perks argued in a speech before his constituents in October 1898 that the Liberal leadership should unequivocally declare that, if returned to office, they would not establish an independent parliament. He drew special attention to Redmond's amendment: 'English electors could not be expected to forget the significant debate on Mr. Redmond's motion on 11th February, when upwards of sixty Irish members declared that "their present idea of Home Rule is now an independent Parliament"'. Adeptly removing home rule from Liberal consideration, Perks argued that if home rule meant an independent parliament the British could not assent to it, while if it implied a more attenuated form of local government the Irish would not accept it. In an endeavour to appeal to the important nonconformist element within Liberalism, he also referred to the repugnant

[7] L. Garvin, 'Parnell and his power', *Fortnightly Rev.*, lxiv (1898), 879; *Westminster Gazette*, 11 and 14 Feb., and 16 March 1898; British Library, Sir Edward Hamilton papers, Additional MS. 48672 fos. 124–5 (Diary, 12 Feb. 1898); F. S. L. Lyons, *John Dillon: a Biography* (1968), p. 187.

[8] *Westminster Gazette*, 15 July 1898; Perks to Rosebery, 29 July 1898, National Library of Scotland, Rosebery papers (hereafter cited as Rosebery papers), MS. 10050 fo. 25r–v. I should like to thank the Trustees of the National Library of Scotland for permission to consult the Rosebery papers.

possibility of an independent parliament installing an Irish Roman Catholic university financed by public funds.[9]

At the opening of parliament in February 1899, Redmond reiterated his appeal for legislative independence, defining this constitutional arrangement as an Irish parliament which in both its sphere and functions would be independent of the Westminster parliament. Again the Liberals could not allow this challenge to go uncontested. Sir Henry Campbell-Bannerman, therefore, who had recently succeeded Harcourt as Liberal Commons leader early in 1899, though reaffirming the Liberal commitment to home rule, adamantly declined to accept any amendment embodying an independent parliament. 'We have always refused', he replied to Redmond, 'to agree to what is known as an independent Parliament'. Haldane put the Liberal case succinctly: 'What he [Redmond] means by this Motion is to lay down something new to what Mr. Parnell meant'. The *Freeman's Journal*, the Dillonite newspaper organ in Ireland, reflected the Irish factions' increasing exasperation with these tactics by ascribing Redmond's conduct to a perverse desire to affront the supporters and assist the adversaries of home rule.[10] Redmond was nonetheless successful in achieving the reunification of the Irish parties at Westminster in the following year: under his leadership the 1885-90 Parnellite policy was revived, and the Irish once again advocated Gladstonian home rule and complete independence from British parties. However, although Redmond's action contributed to the amicable resolution of Irish problems, it engendered intense dissension among Liberals, threatening party cohesion, leading some Liberals to question Gladstonian home rule principles, and finally serving as a primary issue for the leadership debate in the following years.

The outbreak of the Boer War provoked heated discussion within the Liberal party on both imperialism and the Irish question, and eventually divided the party into three groups: the Gladstonians, represented by C.-B., John Morley and Lord Spencer; the Liberal Imperialists, represented by H. H. Asquith, Sir Edward Grey and Richard Haldane; and the Roseberians, with Sir Henry Fowler, Sir Robert Perks and Ronald Munro-Ferguson. The refusal of the war to end in accordance with Unionist expectations furnished the opportunity for Rosebery to resume an active role in Liberal party councils. On 16 December 1901 Rosebery delivered his Chesterfield speech calling for the adoption of a clean slate in domestic politics and a negotiated peace in South Africa. Campbell-Bannerman, succumbing to the pressure Herbert Gladstone, Chief Liberal Whip, and others exerted on him to seek a reconciliation, obtained an interview with Rosebery on 23 December. But the contradictory press reports—doctored for purposes of leadership rather than defining policy—which appeared in the following weeks left Rosebery's position on Ireland unclear.[11]

Any assessment of Rosebery's attitude towards home rule must include a distinction between his public and private views. From his discussion with C.-B., it is evident that Rosebery opposed the creation of a legislative body in Dublin whether subordinate or independent.[12] But once these private opinions were passed on to the Liberal press, Rosebery's personal antipathy was transformed

[9] *Louth and North Lincolnshire News*, 15 Oct. 1898; compare this speech with his statement in the same paper on 15 Jan. 1898.

[10] Hansard, 4, lxvi, cols. 1178, 1183, 1197, 1221; *Freeman's Journal*, 17 Feb. 1899.

[11] For example, *Dundee Advertiser*, 28 and 31 Dec. 1901; *Leeds and Yorkshire Mercury*, 31 Dec. 1901; *Leeds Mercury Weekly Supplement*, 4 and 11 Jan. 1902.

[12] Rosebery memorandum, 23 Dec. 1901, quoted R. O. A. Crewe-Milnes, 1st marquess of Crewe, *Lord Rosebery* (2 vols., 1931), ii. 573-4.

into a public repudiation of home rule. To profess such an opinion made any Liberal leader's position untenable. What gave credibility to this interpretation, of course, was the rhetorical flourish of the phrase, the 'clean slate', which implied the adoption of a more relevant and productive approach to the Irish question rather than a rejection of home rule. Rosebery frequently indulged his vivid imagination on public platforms, a practice which not only produced enigmatic speeches, but which, in this instance, materially contributed to the misconstruction adopted by, and the plausibility given to, the anti-imperialist press reports. In actual fact, Rosebery refused to disavow home rule for the same reason the Gladstonians declined to give a pledge implementing this policy: it was not practical politics.

Rosebery's Liverpool speech on 14 February generated less public interest than his oratorical performance at Chesterfield. His extensive retrospective remarks on Ireland, however, described by one historian as 'standard unionist arguments', merit an examination.[13] In declaring that the Irish alliance had been abrogated, that the resurrection of the home rule bills would be futile, and that the Irish question had been transformed through the Local Government Act, Rosebery simply restated the Liberal Imperialists' arguments. From these same three propositions, Asquith, Grey and Haldane urged the Liberal adoption of an instalment approach, which would gradually prepare for an Irish parliament, whereas Rosebery articulated a widely held sentiment that the disloyalty of the Irish leaders in the war disqualified them from home rule. But this had less importance than his central argument—the changes in the Irish constitutional demand and European dualism. 'The Irish leaders', he contended, 'have at last played their full hand. They have demanded, not what Mr. Gladstone was willing to give them, but an independent Parliament in Dublin'. Probably referring to Dillon's speech in 1898 on Redmond's amendment, he asserted that this demand itself fell short of the ultimate Irish goal of separation. However much the steadfast Gladstonians would dispute the relevance, they could not discount the accuracy of this judgement.[14] What made Rosebery's statement more than just a repetition of the position already marked out by Perks was his attempt, following Gladstone's lead, to view Ireland in a European context.

Among the diverse arguments advanced to support Irish self-government in 1886 was the concept of historical analogy. During a visit to Norway in August 1885 W. E. Gladstone came to view the Norwegian-Swedish constitutional relationship as a conceivable pattern for Anglo-Irish union. Within a week of his return on 8 September he wrote to Lord Hartington expressing his ardent desire 'that our friends will give to the Irish case a really historical consideration', citing both the Norwegian and Austro-Hungarian developments as worthy of study in 'the reconsideration of the whole position'.[15] Gladstone further elaborated on this conviction during the home rule debates in 1886. Arguing that as the strain successfully endured by the Scandinavian countries exceeded that inherent in any scheme the British contemplated, Gladstone maintained that the Norwegian–Swedish association could serve as a useful 'precedent' for Irish self-govern-ment. Gladstone again employed this logic to justify the bill of 1893. Sceptical

[13] *Leeds and Yorkshire Mercury*, 15 Feb. 1902; McCready, p. 331; see also J. A. Spender, *The Life of the Rt. Hon. Sir Henry Campbell-Bannerman* (2 vols., 1923), ii. 26–7.

[14] Hansard, 4, liii, col. 391.

[15] Anna Brassey, Lady Brassey, 'Mr. Gladstone in Norway', *Contemporary Rev.*, xlviii (1885), 494; *British Views on Norwegian–Swedish Problems, 1880–95: Selections from Diplomatic Correspondence*, ed. P. Knaplund (Oslo, 1952), p. xi; Gladstone to Hartington, 8 Sept. 1885, quoted in J. L. Hammond, *Gladstone and the Irish Nation* (1938), pp. 404–5.

critics, however, found Gladstone's refuge in historical analogy indefensible. The Oxford law professor, A. V. Dicey, for example, in his classic unionist study, *England's Case against Home Rule*, devoted almost twenty pages to assailing this proposed emulation of foreign political relationships. The tenuous ties uniting the Scandinavian countries also received press coverage in *The Times* before the introduction of the second bill.[16] Eventually Gladstone's critics found their apprehension confirmed when the harmonious relationship deteriorated in the eighteen-nineties and a prolonged acrimonious debate ensued, finally culminating in the separation of Norway from Sweden in 1905.

Mindful of the danger of allowing his private aversion to home rule to become a Liberal Unionist pronouncement, Rosebery in his Liverpool speech combined the Gladstonian historical analogy and Redmond's demands for an independent legislative body to forestall the consideration of home rule. He alluded to the analogies that had previously been employed between European dualism and Irish home rule, arguing that new problems in the Scandinavian union made it undesirable to put Ireland in a parallel situation. Rosebery refused, however, to be entirely negative. His Irish policy included proposals for an expansion of county government, devolution and the reform of Dublin Castle. He further suggested that it might be possible to grant Ireland a local subordinate legislature as part of a scheme of imperial federation, but that did not, Rosebery re-emphasized, involve an independent parliament.

Rosebery's position was neither Unionist in substance nor opportunistic in intent. As president of the Imperial Federation League he had delivered a speech in October 1888 attacking Austro-Hungarian dualism, and asserting that, as a union of two equal states, it excluded the path to federation. In a memorandum written almost a decade later, noteworthy in itself for demonstrating his entertainment of a home rule solution, Rosebery felt the changing circumstances in Austria and Norway 'should redouble our vigilance in regard to the question of Irish government ...'. The passage of three years increased his doubts, and in his discussion with C.-B. in December 1901 he confessed that the Austrian and Swedish systems 'made me feel that I could never be a party to introducing anything of the kind in Great Britain'. Merely to accuse Rosebery of opportunism, therefore, as one historian has recently done, is to ignore the evolution of his beliefs.[17] Far from exploiting European dualism in an opportunistic way as a tactic for opposing Redmond's demand for an independent parliament, Rosebery was convinced by European affairs that an independent parliament would create parliamentary dualism, which would lead ultimately to separation. Although he had not opposed a subordinate Irish parliament, the tension within his position had brought him to the precipice, beyond which lay Liberal Unionism. Even the Irish construed his speech in this manner: Tweedmouth informed Munro-Ferguson that Redmond did not discern any statement at Liverpool which would 'bar a statutory assembly in Ireland'.[18]

---

[16] *Norwegian-Swedish Problems*, pp. xi–xiv; Hansard, 3, ccciv, cols. 1046–7, 1540–1; *ibid.*, 4, x, cols. 1609–10; A. V. Dicey, *England's Case against Home Rule* (1886), pp. 48–66; *The Times*, 15 Nov. 1892 and 27 Dec. 1893.

[17] *Jour. Imperial Federation League*, iii (1888), 244; Rosebery memorandum, 28 July 1898, Rosebery papers, MS. 10177 fos. 120v–121; Crewe, ii. 573–4; Marley, p. 284. It is interesting that John Morley's biography of Gladstone, published in 1903, disparaged the recourse to foreign analogies, which 'carried little conviction' and were 'rather decorative than substantial' (J. Morley, *The Life of William Ewart Gladstone* (3 vols., 1903), iii. 315–16).

[18] Munro-Ferguson to Rosebery, 9 March 1902, Rosebery papers, MS. 10019 fo. 141v.

The subsequent Rosebery/C.-B. breach—ostensibly the result of differences over home rule and imperialism—leading to the formation of an organization dedicated to advancing the Chesterfield policy is well known. Of the two groups contained in the Liberal League, however, the ideas of the Liberal Imperialists have been more fully analysed than those of the Roseberians. Two themes— Redmond's enlarged demands and Irish disloyalty—dominated the Roseberian speeches and private correspondence. In a lengthy letter to C.-B. on 10 January 1902, Fowler enumerated five factors influencing the Liberal attitude towards home rule, but he gave the greatest weight to a discussion of the Irish challenge to the unlimited superiority of the Westminster parliament. His aversion to the Irish was partly provoked by their disavowal of the constitutional provision ensuring Westminster's supremacy. Fowler contended that the Irish refused to recognize 'any settlement as final until they have secured absolute independence', a belief that reflected less his Liberal Unionist predilections than his exasperation at Irish duplicity.[19] What especially incurred Fowler's anger was the type of conduct Redmond displayed in the Commons on 23 January. After drawing a parallel between Canada and Ireland, Redmond asserted that just as the Canadians refused to be governed by Westminster so would the Irish. Several days later in a letter to Rosebery advising Liberal dissociation from this attitude, Fowler mistakenly attributed Redmond's speech to John Morley.[20] While this may have been inadvertent, it is quite possible that to him and the other League members the pro-Boer Liberals and the treacherous Irish were indistinguishable.

Indeed, in the Roseberian mind their two central tenets were merged in the concept of Irish disloyalty: one response to two similar threats to the integrity of the empire. At home the Irish were assaulting the empire through their demand for an independent parliament, while abroad they were no less assuredly undermining the empire through their support for the Boers. Lord Crewe's speech in the same month exemplified this attitude. Redmond's refusal to accept a subordinate parliament as a settlement of Irish nationalist aspirations, and the Irish alignment with the 'enemies of the empire' required a Liberal reconsideration of the Irish question. To thwart any repetition of the policies of 1886 and 1893, Crewe denounced the Irish demands for a Liberal priority pledge to introduce an independent parliament. The *Leeds and Yorkshire Mercury*'s editorials also emphasized that Irish disloyalty precluded a Liberal alliance. 'Every intelligent Liberal', the paper commented, 'now perceives that no regular co-operation is possible with a party whose leader . . . insists on an absolutely independent Parliament for Ireland' and who anticipated the opportunity 'when, like the Boers, they may take up arms against her [England]'.[21] Apprehension prevailed among the Rosebery faction that the abstract Gladstonian commitment to home rule would lead to a renewal of the alliance if the Liberals lacked an independent majority at the next election.

[19] Fowler to Campbell-Bannerman, 10 Jan. 1902, Brit. Libr., Campbell-Bannerman papers, Add. MS. 41214 fos. 241–245v; for other examples see Perks to Rosebery, 7 Feb. 1902, Rosebery papers, MS. 10050 fos. 216v–217; Reay to Rosebery, 9 Nov. 1901, *ibid.*, MS. 10044 fo. 128; 'Is the Liberal League a conspiracy?', *New Liberal Rev.*, iv (1902), 624, 627; W. Robertson Nicholl, 'How to attain Liberal unity', *ibid.*, p. 345; C. Douglas, 'The Liberal League', *Contemporary Rev.*, lxxxi (1902), 581–2; 'Liberalism and labour', *Liberal League Publications*, x (n.d.), 7–8.

[20] Hansard, 4, cl, col. 713; Fowler to Rosebery, 25 Jan. 1902, Rosebery papers, MS. 10116 fos. 9–10.

[21] *Leeds and Yorkshire Mercury*, 5 Oct. 1901; for Crewe's speech see the *Westminster Gazette*, 24 Jan. 1902; for other examples of hostility to Irish disloyalty see earl of Crewe, 'Ireland and the Liberal party', *New Liberal Rev.*, i (1901), 582–3; 'The present aspect of the Irish Question: a letter by the Rt. Hon. Sir Henry H. Fowler, M.P.', *Liberal League Publications*, xvii (n.d.), 7; Perks to Rosebery, 6 Dec. 1901, Rosebery papers, MS. 10050 fos. 194v–195.

As the Liverpool speech mobilized considerable support, it is important to understand why the Roseberian policy struck such a responsive chord among certain Liberals. Within a week of his declaration Rosebery received the support of the Harmsworth press empire, of which two newspapers—the *Leeds and Yorkshire Mercury* and the Glasgow *Daily Record and Mail*—enunciated the Roseberian Irish policy. Within two months of the formation of the Liberal League a fund of £6,000 existed and grew to £11,000 by November. A dedicated group of journalists, including Sir Thomas Wemyss Reid, formerly both a Gladstonian Liberal and editor of the *Leeds Mercury* for which he continued to write a leader, and E. T. Cook, furnished propaganda through pamphlets and the League's periodical, the *New Liberal Review*.[22]

One conspicuous source of Liberal discontent was the initial adoption of home rule. Thomas Heyck has convincingly argued that the radical conversion to Gladstone's Irish policy was motivated less by ideological convictions than by a purely pragmatic approach to a largely incomprehensible Irish situation. Rosebery himself had epitomized this tendency in 1886. This practical commitment to home rule was also based on the assumption of a conciliation/coercion framework, in which home rule became increasingly seen as the only viable alternative to coercion.[23] Rosebery's opposition to an independent parliament offered these disenchanted Liberals an ideal justification for withdrawing from home rule. For those who embraced Lord Rosebery's policy, the question of a subordinate parliament need not be confronted, and charges of recanting a dubious Liberal principle need never be raised. Wemyss Reid exhibited the tactical element in this policy in a letter to Rosebery in September 1901. 'The Liberal party', he observed, 'got its charter of freedom when Dillon & Redmond made their speeches demanding an independent Parliament in Dublin . . .'. Considering the origin of their conversion, it is not surprising that the Roseberians were sensitive to C.-B.'s accusation that the abandonment of home rule meant the revival of coercion. This policy deflected this criticism. 'If we can show that whilst we shall not touch anything in the nature of an independent Parliament', Reid wrote to Rosebery several weeks earlier, 'we have a policy of our own which is not founded on mere coercion'. Rosebery's followers adopted this policy for diverse reasons. Some, like Fowler, resented the Irish prevarication; others, like Perks, found nonconformist problems impeded by or inconsistent with home rule; while others, like Reid, underlined the mutual advantages of avoiding both a subordinate parliament and coercion.[24] Despite the dissimilarity of their reasons, all concurred in the refusal to resurrect the Irish alliance and to promote a third home rule bill.

Throughout 1902 the subject of a Liberal Irish policy provided ample material for animated discussion. Rosebery delivered three more disclaimers of an independent parliament, but, as his speech in March exemplified, he became increasingly pessimistic about the possibility of granting Ireland a legislative body whose authority would remain circumscribed. Redmond addressed himself to this challenge in a speech in the same month, denying the assertion that the Irish had changed their demands and insisting that home rule was their sole

[22] Harold Harmsworth to Rosebery, 22 Feb. 1902, Rosebery papers, MS. 10168 fos. 34, 35v; Perks to Rosebery, 22 Nov. 1902, *ibid.*, MS. 10051 fo. 29; Reid to Rosebery, 26 Sept. 1900, *ibid.*, MS. 10057 fo. 73. A. W. Roberts, 'Leeds Liberalism and late-Victorian politics', *Northern Hist.*, v (1970), 131–56, discusses the importance of the *Leeds Mercury* as a provincial organ for Liberalism.

[23] T. W. Heyck, *The Dimensions of British Radicalism: the Case of Ireland, 1874–95* (Chicago, 1974), pp. 134, 145, 233–4; R. R. James, *Rosebery: a Biography of Archibald Philip, 5th Earl of Rosebery* (1963), p. 176.

[24] Reid to Rosebery, 24 Aug. and 5 Sept. 1901, Rosebery papers, MS. 10057 fos. 175v, 184.

aspiration.[25] Yet the vacillations of the Irish nationalist press revealed the consternation within the Irish party at this attack. Following the Liverpool speech, the *Freeman's Journal* admitted that the home rule bills were compromises for the 'full claim' of an independent parliament. It swiftly changed this position two days later, however, with the claim that no departure from traditional Irish desires had occurred, but later in the year confessed an inability to discern in Rosebery's statements any obstacle to his supporting a subordinate parliament.[26] Both the Liberal Imperialist and Gladstonian wings also endeavoured to discredit the Roseberian position. The *Westminster Gazette* and the party leadership's *Liberal Magazine* both stressed that Redmond spoke for a mere handful of Irish M.P.s on the two occasions in proposing his amendments, which the Liberals refused to endorse. Redmond had 'proclaimed independence', the *Westminster Gazette* conceded, 'but it is significant that he has never repeated the demand as Leader of the United Irish Party'. Hesitant Liberals would not have received complete reassurance had the paper published a later Redmond speech in October 1901 in which he again described the home rule bills as 'compromises' and the minimum of the Irish demand.[27]

Ultimately the success of the Liberal League was dependent on the size of its parliamentary membership as Edward Hamilton, a life-long friend of Rosebery, realized when he noted that 'quantity helps to form a party better than quality'. Quality was certainly evident with the presence of Asquith, Grey and Haldane, but quantity apparently failed to materialize. From a list of League candidates for the 1906 general election it can be estimated that there were twenty-five sitting M.P.s, probably a reasonable figure, even excluding those individuals who died or retired.[28] Unfortunately numerous problems were encountered in the attempt to read the speeches of these M.P.s to ascertain the relative strengths of the two groups within the League. Nevertheless, seven can be classified as members of the Roseberian wing: Charles Douglas, Sir Henry Fowler, John Fuller, Ronald Munro-Ferguson, Sir Robert Perks, Charles Day Rose and Harold Tennant.[29] An almost equal number were Liberal Imperialists: Asquith, Grey and Haldane along with Rowland Barran, Edward Ellice and Rufus Isaacs.[30] This leaves a group of twelve M.P.s about whom one can speculate, but not confidently classify.[31]

Why did Rosebery, one of the most articulate and dynamic public speakers of his time, fail to translate such assets into parliamentary support? His close friends were convinced that his disinclination to resume office as well as his desire to forward both the Chesterfield policy and the political careers of others irreparably damaged, if not destroyed, his chances of success. 'A hint of this kind

[25] *Leeds and Yorkshire Mercury*, 11 March, 1 Aug. and 3 Nov. 1902; for Redmond's speeches see the *Dundee Advertiser*, 17 March 1902.

[26] *Freeman's Journal*, 15 and 17 Feb., and 2 Aug. 1902.

[27] *Westminster Gazette*, 17 Feb. 1902; *Liberal Magazine*, x (1902), 103–4; for Redmond's speech and the Roseberian reaction see the *Liberal Magazine*, ix (1901), 546; *Leeds Mercury*, 3 Oct. 1901.

[28] Brit. Libr., Hamilton papers, Add. MS. 48679 fo. 41 (Diary, 3 March 1902); Matthew, appendix ii. Rosebery gave a figure of 26 M.P.s in Nov. 1904 (Spender memorandum, 2 Nov. 1904, Brit. Libr., Spender papers, Add. MS. 46387 fo. 53).

[29] Douglas, pp. 581–2; Fowler, *The Times*, 6 May 1902; Fuller, *Wiltshire Times and Trowbridge Advertiser*, 15 March 1902; Munro-Ferguson, *Leith Burgh Pilot*, 13 Sept. 1902; Perks, *Louth and North Lincolnshire News*, 6 Sept. 1902; Rose, *Cambridge Independent Press and Ely Gazette*, 5 Jan. 1906; Tennant, *Berwickshire Advertiser*, 23 Dec. 1902.

[30] Barran, 'Mr. Rowland Barran, M.P., on the North Leeds bye-election', *Liberal League Publications*, xxii (n.d.); Ellice, *St. Andrews Citizen*, 12 Sept. 1903; Isaacs, *Reading Observer*, 16 Dec. 1905.

[31] Andrews, *Leeds and Yorkshire Mercury*, 28 Sept. 1905, adopted a policy of administrative reform. Both Chance, *Carlisle Express and Examiner*, 10 June 1905, and Emmott, *Oldham Evening Chronicle*, 21 Dec. 1905, favoured a system of home rule all round.

takes the heart out of his friends who are much more numerous than he will allow', Hamilton lamented after admonishing Rosebery for this view. One credible explanation for the limited appeal of the League, therefore, was the inscrutable personality of the leader himself. Due in part to Rosebery's indifferent attitude towards his own career prospects, Alfred Harmsworth withdrew his newspaper support to follow a new champion and a new cause, Joseph Chamberlain and tariff reform.[32]

Yet Rosebery himself believed that this reproof was unwarranted, and ironically blamed his so-called 'friends'. Thus, in reply to a similar reproach from Wemyss Reid, Rosebery pathetically described himself as 'digging my grave' for the benefit of the Liberal Imperialists, who eschewed active participation for the more congenial role of interested observers. Clearly, he was alluding to M.P.s of the J. M. F. Fuller type, who, despite professed Roseberian affinities, did not join the League until July 1903, and whose justification for finally joining was irrelevant, if not meaningless. Disregarding his own reservations, Rosebery continued, he acquiesced to those who argued that his leadership would have widespread appeal, but with the expiration of almost nine months the League contained only fifteen M.P.s and an equal number of peers. The resulting despondency he expressed in his sardonic reply to Hamilton: 'It is all very well for you to talk of my many friends. But as far as I can see they don't come tumbling over one another'. In fact, an overwhelming feeling of betrayal permeated Rosebery's attitude to those 'who pushed me forward and then returned home'.[33]

Rosebery's rejoinder to the criticism of Reid and Hamilton, however, can be seen in a different light. While opposition to an independent parliament appealed to a segment of Liberals who found confrontation politics with the Lords a fatal Liberal preoccupation, Rosebery's similar obsession with Irish disloyalty appeared incompatible with Liberal principles. Lord Crewe, Rosebery's son-in-law, included both arguments in his January 1902 speech and should presumably have been disposed towards Rosebery's policy. But, as he informed Rosebery, Crewe declined to join the League because he felt he could exert influence in dissuading Liberals from supporting the pro-Boers. Yet in a discussion with Hamilton, Crewe reacted to the suggestion that the Irish neglected a propitious occasion of drawing a parallel with the loyalty of the self-governing colonies. The Irish, he retorted, 'had found in the past that if they behaved themselves they never got anything done for them'. As a result they were compelled to agitate—legally and illegally—to elicit a positive British response. Alfred Emmott, a League member who advocated gradual reform as the path to imperial federation, echoed this sentiment. He wrote to Rosebery:

The particular point which has caused searchings of heart to me & others whom I know is the stress laid in your [Liverpool] speech on disloyalty as if it were an incurable disease, as compared with the vagueness of your references to remedial measures which ought in time to remove that disloyalty.[34]

[32] Brit. Libr., Hamilton papers, Add. MS. 48680 fos. 19, 34 (Diary, 7 Sept. and 12 Oct. 1902); Reid to Rosebery, 13 Nov. 1902, Rosebery papers, MS. 10058 fos. 69–74; Perks to Rosebery, 8 Oct. 1903, *ibid.*, MS. 10051 fo. 138r–v.

[33] Fuller to secretaries of the Liberal League, 22 July 1903 (copy), Wiltshire Record Office, Fuller papers, MS. 1196/4; Rosebery to Reid, 14 Nov. 1902 (marked never sent), Rosebery papers, MS. 10058 fos. 79–80v; Brit. Libr., Hamilton papers, Add. MS. 48680 fo. 34 (Diary, 12 Oct. 1902).

[34] Crewe to Rosebery, 23 Feb. 1902, Rosebery papers, MS. 10168 fo. 62r–v; Brit. Libr., Hamilton papers, Add. MS. 48679 fo. 16 (Diary, 5 Jan. 1902); Emmott to Rosebery, 23 Feb. 1902, Rosebery papers, MS. 10168 fo. 40v.

One of the reasons the Liberal League did not attract a wider membership derived not from the denunciation of an independent parliament, but from the castigation of Irish behaviour during the war. This is not to say that Rosebery's own testy and erratic character was anything but a liability to the League and to himself, but that other factors also played an important role in the demise of both.

Rosebery's Irish policy originated in part from W. E. Gladstone's endeavour to place Ireland in a European context, and in part from Redmond's demand for what Liberals could not contemplate, an independent parliament. This policy found a receptive audience among those Liberals whose adoption of home rule in 1886 reflected their antipathy to coercion, but whose devotion to this principle never exceeded their own limited understanding of Irish problems. Exclusion from power served only to undermine this feeling. Yet, whereas opposition to an independent parliament could be reconciled with Liberalism, Rosebery's emphasis on Irish disloyalty contradicted a basic Liberal assumption upon which home rule had been predicated. Only a thin line divided the Roseberians from the Liberal Unionists, and to embrace both these ideas would eradicate that distinction. Almost a decade later on the third reading of the home rule bill, two followers of Rosebery, Munro-Ferguson and Tennant, supported this policy, despite Rosebery's inability to follow this course in the Lords. C. M. Douglas, however, had accepted this conclusion by standing as a Liberal Unionist candidate for South Lanarkshire in December 1910. Writing to Alfred Emmott after his defeat, he expressed the sentiment Rosebery himself must have felt:

I have always been less hopeful than you of finding a way of self-government for Ireland which would not injure this country. My last hopes were dissipated in the fate of the Councils Bill.[35]

[35] Douglas to Emmott, 6 Jan. 1911, Nuffield College, Oxford, Emmott papers, MS. 4 fo. 343v. I should like to thank Mrs. Joan Simon, Pendene Road, Leicester, for permission to consult the Emmott collection.

14

IRISH HOME-RULE FINANCE:
A NEGLECTED DIMENSION OF
THE IRISH QUESTION, 1910-14
PATRICIA JALLAND

'**H**ome rule', complained Augustine Birrell, 'is the most *unlucky* cause mortal man was ever associated with. Its path is strewn with ghosts and skeletons — wine, women and money. Now it is money. . . . *Sentiment* is easily kept alive, from one generation to another; it costs nothing but a harp and a song. But *cash* — where is that to come from?'[1] The problem of finance proved to be an insurmountable obstacle to any compromise over Irish home rule at the abortive Irish Convention of 1917-18. By contrast, the struggle over the third home-rule bill from 1912 to 1914 was dominated by the question of Ulster and not finance. The bill was ultimately wrecked by the opposition of the Ulster protestants to any home-rule bill for a united Ireland. Home-rule finance has been overlooked by most historians because it seemed less important and no doubt also because it was immensely complicated.[2] But the problem of finance was a very real difficulty which still confronted politicians even if the objections of the Ulster protestants could be overcome. More important, the complex relationship between Ireland and Britain cannot be fully understood unless the financial dimension is taken into account.

Informed politicians in 1911 believed that the chief obstacle in the path of the third home-rule bill would be the fiscal question. The prime minister, H. H. Asquith, told his liberal cabinet in January 1911 that finance was the supreme problem in view of the bankrupt condition of Ireland. Birrell, who was the chief secretary for Ireland, feared that there would be no home rule unless a satisfactory conclusion could be reached over finance.[3] Several colleagues in the cabinet shared their concern. Walter Runciman believed that home rule would collapse on the problem of finance. John Morley had more experience than most liberals of the pitfalls of Anglo-Irish finance,

[1]Birrell to Lloyd George, 13 Apr. 1914 (H.L.R.O., Lloyd George papers, C/3/8/3). I wish to thank Professor Trevor Lloyd for his numerous helpful and detailed suggestions on an earlier draft of this article.
[2]But see R. B. McDowell, *The Irish Convention, 1917-18* (London, 1970), for an excellent examination of the discussions on finance at the convention.
[3]Pease diary, 20 Jan. 1911 (Nuffield College, Oxford, Gainford papers, Pease diary, vol. i, f. 137); C. P. Scott diary, 2 Feb. 1911 (B.L., Add. MS 50901, ff 1-2); *The Times,* 4 Mar. 1911; *Nation,* 15 Apr. 1911.

and he saw 'the question of money' as the root of the problem facing them 'in the rapids' of the third home-rule bill.[4] The independent Irish nationalist, William O'Brien, warned Asquith that 'finance will either make or mar the bill'. And while the conservatives devoted far more attention to the Ulster question than the liberals, they did not neglect the significance of fiscal matters. Thomas Gibson Bowles, a unionist financial expert, told Bonar Law in November 1911: 'finance is going, I believe, to be for the first time the great difficulty — though indeed it always was one of the greatest'.[5]

They had good reason for such fears. The existing Irish administration was notoriously inefficient and unwieldy. A separate Irish executive was maintained after the union, though the Irish exchequer was abolished in 1817 and an Irish department of finance was not created until the foundation of the Dáil in 1919. After 1817 'both British and Irish revenue was paid alike into the imperial exchequer and Irish expenditure was controlled by the Treasury in Whitehall, subject only to the Westminster parliament's imposition and repeal of Irish taxation'. The usual differences of opinion between Treasury and spending departments were magnified by the existence of the Irish executive and the proliferation of more than forty Irish boards and departments with varying degrees of independence. The size of the financial problem increased as the balance of indebtedness moved against Ireland. The cost of the government of Ireland was already regarded by the Treasury as disproportionately high in 1890, but it escalated over the next twenty years with 'constructive unionism' and new social services.[6]

A cabinet sub-committee was established in 1911 to examine all aspects of the third home-rule bill except for its fiscal clauses. The committee operated in a leisurely fashion, deciding almost by default to follow the Gladstonian home-rule model of 1893. The fiscal aspects were investigated first by a specialist committee of financial experts under Sir Henry Primrose, and later by Herbert Samuel. This method of procedure had distinct disadvantages, since the men working on the main provisions of the bill were not acting in close co-ordination with the financial experts. The result was a measure which combined a reproduction of the 1893 bill with a wholly revised financial scheme. The separate examination of the two sections of the bill was unwise, given the interdependence between financial and other aspects of home rule.

A small specialist committee of financial experts was appointed in January 1911, under the chairmanship of Sir Henry Primrose, to examine the financial relations between England and Ireland and to recommend a

---

[4]Emmott diary, 1 Sept. 1911 (Nuffield College, Oxford, Emmott diary, vol. ii, f. 35); *Newcastle Chronicle,* 19 Jan. 1912; Morley to Carnegie, 25 Oct. 1911 (Bodl., MS film 569).

[5]O'Brien to Asquith, 4 Nov. 1911 (Bodl., MS Asquith 36, f. 9); T. G. Bowles to Bonar Law, 16 Nov. 1911 (H.L.R.O., Bonar Law papers, 24/3/42).

[6]Ronan Fanning, *The Irish department of finance, 1922-58* (Dublin, 1978), p. 4; Pauric Travers, 'The last years of Dublin Castle: the administration of Ireland, 1890-1921' (unpublished Ph.D. thesis, Australian National University, 1981), passim.

fiscal scheme for the home-rule bill. The members of the Primrose committee were mainly English financial experts, with no strong political affiliations though with a decidedly liberal bias. They included W. G. S. Adams, reader in political science at Oxford and recently an official of the Irish department of agriculture; William Plender, president of the Institute of Chartered Accountants; Henry Gladstone, ship-merchant, and F. M. Jackson, exporter, both highly respected in mercantile and banking circles. The cabinet seemed unaware of the need for adequate Irish representation on the committee if the nationalists were to be satisfied with its findings. Birrell, as chief secretary for Ireland, had to plead for the inclusion of an Irish catholic bishop and of Lord Pirrie, the liberal chairman of Harland and Wolff, the famous Belfast shipbuilding firm. Birrell was ridiculed in cabinet,[7] but he won his point, though the nationalist press was far from satisfied with the Irish representation on the committee. The most influential Irish expert was Denis Kelly, Roman Catholic bishop of Ross, a staunch nationalist and remarkably able man, with considerable experience of various bodies concerned with Irish economic development. Birrell prematurely revealed the existence of this finance committee in a public speech in March 1911. Subsequently he refused information on its activities on the grounds that it was 'a purely advisory body for the sole benefit of the cabinet' and not 'a star chamber of mysterious persons armed with all sorts of powers'.[8]

This home-rule finance committee devoted six months' careful study to the financial aspects of the Irish question and interviewed numerous witnesses. They produced a critical actuarial report which was printed for cabinet use in October 1911 and finally issued as a parliamentary paper in April 1912, after considerable controversy regarding its possible publication.[9] This Primrose report provided a critical review of the financial provisions of the first two home-rule bills, outlined significant changes in the financial relationship between England and Ireland since 1896, and finally proposed its own simple and clear solution.

The Primrose committee naturally started by examining the financial provisions of Gladstone's bills. Unlike the liberal cabinet of 1911, Gladstone was fascinated by the fiscal aspects of home rule. He believed that the two main financial questions were the size of the Irish contribution to imperial expenditure and the fiscal powers to be granted to the new Irish parliament. The 1886 bill said that the proposed Irish parliament should receive all the revenue collected in Ireland, including the money raised by excise taxes on spirits, even when they were eventually sold and consumed outside Ireland. From this revenue Ireland was to pay one-fifteenth of the common imperial expenditure. This was opposed by Joseph Chamberlain and other critics who claimed that it was taxation without representation,

[7]Pease diary, 20 Jan. and 1 Mar. 1911 (Gainford papers).

[8]*Hansard 5 (commons)*, xxiii, 2418 (6 Apr. 1911); xxix, 2000-01 (16 Aug. 1911); *The Times*, 4 Mar. 1911.

[9]*Report of the committee on Irish finance* (hereafter cited as *Primrose report*), [Cd. 6153], H.C. 1912-13, xxxiv, 5-40; *Minutes of evidence taken by the committee on Irish finance*, [Cd. 6799], H.C. 1913, xxx, 1-252. See also cabinet paper dated 17 Oct. 1911 (P.R.O., Cab. 37/108/132).

since the Irish were to have no members at Westminster. The Irish fought hard to pay no more than one-twentieth of the total budget for imperial purposes. John Morley, Gladstone's chief secretary for Ireland, later recalled that 'on more than one financial point the conflict went perilously near to breaking down the whole operation'; he believed the Irish might have rejected the bill on this issue, had it ever reached committee stage.[10] It was already clear in 1886 that it was impossible to determine a fair ratio between British and Irish shares of joint imperial expenditure which had any logical statistical basis.[11]

The 1886 bill also provided that customs and excise, which were the principal source of taxation, should continue to be imposed and controlled by the imperial government. The Irish were left only with power to impose direct taxes, but they felt less strongly on this issue in 1886 than in 1911-12. Gladstone's original proposals of March 1886 suggested that the Irish parliament control customs and excise, thus making Irish exclusion more logical and justifiable.[12] But Chamberlain and Hugh Childers protested so strongly about the hostility of British public opinion and business interests that the bill finally retained control of customs at Westminster.[13] The majority of Irish members would have preferred Irish control of customs and excise, but did not feel sufficiently strongly to propose defeating the measure on that issue. Parnell was one of the few nationalists who wanted to fight this point in committee, as he sought the right for Ireland to impose protective tariffs.[14]

Two financial schemes were involved in the 1893 bill, since the original plan was later found to be based on faulty calculations and had to be drastically amended in committee. The first scheme provided that the imperial exchequer should receive the revenue from Irish customs and excise, to cover the Irish contribution to imperial expenditure. All remaining Irish revenue was to be used by the Irish government for local Irish expenditure. This essentially simple plan was unfortunately based on inaccurate calculations which had suggested that the amount collected in Irish customs and excise duties equalled approximately the amount the government felt the Irish ought to contribute. The government was compelled to make the embarrassing admission in committee that the Treasury had over-estimated the yield from Irish excise, and the plan was consequently abandoned. The Primrose committee regretted this decision, for it considered this scheme much superior to that of 1886, or to the one which eventually replaced it in 1893; it decided the difficult question of the

[10]John Morley, *The life of William Ewart Gladstone* (3 vols, London, 1903), iii, 306.

[11]*Government of Ireland bill,* 13 Apr. 1886, pp 6-12 (H.L.R.O., Lloyd George papers, C/19/1).

[12]Ibid.; Gladstone's memorandum to Morley, 29 Mar. 1886 (B.L., Gladstone papers, Add. MS 44647); Cabinet paper on 'Ireland: finance' (P.R.O., Cab. 37/18/33).

[13]Childers to Gladstone, 18 Mar. 1886 (B.L., Gladstone papers, Add. MS 44132); Irish finance committee report, 1 Apr. 1886 (ibid., Add. MS 44647).

[14]*The Times,* 6 Oct. 1885 (Parnell's Wicklow speech); *Hansard 3,* ccciv, 1131 (Parnell, 8 Apr. 1886).

Irish imperial contribution in a simple manner, without reference to insoluble problems of relative taxable capacities or moral obligations.[15]

The revised scheme of 1893 provided that two-thirds of Ireland's revenue would cover local Irish charges, while the remaining one-third would constitute Ireland's contribution to imperial expenditure. For a provisional period of six years the imposition and collection of all Irish taxes would be retained by the imperial government, and arrangements would be revised thereafter. John Redmond expressed the common criticism that this bill did nothing to solve the finance problem, since the scheme was merely provisional. The Primrose committee shared Redmond's disapproval of postponing complex issues to some future date; it also condemned the plan on the grounds that the only practicable way to calculate the imperial contribution was to assign a single head of revenue, rather than a proportion of the total revenue.[16]

Birrell commented that the financial problem was almost insuperable even in Gladstone's day, but by 1911 it was a far greater obstacle, since the balance of indebtedness had moved against Ireland.[17] The Primrose committee analysed the crucial changes which had taken place in the intervening years. In 1886 Irishmen contributed in taxes to the United Kingdom exchequer well over £2 million more than they received from government expenditure.[18] By 1910-11 Irishmen received over £1 million more in benefits, mainly for old age pensions and land purchase, than they paid in taxes. Irish revenue had increased by only 28 per cent between 1896 and 1911, whereas government expenditure in Ireland had soared by 91 per cent. The total increase in government expenditure since 1896 was about £5.4 million. Nearly half of this was accounted for by old age pensions, which amounted to one-third of government spending in Ireland. Estimates presented to the government suggested that expenditure in Ireland would increase by a further £500,000 in 1910-11. The Primrose committee and most Irish nationalist economists disapproved of this steadily rising expenditure, which made Irish self-sufficiency and financial autonomy increasingly unattainable. The financial link with Great Britain entailed in Ireland a scale of expenditure which was beyond the requirements of a largely rural population and beyond the natural resources of the country to supply. The committee also considered it most unwise to saddle the new Irish government with impossible liabilities for imperial expenditure under existing circumstances.[19]

The Primrose committee rejected Gladstone's financial schemes, and proposed instead a radical yet simple plan. The Irish government should be

[15]Cabinet paper 'Irish finance', 14 Dec. 1892 (P.R.O., Cab. 37/32/51); *Primrose report*, p. 19.

[16]*Government of Ireland bill*, 1 Sept. 1893, pp 6-7 (H.L.R.O., Lloyd George papers, C/19/1); *Hansard 4*, viii, 1476-8, xi, 237-8, (Redmond, 14 Feb. and 13 Apr. 1893); *Primrose report*, p. 21.

[17]C. P. Scott diary, 2 Feb. 1911 (B.L., Add. MS 50901, ff 1-2).

[18]*First report of the royal commissioners appointed to inquire into the financial relations of Great Britain and Ireland*, [C. 8262]. H.C. 1896, xxxiii.

[19]*Primrose report*, pp 6-7, 25-6.

given full control over all her own revenue and expenditure, except that the imperial exchequer should meet the Irish deficit by assuming liability for all Irish old age pensions already granted before home rule came into operation. This would be a temporary charge on the British exchequer, which would steadily diminish with the deaths of existing pensioners, forcing Ireland to reduce her inflated expenditure. Moreover, Ireland should not be asked to contribute to imperial expenditure until she had reduced her annual deficit. The committee believed that the granting of full powers of taxation, combined with complete control of expenditure, would remove most points of potential financial friction between the two countries. This plan was expected to promote 'an autonomous Ireland, self-contained and self-sufficing so far as its own local administration and finances are concerned'.[20]

The Primrose committee's report was printed for cabinet use in October 1911, after six months of careful study of Anglo-Irish finance. Its recommendations were very similar to those proposed by Irish nationalist financial experts, such as Thomas Kettle, C. H. Oldham, Thomas Lough and Erskine Childers. Since the 1880s Irish economists increasingly recognised the significance of fiscal control as an instrument of social and economic policy. A vigorous public campaign for fiscal autonomy was waged in Ireland, placing particular emphasis on the demand for Irish control over customs and excise, and arguing that home rule would have no meaning without financial independence. It was obvious that Ireland would suffer financially from fiscal independence, but she would learn to shoulder her own responsibilities, instead of being 'demoralised by British doles'.[21] The nationalists were naturally delighted to learn that the Primrose committee's proposals were so favourable to Irish interests. Bishop Kelly of Ross kept the Irish leaders and the chief secretary informed of the committee's progress. Kelly remained hopeful in 1911 that the committee's generous proposals would be adopted, for 'in the altered circumstances a bold and full measure of home rule has a better chance of success than a half-measure'. T. P. O'Connor, however, was less sanguine, even in July 1911, and doubted whether a scheme so favourable to Ireland would ever be accepted by the Commons.[22]

The Irish chief secretary also agreed with the Primrose committee's proposals. In January 1911 Birrell confided to Sir Walter Blunt that he anticipated great difficulties in persuading certain sections of the liberal party to agree to home rule on generous financial lines. Birrell was also well aware that whilst fiscal independence would give the new Irish government far greater powers, it would lose extensive British subsidies; he told James Bryce, 'Ireland is rather puzzled between other people's money and a

[20]Ibid., pp 29-32, 44.
[21]See e.g. T. M. Kettle, *Home-rule finance* (Dublin, 1911); Erskine Childers, *The framework of home rule* (London, 1911); Lough's letters to *Nation,* 30 Sept. and 11 Nov. 1911; Frank MacDermot's letter to *Nation,* 11 Nov. 1911.
[22]Bishop Kelly to Redmond, 16 Sept. and 6 Oct. 1911 (Denis Gwynn, *The life of John Redmond* (London, 1932), pp 193-4); C. P. Scott diary, July 1911 (B.L., Add. MS 50901, ff 21-2); Birrell to Churchill, 26 Aug. 1911 (Verney papers).

cabinet of its own'.[23] Birrell made several speeches favouring a bold and generous financial settlement, arguing that generosity must 'fringe the footing of justice'. He told Churchill privately in August 1911 that Ireland should be given 'very full powers over her own revenue, taxation and expenditure'.[24]

Unfortunately for the nationalists, the Irish chief secretary was the only minister to support the Primrose committee's recommendation of Irish financial independence. The Primrose committee was merely advisory, and it was not Birrell, but Herbert Samuel, who was delegated to frame the financial provisions of the bill. The postmaster-general was one of Asquith's brilliant young protégés. Precise, accurate and restrained, he was highly respected in the cabinet for his quick mastery of complex material and his general quiet efficiency.[25] The members of the main committee on home rule were only too pleased to leave the financial aspects in Samuel's capable hands. Lord Loreburn, the chairman, admitted to C. P. Scott that he had 'not gone much into' the financial problems of the bill.[26] Thanks to Samuel, finance was the only aspect of the home-rule bill which was thoroughly and efficiently examined in 1911.

In October 1911, Samuel studied the Primrose report, utilised most of its statistics, but entirely rejected its fundamental proposition regarding Irish fiscal autonomy. Samuel worked exceptionally hard on the financial provisions, drafting detailed proposals which were revised time and time again before submission for comment to Robert Chalmers at the Treasury and to his colleagues on the cabinet committee.[27] From the autumn of 1911 he devoted much of his remarkable energy and concentration to his home rule finance scheme. He deluged the leisurely home-rule committee with detailed memoranda on finance, throughout November 1911. His six statements suggested numerous alternative proposals, outlining the advantages of each, and providing subsequent modifications in the light of additional information. The memoranda discussed various methods of meeting the Irish expenditure of £12¼ million and examined every conceivable method of apportioning Irish revenue and expenditure between the two governments.[28] However, Samuel's conscientious devotion to home-rule finance had its limitations. The scheme he ultimately produced

[23]W. S. Blunt, *My diaries: being a personal narrative of events, 1888-1914* (2 vols, New York, 1923), ii, 336 (28 Jan. 1911); Birrell to Bryce, 4 Jan. 1912 (Bodl., Bryce papers, uncatalogued).

[24]*The Times,* 25 Mar. 1911 (Birrell at Manchester Reform Club); Birrell to Churchill, 26 Aug. 1911 (Verney papers); *Nation,* 21 Oct. 1911 (Birrell at Ilfracombe).

[25]The late Mrs Lucy Masterman commented that Samuel 'was not a very good handler of the house'; he did well in the complex financial matters, not fully understood by other people, but he did not manage people well, nor was he particularly sympathetic to their feelings (interview, 3 Feb. 1974).

[26]C. P. Scott diary, 7 Jan. 1912 (B.L., Add. MS 50901, ff 58-9).

[27]See Samuel papers (H.L.R.O., A/41/2-4).

[28]Samuel's six memoranda on 'Irish finance', 6, 13, 14, 22 (two), 23 Nov. 1911 (H.L.R.O., Lloyd George papers, C/20/1/5; P.R.O., Cab. 37/108/141, 145-6); see also Samuel papers (H.L.R.O., A/41/2-4), which include Samuel's drafts and notes.

took account of so many variables that its manifold complexities baffled his colleagues and bored the house of commons. Samuel's plan did not even begin to satisfy the nationalists or the Irish chief secretary. There was never any doubt that he would reject the Primrose recommendation of Irish fiscal autonomy.

Samuel finally presented his proposals to the cabinet on 4 December 1911, and they were incorporated into the latest draft of the home-rule bill on 5 March 1912, though very few changes were made in the interim.[29] Samuel's scheme was extraordinarily elaborate, and involved a far greater degree of British control over Irish finance than the Primrose proposals. For the sake of clarity the provisions are outlined here in their final form, as incorporated into the last draft of the home-rule bill, and including the few changes made at the nationalists' request. Until the £2 million Irish deficit was extinguished, the entire proceeds of all Irish taxes, including customs and excise, were to be paid into the imperial exchequer. A block grant of about £6 million would be transferred annually from the imperial to the Irish exchequer, to cover all purely Irish expenditure, other than the 'reserved services'. The imperial government was to control and pay for the 'reserved services', including old age pensions, national insurance, land purchase and collection of taxes. If the Irish government chose to take over any of the 'reserved services', then the block grant, generally termed the 'transferred sum', would be increased accordingly. The transferred sum would include a surplus of £500,000 per annum for the first three years, to provide a working margin for the Irish government. This surplus would be reduced gradually during the next six years, until it reached £200,000 per annum, at which point it would remain fixed. The financial scheme should be re-examined when Irish revenue exceeded expenditure for three consecutive years. Once Irish solvency was thus established, the imperial parliament would consider imposing a fair Irish contribution to common imperial expenditure. Samuel's decision that Irish customs and excise should remain under imperial control, as in Gladstone's bills, was one of the more controversial points. However, the Irish parliament was granted very limited powers to vary customs and excise duties imposed by the imperial parliament, and could also levy any entirely new taxes other than customs duties. The balance sheet of the Irish government's first proposed budget was outlined as follows:[30]

[29]See 'Irish finance', 4 Dec. 1911 (Bodl., MS Asquith 105, ff 223-8; P.R.O., Cab. 37/108/167).

[30]This is a simplified sketch of an extremely intricate scheme. For details, see 'Irish finance', 4 Dec. 1911 (ibid.); 'Government of Ireland bill', 15 Apr. 1912 (ibid., MS 106, ff 199-222); *Hansard 5 (commons)*, xxxvii, 62-6 (15 Apr. 1912), for Samuel's outline of the provisions; *Outline of the financial provisions of the bill*, [Cd. 6154], H.C. 1912-13, lxix.

Revenue		Expenditure	
Transferred sum	£6,127,000	All purposes not	
Post Office	1,354,000	separately specified	£5,462,000
Fee stamps	81,000	Post Office	1,600,000
Total	£7,562,000		7,062,000
		Surplus	500,000*
		Total	7,562,000

*Subject to reduction to £200,000.

The imperial government's balance-sheet was as follows:

Revenue		Expenditure	
Irish revenue (excluding Post Office and fee stamps)	£9,404,000	Transferred sum	£6,127,000
		Old age pensions	2,664,000
Deficit	2,015,000	National insurance and labour exchanges	191,500
		Land purchase—	
Total	£11,419,000	(1) Land Commission	592,000
		(2) Other charges	169,000
		Constabulary	1,377,500
		Collection of revenue	298,000
		Total	£11,419,000

Birrell's reaction to Samuel's somewhat indigestible statistical material was predictable. He circulated to the cabinet a characteristically informal memorandum in November which provided a refreshing contrast. Birrell pointed out with a touch of sarcasm that Samuel had exhausted the possibilities of the case if it were dealt with by *not* granting Ireland full control of her own revenue. Samuel's approach could be reduced to the basic question of 'how much or how little of revenue can be given to provide the new Irish parliament with useful and educational occupation?'. The chief secretary reserved his strongest criticism for Samuel's proposal that the new Irish parliament should be deprived of control of customs and excise. Birrell believed it was dangerous to focus Irish resentment on the customs issue; an active public opinion throughout Ireland was demanding control of customs from the conviction that 'without customs there is no self-government'. He warned that the support of influential Irishmen, such as Sir Horace Plunkett, would be withheld from any proposals falling short of the Primrose recommendations. The government's scheme would inevitably have a cool reception in Ireland, especially by comparison with the generous Primrose proposals. Birrell appealed to his colleagues to reject Samuel's scheme: 'give Ireland the Primrose report and thus secure her support'.[31]

[31]Memorandum by Birrell on Irish finance, 27 Nov. 1911 (P.R.O., Cab. 37/108/161; H.L.R.O., Lloyd George papers, C/20/1/4).

The chief secretary had little hope of influencing the home-rule committee which seems to have been generally opposed to Irish fiscal autonomy. Sir Edward Grey, Lord Loreburn, John Morley and John Burns all at various times agreed that 'fiscal independence was impossible'.[32] Birrell barely managed to conceal his disappointment, when he sent an untypically terse memorandum to Redmond in December informing him that the Primrose report had been rejected. Birrell explained rather weakly that the decision was due to 'public considerations outside the purely financial aspect of the Irish problem'. He mentioned in particular that complete fiscal autonomy for Ireland must involve the total exclusion of the Irish members from the imperial parliament.[33] But there were strong objections to Irish exclusion. It would be opposed on principle by those liberals who favoured an ultimate scheme of United Kingdom devolution. As *The Times* pointed out in February 1912, 'there is a strong federalist element in the cabinet which sees in Irish fiscal autonomy a bar to the ultimate establishment of a federal system'.[34] At the level of political self-interest, Irish exclusion would also reduce the voting strength of the liberals in the house of commons. The *Nation* subsequently tried to explain the rejection of the Primrose report in terms of 'the strong opposition in England, the violent opposition in Ulster, the reluctance of some liberal members to agree to any scheme not reducible to federal terms, or seeming to threaten in the remotest way the security of free trade'.[35] Some liberals undoubtedly feared also that financial autonomy would eventually lead to demands for an independent foreign policy, and ultimately to complete separation.

Strong objections to the Primrose report certainly existed. Yet it was not the most sensible procedure to appoint a committee of financial experts to advise the government, only to reject their recommendations so completely, especially when they won so much Irish support. Samuel might at least have worked in co-operation with some of the Primrose committee members in an attempt to reach a compromise settlement likely to be more acceptable in Ireland. Instead, Samuel developed a plan entirely independently of the Primrose committee, based on completely different aims and assumptions.

The Irish nationalists detested Samuel's financial provisions and were most unhappy about the rejection of the Primrose report. Redmond and Dillon outlined their response to Samuel's scheme in a memorandum of 29 January 1912, in which they dealt with issues of principle, leaving matters of detail for later consideration. They objected forcefully to imperial control of taxation as a 'distinctively retrograde step', and requested that Ireland be given the power to impose all taxes. They also urged that the Irish parliament's powers to add to the specified customs and excise duties should be much wider.[36] Redmond's misgivings were no doubt increased by

[32]*The Times,* 5 Dec. 1910; C. P. Scott diary, 6-8 Sept. 1911 (B.L., Add. MS 50901, ff 37-40); Burns diary, 5 Feb. 1912 (B.L., Add. MS 46334, f. 4).

[33]Birrell's memorandum, *c.* Dec. 1911 (N.L.I., Redmond papers, MS 15169, seen on Bodl. MS film 1059).

[34]*The Times,* 2 Feb. 1912.   [35]*Nation,* 7 Dec. 1912.

[36]'Memorandum on clauses of the home-rule bill', 29 Jan. 1912, pp 4-6 (P.R.O., Cab. 37/109/8).

the caustic remarks of Bishop Kelly that Ireland was merely left with 'the amusement of adding tags to taxes up to 10 per cent and the game of blind man's buff of going in search of new subjects of taxation'. Opposition in Ireland to Samuel's plan was extensive. Frank MacDermot expressed widespread indignation in a letter to the *Nation* in January 1912 'contesting the propriety of putting aside financial autonomy thus unceremoniously'.[37] L. S. Amery reported to Bonar Law, after a visit to Ireland in January 1912, that there were increasing doubts as to whether the nationalists could accept the fiscal plan for home rule: 'the demand for a complete control of customs and excise is growing and will, so many people think, soon be much too strong for Redmond and Co. to resist, if not this spring at any rate before the two years of possible delay are out'.[38] Redmond was fully aware of the strength of this hostility, and his friend Michael Ennis added the warning in February that the General Council of the Irish County Councils would be forced to oppose inadequate fiscal provisions.[39]

However, Redmond and Dillon decided that they must tolerate Samuel's scheme, rather than risk wrecking home-rule prospects only a few months before the introduction of the bill. Dillon advised Redmond that it would be tactically wiser to accept Samuel's proposals rather than hold out for the full fiscal autonomy recommended by the Primrose report. If it became known in Ireland that the nationalist leaders had pressed for wider powers and been refused, the Irish national convention might endanger the entire bill and discredit the nationalist leaders by demanding radical fiscal amendments.[40] So the nationalist leaders reluctantly acquiesced in the general principles of Samuel's fiscal scheme, though they were prepared to fight over some of the details. They believed they were unlikely to succeed with the cabinet where the Primrose committee and the chief secretary had failed. It seemed tactically wiser to concentrate the full force of their critical attack on other aspects of the home-rule bill, where prospects of obtaining concessions might be greater.

The nationalist leaders, then, were only prepared to contest a few financial points. Samuel had initially intended that the surplus sum needed to provide a working margin for the Irish government should be about £150,000.[41] A series of conferences was held in the last two weeks of March 1912 between the two Irish leaders and Asquith, Lloyd George, Birrell and Samuel to discuss disputed points in the bill.[42] Redmond and Dillon insisted that '£150,000 would be useless. . . It would seem to be absolutely necessary that the surplus should be considerable'.[43] After a cabinet discussion on 2

[37]Bishop Kelly to Redmond (Gwynn, *Redmond*, p. 197); *Nation*, 20 Jan. 1912.

[38]L. S. Amery to Bonar Law, 17 Jan. 1912 (H.L.R.O., Bonar Law papers, 25/1/33).

[39]M. A. Ennis to Redmond, 17 and 20 Feb. 1912 (N.L.I., Redmond papers, MS 15254, seen on Bodl. MS film 1081).

[40]Dillon to Redmond, 14 Jan. 1912 (ibid., MS 15812, seen on Bodl. MS film 1063).

[41]Samuel, 'Irish finance', 6 Mar. 1912 (P.R.O., Cab. 37/110/39).

[42]Harcourt's pencilled notes on cabinet meeting, 14 Mar. 1912 (Bodl., Harcourt papers); Asquith's cabinet letter, 14 Mar. 1912 (Bodl., MS Asquith 6, f. 118); Memorandum by Samuel, 27 Mar. 1912 (H.L.R.O., Samuel papers, A/41/7a).

[43]'The home-rule bill: memorandum on certain points' (H.L.R.O., Lloyd George

April, Birrell reported to Dillon, with relief, that 'the surplus was agreed to (with some grimaces and wry faces)' on the lines of £500,000.[44] The nationalist leaders also succeeded in their request for the removal of the 10 per cent limitation initially imposed on the increase of customs and excise duties on beer and spirits by the Irish parliament. Samuel informed Redmond that this concession was a considerable extension of the powers contemplated in his original scheme.[45]

By 4 April 1912, Samuel was satisfied that the financial clauses of the home-rule bill were 'water-tight'. The postmaster-general worked extremely hard in the last few days before the introduction of the bill, discussing final drafting points in numerous conferences with Birrell and Redmond. Luck favoured him in his tortuous task. The day before the first reading began, Samuel wrote jubilantly to his wife: 'the figures of last year's Irish revenue and expenditure (to April 1st) are in today and show the [deficit] situation to be a million pounds better than had been estimated! So we rejoice.'[46] This recent increase in Irish revenue provided an unexpected bonus for the government. It helped to justify their claims that the Irish deficit, which was expected to reach £1½ million in 1912-13, could ultimately be extinguished.

On the morning of 11 April, Samuel was required 'to go through the finance part of the P.M.'s oration with him'. Later that day, when he introduced the home-rule bill in the house of commons, Asquith outlined the financial proposals. He argued that continuation of the existing method of governing Ireland would 'inevitably increase the current deficit' by further developing Irish resources at British expense. Home rule, on the other hand, would adjust Irish finances to Irish needs and reduce the deficit by giving Irishmen a direct interest in effecting economies. Unfortunately, Samuel's coaching was not entirely effective, as Sir Courtenay Ilbert thought Asquith 'left the financial provisions in some obscurity'.[47] Four days later, Samuel explained his complex scheme at greater length. He emphasised the transformation from a situation of £2 million surplus in 1893 to the £1½ million deficit expected in 1912-13. If the unionists rejected home rule, the existing Irish burden on the British taxpayer would be progressively increased.[48]

The Samuel scheme presented just as many difficulties as the Primrose plan without providing a final solution to the question of Irish finance. It was so complicated that few people other than Samuel ever understood it.

---

papers, C/20/2/13). Samuel's memorandum of 27 Mar. 1912 indicates that this was the joint work of Dillon, Redmond, T. P. O'Connor and J. J. Clancy written *c.*25 Mar. 1912 (H.L.R.O., Samuel papers, A/41/7a).

[44]Birrell to Dillon, 2 Apr. 1912 (N.L.I., Redmond papers, MS 15182, seen on Bodl. MS film 1063).

[45]'Memorandum on certain points' (H.L.R.O., Lloyd George papers, C/20/2/13); Samuel to Redmond, 4 Apr. 1912 (Redmond papers, N.L.I. MS 15224, seen on Bodl. MS film 1071).

[46]Ibid.; Samuel to his wife, 9 and 10 Apr. 1912 (H.L.R.O., Samuel papers, A/157/609-10).

[47]Ibid.; *Hansard 5 (commons)*, xxxvii, 1399-1426 (Asquith, 11 Apr. 1912); Ilbert diary, 11 Apr. 1912 (H.L.R.O.).

[48]*Hansard 5 (commons)*, xxxvii, 62-6 (Samuel, 15 Apr. 1912).

The Times complained that its chief characteristics were 'complexity, entanglement, and obscurity'.[49] The financial scheme provided an easy target for unionist attacks and ridicule. Sir John Marriott declared in the *Nineteenth Century* that 'constitutional independence and financial dependence cannot permanently coexist'. If Ireland wanted to enjoy the advantages of a large degree of self-government, then she should shoulder her own financial responsibilities.[50] The most scathing attacks came from Amery, in the commons and the press. He declared that Ireland should have been given either full fiscal autonomy on Primrose lines, or no taxing powers at all. The worst feature of Samuel's bill was that it provided endless causes of friction between England and Ireland.[51] The unionists also complained that the scheme could not possibly be final, because the humiliating restrictions and dual control of finance would prove intolerable to the Dublin parliament.[52] Carson accused Asquith of attempting to end the union because the poorer country was reaping too much benefit from the richer. Lord Hugh Cecil argued that Ireland's status would be reduced from that of wife to mistress, who was to be kept by John Bull. George Wyndham also believed that an equal union would be replaced by 'a morganatic alliance with a chance of saving something on the pin-money'.[53]

However, the private correspondence of the unionists suggests that they were never really very concerned about the financial aspects of the bill, except so far as they offered easy targets and useful debating points. The opposition had a far more promising line of attack in the Ulster question. In any case, they could rely on the government's own ranks to provide damaging criticism of the finance scheme. During the debates on the first and second readings, Carson and Amery predicted a liberal revolt against the proposed taxing system, but the crisis which developed by November 1912 probably exceeded their expectations.

Many liberal members were far from satisfied by Samuel's intricate system of checks and balances. MacCallum Scott, a Scottish liberal backbencher, noted in his diary in May: 'complete fiscal independence would be better than the complicated fiscal machinery in the bill. It is too

[49]*The Times,* 30 Apr. 1912. On the general failure to understand the financial scheme, see e.g. *Hansard 5 (commons),* xxxvii, 269 (Lough, 16 Apr. 1912); ibid., cols 126-7, 130-31 (Walter Guinness, 15 Apr. 1912); ibid., xxxviii, 132-4 (Barnes, 6 May 1912); ibid., xlvi, 2173-4 (Horner, 15 Jan. 1913): 'there is not one man in this house understands the finances of this bill, and . . . I do not believe that one man in twenty even tried to understand'.

[50]J. A. R. Marriott, 'The third edition of home rule — I: a first impression of the bill' in *Nineteenth Century,* lxxi (May 1912), pp 833, 842-3.

[51]See e.g. L. S. Amery, *The case against home rule* (London, 1912); *Hansard 5 (commons),* xxxvii, 1772-85 (Amery, 30 Apr. 1912); Amery's letter to *The Times,* 20 Apr. 1912.

[52]See e.g. *Hansard 5 (commons),* xxxviii, 248-53 (Austen Chamberlain, 7 May 1912); ibid., cols 145-57 (Locker-Lampson, 6 May 1912); Anon., 'The home-rule bill' in *Quarterly Review,* ccxvii (July 1912), esp. pp 265-74.

[53]*Hansard 5 (commons),* xxxvi, 1432 (Carson, 11 Apr. 1912); ibid., xxxvii, 80-85 (Lord Hugh Cecil, 15 Apr. 1912); ibid., xxxviii, 419-34 (Wyndham, 8 May 1912).

ingenious. It is fancy finance.'[54] By the time the home-rule bill reached the committee stage, the liberal criticism of the finance scheme had focused more specifically on the taxing clauses. Samuel had made minimal concessions to the Irish demands for fiscal autonomy by allowing the Irish parliament to retain only very limited powers to vary customs and excise duties. These were sufficient to provoke a liberal back-bench revolt, supported by more than seventy members, during the committee debate on the financial provisions in October and November 1912. A large proportion of those liberals who consistently abstained or voted against the taxing provisions represented Scottish constituencies. The objections of men like Cathcart Wason, Munro-Ferguson and D. V. Pirie seem to have been genuinely inspired by a conviction that the Irish fiscal provisions could not be reconciled with the future federal organisation of the United Kingdom. These Scottish liberals were among the most enthusiastic supporters of the movement for 'home rule all round', to make the Irish bill the first step in a more ambitious scheme for United Kingdom devolution.[55] Among some of the other speeches, there was more than a hint of resentment at the prospect of Irish people enjoying tea or tobacco taxed at lower levels than in England or Scotland.

Notice was served of the impending attack on 17 October, during the committee debate on clause two, concerning the legislative powers of the Irish parliament. Hayes-Fisher, a unionist, put down an amendment to withdraw the power of varying imperial taxation from the Irish parliament, since he believed the 'grotesque' financial clauses would reduce any future federal scheme to chaos. This led to a preliminary debate on the finance scheme, which was not scheduled for discussion until early November. Two Scottish liberal 'federalists' spoke in favour of the unionist amendment. MacCallum Scott expressed considerable anxiety over the fiscal provisions and stated that his fears were shared by many other members on his side. The second liberal critic, Cathcart Wason, a former liberal unionist, became a prominent leader of the liberal members' revolt. Wason protested against conferring on the Irish parliament even a limited control over customs, particularly the right to reduce customs duties, since this would postpone the Irish imperial contribution even further into the distant future.[56]

The adverse criticism evidently worried the postmaster-general, for it prompted him to circulate a cabinet paper on 22 October, reminding his colleagues of the provisions concerning customs variations, and the reasons for their insertion. Samuel emphasised that the terms of the bill prevented the Irish parliament from practising a protective policy against British goods — a point frequently ignored by the opposition in their eagerness to score debating points. The Irish parliament's power to vary customs and excise duties was already severely restricted. If even this right were revoked, it could raise little revenue as it would be deprived of any effective taxing

[54]MacCallum Scott diary, 15 May 1912.

[55]See Patricia Jalland, 'United Kingdom devolution, 1910-14: political panacea or tactical diversion?' in *E.H.R.*, xciv (1979), pp 757-85.

[56]*The Times*, 18 Oct. 1912.

powers. He further argued that it was wrong to deny the Irish people the right to reduce indirect taxes on tea and sugar, which affected the poorest classes most closely. Samuel also ridiculed fears that such reductions in Irish duties would lead to serious inconvenience in traffic between England and Ireland, or to large-scale smuggling operations. Recognising the implications of the source of the attack on the customs provisions, Samuel carefully distinguished between Scottish and Irish requirements in the event of a future system of devolution. The Irish deficit forced the imperial exchequer to take the normal growth in yield of Irish revenues, so that Ireland must be allowed some taxing powers to meet the normal growth in expenditure. Scotland could not ultimately be granted similar taxing powers, since Scotland and England were physically contiguous, but such rights would not be needed as Scotland had no deficit.[57]

Samuel was well-advised to justify his case, for the attack rapidly gathered momentum. Nineteen liberals who opposed Irish control of customs met to discuss the question on 24 October. MacCallum Scott saw in this the 'makings of a strong movement' which had a real chance of forcing the government's hand.[58] They decided to send a deputation to interview Samuel four days later, to urge that 'in the interests of the federal idea customs and excise should be controlled by the imperial parliament'. The deputation was not satisfied by Samuel's exposition of the relevant provisions, though MacCallum Scott admitted that the minister was 'very glib and knows his stuff'.[59] The *Manchester Guardian* gave substantial support to this group of critics in a leader article on 4 November: 'the whole of the provisions with regard to customs duties appear to us fraught with possibilities of friction'. Samuel's scheme was condemned as 'a half measure that bristles with difficulties'. The *Guardian* suggested instead that control of customs should be withdrawn from the Irish parliament altogether, but in exchange Britain should not force Ireland to pay the balance of her deficit.[60]

The full strength of the liberal opposition to Samuel's finance scheme was revealed in November 1912 when the financial provisions were at last debated in committee. The principles of the scheme were presented to the house first, in the form of a brief resolution, while the detailed provisions were debated later in the month. During the main debate on the finance resolution on 7 November, Lewis Haslam gave the government due notice of the intentions of the group of dissidents. He put down an amendment asking for removal of the Irish parliament's power to reduce customs and excise duties. He declared that 'a great majority' of liberal members disliked this provision, and he knew that seventy or eighty liberal members wanted the power of reduction omitted altogether. Haslam's primary motive was federalist, since he believed that centralisation of customs was an essential prerequisite to United Kingdom devolution. He also objected to the massive

[57]Samuel, 'Variation of customs duties in Ireland', 22 Oct. 1912 (P.R.O., Cab. 37/112/116); Mottistone papers (Nuffield College, Oxford, MS 14, ff 98-9).
[58]MacCallum Scott diary, 24 Oct. 1912.
[59]Ibid., 28 Oct. 1912; *The Times,* 29 Oct. 1912.
[60]'The finance of home rule' in *Manchester Guardian,* 4 Nov. 1912.

cost and practical complications likely to result from differential duties between the two countries, including English hostility to lower prices in Ireland.[61] Haslam thought the majority of liberal members would be reconciled if the Irish parliament's power to vary taxes was confined to the right to increase customs and excise duties.

But a group of liberal dissidents wanted to go even further. Cathcart Wason put down another amendment proposing to deprive the Dublin parliament of all powers to vary customs and excise duties. Wason and his friends circulated a memorial amongst all liberal members justifying their demand for the retention of full imperial control of all customs and excise duties. They argued that Samuel's provisions would establish irritating customs barriers, and that poor people in Britain would bitterly resent the injustice of Ireland enjoying untaxed tea, sugar, tobacco and drink. Secondly, they believed that 'the proposal cuts into the very vitals of any federal system'.[62] The *Manchester Guardian* was sympathetic but not sanguine: 'there is no likelihood that the government will budge on this question. Nor will the effect of Mr Wason's movement be considerable on a division.' *The Times* noted that liberal feeling on the customs provisions was divided, but trusted that 'the federalist liberals who desire that customs and excise should be under complete imperial control will probably not press their views to extremities'.[63]

However, attention was diverted from the actual substance of the finance scheme by a deliberate opposition manoeuvre intended to destroy it altogether in a notorious snap division. Mention of this famous incident is the closest that most histories and biographies of this period get to the finance of home rule, though they rarely explain its context very clearly. When the report stage of the finance resolution was taken on 11 November, the unionists defeated the government on a crucial wrecking amendment moved by Sir Frederick Banbury. He proposed to reduce the transferred sum so drastically as to remove the British subsidy to Ireland. This surprise opposition move caused a dramatic parliamentary crisis marked by severe disorder and great excitement. Unionists were summoned unexpectedly early on a Monday by a code telegram urging them to 'meet me at Marble Arch at four. Susie.' The adverse vote was only rescinded after wild scenes in the house of commons which disrupted the tight home-rule timetable.[64]

In case the government had forgotten the liberal members' grievances over the taxing provisions, a deputation waited on Asquith on 18 November to refresh his memory. The two stages of a slightly-revised finance resolution were taken on 19 and 20 November in a much-subdued house. Damaging criticism of the customs and excise provisions came from five prominent Scottish liberal federalists, led by Cathcart Wason and Munro-Ferguson, repeating previous arguments.[65] There was considerable backbench support for the dissidents. When the divisions on the finance

[61] *Hansard 5 (commons)*, xliii, 1535-7.

[62] *Manchester Guardian*, 7, 8 Nov. 1912; *The Times*, 8 Nov. 1912.

[63] *Manchester Guardian*, 8 Nov. 1912; *The Times*, 11 Nov. 1912.

[64] See Patricia Jalland, *The liberals and Ireland* (Brighton, 1980), pp 106-7.

[65] *Hansard 5 (commons)*, xliv, 147-9 (Cathcart Wason, 19 Nov. 1912); ibid., cols 159-60 (Munro-Ferguson, 19 Nov. 1912); *The Times*, 20 Nov. 1912.

resolution were taken on 19 and 20 November 1912, forty-seven liberals failed to vote on 19 November and fifty-one did not vote the following day at report stage. Of the sixty-four liberals who failed to vote on one or both divisions, more than one-third were federalists and thirteen represented Scottish constituencies.[66]

The Irish nationalists had maintained a remarkable degree of restraint during the debates on the finance scheme which they disliked so intensely. Consequently, the demands of the liberal dissidents for removal of the already limited taxing powers were embarrassing as well as infuriating. On 20 November *The Times* alleged that the government intended to revoke the Irish parliament's power to reduce customs and excise duties, to meet the criticism of 'a formidable section of the party'.[67] Redmond immediately sent an anxious warning to Birrell, that there would be 'an outburst of dissatisfaction' in Ireland if the power to reduce customs was withdrawn: 'if, in the first instance, we had been deprived of this power, Irish public opinion would probably have swallowed it; but to take it from us now, and in consequence of the threatened revolt of some of the liberal members, would have a very serious effect'.[68] But despite Redmond's appeal, the cabinet next day revoked the Irish parliament's power to reduce customs duties. Asquith later informed the king that this was a necessary concession 'in view of the prevailing opinion in the commons'. Birrell explained regretfully to Redmond that Asquith, Lloyd George and Samuel 'were fully persuaded that a parliamentary situation had arisen, which cannot be fairly estimated simply by counting votes in the lobby, and that the concession is really *necessary* if we are to carry the *brains* of our English party with us'.[69]

A government amendment deleting the Irish parliament's power to reduce customs duties was carried by 324 votes to 213 on 26 November. It was already clear that this concession would at least partially satisfy a considerable number of the dissidents. About twenty had passed a resolution at a meeting on 20 November, stating that they would be satisfied by such a concession. They included men like Cathcart Wason, Haslam and Munro-Ferguson. Altogether at least seventeen of the dissident liberals voted for the government amendment the following week. But a sufficiently large proportion of the dissidents remained unappeased to suggest that an unpleasant crisis might have developed without the government's concession. Forty-five liberals failed to vote on the government amendment, twenty-one of whom had also abstained on one or both divisions on the finance resolution. These twenty-one included six federalists and a number of extremists who wanted the powers of variation abolished in both directions.[70]

[66]See *Hansard 5 (commons)*, xliv, 251-6, 443-7, for the two division lists.

[67]*The Times*, 20 Nov. 1912.

[68]Redmond to Birrell, 20 Nov. 1912 (N.L.I., Redmond papers, MS 15169, seen on Bodl. MS film 1059).

[69]Birrell to Redmond, 21 Nov. 1912 (ibid.); Asquith's cabinet letter to king, 21 Nov. 1912 (Bodl., MS Asquith 6, f. 184); Pease diary, 21 Nov. 1912 (Nuffield College, Oxford, Gainford papers, Pease diary, vol. ii, f. 57).

[70]*The Times*, 21 Nov. 1912; *Hansard 5 (commons)*, xliv, 1109-20 (division list on government amendment, 26 Nov. 1912).

Redmond reluctantly agreed to the government amendment, but he had good reason for bitterness. The nationalist leaders had co-operated with the government, despite their opposition to Samuel's finance scheme. Yet the first serious attack from the liberal benches led the cabinet to demand still further fiscal concessions from the nationalists, regardless of the response in Ireland. Redmond's position was not helped by the insensitive comments of the liberal press. The *Westminster Gazette* did not imagine the Irish people would object to the omission of a power to reduce taxes which they would be unable to afford in the foreseeable future. The *Manchester Guardian* even predicted that the nationalists would gladly assent to the alteration, since they valued the reduction powers only as a symbol of fiscal freedom, rather than a practical weapon.[71] Such comments illustrated the failure of most liberals to understand the Irish position. The Dublin correspondent of *The Times* was more accurately informed of the true state of feeling in Ireland. 'Something like consternation' had been provoked by this latest amendment, which intensified the existing discontent in Ireland over the fiscal provisions. The Irish parliament's power to reduce duties was highly valued by the poorer classes as a means of lowering food prices. This amendment destroyed that hope and Ireland would demand an explanation if the nationalist leaders swallowed the amendment without protest. William O'Brien's All-for-Ireland League reached a unanimous decision on 24 November that this amendment wrecked the last vestiges of national self-government in the bill and rendered the fiscal clauses wholly unacceptable.[72] The liberals may have been correct in stating that the proposed Irish government could not afford to reduce duties; but the Irish were justified in their complaint that the customs amendment made such fiscal autonomy as was granted by the bill illusory in the extreme.

Samuel's financial provisions provoked a rebellion on a key issue among about 20 per cent of liberal members. This threatened revolt was responsible for one of the very few amendments of any importance inserted in the bill at committee stage. (The only other important amendment was the abandonment of the nominated senate.) It is significant that this amendment was forced from the government by pressure from its own liberal supporters rather than its nationalist allies. The government could not afford to risk alienating its own followers on any points when the opposition was prepared to make political capital out of the least hint of division in government ranks. But the nationalist leaders felt obliged to acquiesce in the financial provisions as the price of home rule. As a *Quarterly Review* article pointed out in October 1912: 'so long as the ministers keep the home-rule flag flying, it is not from the nationalists that they have any defection to fear'.[73]

After November 1912, however, the serious problems involved in Samuel's finance scheme were obscured by the increasing emphasis on the Ulster question, which rapidly came to dominate the scene. The debate on the remaining financial clauses was an anti-climax. The finance scheme was

[71] *Westminster Gazette,* 21 Nov. 1912; *Manchester Guardian,* 20 Nov. 1912.
[72] *The Times,* 25 Nov. 1912.
[73] Anon., 'The Ulster covenant' in *Quarterly Review,* ccxvii (Oct. 1912), p. 569.

rushed through the house under closure, when members were already exhausted after a lengthy and tiring session. Only five out of the thirteen fiscal clauses were discussed at all thoroughly in committee. The other eight clauses were passed under closure, with little or no debate, accompanied by recurrent protests from the opposition. Eleven clauses were disposed of in the last week of November, and only three of these were adequately discussed. Moreover, the debate on those clauses which did receive attention was not particularly inspired, frequently repetitive, and marked by abysmal ignorance.[74] The only alteration worthy of note other than the change in the customs' provisions, was the government amendment to clause twenty-six, enabling the Irish parliament to secure a revision in the financial arrangements sooner than previously stipulated.

The report stage of the financial clauses was disposed of on 8 January 1913 in a particularly thin and apathetic house. Amery denounced the scheme as a 'miserable, bastard framework of finance. . . It is a finance of odds and ends; it is jumble sale finance.'[75] The unionist *Evening Standard* described the debate in an entertaining, if highly prejudiced manner:

And then nearly everybody went off to tea. For home rule was the subject — a boring topic — and the particular menu of the night was the financial relations between England and Ireland — an appalling prospect. . . At one time even the nationalists slackened down to 14. . . Liberal and radicals totalled 14, and — may it portend nothing! — the entire unionist party numbered 13. Mr Herbert Samuel was the sole guardian of the Treasury bench.

Samuel 'babbled amazing statistics' in defence of his scheme, and in such a fashion 'the muddled finance of the bill was approved'.[76] Not surprisingly, Samuel was immensely relieved 'not to have my share of the burden of that bill any longer on my shoulders'.[77] Under the terms of the 1911 Parliament Act, the financial provisions could not be altered after the first complete passage through the commons, except perhaps as part of an entirely separate agreement over Ulster. Little more was heard of home-rule finance after January 1913, with the increasing gravity of the Ulster situation.

In terms of the Ulster crisis of 1912-14, the most fundamental weakness in Samuel's scheme was that it increased the government's difficulties in making subsequent provision for Ulster. It tied the liberals even more firmly to the original home-rule bill of April 1912, which ignored the Ulster problem. It was clear that Samuel's complicated system of checks and balances would automatically break down if Ulster had to be excluded at any stage. Samuel himself claimed that 'it is difficult to see how any workable financial scheme, of any kind, can be evolved, based upon a fiscal separation between Ulster and the rest of Ireland'.[78] Evidently, Asquith and Lloyd George did not share this view when they agreed to Ulster exclusion

[74]*The Times,* 25 Nov. 1912; J. H. Morgan, 'The home-rule bill reconsidered' in *Nineteenth Century,* lxxiii (Jan. 1913), pp 213-17.

[75]*Hansard 5 (commons),* xlvi, 1218-19 (L. S. Amery, 8 Jan. 1913).

[76]*Evening Standard,* 9 Jan. 1913.

[77]Samuel to his mother, 19 Jan. 1913 (H.L.R.O., Samuel papers, A/156/426).

[78]Samuel, 'A suggestion for the solution of the Ulster question', 18 Dec. 1913 (ibid., A/41/12; P.R.O., Cab. 37/117/95).

in 1914, but the complexities of Samuel's scheme added immensely to their problems in revising the financial provisions.[79] Hostile critics claimed that 'freedom for Ulster walks hand in hand with financial chaos in this particular bill', and even interpreted the finance scheme as a 'crafty device to . . . create a dilemma from which Ulster cannot escape'.[80]

In the course of the negotiations over Ulster in 1913 and 1914, Asquith was prepared to reduce the fiscal powers of the Irish parliament even further as a *quid pro quo* for unionist concessions over Ulster. The Dublin parliament's remaining right to increase customs and excise duties became an incidental counter in the party leaders' bargaining. When Asquith met Bonar Law on 6 November 1913, the prime minister admitted that the taxing provisions would have to undergo considerable modification, which would be unwelcome to the nationalists. The likely nature of this modification was indicated in a note from Samuel to Asquith, six weeks later, discussing methods of compensating the Irish parliament for the total withdrawal of customs variations.[81] Nothing was settled when the cabinet discussed possible arrangements for the temporary exclusion of Ulster early in March 1914. The fixed part of the transferred sum would obviously have to be reduced if the imperial parliament continued to govern Ulster. It was further argued that if exclusion were only to be temporary, it would ease matters if the taxing powers of the Irish parliament were postponed until the expiration of the exclusion period.[82] It was clear that the inevitable result would be the loss of the Irish parliament's remaining taxing powers.

The government's treatment of home-rule finance revealed major weaknesses. It was unwise to commission a committee of financial experts to examine the fiscal question, only to jettison its proposals, especially when these had such firm support within nationalist Ireland. It was unusual procedure to ignore the Primrose report completely and request the postmaster-general to develop an entirely independent scheme, based on different aims and assumptions. Samuel's plan overruled the views of the chief secretary for Ireland, the nationalist leaders, and the Primrose committee, and aroused considerable resentment in Ireland. This intricate system of checks and balances did not even satisfy the government's own liberal supporters, while it increased the problems of devising a subsequent compromise on the Ulster question. The 1912 home-rule bill was a curious combination of the 1893 bill with a totally revised financial scheme. The separate examination of the two sections of the bill was unwise, given the interdependence between financial and other aspects of home rule. A complete reappraisal of the entire measure, such as Samuel applied to the

[79]See e.g. 'Government of Ireland bill: note', early Mar. 1914 (H.L.R.O., Lloyd George papers, C/20/2/8); Draft of white paper, 6 Mar. 1914 (Bodl., MS Asquith 110, f. 216).

[80]*Hansard 5 (commons)*, xxxix, 1108 (Newman, 13 June 1912); Marriott, 'The third edition of home rule', p. 841.

[81]Asquith's notes (Bodl., MS Asquith 39, ff 3-6); Samuel to Asquith, 20 Dec. 1913 (ibid., f. 60).

[82]'Government of Ireland bill: note', early Mar. 1914 (ibid., MS 110, ff 206-14; H.L.R.O., Lloyd George papers, C/20/2/8).

financial provisions, might have been more effective. Instead the 1912 bill ignored Ulster, and put forward a highly complicated fiscal scheme which infuriated enemies and allies alike.

The obsession with the Ulster question, however, obscured the real gravity of the financial problems of home rule from 1912 to 1914. As Sir Almeric Fitzroy noted in July 1913, 'the government have escaped substantial criticism on the financial claims which constitute the real flaw in their constructive statesmanship, and might, if properly exposed, have upset their plans'.[83] While the Ulster problem became more intractable the fiscal expectations of the Irish nationalists had increased. They did not insist very strongly on control of customs in 1886 and 1893, but their sense of its significance rose substantially between 1893 and 1914. By 1917-18, even the more moderate nationalists accepted the view of William Martin Murphy that control of customs was 'the most essential right that a country with any pretence to self-government should possess'. This reflected the rapid movement in Irish public opinion since the Easter rising. But as the nationalists increased their fiscal demands, so the two questions of Ulster and finance became more obviously interwoven. The Ulster unionists left no doubt that control of customs by the imperial parliament was an essential condition for any home-rule compromise. Deadlock was reached over the issue of fiscal autonomy before the convention broached the question of partition.[84] By 1917 fiscal autonomy was as much a matter of fundamental principle concerning Irish nationality as was partition. The gap between nationalists and Ulster unionists could not be bridged on either issue by mutual agreement.

[83]Sir Almeric Fitzroy, *Memoirs* (2 vols, London, 1925), ii, 518 (15 July 1913).
[84]McDowell, *Irish Convention,* pp 108, 118, 122-5, 144 *et passim.*

15

LORD RANDOLPH CHURCHILL AND HOME RULE*

R.E. QUINAULT

'If we wish to maintain the Act of Union we must abide by the conditions of the Act of Union.'
Lord Randolph Churchill 1883[1]

'It is rather in these old speeches that we find instruction than in anything said at the present day.'
Lord Randolph Churchill 1888[2]

I

Controversy has always surrounded the Irish policy of Lord Randolph Churchill. In particular, he played an important part in opposing Gladstone's home rule bill of 1886, when he 'played the Orange card'. But despite this episode there has been much varied speculation about his real attitude towards home rule. Was he a sincere and consistent opponent of home rule, as his son and his friend, Rosebery, claimed, or was he, as Wilfred Blunt alleged, a secret sympathiser with home rule?[3] Alternatively, did Churchill merely adopt an opportunist attitude towards home rule as Robert Rhodes James has implied?[4] In their recent book, entitled *The Governing Passion*, A. B. Cooke and J. R. Vincent have produced a new and idiosyncratic interpretation of Churchill's involvement with Ireland

---

*I wish to thank A. D. Macintyre, of Magdalen College, Oxford, for his comments on an earlier draft of this article and for stimulating my interest in Irish history.

[1] *The Times*, 21 Dec. 1883.

[2] *Both sides of the home rule question: two speeches by Lord Randolph Churchill and John Morley at the Oxford Union* (Oxford, 1888), p. 19.

[3] Winston Churchill, *Lord Randolph Churchill* (2nd ed., London, 1907), pp 470—1. Lord Rosebery, *Lord Randolph Churchill* (London, 1906) pp 21—2. Randolph S. Churchill, *Winston S. Churchill*, ii. companion part i (London, 1969), p. 491.

[4] Robert Rhodes James, *Lord Randolph Churchill* (London, 1969), p. 211.

and home rule in the period 1885-6.[5] The purpose of this enquiry is to re-examine these interpretations, especially Cooke and Vincent's.

Cooke and Vincent depict Churchill as a mercurial opportunist, whose attitude towards Ireland was determined by personal and party ambitions and strategies. Churchill was no exception in this regard since 'the Irish question was the temporary and particular name given in the 1880s to a continuous and permanent existential problem which party managers inflict upon themselves.'[6] This statement forms part of a welter of sinuous prose which merely contends that Westminster politicians only thought of Ireland as a convenient party battleground. Since Cooke and Vincent give no overview of Churchill's Irish policy, their individual (and somewhat contradictory) points may be listed for convenience:

1. Churchill was 'greatly more concerned with party alignments than with Irish unrest.'[7]
2. Churchill understood Irish politics 'probably better than any other British politician.'[8]
3. 'Churchill pushed in turn all possible policies, whether substantively pro-Irish or anti-Irish, whether sensational or irresponsible, so long as they pointed towards some hope of joint action with the liberals or towards an eventual possible reconstruction of the tory party.'[9]
4. 'Churchill's Irish policy, if he had one, was not very evident before July 1885.'[10]
5. 'In Irish terms, Churchill was basically 'green' not 'Orange' in his whole orientation.'[11]

The veracity of these statements will be examined by considering, first, the nature of Churchill's contacts with Ireland and secondly, his actual Irish policies.

Churchill's involvement with Irish politics derived, originally, not from personal initiative, but from his family and social circumstances. He showed no interest in Irish affairs before 1876, when his father, the seventh duke of Marlborough, reluctantly agreed to become lord lieutenant of Ireland, at the invitation of Disraeli.[12] At that time, Lord Randolph was unpopular in fashionable London society, because

---

[5] A. B. Cooke and John Vincent, *The governing passion: cabinet government and party politics in Britain 1885–6* (Brighton, 1974), hereafter cited as Cooke and Vincent.
[6] *Ibid.*, p. 18.   [7] *Ibid.*   [8] *Ibid.*, p. 39.   [9] *Ibid.*, p. 47.
[10] *Ibid.*, p. 76.   [11] *Ibid.*, p. 75.
[12] Marlborough to Disraeli, 22 July 1876 (Hughenden House, Buckinghamshire, Disraeli papers, B/xii/A/138).

of his action about a scandal involving the Prince of Wales.[13] He therefore avoided social ostracism in London by becoming unofficial private secretary to his father in Dublin. By working and travelling with his parents, during 1877-9, Randolph learnt about both the Dublin Castle administration and the troubled rural areas of Ireland.[14] He thus became well aware of both Irish distress and the everyday problems involved in governing Ireland from Dublin. Since Cooke and Vincent admit that politicians who had actually to govern Ireland would not think merely in terms of party advantage, their claim that Churchill was 'more concerned with party alignment than with Irish unrest' appears doubtful.[15] Moreover, they produce no evidence to show that Churchill forgot his Irish government experience when evolving his policies in the 1880s.

It certainly was the case that the Irish contacts Churchill made in the late 1870s proved useful to him in the following decade. In particular, his association with the Irish government's law adviser, Gerald Fitzgibbon, resulted in a life-time's friendship and a host of letters from Dublin relating to current Irish politics. Churchill's Irish correspondents in the 1880s were mostly Tories, particularly Dublin lawyers. He did not correspond regularly with Irish catholics and nationalists. The limited nature of his contacts must inevitably have affected his thinking on Irish affairs.[16] In the late 1870s, when resident in Dublin, Churchill had been intimate with Isaac Butt, the leader of the home rule party and the catholic priest, Father Healy of Little Bray. But these friendships were not indicative of nationalist, anti-tory leanings on Churchill's part as Cooke and Vincent have implied,[17] since Butt was then wooing the tory government in the hope of gaining remedial legislation for Ireland. Hicks Beach, the Irish chief secretary, observed that the tories had 'already received no little advantage from Butt's sympathies being tory rather than whig.'[18] A decade later, Churchill pointed out that there had been a conservative and constitutional element in the early home rule party — citing

[13]Philip Magnus, *King Edward the Seventh* (London, 1964), pp 140—150.
[14]*The Times*, 29 Jan. 1895. Mrs G. Cornwallis-Wst, *Reminiscences of Lady Randolph Churchill* (London, 1908), pp 78—9.
[15]Cooke & Vincent, p. 18.
[16]See Lord Randolph Churchill papers, Churchill College, Cambridge, (hereafter cited as RCHL).
[17]Cooke & Vincent, p. 75.
[18]Beach to Northcote, 1 June 1877 printed in David Thornley, *Isaac Butt and home rule* (London, 1964), p. 355.

Butt, E. R. King-Harman and George Morris as examples.[19] Even less significant was Churchill's intimacy with Father Healy. The latter was essentially non-political and also became friendly with such unbending tories as Arthur Balfour, Lady Salisbury and even the Monaghan Orangeman, Sir John Leslie.[20]

Cooke and Vincent exaggerate the extent to which Churchill was directly involved in Irish affairs.[21] Although he usually attended Fitz-gibbon's annual Christmas party at Howth, he seldom stayed for more than a few days. He only made two other very brief visits to Ireland in 1885—6. He never revisited the disturbed areas of rural Ireland in the 1880s. Nor was he ever directly responsible for the formulation of tory Irish policy. Moreover, many other matters often engaged his attention. A four month visit to India in 1884—5 was followed by his involvement in the Afghan frontier crisis and later by his appointment as Secretary of State for India in Salisbury's tory government. Churchill's knowledge of Irish politics derived from his experience as unofficial private secretary to his father in 1877—9 and from the contacts he made then. This gave him an advantage over most, but by no means all British politicians. In the commons, in the mid-1880s, a number of leading politicians, such as Hartington, Hicks Beach, Lowther, Forster, Trevelyan and Campbell-Bannerman, had formerly been Chief Secretary for Ireland. In the lords, several peers had been Lord Lieutenant of Ireland, in particular Spencer, who had held the post for nine years. Thus, in terms of the extent of his official experience, there is no *prima facie* case to support Cooke and Vincent's claim that Churchill understood Irish politics probably better than any other British politician.[22] But their other assertions about Churchill's Irish policy can only be tested by examining in detail Churchill's views on home rule, Irish govern-ment and Ulster unionism.

II

Cooke and Vincent state that Churchill had no very evident Irish policy before July 1885.[23] But since they do not investigate Churchill's views on Ireland before the formation of the tory government in June

[19]*Both sides of the home rule question*, p. 18
[20]*Memories of Father Healy of Little Bray* (London, 1896), pp 274—86.
[21]Cooke & Vincent, pp 74—5.
[22]*Ibid.*, p. 39.   [23]*Ibid.*, p. 76.

1885 they have no right to make such a claim. In fact, Churchill believed in and advocated a broad but tangible Irish policy long before the tories came to power. That policy may be simply defined as enlightened unionism. He wished to defend the act of union between Britain and Ireland at all costs, but in such a way that Ireland would become reconciled to the arrangement, and profit from it. To understand why Churchill advocated such a policy one has to examine the early influences which affected his Irish thinking. These early influences have been overlooked, not only by Cooke and Vincent, but by such earlier writers as his son Winston and Robert Rhodes James. All these writers have regarded Churchill's Irish policy as something which he evolved individually in response to current circumstances, whereas, in reality, his attitude was largely derived from the existing views of his own family.

Lord Randolph's father, the seventh duke of Marlborough, was a strong upholder of the union between Britain and Ireland. In 1868, he opposed the disestablishment of the Irish church partly on the grounds that it might lead to the repeal of the union.[24] In 1880, Lord Beaconsfield cast his election address in the form of a letter to Marlborough, as lord lieutenant of Ireland, drawing attention to the home rule threat. After Beaconsfield's death in 1881, Marlborough reminded the public of the ex-premier's warning.[25] But the strongest unionist influence on Churchill was probably that of his mother. She was the daughter of the third marquess of Londonderry, the half-brother of the famous politician Robert Stewart, Viscount Castlereagh. The unionist tradition Castlereagh established was maintained by his family in subsequent generations. The third marquess, Randolph's grandfather, published Castlereagh's correspondence, in 1848, to rescue his name from the calumnies of his political opponents.[26] His daughter Frances, duchess of Marlborough, apparently passed on her family's unionist sentiments to her two sons, Blandford and Randolph. The former, though somewhat liberal in politics, was a strong opponent of home rule.[27] Randolph was much influenced by his mother and obtained from her, according to Escott, 'the rudiments of his practical instruction in at least the politics of

[24] *Hansard 3*, cxciii, 35.
[25] *Jackson's Oxford journal*, 20 Oct. 1881.
[26] *Memoirs and correspondence of Viscount Castlereagh, second marquess of Londonderry* ed. Charles Vane, marquess of Londonderry (London, 1848), i, iii.
[27] Marlborough to the editor of an unstated newspaper, 1 Jan. 1886 (RCHL 1/xi/1310).

Ireland.'[28] Certainly Randolph was aware of the unionist tradition of his mother's family. In his famous speech at Belfast in 1886, he declared, 'I like greatly to remember that I can number among my ancestors the great minister Castlereagh, who founded the union between Great Britain and Ireland.'[29] The family's unionist principles were also upheld by the sixth marquess of Londonderry, who was Lord Lieutenant of Ireland in 1886-9 and partly owed his office to his relationship to Churchill who was Londonderry's cousin, not his brother-in-law as stated by Cooke and Vincent.[30] The latter only draw attention to Londonderry's progressive views.[31] They fail to mention that he was a vehement and life-long opponent of home rule. In 1912, when he opposed a home rule bill for the third time, Londonderry told the house of lords: 'My whole political life has been bound up in the union of England and Ireland. I am the collateral descendant of the man who carried the union — I entered parliament as Member for County Down, my only pledge being that I would uphold the union to the best of my ability.'[32]

When M.P. for Down in the late 1870s, the future marquess of Londonderry held similar views on Ireland to those of his cousin Randolph. Both men wanted to strengthen the union by passing remedial Irish legislation. This would undermine the position of the militant home rule M.P.s who were disrupting parliament at that time. Churchill, speaking in his Woodstock constituency in 1877, declared that 'it was inattention to Irish legislation that had produced the obstruction to English legislation.'[33] His remarks were attacked as Parnellite by the *Morning Post* and were disliked by his father, then Lord Lieutenant.[34] But Churchill had only advocated a progressive *unionist* Irish policy and had specifically opposed home rule.[35] As Parnell's influence waxed in Ireland, while that of Butt and the moderate home rulers waned, Churchill's unionist sentiments became more negative. Thus in 1879, he opposed the extension of the Irish borough franchise since he thought it would result in the return of M.P.s pledged to repeal the union. He described Parnell's supporters as 'the ignorant, idle and drunken' unenfranchised part of the

[28] T. H. S. Escott, *Randolph Spencer Churchill* (London, 1895), p. 98.
[29] *The Times*, 23 Feb. 1886.
[30] Cooke & Vincent, p. 448.
[31] *Ibid.*, pp 447—9.
[32] *Hansard 5* (lords), xiii, 636.
[33] *Jackson's Oxford Journal*, 22 Sept. 1877.
[34] Winston Churchill, *Randolph Churchill*, pp 73—5.
[35] *Jackson's Oxford Journal*, 22 Sept. 1877.

population.[36] In his 1880 election address, Churchill declared that the Parnellite party must 'be resisted at all costs.'[37] Speaking at Hull, in 1881, he observed about Parnell that 'no one fears his influence in Ireland more than I do.'[38] At Edinburgh, in December 1883, Churchill devoted the whole of a major speech to the danger of home rule. Like Salisbury, he saw home rule as a strategic threat to Great Britain. Churchill claimed that if England lost control over Ireland she would cease to be a great power.[39]

But, if Churchill was a consistent opponent of home rule he was prepared to co-operate with the home rule party on a range of other matters, including remedial Irish legislation. The latter, he argued, might induce the Parnellite party to abandon its major objective.[40] But Churchill thought that a policy of killing home rule by kindness would only succeed if Ireland was treated on really equal terms with the rest of the United Kingdom. Thus, he opposed a Commons clôture by two-thirds majority vote in 1882, because it would only be used against the home rule party. This would arouse resentment in Ireland which might lead to independence.[41] In his Edinburgh speech in 1883 he expressed the hope that the union would come to repose 'not on force of arms, as it does now, but on force of habit.'[42] It was his desire for a *positive* unionist Irish policy which explains largely why he changed his mind about the wisdom of extending the proposed parliamentary reform act to Ireland in 1884. He had initially opposed such a move on the grounds that it would strengthen the electoral position of the home rule party.[43] But in May 1884, he decided to support the inclusion of Ireland in the reform bill. His *volte-face* was denounced by a few tory M.P.s[44] There is no evidence that his action was prompted by a desire to gain the Irish vote in England at the next election as Lord George Hamilton later claimed.[45] Churchill had previously observed that the Irish vote in England was 'by no means so great as those who wish to dispose of it supposed.'[46] Another tory M.P., St John

---

[36] *Hansard 3*, ccxiii, 1233—4.

[37] Winston Churchill, *Randolph Churchill*, p. 828.

[38] *The Times*, 1 Nov. 1881.

[39] *Ibid.*, 21 Dec. 1883.

[40] *Hansard 3*, cclviii. 197.   [41] *Ibid.*, cclxxiv, 610.

[42] *The Times*, 21 Dec. 1883.

[43] Churchill to H. H. Wainwright, 9 June 1884 (RCHL 1/3/424).

[44] *Hansard 3*, cclxxxviii, 854, 862.

[45] Lord George Hamilton, *Parliamentary reminiscences and reflections 1868-1885* (London, 1916), p. 249.

[46] *Hansard 3*, cclxxxiv, 369.

Broderick, later alleged that Churchill's action had resulted from a private understanding he had made with Parnell.[47] But Churchill made no agreement with Parnell in 1884 and Broderick clearly conflated the events of 1884 with those of 1885.

In fact, Churchill's change of heart reflected the prevailing view in the tory party. In his own words, 'Chaplin's proposals to exclude Ireland from the Bill met with so little favour from the leaders of our party that he wisely declined to press it to a division.'[48] But it was also true that Churchill had reasons of his own for supporting the extension of parliamentary reform to Ireland. If this was effected on equal terms he believed that it would 'sow the seeds of conciliation . . . by sowing the seeds of complete political equality.'[49] His father had declared in 1880 that 'It was most desirable . . . that everything in Ireland should be assimilated to England' and Randolph was simply following that precept.[50] Moreover, Randolph argued that the enfranchisement of the Irish agricultural labourers — who had been neglected by the Land League and were influenced by the catholic hierarchy — would weaken the position of the home rule party.[51] Although this hope did not materialise at the 1885 general election, it was true that the Land League had received little support from the agricultural labourers.[52] Moreover, Churchill soon had doubts whether the extension of the reform act on equal terms to Ireland would not increase the representation of the home rule party. But he argued that it was less dangerous for the Irish to express their views constitutionally than in other ways. He thought that once the real extent of the home rule threat was apparent, there would be more chance of overcoming it.[53]

Much controversy surrounds Churchill's Irish policy in 1885. In particular, his opposition to Irish coercion and his support for a new enquiry into the Maamtrasna murders gave rise to the suspicion that he would do anything to please the nationalist M.P.s — even support home rule. But Churchill's actions in 1885 can only be properly

[47]The earl of Midleton, *Records and reactions 1856-1939* (London, 1939), p. 61.

[48]Churchill to Wainwright, 9 June 1884 (RCHL 1/3/424).

[49]*Hansard 3*, cclxxxviii, 855.

[50]*Ibid.*, cclii, 1322.

[51]*Ibid.*, cclxxxviii, 855—7.

[52]Sam Clark, 'The social composition of the Land League', in *I.H.S.*, xvii, no. 68 (Sept. 1971), pp 455—69.

[53]*The Times*, 9 Oct. 1884.

understood if they are set in the context of his earlier views and policies on Ireland.

Churchill's opposition to extraordinary criminal legislation for Ireland derived from the views of his father in the late 1870s.[54] In 1881, Churchill opposed the introduction of an unlimited coercion bill, arguing that force was not a long-term remedy.[55] In 1882, he expressed the hope that future tory policy towards Ireland would not be confined to negative support for coercion.[56] Thus his opposition to coercion in 1885 was not unprecedented. In May 1885, he pointed out that a renewal of coercion would only convert the new Irish electors into home rulers.[57] Moreover, Churchill was aware that the ailing liberal government, undecided about renewing Irish coercive legislation, contemplated resolving the problem by resignation.[58] Thus the tories would be responsible for the renewal of coercion, which would provoke the ire of the nationalists and the radicals, leaving the tories in a weak position at the forthcoming election.[59] Churchill's opposition to a renewal of coercion was further strengthened by his knowledge that the amount of serious crime in Ireland had recently decreased.[60] When Salisbury formed his tory government in June 1885, Churchill refused to join it unless coercion was abandoned.[61] But Churchill was not directly responsible for persuading the new government to adopt this course. The political situation in general left Salisbury with no choice in the matter. As Churchill later observed, a minority tory government would have had little chance of passing a new coercion bill at the end of a parliament.[62]

The new tory government depended on an understanding with the nationalists in order to survive. Consequently, Churchill had several private discussions with Parnell in order to ensure tory co-operation with the nationalists.[63] But there is no direct evidence that Churchill contemplated buying Parnellite support by a pledge that the tories would adopt home rule. In any case, Churchill was in no position per-

---

[54]Compare, for example, the duke's speech in the lords (*Hansard 3*, ccxxxv, 1309—10) with his son's speech in the commons (*ibid.*, ccliii, 1651).

[55]*Ibid.*, cclvii, 363.

[56]*Ibid.*, cclxxiv, 613—4.

[57]*The Times*, 21 May 1885.

[58]Churchill's memorandum on events in 1885, written c. 1889 and published in Winston Churchill, *Randolph Churchill*, p. 328.

[59]*The Times*, 4 June 1894.

[60]Gorst to Churchill, 28 May 1885 (RCHL 1/5/618).

[61]Churchill's memorandum in Winston Churchill, *op. cit.*, p. 332.

[62]*Ibid.*   [63]Cooke & Vincent, pp 74—5.

sonally to decide such a momentous change in party policy. Many years later, Wilfred Blunt did allege that in May 1885, Churchill had talked of educating his party to accept home rule. But in his account of their conversation, Blunt admitted that Churchill had objected to the phrase 'home rule'.[64] Thus he may have had in mind only popular Irish local government — which he did urge Salisbury to adopt.[65] When Blunt again raised the question of home rule with Churchill, in December 1885, he was told that the tory party would not support it.[66] Churchill later observed that Blunt knew 'as much about Ireland as the man in the moon' and the two men never co-operated on Irish matters.[67] Blunt's allegation that Churchill was contemplating home rule in May 1885, directly conflicts with the evidence of Churchill's public speeches at that time, when he declared that the tory party would maintain the union unimpaired.[68]

Churchill's close contacts with the nationalists did, however, lead some tory back-benchers to view him with suspicion.[69] Once a member of the new government, he refused to be drawn in the Commons on the question of home rule.[70] In September 1885, *The Times* attacked his silence on this matter in a speech at Sheffield,[71] which, in Salisbury's opinion, had left 'nothing to be desired in respect to ministerial caution.'[72] A month later, Churchill explained:

I trust it will not be thought necessary for us to show our hand about local government or to allude to home rule or repeal at all. The nationalists do not expect us to do so and do not want us to do so. Perhaps it might be indicated that perfect similarity of treatment between the two countries as regards local government is our platform, but negatives would I think be most ill-timed.[73]

But Churchill had not abandoned his antagonism to home rule. In October 1885, he told Holmes, the Irish attorney-general, that he had not committed himself to the Parnellites in favour of home rule,

---

[64]W. S. Blunt, *Gordon at Khartoum* (London, 1911), pp 429—30.
[65]Winston Churchill, *Randolph Churchill*, p. 436.
[66]W. S. Blunt, *The land war in Ireland* (London, 1912), p. 9.
[67]*The Times*, 25 Oct. 1887.
[68]*Ibid.*, 21 May, 4 June 1885.
[69]D. C. Savage, 'The origins of the Ulster Unionist party 1885—6', in *I.H.S.*, xii, no. 47 (March 1961), p. 191.
[70]*Hansard 3*, ccxcix, 116—117.
[71]*The Times*, 5 Sept. 1885.
[72]Salisbury to Churchill, 6 Sept. 1885 (RCHL 1/7/860a).
[73]Churchill to Salisbury, 1 Oct. 1885 (Hatfield House, Salisbury papers).

which would be fatal to the tories.[74] Cooke and Vincent claim that his evidence was 'probably based on Holmes's selective memory in later life only, and . . . may reflect anxiety to wipe away any trace of earlier political frailties.'[75] But this is mere supposition, whereas Holmes's memoir is corroborated by Churchill's Birmingham election address, issued only a week after his conversation with Holmes and containing a commitment to support the union[76] more explicit than Salisbury's at Newport a few days before.[77] Churchill also told Lord George Hamilton that in his dealings with the nationalists he had never compromised himself on the question of home rule.[78]

In July 1885, Parnell sought a fresh inquiry into the verdicts in 1882 on the alleged Maamtrasna murders. Hicks Beach, the new tory leader of the commons, intimated that Carnarvon, the lord lieutenant, might reconsider the verdicts which had been upheld by Lord Spencer, the previous lord lieutenant. Churchill seconded his leader's remarks and attacked Spencer's administration.[79] Cooke and Vincent's account of this incident throws no light on Churchill's role but merely states that the action of Hicks Beach and Churchill conflicted with a previous decision of the cabinet.[80] They do not point out that, in 1884, Churchill had voted with the nationalists in favour of a new enquiry.[81] Even Salisbury thought Churchill could not have said much else 'pledged as he was'.[82] Churchill's attacks on Spencer reflected the acrimonious disputes over Irish policy between the latter and Randolph's father, the duke of Marlborough, in preceding years.[83] Spencer later claimed that the remarks of Hicks Beach and Churchill converted him to support home rule, since the Tories were

[74]A. B. Cooke & J. R. Vincent, 'Ireland and party politics 1885—71 an unpublished Conservative memoir', in *I.H.S.*, xvi, no. 62 (March 1968), p. 163.

[75]Cooke & Vincent, p. 479, note 112.

[76]Winston Churchill, *Randolph Churchill*, p. 831.

[77]*The Times*, 8 Oct. 1885.

[78]Lord George Hamilton, *Parliamentary reminiscences and reflections 1886-1906* (London, 1922), p. 20.

[79]*Hansard 3*, ccxcix, 1098—9.

[80]Cooke & Vincent, p. 276.

[81]Winston Churchill, *Randolph Churchill*, p. 355.

[82]Salisbury to Carnarvon, 22 July 1885, printed in Sir A. Hardinge, *The life of Henry Howard Molyneux Herbert, fourth earl of Carnarvon*, 3 vols (London, 1925) iii, 170.

[83]See, for example, the speeches by Marlborough (*Hansard 3*, ccxxxv, 1309, and the speeches by Spencer (ibid., cclii, 85—9 and ibid., cclxi, 389).

clearly going in that direction.[84] But Churchill cannot be held responsible for Spencer's misreading of the situation. Nothing Churchill said indicated that the tories were about to adopt home rule.

The allegation of Robert Rhodes James that Churchill waited until the general election of 1885 before making up his mind about home rule is demonstrably false.[85] Over a month before the election he wrote to Fitzgibbon:

It is to the bishops entirely to whom I look in the future to turn, to mitigate or to postpone the home rule onslaught. Let us only be enabled to occupy a year with the education question. By that time, I am certain, Parnell's party will have become seriously disintegrated . . . and the bishops, who in their hearts hate Parnell and don't care a scrap for home rule, will . . . complete the rout.[86]

His remarks were reminiscent of his mother's in 1877 — that the Irish catholic clergy 'hate home rule in their hearts.'[87] Before the result of the 1885 election was known, Churchill sketched for Salisbury a possible programme for the 1886 parliamentary session. He assumed 'that anything in the future of an Irish parliament is impossible always.'[88] His hostility to home rule was unshaken by the liberal election victory.[89] When Churchill learnt, with surprise, that Carnarvon favoured some kind of home rule, he called for the resignation of the lord lieutenant.[90]

Cooke and Vincent have argued that Churchill took an anti-home rule stance after the elections 'to create a liberal cave and perhaps thereby a tory reconstruction. . . . it was a fusionist tactic aimed as much against Salisbury as against Gladstone.'[91] But since there was nothing new about Churchill's anti-home rule stance, no novel explanation of his action is required. It was not true that Churchill favoured any Irish policy which would result in a tory-liberal coalition. He only supported co-operation with dissident liberals in order to prevent the passage of home rule. During the 1885 election — while the tories still had hopes of winning an overall majority — Churchill lambasted both whigs and Chamberlainites and claimed that

[84]Sir John Ross Bt., *The years of my pilgrimage* (London, 1924), p. 177.
[85]R. R. James, *Randolph Churchill*, p. 211.
[86]Churchill to Fitzgibbon, 14 Oct. 1885 (RCHL 1/8/978).
[87]Duchess of Marlborough to Corry, n.d. (Disraeli papers, B/xx/Ch/87.)
[88]Churchill to Salisbury, Nov. 1885 (RCHL 1/10/1126).
[89]Churchill to Morris, 7 Dec. 1885 (RCHL 1/10/1145).
[90]Churchill to Salisbury, 10 Dec. 1885 (Salisbury papers).
[91]Cooke & Vincent, pp 41—2.

Hartington was supporting Parnell.[92] He would not have used such language had he wished himself to lead a tory-liberal coalition. Before the election result was known, Churchill did privately advocate a coalition, but one with a specific object which would end his own front-bench career. He told Salisbury that the latter would 'never get whig support as long as I am in the government and whig support you must have.' He claimed that a formal whig-tory coalition 'would keep the Parnellites and radicals at bay for years, and after all, that is what must be arrived at.'[93] Once it became clear that Gladstone favoured home rule, Churchill tried publicly to win over Hartington in a speech at Paddington.[94] In the following months, Churchill did his best to cement an alliance between the tories and the dissident liberals by emphasising their common support for the union.[95] There is no evidence to support Cooke and Vincent's contention that Churchill's anti-home rule ardour abated after the early spring of 1886.[96] In his speech against the home rule bill in April, Churchill declared that no M.P. 'would ever be called upon to consider matters more momentous than those which are now before the house of commons.'[97] His June 1886 election address was exclusively devoted to an impassioned attack on Gladstone and his Irish policy.[98] Although Churchill took a holiday during the 1886 election campaign, he was then confident that Gladstone would be heavily defeated.[99]

Much of the credit that Churchill gained in his party for his opposition to home rule was dissipated when he resigned from the tory government in December 1886. But there was a connection between his resignation and his opposition to home rule. Before the 1886 election, Churchill thought that, although the tories would win, the longer term danger of home rule would remain.[100] After the unionist

[92]*The Times*, 7 Nov. 1885.
[93]Churchill to Salisbury, 29 Nov. 1885 (Salisbury papers).
[94]*The Times*, 15 Feb. 1886.
[95]See, for example: *The Times*, 4 March 1886; also, Churchill to Salisbury, 17 April 1886 (RCHL 1/10/1480a) and Churchill to Hartington, 19 June 1886 (RCHL 1/13/1537a).
[96]Cooke & Vincent, p. 77.
[97]*Hansard 3*, cciv, 1317.
[98]Winston Churchill, *Randolph Churchill*, pp 858—62.
[99]*The Times*, 15 Feb. 1886, and Churchill to Hartington, 19 June 1886 (RCHL 1/13/1537a).
[100]Churchill to the duchess of Marlborough, 17 June 1886 (RCHL 1/13/1532).

victory, he complained that 'the allied armies do not understand the necessity of hot pursuit of the routed foe.'[101] In his famous Dartford speech, in October, he warned his party against over-confidence and stressed the need to preserve the unionist alliance.[102] A liberal policy (the Dartford programme) was thus essential, since although the unionist alliance was firm amongst the leaders, this was not the case amongst the rank-and-file.[103] He made the same point, after his resignation, in an explanatory letter to the tory whip, Akers-Douglas:

The primary object of all government at the present moment is to maintain the union, to maintain it not for a session, or for a parliament, but for our time. The maintenance of the union is, to my mind, in no way a question of men, but entirely a question of measures and administration.[104]

Churchill, in other words, believed that his resignation, in itself, would have no deleterious effect on the unionist cause. Indeed, his resignation was partly prompted by his belief that his party was not doing enough to defend the union. He felt that England would only be secured for the union if the government passed progressive legislation.[105] His prediction that Gladstone's home rule policy would otherwise triumph at the next election[106] was fully borne out in 1892.

In his resignation statement, Churchill declared that, when in office, 'I regarded the liberal unionists as a useful kind of crutch and I looked forward to the time, and no distant time, when the tory party might walk alone.'[107] An apparent change in liberal unionism prompted Churchill to change his own attitude, which was not, as has been alleged, inconsistent.[108] Shortly before Churchill resigned, the first 'Round Table Conference' took place at which the terms for a possible liberal re-union were discussed. Chamberlain, who led the

[101]Churchill to Morris, 9 June 1886, printed in Maud Wynne, *An Irishman and his family* (London, 1937), p. 115.
[102]*The Times*, 4 Oct. 1886.
[103]The Queen to Salisbury, 25 Nov. 1886, printed in *The letters of Queen Victoria*, third series, ed. G. E. Buckle (London, 1930), i. 225—6.
[104]Churchill to Akers-Douglas, 1 Jan. 1887, printed in Winston Churchill, *Randolph Churchill*, p. 640.
[105]*Hansard 3*, cccx, 288.
[106]Churchill to Morris, 2 Jan. 1887, printed in Wynne, *An Irishman*, p. 118.
[107]*Hansard 3*, cccx, 289.
[108]M. C. Hurst, *Joseph Chamberlain and Liberal reunion: the Round Table Conference of 1887* (London, 1967), p. 256.

liberal unionist delegation at the conference, was advised by Churchill not re-unite with Gladstone.[109] But, when Chamberlain went ahead with the negotiations, Churchill told the commons that Chamberlain was pursuing 'an erroneous and mistaken course.'[110] When, after the failure of the Round Table Conference, the liberal unionists moved closer to the tories, Churchill, welcomed Hartington's statement that all hopes of liberal reunion must be finally abandoned as 'the cardinal feature of the recess.'[111] Thereafter, he continuously supported the liberal unionists and denounced home rule and the Parnellite party. For example, in his 1892 election address he declared that his opinions on home rule 'are unaltered and unalterable,'[112] and, in the last year of his political career, he made very many speeches against home rule in various parts of Britain.[113] He died as he had lived — true to his un-yielding unionist principles.

III

Churchill's most dramatic involvement in Irish politics was what he himself described as 'playing the Orange card'. Cooke and Vincent have questioned both his sincerity and consistency. More generally they argue that 'Ulster failed to make any impact on events in 1886' since 'British politicians did not think about Ulster.'[114] But this is not true of Churchill who had important links with Ulster before 1886 which were not investigated either by his biographers or by Cooke and Vincent who therefore failed to appreciate the degree to which his 'playing the Orange card' in 1886 was both sincere and consistent with his earlier policy. As a grandson of the marquess of Londonderry, Churchill came partly from Ulster protestant stock. As he pointed out in his 1886 Belfast speech, he was descended from both the McDonnells of Antrim and the Stewarts of Down.[115] His mother spent much of her early life at Mountstewart, her father's seat at New-townards, outside Belfast. Randolph stayed at Mountstewart in 1877, when his father, the lord lieutenant, was paying an official visit to Ulster. The duke of Marlborough considered that his reception in Belfast was the highlight of his career and he pointed towards the

[109] *Ibid.*, p. 114.   [110] *Hansard 3*, cccx, 289.
[111] *The Times*, 16 Dec. 1887.
[112] Winston Churchill, *Randolph Churchill*, pp 862—3.
[113] See, for example, *The Times*, 8, 15, 23 & 27 May 1893.
[114] Cooke & Vincent, p. 162.
[115] *The Times*, 23 Feb. 1886.

loyalty and prosperity of Ulster as an example to the rest of Ireland. He expressed the hope that religious discord in Ireland was now only 'a relic of the past.'[116] His unsectarian unionist outlook was matched by that of his wife's family. The third marquess of Londonderry, Randolph's grandfather, declared in 1850 that he was neither 'an Orangeman or a repealer.'[117] His widow erected a new Roman Catholic chapel at Newtownards.[118] Thus Randolph was brought up in an atmosphere favourable to Ulster unionism, if not to Orangeism as such. It was events in Ulster in 1883, rather than in 1885—6, which convinced Churchill that Orangeism was an indispensable ingredient of Ulster unionism.

By the early 1880s, protestant Ulster was the only part of Ireland which had remained impervious to the appeal of home rule. This hostility to Parnell's party recalled the region's previous opposition to O'Connell's repeal party in the 1830s.[119] Before the summer of 1883, the only part of Ulster to elect a home rule M.P. was County Cavan, which was largely catholic. But when T. M. Healy was elected as the first home rule M.P. for County Monaghan, in June 1883, the Ulster protestants felt a new sense of political insecurity. When the nationalists extended their operations to County Tyrone, which had a larger protestant population, they were opposed by counter-demonstrations organised by the Orange Order.[120] At this juncture, Sir Stafford Northcote, the tory leader in the commons, accepted an invitation to visit Belfast. He was enthusiastically received by loyalists angry at the nationalist 'invasion' of Ulster.[121] Northcote's visit soon acquired an Orange character[122] and Churchill later described it as a 'frightful blunder.'[123] In 1883, Churchill was busy establishing the Primrose League as an inter-denominational association to combat atheism. It had been foreshadowed by the alliance of tories and Irish nationalists against the admission of Bradlaugh to parliament.[124]

[116] *The Belfast News Letter*, 24 July 1877.

[117] *Hansard 3*, cxii, 464.

[118] *The Belfast News Letter*, 25 July 1877.

[119] Angus Macintyre, *The Liberator, Daniel O'Connell and the Irish party 1830-47* (London, 1965), Appendix D.

[120] *The Times*, 27 Sept. 1883.

[121] *Ibid.*, 2—8 Oct. 1883.

[122] Andrew Lang, *Life, letters and diaries of Sir Stafford Northcote, first earl of Iddesleigh* (London, 1891), p. 375.

[123] Churchill to Salisbury, 16 Nov. 1885 (Salisbury papers).

[124] R. E. Quinault, 'The Fourth Party and the Conservative opposition to Bradlaugh', *Eng. Hist. Rev.* ccclix (April, 1976), pp 332—3.

Early in 1884, for example, Healy, the newly elected home rule M.P. for Monaghan, was the teller in a division against Bradlaugh which attracted general tory support.[125] But, although Churchill was anxious to co-operate with the nationalists against the liberal government, he was not unaware of the significance of events in Ulster in 1883. For example, his friend Fitzgibbon had pointed out that, although the Orangemen might be inept politicians, they were indispensable allies in the fight against home rule.[126]

In October 1883, the nationalists began campaigning in Fermanagh 'a county still more deeply tinctured with the traditions of Orangeism' than Tyrone.[127] A nationalist meeting at Roslea provoked a rival Orange meeting there attended by Lord Rossmore, a local landowner who later declared that there would be bloodshed if nationalist demonstrations were allowed to continue. This declaration provoked Spencer, the liberal lord lieutenant, to remove Rossmore from the magistracy, thus making him a loyalist martyr. Support for Rossmore was voiced at a large Belfast meeting which was chaired by Lord Arthur Hill M.P., who invited Churchill to speak.[128] Although he did not attend, Churchill sent a letter to the meeting, declaring that Rossmore's dismissal 'was but one of the many proofs' of the sympathy which existed between the government and the nationalists.[129] He reiterated this charge at the opening session of parliament in 1884.[130] He also defended the Ulster Orangemen's 'vigorous resistance' to the nationalist 'invasion', referring to folk memories of the 1641 catholic massacre of protestants. He pointed out that although Parnell controlled most of Ireland, 'there was one province and one people and one race and one religion' which resisted him.[131] When Churchill later decided to support the extension of the reform bill to Ireland, he tried to persuade the Ulster protestants that the measure would not harm their interests. He pointed out that the protestant minority had already lost power outside Ulster, while inside that province, 'superior wealth, superior enterprise, superior learning and superior intelligence' would enable the protestants to

---

[125]*House of Commons Divisions,* 11 Feb. 1884.
[126]Fizgibbon to Churchill, 11 Oct. 1883 (RCHL 1/2/181).
[127]*The Times,* 17 Oct. 1883.
[128]Lord Rossmore, *Things I can tell* (London, 1912), pp 240—9, Hill to Churchill, 15 Jan. 1884 (RCHL 1/2).
[129]*The Times,* 29 Jan. 1884.
[130]*Hansard 3,* cclxxxiv, 370.
[131]*Ibid.,* 373.

hold their own politically.[132] Such arguments did not convince all protestant Ulstermen, but the *Belfast News Letter* admitted that Churchill was not the only tory M.P. to change his mind on the reform question.[133]

In June 1885, Salisbury formed a minority tory government which bought the neutrality of the nationalists by not renewing coercion. Although it has been suggested that this ministry was not trusted by Ulster tory M.P.s,[134] Churchill claimed that, 'almost without exception, [they] supported the policy of the government.'[135] It has also been claimed that Churchill's support for a new enquiry into the Maamtrasna verdicts offended most Ulster tory M.P.s,[136] but, in the commons debate, only two Ulster M.P.s, C. E. Lewis and J. Macartney, criticised Churchill's attitude. Lewis, who was more out-spoken, was an Englishman who had been the only tory M.P. publicly to criticise the government for abandoning coercion. Churchill, unlike Gorst, had no brush with the Ulster tories during the debate.[137] But, although Cooke and Vincent point out that Churchill repudiated Gorst's remarks in cabinet,[138] they fail to draw the obvious conclusion that he had no wish to alienate the Ulster tories, but argue instead on the evidence of a single letter — to Salisbury in November 1885 — that Churchill was hostile to the Ulster tories. Churchill here remarked that 'these foul Ulster Tories have always ruined our party.[139] But this comment must be placed in context. A month before, Carnarvon, the tory lord lieutenant, had complained to Churchill that internal dis-putes among the Ulster tories might result in seats being lost to the nationalists.[140] Churchill only attacked the Ulster tories because they were co-operating with the whigs: 'The original plan of campaign to carry on the contest on tory lines irrespective of whigs was quite sound, but in order to secure the return of Lord E. W. Hamilton for Tyrone, seats have been given to the whigs. This is too maddening.'[141] Churchill had earlier declared that the Ulster tories would be foolish to

[132]*Ibid.*, cclxxxviii, 858—9.
[133]*The Belfast news Letter*, 21 May, 1884.
[134]Savage, 'Origins of Ulster unionist party', in *I.H.S.*, xii, p. 191.
[135]*The Times*, 5 Sept. 1885.
[136]Winston Churchill, *Randolph Churchill*, pp 356—7; James, *Randolph Churchill*, p. 207, Midleton, *Records and reactions*, p. 64.
[137]*Hansard 3*, ccxclx, 119—230.
[138]Cooke & Vincent, p. 278.   [139]*Ibid.*, p. 160.
[140]Carnarvon to Churchill, 18 Sept. 1885 (RCHL 1/8/903).
[141]Churchill to Salisbury, 16 Nov. 1885 (Salisbury papers).

make an electoral pact with the whigs since he believed that no Irish whig would be returned at the coming election.[142] Thus his letter to Salisbury is further evidence that, contrary to Cooke and Vincent's allegation, he did not pursue a tory-liberal coalition.[143]

Churchill's comments on the Ulster tories must also be seen in the context of his poor relations with the Hamiltons. In his letter to Salisbury, Churchill observed that 'those Hamiltons care about nothing except themselves.'[144] The Churchill and Hamilton families were, to some extent, rivals for preferment within the tory party. Although the marquess of Blandford, the duke of Marlborough's heir, had married a daughter of Abercorn in 1869, he subsequently neglected his wife, preferring an affair with the countess of Alyesford. Consequently, Abercorn's son refused to serve under Marlborough when he was appointed Lord Lieutenant of Ireland.[145] Other differences widened the rift between the two families. In October 1883, Northcote stayed with Abercorn when he visited Belfast. The duke expressed the hope that Northcote would head the next government.[146] Earlier that year, Churchill had risked his whole political position by publicly declaring that Salisbury, rather than Northcote, should lead the next tory government.[147] Then, in 1884, Lord Claud Hamilton, a younger son of Abercorn and a tory M.P. for Liverpool, denounced Churchill for supporting the extension of the reform bill to Ireland.[148] In July 1885, Churchill refused to speak at Liverpool because of the opposition of Lord Claud, who believed that Churchill was in alliance with the Parnellites.[149]

Cooke and Vincent assert that Churchill's adoption of an Orange stance in December 1885 was merely a feint: how could a man in favour of concessions to nationalist sentiment in the fields of local government and catholic education 'throw himself whole-heartedly into vulgar unionism' by sincerely allying with Orange bigots like Saunderson?[150] But there was nothing inconsistent about both opposing home rule by co-operating with Orangemen *and* supporting remedial Irish policies acceptable to the nationalists — the policy of

---

[142]*The Times*, 7 Nov. 1885.   [143]Cooke & Vincent, p. 47.
[144]Churchill to Salisbury, 16 Nov. 1885 (Salisbury papers).
[145]G. Hamilton to Corry, 13 Sept. 1876 (Disraeli papers, B/xii/A/145).
[146]*The Times*, 4 Oct. 1883.
[147]*Ibid.*, 2 April 1883.
[148]*Hansard 3*, cclxxxviii. 862.
[149]See RCHL 1/6/743 & 752—7. See also Savage, *op. cit.*
[150]Cooke & Vincent, pp 296—7.

enlightened unionism which Churchill had always preached. Moreover, not all the Orange leaders were vulgar bigots opposed to
remedial measures. Saunderson, the leader of the Ulster tories in the
commons, had only joined the Orange Order as recently as 1882 and
had formerly been a Liberal M.P. for County Cavan.[151] He claimed
that the opposition to the nationalist 'invasion' of Ulster was a protest
'against revolution, against separation, against crime and against
lawlessness; not against Roman Catholicism.'[152] Ewart, one of the
tory M.P.s for Belfast, also claimed that Orangemen supported civil
and religious liberty for catholics.[153] Lord Rossmore, the leader of the
Monaghan Orangemen, came from a liberal background like Saunderson. His grandmother had been a catholic and his grandfather had
supported catholic emancipation. Rossmore was on good terms with
the local catholic bishop and provided land for a catholic chapel.[154]
Nor were all Orangemen reactionary. In January 1886, Saunderson,
in Churchill's words, 'greatly impressed the House,'[155] when he
pointed out that he had supported the 1870 Land Act and complained that 'the misfortune of all the concessions yet extorted by
Ireland has been that they have been snatched from an unwilling
hand.'[156] His speech may have been partly inspired by Churchill, to
whom he had talked a few days before[157] and he implied that he
would support remedial Irish measures, providing the union and law
and order were maintained. Soon afterwards, Churchill, in Saunderson's words, 'placed himself at my disposal for a meeting in
Ulster.'[158]

Cooke and Vincent argue that Churchill 'sounded the Orange
note' because he wanted to make his peace with the Ulster tory M.P.s;
because he wanted to leave Salisbury stranded on the far right and
'chiefly because other leading tories had decided to stay silent and
Churchill had a chance to engross party orthodoxy.'[159] These arguments are unconvincing. It was not so much Churchill, but Salisbury
and Northcote, the official party leaders, who were viewed with

---

[151]Reginald Lucas, *Colonel Saunderson M.P. a memoir* (London, 1908), pp
65—6.
[152]Edward Saunderson, *Two Irelands, or loyalty versus treason* (London 1883),
p. 31.
[155]*Hansard 3*, ccii 173.   [156]*Ibid.*, 167—8.
[154]Rossmore, *Things I can tell,* pp 19, 38—9.
[155]*Hansard 3*, ccii. 173.   [156]*Ibid.*, 167—8.
[157]Lucas, *Saunderson*, pp 94—6.   [158]*Ibid.*, p. 96.
[159]Cooke & Vincent, p. 77.

suspicion by the Ulster tories.[160] Nor did Churchill leave Salisbury stranded on the far right, since the latter had long been opposed to home rule, while he did not directly associate himself with Ulster unionism until his visit to Belfast in 1893. The silence of the other tory leaders was largely fortuitous. They had collectively supported the union in the Queen's speech and they had no concrete policy to attack before the introduction of Gladstone's home rule bill. Hicks Beach had also been invited to speak at Belfast, but had thought it unnecessary for both himself and Churchill to be 'on the stump in Belfast in the same week.'[161] Churchill's visit to Belfast reflected his real links with Ulster. When he left London he was accompanied by Saunderson, Rossmore and Sir John Leslie. Rossmore had first met Randolph at Dublin Castle in the late 1870s.[162] Leslie, another Monaghan Orangeman, also knew Churchill, since his son had married Churchill's sister-in-law, Leonie Jerome, in 1884. When he landed at Larne, Churchill was greeted by Captain McCalmont, tory M.P. for East Antrim, and by William Johnston, tory M.P. for East Belfast. The former had been aide-de-camp to Churchill's father in Dublin, while the latter had been appointed inspector of Irish fisheries by Marlborough in 1878.[163]

Churchill's visit to Belfast was not exclusively Orange in character. At the Ulster Hall, for example, he received addresses from the Irish Primrose League which was inter-denominational.[164] Although he asked the Orange Order to help to defend the union, he made no more concessions to Orange sentiment than he had done when addressing his Paddington constituents.[165] He did not advocate sectarian confrontation, but appealed to loyal catholics to defend the union. He did not encourage militancy, but merely predicted that if home rule was enacted the conflict would cease to be constitutional in character.[166] Salisbury thought Churchill had 'avoided all shoals and said nothing to which any catholic could object.'[167] *The Times* noted that Churchill's remarks were accepted by liberals as well as by

[160] *The Belfast News Letter*, 16 Nov. 1885.
[161] Beach to Churchill, 12 Feb. 1886 (RCHL 1/12/1376).
[162] *The Times*, 22 Feb. 1886. Rossmore, *Things I can tell*, p. 260.
[163] *The Times*, 23 Feb. 1886 and 27 Nov. 1885. *D..V.B.*, William Johnston (1829—1902).
[164] *The Times*, 23 Feb. 1886.
[165] *Ibid.*, 16 Feb. 1886.
[166] *Ibid.*, 23 Feb. 1886.
[167] Salisbury to Churchill, 24 Feb. 1886 (RCHL 1/12/1390a).

conservatives in Ulster.[168] Nevertheless, Churchill's political opponents were quick to claim that he was fanning the flames of sectarian hatred. This charge appeared to be justified when a letter of Churchill's was published in May 1886. This contained the phrase, 'Ulster will fight, Ulster will be right.' But the true purport of this letter has not been appreciated since only the concluding sentence was quoted in Winston's biography of his father.[169] Significantly, the letter was written to a Glasgow liberal, William Young, who wanted bi-party co-operation to defend the union. Most of Churchill's letter advocated his usual policy of enlightened, egalitarian treatment of Ireland within the union. Churchill pointed out that the readiness of Ulster to fight to save the union recalled the policy of the northern part of the United States which provoked the American civil war.[170] The American analogy would have come readily to Churchill's mind since his father-in-law, Leonard Jerome, the New York financier, had been treasurer of the Union Defence Committee during the civil war.[171] The triumph of the unionist cause in America and the subsequent peace and prosperity of the United States encouraged Churchill to believe that a firm defence of the union with Ireland would be justified by results.

Contrary to what Cooke and Vincent have claimed, Churchill did not abandon his Orange contacts after the spring of 1886.[172] In his 1886 election address, he denounced the 'desertion of our Protestant co-religionists' and praised the Church of Ireland — sentiments which appealed to Orangemen in particular.[173] Shortly before the elections, Saunderson asked Churchill to use his influence to secure the North Belfast tory candiature for Maxwell Somerset.[174] But there was another candidate in the field and Churchill replied:

Any action which could by any possibility imperil a unionist seat and produce the smallest appearance of division among unionists would be fatal . . . A disaster in Belfast would be terrific and would be a sorry reward to English politicians who at some risk of misconception have identified themselves with Ulster. I therefore on the whole implore you to restrain Somerset Maxwell.[175]

[168] *The Times*, 23 Feb. 1886.
[169] Winston Churchill, *Randolph Churchill*, pp 478—9.
[170] *The Times*, 8 May, 1886.
[171] Ralph G. Martin, *Lady Randolph Churchill* (London, 1974), i. 29.
[172] Cooke & Vincent, p 77.
[173] Winston Churchill, *Randolph Churchill*, pp 858—62.
[174] Saunderson to Churchill, 25 June 1886 (RCHL 1/13/1549).
[175] Churchill to Saunderson, 28 June 1886, printed in Lucas, *Saunderson*, pp 104—5.

In August 1886, Saunderson told Churchill that 'I know and all Ulster knows the deep interest you feel in the welfare of Irish loyalists in general and in Belfast in particular.'[176] When Churchill resigned in December 1886, Saunderson expressed his regret and refused to condemn him unheard.[177] Churchill replied, reaffirming his attachment to the union, but arguing that a policy of peace, retrenchment and reform was required to ensure long-term English support for the union. He thought that Saunderson, with his 'sound liberal principles' would concur with this view.[178] Saunderson remained friendly with Churchill, allowing him to take his own back-bench seat in the commons.[179] Churchill, on his part, remained a loyal defender of the Ulster unionists. When Gladstone introduced his second home rule bill, in 1893, Churchill told the commons that Ulster was 'the most important consideration in any measure you may propose for the government of Ireland.'[180] In a speech at Liverpool, he declared that 'I have been a great deal in Ulster and I have family ties in Ulster' and was therefore aware of the strength of Ulster's hostility to home rule.[181] But unlike his son, Winston, he opposed home rule even if Ulster was excluded from its jurisdiction.[182]

IV

Throughout his career, Lord Randolph Churchill was a sincere and consistent opponent of home rule: as his son's biography demonstrates. But, in some respects, Winston's life provides an incomplete and misleading account of his father's involvement with the Irish question. In particular, Winston was apparently unaware of the extent to which Lord Randolph's Irish policy of enlightened unionism was largely a family heirloom which he simply up-dated to meet the circumstances of the mid-1800s. Winston, by ignoring this family dimension, failed to provide an explanation for his father's consistent unionism and underestimated his involvement in Irish politics. Nevertheless, his

[176]Saunderson to Churchill, 10 Aug. 1886 (RCHL 1/14/1653).
[177]Saunderson to Churchill, 12 Jan. 1887 (RCHL 1/19/2333).
[178]Lucas, *Saunderson*, p. 120.
[179]*Ibid.*, p. 124.
[180]*Hansard 3*, viii, 1625—6.
[181]*The Times*, 7 April 1893.
[182]Churchill to Fitzgibbon, 30 April 1893, printed in Winston Churchill, *Randolph Churchill*, p. 808.

biography provides an infinitely more useful and correct account of Lord Randolph's attitude towards home rule than any subsequent study.

In *The Governing Passion,* Cooke and Vincent have presented, *inter alia,* an incomplete, inaccurate and highly misleading account of Churchill's involvement in Irish politics during 1885—6. This is particularly true of their five contentions listed at the beginning of this article. Churchill *was* much concerned with Irish unrest because he believed that if it was left unchecked, it would undermine the union. His desire to mitigate Irish unrest prompted his attitude towards coercion, the clôture, parliamentary reform, denominational education and local government.[183] His Irish policy was not determined merely by a desire for a liberal alliance or a tory reconstruction. Before the 1885 general election and the emergence of home rule as an immediate threat, Churchill's Irish policy was essentially anti-liberal. After the election, Churchill's objective was both to defeat home rule and strengthen the existing tory party, by means of a unionist alliance with a minority of dissident liberals. It is both incorrect and misleading to describe Churchill's Irish policy as 'green' rather than 'Orange'. In terms of his general Irish policy, Churchill, as an enlightened unionist, was neither 'green', nor 'Orange'. He favoured co-operation with the nationalists, on the one hand, and with the Orangemen, on the other, only for Tory and unionist reasons. But on the central question of home rule, Churchill was clearly 'Orange' rather than 'green' when forced to take sides. Cooke and Vincent's use of such simplistic dichotomies as 'Orange' and 'green' and 'pro-Irish or anti-Irish' reflects the superficiality of their approach. These terms imply that Irish politics were clearly polarised. But within the protestant and catholic communities, various hierarchies — clerical, Parnellite, Fenian, Orange and moderate unionist — were rivals for authority and influence. These groups had different concerns and priorities, many of which had little direct relevance to the home rule question. Churchill was aware of these distinctions and his Irish policy reflected this complicated situation.

Cooke and Vincent's erroneous views on Churchill's role in 1885—6 reflect the general methodological shortcomings of their approach. They claim that to understand the crisis of those years,

---

[183]Lack of space has prevented attention being paid to all aspects of Churchill's policy. I hope to rectify this in a subsequent study.

'minute analysis on a day-by-day basis' is essential.[184] But such a study has little value if it is not related to the wider historical context. Cooke and Vincent make no serious attempt to do this. Thus, for example, they examine Churchill's Irish policy in a grossly myopic way, ignoring his views both before and after 1885—6. Even if such a survey was not strictly relevant to their immediate objective, it would have enabled them to obtain a far more profound insight into the mentality of their principal characters. For all politicians approach contemporary problems with attitudes born of previous experience. Cooke and Vincent believe that the public misjudged the leading politicians of the day because they did not appreciate 'the calculations about personal competition which shaped political action.'[185] But the authors' obvious pre-occupation with such alleged calculations lead them to ignore evidence which suggests that politicians did not think merely in terms of personal advancement. For example, they do not mention Churchill's readiness to stand aside if a whig-tory coalition was formed. They also argue that events in 1885—6 were determined by a handful of politicians whose 'conceptions were formed, on a very small factual basis, by interpreting what they read in the newspapers in the light of the opportunities they saw in high politics.'[186] But, even on their own evidence, there is ample proof that Churchill's conceptions, at least, were not merely formed in this way. For example, his family ties and contacts with Ulster meant that he *was* able to estimate the potential seriousness of protestant revolt.[187]

Cooke and Vincent separate their theories from their chronicle of events, claiming that differing views can be derived from their evidence.[188] But the general character of their diary renders it of limited value as a foundation for theoretical enquiry. Although they believe that a day-by-day analysis is essential to understand the period, their diary does not give a complete everyday account. Thus, for example, half the period of Salisbury's first ministry is dismissed in a few pages. Yet the diary does include much trivial information, such as the exact time when Salisbury left for his French holiday.[189] Most of the diary is derived, not from newspapers, but from correspondence between politicians. But this type of information usually does not throw much light on either the general views of politicians, or the wider influences acting upon them. These aspects are often more

[184]Cooke & Vincent, p. xiii.   [185]*Ibid.*, p. 166.
[186]*Ibid.*, p. 161.   [187]*Ibid.*, p. 162.
[188]*Ibid.*, p. xiii.   [189]*Ibid.*, p. 438.

clearly revealed in the speeches of politicians to which Cooke and Vincent pay little attention. Yet the position and influence of politicians were much affected by the character and quality of their speeches, which were usually reported verbatim in the press. Thus Cooke and Vincent neglect evidence of indisputable contemporary importance, preferring to concentrate on, often hypothetical, house-party cabals. For example, they ignore a strongly unionist speech by Churchill on 2 June 1886, but do mention that he was expected to spend the week-end in the company of Ellen Terry at Labouchere's.[190] Such mistaken emphasis accounts for many of the misconceptions which flaw *The Governing Passion.*

Finally, what was the wider significance of Churchill's opposition to home rule? At the personal level, Churchill's fervent unionism had an important effect on his political career. It reinforced his loyalty to the tory party as the principal pillar of the union. Ironically, however, it also prompted him to champion progressive policies (intended to strengthen the union) which helped to alienate him from the other tory leaders after the 1886 general election. His consistent policy of enlightened unionism does not tally with recent interpretations of him as an unprincipled, self-seeking opportunist. At the public level, the importance of Churchill's role in the formulation of tory Irish policy can be exaggerated. He was a cabinet minister for only a year and never had departmental responsibility for Ireland. His unionist sentiments were shared by nearly all his colleagues, while his 'playing of the Orange card' reflected the long established ties between protestant Ulster and the tory party. Nevertheless, Churchill's hostility to home rule *was* of considerable political importance. As perhaps the most popular politician on the tory side in 1886, he had great influence over the British electorate. If he had favoured home rule he would have seriously, if temporarily, compromised his party's unionist image. Instead, he played a key role in creating a united front against home rule. His policy of enlightened unionism reflected the innate conservatism of his outlook. He saw himself as carrying on the traditional tory Irish policy as developed by Pitt, Peel and Disraeli.[191] His policy was as much influenced by the history of Ireland over the previous century as it was by contemporary events. Thus, for example, he believed that the home rule party would collapse, just as O'Connell's repeal party and all other Irish indigenous parties had

---

[190] *Ibid.,* p. 431. *The Times,* 3 June 1886.
[191] *The Times,* 4 June 1885.

withered away.[192] But, although he believed that the home rule threat could be defeated, he did not derive his policy from dry political calculation. For his attachment to the union was a personal sentiment: an article of faith he was never prepared to question.

[192] *Both sides of the home rule question,* p. 27.

16

THE ULSTER LIBERAL UNIONISTS
AND LOCAL GOVERNMENT REFORM, 1885-1898
CATHERINE B. SHANNON

In the mid-1880s English political leaders found it essential to develop new policies for Ireland. While the liberals, led by Gladstone, were converted to the home-rule solution, the tories sought to preserve the union with a two-pronged policy. First, Ireland's economic disorders were to be cured by vigorously developing the system of state-aided land purchase, and by having the imperial treasury assume a large portion of the cost of developing the country's natural resources and industrial potential. This aspect of the policy rested upon the tory conviction that Irish support of home rule would diminish in direct proportion to significant economic and social advance. The second part of the policy called for the establishment of a democratic system of local government which was to be the limit of political concessions to Irish nationalist sentiment.

When Irish local government reform finally was granted in 1898, it was a unionist government backed by strong liberal-unionist support that secured the necessary legislation. In fact, the consistent exertion of liberal-unionist pressure was largely responsible for the progressivism of unionist policy from 1887 to 1892. In the following study, the emphasis will be on the relationship between this liberal-unionist pressure and the government's ultimate extension of democratic local governing institutions to Ireland. Consideration will be given to the genesis of the tory adoption of local government reform and to the effect which this adoption had upon the sensibilities of the Irish and English unionists.

The great parliamentary and administrative reforms of the nineteenth century culminating in the franchise act of 1884 and the redistribution act of 1885, stimulated interest in a similar reform of county administration throughout the United Kingdom. The political motivation to abolish the oligarchic grand juries was reinforced by the pressures which the rapid industrialization of Victorian England had thrust upon local authorities in the realm of public welfare and the maintenance of sanitary conditions. Centralization and uniformity had to be brought to the multifarious and often overlapping organs hitherto entrusted with local affairs. While in Ireland the administrative confusion was equally serious, action was politically imperative because the grand juries were the bastions of the protestant landlord ascendency, and hence entirely out of sympathy with the majority of the population.

Although the liberals had been the first to include local government reform in their 1881 platform, foreign entanglements and the larger parliamentary reforms prevented them from preparing a bill until the spring of 1885. However, the proposal of the local government board for an English reform was never introduced, owing to considerable disagreement in the cabinet between the whigs, led by Lord Hartington, and the radicals led by Joseph Chamberlain, over the extent of powers to be conferred on the proposed local councils. While the latter wanted to provide the local bodies with powers of compulsory land purchase, Hartington and the whigs believed such a provision, if applied to Ireland, might lead to disastrous consequences for the landed classes.[1]

Chamberlain's subsequent efforts to settle the local government question and also satisfy the Irish first by his ' central board' scheme and later by the national councils plan added to the cabinet divisiveness. By the second week of August rumours of a possible split in the liberal party over the latest Chamberlain proposal as well as over Gladstone's proclivities towards home rule, were spreading throughout the parliamentary ranks.[2] Gladstone's failure to denounce Parnell's August speech in which the latter emphatically declared his goal to be an Irish parliament, substantiated the earlier rumours.

The tories were well aware of these whisperings within the liberal camp, and the situation was rapidly progressing to the point where they might steal the liberals' thunder on local government reform. By early autumn, Salisbury was absolutely convinced that Parnell's goal was a Grattan's parliament.[3] Possessed with this information, the conservatives could conveniently abrogate any plans for an alliance

---

[1] S. Gwynn and G. Tuckwell, *The life of Sir Charles W. Dilke* (London, 1917), ii, 11–12.

[2] B. Holland, *The life of Spencer Compton, the eighth duke of Devonshire* (London, 1911), ii, 77–8; C. H. D. Howard, 'The Irish "central board" scheme, 1884–5' in *I.H.S.*, viii, no. 32, (Sept. 1953), pp 324–61.

[3] Salisbury's conviction derived from his interview with Lord Carnarvon following the latter's secret meeting with Parnell in August (*Hansard* 3, cccxxv, 1179).

with the Irish nationalists, and propose the politically less dangerous local government reform. Lord Randolph Churchill's recently publicized plans for ' tory democracy '[4] would make the new conservative policy easy to defend. The stage was thus perfectly set.

On 7 October at Newport Lord Salisbury pledged his party to abolish the grand jury system throughout the United Kingdom. Ireland, he emphasized, presented a difficulty owing to the divisions in the population, and he promised that the integrity of the empire would take precedence over all other matters, including local government.[5] However, the ' Hawarden kite ' of 16 December 1885, and Arthur Balfour's December report to his uncle that Gladstone would have difficulty in withdrawing home rule[6] confirmed in finality that the tory alternative would be local government reform.

Following the official tory announcement in the Queen's Speech on 21 January 1886, Sir Michael Hicks Beach soothed both tory and landlord nerves when he asserted that the Irish reform would have to wait until conditions in Ireland would not enable the majority, either political or social, to tyrannize the minority.[7] However, once the successful mutiny of the Irish party on 26 January placed Gladstone at the head of the government, the Irish members showed little interest in local government now that the liberal leader was publicly pledged to act in accord with the constitutional theories of the Irish parliamentary party.

The story of the first home rule bill need not detain us. It is convenient to turn to August 1886 when Lord Salisbury returned to office, backed by a majority of 118, of whom 74 were former liberals who had deserted the Gladstonian ranks in order to preserve the union. This liberal unionist conservative alliance became the medium through which continuous pressure was exerted upon the more moderate wing of the conservative party to offer a positive Irish policy rather than mere resistance to home rule. Joseph Chamberlain's close relationship with Arthur Balfour,[8] the prime minister's nephew, gave the liberal dissidents convenient political leverage in their attempt to secure comprehensive land legislation and initiate economic revolution in Ireland.

---

[4] *The Times,* 4 June 1885.
[5] *The Times,* 8 Oct. 1885.
[6] B. Dugdale, *Arthur James Balfour* (London, 1936), i, 90.
[7] *Hansard 3,* cccii, 125.
[8] Dugdale, op. cit., i, 101.

Quickly appreciating their newly established influence, the Ulster liberal unionists instructed their delegates to the December conference of liberal unionists in London to impress upon the government that the maintenance of the union depended upon an aggressively positive Irish policy.[9] Encouraged by the discussions which the Ulster delegates had there with Chamberlain regarding local government schemes for Ireland, the Ulster association soon sent a deputation to the Irish chief secretary, Sir Michael Hicks Beach. In addition to asking for an extension of the fair rent clause of the land act of 1881 to leaseholders and town park tenants, the Ulster deputation requested that:

the Ashbourne act should be extended so as to make the abolition of dual ownership a matter of a few years only; that, pending the results of an enquiry of the royal commission on the development of Irish resources, arterial drainage should be undertaken and agricultural developments fostered by the government; that the establishment of light railways and tramways should be undertaken or assisted by the state; and that the local government proposals for England should be extended to Ireland.[10]

This was an ambitious programme indeed. Although the chief secretary favoured such remedial legislation, his failing health and the prime minister's insistence that law and order be restored first, militated against the introduction of any comprehensive programme. Nevertheless, the liberal unionist pressure to redeem the local government pledge was so strong that Gladstone thought it significant.

The government have as you observe promised a measure prescribing for some type of local government in Ireland, and the dissident leaders have made very large declarations in this respect. Six months or more it has taken for consideration. What I contend is that unionists will be bound to produce their measure when parliament has met and above all that the dissidents are bound to make them produce it, which undoubtedly they have the power to do.[11]

Meanwhile in Ireland the steady success of the Plan of Campaign during November caused such uneasiness among the Irish unionists that they clamoured for the application of Salisbury's law and order formula. The first indication of Dublin Castle's intention to vigorously

[9] *The Ulster Liberal Unionist Association: a sketch of its history, 1885-1914* (Belfast, 1914), p. 22; hereafter cited *Ulster Liberal Unionist Association.*

[10] Ibid., p. 22.

[11] Gladstone to Campbell-Bannerman, 16 Dec. 1886 (B.M., Add. MS 41215, f. 27).

fight agrarian disorder came with the resignation of Sir Robert Hamilton, the permanent under-secretary, whose opinions on home rule were too sympathetic for unionist peace of mind. In an effort to appease the Irish landlords and unionists, Hamilton's position was filled by Sir Redvers Buller who had already established a reputation as a firm administrator in the colonial service. When Hicks Beach's resignation transferred the Irish mantle to Arthur Balfour in March, the prime minister's nephew quickly demonstrated that he shared his uncle's conviction of the urgency of restoring respect for the law in rural Ireland. Armed with the famous 'jubilee coercion' act, and encouraged by the Irish loyalists, Balfour launched his first attack on the Plan of Campaign when he persuaded the 12 August cabinet to proclaim the National League as a dangerous organization.[12] For the remainder of the year and well into 1888 Balfour's Irish administration proved very adept in suppressing the widespread agrarian unrest.

Because the essentially moralistic philosophy which governed Balfour demanded that the cause of the agitation be tackled at its roots, the chief secretary did not limit his activities to coercive measures. Viewing the land problem as the seed from which all the agrarian and separatist agitation germinated, Balfour concluded that only the abolition of dual ownership and the establishment of peasant proprietorship could bring peace to Ireland. While the liberal unionists had been continually urging such action, the March report of the Cowper commission stressed the urgency of a rapid conversion to single ownership. Moreover, the agricultural depression of 1885–6 was so serious that drastic revision of rents was essential. Determined to cure Ireland of its historic land sickness, and backed by liberal unionist support, Balfour waged a tedious but successful parliamentary battle for rent reductions.[18] In cabinet discussions on his land programme, Balfour was highly critical of recalcitrant landlords who claimed a violation of property rights. The chief secretary reminded his colleagues that the land scheme

like that which we have proposed (which it be observed, violates no recognized principle of legislation or justice) is an essential part of any plan for the restoration of law and order. The landlords must not consider it in isolation. They must take it in connection with the whole

---

[12] L. P. Curtis, *Coercion and conciliation*, p. 185.
[18] F. S. L. Lyons, ' John Dillon and the Plan of Campaign ' in *I.H.S.*, xiv, no. 56 (Sept. 1965), pp 321–2.

policy of the government; and they must feel that the sacrifice asked of them (if sacrifice it be) is absolutely required if the union, and all the union means to them, is to be maintained.[14]

In the following year peasant purchase increased after Balfour's land legislation secured a reduction in the purchase price, a relaxation in security requirements as well as an additional five million pounds for the land purchase scheme. The introduction of four drainage bills and a light railways bill in the spring of 1889 demonstrated the chief secretary's appreciation of the need to develop Ireland's natural resources and industrial potential. While the light railways bill alone achieved passage, it appears that Balfour's policy was exactly akin to the recommendations which the Ulster liberal unionists had previously made to Hicks Beach.

Despite the significant land measures, the question of local government reform continued to plague the government because the liberal unionist campaign for the reform did not abate in the least. After emerging from more discussions with Chamberlain in October 1887, the Ulster Liberal Unionist Committee looked to the next parliamentary session for the redemption of the 1886 promise.[15] In fact, at this juncture, the cabinet was drafting proposals for the English and Scotch reforms, but the ministers were obdurate in resisting an Irish measure. That the government's resistance had the support of many of the English liberal unionists members is apparent from a letter A. C. Sellars, an English liberal unionist, sent to Hugh de F. Montgomery of Sixmilecross, Co. Tyrone : ' . . . Hartington, nearly all the liberal unionists who have spoken, Salisbury and the government are almost unanimously against an Irish local government measure this session '.[16] Indeed, the cabinet's rejection of the Irish reform, which was the unwanted child of the conservative dissident marriage, turned the Ulster Liberal Unionist Committee into something like a ' nagging wife ', and it was Sellar's opinion that ' . . . we had better give the thing up so far as Ulster is concerned . . .',[17] if the Ulstermen were consistently to hold a pistol to the government's head at every disappointment.

[14] Balfour's cabinet memorandum on land policy, 8 Apr. 1887 (B.M., Add. MS 49822, ff 49–50).

[15] *Ulster Liberal Unionist Association*, p. 83.

[16] A. C. Sellars to Montgomery, 29 Jan. 1888 (P.R.O.N.I., Dod/627/428/218).

[17] Sellars to Montgomery, 13 Mar. 1888 (P.R.O.N.I., Dod/627/428/219).

While the opening of parliament in 1888 brought the promised reforms for England and Scotland, the continued serious agitation sponsored by the Plan of Campaign gave both landlords and unionists the ammunition to fight an Irish reform. In the same session Maurice Healy, Timothy Harrington, Arthur O'Connor, J. L. Carew and Thomas Sexton sponsored a private bill for Irish county councils. It is apparent from the debate accompanying the introduction that the Irish motivation was to embarrass the government and to drive a wedge between the conservatives and the liberal unionists. Although admitting in debate that the grand jury system was indefensible in theory, Balfour echoed the official resistance when he stated: ' different circumstances and different behaviour are essential before local self government can be proposed with hope of success in that country, and the reasons which are against it cannot be described as political '.[18] Chamberlain also opposed the bill but on the grounds that a partial solution of the land question must precede any local government reform.[19]

Meanwhile, the failure of the round table conference prompted more determined effort by the liberal unionists to secure a more progressive government policy.[20] In April, and again in May at the meeting of the Grand Committee of the New Birmingham Association, Chamberlain called for public works schemes in Ireland's congested districts, comprehensive land purchase, and for the establishment of provincial councils to supplement the proposed future county councils.[21] Despite Chamberlain's appeals, cabinet procrastination prevailed as late as January 1889 as is shown by Salisbury's letter to Arthur Balfour.

We are saved from any reproach from our English friends by the fact that we do not at present contemplate setting up county councils in Ireland. The mode of dealing with the difficulty to which we have pledged ourselves here is not available in Ireland.[22]

However, within three months, fear of Chamberlain's scheme of provincial councils awakened unionist interest in Irish local government. Writing to Hugh Montgomery, William Kenny, a prominent

[18] *Hansard 3*, cccxxv, 503.
[19] Ibid., col. 507.
[20] For the fullest account of attempts at liberal reunion see M. Hurst, *Joseph Chamberlain and liberal reunion* (London, 1967).
[21] *The Times*, 29 May 1888.
[22] Salisbury to Balfour, 16 Jan. 1889 (B.M., Add. MS 49689, ff 49–50).

Dublin liberal unionist, described local unionist apprehensiveness over popularly elected provincial councils.

Pim and others rightly fear Chamberlain's ' awful scheme of provincial councils ' and in order to counteract it, wanted to demand a local government bill as soon as possible. We all thought it well that I should communicate with Lord Hartington who replied very freely and frankly saying, ' each delegate should give his own individual view admitting that there was a difference of opinion on the subject in the body he represented. . . .' We have had some small friction with Birmingham and Joe on local government but now smoothed over.[28]

Despite this liberal unionist pressure and a weakening of the land league agitation by mid-1889, Balfour insisted that local government would have to await the passage of a comprehensive land bill, because only then could the government be sure that the national league would not use the councils as weapons to wield against the landlords. Accordingly, the chief secretary devoted his legislative efforts to the abortive land purchase bill of 1890. Throughout the parliamentary consideration, Chamberlain, with Parnell's support, continually urged the government to associate the future local authorities with the land purchase scheme. An indication of the anxiety which this proposal engendered among both Irish and English unionists is shown in A. V. Dicey's letter to Balfour.

The proposal to extend local government to Ireland on what is termed English lines, seems to me in itself absurd. One thing is certain. The state of England is quite different from that of Ireland, and there is not the least presumption that an arrangement which succeeds in Birmingham will succeed say in Limerick. The extension of local government is absolutely inconsistent with the policy of strictly enforcing the law by means of so-called coercion. I have long thought that the dogmas entertained by liberal unionists about local government, were, if any attempt were made to apply them to Ireland, likely to break up the unionist party. That the government should be in any way pledged to

---

[28] Kenny to Montgomery, 21 Apr. 1889 (P.R.O.N.I., Dod/627/428/ 111). Kenny was active in establishing the liberal union of Ireland and in organizing the Hartington and Goschen visit to Ireland in 1887. He sat as a unionist M.P. for Stephen's Green from 1892-7, and was solicitor-general for Ireland, 1895-7 (*Who was Who*, 4th ed., London, 1967, ii, 580-1). Frederic William Pim, another prominent unionist, was chairman of the Dublin and South-Eastern Railway from 1896 to 1917 (*Who was Who*, 4th ed., ii, 840).

the policy of extending local self-government in Ireland, I greatly regret, but even if this is inevitable I do trust it may be found possible to keep apart the question of local government and not to mix the weakest with the strongest point of the unionist programme.[24]

Although Balfour was opposed to Chamberlain's proposal, he rebuked the Oxford professor, maintaining that failure to initiate local government reform in deference to right wing unionists constituted a far greater danger to the party's future than a prompt introduction would. The chief secretary emphasized that he had no choice in the matter because when he took office the government was '. . . already absolutely pledged to it; the liberal unionists have never ceased to press it upon our consideration, and I understand that a not inconsiderable number of liberal unionist electors regard it as a vital question'. Chastizing Dicey even further, Balfour asked '. . . is it worthwhile or right to repudiate the pledges which have been given, and to break up the unionist party rather than attempt to carry a measure to which a most important fraction of the party attach the greatest consequence?'[25]

While ultra-unionist and landlord nerves were momentarily soothed by the defeat of the 1890 land measure, the successful passage of the 1891 land bill meant that local government reform for Ireland ceased to be an academic question. Firstly, Balfour had always promised that reform would immediately follow a comprehensive land measure. Secondly, Balfour genuinely believed that Ireland deserved local government reform. Thirdly, conservative losses in the bye-elections of the previous eighteen months necessitated strong liberal unionist support in the imminent general election. Moreover, by the summer of 1891 prompt action offered an irresistible opportunity for capitalizing on the divisions and disillusionments which the exposure of the Parnell-O'Shea affair engendered within the Irish party and Ireland. Speaking at Plymouth on 10 August 1891, Balfour announced that the Irish legislation would be introduced in the next session.

Immediately following the announcement, Balfour was deluged with letters from irate Irish unionists and landlords who accused the government of gross indifference to the interests of the 'loyal minority', and who predicted that the National League would monopolize the new organs just as they had controlled the poor law

[24] Dicey to Balfour, 29 Apr. 1890 (B.M., Add. MS 49792, f. 182).
[25] Balfour to Dicey, 30 Apr. 1890 (B.M., Add. MS 49792, f. 185).

boards.[26] Loud demands were raised in the unionist press for protective devices such as minority representation or special franchise qualifications.[27] Answering the Honourable St John Broderick, one of the most strenuous objectors to the extension, the chief secretary denied that the councils could raise havoc and drive the main supporters of the union from Ireland. Extremely bitter over the sudden eruption of this unionist opposition, Balfour said:

I consider that I have a real grievance against the party, for the pledge has been given over and over again. It has been introduced in one queen's speech after another, and so far as I know, not a single serious expression of disapproval has been received during all these years by any responsible member of the government. I do not know whether the party take the view that promises are made to be broken, if so, I cannot agree with them.[28]

Writing to the duke of Abercorn a week later, Balfour dashed any unionist hopes of postponement.

. . . even if we desire to retreat, which (so far as I am concerned, at all events), it is not possible for us to do so without the most serious discredit. I think that you will find a good many northern members are strongly in favour of the bill. . . . I have a letter from Waterford strongly approving the government policy. I know Saunderson and Macartney take the same view, and I hope, therefore, that on the whole our friends will be tolerably unanimous in support of the government proposals.[29]

Nevertheless, as the autumn progressed, Dublin Castle received more and more unionist protests against the measure as well as demands for protective devices, and Sir West Ridgeway warned his chief that: 'You will have great difficulty with Ulster unless you

---

[26] It should be noted that the local government board when considering the 1892 local government bill assured the chief secretary that in the past they had enjoyed sufficient power to take effective action against any local body which persisted in passing inflamatory resolutions, or in arousing unlawful activity. The insinuation of the board's minute was that they could and would take action under the new system if necessary (S.P.O., C.S.O., R.P. 1892/4813).

[27] *The Times,* 21 Aug. 1891; *The Spectator,* 15 Aug. 1891.

[28] Balfour to Broderick, 2 Sept. 1891 (B.M., Add. MS 49830 f. 199).

[29] Balfour to duke of Abercorn, 9 Sept. 1891 (B.M., Add MS 49830, ff 229–30).

strengthen and render possible the position of the Protestants in the five counties. . . .'[30]

Despite Ridgeway's advice, Balfour was reluctant to introduce strong safeguards, and he requested the marquess of Waterford, one of his few enthusiastic supporters, to

. . . impress upon your friends that the view (which the more I reflect upon it the more I am convinced is the right one) that any dykes and safeguards in the shape of franchise qualifications and so forth are not only useless but worse than useless. They irritate one party without protecting the other. They destroy all appearance of equality between the treatment of England and Ireland, and they would certainly be swept away in the first storm. I am very anxious for minority representation if that can be obtained as this will ensure some good men upon every county council, which is absolutely on ' democratic lines '.[31]

The support of a very few enlightened unionists such as Lords Waterford, Castletown and De Vesci,[32] as well as the death of Parnell in October, encouraged Balfour to proceed directly with the Irish reform. Writing to Ridgeway, Balfour reported George Lewis's view that ' . . . this was the moment for the government to promote a compromise and that the present men, McCarthy, O'Brien and others, if properly approached would accept almost anything '.[33] This appraisal must have considerably encouraged Balfour because it was not apparent that Parnell's death had left the McCarthy followers as weak and disillusioned as Lewis indicated. Ridgeway replied that a good local government bill was the perfect instrument with which to dish home rule and drive a wedge even deeper into the ranks of Irish nationalists.[34]

Irrespective of Balfour's wishes, the ultra-unionist campaign to secure stringent safeguards was successful, and the measure introduced on 18 February 1892 by Balfour was so halting and inadequate

[30] Ridgeway to Balfour, 19 Oct. 1891 (B.M., Add. MS 49812, f. 199). Ridgeway was probably referring to Cavan, Monaghan, Donegal, Fermanagh and Tyrone where catholics and protestants were more evenly balanced than in the rest of the north.
[31] Balfour to Waterford, 22 Oct. 1891 (B.M., Add. MS 49830, f. 311).
[32] *The Times*, 24 Aug. 1891.
[33] Balfour to Ridgeway, 14 Oct. 1891 (B.M., Add. MS 49830, f. 282). Lewis was Sir George Henry Lewis, 1833–1911, who had represented the nationalists during the investigations of the special commisison, 1888 (*Who was Who*, 3rd ed., London, 1962, i, 428).
[34] Ridgeway to Balfour, 19 Oct. 1891 (B.M., Add. MS 49812, f. 199).

that all the Irish nationalists as well as many English liberals demurred from taking it seriously. The long awaited bill provided for county and district councils, elected on a parliamentary franchise. Grand jury responsibilities relating to road maintenance, sanitation and some appointments to asylum boards were to be transferred to the proposed councils. The administration of local revenues and the striking of the county cess were handed over to the majority of the ratepayers. The three main safeguards included were firstly, a cumulative vote for those paying the highest county cess. Secondly, the grand jury right of traverse was retained enabling any ratepayer to challenge any council presentment before a judge and jury. A storm of indignation arose from the Irish members of parliament over the third and most controversial safeguard, which provided for the dismissal of county and district councils for disobedience to the law, corruption or consistent malversation and oppression. A petition of accusation signed by twenty cesspayers and approved by two judges of assize was sufficient for the dismissal. The fourth and final safeguard, and one entirely without precedent in the English and Scotch system, provided for a joint committee of council members and grand jurors to have a supervisory vote on all capital expenditures as well as on the appointment of all new local government officers.

The reception which the Irish members accorded Balfour's bill was one of universal condemnation. The bill, with all its unprecedented and encumbering safeguards, was useless to the Irish for it did not really abolish the oligarchic grand juries, or their controversial powers of granting compensation for malicious injury. The Irish members regarded it as an insult to the moral and political integrity of the Irish people, and labelled the proposal as nothing more than a coercion bill in disguise.[35] John Redmond, the Parnellite leader called it ' monstrous ',[36] while Colonel Nolan called it ' absurd '.[37] In short, nationalist opinion was entirely and irrevocably opposed to this tory attempt to redeem the local government promise.

While it is conceivable that the bill might have been satisfactorily amended in committee, nationalist support was impossible owing to the increasing possibility of a general election. The Irish could not support any tory local government bill, no matter how liberal its construction, because the recent bye-elections made it almost absolutely certain that the liberals, the party officially pledged to home rule,

---

[35] *Hansard 4*, i, 726–95.
[36] Ibid., col. 726.
[37] Ibid., col. 726.

would emerge victoriously from the impending electoral struggle. In the last days of 1891 and the early months of 1892, Irish members had their sights on a higher goal, and no matter how desirable democratic control of local affairs might be in itself, home rule was still the primary and ultimate aim. If any political energy was to be expended, it would be far better utilized in convincing the English liberal electorate of the justice of the Irish demand. When it was clear that the only support for the proposal came from the liberal unionists, the bill was abandoned.

The return of the conservatives to office in 1895, following three years of liberal rule, dashed for at least five years Irish hopes of attaining home rule. While the Irish parliamentarians used every device available to publicize the justification of their demand, it was imperative that they alter their position to suit the new circumstances resulting from the liberal defeat. Complete concentration upon an object whose attainment had been propelled into the future was tactically and politically impossible. The nationalist attitude would have to be determined by tory inclinations toward Ireland. Fortunately for Ireland, the unionist government was not disposed to renew a coercionist policy. Agricultural prosperity and the political apathy engendered by the internecine rivalry within the Irish party gave a great stimulus to a conciliatory policy, and thus made Gerald Balfour's task of piloting remedial legislation through parliament a bit more tractable than his brother had faced. Moreover, Ireland's freedom from active coercion enabled the Irish members to offer some cooperation with remedial legislation. The Irish were not obliged as in the past to use every discussion of Irish affairs to condemn the government's law enforcement procedures. A growth in the number of Irish unionists who favoured a progressive policy was also of great help to Balfour in his attempt to bring social and economic amelioration to Ireland. The chief secretary came to rely upon the active support of men like Lords Monteagle, Castletown, Waterford as well as Hugh de F. Montgomery, the O'Conor Don and Horace Plunkett. Chamberlain's presence in the cabinet once again gave the liberal unionists a useful channel through which to press for a progressive policy. Indeed, the pressures of fighting the second home rule bill had given Chamberlain greater influence in the conservative wings of the unionist party. In short, by 1895 the unionist ministers responsible for Irish policy had become convinced, as Arthur Balfour was previously, that negative unionism was imposible, and that preservation of the union depended upon significant economic and social improvement. On 19 July 1895, Arthur Balfour forecast the new departure when he criticized past British policy as cruel and stupid, and called upon all unionists to accept their Irish responsibilities.[38]

However, six weeks later, Gerald Balfour's sincere but unfortunate confession that he held a sanguine hope of 'killing home rule by kindness' prevented the largest section of the Irish party from rendering active cooperation and eventually stigmatized many genuinely nonpartisan efforts to bring a better life to the Irish people. The most famous example of nationalist opposition was the hostile reception given to Horace Plunkett's efforts with the Irish Agricultural Society.

Nevertheless the unionist majority was large enough to pass beneficial measures and the cabinet's most trying difficulties were with the reactionary landlords like Lords Ardilaun, Westmeath, Barrymore and Clonbrook who viewed any concessions to the nationalists with jaundiced eyes. Proof of the ministry's newly found benevolence was shown by the prompt action in 1896 to revive the land purchase programme. Sharing his brother's conviction that a more complete solution of the land question was fundamental to Irish pacification, Gerald Balfour freed the 1891 legislation of its elaborate security arrangements[39] and augmented the land purchase funds by thirty-six million pounds in the 1896 act. The rising value of purchase applications from 500,000 pounds in 1895 to 750,000 in 1897, and finally to two million pounds in 1898 was the best indication of the act's success.[40]

Yet the question of Irish local government reform remained. The problem was resurrected in the spring of 1897 as a result of universal Irish indignation over the alleged overtaxation of Ireland. The report of the royal commission on financial relations had prompted all Irish members to press for an equivalent grant from the imperial exchequer for approximately 750,000 pounds in aid of agricultural rating. When the government proposed to dip into these funds for 150,000 pounds to finance the abortive agricultural and industries bill of 1897, a storm of Irish protest arose. When all the Irish unionists joined with the nationalists in supoprt of V. F. Knox's 7 May budget motion which accused the government of gross financial injustice towards

---

[38] *The Times*, 20 July 1895.

[39] Under the 1891 act, prospective tenant buyers had to pay higher rents for five years as security against default (Curtis, *Coercion and conciliation*, p. 351).

[40] J. Pomfret, *The struggle for land in Ireland* (Princeton, 1930), p. 274.

Ireland, the ministry abandoned the agricultural and industries bill, and promised Ireland her full equivalent grant.

The official announcement that Ireland would receive her equivalent grant for agricultural rating along with and conditional to a reform of local government, came on 21 May 1897. In his address, Arthur Balfour emphasized the impossibility of giving any relief to Irish rates without first reforming the antiquated system of local administration, '. . . which we have rejected in England and Scotland, and which the great majority on this side of the house are pledged to reform in Ireland also '.[41] While the prospect of a democratic system of local government was warmly greeted by the Irish nationalists, even the zealous unionist Sir Edward Carson declared that it would be narrow for his party to be antagonistic as long as the government kept its promise of protecting the high rate paying minority.[42]

The cabinet's idea of attaching the financial relief to the local reform was very astute. While it granted the nationalists a decided political advantage, the financial proposals were sufficiently attractive to the landlords to prevent them from opposing their inevitable exile from local administration. The landlords were to be relieved of their former share of the poor rates, and they were now liable for rates only as occupiers, not as owners. In effect, the agricultural equivalent grant had enabled the unionist government to grant democratic local government to Ireland by buying off landlord opposition.

The role of the liberal unionists in redeeming the 1886 promise at this juncture was of no mean importance. While Chamberlain and Devonshire placed continuous pressure upon the cabinet, immediately after the passage of the 1896 land act, the Ulstermen resumed their local government campaign by passing a resolution at their annual meeting in 1897.[43] Moreover, the five Irish liberal unionist parliamentarians were not content with pure resistance to home rule, and consequently, H. O. Arnold Foster, Sir Thomas Lea, T. W. Russell, William Kenny and W. E. H. Lecky continually displayed their progressive unionism by supporting schemes for the agricultural and industrial development of Ireland. Along with all the other liberal unionists, they also wanted democratic local government.

The growing administrative pressure to bring efficiency to the workhouse system further stimulated the government's determination

[41] *Hansard 4,* xlix, 1041.
[42] Ibid., col. 1047.
[43] *Ulster Liberal Unionist Association,* p. 85.

to proceed with the reform. The desired amalgamations and improvements could be better accomplished if the proposed general reform relieved the guardians of their superfluous duties. Lastly, by 1897, the antiquated grand jury system was politically indefensible and procrastination had become intolerable once the land purchase scheme had been passed and the landlords secured in their payments. By placing the incidence of taxation on the occupier, the landlords and unionists were sufficiently protected from financial ruin through excessive taxation.

The local government bill which Gerald Balfour presented on 21 February 1898 eventually established county and district councils, elected triennially on a parliamentary franchise. Those women and peers, who but for their sex and title would have qualified for the parliamentary register, were also given the local government franchise. The application of the one-man one-vote principle to every occupier abolished the plural voting privileges formerly enjoyed by the landlords. Because the only qualification for eligibility for office was the possession of a local government franchise, local politics were now open to all Irishmen, irrespective of wealth, religion or politics. The new councils assumed all the fiscal duties formerly exercised by the grand juries, as well as the administration of certain parliamentary acts formerly executed by the guardians.

The parliamentary reception accorded to Balfour's bill did not give the government any grounds for complaint. The very minute objections brought forth by both nationalists and unionists were solely for appearance sake. Unionists did not want to jeopardize the prospective financial relief. The nationalists, on the other hand, saw the legislation as a step on the road to home rule because they believed the councils would provide useful machinery to further the home rule agitation. Appreciating this possibility, John Dillon spoke of ' . . . that absolute necessity of a limited movement to secure popular control of the county councils . . .',[44] when William O'Brien was planinng the convention of the United Irish League to be held in September 1898.

When the first elections under the Local Government (Ireland) Act, 1898, were held in March 1899, the results expressed an overwhelming confidence in the abilities of the nationalistic Irish to manage their own affairs. It was inevitable that the first elections were fought primarily on political lines. To have expected the Irish

---

[44] Dillon to O'Brien, 8 July 1898 (N.L.I., O'Brien papers, MS 8885/13).

in the first flush of their newly obtained electoral powers to ignore the predominant political issues of the day, whether they be home rule versus unionism, or landlordism versus tenant demands, was asking too much. The final returns gave the nationalists 551 places on the county councils while the unionists could claim only 125, with 86 of these being in Ulster.[45]

The promise to extend democratic local government to Ireland had been largely a direct outcome of the Gladstonian conversion, and as we have seen, its fulfilment was in great measure attributable to the constant pressure which the Ulster Liberal Unionist Committee exerted upon the ministry. While the cabinet positions of Joseph Chamberlain and Lord Randolph Churchill gave the Ulstermen a channel of communication to the highest echelons of the unionist party, their perennial campaign for popular government not only added further confirmation to Arthur Balfour's personal belief in progressive unionism, but also provided both Balfour brothers with the political argument to force their more reluctant conservative colleagues to accept a progressive Irish policy. Arthur Balfour's insistence that democratic local government was necessary, not only because of the unionist alliance, but also because he believed that the act of union demanded equal treatment, was also of crucial significance. It is to his credit that he attempted to redeem the pledge in 1892 in the face of great unionist opposition and cabinet reluctance. His exposition of the benefits of economic and social amelioration to his younger brother Gerald furnished the latter during his tenure in the Irish office with the determination to achieve significant improvements in Ireland's economic, social and political life.

[45] While the issues of home rule and land entered into the 1902 and 1905 county council elections, after 1903 local electors demonstrated an increasing concern for economy and efficiency in local government. See my unpublished M.A. thesis, ' Local government in Ireland : the politics and administration ', University College, Dublin, 1963, ch. 4.

17

THE SOUTHERN IRISH UNIONISTS,
THE IRISH QUESTION, AND BRITISH POLITICS,
1906-1914[1]

P.J. BUCKLAND

The period 1906–14 is often regarded as one of continual disagreement and turmoil in British politics. This may be true; but it is important to understand why. In fact, British politics between 1906 and 1914 were marked by a strong desire to avoid extremes. Developments on the fringe of politics, socialism, syndicalism and suffragism, made a deep impression upon the moderate elements of both major parties and their desire to contain such signs of disturbance was epitomised in the constitutional conference held in 1910. Yet the Irish question frustrated attempts at moderation, embittered politics and hindered the development of a more representative, democratic and social stage in the United Kingdom.

Until 1911 the Irish question allowed a dispute over the powers of the house of lords to dominate politics. In the last analysis the liberals wanted to curb the powers of the lords to allow the passage

[1] This paper is based on the M.A. thesis by P. J. Buckland, 'The unionists and Ireland: the influence of the Irish question upon British politics, 1906–1914', Birmingham University, 1966, hereafter cited as Buckland. The main manuscript sources consulted were: the Austen Chamberlain papers in the Birmingham University Library, AC 1–56; the Arthur James Balfour papers, B.M., Add. MSS 49683–49962; the records of the Irish Loyal and Patriotic Union and (from 1891) of the Irish Unionist Alliance, the southern unionists' political organisation in Ireland, and of the Joint Committee of the Unionist Associations of Ireland, an Irish unionist propaganda organisation. The Irish unionist records are deposited in the P.R.O.N.I., D 989 and D 1327. Also consulted were the Carson papers, the Montgomery papers, and the records of the Ulster Unionist Council in P.R.O.N.I.; the Redmond papers and the personal diaries and journals of Lady Mary Howard of Shelton Abbey, Bray, in N.L.I. Extracts from the more useful (for the purposes of this paper) collections are printed with the kind permission of the librarian, Birmingham University; the trustees of the British Museum; and the deputy keeper of the P.R.O.N.I., respectively.

of a measure such as home rule, while the unionists[2] were anxious to keep the power of forcing a dissolution in order to maintain the union. Thus, by preventing agreement at the constitutional conference, the Irish question caused the liberal government to implement a more radical, though less democratic, scheme for the reform of the relations between the two houses of parliament than might have been achieved by agreement between the two parties.[3] Then, the way having been cleared for the third home rule bill which was introduced in April 1912, the Irish question dominated politics, squeezed out

[2] Until a fusion in 1912 the opposition party after 1906 comprised two wings, the members of the conservative and constitutional associations and those of the liberal unionist organisation, the former being the predominant partners. Although the term unionist was generally applied to this alliance in the early twentieth century, it comprised three broad geographical sections : the British section, primarily conservative; the southern Irish section whose overriding concern was the maintenance of the legislative union between Great Britain and Ireland; and the northern Irish section whose main political interest was also the maintenance of the union. The varied interests of members of these different sections meant that at times the distinction was not clear-cut; but, for the purposes of this paper, the term conservative will apply to the British, the predominant section of the opposition; the term southern unionist to that section of the party with major interests in the three southern provinces of Ireland; and the term Ulster unionist to that section with interests in the northern province of Ireland. When the opposition party as a whole is meant, the epithet unionist will be applied; the term Irish unionist will apply to the two Irish sections taken together.

[3] These points have been argued in Buckland, ch. 7. Though often assumed by historians, the dominance of the Irish question at the constitutional conference has never hitherto been adequately documented. However, a meeting-by-meeting account of the conference recorded by Austen Chamberlain, one of the opposition delegates, and his daily letters to his wife in which he gives his impressions of the final meetings of the conference, do confirm that the Irish question prevented effective discussion of the other issues before the conference and obviated the agreement reached on other matters, such as finance. Chamberlain's account and a supplementary one by Lord Lansdowne, another opposition delegate, are in the Austen Chamberlain papers, AC 10/2/35–65. These accounts resolve an apparent conflict of evidence that has perturbed Mr R. Jenkins (in *Mr Balfour's poodle* (1954), p. 103) and led him to doubt whether there was any chance of agreement at the conference. Contrary to Mr Jenkins's suspicion, the substantial liberal concession over finance was made after the summer recess at the fourteenth and fifteenth sittings, i.e. on 11 and 12 October. For Chamberlain's letters to his wife in November 1910, see AC 6/1/81–3. An attempt to reconstruct the conference has been made in Buckland, pp. 667–95.

progressive measures and attitudes, and brought the United Kingdom to the verge of civil war.[4] It was not just that two armed forces faced each other in Ireland and that English country houses were being prepared to receive (unionist) casualties.[5] Free rein was given to the reactionary elements within the opposition party which hoped to defeat the bill by supporting the Ulster unionists' resistance to home rule.[6] The struggle was thus brought to the centre of politics, with scenes in the house of commons and the formation of armed bands, in the midlands at least, under the cover of Ulster Athletic Clubs.[7] A vicious spiral was created. Plans to amend the mutiny act helped to precipitate the Curragh incident, which led to a further degeneration of British politics in 1914, affecting that give and take of political and social life that lies behind the successful working of parliamentary democracy in Great Britain. In attempting to account for the influence of the Irish question on British politics this paper will emphasise those factors previously underrated, if not ignored completely, viz southern Irish unionism and is especially intimate relationship with the conservative party in Great Britain.

The reason that the Irish question could exercise such an influence on British politics lay in the nature and extent of the disagreement of the two major parties over that issue. Abortive attempts at compromise in 1913–14 on the basis of the exclusion of Ulster from the operation of the third home rule bill only underlined the difference between the parties on the Irish question. For, owing to the organisation of Irish nationalism and of Irish unionism, liberals and conservatives found themselves in fundamental disagreement over Ireland. In the first place the deep divisions of Irish politics, between nationalists and unionists, between catholics and protestants, between the ' Gaels ' and the ' British ', were translated into British politics, thus introducing a degree of intransigence alien to the British political system. Secondly, because of the vitality of the Irish organisations

---

[4] Buckland, ch. 8.

[5] Duchess of Somerset to Sir Edward Carson, 13 Jan. [1914?], Carson papers, P.R.O.N.I.

[6] See e.g. the changing views of Lord Lansdowne in *Official report (house of lords)*, series 5, ix, 10 Aug. 1911, col. 888, and in Lansdowne to A[rthur] J[ames] B[alfour], 6 Mar. 1914, B.M., Add. MS 49730, ff. 268–9.

[7] Lord Willoughby de Broke to Carson, 17 Nov. 1913, enclosing a letter from William Nightingale (the Birmingham agent of the British League for the Support of Ulster and the Union) to de Broke, 13 Nov. 1913, Carson papers, P.R.O.N.I.

taken in conjunction with circumstances, the liberal and conservative attitudes on the Irish question became, or appeared to contemporaries to be, essential to their existence as major political parties.[8]

The essential nature of the attitude of the liberals, in power between 1906 and 1914, has long been noted by their supporters and opponents. The liberals believed in principle in home rule, while dependence upon the Irish nationalists in parliament and in certain British constituencies compelled them to act upon these principles. Despite the consequences for British politics, they refused to govern Ireland by coercion and were committeed to some modification of the union.[9] On the other hand the attitude of the opposition has been accepted rather than explained. The unionist party vigorously and heatedly contested liberal policy towards the government of Ireland. Opposition to liberal Irish policy became their main plank[10] and they were determined to frustrate liberal efforts to modify the union even at the risk of civil war. Indeed opposition to home rule became as much essential to the life of the unionist party as belief in home rule was to the liberal party. To compromise on the union would have split the party; or (what is as important) this is what the opposition leaders feared throughout the period 1906–1914.[11]

For this critical situation within the unionist party, the Irish unionists, particularly of the south and west, were responsible. It is true that considerations of empire and constitution made the opposition, avowedly the constitutional party and by profession the imperial one, reluctant to accept home rule for Ireland; but neither of these objections was sufficiently conclusive to permit intransigence upon the Irish question. What did make for this intransigence, which was by 1913 endangering the empire and the constitution, was Irish unionism. It gave some point to the union when other arguments for its maintenance seemed irrelevant. Irish unionists persuaded the

[8] These points are discussed in Buckland, ch. 1–3.

[9] Buckland, ch. 2. Most helpful for an understanding of the liberal Irish policy are E. P. M. Wollaston, 'The Irish nationalist movement in Great Britain', London M.A. thesis (1958) and H. W. McCready, 'Home rule and the liberal party, 1899–1906', in *I.H.S.*, xiii. 316–48 (Sept. 1963).

[10] The emphasis to be placed by the opposition on the Irish question in this period was indicated in a speech by Balfour, the opposition leader, during the 1906 election campaign, *The Times*, 6 Jan. 1906.

[11] See e.g. Lord Lansdowne (opposition leader in the lords) to A(usten) C(hamberlain), 24 Nov. 1913, AC 11/1/50. For the fears of the leadership in 1906 and 1910 see below.

opposition to accept their own intransigent attitude towards the union and liberal policy : and were in a position to exact condign punishment should the leadership fail them. The way in which the opposition seemed to identify itself with the Ulster section of Irish unionism when the third home rule bill was introduced is well known.[12] Yet, since the protestantism and determination of Ulstermen also made an impact upon British opinion at large,[13] and since the liberals were prepared to consider a compromise on the basis of exclusion,[14] considerations of Ulster unionism do not in themselves account for the opposition's emphasis upon the maintenance of the union. Moreover, as will be suggested later, there seems good reason for doubting the popularity of the cause of the Ulster unionists among conservatives.[15] Rather the opposition in the main took up the Ulster question after 1911 on tactical grounds, hoping that local resistance would defeat home rule and using the Ulster question as a cloak to hide their own intransigence on the Irish question,[16] an intransigence due to concern for the unionists of the three southern provinces of Ireland.

While the strength and determination of the Ulster unionists to resist home rule has never been doubted, the southern unionists have received a bad press. They were a small, scattered, though wealthy, minority in the south of Ireland so that they made little impact upon the generality of British politicians and electors. They never threatened to resist home rule by armed force, or even to do violence to nationalist politicians. The result has been that they have received little attention from historians and have been belittled even by their own former leaders. Lord Midleton, a former chairman of the Irish Unionist Alliance,[17] ousted in 1919 following his acceptance of the principle of home rule in the convention, wrote thus of southern unionists :

With rare exceptions they lacked political insight and cohesion. Contented to air their feelings at intervals, they restricted themselves to the easy task of attending meetings in Dublin and voting strong resolutions which they

---

[12] The best account is in R. Blake, *The unknown prime minister* (1955), ch. VII, IX–XIII.

[13] See e.g. leader in *The Times*, 18 May 1914.

[14] See e.g. Asquith's memorandum to H.M., quoted in R. Jenkins, *Asquith* (1964), pp. 276–7.

[15] See below.

[16] Buckland, pp. 240–59.

[17] See below.

expected the British government to respect. I remember a special meeting at Londonderry House, at a crisis, when after vigorous attacks on the government, of which I happened to be a junior member, the meeting adjourned to a sumptuous luncheon without defining any policy they might accept.[18]

Such an estimate is misleading, for since the 1880s the southern unionists had shown great energy and initiative in safeguarding their interests, interpreted to mean the act of union.

In 1885 was founded the Irish Loyal and Patriotic Union to co-ordinate unionist energies in Ireland in order to maintain the union. Its immediate object, however, had been to combat Parnellites in the three southern provinces in the general election of that year, the first following the extension of the franchise in 1884 and the redistribution of 1885.[19] Fifty-two seats were contested; but the difficulty of electioneering in southern Ireland soon became apparent. Therefore in 1886 the I.L.P.U., limiting itself to ' constitutional means', tried to set up a mass party organisation for all Ireland to maintain a consistent propaganda on behalf of the union in British politics.[20] Though branches were established in all counties in Ireland, save Monaghan,[21] the I.L.P.U. failed to become the one unionist association for all Ireland. The Ulster unionists, separated by religious intensity and social situation from the southern unionists, preferred to maintain their own organisation, so that the I.L.P.U., called after a reorganisation in 1891 the Irish Unionist Alliance (I.U.A.),[22] was by 1893 generally recognised as representative of unionist opinion only in the three southern provinces;[23] and by 1906 southern unionists,

[18] Earl of Midleton, *Records and reactions, 1856-1939* (1939), pp. 226-7.

[19] I.L.P.U. manifesto in *The Times,* 16 Oct. 1885; I.L.P.U. *Prospectus* (1886), copy in Bodleian Library; I.L.P.U., *Annual report 1887,* pp. 1-2, P.R.O.N.I., D 989/46.

[20] *Irish Times,* 9 Jan. 1886 for report of the first annual general meeting of the I.L.P.U., 8 Jan. 1886.

[21] I.L.P.U., Executive council minute book, 1886-9, *passim,* P.R.O. N.I., D 989/1; I.U.A., *Annual reports,* 1901-13, appendices, D 989/36 and 12a/2.

[22] Executive council minute book, 1889-1920.

[23] Balfour's letter to the organisers of a unionist demonstration in Dublin, April 1893, copy in I.U.A., Executive council minute book, 1893-4, 10 Apr. 1893, P.R.O.N.I., D 989/2; ibid., 24 Nov. 1893, for a resolution from the Liberal Union of Ireland to I.U.A., suggesting a Dublin demonstration to be addressed by Joseph Chamberlain. The

seemingly becoming wary of the Ulstermen's intensity,[24] were content with this.[25] Nor did the I.U.A., which in 1913 had a nucleus of some 683 members,[26] ever achieve mass party status, its branches tending to vary in strength as did the density of the protestant population in the south of Ireland.[27] This organisational failure reflected the limited social basis of southern unionism, which tended to be protestant, anglicised, propertied, and aristocratic.[28] Typical of the members of the southern unionist association were men like Sir Thomas Butler, a founder member, and the Shaws. Sir Thomas owned lands in county Carlow valued at his death in 1908 at £82,028, the demense, which contained 937 acres, being assessed at £9,837. Despite mortgages, such holdings enabled him to enjoy a comfortable social and an active public life as one of the leading representatives

unionists of the nine counties of Ulster in the main had little to do with the southern unionist association whose branches in the north were invariably weak, depending on the energy of one or two individuals. Only after the exclusion of six counties of Ulster had become by 1918 the definite policy of the Ulster Unionist Council, did the unionists of the other three counties of Ulster, whose social and religious structure was similar to that of the counties in the southern provinces, throw in their lot wholeheartedly with unionists of the south. In 1919, for instance, the Monaghan Unionist Association was affiliated as a branch of the souhern unionist association. See Montgomery papers, P.R.O.N.I., DOD 627/435 and I.U.A., *Annual report, 1919–20*, P.R.O.N.I., D 989/12a/2.

[24] Midleton to A.J.B., 5 Oct. 1911, B.M., Add. MS 49721, ff. 291–2, complaining of Carsonism and Carson's aggressive language and concluding 'it is of course as impossible to refute Carson publicly as to controvert his silly proposals to march upon Cork etc.'; 'cadet of one of the old Irish Catholic families' writing to *The Times*, 14 Oct. 1912.

[25] I.U.A. resolutions, *D.D.E.*, 30 Aug. 1906, 27 Apr. 1912.

[26] I.U.A., *Annual report, 1912–13*, appendix A, giving the officials and representatives of the local branches of the I.U.A. on the supreme governing body of the association.

[27] See e.g. the diminishing ambitions of the successive constitutions of the association, Executive council minute book, 1889–1920, P.R.O.N.I., D 110/Mic; and compare the numerical strength of the branches of the I.U.A. indicated by *Annual report, 1912–13*, appendix A, with the religious professions of the inhabitants in each county given in *Census of Ireland for the year 1911*, preliminary report, Cd. 5691 (1911), pp. 6–7.

[28] For the qualities that a southern unionist lady required of other southern unionists see Mary ffolliott to H. de F. Montgomery, 14 Mar. 1918, Montgomery papers, P.R.O.N.I., Dod 627/432.

of Irish landowners.[29] The Shaw family seems to have tried to establish a dynasty within the southern unionist organisation. Sir Frederick Shaw, baronet, was an honorary secretary of the association while his son, Herbert, was first an organiser of an Irish unionist anti-home rule campaign in England and then became secretary of the association. Father and son were members of the Dublin branch of the association, with an estate in Dublin county handed down from William Shaw of Hampshire, a soldier of scottish descent who had established himself in Ireland after fighting at the battle of the Boyne.[30]

Though in an age of democracy this narrow social basis was to prove fatal, over a shorter period it was a source of strength. The limited nature of southern unionism meant that its organisation was based upon close social contacts and was itself closely knit;[31] the wealth of the southern unionists meant that what work their association undertook could be adequately financed;[32] and finally their social and financial standing encouraged southern unionists to act in British politics with every hope of success.[33]

The southern unionist association worked on two fronts: in Ireland and in Great Britain, though after 1906 the work done in Ireland only sufficed to give evidence of the fact of southern unionism.[34] Apart from subsidising Ulster unionism, the I.U.A. contested three seats in the south of Ireland, outside of Dublin University, and organised meetings, manifestoes, petitions and tours of the south of Ireland for British electors. By 1914 one or two deputations of between ten and fifteen electors were arriving weekly to inspect certain areas illustrating (alleged) nationalist incompetence

[29] Probate will of Sir Thomas Pierce Butler granted 8 Mar. 1909, P.R.O.I., no. 6034; *Notes from Ireland,* passim.

[30] I.U.A., *Annual reports,* 1901–13, appendices; minute book of the Joint Committee of the Unionist Associations of Ireland, passim, P.R.O. N.I., D 1327/2/1; *Burke's peerage* (1911), p. 1767.

[31] See e.g. the personal diaries and journals of Lady Alice Mary Howard of Shelton Abbey, Bray, in N.L.I., no. 3621.

[32] I.U.A. pamphlet entitled 'The Irish Unionist Alliance: its work and organisation' (1893); I.U.A. Subscription book, 1907–14, P.R.O.N.I., D 989/4/3.

[33] Leader in *D.D.E.,* 9 Jan. 1886.

[34] See e.g. editorial comment upon the reorganisation of the I.U.A. in 1906, *Notes from Ireland,* June 1906.

and terrorism.[35] The success of this work in Ireland, particularly of the tours, depended upon the enthusiasm and self-sacrifice of local unionists in the small towns of Ireland who had to give a great deal of time and trouble to them and who had themselves to interview the visitors and to get other unionists to do so. One such self-sacrificing unionist, selected for commendation by the secretary of the I.U.A.,[36] was a Roman Catholic.[37] He was Michael M'Cann of Newtown-forbes, Longford, who with his wife had ' done as much as anybody in Ireland to convert the radical visitors '. 'A big farmer' and the Longford branch representative on the general council of the I.U.A., he entertained a very great number of tourists at his house and frequently fed them. For his pains he was (allegedly) severely boy-cotted. Another organiser was H. V. McNamara of Ennistymon House, county Clare, honorary secretary of the Clare county branch of the I.U.A. Despite living in ' one of the worst districts in Ireland ' he showed ' the very greatest pluck ', making ' admirable arrange-ments for the reception of tours in Ennis ' and doing ' splendid work in co. Clare during the last year '.[38]

All such work in Ireland, itself a sufficient rebuttal of Midleton's slighting assessment of southern unionists, served to support a continuous campaign in British politics against home rule. Southern unionists recognised the futility of trying to contain the nationalist movement in Ireland, but were still unwilling to accept home rule. Moreover, being a scattered minority, they were unable to consider the use of force to resist the imposition of a home rule bill.[39] Thus southern unionists had to ensure that a bill dissolving the union would

[35] Buckland, pp. 340–59. Apart from the several minute books of the I.L.P.U. and I.U.A., the other useful sources for unionist activity in the south of Ireland are *Notes from Ireland* (a bulletin of Irish political news published regularly by the southern unionist organisation), the *Irish Times* and *D.D.E.*

[36] Shaw to Wicks (Carson's secretary), 15 Jun. 1914, in a file of letters from the I.U.A. to Sir Edward Carson, P.R.O.N.I., D 989/12a/1.

[37] For this reason he was probably singled out for a word of encour-agement, since the I.U.A. hoped to persuade substantial Roman Catholics to become unionists. See e.g. Midleton writing to *The Times*, 21 Oct. 1912.

[38] Shaw to Wicks, 15 Jun. 1914, I.U.A. to Carson, P.R.O.N.I., D 989/12a/1; I.U.A., *Annual report, 1912–13*, appendix A. The relative strength of the county Clare branch of the I.U.A. in 1913 would seem to confirm Shaw's appreciation of McNamara's energy.

[39] *Irish Times*, 9 Jan. 1886.

not be passed by a Westminster parliament or approved by a British electorate. The only constitutional means open to southern unionists was to carry on, mainly through their association, a campaign throughout British politics, organised, owing to the exigencies of party politics, through the conservative opponents of the home rule party.[40]

The campaign was waged in two spheres. In the more restricted sphere of parliamentary and party politics, southern unionists relied upon action in parliament by representatives in both houses, and behind the scenes by correspondence and deputations to unionist leaders and conferences. The campaign in the constituencies was fourfold: the production and distribution of literary propaganda; the organisation of demonstrations; canvassing; and the maintenance of a 'follow-up' service. This work, concentrating on more marginal seats and crystallising around elections, had been carried on by the I.L.P.U. or the I.U.A. ever since 1886; but after 1907 it was done in conjunction with the Ulster Unionist Council, under the auspices of the Joint Committee of the Unionist Associations of Ireland, though the southern unionists bore the greater burden, supervising the work in England and Wales.[41] In fact after 1906 this campaign was all the more insistent and developed as liberal policy towards Ireland evolved, for southern unionists hoped to force a general election on the specific issue of home rule. Seeing that Redmond's position was being challenged in Ireland, but (absorbed in constitutional politics) not appreciating the independence and strength of the extreme nationalist wing, southern unionists were convinced after 1906 of the mystical quality of a third rejection of a home rule bill to kill home rule completely.[42] Therefore all their energies after 1906 were directed to this end.

The extent to which this campaign created an anti-home rule opinion in Great Britain cannot be determined; but there can be no doubt that, organised as the campaign was through the unionist party, it made the opposition aware of the southern unionist viewpoint.[43]

[40] Resolution of the executive committee of the I.U.A., 26 Oct. 1906 in *D.D.E.*, 27 Oct. 1906.

[41] This campaign is dealt with in some detail in Buckland, pp. 355–401 and ch. 6. Apart from newspapers the main sources were the several minute books of the I.U.A. and the minute book of the Joint Committee of the Unionist Associations of Ireland.

[42] *D.D.E.*, 29 Aug. 1908, 27 Apr. 1912.

[43] Some attempt at assessing the impact of the Irish unionist campaign in G.B. has been made in Buckland, pp. 359, 364–5, 387–90, 395–6, 486–7, 493–4, 495, 501, 503–4, 504–6.

This southern unionist success, and some picture of the way their association worked, can be seen in the way southern unionists deterred the unionist leadership from working wholeheartedly in 1913 and 1914 for a compromise on the Irish question on the basis of the exclusion of Ulster from the operation of the third home rule bill.[44]

By the autumn of 1913 the effect of the disagreement of the parties over the Irish question was causing grave concern, and in an effort to avoid possible civil war politicians looked for a compromise on the basis of the exclusion of Ulster. In common with an influential section of the party, including a former leader, Balfour,[45] and the leader of the Birmingham group, Austen Chamberlain,[46] Andrew Bonar Law, the leader of the opposition in the house of commons, genuinely desired a settlement; and in September 1913 in conversation led liberal ministers to believe that some settlement was possible.[47] Meanwhile, however, Lansdowne, leader of the opposition in the lords, a southern Irish landowner[48] and member of the I.U.A.,[49] learning of the drift of such conversations, reminded Law of the southern unionists.[50] Thus, when the king's secretary suggested a conference on the basis of the exclusion of Ulster, Law could only refuse on the ground that ' there would be a wild outburst of resentment against us in the south of Ireland which would be reflected with almost equal violence in England '.[51]

[44] Although the Buckingham Palace Conference was concerned with a compromise based on the exclusion of Ulster, this does not mean that the opposition really wanted such a compromise. They would have preferred a general election and it seems likely that the opposition could not refuse to enter any sort of conference without alienating public opinion, which would have been fatal to a party hoping for an early dissolution of parliament.

[45] K. Young, *Arthur James Balfour* (1963), pp. 119–120; *The Times,* 1 Feb. 1913; A.J.B. memo. on ' the constitutional question ', 1913, B.M., Add. MS 49869, ff. 123–32.

[46] A.C. to Mary (his step-mother), 25 Feb., 23 Mar., 24 Apr., 4 May 1914, AC 4/1/1078, 1098–9, 1124, 1131; A.C. to Lansdowne, 29 Oct. 1913, AC 11/1/46.

[47] Law to Carson, 18 Sept. 1913, quoted in Blake, p. 156; Law to Lansdowne, 29 Sept. 1913, ibid., p. 159; Jenkins, *Asquith,* pp. 286–8.

[48] G.E.C., *The complete peerage* (revised ed., London 1910–59), vii. 436–43. Especially instructive (with reservations) is the survey of estates made in 1883.

[49] I.U.A. Subscription book; I.U.A., *Annual report, 1912–13,* appendix A.

[50] Blake, pp. 157–8.

[51] Law to Stamfordham, n.d., in Blake, p. 159.

The difficulty was that the southern unionists, as a result of persistent organisation and propaganda, had many sympathisers among British conservatives, their lonely plight in the nationalist southern provinces giving some real meaning to the idea of the union.[52] By the beginning of October, though, the situation seemed to have altered. Sir Edward Carson had had an interview with leading southern unionists and reported to Law that they had indicated that they were not prepared to agitate strongly against home rule and that they were afraid of intimidation and damage to their financial and business interests. Thus Law wrote to Lansdowne on 8 October that

I am more hopeful than I was of a settlement of that kind . . . the leading men in Ulster do desire a settlement on the basis of leaving Ulster out, and Carson thinks that such an arrangement could be carried out without any serious attack from the unionists in the south.[53]

When, therefore, Asquith suggested a private meeting with Law, the latter accepted[54]—and, to judge from the above letter to Lansdowne, his mood was not pessimistic.

During the conversations (three took place between October and December), Law's slight optimism disappeared, to be replaced by a deep despondency; for Law thought that Asquith would propose the exclusion of four or six counties of Ulster to settle the Irish question. The trouble was that such a proposal would seem to public opinion so reasonable that the unionist leadership could scarcely take responsibility for rejecting it; yet should they agree a party revolt was likely. Law, therefore, refused to press Asquith upon the issue and the conversations drifted inconclusively.[55]

The reasons behind Law's despondency and drifting are not hard to find. On the one hand there was Ulster. Ulstermen demanded the exclusion of the whole province of Ulster, for their organisation applied to the whole province and after the signing of the covenant the concept of Ulster had, to Ulstermen, achieved an almost mystical

---

[52] See e.g. Sir Charles Petrie, *Walter Long and his times* (1936), p. 176.

[53] Law to Lansdowne, 8 Oct. 1913, copy in B.M., Add. MS 49693, ff. 62–4.

[54] Blake, pp. 160–1.

[55] Blake, pp. 161–7; for A.C.'s comments upon Law's performance, see A.C. to Mary, 11 Feb. 1914, AC 4/1/1069.

significance.[56] Yet had the Ulstermen been the unionist party's only concern, a compromise between the two parties might have been effected, giving Ulstermen less than they ostensibly demanded.[57] They were not, however, for there remained the southern unionists.

In his first conversation with Asquith, Law had pointed out the

> danger of the unionists in the south and west thinking that we had betrayed them, which would make any action on our part impossible if they were unanimous in that view;[58]

and since Law's conversation with Carson southern unionists had clarified their position, announcing their firm determination to defeat home rule. This had been their policy since 1885 and they were keeping to it. Admittedly after 1911 there were complications, for the parliament act ensured that, with a majority for home rule within the house of commons, a home rule bill would become law. Faced with this likelihood one or two southern unionists favoured accommodation with the nationalists;[59] but this attitude was not widespread and the I.U.A. — pledged to the maintenance of the union — actually increased its membership as the third home rule bill progressed under the protection of the parliament act.[60] It is also true that southern unionists did support Ulster's agitation; but they did so only for tactical reasons in the hope of wrecking the bill.[61] The last thing that southern unionists wanted was a settlement in 1913 and 1914. They hoped to prevent the bill from becoming law or from becoming operative by forcing a dissolution of parliament and having the government defeated in an appeal to the electors on home rule.

Accordingly, in the autumn of 1913 the Joint Committee stepped up its campaign in the constituencies;[62] and, just before Law met

[56] Blake, pp. 161–7.

[57] To judge from the ease with which the U.U.C. at a later date accepted and defended the exclusion of only six counties.

[58] Law, 'Notes on conversation with the P.M.', 15 Oct. 1913, quoted in Blake, pp. 161–2.

[59] J. K. P. Newman to Redmond, 3 Jan. 1913, Redmond papers, N.L.I., PC 262 (vi).

[60] Comparison of appendices in I.U.A., *Annual reports*, 1906–13; and the increase in small subscriptions shown in I.U.A. Subscription book would seem to confirm assertions about increasing interest in unionism in the south made at I.U.A. a.g.m., 1913 in *D.D.E.*, 25 Apr. 1913.

[61] J. M. Wilson at I.U.A. a.g.m., 1913, *D.D.E.*, 25 Apr. 1913; minute book of the Joint Committee of the Unionist Associations of Ireland, 25 Mar. 1914.

[62] Ibid., 31 Jul., 5 Sept. 1913.

Asquith for the first of their compromise talks, a letter was published in *The Times* from Lord Barrymore, then chairman of the I.U.A. He complained of the dominance of the Ulster question and demanded that southern unionists, opposed as ever to home rule, ' should have an opportunity of laying the true facts before the British people and taking their verdict at a general election '.[63] This carefully phrased letter was, in fact, a threat to the unionist leadership, for southern unionists had realised what was happening and determined to represent their real viewpoint to the unionist party and leadership. Prior to the publication of Barrymore's letter the vice-chairman of the I.U.A. had written privately to Carson that there was a ' strong feeling amongst a number of the unionists in Dublin, Cork and elsewhere ' that their case was being overlooked,

but we at headquarters here are most anxious that nothing should be done at the present juncture which could in any way embarrass you or Mr Bonar Law. We therefore thought that it would meet the situation and satisfy our people if Lord Barrymore (our chairman) were to write a letter to *The Times* and other leading newspapers reminding their leaders of the position of the unionists of the south and west without . . . in the least complicating the situation for either you or Mr Bonar Law.[64]

This letter epitomises the spirit of southern unionism and its organisation: persistent and determined, yet appealing and tactful; and its protest succeeded in making an impact upon the unionist leadership. Lansdowne wrote to Carson that Barrymore's letter ' will receive a good deal of backing '; and reminded him that although the unionists of the south and west were helpless to organise resistance to home rule in Ireland, ' they are quite powerful enough to provoke a serious outcry against us if we throw them over '.[65]

Law must have been aware of such correspondence. Even should he not have noticed these protests, the energy of the southern unionists in organising demonstrations brought home to him the southern unionist reliance upon the opposition leadership. Earlier in the year Law had been waited upon by a deputation of the I.U.A. and had agreed to address a demonstration in Dublin in the following November.[66] Any doubts about southern unionist determination would have been

[63] *The Times,* 11 Oct. 1913.

[64] G. F. Stewart to Carson, 8 Oct. 1913, Carson papers, P.R.O.N.I.

[65] Lansdowne to Carson, n.d., in I. Colvin, *The life of Lord Carson* (1934), ii. 220-2; see also Lansdowne to A.C., 12 Dec. 1913, AC 11/1/56.

[66] *Notes from Ireland* (1913), p. 38.

dispersed when Law attended on 28 November 'the most impressive and significant demonstration ever held south of the Boyne', as Carson's biographer, none too sympathetic to the southern unionists, described it.[67] Prior to the demonstration Law received protests against home rule from unionists throughout the south and west of Ireland; and it must have been with a twinge of conscience that, in reply to these thirty-one addresses, he declared :

I did not need these addresses to know how strong and how real is the feeling in favour of unionism on the part of those districts of the great country to which you belong.[68]

Southern unionist pressure upon the opposition mounted in 1914, mainly through a sub-committee of the I.U.A. headed by Lord Midleton.[69] He had entered the commons in 1880 and had quickly risen to prominence and to government rank owing to his criticism of Gladstone's Irish policy.[70] Indeed, despite his later alienation of the I.U.A., the defence of the union was the underlying theme of most of his career. Soon after he entered the house of lords, on his father's death in 1907, he became leader of the Irish peers there, and kept their interests to the fore, for example, when the reform of the lords was being discussed in 1910–11.[71] This emphasis upon the Irish question is not surprising, for Midleton derived the greater part of his income from estates in Cork.[72] Closely associated with the I.U.A. until 1919,[73] he assiduously put the southern unionist viewpoint before his conservative colleagues and the press, especially from 1911 onwards when unionism in Ulster seemed to be obscuring the existence of unionist opinion in the south of Ireland.[74] He thus took his duties as head of the I.U.A. sub-committee seriously in 1914 and tried to prevent the 'shadow cabinet' from effecting a compromise based on the exclusion of Ulster.[75] These efforts on behalf of the I.U.A. were

[67] Colvin, p. 247; or rather he accepted such a description.
[68] *Notes from Ireland* (1913), p. 112.
[69] I.U.A. to Carson, P.R.O.N.I., D 989/12a/1.
[70] *D.N.B., 1941–50*, p. 108.
[71] Midleton's memo. on house of lords reform, 21 Mar. 1911, B.M., Add. MS 49721, ff. 255–62.
[72] G.E.C., *Complete peerage*, viii. 701–706.
[73] *Irish Times* 25 Jan. 1919.
[74] Colvin, pp. 249–50; see above.
[75] I.U.A. to Carson, 1914, P.R.O.N.I., D 989/12a/1; Midleton's memo. on the amending bill, 23 Jun. 1914, B.M., Add. MS 49721, ff. 302–5.

complemented by the activities of individual southern unionists, quick to threaten a split in the conservative party should the leadership countenance compromise instead of a general election.[76] This was the unanimity which Law so feared. In face of it the discussions of the 'shadow cabinet' were dominated by considerations of Irish loyalists.[77] All that the opposition could do was to drift towards crisis, putting forward demands for the exclusion of Ulster known to be unacceptable to the government and the Irish nationalists,[78] and taking up the southern unionist cry of dissolution.[79]

Clearly, then, the southern unionists were a significant force in British, if not in Irish, politics. Their efficient and energetic campaign throughout British politics is sufficient to explain why the unionist party should have been more aware of the southern unionist viewpoint than the liberals. But it is another thing to explain why the unionist party was so susceptible to southern unionist pressure as to allow that viewpoint to dominate opposition thinking between 1906 and 1914; and why the party was more responsive to southern unionism than to Ulster unionism. The short answer is that the southern unionists were better placed than the Ulster unionists throughout the unionist party; the fuller explanation is threefold.

(1) In the first place Irish unionists, especially those of the southern provinces, were well represented within the unionist party at all levels. They were well placed in the policy-making section of that party and worked through such leaders to ensure the best presentation of their case. As is well known, unionist policy was at that time determined by a small group of some twenty or thirty leaders comprising the 'shadow cabinet', and an even smaller number was frequently, though informally, consulted by the official leaders of the party in the commons and the lords.[80] Of these the most influential

---

[76] See e.g. Lord Oranmore and Browne's letter in *The Times,* 19 May 1914 protesting against a leader article which held that opposition to home rule (outside Ulster) was no longer practical politics.

[77] See e.g. A.C. to Mary, 4 May 1914, AC 4/1/1131.

[78] See e.g. Colvin, p. 397.

[79] See e.g. Carson's speeches in G.B., especially at Herne Hill, 5 July 1914, Colvin, pp. 402, 414-5.

[80] B. Dugdale, *Arthur James Balfour* (1936), ii. 25; R. T. MacKenzie, *British political parties* (1st ed., London, 1955), p. 75; Sir Charles Petrie, *The life and letters of the rt. hon. Sir A. Chamberlain* (1939), i. 229 *et seq.*; Petrie, *Walter Long*, pp. 171 ff.; Blake, p. 103; A.C. to Mary, 1 Mar. 1912, AC 4/1/765.

were Irish unionists.[81] Among leading unionists in the lords were four southern unionists, the fifth marquis of Lansdowne, the ninth Viscount Midleton, the first Baron Ashbourne and the eighth and ninth dukes of Devonshire; and one Ulsterman, the sixth marquess of Londonderry. In the commons there were two southerners, Sir Edward Carson and Walter Long (who regarded himself as a southern unionist);[82] and Law, who may by origin and outlook be classed as an Ulsterman.[83] Such leaders constantly urged the Irish unionist viewpoint upon their colleagues. Lansdowne and Midleton were associated with the I.U.A.;[84] both derived the greater part of their income from estates in the south of Ireland;[85] and it has been suggested how active they were on behalf of the southern unionists.[86]

The Irish unionists were also important to the unionist opposition in both houses of parliament. In 1914, though only two unionists sat for southern Irish constituencies, the fact that southern unionists had close British connections enabled eighteen southerners to sit for British constituencies, while there were eighteen Ulstermen in sixteen Ulster and two British seats.[87] The very number of Irish unionists in the commons was significant. After 1906 the numerical weakness of the opposition made the solid support of the Irish unionists seem more important than ever;[88] and after the closely fought elections of 1910 their importance was enhanced, for without the Irish unionists the differences between the two major parties in the commons would have been greater.[89] But their importance and influence really depended upon the way in which they worked within the party.

[81] Buckland, pp. 514–45.

[82] Between the I.U.A. and Long there existed a mutual admiration society. See e.g. reports of I.U.A. meetings attended by Long, in *D.D.E.*, 4 Jan., 30 Aug. 1906.

[83] Blake, pp. 17–22.

[84] I.U.A., *Annual reports,* 1906–13, appendix A; see above.

[85] G.E.C., *Complete peerage,* vii. 436–43, viii. 701–706.

[86] See above.

[87] Figures based upon information in *Dod's parliamentary companion, 1914.*

[88] See e.g. A.C.'s comment on the death of Col. Saunderson, M.P., the leader of the Irish unionist M.P.s, in A.C. to Mary, 27 Oct. 1906, AC 4/1/111 : 'He is a real loss, especially at this time, as he exercised some influence over that very wild body of men, the Irish unionist M.P.s.'

[89] See e.g. W. Long to A.J.B., 3 Apr. 1910, B.M., Add. MS 49777, ff. 65–7. That Balfour appreciated their importance is shown in Sandars to A.J.B., 14 Feb. 1911, B.M., Add. MS 49767, ff. 99–110.

By assiduously courting the unionist party, personal contacts reinforcing the political propaganda of the I.U.A. and Joint Committee of the Unionist Associations of Ireland, Irish unionists created between Irish unionists and British conservative parliamentarians an attachment which could never have been achieved between the liberals and the nationalists, the latter insisting on holding themselves aloof from the intimate side of British politics. The success of Walter Long's Union Defence League testifies to this;[90] but in this respect southern unionists attained more influence than did the Ulster unionists, as perhaps is indicated by the greater number of marriages of British conservative M.P.s into southern, rather than Ulster, unionist families.[91] Although the political support of the Ulster unionists was regarded as valuable,[92] their ' prejudice and intolerance '[93] caused personal revulsion among many British conservatives, especially when that fanaticism had political consequences, such as leading the Ulstermen to vote against the party as in 1908. In that year Ulster unionists complained that some conservative by-election candidates were paying insufficient attention to the Irish question; while on May 4, some Ulster members voted against the party upon the licensing bill. The result was that their complaints about candidates fell upon unfavourable ground, Balfour's secretary, Sandars, tartly recording:

Moreover . . . the action of the north of Ireland members in the division on the licensing bill last night is not calculated to recommend their advocacy of unionist interests in Ireland to the English electorate. It would have been regrettable that they should *abstain* on a matter of such interest to the party as the licensing bill, but that they should deliberately vote against their party in respect of a bill which applies to England but does not apply to Ireland is outrageous. They had to listen to some very straight talk last evening.[94]

---

[90] W. Long, *Memories* (1923), passim, though he exaggerates the League's electoral work. See also A. M. Gollin, *Proconsul in politics* (1964), pp. 185–7, 190; and Buckland, pp. 456–8, 461–2.

[91] *Dod*, 1914. There appear to have in 1914 seven British M.P.s married into southern unionist families and only two into Ulster unionist families.

[92] Lord Cawdor to Sandars, 1 Feb. 1909, B.M., Add. MS 49709, ff. 63–4.

[93] Sandars to A.J.B., 13 Jan. 1907, B.M., Add. MS 49765, ff. 5–8.

[94] Ibid., 5 May 1908, ff. 148–51.

Even apart from such issues, the Ulster unionists lacked tact.[95] On the other hand, southern unionists, ever aware of the wider issue of the union,[96] always acted with the unionist party, moving easily, like Walter Guinness[97] or Edward Goulding, within the party, merging into the main body of unionist M.P.s and becoming active and influential on the back-benches in a non-controversial way. Of Edward Goulding, D.L. for county Cork, J.P. for London, member for Worcester, friend of Austen Chamberlain and Bonar Law and leader of many sorties against the government on divers issues,[98] Robert Blake has truly said that he was

one of those back benchers who are never serious aspirants for office, but who, by their hospitality, their energy in party manoeuvres, their love of gossip, and of intrigue in the better sense of the word, exercise an influence upon party politics which is apt to be overlooked by the historian.[99]

More significantly, perhaps, although he was a leading tariff reformer, Goulding was prepared in 1912–13 to subordinate his fiscal views to the cause of the union.[100]

More politically important, after 1906, when the unionist party relied upon the house of lords to redress the verdict of the constituencies, was the Irish unionist representation in the house of lords. Again the southern, as opposed to the Ulster, unionists predominated. In 1914, for instance, 104 peers had Irish interests, 28 being Irish representative peers; and of the total, 86 had interests in the south of Ireland, their influence being increased by connections through marriage.[101] This group of Irish peers, led after 1907 by Lord Midleton, had their own organisation[102] and had in the past secured

[95] See e.g. letter of complaint from the secretary of the British League for the Support of Ulster and the Union, T. Comyn Platt to Bates (sec. of U.U.C.), 6 Apr. 1914, P.R.O.N.I., D 1327/4/2.
[96] I.U.A., *Annual report, 1907–8,* pp. 9–10.
[97] A.C. to Mary, 21, 30 Nov. 1906, 16, 18 May 1908, 17 June 1909, AC 4/1/120, 122, 272, 273, 444.
[98] *Dod, 1908*; Sandars to A.J.B., 10 Mar. 1910, B.M., Add. MS 49766, ff. 161–73, and 18 Jan. 1911, ibid., 49767, ff. 86–9; Blake, ch. V.
[99] Blake, p. 52.
[100] A. M. Gollin, *The Observer and J. L. Garvin* (1960), pp. 380–3.
[101] *Dod, 1914.*
[102] Midleton's memo. on house of lords reform, 21 Mar. 1911, B.M., Add. MS 49721, ff. 255–62. He says that Irish peers 'have a good organisation, a strong sense of grievance and a scant belief in protection by the front bench and by English colleagues'.

the defeat of Salisbury's government.[103] Their very number made Irish peers important. For instance, when in 1911 two different sections of the opposition were whipping up support for their respective views on the parliament bill, special efforts were considered to win over these Irish peers.[104] Apart from number, though partly because of it, peers with Irish interests provided some of the most prominent and active members of the unionist party in the house of lords. In addition to leaders like Lansdowne and other members of the ' shadow cabinet ', the Irish unionists—though the evidence for this is scanty[105] —appear to have been the mainsprings of what means existed for consultation between front and back bench opposition peers on matters of high policy. This was through the ' so-called Donoughmore committee ', dominated, it would appear, by Lord Donoughmore, an active member of the I.U.A.[106]

Irish unionists also possessed considerable influence in the constituency organisations. This can be partly attributed to the close connections that they maintained with Great Britain through family and property;[107] but more politically impelling was the effect of the anti-home rule campaign waged by Irish unionists at a time when conservative organisation was defective. The state of British conservative organisation was such that the central office could offer little assistance by way of speakers or other workers to local associations, who thus felt neglected and disgruntled, especially when confronted with what they regarded as an efficient radical machine.[108] Into this unhappy situation entered the Irish unionists. They offered to arrange and to publicise meetings and to provide speakers, canvassers and literature, especially at election time, in those areas where a little extra

[103] R. B. McDowell, *British conservatism, 1832–1914* (1959), p. 117.

[104] Selborne to Carson, 26 July 1911, Carson Papers, P.R.O.N.I.

[105] Consisting of a letter from Lansdowne to Sandars relating to unionist policy and house of lords reform, 2 May 1911, B.M., Add. MS 49730, ff. 236–7.

[106] *Dod, 1910*; *D.D.E.*, 24 Apr. 1910; I.U.A., *Annual reports, 1906–1913*, appendices.

[107] E.g. Midleton, whose family had long held estates in Cork and Surrey, appears to have been in touch with the Surrey M.P.s. See Midleton to Carson, 11 Nov. 1913, quoted in Colvin, pp. 249–50.

[108] For state of conservative organisation see Sandars to A.J.B., 11 Oct. 1909, B.M., Add. MS 49766, ff. 15–6; 19, 21 Jan., 18 Mar., 24 Sept. 1910, ibid., 49766, ff. 71–4, 75–80, 186–95, 247–9; 19 Dec. 1910, ibid., 49767, ff. 44–9; Sandars to Lansdowne, 6 Nov. 1909, ibid., 49730, ff. 21–6.

effort might possibly secure the return of the conservative candidate.[109] All this was done at very little cost to the local association, who got the credit for their cooperation and who could feel that they were no longer neglected but rather part of a larger cause.

Throughout the period 1906–14 the services of the I.U.A. and then of the Joint Committee of the Unionist Associations of Ireland were in constant demand by local British conservative associations,[110] with the result that the unionist party became tied at grass roots level to the cause of the Irish unionists. The campaign ensured that conservative organisations and candidates maintained a firm opposition to the various stages of liberal policy towards Ireland;[111] but more than this the defective state of conservative organisation in Great Britain and the efficiency and persistence of Irish unionist campaigning created a feeling among local conservatives that their success was dependent in large part upon the Irish unionists. After the second general election of 1910, in which the Joint Committee had sent 278 workers into 282 British constituencies and had circulated almost three million pamphlets and leaflets,[112] the conservative eastern district agent in England wrote to the acting secretary of the I.U.A.:

Let me thank you and those with you for the immense help you have given us; my only sorrow being that the results appear perhaps to you so meagre. But let me assure you that without your help the conservative party at the present moment would not be nearly so strong as they are.[113]

Even when conservative candidates were unsuccessful the Irish unionists reaped benefit, sometimes receiving very fulsome letters from

[109] I.L.P.U., Executive council minute book, 1886–9, 25 June, 6 Aug. 1886, 30 Sept. 1887; I.U.A., *Annual report, 1906–7*, pp. 16–17; I.U.A., Finance committee minute book, 2, 15 Apr. 1907, P.R.O.N.I., D 989/4/1; minute book of the Joint Committee of the Unionist Associations of Ireland, passim.

[110] See e.g. minute book of the Joint Committee of the Unionist Associations of Ireland, 31 Dec. 1908, 19 Oct. 1911.

[111] E.g. after the Joint Committee had decided to step up its campaign in 1913–14, particularly in respect of the distribution of (free) literature, the U.A.I.'s eastern agent was able to report that 'a good many of the Secretaries' of conservative clubs and reading rooms had undertaken to 'have prominently displayed' the U.A.I.'s literature and that 'many agents . . . are at present engaged in making a special anti-home rule campaign in their division', minute book of the Joint Committee of the Unionist Associations of Ireland, 20 Feb. 1914.

[112] Bate's report on general election work, ibid., 4 Jan. 1911.

[113] Quoted in Ball's report, ibid., 4 Jan. 1911.

grateful candidates or their agents asking the organisation to 'keep yourself in readiness against future demands by me '.[114]

What these and similar letters[115] signify is that the Irish unionists had the organisation and good will in a good number of British constituencies to convert,[116] with the help of their power in the unionist parliamentary party, that dislike of compromise, normal in constituency politics, into a party revolt, should the unionist leadership consider a policy not acceptable to them.

(2) It was not, however, that the unionist party's attitude on the Irish question was a mere cynical response to the persistent political pressures of Irish unionism. A second reason for the opposition's attachment to the Irish unionist cause was that that cause was acceptable to British conservatives. The Irish unionist case appealed to the more imperially-minded members of the opposition, for Irish unionists were careful to link home rule with the disintegration of the empire.[117] This was to the benefit of Irish unionists in general; but the southern unionist case made an especial appeal to the opposition. Whereas the Ulster case undoubtedly made a direct appeal to men like Law[118] and to Scottish nonconformists,[119] the southern unionist case had a wider appeal to those landed British conservatives who comprised the most effective part of the entire opposition party.[120]

---

[114] Letter from the defeated unionist candidate in the West Lothian by-election, 1913, quoted in Bates's scottish report, minute book of the Joint Committee of the Unionist Associations of Ireland, 18 Nov. 1913.

[115] See e.g. ibid., 18 Jan. 1911, 4 Aug. 1914.

[116] In England from September 1911 to the middle of July 1914 the Joint Committee of the Unionist Associations of Ireland organised over 5,000 meetings, canvassed 1,246,225 doubtful voters in over 200 constituencies and assisted at 23 contested elections. In the same period in Scotland 3,843 meetings were held, 205,654 doubtful voters were canvassed and aid was given in 10 by-elections. An estimated 6 million booklets, leaflets and pamphlets were distributed throughout Great Britain in these months. See minute book of the Joint Committee of the Unionist Associations of Ireland, passim.

[117] See e.g. the speech by Chamberlain's theorist, Professor Hewins, at I.U.A. a.g.m., 1913, *D.D.E.*, 25 Apr. 1913.

[118] Blake, p. 17–22.

[119] See e.g. report of the activity of the Unionist Associations of Ireland at the Leith by-election in *The Times*, 26 Feb. 1914.

[120] W. L. Guttsmann, 'The changing social structure of the British political elite, 1886–1935 ', *British Journal of Sociology*, ii (1951), pp. 122–4; Guttsmann, 'Aristocracy and middle classes in the British political

There existed between the landed and aristocratic southern unionists and British conservatives a general sympathy symbolised in the close attachment of Walter Long, the epitome of the English country gentleman,[121] to the southern unionist cause. In the twentieth century this sympathy was all the stronger when the landed classes in both Great Britain and Ireland felt under pressure. Southern unionists, fearing that under home rule their estates would be heavily taxed, if not confiscated, insisted upon identifying the union as the barrier to socialism.[122] Put this way, their appeal could hardly fail to arouse a warm response among landed men like Walter Long, who was under pressure and having to sell part of his estates,[123] and among old conservatives such as the fifth marquis of Salisbury, who was anxious to rally 'cautious men who will join me in resistance to restless change'.[124]

(3) A third reason is, however, necessary to complete the explanation of how the Irish unionist viewpoint could dominate the thinking of a major British party after 1906, even at times when the liberal government were trying to avoid the Irish question. Were there not any other British issues upon which the unionist party could take a united and fruitful stand? The plain truth was that there were not. British conservatism was split, if not exhausted, by an internecine dispute over the question of tariff reform; but neither faction was sufficiently in sympathy with the liberals to desert completely the unionist party, and both were determined to convert the undecided mass of the party to their respective viewpoints. There were, therefore, two factions, both in different degrees on the defensive, and a party leader searching for common ground. Such circumstances provided a splendid opportunity for a well-organised and well-placed body with a clearly defined object and a simple and acceptable appeal to insinuate itself and its views into the party and to become dominant.

elite, 1886–1916', ibid., v (1954), pp. 12–32. For an interesting illustration of such statistical evidence see Ld. Mount-Edgecombe to A.C., 18 Jan. 1909, and A.C. to Mount-Edgecombe, 19 Jan. 1909, AC 17/3/75–6.

[121] See Petrie, *Walter Long*, passim; Long to A.C., 6 June, 6, 7 July 1905, AC 16/3/62–3, 65, concerning the working of the 1903 land act on terms favourable to the Irish unionists.

[122] Lords Ardilaun and Longford reported in *D.D.E.*, 29 Aug. 1908, 23 Apr. 1910.

[123] F. S. L. Thompson, *English landed society in the nineteenth century* (1963), p. 322.

[124] Salisbury to A.C., 12 Feb. 1910, AC 8/5/10.

Licensing and denominationalism were the two other issues which separated the conservatives from the liberals; but, though it is ironic to note that without the home rule question the nationalists would have been inclined to vote with the conservatives on these two other issues, both interests had political or electoral drawbacks. Irish unionism on the other hand had organisation, power throughout the party and a generally acceptable appeal to take advantage of the vacuum created by the fiscal dispute.[125]

Although Irish unionists in the main accepted the need for fiscal change, their prime concern was the maintenance of the union. As a body they did not take any part in the controversy over the merits of fiscal reform, but concentrated on keeping the party united and rallied to its leaders. This they did in two related ways: by encouraging the unionist leaders to avoid either extreme; and by ensuring that no reliable or talented opponents of the liberal government were excluded from the party or from parliament on account of their fiscal views. Their hope was that both free traders and tariff reformers 'would declare fully for the maintenance of the union and unionist principles first'.[126] This expectation was realised, for the Irish unionists came to be regarded as a useful body of support in the party and the middle fiscal course was hardly a platform. Thus the net result of their mediation was that the Irish unionists succeeded in attaching not only both fiscal wings, but also the whole party, to their cause.

There are many instances of this process of attachment,[127] but the best documented example of the way in which Irish unionists ensured that their views would prevail and of the way in which the divisions of British conservatism assisted them is the Kendal by-election of 1913. The fact that this by-election occurred in the midst of the struggle over the third home rule bill only increases its significance as committing the opposition to the Irish unionist interpretation of the Irish question.

[125] See Buckland, pp. 576–605.

[126] *The Times*, 2 Nov. 1905; see also Londonderry to A.C., 5 Nov. 1905, AC 17/3/14, 16; Londonderry to A.J.B., 5 Nov. 1905, B.M., Add. MS 49802, ff. 101–2.

[127] See e.g. the way in which Long helped Balfour to avoid fiscal amendments to the Address, A.J.B. to A.C., 9 Feb. 1907, AC 7/6/18; the way Irish unionists rallied support for Law's leadership in 1912–13, Buckland, pp. 595–8; and the way in which Long negotiated between unionist free trade candidates and the party organisation, Long to A.J.B., 29 Dec. 1907, B.M., Add. MS 49776, ff. 229–34, and R. Cecil to A.J.B., 16, 21 Mar. 1909, ibid., 49737, ff. 90–1, 92–4.

Colonel Weston was selected on 8 March 1913 as conservative candidate for the vacancy in the Kendal division of Westmoreland, caused by the death of the sitting conservative member, Colonel Bagot. He was chosen as an influential and active local man, for years interested in local government and affairs and a large employer of labour in the district. Appealing as 'Westmoreland born and bred', and fighting the government on its declared policy as a whole, he seemed to be an ideal candidate.[128] The only difficulty was that he was a free trader, in favour of the then existing fiscal system. Local conservative leaders were aware of this and not at all perturbed. 'By postponing tariff reform we have knocked our radical friends off their perch', was the racy comment of the chairman of the local executive.[129]

The central organisers of the conservative movement in Great Britain did not see it this way. Only in December had the party been brought to a standstill over the tariff question, and a compromise had been patched up. The ardent tariff reformers, not pleased with that compromise, were fuming within the party and tempers were mounting.[130] Should the unionist leadership countenance further withdrawals from the policy of tariff reform, the effects upon the party were unpredictable. Therefore since the selection of Colonel Weston and the publication of his fiscal views, the central office had been negotiating with the local leaders in the hope of devising a means of escape.[131] Colonel Weston was not, however, willing to declare himself in agreement with the party on the fiscal question; and his committee stood by him. Therefore the central office repudiated Weston, its three agents and twenty speakers, sent before his fiscal views were known, being withdrawn.[132]

This repudiation and withdrawal left only the twenty workers of the Unionist Associations of Ireland, who had been at work in the constituency since the opening of the campaign. The Irish unionists did not judge a candidate by his fiscal views and were anxious to

[128] *The Times,* 8, 12 Mar. 1913.

[129] Ibid., 12 Mar. 1913.

[130] See e.g. A.C. to Mary, for Jan. and Feb., but especially 8–9, 16 Mar. 1913, AC 4/1/942, 948.

[131] Speech by Law (ironically) at Manchester Free Trade Hall on 18 Mar., reported in *The Times,* 19 Mar. 1913; also election report, ibid., 15 Mar. 1913.

[132] *The Times,* 14, 15 Mar. 1913.

prevent the return of home rule candidates.[133] 'The simple fact that Colonel Weston was opposed to the government made him worthy of support', commented one Irish unionist.[134] Therefore the Joint Committee's workers under the northern agent remained as Weston's 'mainstay in speakers and canvassers'. Weston appreciated this help and on 17 March, four days after the withdrawal of central office support, wrote to the headquarters of the association in Dublin thanking them for their assistance and declaring that he would regard his return as a victory for the union.[135]

The sequence of events is most important. Weston had begun his campaign as a free trader, allegedly as an advocate of the settlement of home rule by consent, taking as his main plank compulsory military training. At first the contest revolved around this issue; even the Irish nationalist M.P., who came to speak for the liberal candidate, took as his text not the blessings of home rule, but the evils of conscription barrack-life on the continent.[136] Then on 13 March the central office withdrew its workers from the constituency. After he became thus dependent upon Irish unionist support, Weston adopted as his chief plank opposition to home rule. He was returned with a majority of 581 and the Irish unionists duly reaped their reward—notice that he wrote to the southern unionist office—Weston declaring 'if with God's help my return should assist the loyalists of Ireland, I shall indeed be truly thankful'.[137] Although those who disliked the 'whole-hoggers' were pleased at the Irish unionists' independent support for Weston,[138] it must be admitted that the policy was not without its dangers for Irish unionist relations with the tariff reformers.[139] Weston's success, however, offset any hostility that might have spread, the mass of the unionist party being grateful for the Irish unionists' contribution to the party's success.[140] Clearly the fiscal dispute gave Irish unionists an opportunity which they were quick to grasp.

[133] *Irish Times,* 18 Mar. 1913.
[134] *The Times,* 20 Mar. 1913.
[135] *The Times,* 18 Mar. 1913.
[136] Ibid., 12, 13 Mar. 1913.
[137] *The Times,* 20 Mar. 1913; minute book of the Joint Committee of the Unionist Associations of Ireland, 21 Apr. 1913.
[138] Sandars to A.J.B., 23 Mar. 1913, B.M., Add. MS 49768, ff. 42–5.
[139] A.C. to Mary, 16 Mar. 1913, AC 4/1/948.
[140] See e.g. leader comment in *The Times,* 20 Mar. 1913.

Another circumstance assisted the Irish unionists when the third home rule bill was being discussed. In 1911 the unionist party had allowed the parliament bill to pass through the house of lords, an action characterised by some as surrender. The result was to increase that feeling of futility engendered by the fiscal dispute and to intensify a determination on the part of a significant section of the unionist party not to compromise on home rule.[141]

Just in case any unionist did flirt with home rule, there was an incident to remind him of the influence that Irish unionists could, and would, exert within the party, should they feel that they were being betrayed. This was the famous 'devolution crisis' or 'MacDonnell mystery', which, if it did not bring down Balfour's government in 1905, certainly paralysed the opposition in 1906.[142] Balfour clearly remembered the incident[143] and it is a tribute to the power of the Irish unionists that, when in 1910 a few members of the opposition were canvassing federalism, Balfour forwarded to Austen Chamberlain 'a pair of Irish unionist letters—the first drops in the storm which will assuredly break over us if any new departure be admitted'.[144]

Of these Irish unionists the southern unionists were the more influential in terms of conservative politics, giving the conservative party in Great Britain a politically impelling commitment on the Irish question. This fact had serious consequences for British and Irish politics, and helps to explain the so-called failure of British statesmen to solve the Irish question for many years. The agitation of the southern unionists in British politics delayed the most rational solution to the problem of reconciling the aspirations of the larger nationalist majority in Ireland with the prejudices and interests of the Ulster protestants. Furthermore, since the liberals had an equally impelling but opposite commitment on the Irish question, the existence of an united and active unionist opinion in the south of Ireland allowed the Irish question to influence and embitter British politics, especially after 1912. Anxious to defend the southern unionists, and feeling magnanimous in their defence, the conservative party in Great Britain

[141] Law, 'Notes on conversation with the P.M.', 15 Oct. 1913, quoted in Blake, pp. 161–2.

[142] Buckland, pp. 607–20, based mainly upon a file of letters relating to the 'mystery' among A.C.'s correspondence, AC7/4 passim, and Sandars to A.J.B., B.M., Add. MS 49764, passim.

[143] A.J.B. to Cawdor, 7 Jan. 1909, B.M., Add. MS 49709, ff. 59–60.

[144] A.J.B. to A.C., 27 Oct. 1910, AC 10/2/10.

was willing to condone the direct action of the Ulster unionists and to countenance other scarcely constitutional steps. Only with the altered conditions of British political life after the war and with the disunity of southern unionists could the partition of Ireland become practical politics and the Irish question be taken out of British politics.

INDEX

Abercorn, Duke of, 337, 356
Acland, A.H.D., 251, 269, 271
Adams, W.G.S., 299
agricultural labourers, 23, 182-3, 214, 326
agricultural problems (depression, distress), 24, 33, 35, 37, 42, 59, 65
Akers-Douglas, A., 332
'All-for-Ireland League', 195, 314
'All Ireland' Catholic Association, 190, 194
Amery, L.S, 307, 309, 315
Amnesty Association, 38, 42, 45
Ancient Order of Hibernians, 194-5
Anderson, R., 22-3
Annual Register, 7, 14
anthem, 6-8, 15-19
Anti-Contagious Acts Association, 240
Anti-Corn Law League, 244, 252, 260
Anti-Parnellites, 187-8
Antonelli, Cardinal, 122, 141, 157, 160-1
Ardilaum, Lord, 360
Arnold, A., 279
Arnold, M., 240
Arnold Forster, H.O., 361
'Articles Club', 269
Ashbourne Act (1885), 350
Ashbourne, Baron, 380
Asquith, H.H., 269, 281, 285, 288-9, 293, 297-8, 303, 307-8, 312-13, 315-16, 375-6
athletics, 95-9, 101, 105, 107-9

Bagehot, W., 223
Bagot, Colonel, 388
Balfour, A.J., 115, 238, 322, 349, 351-61, 363, 374, 381, 390
Balfour, G., 359-60, 363
Ballot Act (1872), 33-5, 37, 49, 51, 55-9
Banbury, Sir F., 312
Baptist, The, 259, 266-7
Barran, R., 293
Barry, W., 102
Barrymore, Lord, 360, 377
Bear, W.E., 242
Belfast Catholic Association, 190-1
Belfast News-Letter, 336
Bendix, R., 63
Bennett, E., 112-14
Berrington, H., 264

Biggar, J., 101
Birrell, A., 192-4, 269, 297, 301-8, 313
Blake, R., 382
Blennerhassett, R.P., 49-54
Blennerhassett, Sir R., 55
Blunt, Sir W., 302, 319, 328
Boer War, 286, 288, 294
Boland, J., 97
Borrow, G., 36
Bourne, Archbishop F., 192
Bowles, T.G., 298
Bracken, J.K., 97, 102, 104, 106-7, 112
Bradlaugh, C., 278, 280, 334
Bradley, J.A., 113
Bright, J., 51, 147, 149, 161, 164, 213, 223-4, 252, 256, 265
Broderick, St. J. (Lord Midleton), 324-5, 356, 368-9, 372, 378, 380, 382
Brotherhood of St. Patrick, 123-4
Browne, Bishop, 120
Browne, G., 45
Bryce, J., 193, 271, 302
Buckingham Palace Conference, 374
Buller, Sir R., 351
Bunting, P., 271
Burns, J., 266, 306
Burt, T., 280
Butler, Bishop, 144
Butler, J., 104
Butler, Sir T., 370
Butt, I., 38-9, 42-3, 46, 48-9, 58, 83-4, 234, 321-2, 324
Buxton, S., 269

Caine, W.S., 249, 263, 272, 276
Cairnes, J.E., 206, 209, 220, 222, 228-9
Callan, P., 45
Campbell, G., 234-5
Campbell-Bannerman, Sir H., 247, 255, 288, 291-2, 322
Carew, J.L., 353
Carnarvon, Lord, 329-30
Carson, Sir E., 309, 361, 375-8, 380
Castledown, Lord, 357, 359
Castlereagh, Viscount, 323-4
Castlerosse, Lord, 52
Catholics, catholicism, 5-6, 10, 13, 16, 37-8, 43-4, 48, 50, 56-8, 64, 66-9, 73, 120-4, 127, 135-7, 141, 143-4, 150, 157, 162, 165, 168, 191-2, 196, 199,

217, 220-1, 321, 334, 339, 342, 366
Catholic Association, 67
Catholic Church, 36, 42, 47, 59, 67, 73, 143,
    156-7, 159, 161, 164, 168-9, 176, 181,
    187-8, 192, 195, 197, 201-3, 207, 220,
    338
Catholic Emancipation, 10-11, 57, 73, 119,
    206-7, 338
Catholic Young Men's Society, 31-2
Causton, R.K., 272
Cecil, Lord H., 309
Celtic Times, 107
Centenary of 1798 Rebellion, 287
Central Board Scheme, 348
Chalmers, R., 303
Chamberlain, A., 374, 382, 390
Chamberlain, J., 240-3, 245, 249, 251-3,
    259, 262, 265, 267-70, 279, 283, 287,
    294, 299-300, 330, 332, 348-50, 352-5,
    359, 361, 363
Chaplin, H., 326
Childers, E., 302
Childers, H., 300
Churchill, B., 323, 337
Churchill, Lord R., 319-45 *passim,* 349,
    363
Churchill, Sir W.S., 303, 323, 340-2
citizen army, 15, 17
Clerkenwell explosion, 211-12
Clonbrook, Lord, 360
Cobden, R., 244
coercion, 66, 239, 263, 292, 295, 327,
    336, 342, 359, 367
Confederation of Kilkenny, 5
Coffey, Bishop, 172
Cole, G.D.H., 259
Collings, J., 250
Collins, Sergeant, 114
Compensation for Tenants' Improvements,
    130-1, 133, 137, 139, 145, 147-8, 155,
    206, 210, 214, 229, 235
Congested Districts Board, 169, 172
Connaught Telegraph, 71
conscription, 201
Conservative(s), party, 38, 40-50, 52, 55-7,
    84, 118-19, 131, 134, 144, 148-9, 155-
    7, 163, 165, 178, 190, 192-3, 217-18,
    223, 227, 229, 230, 239, 242, 261, 278,
    298, 321, 325, 328-32, 336-40, 342-4,
    347-9, 352-3, 355, 358-9, 366-8, 373,
    379, 381, 383-8, 390
Constructive (Enlightened) Unionism, 323,
    325, 340-2, 344, 347
Contemporary Review, 251
Cooke, E.T., 292

Co-operative Movement, 167, 170-8,
    180-5
Cork Examiner, 12, 113, 175
Cork Exhibition, 171
Cornford, J., 265
Corrigan, Sir D., 44
Councils Bill (1907), 193, 295
Cowper Commission, 351
Crewe, Lord, 291, 294
Croke, Archbishop T., 96-7, 100-1, 103-
    5, 107, 109, 111, 114, 187
Cullen, Cardinal P., 21, 47, 117-18, 120,
    123-38, 140-7, 149-65
Cunningham Graham, R.B., 266
Curragh Incident, 366
Curtis, L.P., Jr., 239
Cusack, M., 95-100, 102-3

Dahrendorf, R., 63, 74
Daily News, 225, 227-9
Daily Record and Mail, 292
Daly, J. (Limerick), 25
D'Arcy, M., 56
Daunt, W.J.O'N., 21, 35
Davies, J., 62, 64-5
Davin, M., 96, 98, 102-5, 107, 109, 112-
    13
Davis, T., 7, 95, 127, 196
Davitt, M., 69-70, 73, 96, 101, 104-5, 111,
    178, 196
Dawson, C., 11-12, 14
Dease, E., 50-1, 53, 55
Delane, J.T., 224, 231
Democratic Labour Federation, 182
Denieffe, J., 24
Denny, Mr., 53
Denvir, Dr., 130
Department of Agriculture and Technical
    Instruction, 171
Derby, Lord, 148, 152, 210
Deutsch, K., 63
Devlin, J., 194
Devoy, J., 22-4, 69
Dicey, A.V., 290, 354-5; *England's Case
    Against Home Rule,* 290
Discontent Thesis, 62-6, 74-5
Digby, K., 55
Digby, M., 173, 175, 179
Dilke, Sir C., 269
Dillon, J.B., 126, 128-30, 133, 137-9, 141,
    146-8, 155
Dillon, J., 178, 187, 194-5, 202, 186-7,
    189, 292, 306-8, 362
Dineen, F.B., 104, 106, 108, 113
Disestablishment, 125, 127, 130-1, 136,

141-2, 144, 146, 149-50, 153, 155-7, 159-63, 213, 323

Disraeli, B., 32, 165, 210, 231, 320, 323, 344
Donoughmore, Lord, 383
Dorrian, Dr., 130, 133, 138-9, 146
Doughty, G., 287
Douglas, C., 293, 295
Downing, M., 38, 48, 138
Drummond, T., 131
Dublin Castle, 8, 22, 26, 101-2, 108, 151-3, 290, 321, 339, 350, 356
Dublin City flag, 14, 19
Dublin Corporation, 13-14
Dublin Evening Mail, 44
Dublin National Exhibition (1882), 3, 11
Dublin Review, 127
Dufferin, Lord, 46, 229
Duffy, C.G., 129, 135, 139
Duggan, Bishop, 97
Dunbar, J., 103
Dwyer, Bishop, 172, 183, 191-3, 198-9

Easter Monday (1916), 198
Easter Rising (1916), 15-16, 18, 197-8, 202, 317
Eastern Question, 245, 249
Ecclesiastical Titles Bill, 119, 125, 141
Economist, The, 223, 225, 227-8
education, 42-3, 46-8, 50-1, 55, 82, 120, 125, 127-8, 130, 141, 145-6, 149, 150, 153, 155, 157-62, 190-4, 199, 200, 207, 220, 288, 337, 342
Education Act (1870), 243
Edwards, F., 276
Edwards, O.D., 6
Edwards, R.D., 118
Eighty Club, 192-3
Elections (Ireland), 35-6, 38-41, 43, 45-58, 70, 80-1, 84-6, 89, 141, 148-9, 162, 199, 201-2
Ellice, E., 293
Ellis, T., 269-71
Emmott, A., 294-5
Empire, 207, 209, 212, 217
English Amateur Athletic Association, 95
Ennis, M., 307
Ensor, Sir R., 33, 42
Escott, T.H.S., 323
Esmonde, Sir J., 55
Established Church (Church of Ireland), 156-8, 160-1, 227, 231
Evans, H., 261
Evening Standard, 315
evictions, 61-2, 64-6, 74, 163
Extension of the Franchise Bill (1866), 147-8

Eyre, E.J., 212

Fabians, 253, 269, 273, 279
farmers, tenant farmers, 23-4, 31, 54, 61-2, 64-74, 80, 83, 86-9, 92-3, 163, 172-3, 175-7, 179-83, 205, 208-10, 214-17, 222, 224, 227, 230, 232-3, 235
Feierabend, I. and R., 62, 64, 75
Fenian(s), Fenianism, 3-4, 6-8, 21-33, 35-42, 45-6, 48, 50-2, 55, 58, 69-70, 95-7, 100-15, 117-26, 128-30, 132, 141-3, 145, 147, 149, 151-4, 156, 158-9, 161, 164, 197, 201, 205-11, 214, 216-17, 224, 228, 342
Fermoy, Lord, 30
festivals, 8-9
Finlay, Fr., 173-4
Firth, J.F.B., 277
Fitzgerald, P.N., 96, 104, 108, 110-15
Fitzgerald, V., 47
Fitzgibbon, G., 321-2, 335
Fitzroy, Sir A., 317
Fogarty, Bishop M., 198
Ford, J.C., 112
Forster, W.E., 322
Fortescue, C., 39, 210, 230
Fortnightly Review, 235
Fowler, H.H., 243-4, 256, 269
Fowler, Sir H., 288, 291-3
Fox, C.J., 250
Freeman, T.W., 66
Frewen, R.J., 106, 113
Fuller, J., 293-4
Furlong, Dr., 149

Gael, The, 107
Gaelic Athletic Association, 31, 95-115
Gaelic League, 97, 193, 196
Gallagher, P., 175, 177
Garibaldi, G., 125, 142-3, 151, 154
General Post Office, Dublin, 16
George, H., 276
Geschwender, J., 62
Gilloohy, Bishop, 120, 130
Gilmartin, Archbishop, 202
Gladstone, Henry, 299
Gladstone, Herbert, 253, 257, 288
Gladstone, W.E., 35, 37, 41, 43, 46, 48, 55, 117, 121, 142, 155, 160-5, 209, 220, 224, 229-31, 234-5, 239-41, 243-6, 248-60, 262-3, 274, 280, 282-3, 285-7, 289-93, 295, 298-301, 304, 319, 332-3, 339, 341, 347-50, 363, 378
Gorst, J.E., 336
Governing Passion, The, 319, 342, 344
Goulding, E., 382

Grand juries, 79, 81-2, 347-9, 354-5
Grattan, H., 3-4, 10, 12, 196
Grattan's Parliament, 10, 12
Gray, E.D., 14, 107
Gray, Sir J., 10, 126, 132, 234
Greville-Nugent, G.F., 44
Greville-Nugent, R., 41-2
Grey, Lord, 250
Grey, Sir E., 269, 285, 288-9, 293, 306
Guinness, W., 382
Gurr, T., 62
Gwyn, W.B., 34

Haldane, R.B., 250-1, 258, 269, 278-80,
    285-6, 288-9, 293
Hamer, D.A., 259, 268
Hamilton, Lord C., 337
Hamilton, Lord E.W., 336
Hamilton, Sir E.W., 293-4
Hamilton, Lord G., 325, 329
Hamilton family, 337
Hamilton, Sir R., 351
Hammond, J.L., 34
Hanham, H.J., 34, 239-40
Harcourt, Sir W., 253-5, 282-3, 286-7
harp, 5, 16, 19
Hardie, K., 266
Hardy, G., 230-1
Harmsworth, A., 294
Harrington, T.C., 253
Hartigan, J., 27
Hartington, Lord, 39, 42, 45, 50-1, 55, 241,
    289, 322, 331, 333, 348, 354, 361,
    380
Harrison, F., 268
Haslam, L., 311-13
Hauser, P., 75
Hawarden Kite, 349
Hayes, C., 18
Healy, Fr., 321-2
Healy, Archbishop J., 189, 191
Healy, M., 353
Healy, T.M., 188-9, 194-5, 334-5
Henry VIII, 5
Henry, Bishop H., 190-1
Henry, M., 47, 49
Hern, D.C., 40
Heyck, T.W., 292
Hibernian Bank, 13
Hicks Beach, Sir M., 321, 329, 339, 349-
    52
Hill, Lord A., 335
Hinds, J.T., 37
Hoctor, P.T., 96, 104, 106, 110-14
Hocker, P., 104

Hogan, Alderman, 110, 113
Holmes, H., 328-9
Home Government Association (League), 42-3,
    45-7, 55-6, 58, 84
Home Rule, 191, 193-4, 197-8, 237-8, 244-55,
    257-60, 262-4, 266-9, 271-93, 295, 297-
    315, 319-20, 324-33, 335, 339, 341-2,
    344-5, 347-9, 358-60, 365-8, 372-3,
    375-9, 386-7, 389-90
Home Rule Bill (1886), 246, 272, 299-300,
    304, 319-20, 339, 349
−, (1893), 255, 257, 289-90, 298-301, 304,
    316, 341
−, (1912/1914), 195, 200, 295, 297-8, 301-
    17, 325, 365-6, 368, 374, 376, 387, 390
Home Rule finance, 297-317
Home Rule Movement (Association, League),
    2-3, 7, 39, 43-5, 47-9, 51-8, 82
House of Commons, 9, 14, 40, 117, 133, 146,
    154, 160-1, 163, 206-9, 218, 220-1,
    223, 226, 229-33, 247, 255, 262, 273, 280,
    283, 286, 291, 309, 312-13, 315, 325, 338,
    378, 380, 383
House of Lords, 192, 255-7, 260, 267-8, 275,
    282, 286, 294-5, 364, 390
Howell, G., 261
Hughes, T., 211, 219, 223-4
Hughes, T., 211, 219, 223-4
Hyde, D., 196

Ilbert, Sir C., 308
Imperial Federation League, 290
Incumbered Estates Bill, 206
Independent Brigade, 37
Independent Irish Party (1850s), 120, 129, 132,
    135-6, 140
Invincibles, 108
Irish Agricultural Organisation Society, 171-4,
    179, 360
Irish Amateur Athletic Association, 99-101,
    105
Irish Athletic Association, 99
Irish Catholic, 171
Irish Church Act (1869), 33, 36, 42
Irish College, Rome, 120, 141
Irish Convention (1917), 200-1, 297
Irish Co-operative Dairy and Agricultural
    Societies, 173
Irish Cycling Association, 99
Irish Ecclesiastical Record, 156
Irish Felon, 46
Irish Football Association, 98
Irish Freedom, 17
Irish-Ireland, 196-7, 201
Irish Labour Movement, 15, 29

Irish Land, The, 235

Irish Loyal and Patriotic Union, 369, 373

Irish Party, 2-4, 6-13, 15, 17-19, 34-5, 52, 52, 54, 59, 67, 81, 83, 117-19, 158-9, 187-9, 191-2, 194-202, 237, 286-7, 293, 325-6, 328-9, 333, 336, 349, 360, 373, 389

Irish People, 24, 27, 29, 31, 130, 132, 135, 143

Irish Times, 44, 136

Irish Transport and General Workers' Union, 15

Irish Unionist Alliance, 368-74, 376-8, 380, 383-4

Irish Volunteers, 3, 17, 197-8

Irish vote, in Britain, 237, 325, 367

Irishman, 30, 51, 98

Isaacs, R., 293

Italy, 119, 141-2, 153-4, 159

Jackson, P.M., 299

James, I., 5

James, R.R., 319, 323, 330

Jerome, L., 339

Johnson, W., 339

Joint Committee, Unionist Associations of Ireland, 381, 384, 388-9

Joyce, J., author, 95

Jubilee Coercion Act, 351

Kavanagh, J., 125

Keane, Bishop, 121, 130, 138, 146

Keegan, G., 109, 113

Kellas, J., 271

Kelly, Bishop D., 170, 195, 299, 302, 307

Kelly, Colonel, 153

Kelly, P.C., 104

Kelly, P.J., 97

Kenmare, Lord, 50-4

Kennedy, J.E., 102, 106, 112

Kenny, W., 353, 361

Keogh, Justice, 49, 130, 135, 136

Kettle, T., 302

Kickham, C.J., 29, 31, 41, 95, 103, 111

Kilduff, Bishop, 130

Kilmainham Treaty, 87

Kimberley, Lord, 210

King Harmon, E.R., 44, 48, 322

Kirby, Mgr., 118, 120, 126, 128, 133, 141-2,

Knox, Major, 44

Knox, V.F., 360

Kornhauser, W., 63

Labour Party, 253

Labouchere, H., 255, 268-9, 280, 344

Lampson, G. Locker, 65-6

Land Act (1870), 33, 36, 42, 163, 224, 234-5, 338

—, (1881), 80-1, 163, 350

Land Bill (1866), 231

—, (1867), 156

—, (1891), 355

Land League, 62, 70-1, 73, 81, 85, 87, 100, 102, 163, 182, 326

Land Purchase Act (1903), 189, 191, 194

Land question, 145-7, 149, 153, 155, 159, 162, 169, 182, 189, 196, 207-10, 213-15, 217, 221-5, 227-35, 237, 351, 353

Land Tenure Reform Association, 270

Land War, 61-2, 64-8, 73-5, 80, 87

landlords, 30-1, 35, 40, 44-5, 48-54, 57-9, 61-2, 64-7, 69, 73-4, 79-81, 83, 85-7, 89, 92-3, 205-10, 213-16, 223-4, 227, 229-33, 348, 351-2, 354-5, 361-2, 371

language revival, 196-7

Lansdowne, Lord, 374-5, 377, 380, 383

Larkin, E., 73, 176

Lavelle, Fr. P., 123-4

Law, A.B., 297-8, 306, 309, 314-17, 322, 374-80, 382, 385

Layard, A.H., 141

Lea, Sir T., 361

Leader, The, 196

Leahy, Bishop, 130

Lecky, W.E.H., 361

Leeds and Yorkshire Mercury, 291-2

Leslie, Sir J., 322, 339

Lewis, C.E., 336

Lewis, G., 357

Lewis, G.C., 66

Lewis, H., 276

Lewis, H.O., 48

Liberal Central Association, 269-70, 272

Liberal Gazette, 293

Liberal League, 291-5

Liberal(s), Party, 36-53, 55-8, 84, 117, 119, 125, 131, 134-5, 140-2, 144, 146-9, 156, 163-4, 185, 191-2, 194-5, 199, 202, 208, 213, 217-18, 220, 223-4, 227, 229, 231, 238-95, 297-9, 306, 309-16, 327, 330-3, 335-9, 342-3, 347-8, 358, 364, 366-9, 381, 386-7, 390

Liberal Publications Department, 271

Liberal Unionists, 250, 258, 287, 291, 295, 332-3, 349-55, 359, 361

Liberation Society, 240, 261, 270

Lichfield House Compact, 57
Lloyd George, D., 192, 276, 307, 313, 315
Local Government Act (1898), 79, 81-2, 93,
    286, 289, 347, 362
Local Government Board, 82
local self-government, 12, 79, 81, 94, 237,
    286-7, 290, 328, 337, 342, 347-50,
    352-63
Loewenstein, K., 19
Logue, Archbishop M., 188, 190-1, 195, 199,
    201-2
Londonderry, Marquess of, 324, 334, 380
Long, W., 380-1, 386
Loreburn, Lord, 303, 306
Lough, T., 302
Lowe, R., 36, 231-2
Lowther, J., 322
Lucas, F., 135
Lucy, T.C., 21-2, 24-5
Lynam, J., 97

Maamtrasna Case, 326, 329, 336
Macartney, J.E., 56, 336
MacDermot, F., 307
MacHale, Archbishop J., 11, 37-8, 42, 49-50,
    119-20, 123-4, 129, 132, 138-40, 144-6,
    157-8, 163, 196
Macintyre, A., 66
Macken, Rev. T.F., 170
Mackey, A., 104
MacManus, T.B., 119, 122, 124, 154
MacNeill, E., 196
Madden, J., 48
magistrates, 86-7
Maguire, J., 48
Maguire, J.F., 126, 229
Mallon, J., 32
Manchester Guardian, 227, 311-12, 314
Manchester martyrs, 7-9, 19, 33, 153-5,
    211
Mannheim, K., 63
Manning, Cardinal H.E., 118, 127, 142-3,
    156, 159-60
Marlborough, Duke of, 320, 322-3, 326-7,
    333, 337, 339
Marlborough, Duchess of, 323-4, 329-30,
    333
Marriott, Sir J., 309
Martin, J., 22, 41-2, 46, 49, 119, 129, 147
Marx, K., 63
Mathew, Fr. T., 29
Maxwell, General, 198
Maynooth, 127, 138, 162, 202
Mayo, Lord, 159, 229, 231
McCaffrey, L.J., 34, 69

McCalmont, Captain, 339
McCann, M., 372
McCarthy, J., 357
McCarthy, J.P., 97
McCarthy, St.G., 97
McEvilly, Archbishop, 169
McGee, T. d'A., 21
McHugh, Bishop C., 199
McInerney, P.J., 108
McKay, J., 97, 99, 102
McMahon, Fr., 100
McNamara, H.V., 372
M'Swiney, Rev. E., 182
M'Swiney, P.P., 125, 137, 155
Meagher, T., 95
Menton, J., 96
Methodist Times, 266
Mill, J.S., 205-36 *passim*
–, *Autobiography*, 211, 216, 232-4
–, *Considerations on Representative Govern-
    ment*, 205-6, 212, 218, 221
–, *England and Ireland*, 205, 211, 213-14,
    216, 219-22, 224, 226-8, 231, 233-4
–, *On Liberty*, 220
–, *Principles of Political Economy*, 205-6,
    208-9, 214, 222, 228, 233, 235
–, *Thoughts on Parliamentary Reform*, 212
Mobilisation Thesis, 69, 72, 74-5
Moloney, Fr., 112
Moloney, F.R., 97, 103-4, 106-7
Monsell, W., 39, 47, 50, 121, 156, 158
Monteagle, Lord, 359
Montgomery, H. de F., 352-3, 359
Moore, G.H., 37-40, 42-3, 47, 58, 129,
    140
Moran, Bishop, 157
Moran, D.P., 196
Moran, Fr. P.F., 128
Moriarty, Bishop, 39, 50-1, 54, 121-2, 145,
    156-8, 161
Morley, A., 270-1, 283
Morley, J., 34, 238-9, 243-4, 247, 256, 258,
    266, 268-9, 272, 278-80, 282-3, 288,
    291, 297-8, 300, 306
Morley, S., 265
Morning Post, 324
Morris, G., 322
Mundella, A.J., 280-1
Municipal Corporations Act, 94
Municipal Reform League, 277
Munro-Ferguson, R., 288, 290, 293, 295, 310,
    312-13
Murphy, Fr., 100
Murphy, J.F., 102, 108
Murphy, W.M., 317

Murtagh, J., 42

Naas, Lord, 210
Nagle, P., 26-9
Nally, J., 113
Nation, 6, 46, 73, 84, 140, 306-7
National Association, 117-18, 124-5, 128, 130-41, 145-8, 155-6, 158, 162, 164
National Education League, 240, 261, 270
National Flag, 3-7, 9, 15, 18-19, 101
National League, 3, 7-9, 84-5, 100, 102, 108, 111, 113, 354-5
–, (1860s), 119, 147
National Liberal Federation, 241-3, 247, 249-50, 254, 260, 271-2, 281-3
National organisation, 17, 57-8, 63, 67, 74, 87
National Radical Union, 263
National Reform Union, 244
National symbols, 1-20
Nationalist(s), nationalism, 3, 8, 12-14, 43, 46-8, 56, 58, 70-1, 74, 84, 101, 128, 168, 185 193, 196, 210, 217, 220, 237, 247, 299, 304, 321, 327, 335, 337, 358, 360-3, 371, 376, 379, 381, 387, 390
Neate, C., 230-1
New Liberal Review, 292
Newry, Viscount, 47
Nineteenth Century, 249, 309
Nipperdey, T., 18
Nolan, J.P., 49-50, 53
Northcote, Sir S., 334, 337-8
Nulty, Bishop, 130, 132, 138, 145, 147

Oberschall, A., 63
O'Brien, C.C., 34, 239
O'Brien, P. (Nenagh), 113
O'Brien, R.B., 33
O'Brien, Rev. R., 31-2
O'Brien, W., 79-81, 83, 86-7, 111, 113-14, 187-8, 194-5, 298, 314, 357, 362
O'Connell, D., 3, 10-14, 19, 42, 57, 59, 67, 125-6, 130-1, 137, 196, 334, 344
O'Connell, Sir J., 53
O'Connor, A., 353
O'Connor, T.P., 302
O'Connor Don, The (elder), 55
O'Connor Don, The (younger), 359
O'Crowley, F., 99, 102, 104
O'Donnell, Bishop, 172-3, 189, 191, 195, 200, 202
O'Hagan, T., 135
O'Hea, Bishop, 130
O'Kelly, Major, 110
O'Keefe, P.J., 104

Oldham, C.H., 302
O'Leary, C., 34
O'Leary, Fr., 120-1
O'Leary, J., 21, 103-5, 111
O'Neill, H., 196
O'Neill, M., 23
Orangemen, 10, 16, 38, 41, 43-4, 46, 48-9, 143, 220, 319-20, 334-5, 337-40, 342
Orange Card, 319, 333-4
O'Reilly, J.B., 104, 108, 113
O'Riordan, T., 104, 106, 112-13
Ortega y Gasset, J., 63
O'Shea, K., 34
O'Shea, P., 113
Ostrogorski, M., 243, 264
O'Sullivan, Rev. E., 54

Pall Mall Gazette, 223, 226-7, 234
Palmerston, Lord, 120, 122, 131, 141-2, 205
Parnell, C.S., 3, 8-12, 14, 33-4, 40, 45, 49, 52, 55, 57-9, 69-70, 73, 81, 84-5, 87, 96, 101-2, 104-5, 107, 111, 115, 174, 187-8, 195-6, 254-8, 280, 286-7, 300, 324-7, 330-1, 335, 348, 354-5, 357
Parnellite(s), 86-7, 89, 187-8, 283-4, 286, 324-5, 327, 337, 369
Paul-Dubois, L., 169
Peace Preservation Act (1871), 42, 45-6
–, (1881), 70-1, 81, 87
Peace Society, 270
Pelling, H., 260, 267
Penal Code, 120
Perks, Sir R., 287-9, 292-3
Phoenix Society, 26, 29, 32
Pim, J., 44
Pinard, M., 63
Pirie, D.V., 310
Pirrie, Lord, 299
Pitt, W., 344
Plan of Campaign, 89, 113, 350-1, 353
Plender, W., 299
Plunkett, G., 46-7
Plunkett, Sir H., 171-3, 175, 178-9, 184, 305, 359-60
police, 22, 28, 30, 45, 106, 108-9, 112, 197
Poor Law, 150
Poor Law Commission, 82
Poor Law Guardians, 3, 80-94, 355-6, 362
Power, J.W., 97, 102-4
Powis Commission, 157
Primrose Committee, 299-310, 316
Primrose, Sir H., 298
Primrose League, 334, 339

Pro-Boers, 291, 294
Protestant(s), 6, 10, 13, 16, 48, 50, 56-8, 64,
   66-7, 69, 84, 144, 150-1, 168-9, 181, 190,
   195, 200, 217, 220, 342, 348, 366
Protestant Vigilance Committee, 129-30

Quarterly Review, 314

Radical Programme (1885), 277
Redmond, J.E., 4, 188, 190-2, 194-5, 197-200,
   285-7, 289-93, 295, 301, 307-8, 313-14,
   358, 373
Reform Act (1867), 205-6, 223
Reform League, 212
Reform Union, 261
Reid, T.W., 271, 292, 294
Reilly, Constable, 114
Rendel, S., 276
Repeal (association), 10-12, 32, 56-7, 67, 69,
   119-21, 129, 158, 323-4, 334, 344
rents, 61-2, 64-6, 74, 233
Rerum Novarum, 168
Ribbonism, 42, 45
Ridgeway, Sir W., 356-7
Ridker, R.G., 75
Ripon, Lord, 250, 254
Rising (1798), 17
—, (1867), 22, 35-7, 39, 151-4, 209
Ronayne, J.P., 55
Rosa, J.O'D., 26-7, 39-41, 57
Roscommon Journal, 71-2
Rose, C.D., 293
Roseberry, Lord, 247, 249-50, 255-8, 269,
   275, 282, 285, 287-95, 319
Rossmore, Lord, 335, 338
Round Table Conference, 332-3, 353
Royal Irish Constabulary, 7-8, 25, 27, 29-
   30, 104
Royal University, 144
Runciman, W., 297
Russell, Dr (Maynooth), 158
Russell, G., 185
Rusell, G.W.E., 247
Russell, Lord J., 119, 122, 131, 141, 148,
   154, 207, 220
Russell, T.W., 361
Ryan, P.J., 97

Sadleir, W., 135-6
Salisbury, Lady, 322
Salisbury, Marquiss of, 286, 322, 325, 327-
   39, 336, 338-9, 343, 348, 350-3, 383,
   386
Sandars, J., 381
Saturday Review, 225-6, 228

Saunderson, E., 337-41
Scanlan, Fr., 110-11
Schnadhorst, F., 270-1, 273-4
Schramm, P.E., 1
Scott, C.P., 303
Scott, M., 309-11
Seager, R., 272
Secularists, 192, 195
Sellars, A.C., 252
Sexton, T., 353
Shaw, family, 370-1
Shaw, W., 45
Shaw-Lefevre, G., 246
Sinn Fein, 15, 17, 194, 200, 346
Smyth, P.J., 45, 47, 49
Somerset, M., 340
Southern Irish Unionists, 200, 366-70, 372-
   82, 386, 390, 391
Special Commission (1888), 33
Spectator, 211, 227-8
Spencer, Lord, 229-30, 248, 288, 322, 335
Spender, J.A., 286
Stack, W., 100
Stanley, Lord, 35-6, 154, 236
'Step by Step' policy, 285-6, 289
Stephens, J., 22, 24-7, 122
Steward, J., 102
Strauss, E., 34, 238
Stuart, J., 271-2, 277
Sullivan, A.M., 22, 124-5, 132, 140
Sweeney, J., 97
Swift, J., 196
Synder, D., 63

Talbot, Mgr., 141
Tandy, N., 95
Temperance, 29, 249, 254, 276
Tenant Right (League), 36, 42, 46, 48, 55-6,
   67, 70, 118, 120, 124, 130, 132, 145,
   147, 150, 155, 205, 235
Tennant, H., 293, 295
Tenure and Improvement of Land Bill
   (1866), 148, 155
Terry, E., 344
Thom's Directory, 86, 89
Thomas, D.A., 276
Thornley, D., 34
Tilly, C., 62-3
Times, The, 39, 143, 161, 224-6, 228, 231,
   290, 306, 308, 312-14, 328, 339, 377
Tims, J., 273
tithes, 66
Tocqueville, A. de, 62
Todd, J.H., 127
Toibin, M., 16

Tone, Wolfe, 95
Torley, J., 114
Treasury, 121, 298, 300, 302-3, 347
Trench, Archbishop, 150
Trench, E. le Poer, 50
Trevelyan, G.O., 263, 322
Troy, W., 113

Ulster, 4, 10, 13, 56, 62, 84, 93, 130,
    194, 197, 200, 297-8, 306, 309,
    314-17, 322, 333-6, 340-1, 343-4, 346,
    356, 368, 370, 374-9, 381, 390
Ulster Athletic Clubs, 366
Ulster Custom, 235
Ulster Liberal Unionist Committee, 351,
    363
Ulster Unionist Council, 373
'Unauthorized Programme', 245, 259
Union Defence League, 381
Unionist(s), Party, 13-14, 45, 56-7, 190,
    199, 267, 272, 276, 286, 288-90, 297,
    308-9, 312, 317, 322-4, 331-2, 334,
    339, 341-2, 344, 347, 350-2, 355-6,
    359-60, 362-3, 366-9, 371-3, 375-91
United Ireland, 79, 95-7, 100-1
United Irish League, 188-9, 194, 362
United Irishmen, 3-5
United Kingdom Alliance, 240, 270
United Trades Association, 29
Universities Act (1908), 194
University Bill (1873), 43, 46, 55, 163-4

Valera, E. de, 202
Vere, A. de, 156

Vesci, Lord de, 357
Victoria, Queen, 32, 148, 152
Vincent, J.R., 319-24, 329-31, 333,
    336-8, 340, 342-4

Wales, Edward, Prince of, 3, 8, 14, 45,
    161-2, 321
Walsh, Archbishop W., 187-8, 190, 194-5,
    199, 202
Walters, Inspector, 102
Ward, W., 127
Watson, C., 310, 312-13
Waterford, Lord, 357, 359
Webb, S., 253, 273-4
Weldon, J., 113
Westmeath, Lord, 360
Westminster Gazette, 286-7, 293, 314
Weston, Colonel, 388-9
Whateley, Archbishop, 128
White, Dean, 170, 175-6
Whyte, J.H., 34, 40
William III, king of England, 4
Wilson, H.J., 265
Wilson, J.H., 266
Women's Suffrage Association, 240
Woods, S., 266
Wyndham, G., 309
Wynne, Mr., 54

Young Ireland (ers) Movement,
    3-4, 7, 16, 24, 37, 67, 119, 128,
    149
Young, W., 340